Tolley's Self-Assessment

by

Janek Matthews MA(Cantab), FCA,
Barrister of Pump Court Tax Chambers

Nigel Eastaway FCA, FCCA, FCMA, FCIS,
FTII, FHKSA, FTIHK, FOI, TEP, AIIT
of Moores Rowland, Chartered Accountants

Tolley Publishing Company Ltd

A United News & Media publication

Published by
Tolley Publishing Company Limited
Tolley House
2 Addiscombe Road
Croydon
Surrey
CR9 5AF
0181–686 9141

Typeset in Great Britain by
Phoenix Photosetting, Chatham, Kent

Printed in Great Britain by
The Bath Press, Bath

ISBN 1 86012 287–6

Preface

The first edition of this book was called Simplified Assessing which was the Inland Revenue's title for the current year basis of assessment for the self employed and the move towards the goal of self-assessment. The complexity of the legislation necessary to preserve equality among taxpayers and deemed necessary to protect the Exchequer led to the title becoming inappropriate and the Simplified Assessing Consultative Committee, and this book, have been retitled as Self-Assessment. The result is the most fundamental change in the tax system in the last 70 years.

However, we would like to thank all who contributed to the meetings of the Self-Assessment Consultative Committee, both from the ranks of the Revenue so ably led by Roger Hurcombe and what now appear to be called the customers' representatives.

We would also like to thank our colleagues at Pump Court Tax Chambers and Moores Rowland for their help and advice, and in particular Paula Higgleton ATII, ATT for checking the manuscript and to Kate Young and Elaine Beauchop for typing it and coping with our voluminous amendments and indecipherable handwriting.

The law and practice is stated up to the date of the *Finance Act 1996*.

Jan Matthews
Nigel Eastaway

Contents

Section

Section

Table of Cases

Table of Statutes

Chapter 1

Introduction

Background, consultative documents and consultation process

1.1 On 14 August 1991 the Inland Revenue published their first Consultation Paper 'A Simpler System for Taxing the Self Employed', seeking views on proposals for simplifying and streamlining the way the self-employed were taxed. This followed the new corporation tax system under 'Pay and File'. The expressed main objectives were to:

(*a*) make it easier for taxpayers to understand;

(*b*) make it simpler and more efficient to administer;

(*c*) make it possible for the Revenue normally to accept the tax return and accounts without further correspondence;

(*d*) make it possible for taxpayers normally to pay the right amount of tax at the right time without Revenue intervention by a self-assessment system; and

(*e*) open up the way to further reforms to simplify and improve the personal tax system.

1.2 The preceding year ('PY') basis of assessment for the self-employed had been part of the UK tax system for 70 years following the recommendations of the 1920 Royal Commission. It was open to the criticism that the total profits assessed over the life of a business were not in general the same as the profits earned. Moreover, taxpayers frequently found the rules difficult to understand and to apply, which led to a lack of confidence in the fairness of the system, and put burdens upon taxpayers, their advisers and the Revenue in trying to apply the rules correctly.

1.3 The Consultation Paper put forward two alternative proposals to replace the PY basis of assessment for the self-employed. The first was a current year ('CY') basis, whereby tax would continue to be calculated and paid for income tax years, but it would be based upon the profits for the accounts ending in the actual year rather than the preceding year, leaving the taxpayer free to choose his own accounting period. The second was an accounting period ('AP') basis, whereby larger businesses could continue to choose their accounting periods and pay tax by reference to those accounting periods, similar to corporation tax for companies, but smaller businesses would have to make up accounts to a date close to the tax year end, and pay tax by reference to the actual profit earned in a fiscal year.

1.4 This Consultation Paper attracted a wide response, with most accepting the need for reform, and more than two out of three in broad agreement with the proposals for the CY basis and for self-assessment. A subsequent Consultative Document 'A Simpler System for Assessing Personal Tax' was then issued in November 1992. This document developed the idea that the new system should extend beyond the self-employed, to cover employees who paid tax by assessment and those who received investment income. Under the revised proposals:

(*a*) all income would be taxed on a CY basis; and

(*b*) taxpayers who were sent tax returns could choose whether to self-assess or to continue to allow the Revenue to work out their liability. In the latter case returns would have to be filed with the Revenue earlier to enable the Revenue to work out the tax.

1.5 Those who had responded to the previous discussion document generally preferred the CY basis to the AP basis, although the latter was considered to be simpler in some aspects. The later discussion document took the CY basis further forward. It also assumed that all income taxed by assessment would be included in the new system, and that the schedular machinery of assessment would be done away with. Partners would also be assessed separately rather than on a joint basis. But there was no intention to make any radical changes for employees, most of whom were not sent tax returns and for whom PAYE worked out the correct tax liability.

1.6 Following these two Consultative Documents, and the representations made to the Revenue, in early 1993 the Revenue established committees with representative bodies for the taxpayer. A series of discussion papers were prepared dealing with different topics, and the issues were debated in subsequent committee meetings which continue to be held, which also considered the earlier drafts of the legislation. The authors participated in these proceedings on behalf of the Chartered Institute of Taxation. Further consultative documents covering different areas of taxation and administration have been issued over the years, including papers on employers and employees, transitional year anti-avoidance provisions, post-transaction and pre-transaction rulings. There has also been consultation over the form of the tax return and supplementary pages.

1.7 This is the first time in the history of tax legislation that there has been such a lengthy dialogue between the Revenue and representatives of the body of taxpayers before the introduction of the relevant legislation. It reflected acceptance by the Revenue that such a radical change could not simply be imposed upon taxpayers without a full consultation process, and without the co-operation of the taxpayer's professional advisers. Clearly the Revenue were also mindful of a possible fall in tax revenue during the transitional period in the event that the system did not work properly, and were concerned that it might break down unless it received an element of consensus.

1.8 Many of the representations made by the taxpayer bodies have been accepted by the Revenue and incorporated in the subsequent legislation. To this extent the consultation procedure had positive results. In particular, the Revenue were persuaded not to impose fiscal accounting, and to remove some of the more draconian aspects of the surcharges and penalty provisions. Other representations were noted by the Revenue but regrettably not accepted. Sadly, what was perhaps the major concern of the representative bodies, that the changes appeared to do little to achieve the principal objective of simplification for the average taxpayer, has been little heeded. This is a criticism perhaps to be levelled more at the Parliamentary draftsman than the Revenue. But the Revenue's concern with tax avoidance has always been present, and must have contributed to the length and complexity of the legislation.

Timing for introduction of self-assessment

1.9 The primary legislation introducing the new system, initially described as 'Simplified Assessing', is contained in the *Finance Acts 1994* and *1995*, with some amendments and additions in *FA 1996*. The changes are largely implemented by amending *TMA 1970* and *TA 1988*. The change from the PY to CY basis takes effect for new businesses commencing after 5 April 1994. For existing businesses, 1996/97 is a transitional year with its own rules, whilst the full CY basis comes into force in 1997/98. Self-assessment comes into force from 1996/97. The provisions for the taxation of rents under Schedule A are recast for 1995/96.

1.10 There is to be a further tranche of secondary legislation in Statutory Instruments, which will cover the remaining aspects of the new system, notably the details for employers and employees. There will also be a number of practice statements and codes of practice setting out the Revenue's policy for dealing with specific aspects of the legislation, such as the Schedule A transitional rules and the taxation of non-residents trading in the UK.

Current year basis

1.11 Under the CY system, self-employed persons will generally be charged to tax on the profits made in the accounting period which ends in the year of assessment. So where accounts are made up annually to 30 June, the liability for 1998/99 will be based on the profits in the accounts for the year to 30 June 1998. In the year of commencement the profits assessed will be those which actually arise from the date of commencement to the following 5 April. Hence where a business commences on 1 July 1996 and makes up its accounts to 30 June 1997, the assessment for 1996/97 will be based upon three-quarters of the profits shown in the accounts for the year to 30 June 1997.

1.12 In the year of cessation the profits will be those from the end of the basis period assessed in the preceding year to the cessation date. So assuming that a business which has made up accounts to 30 September ceases on 30 June 2000, the profits assessed in 2000/2001 will be those between 1 October 1999 and 30 June 2000. However, the expressed objective of the new rules is to tax the actual profits which are generated by a business during its lifetime. Accordingly any profits which are taken into account more than once will be eligible for 'overlap relief', either when the business ends, or for an earlier period for which the basis period is longer than a year. So in this example, the profits of the final period may be adjusted to take into account any available overlap relief. There are also special rules where a business changes its accounting date, the general principle being to tax at least twelve months profits in a year.

Transitional arrangements

1.13 For businesses which are in existence on 5 April 1994 there are special rules in the transitional year 1996/97. In the usual case, where accounts are made up to the same date, the profits assessed to tax will be 50 per cent of those for the two years ending in 1996/97. Thus a business which makes up its accounts to 30 June will be assessable in 1995/96 on the profits of the year ending on 30 June 1994. For 1996/97, the profits for the two years to 30 June 1995 and 30 June 1996 will be aggregated, and tax payable on half of the total sum. Taxpayers can either prepare a single account for the whole two-year period or draw up separate accounts for each year. In the latter case, the results should be aggregated to arrive at a single figure for taxable profits. Losses arising in this period will be allowed in full and it may therefore be beneficial to draw up separate accounts if a loss is incurred. There are anti-avoidance provisions in *FA 1995* to counter attempts to take advantage of these transitional rules.

1.14 The transitional arrangements apply in most circumstances. However some self-employed taxpayers will need to make a return of their business profits for 1995/96. This applies where profits are assessable for 1995/96 on a current year basis (likely only if the business started after 5 April 1994, or ceases in 1995/96); or where a claim is made to offset trading losses suffered in a period ending in the tax year 1995/96 against other income for that or earlier years.

Partnerships

1.15 From 1997/98 there will no longer be a joint assessment, but each partner will be assessed individually on his or her share of the partnership profits. This share will be allocated by reference to the period of account rather than the year of assessment. A change of partner, where at least one partner carries on the business before and after the change, is not regarded as a cessation.

Losses

1.16 As part of the introduction of a CY basis, there are a number of consequential amendments to the provisions regarding losses. In particular relief for trading losses is to be given against other income of the year of the loss, or the preceding year (rather than the following year).

Capital allowances

1:17 From 1997/98 capital allowances are generally to be treated as trading expenses, and balancing charges as trading receipts, similar to corporation tax.

Self-assessment

1.18 At the heart of the new system is self-assessment for individuals and trustees. The present tax return is to be altered to dovetail in with self-assessment, and its format is currently being determined. The tax return, together with a self-assessment of the taxpayer's income tax and CGT liability, is generally to be filed by 31 January following the end of the tax year. Provision is made for the possibility of the Revenue correcting any obvious errors or mistakes, known as 'repairs'. The taxpayer who submits his return on time also has a year from the filing date to make any amendments to the return, which corresponds with the period during which the Revenue can give notice of its intention to audit the return. Thereafter, subject to certain Revenue powers of discovery and the taxpayer's ability to make a claim for relief for error or mistake, the return and the tax liability becomes final and conclusive.

1.19 However, those not wishing to self-assess can leave the calculation of their tax liability and the raising of the assessment to the Revenue, but the return must then generally be filed by 30 September following the end of the tax year. Moreover, in those cases where the filing date has passed without the return and self-assessment having being submitted, the Revenue are empowered to make their own determination of the tax due. The tax so determined then becomes payable, but the determination is superseded if the return and self-assessment are later filed.

Revenue audit and data retention

1.20 Policing of the self-assessment system is implemented by giving the Revenue wide powers of enquiring into returns, with the ability to call for documents, accounts and other information. This right of 'random audit' generally expires once twelve months have elapsed from the filing date. To assist the Revenue in such enquiries, taxpayers are required to maintain comprehensive records for possible review, generally for five years after the filing date for those engaged in a business, and for twelve months in other cases.

Discovery and finality

1.21 After the twelve-month period has elapsed during which Revenue enquiries can be raised, a taxpayer's liability can only be increased if the Revenue 'discover' that there has been an under-assessment. The rules for discovery were based upon a mixture of statute, case law and Revenue practice. Under the new statutory provisions, the Revenue can generally only make a discovery assessment if there has been fraud or neglect by the taxpayer, or inadequate disclosure was made.

Payment of tax

1.22 Payments on account of income tax, described as interim payments, are to be made by 31 January in the year of assessment and 31 July immediately following the year of assessment. These are normally based on the liability of the preceding year, with each payment amounting to 50 per cent thereof. The taxpayer has the right to reduce the interim payments if he considers that his actual liability will be less. Interim payments will also not be required where substantially all of the taxpayer's liability is deducted at source, for example under PAYE.

1.23 Payment of the balance of the taxpayer's income tax liability, together with the whole of any CGT liability, is then to be made by 31 January following the end of the year of assessment, i.e. when the taxpayer's return and self-assessment is to be filed.

Surcharges and interest for late payment

1.24 In the event that payment of the final instalment is more than 28 days late, there is an automatic 5 per cent surcharge. There is a further 5 per cent surcharge if payment has not been made by the end of the following six months. In addition interest runs if the interim payments or the final payment are made after the due dates.

Penalties

1.25 If a tax return is submitted late, there is an automatic £100 penalty, which is increased by a further £100 after six months. However both of these penalties are limited to the amount of tax due for the period. After a year's default, the penalty can be as much as the tax liability itself. The Revenue can also apply to the Commissioners for the imposition of further penalties up to £60 per day.

Appeals

1.26 The present procedure for appeals to the General or Special Commissioners is preserved for cases where assessments are made by the Revenue, or where the Revenue seek to amend the taxpayer's self-assessment.

References

1.27 The *Finance Acts 1994*, *1995* and *1996* make numerous amendments to existing legislation, particularly in the *Taxes Management Act 1970* and the *Taxes Act 1988*. References are to the legislation as amended unless otherwise specified. Where it would be helpful for clarity reference is made to 'amended' or 'substituted' *sections,* meaning as amended or substituted by the provisions of the *Finance Act 1994*, *1995*, or *1996* or to 'original enactment' referring to the legislation prior to those *Finance Acts*.

Chapter 2

Schedule D, Cases I and II

Accounting issues

2.1 The change to self-assessment does not of itself affect the way in which a business keeps its books or makes up its accounts. The business is still free to make up its accounts to any date within the fiscal year, and as long as these accounts are prepared on a consistent basis in accordance with generally accepted accounting principles they will form the starting point for the taxable profits. [*Heather v P-E Consulting Group (1973) 48 TC 293, Threlfall v Jones; Gallagher v Jones (1993) STC 537, Odeon Associated Theatres Ltd v Jones (1971) 48 TC 257, Johnston v Britannia Airways Ltd (1994) STC 763*].

Under the current year basis rules any reference to a trade includes a reference to a profession, vocation, employment or office, under *FA 1994, s 218(2)*. Appendix B sets out SSAP2, the statement of the ICAEW relating to accounting policies.

2.2 The Revenue pronouncements on the circumstances in which a cash or conventional (rather than an earnings) basis will be acceptable remain applicable, such as SP A27 'Accounts on a cash basis' which provides as follows:

> 'A company, whether limited or unlimited, is normally required to prepare accounts for tax purposes on an earnings basis, as defined in *TA 1988, s 110(3)*. An individual or a partnership carrying on a trade is similarly required to prepare accounts on an earnings basis, but in the circumstances set out below, accounts prepared on a cash basis, or on a conventional basis such as bills issued or work completed which is neither full "earnings" nor pure "cash", may be accepted from an individual or partnership carrying on a profession or vocation.
>
> Where a profession or vocation is newly set up, or is treated as new for tax purposes under *TA 1988, s 113(1)*, the profits of the first three years from the date of setting up or of the change to which *TA 1988, s 113(1)* applies, are required to be computed on the earnings basis (as defined in *TA 1988, s 110(3)*) in determining all tax liabilities affected by the profits of these years.
>
> The computation of subsequent profits will continue on the earnings basis until the taxpayer asks to change to a cash or other conventional basis. Such a change will be accepted if the new basis seems likely to

provide a reasonable measure of the taxpayer's profit. This is interpreted as meaning that the profits computed on the new basis will not, taking one year with another, differ materially from the profits computed on the earnings basis.

The change must also be a complete one. For example, receipts after the change for work done before the change must be brought into the computation of profits on the cash basis notwithstanding that they have already been brought into account in the computation on the earnings basis; similarly, expenses accrued due but unpaid which were debited in the accounts on the earnings basis may again be debited in the subsequent accounts on the cash basis when they are paid.

A further condition is that the taxpayer wishing to make such a change is required to give a written undertaking that he will issue bills for services rendered or work done (that is in the normal way, completed work but also including work in progress where interim payments or payments on account are contemplated by the terms of the contract or are customary) at regular and frequent intervals. The intervals may be chosen by the taxpayer but they should be quarterly or more often, and they should be specified in the undertaking.

Attention is drawn to the possibility of liability under *TA 1988, s 104*, wherever accounts are prepared on a basis other than earnings: in computing such liability there is no provision for any relief in respect of any profits which may have been brought into the computation twice when the change from the earnings basis was made.

Where accounts are prepared on a cash or other conventional basis and it is desired to change to an earnings basis, no objection will be raised but attention is again drawn to the liability that will arise under *TA 1988, s 104*. A subsequent claim to revert to a conventional basis would not be accepted.'

2.3 This practice statement is not applicable to barristers, to whom the provisions of SP A3 apply, which continues unchanged and basically allows barristers to be assessed on a cash basis from commencement.

2.4 Businesses already on a cash basis or bills delivered basis may continue to be so taxed and the post-cessation receipts provisions in *TA 1988, ss 103–110* continue in force.

Adjustments to accounts

2.5 The profits as shown by the accounts will, as at present, require adjustment for tax purposes by adding back expenses shown in the accounts that are disallowed for tax purposes or dealt with as annual payments, and excluding income assessed under other heads such as rents received under Schedule A, untaxed interest under Schedule D, Case III, income from foreign securities or possessions under Schedule D, Cases IV and V, sundry sources of income under Schedule D, Case VI, income from offices or employments taxed under Schedule E, investment income subject to tax at source, or capital profits subject to capital gains tax. The main substantive change to Schedule D, Case I or II computations will be that capital allowances under the current year basis are to be deducted as trading expenses instead of being subject to separate claims. The capital allowances changes are dealt with in Chapter 4. Relief for pre-trading expenditure under *TA 1988, s 401* is, for trades set up and commenced after 6 April 1995, given by treating the expenditure as having been incurred on the first day of trading, instead of as a notional loss as previously. (*FA 1995, s 120*).

2.6 Normally only Schedule D, Cases I and II income is chargeable on a current accounting year basis, with other forms of income and chargeable gains charged on a strict fiscal year basis. The exceptions are partnership income which includes peripheral income, considered in Chapter 12, and income from overseas trades and professions which, although assessed under Schedule D, Case V, is charged on the current accounting year basis applicable to Schedule D, Cases I and II (see Chapters 5 to 8).

Introduction to the current year basis

2.7 The fundamental principles behind the current year basis are that the adjusted profits of a business should, over its life, equate with the amount on which it is taxed, and that at least twelve months profits should be assessed in each full fiscal year during which a business is in existence. It was also a requirement that there should be no loss to the Exchequer on the change from the preceding year basis of assessment to the current year basis.

2.8 The effect is that the system is a lot more complex than originally envisaged in the Consultation Papers. It results in some of the profits being assessed twice on commencement, or on a change of accounting date to a date ending earlier in the fiscal year. The preceding year basis applicable to existing businesses also resulted in a multiple assessment on the opening period profits. To compensate for such 'double' assessments there is a relief on cessation for what are described as 'overlap profits', and partial relief on a change of accounting date to a date later in the fiscal year, which involves charging to tax profits for a period in excess of twelve months.

2.9 As well as adjusting for the overlap the new rules have to cater for the transition from the preceding year basis for existing businesses. This is done through a transitional year in 1996/97, which broadly is taxed on half the combined profits of the two years ending with the accounting year ending in 1996/97, with the interval from the end of the 1996/97 basis period to 5 April 1997 being an additional overlap period. The averaging of profits in this way gives rise to an apparent opportunity for saving tax by maximising the profits in the transitional period. This potential is clearly recognised by the Revenue, who intend to discourage such activities by anti-avoidance measures containing a significant penalty element. The detailed anti-avoidance provisions are contained in the *Finance Act 1995*. Planning and anti-avoidance is dealt with in Chapter 24.

2.10 A further complication is that the double charging of profits requires the double allowance of foreign tax credits in the opening period. The transitional arrangements require foreign tax credits to be abated under the averaging provisions. This makes the calculation of any excess credit on cessation a complex matter which is dealt with in Chapter 11. Moreover, not all businesses are profitable all the time and losses have to be catered for. The double counting of profits on commencement and on a change to an accounting period ending earlier in the fiscal year in turn requires amendment to prevent the double allowance of the same loss. Furthermore the transitional provisions have to provide that losses do not go unrelieved. These provisions are dealt with in Chapter 3.

2.11 In the explanations which follow there is a series of continuing examples which sets out the rules for determining the basis periods on commencement and subsequent years. These are set out initially in narrative form, then with fully worked figures after 2.23 and 2.35 below. Moreover, there is a flow chart in Appendix A 'Hunt the Basis Period' which is designed to assist taxpayers and their advisers in their quest for the basis period for any year of assessment.

Definitions

2.12 For the purpose of the new provisions there are a number of definitions as follows.

'Accounting date' is defined as the date in a year of assessment to which accounts are made up; or where there are two or more such dates because a set of accounts is produced for a short period, and both periods end in the same fiscal year; the latest of those dates. The 'commencement date' and the 'commencement year' are also defined respectively as the date on which, and the fiscal year in which, the trade, profession or vocation is set up and commenced. [*TA 1988, s 60(5); FA 1994, s 200*].

The profits which are included in the computations of two successive years of assessment are known as 'overlap profits' and the 'overlap period' means the number of days in the period in which the overlap profit arose, i.e. those days included in more than one basis period. [*TA 1988, s 63A(5); FA 1994, s 205*]. See 2.37 to 2.41.

Commencement

First year of assessment

2.13 The current year basis applies to a new business commencing on or after 6 April 1994, or deemed to commence on a partnership change on or after that date where an election for continuation is not made under *TA 1988, s 113(2)*. [*FA 1994, s 218(1)*]. The profits or gains for the first year of assessment are charged for the period from commencement to the following 5 April. So the position is the same as under the existing preceding year basis rules. [*TA 1988, s 61(1); FA 1994, s 201*]. Accounts are split on a time basis as necessary to arrive at the profits for this period [*FA 1994, s 201; TA 1988, ss 72, 834(4)*] unless apportionment on some other basis, for example by reference to specific deals falling in each period, would produce a more accurate method of apportioning profits to each period, *Marshall Hus & Partners Ltd v Bolton* [*1981*] *STC 18*. It is unlikely that the Revenue will use anything other than a time basis unless the circumstances are exceptional.

Examples 1–3 (continuing) (following 2.23)

Mr Mil started business on 1 August 1998 and produced accounts to 5 April 1999. These form the basis period for 1998/99. (*Example 1*)

Mr Molniya started business on 1 August 1998 and produced accounts to 31 July 1999. The (time apportioned) period to 5 April 1999 (248/365) forms the basis period for 1998/99. (*Example 2*)

Mr Moscvich started business on 1 August 1998 and produced accounts to 31 December 1998 and annually thereafter. His basis period for 1998/99 is 1.8.98 to 31.12.98, 153 days, plus (95/365) of the year to 31 December 1999, i.e. from commencement to the following 5 April. (*Example 3*)

Strictly, apportionment should be by days in the respective periods [*TA 1988, s 72(2); FA 1995, s 121*] although in practice apportionment in months or days may be accepted. The examples are worked in days or months as appropriate to illustrate the principles involved as clearly as possible. Although 1996 is a leap year, this is ignored in certain examples for clarity.

Second year of assessment

Where there is a twelve-month accounting period ending in year

2.14 If an accounting period ends in the second year of assessment and the accounting date is twelve months or more from the commencement, the assessment is based on the profits for the twelve-month period ending with that accounting date. [*TA 1988, s 60(3)(a); FA 1994, s 200*]. This will be the most typical case. Note that the accounting date is not necessarily the first accounting date but the first accounting date that falls twelve months or more after commencement.

Examples 1–3 and 5 (continuing) (following 2.23)

Mr Mil who started business on 1 August 1998 and produced his first accounts to 5 April 1999 makes up his annual accounts in the second year to 5 April 2000. They end more than twelve months from commencement and so form the basis period for 1999/2000. (*Example 1*)

Mr. Molniya started business on 1 August 1998 and produced accounts to 31 July 1999, i.e. for a period of twelve months. The basis period for 1999/2000 is the year ended 31 July 1999, i.e. the first (twelve-month) accounting date ending in the second year of assessment. (*Example 2*)

Mr Moscvich who started business on 1 August 1998 produced accounts to 31 December 1998. He makes up his annual accounts to the same date in the second year, i.e. 31 December 1999, which forms the basis period for 1999/2000. (*Example 3*)

Mr Nesterov started business on 1 August 1998 and produced accounts to 31 December 1999, i.e., for a period of more than twelve months. The basis period for 1999/2000 is the year ended 31 December 1999, i.e. 12/17 of the period 1.8.1998 to 31.12.1999. (*Example 5*)

Where there is no twelve-month accounting period ending in year

2.15 If there is not a twelve-month accounting date ending in the second year of assessment the basis period is the twelve months from commencement [*TA 1988, s 61(2)(a); FA 1994, s 201*] save where the unusual circumstances in 2.19 apply. This preserves the principle that at least twelve months profits are to be assessed in a year of assessment.

Example 4 (continuing) (following 2.23)

Mr Nikitin started business on 1 August 1998 and produced accounts to 30 June 1999, i.e. for a period of less than twelve months ending in the second year of assessment. The basis period for 1999/2000 is the year ended 31 July 1999 (being the first twelve months from commencement) computed as the profits for the period from 1.8.1998 to 30.6.1999 and 31/365 of the profits for the year ended 30.6.2000.

Where no accounting period in year and a change of accounting date in third year

2.16 If there is a change of accounting date in the third year of assessment, with accounts made up to a date different from the accounting date in the first year of assessment, and there is no accounting date ending in the second year of assessment, the accounting date change is deemed under the change of accounting date rules (see 2.24 *et seq*. below) to have taken place twelve months before the actual change. This may give a deemed accounting date in the second fiscal year less than twelve months from commencement, in which case the profits for the second fiscal year are charged by reference to the twelve months from commencement. [*TA 1988, s 61(2)(b); FA 1994, s 201*].

Example 7 (continuing) (following 2.23)

Mr Moskalev started business on 1 August 1998 and produced accounts to 5 April 1999 and then to 30 June 2000, i.e. a change of accounting date. There is no accounting period ending in 1999/2000. Therefore under the change of accounting date rules the change to the new accounting date of 30 June is deemed to take place one year earlier, i.e. 30 June 1999. This is less than twelve months from commencement so the basis period for the second year is the twelve months from commencement, i.e. 1.8.1998 to 5.4.1999 plus 117/451 of the period 6.4.1999 to 30.6.2000.

Where there is a change in accounting date less than 12 months from commencement

2.17 If there is a change of accounting date in the second year of assessment, i.e. accounts are made up for a date different from the accounting date in the first year of assessment, but for a period ending less than twelve months from commencement, the basis period for the second year is the profits for the first twelve months. [*TA 1988, s 61(2)(b); FA 1994, s 201*].

Example 8 (continuing) (following 2.23)

Mr Bakshayev started business on 1 August 1998 and produced accounts to 31 December 1998 and then to 30 April 1999 and annually thereafter. The basis period for 1999/2000 is the period 1.8.1998 to 31.12.1998, plus 1.1.1999 to 30.4.1999, plus 1.5.1999 to 31.7.1999, i.e. 92/365 of year ended 30.4.2000; that is the profits for the first twelve months.

Where there is a change in accounting date more than twelve months from commencement

2.18 If the accounting date change is more than twelve months from commencement, the second year basis period is the year to the new accounting date. [*TA 1988, s 60(3)(a); FA 1994, s 200*].

Example 9 (continuing) (following 2.23)

Mr Gudkov started business on 1 August 1998 and produced accounts to 31 December 1998 and then to 30 September 1999 and annually thereafter. The new accounting date of 30 September 1999 is more than twelve months from commencement, therefore the basis period is the twelve months ending on the new accounting date; i.e. 92/153 of the five-month period to 31 December 1998 plus the nine months to 30 September 1999.

Where there is no accounting date in first or second year

2.19 If there is no accounting date in either the first or second fiscal years (perhaps because the business commenced towards the end of a fiscal year) and accounts are made for a long period to an accounting date early in the third fiscal year, the basis period for the second year is the fiscal year itself. [*TA 1988, s 60(1); FA 1994, s 200*]. This sub-section always applies where no other provisions give an alternative basis period for a year of assessment.

Example 6 (continuing) (following 2.23)

Mr Lisunov started business on 1 August 1998 and produced accounts to 30 June 2000, i.e. for a period of more than twelve months ending in the third fiscal year. As there is not an accounting period in 1999/2000, no change of accounting date and no other provisions apply, the basis period for the second fiscal year, 1999/2000, is the fiscal year ended 5 April 2000; i.e. 365/700 of the period 1.8.1998 to 30.6.2000.

Third year of assessment

Where first twelve-month accounting period is in third year

2.20 In the third fiscal year the basis period will be the twelve months ending with the accounting date if this is the first accounting date ending twelve months or more after commencement, i.e. ignoring any accounting dates less than twelve months from commencement. [*TA 1988, s 60(3)(a); FA 1994, s 200*].

Example 6 (continuing) (following 2.23)

Mr Lisunov started business on 1 August 1998 and produced accounts to 30 June 2000 and annually thereafter. The basis period for the third fiscal year, 2000/01, is the twelve months to 30 June 2000, i.e. 365/700 of the period 1.8.1998 to 30.6.2000.

Where first twelve-month accounting period is in second year

2.21 If the first accounting date ending twelve months or more after commencement fell in the second fiscal year, the basis period for the third fiscal year is the period of twelve months beginning immediately after the end of the basis period in the second year of assessment. If accounts are made up on an annual basis this would be the accounts for the year ending in the third fiscal year, which would be the normal position. [*TA 1988, s 60(3)(b); FA 1994, s 200*].

Example 1–3 (continuing) (following 2.23)

Mr Mil started business on 1 August 1998 and produced accounts to 5 April 1999 and annually thereafter. The basis period for 2000/01 is the year ended 5 April 2001, the accounting year ending in the fiscal year. (*Example 1*)

Mr Molniya started business on 1 August 1998 and produced accounts to 31 July 1999 and annually thereafter. The basis period for 2000/01 is the year ended 31 July 2000, the accounting year ending in the fiscal year. (*Example 2*)

Mr Moscvich started business on 1 August 1998 and produced accounts to 31 December 1998 and annually thereafter. The basis period for 2000/01 is the year ended 31 December 2000, the accounting year ending in the fiscal year. (*Example 3*)

Subsequent years of assessment

2.22 In the fourth and subsequent fiscal years the basis period continues to be the period of twelve months after the end of the basis period for the preceding year of assessment. Again, so long as accounts are made up for a twelve-month period, this will normally result in the accounts for the year ending in the fiscal year forming the basis period for that year. [*TA 1988, s 60(3)(b); FA 1994, s 200*].

Examples 2 and 3 (continuing) (following 2.23)

Mr Molniya started business on 1 August 1998 and produced accounts to 31 July 1999 and annually thereafter. The basis period for 2001/02 is the year ended 31 July 2001, the accounting year ending in the fiscal year. (*Example 2*)

Mr Moscvich started business on 1 August 1998 and produced accounts to 31 December 1998 and annually thereafter. The basis period for 2001/02 is the year ended 31 December 2001, the accounting year ending in the fiscal year. (*Example 3*)

2.23 This basic rule can be displaced on a change of accounting date under the rules dealt with in 2.24 to 2.34 below. The fall back basis period of the fiscal year (see 2.19) does not apply since these latter rules fix an alternative basis period applicable to the fiscal year. [*TA 1988, s 60(1)(2); FA 1994, s 200*].

Example 1

Fiscal year accounting

Mr Mil started business on 1 August 1998 and produced accounts to 5 April 1999, i.e. to the end of the fiscal year, and annually thereafter.

Profits (as adjusted for tax purposes)	
1.8.98 to 5.4.99	£8,000
y/e 5.4.2000	£18,000
y/e 5.4.2001	£24,000
y/e 5.4.2002	£30,000

Taxable			
1998/99	1.8.98 to 5.4.99	£8,000	(*a*)
1999/00	y/e 5.4.2000	£18,000	(*b*)
2000/01	y/e 5.4.2001	£24,000	(*c*)
2001/02	y/e 5.4.2002	£30,000	(*d*)

Notes

(*a*) *TA 1988, s 61(1); FA 1994, s 201*, commencement to 5 April.

(*b*) *TA 1988, s 61(2); FA 1994, s 201* is inapplicable, as period from commencement, 1.8.1998 to accounting date, 5.4.2000 is not less than twelve months. Therefore, *TA 1988, s 60(3)(a); FA 1994, s 200* applies as this is the first year of assessment in which the accounting date falls not less than twelve months after commencement.

(*c*) *TA 1988, s 60(3)(b); FA 1994, s 200.*

(*d*) *TA 1988, s 60(3)(b); FA 1994, s 200.*

Example 2

First accounts for twelve months

Mr Molniya started business on 1 August 1998 and produced accounts to 31 July 1999, i.e. for a period of twelve months, and annually thereafter.

Profits (as adjusted for tax purposes)	
y/e 31.7.1999	£14,000
y/e 31.7.2000	£20,000
y/e 31.7.2001	£26,000

Taxable			
1998/99	(1.8.98 to 5.4.99 248/365 × £14,000)	£9,512	(*a*)
1999/00	y/e 31.7.1999	£14,000	(*b*)
2000/01	y/e 31.7.2000	£20,000	(*c*)
2001/02	y/e 31.7.2001	£26,000	(*d*)

Notes

(*a*) *TA 1988, s 61(1); FA 1994, s 201*, commencement to 5 April.

(*b*) *TA 1988, s 61(2); FA 1994, s 201* inapplicable as period from commencement 1.8.98 to accounting date 31.7.99 is not less than twelve months. [*TA 1988, s 61(2)(a); FA 1994, s 201*]. Therefore, the basis period for the first year of assessment in which there is an accounting period under *TA 1988, s 60(3)(a); FA 1994, s 200* is the year ended 31.7.99.

(*c*) *TA 1988, s 60(3)(b); FA 1994, s 200.*

(*d*) *TA 1988, s 60(3)(b); FA 1994, s 200.*

The period from commencement on 1.8.98 to 5.4.99 is taxed both for 1998/99 and 1999/00 and is therefore an overlap period relievable under *TA 1988, s 63A; FA 1994, s 205* resulting in overlap profits of £9,512 (see 2.37 *et seq.* below).

Example 3

First accounts for less than twelve months ending in first fiscal year

Mr Moscvich started business on 1 August 1998 and produced accounts to 31 December 1998, i.e. for a period of less than twelve months ending in the fiscal year of commencement, and annually thereafter.

Profits (as adjusted for tax purposes)	
1.8.98 to 31.12.98	£5,000
y/e 31.12.1999	£16,500
y/e 31.12.2000	£22,500
y/e 31.12.2001	£28,500

Taxable			
1998/99	1.8.98 to 5.4.99		
	£5,000 + (95/365 × £16,500)	£9,295	(*a*)
1999/00	y/e 31.12.99	£16,500	(*b*)
2000/01	y/e 31.12.00	£22,500	(*c*)
2001/02	y/e 31.12.01	£28,500	(*d*)

Notes

(*a*) *TA 1988, s 61(1); FA 1994, s 201* commencement to 5 April.

(*b*) *TA 1988, s 61(2); FA 1994, s 201* does not apply, although the second year of assessment, as the period from commencement 1.8.98 to the accounting date given by *TA 1988, s 60(5); FA 1994, s 200* of 31.12.99, is not less than twelve months. Therefore, this is the first year of assessment in which there is an accounting date which falls not less than twelve months after the commencement date and the basis period is fixed by *TA 1988, s 60(3)(a); FA 1994, s 200.*

(*c*) *TA 1988, s 60(3)(b); FA 1994, s 200.*

(*d*) *TA 1988, s 60(3)(b); FA 1994, s 200.*

The period from 1.1.99 to 5.4.99 is taxed both for 1998/99 and 1999/00 and is therefore an overlap period relievable under *TA 1988, s 63A; FA 1994, s 205* resulting in overlap profits of £4,295 (95/365 × £16,500).

Example 4

First accounts for less than twelve months ending in second fiscal year

Mr Nikitin started business on 1 August 1998 and produced accounts to 30 June 1999, i.e. for a period of less than twelve months ending in the fiscal year following that of commencement, and annually thereafter.

Profits (as adjusted for tax purposes)	
1.8.98 to 30.6.99	£12,500
y/e 30.6.2000	£19,500
y/e 30.6.2001	£25,500

Taxable			
1998/99	1.8.98 to 5.4.99		
	(248/334 × £12,500)	£9,281	(*a*)
1999/00	1.8.98 to 31.7.99		
	£12,500 + (31/365 × £19,500)	£14,156	(*b*)

2000/01	y/e 30.6.2000	£19,500	(*c*)
2001/02	y/e 30.6.2001	£25,500	(*d*)

Notes

(*a*) *TA 1988, s 61(1); FA 1994, s 201*, commencement to 5 April.

(*b*) *TA 1988, s 61(2)(a); FA 1994, s 201* does apply on the second year of assessment, because the period from commencement 1.8.98 to the accounting date is less than twelve months. The basis period given by *TA 1988, s 61(2)(a); FA 1994, s 201* is the twelve months from commencement i.e. 1.8.98 to 31.7.99. This conforms to the requirement for at least twelve months profits to be taxed in every year other than that of commencement or cessation.

(*c*) *TA 1988, s 60(3)(a); FA 1994, s 200* applies as 30.6.2000 is the first accounting date which falls not less than twelve months after commencement.

(*d*) *TA 1988, s 60(3)(b); FA 1994, s 200.*

The period from commencement on 1.8.98 to 5.4.99 is taxed both in 1998/99 and 1999/00 and is therefore an overlap period relieved under *TA 1988, s 63A; FA 1994, s 205* with overlap profits of £9,281. The period from 1.7.99 to 31.7.99 is taxed both in 1999/00 and 2000/01 and is therefore an overlap period relievable under *TA 1988, s 63A; FA 1994, s 205* resulting in overlap profits of £1,656 (31/365 × £19,500) increasing the overlap profits to £10,937.

Example 5

First accounts for more than twelve months ending in second fiscal year

Mr Nesterov started business on 1 August 1998 and produced accounts to 31 December 1999, i.e. for a period of more than twelve months ending in the fiscal year following that of commencement, and annually thereafter.

Profits (as adjusted for tax purposes)

1.8.98 to 31.12.99	£21,500
y/e 31.12.2000	£22,500
y/e 31.12.2001	£28,500

Taxable

1998/99	1.8.98 to 5.4.99		
	(248/518 × £21,500)	£10,293	(*a*)
1999/00	1.1.99 to 31.12.99		
	(365/518 × £21,500)	£15,150	(*b*)
2000/01	y/e 31.12.2000	£22,500	(*c*)
2001/02	y/e 31.12.2001	£28,500	(*d*)

Notes

(*a*) *TA 1988, s 61(1); FA 1994, s 201* commencement to 5 April.

(*b*) *TA 1988, s 60(3)(a); FA 1994, s 200* applies, twelve months to first accounting date. *TA 1988, s 61(2); FA 1994, s 201* does not apply as the accounting period is not less than twelve months.

(*c*) *TA 1988, s 60(3)(b); FA 1994, s 200.*

(*d*) *TA 1988, s 60(3)(b); FA 1994, s 200.*

The period from 1.1.99 to 5.4.99 is taxed both in 1998/99 and 1999/00 and is therefore an overlap period relievable under *TA 1988, s 63A; FA 1994, s 205* resulting in overlap profits of £3,943 (95/518 × £21,500).

Example 6

First accounts for more than twelve months ending in third fiscal year

Mr Lisunov started business on 1 August 1998 and produced accounts to 30 June 2000, i.e. for a period of more than twelve months ending in the second fiscal year following the year of commencement, and annually thereafter.

Profits (as adjusted for tax purposes)

1.8.1998 to 30.6.2000	£32,000
y/e 30.6.2001	£25,500

Taxable

1998/99	1.8.98 to 5.4.99 (248/700 × £32,000)	£11,337	(*a*)
1999/00	6.4.99 to 5.4.00 (365/700 × £32,000)	£16,686	(*b*)
2000/01	1.7.99 to 30.6.00 (365/700 × £32,000)	£16,686	(c)
2001/02	y/e 30.6.2001	£25,500	(*d*)

Notes

(*a*) *TA 1988, s 61(1); FA 1994, s 201* commencement to 5 April.

(*b*) *TA 1988, s 60(1); FA 1994, s 200* applies on the fiscal year basis as there is no accounting period ending in the second year of assessment, therefore *TA 1988, s 60(3); FA 1994, s 200* cannot apply, and therefore *TA 1988, s 61; FA 1994, s 201* cannot apply either in view of *TA 1988, s 61(2)(a); FA 1994, s 201*.

(*c*) *TA 1988, s 60(3)(a); FA 1994, s 200* applies, twelve months to first accounting date. *TA 1988, s 61(2); FA 1994, s 201* does not apply as it is the third year of assessment, nor does *TA 1988, s 60(3)(b); FA 1994, s 200* as *TA 1988, s 60(3)(a); FA 1994, s 200* applies.

(*d*) *TA 1988, s 60(3)(b); FA 1994, s 200.*

The period from 1.7.99 to 5.4.00 is taxed in both 1999/00 and 2000/01 and is therefore an overlap period relievable under *TA 1988, s 63A; FA 1994, s 205* resulting in overlap profits of £12,800 (280/700 × £32,000).

Example 7

Change of accounting date in third year

Mr Moskalev started business on 1 August 1998 and produced accounts to 5 April 1999 and then to 30 June 2000, i.e. a period ending in the third year and not for twelve months from the first accounting date and within two years of commencement.

Profits (as adjusted for tax purposes)			
1.8.98 to 5.4.99		£11,000	
p/e 30.6.2000		£21,000	
y/e 30.6.2001		£25,500	
Taxable			
1998/99	1.8.98 to 5.4.99	£11,000	(*a*)
1999/00	1.8.98 to 31.7.99		
	£11,000 + 117/452 × £21,000	£16,436	(*b*)
2000/01	1.7.99 to 30.6.2000		
	(366/452 × £21,000)	£17,004	(*c*)
2001/02	y/e 30.6.2001	£25,500	(*d*)

Notes

(*a*) *TA 1988, s 61(1); FA 1994, s 201* commencement to 5 April.

(*b*) *TA 1988, s 61(2)(b); FA 1994, s 201* first twelve months.

(*c*) *TA 1988, s 62(2)(b); FA 1994, s 202* applies, twelve months to new accounting date.

(*d*) *TA 1988, s 60(3)(b); FA 1994, s 200.*

The period from 1.8.98 to 5.4.99 is taxed in both 1998/99 and 1999/00 and is therefore an overlap period relievable under *TA 1988, s 63A; FA 1994, s 205* resulting in overlap profits of £11,000. The period from 1.7.99 to 31.7.99 is taxed in both 1999/00 and 2000/01 and is therefore a further overlap period resulting in additional overlap profits of £1,440 (31/452 × £21,000).

Example 8

Change of accounting date in second year

Mr Bakshayev started business on 1 August 1998 and produced accounts to 31 December 1998 and then to 30 April 1999 and annually thereafter.

Profits (as adjusted for tax purposes)

1.8.98 to 31.12.98	£10,000
1.1.99 to 30.4.99	£6,000
y/e 30.4.2000	£30,000
y/e 30.4.2001	£40,000

Taxable (subject to overlap relief under *TA 1988, s 63A; FA 1994, s 205*)

1998/99	1.8.98 to 5.4.99	£14,750	(*a*)
1999/00	1.8.98 to 31.7.99	£23,561	(*b*)
2000/01	y/e 30.4.00	£30,000	(*c*)
2001/02	y/e 30.4.01	£40,000	

Notes

(*a*) *TA 1988, s 61(1); FA 1994, s 201* actual basis for year of commencement £10,000 + (95/120 × £6,000) = £14,750.

(*b*) *TA 1988, s 61(2)(b); FA 1994, s 201* first twelve months. £10,000 + £6,000 + (92/365 × £30,000) = £23,561.

(*c*) *TA 1988, s 60(3)(a); FA 1994, s 200* year ended on accounting date.

The period from 1.8.98 to 5.4.99 is taxed in 1998/99 and 1999/2000. The period from 1.5.99 to 31.7.99 is taxed in 1999/2000 and 2000/01. The overlap period relievable under *TA 1988, s 63A; FA 1994, s 205* is therefore 248 days and 92 days, a total of 340 days and the overlap profits of £14,750 and (92/365 × £30,000) £7,561 a total of £22,311.

Example 9

Change of accounting date in second year more than twelve months from commencement

Mr Gudkov started business on 1 August 1998 and produced accounts to 31 December 1998 and then to 30 September 1999 and annually thereafter.

Profits (as adjusted for tax purposes)

1.8.98 to 31.12.98	£10,000
1.1.99 to 30.9.99	£27,000
y/e 30.9.2000	£35,000
y/e 30.9.2001	£40,000

Taxable (subject to overlap relief under *TA 1988, s 63A; FA 1994, s 205*)

1998/99	1.8.98 to 5.4.99	£19,396	(*a*)
1999/00	y/e 30.9.99	£33,013	(*b*)
2000/01	y/e 30.9.00	£35,000	(*c*)
2001/02	y/e 30.9.01	£40,000	(*d*)

Notes

(*a*) *TA 1988, s 61(1); FA 1994, s 201* actual basis for year of commencement. £10,000 + (95/273 × £27,000) = £19,396.

(*b*) *TA 1988, s 60(3)(a); FA 1994, s 200*, twelve months to new accounting date. £27,000 + (92/153 × £10,000) = £33,013.

(*c*) *TA 1988, s 60(3)(b); FA 1994, s 200.*

(*d*) *TA 1988, s 60(3)(b); FA 1994, s 200.*

The period from 1.10.98 to 5.4.99 is taxed in 1998/99 and 1999/2000. The overlap period relievable under *TA 1988, s 63A; FA 1994, s 205* is therefore 187 days and the overlap profits are 92/153 × £10,000 and 95/273 × £27,000 – a total of £15,409.

Change of accounting date and basis period

Introduction of statutory code

2.24 Under the preceding year basis of assessment changes of accounting date for unincorporated businesses were dealt with in accordance with the Revenue practice explained in Booklet IR 26 (see Appendix D) and, for changes where there is no accounting date ending in 1994/95, the new accounting date ending in 1995/96, Inland Revenue Tax Bulletin No 18, August 1995, page 242 and No 20, December 1995, page 271 (see Appendix F). Although this procedure had no statutory authority it was approved in *CIR v Helical Bar Ltd 1972 48 TC 221* (see Chapter 24). This is however replaced for the current year basis of assessment by *FA 1994, s 202* introducing substituted *TA 1988, s 62* which is designed to prevent taxpayers obtaining any benefit from deferral of tax on a change of accounting date. Otherwise, for example, an accounting date could be brought forward to defer recognition of profit, or doubly tax a period of abnormally low profit, or defer the accounting date to advance recognition of a loss.

Requirements for valid change

2.25 The statutory revised change of accounting date rules in *TA 1988, s 62* will only apply to changes which meet the requirements of *TA 1988, s 62A; FA 1994, s 203*, except in the case of changes made in the second or third fiscal years. This exception for the second and third years allows a new business complete freedom to change its accounting date where the original date selected has turned out to be inconvenient. As regards partnerships, these requirements are to be applied at the level of the partnership, and not the individual partner, under *TA 1988, s 111(4)(d)* and *(6); FA 1995, s 117(2)*.

2.26 These requirements are:

(*a*) that the accounting period to the new accounting date does not exceed a period of 18 months [*TA 1988, s 62A(1)(2); FA 1994, s 203*]; and

(*b*) notice of the change of accounting date is given to the Revenue by 31 January following the year of assessment in which the accounting change is deemed to take place under substituted *TA 1988, s 62(5)* [*TA 1988, s 62A(3); FA 1994, s 203*] (failure to give notice makes the change ineffective for tax purposes); and either

(*c*) no accounting date change which has been effective for tax purposes has been made in any of the preceding five years of assessment, other than in the opening years under substituted *TA 1988, ss 60* or *61* [*TA 1988, s 62A(4); FA 1994, s 203*]; or

(*d*) there has been a change for tax purposes in the preceding five years of assessment but the notice of change of accounting date sets out the reasons for the change, and the Revenue Officer is satisfied that the change is made for *bona fide* commercial reasons, or he does not object to the change within 60 days of receiving the notice. [*TA 1988, s 62A(5); FA 1994, s 203*].

Invalid change of accounting date

2.27 The first two and either the third or fourth of these conditions must be met in order to make the accounting date change effective for tax purposes. If the change is not effective, the new accounting date is ignored in the fiscal year in which it is adopted [*TA 1988, s 62(3); FA 1994, s 202*] and the basis period for tax purposes for the year is twelve months from the end of the previous basis period under *TA 1988, s 60(3)(b); FA 1994, s 200* (*Example 16*, following 2.35).

2.28 If a change is thus ineffective in one year, but the new accounting date continues to be used, there is deemed to be a change in the following fiscal year, and each subsequent year, until the change satisfies the requirements in 2.26 and becomes effective, if ever. [*TA 1988, s 62(4); FA 1994, s 202*]. An example would be where the change was not effective because of an earlier change within the five year 'close' season, but became so following the end of that period.

2.29 Moreover, in applying *TA 1988, s 62(1); FA 1994, s 202* the Revenue have confirmed that (for the purposes of the 18-month rule) the 'new date' in the year following the actual date of change is the new accounting date and that the actual accounting period (which is defined by *TA 1988, s 62(1)(a); FA 1994, s 202* as the actual period to which accounts are made up) is the period to the new accounting date which is for 12 months and which does not fail the 18-month maximum period test.

This is explained in the following two examples, and also by *Example 15* after 2.35 below.

Example 10

Accounts are made up to 30 June each year until the year 2000. In 2001 the accounting period is extended to 30 April 2002 which is a 22-month accounting period. This therefore fails the 18-month restriction in *TA 1988, s 62A(2); FA 1994, s 203* and the basis period for tax purposes in 2001/02 is the twelve months to 30 June 2001. Similarly there is no valid change in 2002/03 and the basis period is the twelve months to 30 June 2002 (twelve months from the end of the last basis period). In 2003/04 there is a valid change as the actual accounting period is the year ended 30 April 2003 and the basis period is the twelve-month period from 1 May 2002 to 30 April 2003, with an additional overlap period from 1 May 2002 to 30 June 2002.

Example 11

Accounts are made up to 30 June each year until the year 2000. In 2001 the accounting period is extended to 31 March 2002 which is a 21-month accounting period. This therefore fails the 18-month restriction in *TA 1988, s 62A(2); FA 1994, s 203* and the basis period for tax purposes in 2001/02 is the twelve months to 30 June 2001. If accounts continue to be made up to 31 March in each year, in the year ended 31 March 2003 there is another opportunity to change the accounting date and provided that the remaining conditions are met the basis period for 2002/03 is the period from the end of the basis period in 2001/02, i.e. 1 July 2001 to the new accounting date 31.3.2003.

Appeals

2.30 An appeal may be made against the Revenue rejection of a change of accounting date on *bona fide* commercial grounds within 30 days of the date of the notice that the Revenue is not satisfied with the reasons for the change. [*TA 1988, s 62A(6); FA 1994, s 203*]. The appeal would be to the Commissioners under the normal procedure as if it were an appeal against an assessment to tax [*TA 1988, s 62A(7); FA 1994, s 203*], but the powers of the Commissioners are amended to give them specific power merely to set aside the Inspector's notice of dissatisfaction if they consider that the change was for *bona fide* commercial reasons, otherwise they have to confirm the notice. [*TA 1988, s 62A(8); FA 1994, s 203*].

2.31 Obtaining a tax advantage is not regarded as a *bona fide* commercial reason for a change of accounting date. [*TA 1988, s 62A(9); FA 1994,* *s 203*]. Tax advantage for this purpose is not defined. It is a term used in *TA 1988, s 709(1)*, but only for the purposes of transactions in securities under *TA 1988, ss 703–709*. Tax advantage therefore is given a wide general meaning and would include a cash flow advantage arising from deferment of tax.

Extended accounting period skipping a fiscal year

2.32 An accounting period for determining changes in accounting date is a period to which accounts are made up. [*TA 1988, s 62A(10); FA 1994, s 203*]. A change of accounting date is deemed to take place either in the fiscal year in which the new date falls, or, if this results in there being no accounting date in the preceding fiscal year, twelve months before the new date. This prevents a fiscal year not being charged to tax on the grounds that there is no accounting date in the fiscal year, which would otherwise have been covered by making the fiscal year itself the basis period under *TA 1988, s 60(1); FA 1994, s 200*. [*TA 1988, s 62(5); FA 1994, s 202*].

Example 12 (continuing) (following 2.35)

Mr Bisnovet produced accounts to 5 April each year until 2001 when the accounting date was extended to 30 June 2002 and annually thereafter. There is no accounting period ending in 2001/02 so the change on 30 June 2002 is deemed to take place on 30 June 2001. The 2001/02 basis period is the twelve months to 30 June 2001, the new accounting date.

Shortened accounting period

2.33 If the accounting period from the end of the previous basis period to the new accounting date or deemed accounting date is less than twelve months, or if the year is the year ending in the second fiscal year, the new basis period is the period of twelve months ending with the new accounting date or deemed accounting date. [*TA 1988, s 62(2)(a); FA 1994, s 202*]. If however the new accounting date in the second fiscal year is less than twelve months from commencement, *TA 1988, s 61(2)(b); FA 1994, s 201* applies as explained in 2.16 above. The application of these rules is likely to result in additional overlap profits for an overlap period which would be eligible for overlap relief, dealt with in 2.37 *et seq*. below.

Example 13 (continuing) (following 2.35)

Mr Grigorovich produced accounts to 5 April each year until 5 April 2001 after which the accounting date was brought forward to 30 June 2001 and annually thereafter. The basis period for 2001/02 is the twelve months to 30 June 2001, the new accounting date, with an additional overlap period from 1 July 2000 to 5 April 2001.

Extended accounting period ending in next fiscal year

2.34 If the period from the end of the previous basis period to the new accounting date is in excess of twelve months the whole of the profit for the period to the new accounting date is assessed, unless this period ends in the second fiscal year, in which case the position is as described in 2.16. [*TA 1988, s 62(2)(b); FA 1994, s 202*].

Example 14 (continuing) (following 2.35)

Mr Beriev produced accounts to 31 July each year until 31 July 2000 when the accounting date was extended to 31 January 2002 and annually thereafter. No accounts were prepared for the year ended 31 July 2001. The basis period for 2001/02 is from the end of the previous basis period, i.e. 1 August 2000 to the new accounting date 31 January 2002.

Two accounting periods ending in fiscal year

2.35 Where it is intended to change the accounting date in a manner which would result in an accounting period of more than 18 months it would not be an effective change and therefore an account might be prepared for twelve months and a short period of, say, nine months. If both accounting periods ended in the same fiscal year they would be amalgamated under *TA 1988, s 60(5); FA 1994, s 200* (see 2.12 above) and the basis period would be the extended period covering both accounts under *TA 1988, s 62(2)(b); FA 1994, s 202*.

Example 15 (continuing) (following 2.35)

Mr Samsonov produced accounts to 31 July each year until 31 July 2001 when the accounting date was changed to 31 March 2002 and annually thereafter. Accounts were prepared for the year ended 31 July 2001 which are amalgamated with those to 31 March 2002. The basis period for 2001/02 is from the end of the previous basis period, i.e. 1 August 2000 to the new accounting date 31 March 2002.

Example 12

Extended accounting period skipping a fiscal year (see 2.32)

Mr Bisnovet started business on 1 August 1998 and produced accounts to 5 April each year until April 2001 when the accounting date was extended to 30 June 2002 and annually thereafter. The requirements of *TA 1988, s 62A; FA 1994, s 203* were met.

Profits (as adjusted for tax purposes)

1.8.98 to 5.4.99	£8,000
y/e 5.4.2000	£18,000
y/e 5.4.2001	£24,000
p/e 30.6.2002	£37,500

Taxable

1998/99	1.8.98 to 5.4.99	£8,000	(*a*)
1999/00	y/e 5.4.2000	£18,000	(*b*)
2000/01	y/e 5.4.2001	£24,000	(*c*)
2001/02	y/e 30.6.2001 (9/12 × £24,000 + 3/15 × £37,500)	£25,500	(*d*)
2002/03	y/e 30.6.2002 (12/15 × £37,500)	£30,000	(*e*)

Notes

(*a*) *TA 1988, s 61(1); FA 1994, s 201.*

(*b*) *TA 1988, s 60(3)(a); FA 1994, s 200.*

(*c*) *TA 1988, s 60(3)(b); FA 1994, s 200.*

(*d*) *TA 1988, s 62(5); FA 1994, s 202* makes this the year in which the accounting date is deemed to change as there is no accounting date in the fiscal year. The period is less than twelve months from the end of the previous accounting date (5.4.2001), therefore *TA 1988, s 62(2)(a); FA 1994, s 202* determines the basis period as twelve months ending with the new accounting date. The period 1.7.2000 to 5.4.2001 is taxed in both 2000/01 and 2001/02 and therefore there is an overlap period relievable under *TA 1988, s 63A; FA 1994, s 205* resulting in overlap profits of £18,000 (9/12 × £24,000).

(*e*) *TA 1988, s 60(3)(b); FA 1994, s 200.* Although this is the year in which the new accounting date actually falls, the change is deemed to take place in 2001/02 under *TA 1988, s 62(5); FA 1994, s 202* (see above), therefore the basis period is twelve months from the end of the basis period for the previous year.

Example 13

Shortened accounting period (see 2.33)

Mr Grigorovich started business on 1 August 1998 and produced accounts to 5 April each year until 2001 when the accounting date was brought forward to 30 June and annually thereafter. The requirements of *TA 1988, s 62A; FA 1994, s 203* were met.

Profits (as adjusted for tax purposes)

1.8.98 to 5.4.99	£8,000
y/e 5.4.2000	£18,000
y/e 5.4.2001	£24,000
p/e 30.6.2001	£7,500
y/e 30.6.2002	£30,000

Taxable

1998/99	1.8.98 to 5.4.99	£8,000	(*a*)
1999/00	y/e 5.4.2000	£18,000	(*b*)
2000/01	y/e 5.4.2001	£24,000	(*c*)
2001/02	y/e 30.6.2001		
	(9/12 × £24,000 + £7,500)	£25,500	(*d*)
2002/03	y/e 30.6.2002	£30,000	(*e*)

Notes

(*a*) *TA 1988, s 61(1); FA 1994, s 201.*

(*b*) *TA 1988, s 60(3)(a); FA 1994, s 200.*

(*c*) *TA 1988, s 60(3)(b); FA 1994, s 200.*

(*d*) *TA 1988, s 62(5); FA 1994, s 202* makes this the year in which the accounting date is deemed to change as accounts are made up to a new date in the fiscal year. The period is less than twelve months from the end of the previous accounting date (5.4.2001), therefore *TA 1988, s 62(2)(a); FA 1994, s 202* determines the basis as twelve months ending with the new accounting date. The period 1.7.2000 to 5.4.2001 is taxed in both 2000/01 and 2001/02 and therefore there is an overlap period under *TA 1988, s 63A; FA 1994, s 205* resulting in overlap profits of £18,000 (9/12 × £24,000).

(*e*) *TA 1988, s 60(3)(b); FA 1994, s 200.*

Example 14

Extended accounting period ending in next fiscal year (see 2.34)

Mr Beriev started business on 1 August 1998 and produced accounts to 31 July each year until 2001/02 when the accounting date was extended to

31 January 2002 and annually thereafter. The requirements of *TA 1988, s 62A; FA 1994, s 203* were met.

Profits (as adjusted for tax purposes)

y/e 31.7.1999	£14,000
y/e 31.7.2000	£20,000
p/e 31.1.2002	£41,000
y/e 31.1.2003	£30,000

Taxable

1998/99	1.8.98 to 5.4.99	£9,512	(*a*)
1999/00	y/e 31.7.99	£14,000	(*b*)
2000/01	y/e 31.7.00	£20,000	(*c*)
2001/02	1.8.00 to 31.1.02 (£41,000 – £7,057)	£33,943	(*d*)
2002/03	y/e 31.1.03	£30,000	(*e*)

Notes

(*a*) *TA 1988, s 61(1); FA 1994, s 201* 248/365 × £14,000 = £9,512.

(*b*) *TA 1988, s 60(3)(a); FA 1994, s 200* overlap 1.8.98 to 5.4.99 = £9,512.

(*c*) *TA 1988, s 60(3)(b); FA 1994, s 200.*

(*d*) *TA 1988, s 62(5); FA 1994, s 202* makes this the year in which the accounting date is deemed to change as accounts are made up to a new date in the fiscal year. The period is more than twelve months from the end of the previous basis period (31.7.00), therefore *TA 1988, s 62(2)(b); FA 1994, s 202* determines the basis as the period ending on the new accounting date (i.e. 31.1.02 falling in the fiscal year ended 5.4.02). This is an 18-month accounting period, subject to overlap relief under *TA 1988, s 63A; FA 1994, s 205*, see 2.37 to 2.41 below, of the appropriate proportion of the overlap relief brought forward, i.e.

$$A \times \frac{B - C}{D}$$

$$£9{,}512 \times \frac{549 - 365}{248} = £7{,}057$$

leaving £9,512 – £7,057 = £2,455 to continue to be carried forward under *TA 1988, s 63A; FA 1994, s 205.*

(*e*) *TA 1988, s 60(3)(b); FA 1994, s 200.*

Example 15

Two accounting periods ending in fiscal year (see 2.35)

Mr Samsonov started business on 1 August 1998 and produced accounts to 31 July each year until 2001/02 when the accounting date was changed to 31 March 2002 and annually thereafter. The requirements of *TA 1988, s 62A; FA 1994, s 203* were met by preparing an account to 31 July 2001 and an eight-month account to 31 March 2002.

Profits (as adjusted for tax purposes)

y/e 31.7.1999	£28,000
y/e 31.7.2000	£40,000
y/e 31.7.2001	£50,000
1.8.2001 to 31.3.2002	£35,000
y/e 31.3.2003	£60,000

Taxable

1998/99	1.8.98 to 5.4.99	£19,025	(*a*)
1999/00	y/e 31.7.99	£28,000	(*b*)
2000/01	y/e 31.7.00	£40,000	(*c*)
2001/02	1.8.00 to 31.3.02 £50,000 + £35,000 − £18,641 =	£66,359	(*d*)
2002/03	y/e 31.3.03	£60,000	(*e*)

Notes

(*a*) *TA 1988, s 61(1); FA 1994, s 201*. 248/365 × £28,000 = £19,025.

(*b*) *TA 1988, s 60(3)(a); FA 1994, s 200*, overlap 1.8.98 to 5.4.99 = £19,025.

(*c*) *TA 1988, s 60(3)(b); FA 1994, s 200.*

(*d*) *TA 1988, s 62(2)(b); FA 1994, s 202*. The change of accounting date takes effect in 2001/02, the first year of assessment in which accounts are made up to the new date under *TA 1988, s 62(5); FA 1994, s 202*. *TA 1988, s 60(5); FA 1994, s 200* amalgamates the two accounting periods and *TA 1988, s 62(2)(b); FA 1994, s 202* applies to fix the basis period as the period from the end of the basis period in the previous fiscal year to the new accounting date. This is a 20-month basis period, subject to overlap relief under *TA 1988, s 63A; FA 1994, s 205* of the appropriate proportion of the overlap relief brought forward, i.e.

$$A \times \frac{B - C}{D}$$

$$£19,025 \times \frac{608 - 365}{248} = £18,641$$

leaving £384 to continue to be carried forward under *TA 1988, s 63A; FA 1994, s 205*.

(*e*) *TA 1988, s 60(3)(b); FA 1994, s 200.*

Example 16

Requirements for change not met (see 2.27)

Mr Hackel started business on 1 August 1998 and produced accounts to 31 July each year until 2001/02 when the accounting date was changed to 31 March 2002 and annually thereafter. The requirements of *TA 1988, s 62A; FA 1994, s 203* were not met as the accounting period was 20 months to 31 March 2002. The remaining conditions were met so there was a deemed change at 31 March 2003 under substituted *TA 1988, s 62(4); FA 1994, s 202*.

Profits (as adjusted for tax purposes)	
y/e 31.7.1999	£28,000
y/e 31.7.2000	£40,000
1.8.2000 to 31.3.2002	£85,000
y/e 31.3.2003	£60,000

Taxable			
1998/99	1.8.98 to 5.4.99	£19,025	(*a*)
1999/00	y/e 31.7.99	£28,000	(*b*)
2000/01	y/e 31.7.00	£40,000	(*c*)
2001/02	y/e 31.7.01	£51,000	(*d*)
2002/03	1.8.01 to 31.3.03 (£94,000 – £18,641)	£75,359	(*e*)

Notes

(*a*) *TA 1988, s 61(1); FA 1994, s 201*. 248/365 × £28,000 = £19,025.

(*b*) *TA 1988, s 60(3)(a); FA 1994, s 200*, overlap 1.8.98 to 5.4.99 = £19,025.

(*c*) *TA 1988, s 60(3)(b); FA 1994, s 200.*

(*d*) *TA 1988, s 60(3)(b); FA 1994, s 200*, 12/20 × £85,000 = £51,000. Twelve months from end of previous basis period as not a valid change of accounting date for tax purposes to 31.3.2002 (see 2.24).

(*e*) *TA 1988, s 62(2)(b); FA 1994, s 202*, 8/20 × £85,000 = £34,000 + £60,000 total £94,000. This is a 20-month basis period, subject to overlap relief under *TA 1988, s 63A; FA 1994, s 205* of the appropriate proportion of the overlap relief brought forward, i.e.

$$A \times \frac{B - C}{D}$$

$$£19{,}025 \times \frac{608 - 365}{248} = £18{,}641$$

leaving £384 to continue to be carried forward under *TA 1988, s 63A; FA 1994, s 205*.

Discontinuance

2.36 In the fiscal year in which cessation takes place the basis period is from the end of the basis period ending in the preceding fiscal year to the date of discontinuance. [*TA 1988, s 63(b); FA 1994, s 204*]. Where the cessation takes place in the second fiscal year the basis period is from 6 April to the date of cessation. [*TA 1988, s 63(a); FA 1994, s 204*]. Overlap relief may be available as explained below.

Example 17

Mr Lavochkin had been in business many years and made up his accounts to 30 April each year. He ceased to trade on 31 December 2002.

Profits (as adjusted for tax purposes)

y/e 30.4.2001	£30,000
y/e 30.4.2002	£20,000
p/e 31.12.2002	£5,000

Taxable (subject to overlap relief under *TA 1988, s 63A*)

2001/02	y/e 30.4.2001	£30,000	(*a*)
2002/03	p/e 31.12.2002	£25,000	(*b*)

Notes

(*a*) *TA 1988, s 60(3)(b); FA 1994, s 200.*

(*b*) *TA 1988, s 63(b); FA 1994, s 204* beginning on 1.5.2001 immediately after the basis period for the preceding year of assessment (2001/02, 30.4.2001) and ending at the date of cessation, 31.12.2002.

Overlap relief

General position

2.37 The double charge to tax which results from the inclusion of the profits in more than one basis period is partially relieved if there is a change of accounting date to a date later in the fiscal year, resulting in a basis period in excess of twelve months. Any remaining relief is given on cessation. The relief given on a change of accounting date depends on the overlap period doubly charged and the extent to which the extended accounting period exceeds twelve months. See 2.12 above for the definition of 'overlap profits' and 'overlap period'.

Overlap formula

2.38 The proportion of the overlap profits relieved is found by applying the statutory formula [*TA 1988, s 63A(1); FA 1994, s 205*]:

$$A \times \frac{(B - C)}{D}$$

where

A is the aggregate amount of the overlap profit which has not previously been allowed as an overlap adjustment;

B is the number of days in the basis period, which for the formula to apply at all must be more than 365;

C is the number of days in the year of assessment, either 365 or 366 in the case of a leap year; and

D is the aggregate of the overlap periods of any overlap profits arising on commencement or on an earlier change of accounting date or on transition to the current year basis less any overlap periods already relieved on previous occasions.

[*TA 1988, s 63A(2); FA 1994, s 205*].

Overlap relief and change of accounting date

2.39 It will be appreciated that an overlap period can arise not only on commencement, but also on a change of accounting date resulting in an accounting period of less than twelve months for which the basis period is extended to twelve months under *TA 1988, s 62(2)(a); FA 1994, s 202* and under the transitional provisions of *FA 1994, 20 Sch 2(4)*.

Example 18 (continuing) (following 2.40)

Mr Nieman started business on 1 August 1998 and produced accounts to 31 July each year until 2001/02 when the accounting date was extended to

31 January 2002 and annually thereafter. The requirements of *TA 1988, s 62A; FA 1994, s 203* were met.

Profits (as adjusted for tax purposes)			
y/e 31.7.1999		£28,000	
y/e 31.7.2000		£40,000	
p/e 31.1.2002		£82,000	
y/e 31.1.2003		£60,000	
Taxable			
1998/99	1.8.98 to 5.4.99	£19,025	(*a*)
1999/00	y/e 31.7.99	£28,000	(*b*)
2000/01	y/e 31.7.00	£40,000	(*c*)
2001/02	1.8.00 to 31.1.02 (£82,000 − £14,115)	£67,885	(*d*)
2002/03	y/e 31.1.03	£60,000	(*e*)

Notes

(*a*) *TA 1988, s 61(1); FA 1994, s 201*. 248/365 × £28,000 = £19,025.

(*b*) *TA 1988, s 60(3)(a); FA 1994, s 200*, overlap 1.8.98 to 5.4.99 = £19,025.

(*c*) *TA 1988, s 60(3)(b); FA 1994, s 200.*

(*d*) *TA 1988, s 62(5); FA 1994, s 202* makes this the year in which the accounting date is deemed to change as accounts are made up to a new date in the fiscal year. The period is more than twelve months from the end of the previous basis period (31.7.00), therefore *TA 1988, s 62(2)(b); FA 1994, s 202* determines the basis as the period ending on the new accounting date, i.e. 31.1.02 falling in the fiscal year ended 5.4.02. This is an 18-month accounting period, subject to overlap relief under *TA 1988, s 63A(2); FA 1994, s 205* of the appropriate proportion of the overlap relief brought forward.

$$A \times \frac{(B - C)}{D}$$

$$£19{,}025 \times \frac{549 - 365}{248} = £14{,}115$$

A = overlap profit £19,025 as in (*b*) above
B = long accounting period 1.8.2000 to 31.1.2002 = 549 days
C = days in 2001/02 = 365
D = overlap period available, 1.8.98 to 5.4.99 = 248 days

(*e*) *TA 1988, s 60(3)(b); FA 1994, s 200.*

Overlap relief on cessation

2.40 On cessation the overlap relief is the aggregate of any overlap profits, i.e. the amount doubly charged, less any overlap relief previously given on a change of accounting date. [*TA 1988, s 63A(3); FA 1994, s 205*].

Example 18

In the previous example, following 2.39, Mr Nieman ceased to trade on 30 June 2003.

Profit (as adjusted for tax purposes)		
p/e 30.6.03	£45,000	
Taxable		
2003/04 p/e 30.6.03		
(£45,000 – £4,910)	£40,090	(*f*)

Note

(*f*) *TA 1988, s 63; FA 1994, s 204*, 1.2.03 to 30.6.03 less overlap relief under *TA 1988, s 63A(3); FA 1994, s 205* = £19,025 ((*b*) above) less relief on change in accounting date ((*d*) above) £14,115 leaving £4,910 overlap relief against the profits for the final period. If the relief exceeds the profits a loss will result, relievable in the normal way or as a terminal loss.

Losses and overlap relief

2.41 If a loss making period is included in the basis periods for two successive fiscal years it is only included in the first such period. The loss is treated as nil in the second period to avoid giving excess relief. [*TA 1988, s 63A(4); FA 1994, s 205*]. See Chapter 3.

Transitional provisions

General

2.42 Where a business was in existence prior to 6 April 1994, it continues to be assessed under the old provisions for 1994/95 and 1995/96. There is then a transitional year 1996/97 before the new rules take effect in 1997/98. The transitional provisions are set out in *FA 1994, 20 Sch 1–3*. Businesses ceasing before 6 April 1997 are dealt with entirely under the old rules. [*FA 1994, 20 Sch 3(1)*].

Basis period for 1996/97 and 1997/98

2.43 Where there is an accounting date in 1996/97 the basis period for 1996/97 is that twelve-month period ending with the latest accounting date falling in the year. [*FA 1994, 20 Sch 1(2)(a)*]. This is the 'primary' basis period. But if there is no accounting period ending in 1996/97 the basis period is the fiscal year itself. [*FA 1994, 20 Sch 1(2)(b)*].

2.44 The primary basis period for 1997/98 will be the twelve months from the end of the basis period for 1996/97. [*TA 1988, s 60(3)(b); FA 1994, s 200*]. Where the fiscal year is the appropriate basis period for 1996/97, as a result of a change in accounting date, *TA 1988, s 62; FA 1994, s 202* is applied as if the accounting change were made in the first year of assessment in which accounts are made up to the new date. If the accounting date falls in 1997/98 therefore, the basis period for that year would be the twelve months ending with the new accounting date.

Assessment for 1996/97 where 1995/96 on actual basis

2.45 Where the profits for 1995/96 are assessed on an actual basis under existing *TA 1988, ss 61(4), 62(2)* or *(4)*, the assessment for 1996/97 is also on a fiscal year basis. [*FA 1994, 20 Sch 2(3)*].

Assessment for 1996/97 in all other cases – averaging

2.46 In other cases the assessment for 1996/97 is based on the 'appropriate percentage' of the total of (*a*) the amount of profits or gains of the 'primary' basis period (see 2.43 above) as calculated under substituted *TA 1988, ss 60–63A*, and (*b*) the amount of profits or gains of the 'relevant period'. [*FA 1994, 20 Sch 2(2)*]. The relevant period begins immediately after the end of the basis period for 1995/96 computed under the old rules and ends immediately before the beginning of the primary basis period for the year 1996/97 computed under the new rules. The appropriate percentage is 365 divided by the total number of days in the basis period for 1996/97 (which will be 365 or 366 under *FA 1994, 20 Sch 1(2)*) plus the number of days in the relevant period.

2.47 The transitional profit assessed is therefore the annualised profits for the period from the end of the basis period for 1995/96, on the old rules, to the end of the basis period for 1996/97, on the new rules. [*FA 1994, 20 Sch 2(5)*]. Simply stated, this means that in the case of an established business with annual accounts made up to the same date in 1995/96 and 1996/97, the taxable profit for 1996/97 will be 50 per cent of the aggregate profits for the two years.

Example 19 (continuing) (following 2.48)

Mr Mikoyan produces accounts to 5 April each year. The assessment for 1996/97 is on half the combined profits for the years ended 5 April 1996 and 5 April 1997.

Example 20 (continuing) (following 2.48)

Mr Gurevich produces accounts to 30 September each year. The assessment for 1996/97 is on half the combined profits for the years ended 30 September 1995 and 30 September 1996.

Example 21 (continuing) (following 2.48)

Mr Myasishchyev produces accounts each year to 30 April. The assessment for 1996/97 is on half the combined profits for the years ended 30 April 1995 and 30 April 1996.

Example 22 (continuing) (following 2.48)

Mr Yakovlev started business on 1 April 1994 and produced accounts each year to 31 December. The assessment for 1995/96 is on the first twelve months to 31 March 1995. The basis period for 1996/97 is the year ended on the accounting date in the fiscal year, i.e. 31 December 1996. The relevant period is from the end of the basis period for 1995/96, i.e. 1 April 1995 to the beginning of the primary basis period for 1996/97, i.e. 31 December 1995. The assessment for 1996/97 is on $\frac{365}{365 + 275}$ (days in the combined period) of the combined profits of the basis period (y/e 31.12.96) and the relevant period (1.4.95 to 31.12.95).

If Mr Yakovlev elects for the actual basis for 1994/95 and 1995/96, 1996/97 is on the actual profits of the fiscal year with no averaging. The 1997/98 assessment is however based on the year ended in the accounting period, i.e. the year ended 31 December 1997, being twelve months from the end of the primary basis period for 1996/97, the year ended 31 December 1996.

Example 23 (continuing) (following 2.48)

Mr Sikorsky produces accounts to 31 December each year until 1996/97 when the accounting date is changed to 31 March. The primary basis period for 1996/97 is the year ended 31 March 1997. The primary period for 1995/96 is the year ended 31 December 1994. The relevant period is from the end of the basis period for 1995/96, i.e. 1 January 1995 to the beginning of the primary basis period for 1996/97, i.e. 31 March 1996. The assessment for 1996/97 is on $\frac{365}{365 + 455}$ (days in combined period) of the combined profits of the primary basis period (y/e 31.3.97) and the relevant period (1.1.95 to 31.3.96).

Transitional overlap

2.48 If the basis period for the year 1997/98 begins prior to 6 April 1997, which it would do in most cases other than where accounts are made up for the fiscal year, there is an additional overlap profit relievable on cessation or on a change of accounting date resulting in a basis period in excess of twelve months [*FA 1994, 20 Sch 2(4)*], amounting to the profits of the period which fall before 6 April 1997 and after the end of the basis period for 1996/97, *FA 1995, s 122(2)*.

Where there is a change of accounting date resulting in an accounting period of less than twelve months ending in 1997/98, the basis period is twelve months to the new accounting date under *TA 1988, s 62(2)(a)*. The proportion of the profits for the twelve months to the new accounting date which falls into the basis period for 1996/97 would result in a standard overlap profit within *TA 1988, s 63A(5)*. The transitional overlap relief under *FA 1994, 20 Sch 2(2)* being the proportion of the profits assessable for 1997/98 falling prior to 6 April 1997 is limited to that proportion of the profits which falls after the end of the basis period for 1996/97, as otherwise there would be a double overlap of the same profits. These rules are illustrated in example 24 below.

Where profits are assessable under Schedule D, Case V, the statutory basis requires income to be assessed by reference to the fiscal year and this problem cannot therefore arise. Where, by concession, Schedule D, Case V income has been assessed by reference to an accounting period ending in the preceding year basis of assessment, it is understood that the Revenue will apply transitional relief on the same basis as for Schedule D, Cases I and II.

Example 19 (continuing) (see below)

Mr Mikoyan produces accounts to 5 April. The 1997/98 basis period is the year ended 5 April 1998, no part of which falls before 6 April 1997 so there is no transitional overlap.

Example 20 (continuing) (see below)

Mr Gurevich produces accounts to 30 September. The 1997/98 basis period is the year ended 30 September 1997. The transitional overlap period is from 1.10.96 to 5.4.97.

Example 21 (continuing) (see below)

Mr Myasishchyev produces accounts to 30 April. The 1997/98 basis period is the year ended 30 April 1997. The transitional overlap period is from 1.5.96 to 5.4.97.

Example 22 (continuing) (see below)

Mr Yakovlev produces accounts to 31 December. The 1997/98 basis period is the year ended 31 December 1997. The transitional overlap relief period is from 1.1.97 to 5.4.97.

Example 23 (continuing) (see below)

Mr Sikorsky produces accounts to 31 March. The 1997/98 basis period is the year ended 31 March 1998. The transitional overlap period is from 1.4.97 to 5.4.97.

Example 19

Mr Mikoyan has been in business for many years and produces accounts each year to 5 April.

Profits (as adjusted for tax purposes)

y/e 5.4.94	£20,000
y/e 5.4.95	£22,000
y/e 5.4.96	£26,000
y/e 5.4.97	£24,000

y/e 5.4.98	£30,000
y/e 5.4.99	£28,000

Assessable/taxable

1994/95	preceding year basis	£20,000	(*a*)
1995/96	preceding year basis	£22,000	(*b*)
1996/97	transitional year	£24,966	(*c*)
1997/98	current year basis	£30,000	(*d*)
1998/99	current year basis	£28,000	(*e*)

Notes

(*a*) *TA 1988, s 60(3)* (original version).

(*b*) *TA 1988, s 60(3)* (original version).

(*c*) Primary basis period for 1996/97 under *TA 1988, s 60(3)(b); FA 1994, s 200* — £24,000

Relevant period under *FA 1994 20 Sch 2(2)(b), (5)* i.e. 6.4.95 to 5.4.96 — £26,000

Aggregate, *FA 1994, 20 Sch 2(2)* — £50,000

Appropriate percentage under *FA 1994, 20 Sch 2(5)*

$$£50{,}000 \times \frac{365}{366 + 365} = £24{,}966$$

There is no transitional overlap period under *FA 1994, 20 Sch 2(4)* as the basis period for 1997/98 begins on 6 April 1997 under *TA 1988, s 60(3)(b); FA 1994, s 200*.

(*d*) Substituted *TA 1988, s 60(3)(b); FA 1994, s 200*.

(*e*) Substituted *TA 1988, s 60(3)(b); FA 1994, s 200*.

Example 20

Mr Gurevich has been in business for many years and produces accounts each year to 30 September.

Profits (as adjusted for tax purposes)

y/e 30.9.93	£20,000
y/e 30.9.94	£22,000
y/e 30.9.95	£26,000
y/e 30.9.96	£24,000
y/e 30.9.97	£30,000
y/e 30.9.98	£28,000

Assessable/taxable

1994/95	preceding year basis	£20,000	(*a*)
1995/96	preceding year basis	£22,000	(*b*)
1996/97	transitional year	£24,966	(*c*)
1997/98	current year basis	£30,000	(*d*)
1998/99	current year basis	£28,000	(*e*)

Notes

(*a*) *TA 1988, s 60(3)* (original version, accounting year ending in preceding fiscal year).

(*b*) *TA 1988, s 60(3)* (original version).

(*c*) Basis period for 1996/97 under *TA 1988, s 60(3)(b); FA 1994, s 200* (accounting year to 30.9.96 ending in current fiscal year) £24,000

Relevant period under *FA 1994, 20 Sch 2(2)(b), (5)* i.e. 1.10.94 to 30.9.95 £26,000

Aggregate, *FA 1994, 20 Sch 2(2)* £50,000

Appropriate percentage under *FA 1994, 20 Sch 2(5)*

$$£50{,}000 \times \frac{365}{366 + 365} = £24{,}966$$

Overlap period under *FA 1994, 20 Sch 2(4)*: part of basis period for 1997/98, year ending 30 September 1997, which falls before 6 April 1997 and after 30 September 1996, i.e. 1.10.96 to 5.4.97, i.e. 187 days,

$$\text{overlap profits } £30{,}000 \times \frac{187}{365} = £15{,}370$$

(*d*) Substituted *TA 1988, s 60(3)(b); FA 1994, s 200.*

(*e*) Substituted *TA 1988, s 60(3)(b); FA 1994, s 200.*

Example 21

Mr Myasishchyev has been in business for many years and produces accounts each year to 30 April.

Profits (as adjusted for tax purposes)

y/e 30.4.93	£20,000
y/e 30.4.94	£22,000
y/e 30.4.95	£26,000

y/e 30.4.96	£24,000	
y/e 30.4.97	£30,000	
y/e 30.4.98	£28,000	
Assessable/taxable		
1994/95 preceding year basis	£20,000	(*a*)
1995/96 preceding year basis	£22,000	(*b*)
1996/97 transitional year	£24,966	(*c*)
1997/98 current year basis	£30,000	(*d*)
1998/99 current year basis	£28,000	(*e*)

Notes

(*a*) *TA 1988, s 60(3)* (original version, accounting year ending in preceding fiscal year).

(*b*) *TA 1988, s 60(3)* (original version).

(*c*) Basis period for 1996/97 under *TA 1988, s 60(3)(b); FA 1994, s 200* (accounting year to 30.4.96 ending in current fiscal year) £24,000

Relevant period under *FA 1994, 20 Sch 2(2)(b), (5)* i.e. 1.5.94 to 30.4.95 £26,000

Aggregate, *FA 1994, 20 Sch 2(2)* £50,000

Appropriate percentage under *FA 1994, 20 Sch 2(5)*

$$£50,000 \times \frac{365}{366 + 365} = £24,966$$

Overlap period under *FA 1994, 20 Sch 2(4)*: part of basis period for 1997/98, year ending 30 April 1997, which falls before 6 April 1997 and after 30 April 1996, i.e. 1.5.96 to 5.4.97, i.e. 340 days, overlap profits

$$£30,000 \times \frac{340}{365} = £27,945$$

(*d*) *TA 1988, s 60(3)(b); FA 1994, s 200.*

(*e*) *TA 1988, s 60(3)(b); FA 1994, s 200.*

Example 22

Mr Yakovlev started business on 1 April 1994 and made up his accounts to 31 December each year.

Profits (as adjusted for tax purposes)

1.4.94 to 31.12.94	£12,000
y/e 31.12.95	£14,000
y/e 31.12.96	£6,000
y/e 31.12.97	£24,000
y/e 31.12.98	£21,000

Assessable/taxable

1993/94	1.4.94 to 5.4.94 5/275 × £12,000	=	£218	(*a*)
1994/95	1.4.94 to 31.3.95 £12,000 + £3,500 (3/12 × £14,000)	=	£15,500	(*b*)
1995/96	1.4.94 to 31.3.95 £12,000 + £3,500 (3/12 × £14,000)	=	£15,500	
1996/97	Transitional year		£9,395	(*c*)
1997/98	y/e 31.12.97		£24,000	
1998/99	y/e 31.12.98		£21,000	

Notes

(*a*) *TA 1988, s 61(1)* (original version, profits from commencement to next 5 April).

(*b*) *TA 1988, s 60(4)* (original version, no accounting years ending in previous fiscal year, usual Revenue choice of twelve-month period).

(*c*) Basis period for 1996/97 under *TA 1988, s 60(3)(b); FA 1994, s 200* (accounting year to 31.12.96 ending in current fiscal year) £6,000

Relevant period under *FA 1994, 20 Sch 2(2)(b), (5)* i.e. 1.4.95 to 31.12.95 9/12 × £14,000 £10,500

Aggregate *FA 1994, 20 Sch 2(2)* £16,500

Appropriate percentage under *FA 1994, 20 Sch 2(5)*

$$£16{,}500 \times \frac{365}{366 + 275} = £9{,}395$$

Overlap period under *FA 1994, 20 Sch 2(4)*: part of basis period for 1997/98, year ended 31 December 1997, which falls before 6 April 1997 and after 31 December 1996, i.e. 1.1.97 to 5.4.97, i.e. 95 days, overlap profits

$$£24{,}000 \times \frac{95}{365} = £6{,}247$$

Mr Yakovlev has the option to elect for the second and third years of assessment to be charged on an actual basis under *TA 1988, s 62; FA 1994, s 202*. If he so elects the figures become:

Assessable/taxable

1993/94	1.4.94 to 5.4.94			
	5/275 × £12,000 =		£218	(*a*)
1994/95	6.4.94 to 5.4.95			
	270/275 × £12,000 =	£11,782		
	95/365 × £14,000 =	£3,644	£15,426	(*b*)
1995/96	6.4.95 to 5.4.96			
	270/365 × £14,000 =	£10,356		
	96/366 × £6,000 =	£1,574	£11,930	(*c*)
1996/97	6.4.96 to 5.4.97			
	270/366 × £6,000 =	£4,426		
	95/365 × £24,000 =	£6,246	£10,672	(*d*)
1997/98	y/e 31.12.97		£24,000	(*e*)
1998/99	y/e 31.12.98		£21,000	(*f*)

Notes

(*a*) *TA 1988, s 61(1)* (original version) profits from commencement to next 5 April.

(*b*) *TA 1988, s 62(2)* (original version) profits on actual basis for fiscal year.

(*c*) *TA 1988, s 62(2)* (original version) profits on actual basis for fiscal year. The total for 1994/95 and 1995/96 on actual basis is £27,356 £15,426 + £11,930) compared with £31,000 (£15,500 + £15,500) on the original basis so the election is likely to be made.

(*d*) *FA 1994, 20 Sch 2(3)*, as 1995/96 is assessed on an actual basis so is 1996/97 instead of the usual transitional provisions.

(*e*) *TA 1988, s 60(3)(b); FA 1994, s 200.*

(*f*) *TA 1988, s 60(3)(b); FA 1994, s 200.* The overlap period and overlap profits under *FA 1994, 20 Sch 2(4)* remain unchanged.

Example 23

Mr Sikorsky produces accounts to 31 December each year until 1996/97 when the accounting date is changed to 31 March as a result of a 15-month accounting period.

Profits (as adjusted for tax purposes)

y/e 31.12.94	£25,000
y/e 31.12.95	£30,000
1.1.96 to 31.3.97	£45,000
y/e 31.3.98	£40,000

Assessable/taxable

1995/96	preceding year basis	£25,000	(*a*)
1996/97	transitional year	£33,345	(*b*)
1997/98	current year basis	£40,000	(*c*)

Notes

(*a*) *TA 1988, s 60(3)* (original version).

(*b*) Primary basis period for 1996/97 under *FA 1994, 20 Sch 1(2)(a)* (twelve months to 31.3.97)

$\frac{12}{15} \times £45{,}000 =$ £36,000

Relevant period under *FA 1994, 20 Sch 2(2)(b)*, i.e. 1.1.95 to 31.3.96

1.1.95 to 31.12.95	£30,000
1.1.96 to 31.3.96 3/15 × £45,000	£9,000
Aggregate, *FA 1994, 20 Sch 2(2)*	£75,000

Appropriate percentage under *FA 1994, 20 Sch 2(5)*

$£75{,}000 \times \frac{365}{365 + 456} =$ £33,345

Overlap period under *FA 1994, 20 Sch 2(4)*; part of basis period for 1997/98, year ended 31 March 1998, which falls before 6 April 1997 and after 31 March 1997, i.e. 1.4.97 to 5.4.97, i.e. 5 days overlap profits.

$£40{,}000 \times \frac{5}{365} = £548$

(*c*) *TA 1988, s 60(3)(b); FA 1994, s 200.*

Example 24

Mr Khioni produces accounts to 31 December each year until 31 December 1996. He then produces accounts for the six months to 30 June 1997.

Profits (adjusted for tax purposes)

y/e 31.12.95	£30,000
y/e 31.12.96	£40,000
p/e 30.6.97	£24,000

Assessable/taxable

1996/97	£34,952	(*a*)
1997/98	£44,000	(*b*)

Notes

(*a*) Basis period for 1996/97 under *TA 1988, s 60(3)(b); FA 1994, s 200*:

Accounting year to 31.12.96 ending in current fiscal year	£40,000
Relevant period under *FA 1994, 20 Sch 2(2)(b), (5)* i.e. 1.1.95 to 31.12.95	£30,000
Aggregate, *FA 1994, 20 Sch 2(2)*	£70,000

Appropriate percentage under *FA 1994, 20 Sch 2(5)*

$$£70{,}000 \times \frac{365}{366 + 365} = \quad £34{,}952$$

Overlap period under *FA 1994, 20 Sch 2(4)*: part of basis period for 1997/98, year ended 30 June 1997, which falls before 6 April 1997 and after end of basis period for 1996/97, 31 December 1996, i.e. 1.1.97 to 5.4.97, i.e. 95 days, overlap profits

£24,000 × 95/181 = £12,597

(*b*) *TA 1988, s 62(5); FA 1994, s 202* makes this the year in which the accounting date is deemed to change as accounts are made up to a new date in the fiscal year. The period is less than twelve months from the end of the previous basis period (31.12.96), therefore *TA 1988, s 62(2)(a); FA 1994, s 202* determines the basis as twelve months ending with the new accounting date, i.e. £40,000 × 6/12 + £24,000 = £44,000, year ended 30 June 1997. The period 1.7.96 to 31.12.96 is taxed in both 1996/97 and 1997/98 and therefore there is a standard overlap period under *TA 1988, s 63A; FA 1994, s 205*, resulting in overlap profits of £20,000 (6/12 × £40,000).

Cessation pre-6 April 1998

2.49 In order to prevent exploitation of the preceding year basis of assessment by avoiding Revenue adjustments on cessation by delaying the cessation until after 5 April 1997, anti-avoidance provisions are introduced. If the cessation was prior to 6 April 1997 the old rules continue to apply. [*FA 1994, 20 Sch 3(1)*]. If the cessation took place in 1997/98 the Revenue may direct that the old rules continue to apply. In the first instance the self-assessment provisions will apply to 1996/97 under the normal transitional rules, but the Revenue may make a direction for the old rules to apply if the profits or gains chargeable for 1995/96 and 1996/97 are increased by adjusting the assessments to an actual basis. [*FA 1994, 20 Sch 3(2)*].

2.50 This has the effect of charging the final year 1997/98 on the actual basis, not on the new basis, with overlap relief in spite of the Revenue's

Tax Bulletin No 10, February 1994, page 112 which incorrectly states that 1997/98 is not affected by the direction.

Example 25

Mr Antonov had been in business for many years and produced accounts to 30 June each year until 31 January 1998 when he ceased to trade.

Profits (as adjusted for tax purposes)		
y/e 30.6.93	£36,000	
y/e 30.6.94	£30,000	
y/e 30.6.95	£24,000	
y/e 30.6.96	£18,000	
y/e 30.6.97	£12,000	
p/e 31.1.98	£5,000	
Assessable/taxable		
1994/95 preceding year basis	£36,000	(*a*)
1995/96 preceding year basis	£30,000	(*b*)
1996/97 transitional year	£20,971	(*c*)
1997/98 year of cessation	£8,822	(*d*)

Notes

(*a*) *TA 1988, s 60(3)* (original version) accounting year ending in preceding year of assessment.

(*b*) *TA 1988, s 60(3)* as above.

(*c*) Basis period for 1996/97 under *TA 1988, s 60(3)(b); FA 1994, s 200*, accounting year, ending 30 June 1996 in fiscal year. £18,000

Relevant period under *FA 1994, 20 Sch 2(2)(b)(5)* i.e. 1.7.94 to 30.6.95 £24,000

Aggregate, *FA 1994, 20 Sch 2(2)* £42,000

Appropriate percentage under *FA 1994, 20 Sch 2(5)*

$$£42{,}000 \times \frac{365}{366 + 365} = £20{,}971$$

(*d*) *TA 1988, s 63; FA 1994, s 204*, period from end of basis period for 1996/97, 1 July 1996 to date of cessation 31 January 1998, i.e. £12,000 year ended 30 June 1997 plus £5,000 period ending 31 January 1998, i.e. £17,000 less overlap relief under *TA 1988, s 63A(3); FA 1994, s 205* £8,178 (see below) = £8,822.

Overlap period under *FA 1994, 20 Sch 2(4)*, part of basis period for 1997/98 which falls before 6 April 1997, 1.7.96 to 5.4.97 i.e. 279 days

overlap profits £17,000 × $\frac{279}{580*}$ = £8,178

* period 1.7.1996 to 31.1.1998 365 + 215 days.

Revenue direction

The Revenue may direct that the new rules do not to apply under *FA 1994, 20 Sch 3(2)*.

1994/95	preceding year basis	£36,000	(*a*)
1995/96	preceding year basis	£30,000	(*b*)
1996/97	preceding year basis	£24,000	(*c*)
1997/98	6 April to date of cessation	£8,000	(*d*)

Notes

(*a*) *TA 1988, s 60(3)* (original version).

(*b*) *TA 1988, s 60(3)* (original version).

(*c*) *TA 1988, s 60(3)* (original version).

(*d*) *TA 1988, s 63(1)(a)* (original version), i.e. £3,000 (3/12 × £12,000) + £5,000. The total of 1996/97 and 1997/98 on this basis is £32,000 (£24,000 + £8,000) compared with £29,793 (£20,971 + £8,822) on the new basis so the Revenue are likely to make this direction.

The Revenue have a further option to compute 1995/96 and 1996/97 on an actual fiscal year basis under *TA 1988, s 63(1)(b)* (original version).

1995/96 actual basis		
3/12 × £24,000 =	£6,000	
9/12 × £18,000 =	£13,500	
		£19,500
1996/97 actual basis		
3/12 × £18,000 =	£4,500	
9/12 × £12,000 =	£9,000	
		£13,500
		£33,000

However, this is less than as originally computed under the old rules which amounted to £54,000 (£30,000 + £24,000) and this further option would not be exercised in this instance.

Extra statutory concession A7, which prevents the cessation provisions of the preceding year basis of assessment applying unfairly where a business or other source of income passes on death to the spouse of the deceased, is withdrawn. With the introduction of the current year basis of assessment, the precise profits of a business will be taxed over the life of the business and the provisions of ESC A7 are no longer required. Withdrawal, effective from 6 April 1995 for businesses or other sources of income which commenced after 5 April 1994, and for those in existence on 5 April 1994, withdrawal will be effective from a date yet to be announced but not before 6 April 1997. (Inland Revenue press release, 4 April 1995).

Cessation in 1998/99

2.51 Where the cessation takes place in 1998/99 and the profits which would have been charged to tax for 1996/97, had they been calculated on an actual basis, exceed those charged under the transitional provisions, or would have done had it not been for the losses brought forward under *TA 1988, s 385*, the Revenue may make a direction for 1996/97 to be assessed on an actual basis instead of following the transitional year rules. Losses can be brought forward against the recalculated profits. [*FA 1994, 20 Sch 3(3), (4)*]. Note that the direction does not disapply the new rules for 1996/97, as stated incorrectly in the Revenue's Tax Bulletin No 10, page 112. 1996/97 is charged on the fiscal year basis under *FA 1994, 20 Sch 3(4)*.

2.52 Any adjustments arising from the direction should be made by an additional assessment or a reduction or discharge, as necessary. [*FA 1994, 20 Sch 3(5)*].

Example 26

Mr Adler had carried on trading for many years, making up his accounts to 30 June each year until he ceased to trade on 31 December 1998.

Profits (as adjusted for tax purposes)

y/e 30.6.94	£30,000
y/e 30.6.95	£28,000
y/e 30.6.96	£24,000
y/e 30.6.97	£22,000
y/e 30.6.98	£16,000
1.7.98 to 31.12.98	£3,000

Assessable/taxable

1995/96	preceding year basis	£30,000	(*a*)
1996/97	transitional year	£25,964	(*b*)
1997/98	current year basis	£22,000	(*c*)
1998/99	year of discontinuance	£2,184	(*d*)

Notes

(*a*) *TA 1988, s 60(3)* (original version).

(*b*) Basis period for 1996/97
y/e 30.6.96 [*FA 1994, 20 Sch 2(2)(a)*] £24,000

Relevant period under *FA 1994, 20 Sch 2(2)(b)*
y/e 30.6.95 £28,000

Aggregate *FA 1994, 20 Sch 2(2)* £52,000

Appropriate percentage under *FA 1994, 20 Sch 2(5)*

$$£52{,}000 \times \frac{365}{366 + 365} = £25{,}964$$

(*c*) *TA 1988, s 60(3)(b); FA 1994, s 200*, y/e 30.6.97

(*d*) *TA 1988, s 63(b); FA 1994, s 204* y/e 30.6.98 = £16,000
+ p/e 31.12.98 £3,000, total £19,000
less overlap relief, overlap period
1.7.96 to 5.4.97, overlap profits
279/365 × £22,000 = £16,816
final assessment £19,000 − £16,816 = £2,184

Possible Revenue direction under *FA 1994, 20 Sch 3(3), (4)*. 1996/97 on transitional rules (as above) £25,964

1996/97 on actual basis	
3/12 × y/e 30.6.96 (£24,000)	£6,000
9/12 × y/e 30.6.97 (£22,000)	£16,500
	£22,500

As this is less than the amount assessed for 1996/97 under the transitional rules there would be no Revenue direction.

Example 27

Mr Bartini had been in business for many years and produced accounts to 30 September each year until 30 September 1998 when he ceased to trade.

Profits (as adjusted for tax purposes)

y/e 30.9.94	£20,000
y/e 30.9.95	£25,000
y/e 30.9.96	£30,000
y/e 30.9.97	£60,000
y/e 30.9.98	£20,000

Assessable/taxable

1995/96	y/e 30.9.94	£20,000	(*a*)
1996/97	transitional year, or	£27,462	(*b*)
	on Revenue direction	£45,000	
1997/98	y/e 30.9.97	£49,260	(*c*)
1998/99	y/e 30.9.98	£Nil	(*d*)

Notes

(*a*) *TA 1988, s 60(3)* (original version).

(*b*) Basis period for 1996/97 under *TA 1988, s 60(3)(b); FA 1994, s 200* accounting year ending 30 September 1996 in fiscal year under *FA 1994, 20 Sch 2(2)(a)* £30,000

Relevant period under *FA 1994, 20 Sch 2(2)(b), (5)* i.e. 1.10.94 to 30.9.95 £25,000

Aggregate, *FA 1994, 20 Sch 2(2)* £55,000

Appropriate percentage under *FA 1994, 20 Sch 2(5)*

$$£55{,}000 \times \frac{365}{366 + 365} = \quad £27{,}462$$

but see Revenue option below.

Overlap period under *FA 1994, 20 Sch 1(4)* part of basis period for 1997/98 which falls before 6 April 1997, i.e. 1.10.96 to 5.4.97, 187 days, overlap profits

$$£60{,}000 \times \frac{187}{365} = £30{,}740.$$

(*c*) *TA 1988, s 60(3)(b); FA 1994, s 200*, accounting year ending in fiscal year, £60,000 y/e 30.9.97, less overlap relief under *TA 1988, s 63A(4); FA 1994, s 205* carried back as a loss under substituted *TA 1988, s 380 (1)(b)* £10,740 (£30,740 less relieved in 1998/99 £20,000).

(*d*) Substituted *TA 1988, s 63; FA 1994, s 204* period from end of previous basis period, i.e. 1.10.97 to date of cessation 30.9.98, i.e. £20,000 less overlap relief as above £30,740, excess overlap relief available for loss relief £10,740, as above.

Revenue direction
Under *FA 1994, 20 Sch 3(3)(4)* the Revenue may direct the substitution of the actual profits in the fiscal year 1996/97 for those assessed where there is a cessation prior to 6 April 1999. The actual profits for 1996/97 would be:

6/12 × £30,000 (y/e 30.9.96)	£15,000
6/12 × £60,000 (y/e 30.9.97)	£30,000
	£45,000

As £45,000 is greater than the amount charged under the transitional year provisions of £27,462, the Revenue should make the direction and assess £45,000 for 1996/97.

Transitional anti-avoidance measures

2.53 The measures to prevent tax avoidance via exploitation of the transitional rules are necessarily complex because of the numerous ways in which these rules could be so exploited. These include a change of accounting policies, deferment of expenses, an acceleration of income or a change of accounting date in the transitional period, all with a view to maximising the profits falling in the transitional period which are averaged down to the annual equivalent under the transitional rules (see Chapter 24).

Lloyd's underwriters

2.54 Lloyd's underwriters are assessed on a calendar year basis and the calendar year is coterminous with the fiscal year in which it ends. Therefore an underwriter commencing on 1 January 1994 is deemed to have commenced on 6 April 1994, which under the old rules would have been assessed for 1994/95. This does not however work for self-assessment and it is in future provided that the year in which the underwriting results are declared will be the fiscal year in respect of which they are taxed.

2.55 Because Lloyd's currently runs a three-year rolling account, the 1994 calendar year is not closed until 31 December 1996 and the results for that year would be declared in May 1997. These figures therefore form the basis of assessment for 1997/98 under *FA 1994, s 218(3)*. The detailed amendments for Lloyd's underwriters are contained in *FA 1994, ss 219–230* and *21 Sch*, and are outside the scope of this work.

Farmers

2.56 Following the recent concern over BSE, for accounts purposes some farmers have attempted to put nil or nominal valuations on their cattle. The Revenue do not accept that nil or nominal valuations are appropriate and have set special rules for the valuation of cattle for farmers with accounting dates falling between 20 March and 31 May. For farmers who normally prepare accounts to March, March 1996 will fall halfway through the two-year basis period for 1996/97 and the Revenue would rather such farmers avoided the valuation problem by preparing a single, two-year account to March 1997 rather than separate accounts for each year. However, if the valuation is so low as to produce a loss for one year, the farmer would do better to produce two separate accounts because under the transitional rules, if one year shows a profit and the other a loss, the profit is averaged but full relief may be claimed for the loss. (Inland Revenue Press Release 29 April 1996, see Appendix C).

Chapter 3

Loss Relief

Introduction

3.1 Under the existing provisions of *TA 1988, s 380* losses arising in a fiscal year, or by Revenue practice, losses in respect of an accounting year ending in a fiscal year, can be set against the total income of that year. This will include the profits of the preceding year assessed in that year under the normal preceding year basis. Alternatively, losses can be carried forward against the total income of the following year. The provisions are recast to reflect the current year basis while preserving the intention behind the existing legislation. As capital allowances are given as a trading expense there is no need to include capital allowances separately and *TA 1988, s 383* becomes unnecessary. The trade must have been carried on on a commercial basis with a view to the realisation of profit, *TA 1988, s 384*.

Set-off

3.2 As profits are assessed on the basis of the accounting year ending in the fiscal year, a loss may be set against the total income of the preceding fiscal year, thus preserving the one-year carry back, or set against total income for the year in which the losses arise.[*TA 1988, s 380(1); FA 1994, s 209(1)*]. The loss is computed in the same way as a profit by reference to the accounting year ending in the fiscal year, not by apportioning the loss over the fiscal year, as under the previous statutory provisions. [*TA 1988, s 382(3); FA 1994, s 209(3)*]. Relief cannot be given for the same loss twice and it is not possible to claim part of the loss except to the extent that it exceeds available income.

3.3 A claim must be made within one year of the filing date of 31 January following the end of the year of assessment in which the loss arises. The taxpayer may determine whether he prefers to set the loss against the income of the year of the loss before carrying back any balance to the preceding year, or claim relief so far as possible against the income of the preceding year and any balance in the year of the loss. Relief given for a loss arising in the current year takes precedence over a loss arising in a succeeding period carried back. [*TA 1988, s 380(2); FA 1994, s 209(1)*]. The loss is claimed against the current year income under *TA 1988, s 380(1)(a); FA 1994, s 209(1)* and against the preceding year under *TA 1988, s 380(1)(b); FA 1994, s 209(1)*. A loss sustained in 1995/96 can be set against total income for 1995/96 or 1996/97 under *FA 1994, s 209(7)* as amended by *FA 1995, s 118*.

Example 1 (continuing) (following 3.8)

Mr Kamov started business on 1 August 1998 and produced accounts to 31 December 1998 and annually thereafter. He made a loss in the year ended 31 December 2000 which could be claimed against any other income in 2000/01 and/or carried back and set against total income for 1999/2000.

Loss in early years of trade

3.4 *TA 1988, s 381* allows relief for losses in the first four fiscal years of a trade to be carried back against total income of the three preceding years, using the earliest available income first. There is a minor amendment to these provisions to make it clear that the loss relief is available against the whole of the claimant's income up to the amount of the loss. Apparently, it was considered that the existing wording might not cover the situation where the loss exceeded the claimant's income, although this was not a point which the Revenue have taken or would take in practice. [*FA 1994, s 209(2)*].

Example 2 (continuing) (following 3.8)

Mr Yuriev started business on 1 August 1998 and made up accounts to 31 July 1999 and annually thereafter. The first year's accounts showed a loss. The loss for 1998/99 (proportion to 5 April 1999 as first year) can be set against total income for 1998/99 and/or 1997/98 under *TA 1988, s 380; FA 1994, s 209(1)* and the balance of the loss which falls in 1999/2000 (6 April 1999 to 31 July 1999) can be set against total income for 1999/2000 and/or 1998/99.

However as the loss arises in the first four years of trading it may, under *TA 1988, s 381; FA 1994, s 209(2)*, be carried back. The loss for 1998/99 can be set against total income for 1995/96 (carried back three years) with any excess against total income for 1996/97, and any further excess against total income for 1997/98. Any remaining balance can be set against 1998/99 under *TA 1988, s 380(1)(a); FA 1994, s 209(1)*.

The loss for 1999/2000 can similarly be set against any remaining total income for 1996/97, then 1997/98, then 1998/99 under amended *TA 1988, s 381; FA 1994, s 209(2)* with any balance claimed in 1999/2000 under *TA 1988, s 380(1)(a); FA 1994, s 209(1)*.

No double counting of losses

3.5 Where a loss would be included in the computation of two successive years of assessment, for example, under the opening provisions or on a change of accounting date, the loss is only given in the first year in which it is available and is treated as zero in the second year. [*TA 1988, s 382(4); FA 1994, s 209(3)*].

Example 3 (continuing) (following 3.8)

Mr Zhukovsky had produced accounts for the year to 5 April up to and including the year 2000/01 which produced a loss. He then produced accounts for a short period to 30 June 2001 and annually thereafter. The assessment for 2001/02 would be the twelve months ending on the new accounting date 30 June 2001, which includes nine months of the loss for the year ended 5 April 2001. As the loss has been included in 2000/01 however it is treated as nil in 2001/02 to prevent double counting.

Loss carry forward

3.6 The loss carry forward provisions of *TA 1988, s 385* are largely recast to take account of the fact that losses are calculated on the same basis as profits and therefore under the current year basis include capital allowances as a trading expense. *TA 1988, s 385(1); FA 1994, s 209(4)* provides that where a loss has been sustained in a trade, profession or vocation carried on alone or in partnership and relief has not otherwise been given, a claim may be made for the unrelieved loss to be carried forward and set off against the income of the trade, profession or vocation for subsequent years of assessment. Losses must be set against the first available profit and reduce the taxable income by the amount of the loss brought forward. It is no longer necessary to claim for the unrelieved loss for each profitable year, as under the old rules. A single claim will suffice if made within six years of the end of the year of assessment in which the loss arises, or five years from the filing date under *FA 1994, 19 Sch 14* from 1996/97. [*FA 1994, s 209(4)(5)*]. The carry forward of losses against income from a company on a transfer of the business of the company under *TA 1988, s 386* continues with amendments.

Example 1 (continuing) (following 3.8)

Mr Kamov, making up his accounts to 31 December each year, suffered a loss in the calendar year 2000. A loss remained unrelieved after setting the loss against total income in 2000/01 and carrying back so far as possible. The balance of the loss unrelieved can be carried forward under *TA 1988, s 385; FA 1994, s 209(4)(5)* and set-off against future profits of the same trade, profession or vocation.

Terminal losses

3.7 A minor alteration is made to the terminal loss provisions of *TA 1988, ss 388* and *389* to enable terminal loss relief to be available for the final year of assessment as well as for the three preceding fiscal years. [*FA 1994, s 209(6)*].

Example 4

Mr Grushin made up his accounts to 30 November each year until 31 August 2003 when the business ceased. He had no other income until 1 January 2004 when he took a job which produced earnings of £10,000 in 2003/04. The results (as adjusted for tax purposes) were as follows:

y/e 30.11.1999	£85,000
y/e 30.11.2000	£65,000
y/e 30.11.2001	£50,000
y/e 30.11.2002 loss	(£20,000)
1.12.2002 to 31.8.2003 loss	(£110,000)

Assessable/taxable before loss relief

1999/00	current year	£85,000
2000/01	current year	£65,000
2001/02	current year	£50,000
2002/03	current year	£Nil
2003/04	current year	£Nil

Loss relief available

2001/02 current year	£50,000
Less loss carried back under *TA 1988, s 380(1)(b); FA 1994, s 209(1)*	£20,000
Amended assessment	£30,000

Terminal loss

2003/04 loss in last twelve months of trading	
1.12.2002 to 31.8.2003	£110,000
1.9.2002 to 30.11.2002	
	£Nil
(already relieved under *TA 1988, s 380(1)(b); FA 1994, s 209(1)*)	
Total terminal loss	£110,000
Set-off against income in 2003/04	£10,000
Loss carried back	£100,000
Set-off against income in 2002/03	£Nil
Loss carried back	£100,000

Set-off against income in 2001/02	£30,000
Loss carried back	£70,000
Set-off against income in 2000/01	£65,000
Loss unrelieved	£5,000

Commencement date for new rules

3.8 The new rules for loss relief apply in full from 1997/98 and subsequent years of assessment for businesses which commenced prior to 6 April 1994 so that the averaging provisions of the transitional year 1996/97 do not restrict the relief available. [*FA 1994, s 209(7)(8); FA 1995, s 118(7)*].

Example 5 (continuing) (see below)

Mr Groppius made up his accounts to 30 September each year. He had no other income. He incurred a loss in the year ended 30 September 1996, the 'primary' basis period for the transitional year 1996/97. The transitional year assessment is calculated by treating the profits and gains for the year ended 30 September 1996 as nil, as there are no such profits or gains. The transitional year is therefore half the income for the year ended 30 September 1995. The loss relief is then given under the existing loss relief provisions of *TA 1988, s 380* for the loss falling in 1995/96 and 1996/97, the loss for the year ended 30 September 1996 being apportioned over those two years on the strict old rule basis.

Example 1

Set-off and carry forward

Mr Kamov started business on 1 August 1998 and produced accounts to 31 December 1998, i.e. for a period of less than twelve months ending in the fiscal year of commencement, and annually thereafter. He also had investment income of £2,000 a year.

Profits and losses (as adjusted for tax purposes)

1.8.98 to 31.12.98	£5,000	
y/e 31.12.99	£16,500	
y/e 31.12.2000 (loss)	£(22,500)	
y/e 31.12.2001	£28,500	
Taxable – subject to loss relief		
1998/99 1.8.98 to 5.4.99		
£5,000 + (3/12 × £16,500)	£9,125	(*a*)

1999/00 y/e 31.12.99	£16,500	(*b*)
2000/01 y/e 31.12.00	Nil	(*c*)
2001/02 y/e 31.12.01	£28,500	(*d*)

Notes

(*a*) *TA 1988, s 61(1); FA 1994, s 201* commencement to 5 April.

(*b*) *TA 1988, s 61(2); FA 1994, s 201* does not apply, although the second year of assessment, as the period from commencement 1.8.98 to the accounting date given by *TA 1988, s 60(5); FA 1994, s 200*, 31.12.99, is not less than twelve months. Therefore, this is the first year of assessment in which there is an accounting date which falls not less than twelve months after the commencement date and the basis period is fixed by *TA 1988, s 60(3)(a); FA 1994, s 200.*

(*c*) *TA 1988, s 60(3)(b); FA 1994, s 200.*

(*d*) *TA 1988, s 60(3)(b); FA 1994, s 200.*

The period from 1.1.99 to 5.4.99 is taxed both for 1998/99 and 1999/00 and is therefore an overlap period relieved under *TA 1988, s 63A; FA 1994, s 205* resulting in overlap profits of £4,125 (3/12 × £16,500).

Loss relief available
The loss for the year ended 31 December 2000 is £22,500. This may be relieved as follows (ignoring relief under *TA 1988, s 381; FA 1994, s 209(2)*):

Against investment income in 2000/01 [*TA 1988, s 380(1)(a); FA 1994, s 209(1)*]		£2,000
Against trading profits and investment income in 1999/00 [*TA 1988, s 380(1)(b); FA 1994, s 209(1)*]		£2,000 £16,500
Against trading profits for the year ended 31 December 2001 (balance) [*TA 1988, s 385; FA 1994, s 209(4)(5)*]		£2,000
		£22,500

However, as the investment income in 2000/01 is covered by personal allowances, it is probably better not to claim relief against total income in that year (i.e. not to claim under *TA 1988, s 380(1)(a); FA 1994, s 209(1)*) which would increase the loss carried forward against the profits for the year ended 31 December 2001 to £4,000.

Example 2

Set-off, carry forward and early year losses

Mr Yuriev started business on 1 August 1998 and produced accounts to 31 July 1999, i.e. for a period of twelve months, and annually thereafter. He also had investment income of £3,000 a year and a salary of £6,000 p.a. up to 31.3.1998.

Profits and losses (as adjusted for tax purposes)		
y/e 31.7.1999 (loss)	£(14,000)	
y/e 31.7.2000	£20,000	
y/e 31.7.2001	£26,000	
Taxable – subject to loss relief		
1998/99 (1.8.98 to 5.4.99 8/12 × (£14,000))	Nil	*(a)*
1999/00 y/e 31.7.1999	Nil	*(b)*
2000/01 y/e 31.7.2000	£20,000	*(c)*
2001/02 y/e 31.7.2001	£26,000	*(d)*

Notes

(*a*) *TA 1988, s 61(1); FA 1994, s 201*, commencement to 5 April.

(*b*) *TA 1988, s 61(2); FA 1994, s 201* inapplicable as period from commencement 1.8.98 to accounting date 31.7.99 is not less than twelve months *TA 1988, s 61(2)(a); FA 1994, s 201*. Therefore, the basis period for the first year of assessment in which there is an accounting period under *TA 1988, s 60(3)(a); FA 1994, s 200* is the year ended 31.7.99.

(*c*) *TA 1988, s 60(3)(b); FA 1994, s 200.*

(*d*) *TA 1988, s 60(3)(b); FA 1994, s 200.*

The period from commencement on 1.8.98 to 5.4.99 is taxed both for 1998/99 and 1999/00 and is therefore an overlap period relieved under *TA 1988, s 63A; FA 1994, s 205* but no overlap profits.

Loss relief available
The loss of £14,000 for the year ended 31 July 1999 may be relieved as follows (ignoring relief under *TA 1988, s 381; FA 1994, s 209(2)*):

Against investment income in 1997/98 on the basis of the loss in 1998/99 of £9,333 (8/12 × £14,000 for 1.8.98 to 5.4.99) limited to total income [*TA 1988, s 380(1)(b); FA 1994, s 209(1)*]	£9,000
Against investment income in 1998/99 on loss as above unrelieved (£9,333 − £9,000) limited to total income of £3,000 [*TA 1988, s 380(1)(a); FA 1994, s 209(1)*]	£333

Against the same income in respect of the loss for the year ended 31 July 1999 [*TA 1988, s 380(1); FA 1994, s 209(1)*] £4,667 limited to total income (£3,000–£333)	£2,667
Against future profits from the same trade under *TA 1988, s 385; FA 1994, s 209(4)(5)* £14,000 less relieved £12,000 leaving to be claimed against profits for the year ended 31 July 2000	£2,000
	£14,000

Example 2 as above, but giving loss relief under *TA 1988, s 381; FA 1994, s 209(2)*.

Loss for 1998/99		£9,333	
Loss for 1999/00		4,667	
Total losses available for relief		£14,000	
Loss relief			£
1995/96	Earned income		6,000
	Investment income		3,000
			9,000
	Loss arising 1998/99 £9,333 (limited to total income)		(9,000)
	(balance £333 c/f to 1996/97)		
	Chargeable to tax		Nil
1996/97	Earned income		6,000
	Investment income		3,000
			9,000
	Balance of loss arising 1998/99 (£9,333 − £9,000)		(333)
	Loss arising 1999/00		(4,667)
	Chargeable to tax		£4,000

Example 3

Losses on change of accounting date

Mr Zhukovsky started business on 1 August 1998 and produced accounts to 5 April each year until 2001 when the accounting date was brought forward to 30 June and annually thereafter. The requirements of *TA 1988, s 62A; FA 1994, s 203* were met. He had no other income.

Profits and losses (as adjusted for tax purposes)

1.8.98 to 5.4.99	£8,000
y/e 5.4.2000	£20,000
y/e 5.4.2001 (loss)	£(24,000)
p/e 30.6.2001	£7,500
y/e 30.6.2002	£30,000

Taxable – subject to loss relief

1998/99	1.8.98 to 5.4.99	£8,000	(*a*)
1999/00	y/e 5.4.2000	£20,000	(*b*)
2000/01	y/e 5.4.2001	£Nil	(*c*)
2001/02	y/e 30.6.2001		
	9/12 × £nil + £7,500	£7,500	(*d*)
2002/03	y/e 30.6.2002	£30,000	

Notes

(*a*) *TA 1988, s 61(1); FA 1994, s 201.*

(*b*) *TA 1988, s 60(3)(a); FA 1994, s 200.*

(*c*) *TA 1988, s 60(3)(b); FA 1994, s 200.*

(*d*) *TA 1988, s 62(5); FA 1994, s 202* makes this the year in which the accounting date is deemed to change as accounts are made up to a new date in the fiscal year. The period is less than twelve months from the end of the previous accounting date (5.4.2001), therefore *TA 1988, s 62(2)(a); FA 1994, s 202* determines the basis as twelve months ending with the new accounting date. The loss is counted as nil in the apportionment as it has already been taken into 2000/01, and *TA 1988, s 382(4); FA 1994, s 209(3)* excludes it from being included twice. The period 1.7.2000 to 5.4.2001 is taxed in both 2000/01 and 2001/02 and therefore there is an overlap period under *TA 1988, s 63A; FA 1994, s 205*, but no overlap profits in view of the overall loss for the period.

Loss relief available

The loss for the year ended 5 April 2001 is £24,000. This may be relieved as follows (ignoring relief under *TA 1988, s 381; FA 1994, s 209(2)*):

Against profits for the year ended 5 April 2000 [*TA 1988, s 380(1)(b); FA 1994, s 209(1)*]	£20,000
There is no other income in 2000/01 so no relief under *TA 1988, s 380(1)(a); FA 1994, s 209(1)*.	

The relief to carry forward of (£24,000 – £20,000) £4,000 is used against the profits for the year ending 30 June 2001 of £7,500 reducing them to £3,500 under *TA 1988, s 385; FA 1994, s 209(4)(5)*	£4,000
	£24,000

Example 5

Loss in 1996/97

Mr Groppius made up his accounts to 30 September each year. He had no other income. The results, as adjusted for tax purposes, were as follows:

y/e 30.9.94	£6,000
y/e 30.9.95	£25,000
y/e 30.9.96 (loss)	(£35,000)
y/e 30.9.97	£8,000
y/e 30.9.98	£28,000

Assessable/taxable – before loss relief

1995/96	preceding year basis	£6,000	
1996/97	transitional year	£12,483	(*a*)
1997/98	current year basis	£8,000	
1998/99	current year basis	£28,000	

Notes

(*a*) Primary basis period 1996/97

y/e 30.9.96 [*FA 1994, 20 Sch 1(2)(a) and 2(2)(a)*]	Nil
Relevant period [*FA 1994, 20 Sch 2(5)*] y/e 30.9.95	£25,000
Aggregate	£25,000

Appropriate percentage *FA 1994, 20 Sch 2(2)*

$$£25{,}000 \times \frac{365}{366 + 365} = \qquad £12{,}483$$

Loss relief available

Loss in year ended 30.9.96 £35,000, apportioned to 1996/97 6/12 = £17,500, 1995/96 6/12 = £17,500

1995/96 assessable income	£6,000
loss relief under *TA 1988, s 380(1)* (original enactment)	£6,000
Assessment	Nil
Loss relief carried forward	
1995/96 loss £17,500 − £6,000 =	£11,500
1996/97 assessable income	£12,483
Loss relief under *TA 1988, s 380(2)* (original enactment)	£11,500
	£983
Loss relief under *TA 1988, s 380(1)* (original enactment)	£983
Assessment	Nil
Loss relief carried forward	
1996/97 loss £17,500 − £983	£16,517
1997/98 assessable income	£8,000
Less loss relief brought forward under *TA 1988, s 385; FA 1994, s 209(4)(5)*	£8,000
Assessment	Nil
Loss relief carried forward	
£16,517 − £8,000	£8,517
1998/99 assessable income	£28,000
Less loss relief brought forward under *TA 1988, s 385; FA 1994, s 209(4)(5)*	£8,517
Assessment	£19,483

Example 6

Loss 1997/98

Mr Isacco made up his accounts to 30 April each year. He had no other income.

The results, as adjusted for tax purposes, were as follows:

y/e 30.4.94	£18,000
y/e 30.4.95	£20,000
y/e 30.4.96	£15,000
y/e 30.4.97 (loss)	(£30,000)
y/e 30.4.98	£22,000

Assessable/taxable – before loss relief		
1995/96 preceding year basis	£18,000	
1996/97 transitional year	£17,476	(*a*)
1997/98 current year basis	Nil	
1998/99 current year basis	£22,000	

Notes

(*a*) primary basis period 1996/97 y/e 30.4.96 [*FA 1994, 20 Sch 1(2)(a) and 2(2)(a)*]	£15,000
Relevant period [*FA 1994, 20 Sch 2(5)*]	£20,000
Aggregate	£35,000

Appropriate percentage *FA 1994, 20 Sch 2(2)*

$$£35{,}000 \times \frac{365}{366 + 365} = £17{,}476$$

Loss relief available	
1996/97 assessable income	£17,476
loss carried back under *TA 1988, s 380(1)(b); FA 1994, s 209(1)*	£17,476
Assessment	Nil

Loss carried forward £30,000 less relieved £17,476 = £12,524.

1997/98 assessable income therefore no loss relief available	Nil
1998/99 assessable income	£22,000
Less loss relief brought forward under *TA 1988, s 385; FA 1994, s 209(4)(5)*	£12,524
Assessment	£9,476

Transitional rules

3.9 There are no particular transitional provisions relating to losses except that *FA 1994, 20 Sch 8* confirms that the time limit for lodging claims for loss relief for losses sustained in 1994/95 and 1995/96 remains two years from the end of the year of assessment and not one year from the filing date of 31 January following the end of the year of assessment, which applies from 1996/97 onwards. The rules for adding capital allowances to losses under *TA 1988, s 383* for 1995/96 are explained in Inland Revenue Tax Bulletin No 21, February 1996, page 286 (see Appendix F). If the trade or profession commenced on or after 6 April 1994 *TA 1988, s 383* is irrelevant because the new self-assessment rules apply from commencement.

3.10 However, *TA 1988, ss 380, 381* and *388*, as modified for self-assessment, also apply for 1996/97. [*FA 1994, s 209(7); FA 1995, s 118*]. This enables the clarification to *TA 1988, s 381* referred to in 3.4 to be applied for 1996/97 and the anomaly in the terminal loss provisions referred to in 3.7 to be removed. The basic loss provisions under *TA 1988, s 380* can give relief for the same years under the old and new rules. Under the old rules a loss for a period of account ending in 1995/96 could be relieved in that year and 1996/97. Under the new rules a loss for a period of account ending in 1996/97 could be relieved in 1996/97 or 1995/96, see paras 3.1 and 3.2. A loss for a period of account ending in 1997/98 *et seq.* will be dealt with entirely under the new rules. The Revenue's draft notes explaining the self-employment pages of the Tax Return (2/96) Help Sheet 3.11, examples 3(b) and (c) are unhelpful in bringing losses into the transitional year averaging calculation without making clear that the losses unclaimed in the calculation are available for loss claims generally and that losses already relieved cannot be used again. [*TA 1988, s 382(4)*]. A further working of the examples is shown in examples 7 to 9 below. Apportionment can include losses to arrive at the net result of either the previous loss period or the relevant period, *TA 1988, s 72(1)*, but if the net result for either period is a loss it is treated as nil in the computation as only a net gain is included for either period under *FA 1994, 20 Sch 2(2)* which refers to profits on gains.

Example 7. Loss in 1996/97 and change of accounting date (Draft IR Helpsheet 3.11 example 3(b))

Mr Omos made up his accounts to 30 April until 1997 when he changed his accounting date to 5 April. He had no other income. The results, as adjusted for tax purposes, were as follows:

y/e 30.4.94	£12,000
y/e 30.4.95	£14,000
y/e 30.4.96 (loss)	(£6,000)
p/e 5.4.97	£7,000
y/e 5.4.98	£13,500

Assessable/taxable – before loss relief

1995/96	preceding year basis	£12,000	
1996/97	transitional year	£6,690	(*a*)
1997/98	current year basis	£13,500	

Notes

(*a*) Primary basis period 1996/97 y/e 5.4.97 [*FA 1994, 20 Sch 1(2)(a), 2(2)(a); TA 1988, s 72(1)*]

6.4.96 to 30.4.96 (25 days) (loss) 25/366 × £6,000	£(410)
1.5.96 to 5.4.97 (340 days)	£7,000
	£6,590

Relevant period [*FA 1994, 20 Sch 2(2), (5); TA 1988, s 382(4)*]

1.5.94 to 5.4.95 340/365 × £14,000		£13,041
6.4.95 to 5.4.96 (loss) (claimed 1995/96 *TA 1988, s 380(1)*)		
25/366 × £14,000	£956	
341/366 × £6,000	(£5,590)	
		Nil
		£19,631

Aggregate

Appropriate percentage *FA 1994, 20 Sch 2(2)*

$$£19,634 \times \frac{365}{365+366+340\ (1,071)} = £6,690\ (34.08\%\ £19,631)$$

Loss relief available, included above [*TA 1988, s 72(1)*]

£410 × 365/1,071 =	£140
£14,000 × 25/366	£956

Loss in year ended 30.4.96 £6,000, apportioned to 1996/97 [*TA 1988, s 382(4)*]

$$25/366 \times £6,000 \times \frac{(1,071-365)\ (706)}{1,071} = \quad £270$$

apportioned to 1995/96 and claimed under *TA 1988, s 380(1)*

341/366 × £6,000 =	£5,590	
Less profit apportioned to 1995/96		
25/366 × £14,000	956	4,634
		£6,000

The loss apportioned to 1995/96 can be deducted from the taxable income of £12,000, under *TA 1988, s 380(1)* (original version) leaving £7,366 (£12,000 – £4,634).

The loss apportioned to 1996/97 can be deducted from the taxable income of £6,691 under *TA 1988, s 380(1)* leaving £6,420. (£6,690 – £270).

If no part of the loss for the year ended 30 April 1996 is claimed in 1995/96 under *TA 1988, s 380(1)*, the transitional year calculation becomes:

Primary basis period, as above		£6,590
Relevant period [*FA 1994, 20 Sch 2(2), (5)*]		
y/e 30.4.95	£14,000	
1.5.95 to 5.4.96		
341/366 × (£6,000)	(£5,590)	
		£8,410
Aggregate		£15,000

Appropriate percentage *FA 1994, 20 Sch 2(2)*

$$£15{,}000 \times \frac{365}{365 + 366 + 340\ (1{,}071)} = £5{,}112\ (34.08\%\ £15{,}000)$$

Loss relief available, included above [*TA 1988, s 72(1)*]		
£410 × 365/1,071 =		£140
£5,590 × 365/1,071 =		£1,905
Available for claim in 1996/97 under *TA 1988 s 380(1)*	£6,000	
Less relieved, *TA 1988, s 382(4)* £140 + £1,905 =	£2,045	
		£3,955
		£6,000

The loss apportioned to 1996/97 can be deducted from the taxable income of £5,112 under *TA 1988, s 380(1)* leaving £1,157 (£5,112 – £3,955).

Example 8. Loss in 1996/97 and change of accounting date (Draft IR Help-sheet 3.11 example 3(c))

Mr Petrov made up his accounts to 30 April until 1997 when he changed his accounting date to 5 April. He had no other income. The results, as adjusted for tax purposes, were as follows:

y/e 30.4.94	£10,000
y/e 30.4.95	£5,000
y/e 30.4.96 (loss)	(£8,000)
p/e 5.4.97	£6,000
y/e 5.4.98	£7,500

Assessable/taxable – before loss relief

1995/96	preceding year basis	£10,000	
1996/97	transitional year	£3,446	(*a*)
1997/98	current year basis	£7,500	

Notes

(*a*) Primary basis period 1996/97 y/e 5.4.97 [*FA 1994, 20 Sch 1(2)(a), 2(2)(a); TA 1988, s 72(1)*]

6.4.96 to 30.4.96 (25 days) (loss) 25/366 × £8,000	£(547)
1.5.96 to 5.4.97 (340 days)	£6,000
	£5,453

Relevant period [*FA 1994, 20 Sch 20(2), (5); TA 1988, s 382(4)*]

1.5.94 to 5.4.95 340/365 × £5,000		£4,658
6.4.95 to 5.4.96 (loss) (claimed 1995/96 *TA 1988, s 380(1)*)		
25/365 × £5,000	£342	
341/366 × £8,000	(£7,453)	
		Nil
		£10,111

Aggregate

Appropriate percentage *FA 1994, 20 Sch 2(2)*

$$£10{,}111 \times \frac{365}{365 + 366 + 340\ (1{,}071)} = £3{,}446\ (34.08\%\ £10{,}111)$$

Loss relief available, included above [*TA 1988, s 72(1)*]

£547 × 365/1,071 =	£186
£5,000 × 25/366	£342

Loss in year ended 30.4.96 £8,000, apportioned to 1996/97 [*TA 1988, s 382(4)*]

$$25/366 \times £8{,}000 \times \frac{(1{,}071 - 365)\ (706)}{1{,}071} = £361$$

apportioned to 1995/96 and claimed under *TA 1988, s 380(1)*

341/366 × £8,000 =	£7,453	
Less profit apportioned to 1995/96		
25/365 × £5,000	(342)	£7,111
		£8,000

The loss apportioned to 1995/96 can be deducted from the taxable income of £10,000, under *TA 1988, s 380(1)* (original version) leaving £2,889 (£10,000 – £7,111).

The loss apportioned to 1996/97 can be deducted from the taxable income of £3,446 under *TA 1988, s 380(1)* leaving £3,085. (£3,446 – £361).

If no part of the loss for the year ended 30 April 1996 is claimed in 1995/96 under *TA 1988, s 380(1)*, the transitional year calculation becomes:

Primary basis period, as above		£5,453
Relevant period [*FA 1994, 20 Sch 2(2), (5) TA 1988, s 382(4)*]		
y/e 30.4.95	£5,000	
1.5.95 to 30.4.96		
£8,000 × 341/366 =	£(7,453)	
Net loss treated as [*FA 1994, 20 Sch 2(2)*]		Nil
Aggregate		£5,453

Appropriate percentage *FA 1994, 20 Sch 2(2)*

$$£5,453 \times \frac{365}{365 + 366 + 340\ (1,071)} = £1,858\ (34.08\%\ £5,453)$$

Loss relief available, included above [*TA 1988, s 72(1)*]

£547 × 365/1,071 =		£186

Loss in year ended 30.4.96 £8,000, used in 1996/97 relevant period calculation [*TA 1988, s 382(4)*]

£5,000 × 365/1,071 =		£1,704
Claimed in 1996/97 under *TA 1988, s 380(1)*	£8,000	
Less claimed [*TA 1988, s 382(4)*]	(£1,890)	
(£186 + £1,704) =		£6,110
		£8,000

The loss claimed in 1995/96 can be deducted from the taxable income of £1,858 under *TA 1988, s 380(1)* reducing the taxable income to nil, assuming no other income, and leaving £4,252 (£6,110 − £1,858) to carry forward under *TA 1988, s 385*.

The loss brought forward may be claimed in 1997/98 against the profits of £7,500, leaving £3,248 (£7,500 − £4.252).

The income assessable/taxable becomes:

1995/96	preceding year basis	£12,000
1996/97	transitional year	Nil
1997/98	current year basis	£5,749

Example 9. Loss in 1996/97 and change of accounting date

Mr Alexandrov made up his accounts to 30 April until 1997 when he changed his accounting date to 5 April. He had no other income. The results, as adjusted for tax purposes, were as follows:

y/e 30.4.94	£14,000
y/e 30.4.95 (loss)	(£3,750)
y/e 30.4.96 (loss)	(£8,000)
p/e 5.4.97	£300
y/e 5.4.98	£9,400

Assessable/taxable – before loss relief

1995/96	preceding year basis	£14,000	
1996/97	transitional year	Nil	(*a*)
1997/98	current year basis	£9,400	

Notes

(*a*) Primary basis period 1996/97 y/e 5.4.97 [*FA 1994, 20 Sch 1(2)(a), 2(2)(a); TA 1988, s 72(1)*]

6.4.96 to 30.4.96 (25 days) (loss) 25/366 × £8,000	£(546)
1.5.96 to 5.4.97 (340 days)	£300
	Nil

Relevant period [*FA 1994, 20 Sch 2(2), (5); TA 1988, s 382(4)*]

y/e 30.4.95 (loss £3,750)	Nil
1.5.95 to 5.4.96 (loss) (claimed 1995/96 *TA 1988, s 380(1)*)	Nil
	£Nil

Aggregate

Appropriate percentage *FA 1994, 20 Sch 2(2)*

$$\text{£Nil} \times \frac{365}{365 + 366 + 340\ (1{,}071)} = 34.08\% \qquad \text{£Nil}$$

Loss relief available, included above (*TA 1988, s 72(1)*)

Used in primary basis period, £300 × 34.08% =	£102
Balance £546 − £102	444
Loss brought forward	£3,750
Loss apportioned to 1995/96 341/366 × £8,000	£7,454
Loss carried forward	£11,648
Loss utilised	102
	£11,750
Loss incurred y/e 30.4.95	3,750
y/e 30.4.96	8,000
	£11,750

Farming losses

3.11 The restriction for farming losses where there have been losses in the five preceding years under *TA 1988, s 397* has been based on losses before capital allowances. In order to preserve the status quo in determining whether such losses can be set against other income, it is provided by *FA 1994, s 214(3)* that the results are to be computed without reference to capital allowances in order to determine whether there has been a loss in each of the previous five years. Otherwise by treating losses as trading expenses the comparison of results would automatically have been after capital allowances which would have had a material effect on the calculation in many cases.

Relief for losses on unquoted shares

3.12 *TA 1988, s 574* is re-enacted by *FA 1994, s 210* to mirror the changes introduced in *TA 1988, s 380* by *FA 1994, s 209(1)*. The loss as computed for capital gains tax purposes on the shares in an unquoted trading company subscribed for may be set against the total income for the year in which the loss arises under *TA 1988, s 574(1)(a); FA 1994, s 210*, or against the total income of the preceding year under *TA 1988, s 574(1)(b); FA 1994, s 210*. The claim must be made within twelve months from 31 January following the fiscal year in which the loss arises. It is not possible to claim relief twice for the same loss, or to claim a capital gains tax loss relief in respect of the loss claimed for income tax purposes. A loss sustained in 1993/94 can be relieved against total income in 1994/95 as well as 1993/94 under *FA 1994, s 210* as amended by *FA 1995, s 119*.

3.13 A loss claimed against income for the current year is given in priority to relief brought back from the following year under the carry back provisions. [*TA 1988, s 574(2); FA 1994, s 210*]. Relief is given in priority to relief for trading losses under *TA 1988, s 380* or *381*. This would normally be in the taxpayer's favour as such trading losses could be carried forward under *TA 1988, s 385* if the income was insufficient to absorb all the losses available for relief.

Example 10

Mr Kolpakov sustained a capital loss on the disposal of shares subscribed for in Komta Ltd of £23,000 on 1 May 1999. His total income for 1999/2000 was £18,000 and for 1998/99, £20,000. He claimed relief as follows:

Against 1998/99 under *TA 1988, s 574(1)(b); FA 1994, s 210*, £20,000 reducing his taxable income for that year to nil.

Against 1999/2000 the balance of the loss under *TA 1988, s 574(1)(a); FA 1994, s 210* (£23,000 – £20,000) £3,000 reducing his taxable income from £18,000 to £15,000.

Chapter 4

Capital Allowances

Introduction

4.1 The self-assessment rules do not change the assets eligible for capital allowances, nor do they make any fundamental change in the way the allowances are calculated. They do however make a fundamental change to the way in which the allowances are actually given and the chargeable period for which they are given.

Commencement date for new rules

4.2 The new arrangements apply to new businesses commencing on or after 6 April 1994, but not until 1997/98 for businesses already in existence at that date, i.e. after the transitional year 1996/97 to ensure that there is no loss of relief. [*FA 1994, s 211(2)*]. See 4.25 and 4.26 for transitional overlap relief. The transitional rules for adding capital allowances to losses for claims under *TA 1988, s 383* in 1995/96 are explained in 3.9 above and in Inland Revenue Tax Bulletin No 21, February 1996, page 286 (see Appendix F).

Trading expense

4.3 Under the new arrangements capital allowances are treated as a trading expense instead of an allowance for which a separate claim is necessary. This applies to capital allowances on industrial buildings and structures, machinery and plant, dwelling houses let on assured tenancies, mineral extraction assets, agricultural buildings and works, and dredging. [*CAA 1990, s 140(1); FA 1994, s 211*]. Allowances given by way of discharge or repayment of tax which are available primarily against a specified class of income are deductible by reference to a period of account and not for the fiscal year.

4.4 Writing-down allowances, initial allowances and balancing charges are given by treating the allowances as a trading expense in the period of account, or in the case of a balancing charge as a trading receipt in that period, under *CAA 1990, s 140(2); FA 1994, s 211*. This brings the basis for unincorporated businesses onto a similar treatment to that of companies under *CAA 1990, s 144*. The claim for capital allowances is made in the tax return and not as a separate claim under *TMA 1970, s 42* which is repealed for such claims which relate to a trade under *CAA 1990, s 140(3); FA 1994, s 211*.

4.5 Scientific research allowances have always been allowed as a deduction in computing the profits of a trade, and continue to be treated as trading expenses in the same way as other capital allowances, under *CAA 1990, s 140(5); FA 1994, s 211*.

4.6 The revised arrangements for capital allowances apply to professions, vocations, employments and offices as they apply to trades [*CAA 1990, s 140(4); FA 1994, s 211*] and a toll road undertaking is deemed to be a trade for industrial buildings allowance purposes, [*CAA 1990, s 140(6); FA 1994, s 211*], as are Schedule A businesses, *FA 1995, 6 Sch 29–35*.

Example 1

Mr Kazlov made up accounts to 30 June annually. In the year ended 30 June 1999 he incurred expenditure on plant and machinery of £40,000. His capital allowances pool brought forward was £100,000 and he had disposals of £4,000. His profits before capital allowances, but otherwise as adjusted for tax purposes were £52,000.

Capital allowances for y/e 30.6.99	
Written down value brought forward	£100,000
Less disposals	£4,000
	£96,000
Additions	£40,000
	£136,000
Writing-down allowance at 25% p.a.	£34,000
Written down value carried forward	£102,000
Profits for accounting period	£52,000
Less capital allowances	£34,000
Taxable profit	£18,000

The adjusted profit of £18,000 for the y/e 30 June 1999 is assessed for 1999/2000 on the current year basis.

Chargeable period

4.7 The basis period rules for capital allowances are abolished under the self-assessment rules and replaced by a revised definition of chargeable period in *CAA 1990, s 161(2); FA 1994, s 212(2)*. The chargeable period is, in the case of an unincorporated business, the period of account which is the period for which accounts are made up [*CAA 1990, s 60(1)(2); FA 1994, s 212(1)*], subject to gaps and overlaps dealt with in 5.8 to 5.10 below. The chargeable period for capital allowances purposes may fall into one or more basis periods for income tax purposes but it is the profit after capital allowances which is doubly charged, giving rise to overlap relief in due course.

Example 2

In the previous example, had Mr Kazlov started business on 1 July 1998 and incurred expenditure on plant of £140,000, less disposals of £4,000 the computation would have been:

Plant additions	£140,000
Less disposals	£4,000
	£136,000
Writing-down allowance at 25% p.a.	£34,000
Written down value carried forward	£102,000
Profit for accounting period	£52,000
Less capital allowances	£34,000
Adjusted profit	£18,000

Assessable/taxable

1998/99 1.7.98 to 5.4.99 9/12 × £18,000 =	£13,500
Commencement to next 5 April *TA 1988, s 61(1); FA 1994, s 201*	
1999/2000 y/e 30.6.99 =	£18,000
Twelve months to accounting date, *TA 1988, s 60(3)(a); FA 1994, s 200*, overlap relief £13,500 for overlap period 1.7.98 to 5.4.99	

Overlap

4.8 Where there is an overlap of two periods of account the period common to both is deemed to fall in the first period of account only, which means that assets qualifying for capital allowances would be treated as being acquired in the first period of account and not the second. An overlapping of two periods includes the coincidence of the two periods and the inclusion of one period in another. [*CAA 1990, s 160(6); FA 1994, s 212(1)*].

4.9 It would be most unusual for two periods of account to overlap but it could happen; for example, where a partner retired or died, and accounts were made up to the date of his leaving in order to arrive at the amount due to him on dissolution. The remaining partners might continue to prepare an annual set of accounts to the normal accounting date, which would mean that the period to the date the partner left would appear in two sets of accounts. [*CAA 1990, s 160(3)(a); FA 1994, s 212(1)*].

4.10 It should be noted that these rules only apply where the same period appears in two sets of accounts, not where there is an overlap in basis periods, i.e. where the same profits after capital allowances are charged to tax more than once on the transition to self-assessment on a commencement, or on a change of accounting date under the new rules, and which would be relieved by way of overlap relief on a cessation or change of accounting date under the provisions of substituted *TA 1988, ss 60–63A*.

Example 3

Pashinin and Porokhovshchikov were in partnership, making up accounts to 31 December annually until 1999 when Porokhovshchikov died on 30 June. Accounts were prepared to the date of death and for the year ended 31 December 1999.

The capital allowances pool at 1.1.1999 was £120,000 and there were acquisitions of plant and machinery of £9,000 and £12,000 in each half year and disposals of £1,000 and £2,000 respectively.

The capital allowances are:

1.1.99 to 30.6.99	
Written down value brought forward at 1.1.99	£120,000
Additions 1.1.99 to 30.6.99	£9,000
	£129,000
Disposals 1.1.99 to 30.6.99	£1,000
	£128,000
Writing-down allowance £128,000 × 25% × 6/12 =	£16,000
Written down value at 30.6.99	£112,000
Additions 1.7.99 to 31.12.99	£12,000
	£124,000
Disposals 1.7.99 to 31.12.99	£2,000
	£122,000
Writing-down allowance £122,000 × 25% × 6/12 =	£15,250
Written down value at 31.12.99	£106,750

Gap

4.11 The converse of the same period falling in two sets of accounts is a gap between two sets of accounts, which would again be a most unusual situation. It is however catered for in substituted *CAA 1990, s 160(3)(b)* by providing that any interval between sets of accounts is deemed to be part of the first period of account. Therefore any acquisitions or disposals in the interval are related to the earlier period. This rule would appear to apply where there was a suspension of trading, for example, on a farmer selling one farm and after a short period acquiring a new farm. It is likely that the Revenue would agree that the farming trade continued throughout [*TA 1988, s 53*], but accounts would probably be prepared to the date of sale of the first farm and from the acquisition of the second farm.

Capital allowances – basis periods

4.12 Under the previously applying basis period rules in the original *CAA 1990, s 160* the basis period for capital allowances was the same as the basis period for income tax, except in the opening and closing years of assessment where special rules applied. Where two basis periods overlapped the period common to both fell in the first basis period only. If there was a gap between basis periods for example, on a change of accounting date, the interval fell into the second basis period except where that period was one in which the trade was permanently discontinued, in which case the interval was added to the first basis period. A full year's writing-down allowance was given in each basis period except for the opening period and period of cessation, in which case a proportionate part of the writing-down allowances was given.

Example 4

Mr Laville commenced business on 29 December 1988 and ceased 17 August 1996. Accounts were made up to 30 April each year.

	Income tax basis period	*Capital allowances basis period*
1988–89	29.12.88 – 5.4.89	29.12.88 – 5.4.89
1989–90	29.12.88 – 28.12.89	6.4.89 – 28.12.89
1990–91	29.12.88 – 28.12.89*	no basis period
1991–92	1.5.89 – 30.4.90	29.12.89 – 30.4.90
1992–93	1.5.90 – 30.4.91	1.5.90 – 30.4.91
1993–94	1.5.91 – 30.4.92	1.5.91 – 30.4.92
1994–95	1.5.92 – 30.4.93	1.5.92 – 30.4.93
1995–96	1.5.93 – 30.4.94	1.5.93 – 5.4.96
1996–97	6.4.96 – 17.8.96	6.4.96 – 17.8.96

* Probable Revenue selection, although the Revenue have power under *TA 1988, s 60* to choose any twelve-month period ending in 1990/91.

Had an election been made for the actual basis of assessment for the two years following commencement under *TA 1988, s 62* and also the Revenue applied the actual basis on discontinuance under *TA 1988, s 63*, the capital allowances basis period would have been as follows:

	Income tax basis period		*Capital allowance basis period*	
1988–89	29.12.88	– 5.4.89	29.12.88	– 5.4.89
1989–90	6.4.89	– 5.4.90	6.4.89	– 5.4.90
1990–91	6.4.90	– 5.4.91	6.4.90	– 5.4.91
1991–92	1.5.89	– 30.4.90	no basis period	
1992–93	1.5.90	– 30.4.91	6.4.91	– 30.4.91
1993–94	1.5.91	– 30.4.92	1.5.91	– 30.4.92
1994–95	6.4.94	– 5.4.95	1.5.92	– 5.4.95
1995–96	6.4.95	– 5.4.96	6.4.95	– 5.4.96
1996–97	6.4.96	– 17.8.96	6.4.96	– 17.8.96

In both cases a full year's writing-down allowance would be made for all years other than 1988–89 and 1996–97 which would be time apportioned. Balancing allowances and charges would fall into the appropriate basis periods in which disposals took place.

If Mr Laville commenced a new and separate trade on 29 December 1996 making up accounts to 30 April each year, the capital allowances by reference to each accounting period would be given in the computation adjusting the profits for that period as if they were trading expenses, and then the resultant net profit, as adjusted for tax purposes, would be allocated to the income tax basis period. These would be:

1996/97 29.12.1996 to 5.4.1997 [*TA 1988, s 61(1); FA 1994, s 201*]
1997/98 29.12.1996 to 28.12.1997 [*TA 1988, s 61(2)(a); FA 1994, s 201*]
1998/99 1.5.1997 to 30.4.1998 [*TA 1988, s 60(3)(a); FA 1994, s 200*]
1999/2000 1.5.1998 to 30.4.1999 [*TA 1988, s 60(3)(b); FA 1994, s 200*]

Amount of allowances

4.13 Under the old rules a full year's writing-down allowances were given for each fiscal year, irrespective of the length of the capital allowance basis period, other than in the years of commencement or cessation. However, under self-assessment if the period of account in which the expenditure is incurred is for less than or more than twelve months, as it could be, not only on commencement or cessation, but also on a change of accounting date to a period earlier or later in the fiscal year, the writing-down allowance is adjusted pro rata in accordance with the length of the accounting period. [*FA 1994, s 213(3)–(10)*]. For example, if the rate of writing-down allowance is 25 per cent per annum and the accounting period is for 15 months, the effective rate of writing-down allowances becomes 31.25 per cent (25 × 15/12). Conversely if the accounting period is nine months the writing-down allowance becomes 18.75 per cent (25 × 9/12). However, no period of account may exceed 18 months and an accounting period of greater length is divided into twelve-month (or less) periods of account. [*CAA 1990, s 160(4); FA 1994, s 212(1)*]. This rule is modified by *FA 1994, s 218(1A)* (inserted by *FA 1995, s 102*). Where a company commenced trading after 5 April 1994, writing-down allowances and balancing adjustments will only be time-apportioned in the normal way if the company does not in fact commence trading until after 5 April 1995. This modification also applies to writing-down allowances and balancing adjustments in respect of mineral extraction and to allowances for expenditure on patent rights and on the disposal of know-how.

Example 5

Mr Bedunkovich made up accounts each year to 31 December until 1999 when he produced a short set of accounts to 30 June which was a valid change of accounting date for tax purposes and annually thereafter. In the six months to 30 June 1999 he incurred expenditure on plant and machinery of £25,000. His capital allowances pool brought forward was £80,000 and disposals in the period realised £5,000.

Capital allowances for six-month period ending 30.6.99:

Pool value brought forward	£80,000
Less disposals	£5,000
	£75,000
Additions in period 1.1.99 to 30.6.99	£25,000
	£100,000
Writing-down allowances at 25% p.a. for six months $(25 \times \frac{6}{12})$	£12,500
Written down value carried forward at 30 June 1999	£87,500
Adjusted pre-capital allowances profits were:	
y/e 31.12.98	£60,000
1.1.99 to 30.6.99	£27,500
Capital allowances for y/e 31.12.98 were £20,000	
Assessable/taxable	
1998/99 y/e 31.12.98	£40,000
(£60,000 less capital allowances £20,000)	
1999/2000 year to new accounting date 1.1.99 to 30.6.99	£15,000
(£27,500 less capital allowances £12,500)	
1.7.98 to 31.12.98 (£40,000 × 6/12)	£20,000
Assessment	£35,000

Example 6

Mr Lisichkin made up accounts each year to 30 June until 1999 when he produced a long set of accounts to 31 December, which was a valid change of accounting date for tax purposes, and annually thereafter. In the 18 months to 31 December 1999 he incurred expenditure on plant and machinery of £50,000. His capital allowances pool was £110,000 and disposals in the period realised £8,000.

Capital allowances for 18-month period ending 31.12.99:

Pool value brought forward	£110,000
Less disposals	£8,000
	£102,000
Additions in period 1.7.98 to 31.12.99	£50,000
	£152,000
Writing-down allowances at 25% p.a. for 18 months $(25 \times \frac{18}{12})$	£57,000
Written down value carried forward at 31 December 1999	£95,000
Adjusted pre-capital allowances profits were:	
y/e 30.6.98	£80,000
1.7.98 to 31.12.99	£95,000
Capital allowances for y/e 30.6.98 were £30,000	

Assessable/taxable

1998/99 y/e 30.6.98	£50,000
(£80,000 less capital allowances £30,000)	
1999/2000 period 1.7.98 to 31.12.99 (£95,000 less capital allowances £57,000)	£38,000

Subject to overlap relief under *TA 1988, s 63A; FA 1994, s 205*, ignored in this example.

Non-traders

4.14 Where a person is not carrying on a trade, profession or vocation but is still entitled to capital allowances, for example, a landed estate where the allowances are given by way of discharge or repayment, the period of account means the year of assessment. [*CAA 1990, s 160(5); FA 1994, s 212(1)*].

Chargeable period – amendments

4.15 Legislative changes to the *Capital Allowances Act 1990* are made by *FA 1994, s 213*. This makes a number of amendments, including deleting references to basis period throughout the *Capital Allowances Act*, which leaves such references as referring to the chargeable period, i.e. the period of account as redefined by *CAA 1990, s 161(2); FA 1994, s 212(2)*.

4.16 *FA 1994, s 213(3)(a)* deletes the references to years of assessment and basis periods for industrial buildings allowance purposes in *CAA 1990, s 8* which results in such allowances being due at the end of the chargeable period as redefined. The provisions relating to long as well as short periods of account for industrial buildings allowances are brought into effect by *FA 1994, s 213(2)*, amending *CAA 1990, s 3(2)*; those for plant by *FA 1994, s 213(4)*, amending *CAA 1990, s 24(2)(a)(ii)*; those for motor cars used for the purpose of a trade costing more than £12,000, where it is necessary to provide for the maximum annual allowance of £3,000 per annum, to be adjusted pro rata for long and short periods, by *FA 1994, s 213(5)*, amending *CAA 1990, s 34(3)(a),(b)*. The corresponding rules relating to contributions for such cars are covered in *FA 1994, s 213(6)*, amending *CAA 1990, s 35(1)(b)*.

4.17 Similar provisions relating to dwelling houses let on assured tenancies are covered in *FA 1994, s 213(7)*, amending *CAA 1990, s 85(2)*; for mineral extraction allowances by *s 213(8)*, amending *CAA 1990, s 98(6)*; for dredging by *s 213(9)* amending *CAA 1990, s 134(1)* and for scientific research allowances by *FA 1994, s 213(10)*, amending *CAA 1990, s 137(5)–(7)*. The scientific research allowance provisions are considerably simplified by this amendment, which also provides that the relevant chargeable period is to be the chargeable period in which the expenditure was incurred, or in the case of pre-trading expenditure, in the chargeable period beginning with the commencement of the trade. Finally, *FA 1994, s 213(11)* amends *CAA 1990, s 161(5)* by providing that any reference to capital allowances being made in taxing a trade is a reference to them being made in computing the trading income for corporation tax or income tax purposes.

Crown property

4.18 If an industrial building is owned by the Crown, or a person not within the charge to UK tax, the residue of expenditure is calculated as if the owner were entitled to all the normal allowances. The owner is assumed for this purpose to have a fiscal year accounting period which ended immediately before the beginning of the next following year of assessment. [*Substituted CAA 1990, s 8(13)(d)*]. This enables the residue of expenditure to be calculated as the starting point for the purchaser's industrial buildings allowances.

Losses

4.19 The extension of loss relief to include capital allowances becomes unnecessary where the allowances are treated as trading expenses and for the purpose of the loss relief restriction under *TA 1988, s 384* and the inclusion of capital allowances in terminal loss relief. The necessary alterations are made by *FA 1994, s 214(1)(b)–(e)*. The anti-avoidance provisions to prevent the exploitation of capital allowances through the leasing of assets such as narrow boats and containers are retained subject to the necessary amendments in *TA 1988, s 384(6)* introduced by *FA 1994, s 214(2)*.

Farming

4.20 Farm profit averaging in *TA 1988, s 96* used to be on the basis of the profits before capital allowances. However, by treating capital allowances as a trading expense averaging will be by reference to the profits after capital allowances. [*FA 1994, s 214(1)(a)*]. This will affect new businesses from 6 April 1994, but for existing trades the new rules do not come into effect until 1997/98, which means that farm profit averaging for the years up to and including 1995/96, with 1996/97, will be done under the old rules before capital allowances are deducted. The averaging for 1996/97 with 1997/98 and any later pair of years will be done under the new rules after deducting capital allowances. [*FA 1994, s 214(7)*, Inland Revenue Tax Bulletin No 21, February 1996, page 282 (see Appendix F)].

Example 7

Mr Putilov farmed in East Anglia and produced the following results:

Year ended 30 September	*Adjusted profit before capital allowances*	*Capital allowances*		*Adjusted profit after capital allowances*
	£		£	£
1994	100,000	95/96	10,000	
1995	80,000 }			
1996	40,000 }	96/97	8,000	
1997	112,000 }		12,000	100,000
Assessable/taxable				
1995/96				
y/e 30.9.94				100,000
1996/97				
primary basis period				
y/e 30.9.96	£40,000			
Relevant period				
y/e 30.9.95	£80,000			
Aggregate	£120,000			

Appropriate proportion	
$\frac{365}{365 + 365}$	£60,000
Total for two years	£160,000

1996/97 is less than 70% of 1995/96
Therefore, applying farm profit averaging under *TA 1988, s 96*

1995/96 becomes	£80,000
Less capital allowances	£10,000
	£70,000
1996/97 becomes	£80,000
Less capital allowances	£8,000
	£72,000
1996/97, as before	£72,000
1997/98 y/e 30.9.97 (after capital allowances)	£100,000
1996/97 is between 70% and 75% of 1997/98, therefore applying farm profit averaging under *TA 1988, s 96* (marginal relief)	
Difference (£100,000 − £72,000) =	£28,000
multiplied by three	£84,000
Less 3/4 of £100,000	£75,000
	£9,000
Final assessment 1996/97 £72,000 + £9,000 =	£81,000
Assessment 1997/98 £100,000 − £9,000 =	£91,000

which might change if averaged with 1998/99 in due course.

Patents and know-how

4.21 Patent rights qualify for capital allowances with a writing-down allowance of 25 per cent per annum. This requires amendment to cater for long periods of account of more than twelve months as well as short periods of account, and this is achieved by amending *TA 1988, s 520(4)(a)(ii)* by *FA 1994, s 214(4)*. The supplementary provisions relating to capital expenditure on patent rights in *TA 1988, s 521* will be by reference to the chargeable period, not the basis period, as a result of *FA 1994, s 214(5)*, amending *TA 1988, ss 521, 528* and *530*.

4.22 The provisions relating to capital allowances on know-how, extending the allowance pro rata for an accounting period in excess of twelve months, is achieved by an amendment to *TA 1988, s 530(2)(a)(ii)* by *FA 1994, s 214(6)*.

Transitional provisions

4.23 Any unused capital allowances carried forward under *CAA 1990, s 140(4)* which have not been relieved in 1996/97 or earlier periods are treated as due in the first period of account ending after 5 April 1997. [*FA 1994, 20 Sch 9*]. The effect of this is that if the allowances are not relieved in 1997/98 they would be included in the figure for losses carried forward under *TA 1988, s 385; FA 1994, s 209(4)(5)*.

Example 8

Mr Shchyerbakov had agreed tax losses at 5.4.97 of £27,000 and unused capital allowances of £19,000 at the same date. In the year ended 30 September 1997, to which date he made up his annual accounts, the profit as adjusted for tax purposes after capital allowances, amounted to £40,000.

Assessable/taxable 1997/98

y/e 30.9.97		£40,000
Less brought forward		
losses	£27,000	
capital allowances	£19,000	
		£46,000
Assessment		Nil
Losses carried forward £46,000 – £40,000		£6,000

4.24 Because the new rules do not apply for existing businesses until 1997/98 the transitional period 1996/97 is dealt with under the old rules which means that the capital allowances basis period for 1996/97 is from the end of the basis period for 1995/96 to the beginning of the basis period for 1997/98.

Example 9

If in the earlier example 4 Mr Laville had not ceased business on 17 August 1996 but had continued to trade, the position would have been as follows:

	Income tax basis period	*Capital allowances basis period*
1995–96	1.5.93 – 30.4.94	1.5.93 – 30.4.94
1996–97 ½	(1.5.94 – 30.4.96)	1.5.94 – 30.4.96
1997–98	1.5.96 – 30.4.97	no separate basis period, deducted as expense in period 1.5.96 – 30.4.97

Note that all purchases in the lengthened period 1.5.1994 to 30.4.1996 would qualify for a writing-down allowance in 1996/97. However this is one years writing-down allowance under the old rules, irrespective of the length of the capital allowance basis period.

Transitional overlap relief

4.25 Under self-assessment the old capital allowances rules apply up until 1996/97 in order to avoid any loss of allowances on transitional averaging and are applied as an expense in computing the taxable profit for 1997/98. However, in addition to transitional averaging for 1996/97 the balance of the opening year double assessment is relieved by means of transitional overlap relief. Transitional overlap relief gives an additional overlap for that part of the 1997/98 profit which falls after the end of the 1996/97 basis period and prior to 6 April 1997. Inserted *FA 1994, 20 Sch 2(4A)* (*FA 1995, s 122(3)*) provides that the transitional overlap relief is calculated before deducting capital allowances for 1997/98. This ensures that over the life of the business capital allowances are given for the full cost of expenditure less disposable proceeds on qualifying assets. Under the rules for capital allowances under *CAA 1990, s 160*, (original version) gaps and overlaps in basis periods were fully catered for and this worked through the transitional period giving one year's allowances on the net expenditure in the whole of the transitional period, but would have been spoilt by the effective reduction in capital allowances on computing transitional overlap relief on the profits after capital allowances profits for 1997/98.

Example 10

Mr Kudashyev made up accounts each year to 30 September until 31 July 2000 when he ceased to trade.

His capital allowances pool at 1 October 1994 was £60,000 with net additions in the two years ended 30 September 1996 of £40,000. There were no other additions or disposals of plant the balance of which was sold on cessation for £20,000.

Profits as adjusted for tax purposes; before capital allowances.

y/e 30.9.1994	£28,000
y/e 30.9.1995	£30,000
y/e 30.9.1996	£36,000
y/e 30.9.1997	£40,000
y/e 30.9.1998	£45,000
y/e 30.9.1999	£48,000
p/e 31.7.2000	£32,000

Assessable/taxable

1995/96 preceding year basis	£23,000	(*a*)
1996/97 transitional year	£8,000	(*b*)
1997/98 current year basis	£21,250	(*c*)
1998/99 current year basis	£30,938	(*d*)
1999/2000 current year basis	£37,319	(*e*)
2000/2001 cessation period	£Nil	(*f*)

(*a*) *TA 1988, s 60(3)* (original version accounting year ending in preceding year fiscal year) £28,000
Less capital allowances (say) £5,000
£23,000

(*b*) Basis period for 1996/97 under *TA 1988, s 60(3)(b); FA 1994, s 200* (accounting year to 30.9.96 ending in current fiscal year) £36,000

Relevant period under *FA 1994, s 20, 2 Sch (2)(b), (5)* i.e. 1.10.94 to 30.9.95 £30,000

Aggregate, *FA 1994, 20 Sch 2(2)* £66,000

Appropriate percentage under *FA 1994, 20 Sch 2(5)*

$$£66{,}000 \times \frac{365}{365 + 365} = £33{,}000$$

Capital allowances

Written down value brought forward at 1.10.94	£60,000
Net additions in period ending 30.9.96 (*CAA 1990, s 160* original version)	£40,000
	£100,000
Writing down allowances of 25%	£25,000
Written down value carried forward	£75,000
Assessable £33,000 less £25,000 =	£8,000

Overlap period under *FA 1994, 20 Sch 2(4)* part of basis period for 1997/98, year ending 30 September 1997, which falls before 6 April 1997, i.e. 1.10.96 to 5.4.97 i.e. 187 days overlap profits (before capital allowances).

$£40{,}000 \times \frac{187}{365} =$		£20,493

(*c*) *TA 1988, s 60(3)(b); FA 1994, s 200*

y/e 30.9.97		£40,000
Less capital allowances		
w.d.v. brought forward	£75,000	
w.d.a. 25%	£18,750	£18,750
w.d.v. carried forward	£56,250	£21,250

(*d*) *TA 1988, s 60(3)(b); FA 1994, s 200*

y/e 30.9.98		£45,000
Less capital allowances		
w.d.v. brought forward	£56,250	
w.d.a. 25%	£14,062	£14,062
w.d.v. carried forward	£42,188	£30,938

(*e*) *TA 1988, s 60(3)(b); FA 1994, s 200*

y/e 30.9.99		£48,000
Less capital allowances		
w.d.v. brought forward	£42,188	
w.d.a 25%	£10,547	£10,547
w.d.v. carried forward	£31,641	£37,453
Less terminal loss (see (*f*) below)		£134

(*f*) *TA 1988, s 63; FA 1994, s 200*

1.10.99 to 31.7.2000		£32,000
Less capital allowances		
w.d.v. brought forward	£31,641	
sale proceeds	£20,000	
balancing allowances	£11,641	£11,641
		£20,359
Less transitional overlap relief (*b*)		£20,493
Loss available to carry back under *TA 1988, s 388* as terminal loss		£134

Had the transitional overlap been calculated on the profits after capital allowances, as originally drafted, it would have been:

$£21{,}250(c) \times \frac{187}{365} =$		£10,887

instead of £20,493, a loss of £9,606, (187/365 × £18,750 (capital allowances in 1996/97)) which would effectively result in a loss of part of the capital allowances in 1996/97 resulting in less than full relief being given for the cost of each asset over its life.

4.26 As partners are treated as sole traders the calculations of transitional overlap relief on the pre-capital allowance profits for 1997/98 applies. However, where there is a partnership in which a company is a partner, *TA 1988, s 114(3)* (original version) applies for 1996/97. Under this provision the capital allowances for the business are calculated on a current year basis and then apportioned over the fiscal year for individual partners, which means that individual partners will have their capital allowances for 1996/97 based on their proportionate share of the allowances for the accounting periods apportioned to the fiscal year. In 1997/98 capital allowances are treated as a deduction in computing the profit for individuals in partnership with companies under substituted *CAA 1990, s 140, FA 1994, s 211*. This means that full allowances are given for the current year basis assessed in 1997/98 and the transitional overlap relief as originally drafted gave the right results. *FA 1994, 20 Sch (2)(4B)* (*FA 1995, s 122(3)*) therefore disapplies the calculation of the transitional overlap relief on the pre-capital allowances figures for individuals in partnership with companies.

Example 11

Kostovich Ltd carries on business in partnership with Mr Mozhaisky (an individual) and the partnership accounts are made up to 30 September annually. The partners share profits and losses in the ratio of 2:1 respectively. The following results are obtained:

Year to 30 September	Profits (Losses)	Capital allowances
	£	£
1995	18,000	4,500
1996	(9,000)	6,000
1997	30,000	3,000
1998	36,000	7,500

These are attributable as follows:

	Kostovich Ltd		Mr Mozhaisky	
Year to 30 September	Profit (Loss)	Capital allowances	Profit (Loss)	Capital allowances
	£	£	£	£
1995	12,000	3,000	6,000	1,500
1996	(6,000)	4,000	(3,000)	2,000
1997	20,000	2,000	10,000	1,000
1988	24,000	5,000	12,000	2,500

Corporation tax assessments Kostovich Ltd

Accounting period to

		£
30.9.95	Profit	12,000
	Deduct: Capital allowances	3,000
	Offset by loss of accounting period to 30.9.96	9,000
30.9.96	Loss	6,000
	Add: Capital allowances	4,000
		10,000
	Carried back to y.e. 30.9.95	9,000
	Carried forward	1,000
30.9.97	Profit	20,000
	Deduct: Capital allowances	2,000
		18,000
	Deduct: Losses brought forward	1,000
		17,000
30.9.98	Profit	24,000
	Deduct: Capital allowances	5,000
		19,000

Income tax assessments, Mr Mozhaisky

1996/97

	£
Primary basis period, y/e 30.9.96 *FA 1994, 20 Sch 1(2)(a)*	Nil
Relevant period under *FA 1994, 20 Sch 2(2)(B), (5)* i.e. 1.10.94 to 30.9.95	6,000

Appropriate percentage under *FA 1994, 20 Sch 2(5)*

$$£6{,}000 \times \frac{365}{365 + 365} = \qquad 3{,}000$$

Less capital allowances *TA 1988, s 114(3)* apportioned to 1996/97

	£
y/e 30.9.96 $\frac{6}{12} \times £2{,}000 =$	1,000
y/e 30.9.97 $\frac{6}{12} \times £1{,}000 =$	500
	1,500
Assessable £3,000 – £1,500	1,500

Loss claim set-off under *TA 1988, s 380* (original version) strict basis.

1995/96 ½ loss y/e 30.9.96 £3,000	1,500
1996/97 ½ loss y/e 30.9.96 £3,000	1,500

1997/98 substituted *TA 1988, s 60(3)(b)*
FA 1994, s 200

	£
y/e 30.9.97 Profit	10,000
Less capital allowances	1,000
	9,000

Overlap period under *FA 1994, 20 Sch 2(4)* and *(4B)* part of basis period for 1997/98 which falls after 30 September 1996 and before 6 April 1997, i.e. 1.10.96 to 5.4.97, 187 days.

	£
Overlap profits £9,000 × $\frac{187}{365}$ =	4,611

1998/99 substituted *TA 1988, s 60(3)(b), FA 1994, s 200*

y/e 30.9.98	
Profit	12,000
Less capital allowances	2,500
	9,500

Chapter 5

Income From Land in the UK: Schedule A

Introduction

5.1 Whilst self-assessment has not been seen as an opportunity to end the outdated schedular system of taxation, the occasion has been taken to rationalise the Schedule A rules for income tax purposes. The corporation tax rules remain largely unchanged, although in due course they may be brought in line with those for income tax. The reason given for retaining the existing corporation tax provisions is that companies have scope for sideways relief against other income for some property related expenses, e.g., interest, through the charges and management expenses rule. The new Schedule A rules could mean that companies would have all their property expenditure ring fenced as a Schedule A deduction, so they would lose their present flexibility. However, the Revenue have confirmed that where a company produces annual accounts, including a balance sheet, no objection will be made to accepting computations based on the accounts figure. They will usually include accruals for rent receivable and expenses payable. This will remain subject to *TA 1988, ss 33A* and *33B*, dealing with connected landlords and tenants.

5.2 The timing and essential features of the new income tax system are as follows:

(*a*) the new rules generally apply from 1995/96 and are set out in the Inland Revenue's booklet IR 150 entitled 'Taxation of Rents – A guide to property income – Schedule A for income tax 1995/96 and later years' issued in March 1996;

(*b*) 1994/95 is the transitional year, for which there are no statutory rules, but instead non-statutory guide lines contained in an Inland Revenue Press Release of 10 February 1995 (Appendix C) and Tax Bulletin No 20, December 1995, page 268 (Appendix F);

(*c*) the tax payer is treated as carrying on a business, with Schedule D, Case I computation rules, notably the accruals basis for income and expenditure;

(*d*) the charge is on the profits of the current fiscal year, 6 April–5 April;

(*e*) all income and expenditure is pooled, with no differentiation for different kinds of property or different leases;

(*f*) furnished lettings and furnished holiday lettings are included;

(*g*) interest, including overdraft interest, is an allowable expense in computing profit;

(*h*) capital allowances are likewise treated as an allowable expense. The renewals basis, or wear and tear allowances, for furnished lettings, is maintained;

(*i*) losses brought forward will be set against the new pooled income and any excess can be carried forward against future Schedule A income;

(*j*) notwithstanding Schedule D, Case I treatment, property income will still be treated as investment income; and

(*k*) taxable income from property situated outside the UK is determined as for income from UK property.

Timing for introduction of new rules

5.3 The new rules generally apply from 1995/96 both for existing and any new Schedule A source. If the income first arose in 1994/95, the new rules may also be applied for that year. In so far as any of the new provisions relate to corporation tax, they are applicable to accounting periods ending on or after 31 March 1995. [*FA 1995, s 39(4)*].

5.4 If the source of income ceases in 1995/96 the old rules will continue to be applied, provided that the taxpayer was chargeable under Schedule A or Schedule D, Case VI in respect of the same source for 1994/95 and has no other Schedule A income in 1995/96. [*FA 1995, s 39(5)*]. Thus if a taxpayer has three properties generating Schedule A income and one is sold in 1995/96 the new rules will apply in that year. But if all three are sold in that year, there will have been a complete cessation and the old rules will apply.

Scope of charge and charging sections

5.5 The original Schedule A section numbers are retained, but with substituted provisions. This is even more confusing than the retention of the same Schedule D section numbers, in that not only will different rules apply for different years but the same section numbers will have different provisions for income tax and for corporation tax purposes. A substituted *TA 1988, s 15* is applied for income tax purposes from 1995/96 by *FA 1995, s 39(1)*, with detailed rules of computation in *FA 1995, 6 Sch*.

5.6 Income tax under Schedule A is charged on the annual profits or gains of a business carried on for the exploitation, as a source of rent or other receipts, of any estate, interest or rights in or over any land in the UK. Any transaction entered into to this end is deemed to have been entered into in the course of such a business. [*TA 1988, s 15, A Schedule 1(1), 2*].

Persons chargeable

5.7 Tax is charged on and paid by the persons receiving or entitled to the income in question. [Substituted *TA 1988, s 21(1); FA 1995, s 39(2)*]. The new rules do not apply for corporation tax purposes. [Substituted *TA 1988, s 21(8)*]. Hence the new rules apply to individuals, trustees, personal representatives, and non-resident companies with no UK trading activities but UK source rental income.

Receipts chargeable

5.8 The Revenue consider that the restructuring of Schedule A does not exclude any categories of receipt that were previously chargeable. Rather Schedule A is extended to include furnished lettings and rents from caravans and houseboats, previously within Schedule D, Case VI. Items of a capital nature remain excluded by the continued use of the words 'annual profits or gains'.

5.9 Taxable receipts within Schedule A specifically include the following:

(*a*) any payment in respect of any licence to occupy or otherwise use any land;

(*b*) any payment in respect of the exercise of any other right over land;

(*c*) rent charges, ground annuals, feu duties and any other annual payments reserved in respect of, or charged on or issuing out of, that land [substituted *TA 1988, s 15, A Schedule 1(3)*];

(*d*) income from furnished lettings, including furnished holiday lettings. Hence any money which a tenant pays for the use of furniture is within Schedule A, the former right to elect for a split of rent between the property itself and the furniture being abolished. [*FA 1995, 6 Sch 1*]. If unusually the furniture rental forms part of a trade, it remains chargeable under Schedule D, Case I [*TA 1988, s 15, A Schedule 4(1), (2)*];

(*e*) income from caravans or houseboats (including any amounts for the use of any furniture) where the use is confined to use at one location in the UK. The definitions of caravans and houseboats respectively are such that they are essentially used as a place of human habitation [*TA 1988, s 15, A Schedule 3(1), (2), 4(4)*]; and

(*f*) all sporting rights' income and expenses; the sporting rights rules of *TA 1988, s 29* being disapplied. [*FA 1995, 6 Sch 4(b)*].

Lease premiums, assignments, sales with right to reconveyance

5.10 Since none of the sources of income previously chargeable under Schedule A escape the amended Schedule A charge the lease premium provisions of *TA 1988, s 34*, which bring into charge premiums paid on the grant of leases under 50 years, less a deduction of 2 per cent for every year for the term of the lease other than the first, are retained with appropriate modifications to tie in with the concept of a Schedule A business. The notional rent will hence be a receipt of a Schedule A business. Premiums which are received by a person other than the landlord are likewise treated as Schedule A income (previously Schedule D, Case VI). But any deemed premium for work done by the tenant which would have been deductible as an expense of a Schedule A business carried on by the landlord, if incurred by him, is excluded from the definition of lease premium. [*FA 1995, 6 Sch 9*].

5.11 An intermediate landlord who has paid a premium to a head landlord may deduct the chargeable amount of such premium over the period of the lease as if it were an expense of the property. [*TA 1988, s 37; FA 1995, 6 Sch 12*]. A double allowance for the same expenditure is prevented by *FA 1995, 6 Sch 14*, which disapplies *TA 1988, s 87*, which would have given relief to the lessee on the payment of the premium over the life of the lease as a result of Schedule A income being computed under Schedule D, Case I rules.

5.12 The charge imposed by *TA 1988, s 35* on certain assignments of leases for less than 50 years granted at an undervalue, where the grantor could have charged a premium, is also included in the profit of a Schedule A business. [*FA 1995, 6 Sch 10*]. Likewise the charge under *TA 1988, s 36*, where land is sold on terms that it be reconveyed to the vendor or a connected person at a later date is retained. [*FA 1995, 6 Sch 11*].

Furnished holiday lettings

5.13 Although profits from furnished holiday lettings are charged under new Schedule A as a Schedule A business, the activity is treated as a trade for the purposes of relief for losses against other income, pre-trading expenditure, capital expenditure etc. [*FA 1995, 6 Sch 21* amending *TA 1988, ss 503 and 504*]. The substance of the existing tax position is thus preserved. Moreover the various CGT reliefs on the disposal of business assets are preserved for gains attributable to properties used for furnished holiday lettings; see 10.7.

Exclusions from charge

5.14 There are a number of specific exclusions from the Schedule A charge as follows [substituted *TA 1988, s 15, A Schedule 3*]:

(i) yearly interest;

(ii) profits from commercial woodland (which are not charged to tax);

(iii) farming and market gardening profits within *TA 1988, s 53*;

(iv) profits charged under *TA 1988, s 55*, being:

(*a*) mines and quarries;

(*b*) ironworks, gasworks, salt springs, alum mines and waterworks;

(*c*) canals, inland navigation, docks, drains or levels;

(*d*) fishings;

(*e*) rights of market and fairs, tolls, bridges and ferries;

(*f*) railways;

(*g*) other concerns of a like nature;

and rents related thereto under *TA 1988, s 119*, and electric line way-leaves under *TA 1988, s 120*; and

(v) lettings of tied premises by traders falling within *TA 1988, s 98*.

5.15 Moreover, the deduction at source provision relating to rents from mines, quarries and other concerns under *TA 1988, s 119* ceases to have effect in relation to payments made on or after 1 May 1995 under *FA 1995, s 145*. But the rents which are received for electric line way-leaves (in respect of electric, telegraphic or telephonic wires or cables) are still payable net of basic rate tax, under *TA 1988, s 120*.

Business

5.16 'Business' is not defined. Indeed it has not hitherto been a term generally used in income tax legislation, where business activities have been charged, if at all, under the heading of 'trade, profession or vocation'. But the term is used in VAT legislation, where it has been accorded a wide meaning. The Schedule D, Case I charge is specifically extended to single transactions by the definition of 'trade' in *TA 1988, s 832(1)* as including an adventure or concern in the nature of trade.

5.17 Case law might suggest that the mere receipt of rents does not constitute a business, notably the following observations by Lord Diplock in *American Leaf Blending Co v the Director General of Inland Revenue 1978 STC 561* at page 565:

> 'In the case of a private individual it may well be that the mere receipt of rent from property that he owns raises no presumption that he is carrying on a business.'

This issue has seemingly been addressed by *paragraph 1(2)* of the new provisions in substituted *TA 1988, s 15*, which bring within the ambit of a Schedule A business any transaction to generate income from land, i.e. a single transaction. Certainly the Revenue consider that the Schedule A charge extends to one off or casual lettings that may not have the degree of organisation normally associated with a business; see SAT1 (1995) para 9.19. For practical purposes therefore it must be assumed that any receipt of an income nature relating to land will fall to be regarded as a receipt of a Schedule A business.

5.18 Even though Schedule A income is treated as derived from a business and Schedule D, Case I computation rules are applied, Schedule A income is not entirely assimilated to that of a trade. This means that the full loss relief rules of *TA 1988, s 380* do not apply, nor is roll-over relief and retirement relief generally available for CGT purposes.

Computation of profit

General

5.19 Tax is charged on the full amount of profits or gains arising in the year of assessment, so the basis of assessment is the current fiscal year (6 April–5 April). [Substituted *TA 1988, s 21(2); FA 1995, s 39(2)*]. The profits or gains are to be computed as if the Schedule A business were a trade carried on under Schedule D Case I, unless the contrary is expressly provided. [Substituted *TA 1988, s 21(3)*]. Accordingly, Schedule D, Case I principles are to be applied, in particular the accruals concept. However, because profits must be determined on a fiscal year basis, the Schedule D, Case I basis period rules do not apply, and a different accounting period cannot be chosen as the basis for computing profit. From 1995/96 the rating of previous practices using accounting periods ending in the year of assessment are not acceptable.

5.20 In determining taxable profits, some of the more important aspects will be the following:

(*a*) Rents in arrears are to be included; rents paid in advance excluded.

(*b*) Expenses accrued but not paid are likewise to be included; prepaid expenses excluded.

(In small cases, where fiscal year accounts have been prepared in the past, a receipts and payments basis of accounting may still be acceptable; see Inland Revenue Press Release of 10 February 1995 (Appendix C) setting out the transitional proposals.)

(*c*) Any business expense will be deductible unless precluded by the general Case I rules of *TA 1988, s 74(1)*, i.e. where it is capital in nature or not 'wholly and exclusively' incurred for the business. This replaces the former 'prescriptive' approach with an expense only deductible if expressly allowed by statute. Hence the former Schedule A and Schedule D, Case VI deduction rules is disapplied. [*FA 1995, 6 Sch 4*].

(*d*) Although 'private' expenditure will thus be excluded, the Revenue will allow an apportionment between 'business' and 'private' as for Case I.

(*e*) The Case I bad debt rules will apply in determining whether a deduction can be made for unpaid rent. So relief may be available either for a normal bad debt write off or by creating a specific reserve.

(*f*) The commercial profits will be adjusted by applying any relevant tax rules.

(*g*) The post-cessation receipts provisions, including the ability to elect to carryback in *TA 1988, ss 103–106* and *108*, apply. [*TA 1988, s 21(5)*]. Similarly relief is available for post-cessation expenditure under *TA 1988, s 109A*. [*FA 1995, s 90*].

(*h*) Relief is available for pre-trading expenditure under *TA 1988, s 401*. [*FA 1995, 6 Sch 20*].

(*i*) Relief is available for statutory redundancy payments for staff employed on maintaining or managing a property and the costs of certain employee training courses and counselling services under *TA 1988, ss 579(4), 588(4A)* and *589 (9A)*. [*FA 1995, 6 Sch 23, 24* and *25*].

(*j*) The averaging relief for falling profits in *TA 1988, s 96* is not applicable.

(*k*) The anti-avoidance rules relating to rents payable between connected persons contained in *TA 1988, ss 33A* and *33B* are repealed for income tax purposes. [*FA 1995, 6 Sch 4(e)*].

Pooling of income and expenses/repairs

5.21 Under the old rules contained in *TA 1988, s 25(3)–(8)*, let property was divided into three categories:

(*a*) those let at full rents and not on tenants' repairing leases;

(*b*) those let on tenants' repairing leases; and

(*c*) those let at less than a full rent.

Income and expenses from properties within each category were ring fenced, with restrictions on the availability of relief for losses arising from the excess of expenditure over income on any particular category of property. Moreover, a deduction was precluded for expenditure on repairs incurred by reason of dilapidations attributable to a period before the owner acquired the property.

5.22 These rules cease to be applicable from 6 April 1995. [*FA 1995, 6 Sch 4(a)*]. Thereafter all businesses and transactions by any particular person or partnership chargeable under Schedule A are treated as entered into in the course of carrying on a single business. [*FA 1995, s 39(2); TA 1988, s 21(4)*]. Accordingly, income and expenses from all types of property letting in the UK, whether residential, commercial or industrial etc., and whatever the repairing or other obligations under the terms of the lease and the levels of rent, are to be pooled. The effect is that any loss arising from one property will be relieved automatically from profits derived from another. So the loss relief provisions considered in 5.44 *et seq*. below will only be in point if the Schedule A computation produces a net overall loss. It is to be noted, however, that a business carried on by a person in partnership with others is a different business from one he carries on on his own account. So a loss in a private business cannot be set against a profit in a partnership business; see 12.12.

5.23 Moreover, there is no restriction on the cost of repairs incurred shortly after acquisition that fall within the principles of *Odeon Theatres Ltd v Jones (1971) 48 TC 257* rather than *Law Shipping Co Ltd v CIR (1923) 12 TC 621*. The distinction is between acquisition in a state where the property is fit for use, but in need of repair and redecorating, and the purchase price is not materially reduced as a result of the condition, compared with a property acquired in such a dilapidated condition that it was incapable of use as purchased and this was reflected in the acquisition price. ESC A21 allowed relief for repairs where property passed on death between husband and wife and the dilapidations arose prior to the death. This concession has been withdrawn on the basis that it is considered unnecessary. Accordingly any person who succeeds to a property on death, or by *inter vivos* gift, should be entitled to a deduction for the cost of repairs even if carried out shortly after acquisition. (Inland Revenue Press Release 4 April 1995).

5.24 However, such pooling will only apply to the total Schedule A income and expenditure of a particular person or partnership. It follows that a partner in a Schedule A business is not able to aggregate his share of that income and expenditure with that of any separate business carried on alone, or in another partnership. In such a case the taxpayer is treated as having two distinct Schedule A businesses, one carried on by him alone, the other (effectively a share) carried on in partnership. Likewise income treated in a representative capacity is charged separately. As set out below, any loss arising from one Schedule A business cannot be set against a profit derived from the other. This is of course in contrast with the ability to set off a Case I loss sideways against other income.

Property let at an undervalue

5.25 Given the general pooling provisions, the question may arise whether there are any limitations on relief where a particular property is let at less than a full market rent. Except in the context of one estate elections, considered at 5.61 *et seq.* below, there are no specific provisions requiring any uplift in the rent in a Schedule A computation. Although in the computation of trading profits under Schedule D, Case I the *Sharkey v Wernher (1955) 36 TC 275* principle requires goods appropriated from trading stock to private use to be brought into account at market value, this should not apply to Schedule A. In particular, *Sharkey v Wernher* seems to be confined to actual trading stock; see, for example, *Mason v Innes (1967) 44 TC 326*. It is understood that the Revenue accept that there is no requirement to bring in a notional market rent.

5.26 But there may not be complete freedom to offset expenses relating to properties let at an undervalue against surplus income from fully let properties. Thus, expenses are only deductible if they are incurred wholly and exclusively for the purposes of the letting business. Where, for example, property is let at a substantial undervalue to a relative this requirement may well not be satisfied, in that there would be a duality of motive for the expenditure. The Revenue can be expected to scrutinise such cases and only permit an allowable loss where the parties are at arm's length, or where, say, there is an interval between normal lettings, and a relative is in temporary, 'care taking' occupation. This may particularly arise where a substantial deduction for interest is claimed.

Travel expenses

5.27 Travel expenses may be deductible under the 'wholly and exclusively' rule for visits to the property to carry out or supervise repairs or collect rents. But if the landlord's home is located some distance from the property the question may arise whether the expense is properly connected with the letting business. The question may also arise whether the landlord's home may be regarded as his business base, where general management and administration is carried out, so that travel from that base is allowable, on the lines of the trading rules and the dicta in *Horton v Young (1971) 47 TC 60*.

5.28 The point is likely to arise most acutely in the context of furnished holiday lettings, especially for seaside properties where the owner lives some distance away. It is understood that the Revenue's view is that the starting point should not be a consideration of where any 'base' is situated. The need to travel may arise not so much from the letting of the property itself but rather because of the personal preference of the landlord to live in his particular home. Alternatively it may be dictated by the requirements of his employment or other business activities. But where the location of the notional trade seems rational given the geographical spread of the properties, travelling expenses may be allowed. In particular where the let properties are concentrated in one area, and the landlord lives in the same area, travelling expenses may well be regarded as incurred wholly and exclusively for the purposes of the letting activity conducted from a business base in a landlord's home. Much will turn on the precise facts of the case.

Interest

General

5.29 The computation of Schedule A income on Schedule D, Case I lines means that interest will rank as a deductible expense, again on an accruals basis, provided that it is incurred wholly and exclusively for the Schedule A business. This will apply irrespective of the time when the loan was made, and whether or not the property is let throughout the year of assessment. Interest paid on an overdraft, as well as on a loan, will qualify for a deduction. These rules are in contrast to the previous ones, whereby interest was only deductible in respect of a property if:

(*a*) that property was let at a commercial rent for more than 26 weeks in a year and when not let was available for letting or used as the main residence of the borrower, and

(*b*) the interest was payable on a loan taken out to acquire or improve the property.

5.30 Under the new rules interest paid on a borrowing to fund repairs or other revenue expenditure should be deductible. Relief should also be available for interest paid on a borrowing for building or refurbishment during the course of the construction or refurbishment and prior to letting. Relief will also be available in respect of holiday or second homes, although there will then have to be an apportionment for any private use. As a corollary the existing relief for interest paid on a loan to buy or improve let property under *TA 1988, s 355(1)(b)* is abolished in respect of interest paid on or after 6 April 1995. [*FA 1995, s 42(1)–(3)*].

5.31 Where an individual has substantial capital tied up in a letting business it is understood that the Revenue will allow relief in respect of interest on new or increased overdrafts arising from:

(i) losses which were incurred, provided no drawings were taken;

(ii) drawings during periods when the business broke even, provided such drawings were in accordance with previous established practice; and

(iii) improvements to a property or the purchase of new property.

It is understood that relief will also be available for an overdraft to fund periodic drawings taken in accordance with previous practice provided the capital account remains in surplus.

5.32 The new rules apply to interest paid on or after 6 April 1995. However, where the Schedule A source of income ceases entirely in 1995/96 the old rules continue to apply. [*FA 1995, s 42(3)* and *(4)*].

Interest paid in prior years

5.33 To the extent that there is any 'excess' interest arising pre-1995/96, i.e. interest for which relief has not been obtained against letting income, such excess cannot be deducted as such from letting income in 1995/96 (unless the source ceases entirely in 1995/96 when the old rules apply) or subsequent years. However, it would instead be carried forward as a Schedule A loss. Claims to establish such a loss for 1995/96 have to be made before 6 April 1998. [*FA 1995, s 42(5)* and *6 Sch 19(3)* and *(4)*].

Loans qualifying for mortgage interest relief/MIRAS

5.34 In certain cases, the interest will qualify for mortgage interest relief as well as being deductible for Schedule A purposes, e.g. a person living in job-related accommodation paying interest on a loan to buy a house which is let but which is intended in future to be his main residence. The borrower can then choose the form of relief which is preferred. If the loan is not eligible for MIRAS he may choose each year how the relief is to be claimed, whether as a Schedule A business expense or as mortgage interest relief. But interest can only be relieved in one way, there can be no double relief. [*TA 1988, ss 368(3)* and *(4)*]. (See Inland Revenue Tax Bulletin, 17 June 1995, page 221 (Appendix F).)

5.35 If the loan is eligible for MIRAS the borrower has to make an election if he wishes to obtain a Schedule A deduction instead. Otherwise he cannot obtain such deduction. [*TA 1988, s 369(3)*]. However, by concession the mortgage interest relief on a loan may be apportioned between the part of the loan attributable to residential use and the part attributable to business use; see ESC A27/95.

5.36 An election to obtain a Schedule A deduction instead of MIRAS would remove the £30,000 mortgage ceiling and provide relief for the taxpayer at his marginal rate, rather than 15 per cent, so it would be advantageous where the mortgage was substantial and the rent was likewise substantial. Moreover, even if the rent was not substantial, there could also be a benefit for a taxpayer if he had other rental properties, since the interest could then be included in the pool of expenditure. The taxpayer must give notice to the Revenue that he is carrying on or proposes to carry on a Schedule A business, that interest is to be deducted in a Schedule A computation and he must state the date when MIRAS is not to apply. The election has to be made within 22 months from the end of the year of assessment when it is first to have effect. So if the notice is to take effect from 6 April 1996 it must be given before 5 February 1999. Once given, the election is irrevocable, but the taxpayer may still choose to claim mortgage interest relief outside MIRAS, limited to £30,000 at 15 per cent, or make a deduction in computing the profits of the Schedule A business.

5.37 The Revenue are then obliged to notify both the lender and the borrower, giving the date from which the MIRAS scheme will cease to apply, being the later of the date specified by the taxpayer and that on which the notice is given by the Revenue to the lender. In the event of a gap between the date of the borrower's election and the date given in the Revenue's notice, the lender can claim from the Revenue any amount deducted by the borrower from the interest payments during the period, and the Revenue can recover the amount from the borrower by assessment. The loan may be brought back within MIRAS if the property ceases to be let for a Schedule A business. [*TA 1988, s 375A* as amended by *FA 1995, 6 Sch 18*].

Sundry amendments

5.38 Interest which is deductible under Schedule A cannot also be claimed as a charge on income under *TA 1988, s 353*. [*TA 1988, s 368* as amended by *FA 1995, 6 Sch 17*]. The provisions in *TA 1988, s 82* relating to interest paid to non residents are disapplied for Schedule A purposes, as this section could otherwise restrict interest relief on overseas borrowings. [*TA 1988, s 82(6), FA 1995, 6 Sch 13*]. Interest paid to a non resident is, however, non deductible to the extent that it exceeds a reasonable commercial rate. [*TA 1988, s 74(1)(a)*].

Capital expenditure and allowances

New system

5.39 Under the old rules, taxpayers who let property were entitled to allowances for certain capital expenditure. Although the rules for calculating these allowances remain, so, where appropriate, allowances are given by reference to the date when the expenditure was incurred, the method of giving the allowances has changed (see 5.40). Writing-down allowances will be available in respect of the balance of expenditure at the end of the chargeable period for which the allowances are made, together with any balancing allowance or charge on disposals. Under the new system the chargeable period will be the tax year itself, i.e. 6 April to the following 5 April, because the accounting period has to coincide with the fiscal year under Schedule A, except for partnerships, see 12.12. This is in contrast to Schedule D, Case I, where allowances are given by reference to expenditure and disposals in the period of account ending in the fiscal year.

5.40 The method of giving the allowances has changed. Previously the allowances were given by way of discharge or repayment of tax. Under the new rules the allowances are treated as an expense of the Schedule A business in determining the profit of that business. Likewise any balancing charges are treated as a Schedule A receipt. This treatment also applies to the letting of furnished holiday accommodation deemed to be a Schedule A business [*FA 1995, 6 Sch 31*] and dwelling houses let on assured tenancies. [*CAA 1990, s 92; FA 1995, 6 Sch 34*].

Qualifying expenditure

5.41 Capital allowances may be given as a business expense in respect of expenditure on the following, computed under the normal rules set out in *CAA 1990*.

(*a*) Plant and machinery provided for use or used for the purposes of a Schedule A business. This covers such items as cleaning machinery for common areas and security systems. [*TA 1988, s 32; FA 1995, 6 Sch 8(1)* and *(2)*].

(*b*) Leased plant and machinery. Plant let for use in a dwelling is not eligible for allowances except where the letting is a furnished holiday letting. In such case a wear and tear allowance may be available in lieu, see 5.39 [*CAA 1990, s 61; FA 1995, 6 Sch 8(3)*].

(*c*) Thermal insulation. These allowances are also given on unlet property by deeming this to be a Schedule A business. [*CAA 1990, s 67; FA 1995, 6 Sch 32*].

(*d*) Industrial buildings. During a period of temporary disuse the landlord is still deemed to carry on a Schedule A business and hence be eligible for allowances. Initial allowances are available before a building is let. [*CAA 1990, s 9(1A)(a)* and *(b); FA 1995, 6 Sch 29* and *30*].

(*e*) Agricultural buildings. [*CAA 1990, s 132; FA 1995, 6 Sch 35*].

Furnished lettings – wear and tear allowances

5.42 No capital allowances are available for expenditure incurred in connection with the furnished letting of a dwelling house [*CAA 1990, s 61(2)*]. But, as has been the long established position in the past, the Revenue will allow relief under the renewals basis, or alternatively a wear and tear allowance may be claimed under ESC B47. The latter is calculated at 10 per cent of the net rent for the year, namely the rent due less any amount included in the rent towards Council Tax, water rates or any services normally borne by the tenant.

5.43 Under the old rules, where the capital allowances exceeded the property income, any excess could be set against other income. Under the new rules this will create a Schedule A loss which is generally not available for sideways set off against other income. To preserve the existing relief an exception is accordingly made for losses created by excess capital allowances or agricultural expenses; see 5.46.

Example 1

	Expenses Payable For Year £	*Income Receivable For Year* £
I Yuriev		
Year ended 5 April 1996		
Income from property		
Address of property let		
'Domodedevo'		
West Bank Road		
Bambers Green		
Essex CM22 6PB		
Gross rents and other income		12,000
Expenses:		
Repairs and maintenance	1,771	
Plant hire and fuel	902	
Electricity	86	
Insurance	880	
Postage and stationery	200	
Accountancy	400	
Interest	2,600	
		(6,839)
Gross income *less* expenses		£ 5,161

Example 2

	Expenses Payable For Year £	*Income Receivable For Year* £
A Lazarev		
Year ended 5 April 1996		
Rental income and expenses		
Statement for 12 Riverside Mews, SW9		
Rents receivable (furnished)		26,970
Less expenses:		
Service charge and ground rent	2,371	
Insurance	179	
Repairs and maintenance	366	
Wear and Tear allowance 10% × £26,970 − £2,371	2,460	
Advertising	200	
Alarm rental and charges	314	
Maintenance contracts	68	

Inspections	175	
Loan interest	795	
Cleaning charges	80	
Inventory check	85	
Gas and electricity charges	31	
Accountancy	575	
Agency commission	3,972	
Tenancy agreement legal charges	500	
Sundries	100	
		(12,271)
Net income		£14,699

Losses

General

5.44 New Schedule A loss relief provisions are contained in *TA 1988, s 379A*, introduced by *FA 1995, 6 Sch 19*, which provide relief for a Schedule A business whether carried on solely or in partnership. A Schedule A loss is to be computed on the same basis as profits are computed. [*TA 1988, s 379A(7)*]. Any loss so determined is automatically carried forward without the necessity for a claim, and set against Schedule A profits for the following year. If those profits are insufficient to absorb the losses, they may be carried forward to the next following year, and so on indefinitely. However, except for losses attributable to excess capital allowances and agricultural expenses there is no 'sideways' relief. Moreover, because a partnership business is distinct from a business carried on by an individual in his own capacity, a loss on one cannot be set against a profit in another. [*TA 1988, s 379A(1)*].

5.45 Schedule A losses are therefore effectively ring fenced and cannot generally be set against other income. This is the main reason given for not aligning the Corporation Tax rules with the Income Tax rules. It was thought that companies would prefer the existing arrangements whereby interest paid in respect of a Schedule A source may be set against other income as a charge on income. This seems a rather specious argument, in that it would be perfectly possible to apply the Schedule D, Case I computation rules for Corporation Tax, while leaving interest to be dealt with as a charge on income.

Example 3

Mr Klimov has income from a residential investment, and is not entitled to any capital allowances. Profits and losses are as follows:

1995/96	Loss	£6,000
1996/97	Profit	£5,000
1997/98	Loss	£2,000
1998/99	Profit	£7,000

His Schedule A liability will be:

1995/96	nil	*(a)*
1996/97	nil	*(b)*
1997/98	nil	*(c)*
1998/99	£4,000	*(d)*

Notes

(a) Loss £6,000 carried forward: *s 379A(1)(a)*.

(b) Balance of loss £1,000 carried forward (£6,000 − £5,000): *s 379A(1)(b)*.

(c) Loss of £3,000 carried forward (£1,000 brought forward + £2,000 loss for the year).

(d) Profit for year £7,000 less £3,000 loss carried forward.

Losses attributable to excess capital allowances and agricultural expenses

5.46 Although there is no general sideways set off against other income for excess Schedule A losses, an exception is provided for that part of the loss which is attributable to capital allowances and to excess allowable agricultural expenses of an agricultural estate. [*TA 1988, s 379A(2)* and *(3)*]. Allowable agricultural expenses are defined as those in respect of maintenance, repairs, insurance or management of the estate, excluding loan interest, attributable to the farmed portion of the estate. [*s 379A(8)(9)* and *(10)*]. This effectively preserves the relief given by the previous rules under *CAA 1990, s 141* and *TA 1988, s 33*. Relief is available against general income of the year in which the loss occurred and the year following.

5.47 Relief is limited to the smallest of:

(a) The relievable income (defined as the taxpayer's income for the year after deducting any Schedule A losses brought forward under *s 379A(1)* and those brought forward and set sideways against general income under *s 379A(3)*. [*s 379A(6)*]. The net effect is that losses that cannot be set off sideways in later years are used before losses that can.

(b) The Schedule A loss for the year.

(c) The allowable part of the loss, being the net capital allowances, (after setting against any balancing charge or agricultural expenses or the total thereof). [*s 379A(4)*].

5.48 Where sideways relief is claimed for the tax year in which the loss was made and the year after, the total relief for the two years taken together cannot exceed the smallest of any of these amounts. [*s 379A(5)*]. A claim has to be made for this sideways relief by the second 31 January after the end of the year of assessment; i.e. twenty-two months after the end of the tax year. Thus a claim for relief for 1997/98 must be made by 31 January 2000. [*s 379A(3)*].

Example 4

Mr Ushakov incurs exceptional repair expenditure on his let properties, part of which relate to let portions of his agricultural estate, as a result of which he incurs a Schedule A loss in 1998/99 of £40,000.

This includes:

balancing charges	£20,000
capital allowances	£25,000
agricultural expenses	£18,000

The loss claimable against other income under *TA 1998, s 379A(3)* is:

net capital allowances (£25,000 – £20,000)	£5,000
agricultural expenses	£18,000
	£23,000

Leaving a balance of £17,000 (£40,000 – £23,000) to carry forward against future Schedule A income under *TA 1988, s 379A(1)* by *TA 1988, s 379A(3)(b)*.

Example 5

Miss Malyutka incurred a normal Schedule A loss in 1997/98 of £10,000 which she carried forward. In 1998/99 she incurred excess agricultural expenses of £18,000 and had no other income so she carried this forward to set against general income for 1999/2000 in which year she had net rental income of £6,000 and other income of £15,000.

In 1999/2000 loss relief is claimable as follows:

Sch A income	£6,000
Less losses brought forward under *TA 1988, ss 379A(1)* and *379A(6)(a)*	£10,000
Assessable	NIL
Sch A loss carried forward	£4,000

Other income	£15,000
Less excess agricultural expenses for 1998/99 brought forward under *TA 1988, s 379A(3)*	£18,000
Assessable	NIL
Excess carried forward as Sch A loss	£3,000
Total Sch A loss carried forward under *TA 1988, s 379A(1)* and *379A(3)(b)* £4,000 *plus* £3,000 =	£7,000

Example 6

Mr Kalpokov has excess Schedule A capital allowances of:

£16,000 from 1997/98
£14,000 from 1998/99

His total income from 1998/99 is £25,000

Loss relief is available:	
brought forward and set off under *TA 1988, ss 379A(3)* and *379A(6)(b)*	£16,000
1998/99 (£14,000 – £5,000)	£9,000
	£25,000
Assessable	NIL

The £5,000 unrelieved loss may be carried forward against total income in 1999/2000 under *TA 1988, s 379A(3)* or as a Schedule A loss in 2000/01 onwards under *TA 1988, s 379A(1)* and *s 379A(3)(b)*.

Example 7

Mr Kombine has a Schedule A loss in 1998/99 of £5,000 after capital allowances of £12,000 and balancing charges of £2,000.

His total income in 1998/99 is £22,000 less allowable Schedule A loss of £5,000, taxable £17,000. The whole of the Schedule A loss consists of excess capital allowances offsetable against total income under *TA 1988, s 379A(3)* limited to the amount of the loss under *TA 1988, s 379A(4)*.

Losses carried forward under old rules

5.49 Where there is an unrelieved Schedule A deficit brought forward at 1 April 1995, computed under the old rules, this may be carried forward to 1995/96 and later years. This encompasses Schedule D, Case VI losses in respect of furnished lettings previously allowable against Schedule D, Case VI income under *TA 1988, s 392*, and any excess interest. [*FA 1995, 6 Sch 19(2)* and *(3)*].

Furnished holiday lettings

5.50 So far as furnished holiday lettings are concerned, the existing rules in *TA 1988, s 503* permit any losses to be relieved as trading losses, i.e. sideways or backwards. The rules are preserved under the new Schedule A by *FA 1995, 6 Sch 21*. Any losses from furnished holiday lettings on a commercial basis, *Walls v Livesey (1975) STC (SCD) 12,* included within the total Schedule A source may be relieved sideways or backwards against general income. Subject thereto the loss will be relieved against any other Schedule A profits for the year, with any surplus carried forward and set against Schedule A profits of subsequent years.

Example 8

Mr Anatra incurred a net Schedule A loss of £20,000 in 1998/99 which included £12,000 from furnished holiday lettings and £2,000 from net capital allowances.

His total income for 1997/98 was £30,000, for 1998/99, £35,000 and for 1999/2000, £45,000 including Schedule A £5,000.

He claimed for relief as follows:

1997/98 – furnished lettings loss under *TA 1988, s 380(1)(b)*	£12,000
1998/99 – excess capital allowances under *TA 1988, s 379A(3)*	£2,000
1999/2000 – Schedule A balance of loss under *TA 1988, s 379A(1)*	£6,000
Total loss claimed	£20,000

Transitional provisions (1994/95)

General

5.51 Schedule A income has been assessed on a wide variety of bases over the years. With the change to strict fiscal year accounting, and the introduction of amended computation rules, it has been decided that 1994/95 should be the transitional year, to give as long as possible to iron out any problems well before the 31 January 1998 filing date for the 1996/97 self assessment return.

5.52 Taxpayers may either compute 1994/95 Schedule A income on a strict basis by applying the old Schedule A rules ignoring any gaps or overlaps, or the procedure published in the Inland Revenue Press Release of 10 February 1995 (Appendix C) and Inland Revenue Tax Bulletin No 20, December 1995, page 268 (Appendix F) may be applied. This sets out the instructions to inspectors for dealing with the transitional period, and follows extensive discussions with the professional bodies representing taxpayers on the Self Assessment Consultative Committee. These new rules do not apply if the Schedule A source ends in 1995/96, or it is clear that the source is likely to end shortly after. In both of these cases the old rules still apply.

Computation under Inland Revenue transitional proposals

5.53 The principle of these transitional provisions is to leave 1993/94 on whatever basis has been consistently applied in the past and to bring into the 1994/95 computation the whole of the income from the end of the 1993/94 basis period up to 5 April 1995, deducting any income that will be included in 1995/96 on an accruals basis, and adding back any expenses that relate to the period after 5 April 1995. Where a fiscal year basis of assessment has previously applied this will be the only adjustment. Moreover, the Revenue has also stated that in small cases, where accounts have been drawn up to 31 March or 5 April on a receipts and payments basis, these may well be acceptable without amendment for the new Schedule A.

5.54 However, in cases where 1993/94 letting accounts have not been prepared to 31 March or 5 April, but have instead been prepared on a quasi Schedule D, Case I basis, to an accounting date ending in the preceding fiscal year, such as the year to 31 December 1992, the period from the end of the 1993/94 basis period to 5 April 1995 will be well in excess of twelve months. The amount assessable will then be a twelve-month proportion of the income for the entire period. So in this example where the period between 1 January 1993 and 5 April 1995 is twenty-seven months, 12/27 of the net profit (after adjusting for accruals) will be assessable.

5.55 Should the taxpayer and the inspector disagree about the application of these transitional provisions, in the case of furnished lettings if the figures over the lifetime of the business are available and it is clear that the provisional arrangements would be unfair, the inspector is to use his discretion under *TA 1988, s 69* to select any twelve months out of the period from the end of the 1993/94 basis period to 5 April 1995 that gives the fairest result. In Schedule A cases, an attempt is to be made to agree a similar approach. If no such agreement is possible the inspector is to determine the Case VI basis period under *TA 1988, s 69* to correspond to the fairest possible result, and assess Schedule A by reference to the profits of the fiscal year 1994/95, in both cases by apportioning the profits of different accounting periods if necessary. Since the General or Special

Commissioners only have jurisdiction to apply the law on a strict basis on an appeal, should the taxpayer still be dissatisfied his remedy is to take any dispute to the Revenue head office and ultimately to the Revenue Adjudicator.

5.56 When the transitional proposals were published in the Inland Revenue Guide to the new basis of assessment, SAT 1, in July 1995 it was stated in a note to paragraph 9.112 that where 1994/95 had already been assessed and become final, 1994/95 should not be reopened and the transition should be dealt with in the 1995/96 assessment. Seemingly this note was misunderstood since in certain cases inspectors were seeking to treat 1995/96 as the transitional year for the purposes of calculating any adjustment. The concern was expressed that this could operate to penalise taxpayers whose affairs were up-to-date, as they would then not be entitled to any deduction in tax for 1994/95 that might arise if the transitional proposals had been applied for that year. This could be the case where there were falling profits in 1994/95 and increasing profits in 1995/96. The Revenue have now confirmed that in all cases the transitional year is 1994/95 for the purposes of calculating any transitional relief and where the relief, in terms of tax, cannot be given in 1994/95 because that year is closed, it will be given in 1995/96 in accordance with the original intention, (Inland Revenue Press Release 10 February 1995, para 29 Appendix C).

Capital allowances

5.57 As set out more fully in 5.39 *et seq.* capital allowances are generally given as an expense in computing new Schedule A income from 1995/96. For 1994/95, in cases where assessments have previously been based on a period other than the strict fiscal year, the starting point is to take the balance of any qualifying expenditure brought forward from the 1993/94 computation. To this is added qualifying expenditure in the whole of the period to 5 April 1995, less disposals. A twelve-month writing-down allowance is then given on the net figure, irrespective of the length of the period. For furnished lettings, the 10 per cent wear and tear allowance is available as set out in 5.42.

Interest – 1995/96

5.58 Interest paid in 1994/95 would have qualified for relief under *TA 1988, s 353* provided that the qualifying conditions in *s 355(1)(b)* had been satisfied. As set out in 5.29 *et seq.* interest will from 1995/96 be relieved instead as expense in computing the profits of the deemed Schedule A business. This may result in a mismatch for 1995/96, resulting in full relief not being obtained for the total interest paid over the life of a loan where the interest was payable, say, half-yearly in arrears. In such cases additional interest may be allowed in 1995/96 to ensure that over the life of the loan the whole of the interest will broadly be allowable. Such additional relief will only be given if it is fair to do so, taking into account all the circumstances, including any double charge to income on moving to a preceding year basis originally and any drop out as a result of applying the transitional provisions in 1994/95. There is no corresponding anti-avoidance provision to prevent a double allowance of interest paid in advance which would be allowed in 1994/95 on the basis of payments made as a charge on income and in 1995/96 on the interest payable for the fiscal year.

Example 9

Mr Lem received rents from an unlet property in England in advance on the usual quarter dates. He prepared accounts to 5 April 1994 which included four quarters' rent at £2,000 per quarter. Expenses were claimed as incurred, i.e. on an accounts basis. Interest was payable in arrears at £500 per quarter ended 31 March, 30 June, 30 September and 31 December.

The tax computations were:

	1993/94	*1994/95*	*1995/96*
	£	£	£
Rent receivable	8,000	8,000	8,000
Less adjustment for receipt in advance 6 April to 24 June 1995 – 79 days £8,000 × 79/365		1,732	
		6,268	
Less expenses (say)	1,400	1,450	1,500
Interest			2,000
Schedule A income	6,600	4,818	4,500
Less charge on income – interest (*TA 1988, ss 353–354* and *355(1)(b)*)	2,000	2,000	
	4,600	2,818	

Example 10

Mr Belyakov let a property furnished and by agreement with his local Inspector of Taxes, prepared accounts on a calendar year basis and adopted an informal preceding year basis of assessment. Interest of £1,600 per annum was payable half-yearly in arrears on 30 June and 31 December. Rent of £3,600 per annum was payable monthly in advance on the first of each month since 1 March 1981 when the property was acquired.

1993/94

	£	£
Rent receivable in year ended 31 December 1992		3,600
Wear and tear allowance 10%	360	
Agent's commission	540	
Other expenses excluding interest	100	
		1,000
		2,600
Less charge on income – interest paid 30.6.93 and 31.12.93		1,600
Assessable		£1,000

1994/95

	£	£
Rent receivable in period from 1.1.93 to 5.4.95 – 27 months		8,100
Wear and tear allowance 10%	810	
Agent's commission	1,215	
Other expenses excluding interest	225	
		2,250
		£5,850
12/27ths thereof		2,600
Less charge on income – interest paid 30.6.94 and 31.12.94		1,600
Assessable		£1,000

However, the taxpayer argued that in 1980/81 he had paid tax on the rent received on 1 March and 1 April of £600 with no deduction for interest but an allowance for 10 per cent wear and tear allowance and 15 per cent agent's commission totalling £150, and therefore paid tax on £450 × 25/61 = £184 rent in advance. He also argued that in 1981/82 he had obtained relief for four month's interest on 30 June 1981 and six month's interest on 31 December 1981. As a result he had never received relief for interest due from 1 January 1995 to 5 April 1995, i.e. 3/12 × £1,600, £400. The 1981/82 assessment was on the net rents for the year ended 28 February 1982 (first twelve months) and 1982/83 on the same amount. The assessment for 1983/84 was on the net rents for the year ended 31 December 1982. 31 December was the accounting date for the following years.

The Revenue accepted the taxpayer's computation of income and unrelieved expenses and reduced the 1994/95 assessment by £584 from £1,000 to £416.

1995/96

	£	£
Rent receivable for year ended 5 April 1996		3,600
Wear and tear allowance 10%	360	
Agent's commission	540	
Interest for year	1,600	
Other expenses	100	
		2,600
Assessable		£1,000

Summary	*Net Profit* £	*Net Rents* £	*Interest* £	*Assessed* £
1980/81 (£450 − 184 − 133 1 month's interest)	133	450	—	450
1981/82	1,000	2,600	1,333 (10 mths)	1,267
1982/83	1,000	2,600	1,600	1,000
1983/84	1,000	2,600	1,600	1,000
1984/85	1,000	2,600	1,600	1,000
1985/86	1,000	2,600	1,600	1,000
1986/87	1,000	2,600	1,600	1,000
1987/88	1,000	2,600	1,600	1,000
1988/89	1,000	2,600	1,600	1,000
1989/90	1,000	2,600	1,600	1,000
1990/91	1,000	2,600	1,600	1,000
1991/92	1,000	2,600	1,600	1,000
1992/93	1,000	2,600	1,600	1,000
1993/94	1,000	2,600	1,600	1,000
1994/95	1,000	2,600	1,600	416
Adjustment			(584)	
1995/96	1,000	2,600	1,600	1,000
	£15,133			£15,133

Partnerships

5.59 The new current year basis rules applicable to partnerships are applied to a Schedule A business carried on by the firm. This means that each partner will be assessed on his share of the Schedule A income, and there will be no deemed cessation on a change of partner. It also means that the strict fiscal year basis for Schedule A is modified, so that there is a deemed second Schedule A trade coterminus with the Schedule D, Case I trade; see Chapter 12. [Substituted *TA 1988, s 21(6)* and *(7); FA 1995, s 39(2)*]. As indicated in 12.11 a partnership business is distinct from one separately carried on by an individual alone, so profits from one cannot be set against losses of the other (confirmed by Sir George Young, Hansard, 9 February 1995 col. 167 and Inland Revenue Tax Bulletin No 20, December 1995, page 271 (Appendix F). Likewise if an individual is a member of two partnerships with Schedule A income, these will be treated as distinct and separate businesses.

Joint ownership

5.60 As explained in 12.12 the mere joint ownership of property does not constitute a partnership and each joint owner has to self-assess on his share of the joint income of his own Schedule A business, Tax Bulletin No 20, December 1995, page 271 (Appendix F). Where the joint ownership of property does not amount to a partnership the Revenue will not go so far as to treat the co-ownership as a quasi partnership but would avoid making enquiries into the co-ownership property income by way of enquiry through a passive co-owner. Enquiries would therefore be addressed to the managing co-owner who would be required to provide the relevant information although it will naturally be necessary to inform the remaining co-owners that their returns are under enquiry because of enquiries into the co-owned property. The procedure to be adopted will be explained at a forthcoming Tax Bulletin article.

Land managed as one estate

5.61 Provisions contained in *TA 1988, s 26* allow a 'one estate election', which effectively enables relief to be obtained for the cost of the owner occupied part, notably the upkeep of the estate manor, against total estate income. These provisions are continued under the new Schedule A, but the application of Schedule D, Case I principles may provide additional relief for, say, specific provisions and accruals, and it may even be possible to obtain relief for interest on, say, a borrowing to improve or refurbish the principal house as an expense.

5.62 Where land has been managed as one estate continuously since 1962/63 and part of the estate is unlet or let at a rent below the annual value, the annual value is deemed to be the rent receivable in the Schedule A computation. The annual value is defined by *TA 1988, s 837* and Extra Statutory Concessions A56 and B30 as equivalent to the old gross rateable value, which is normally a very low figure compared with the market rent. The estate disbursements and expenses may be set against the deemed income and the actual income of the entire estate. This has the effect of relieving the excess expenditure relating to the unlet or reduced rent portion of the estate over the annual value. However, a deficit arising from excess maintenance expenditure on the unlet or reduced rent portion is effectively ring fenced. It is not treated as a Schedule A loss, but may be carried forward against future income from the estate. But excess expenditure on the fully let portion of the estate may create a Schedule A loss deductible under *TA 1988, s 379A* against other Schedule A income. This may be particularly helpful in the case of interest relief relating to the fully let properties. [*FA 1995, 6 Sch 5*].

5.63 In order to apply the single estate treatment it is necessary for an election to be made within twelve months of the end of the fiscal year in which a change of ownership takes place; *TA 1988, s 26(3)*. The application of these rules to land held in trust is unclear although it would seem that the Revenue regard a change in the trustees or a change of life tenant as an occasion requiring an election. In a case of a strict settlement under the *Settled Land Act 1925*, it is arguable that a change in the *Settled Land Act* trustees would not be a change of owner, although a change of life tenant treated as the statutory owner in whom the legal estate vests would be a change requiring a further election. The Revenue strictly enforce the time limit for such elections.

Example 11

Lord Kukuracha owns a landed estate in Lincolnshire in respect of which an election under *TA 1988, s 26* has been made. The annual value of the manor house in which he lives and surrounding amenity land is £1,800 per annum. The net rents before repairs for the let portion of the estate amounts to £40,000 in 1998/99. The repair expenditure amounts to £25,000 on the manor house and grounds and £6,000 on the let properties.

The Schedule A assessment for 1998/99 is:		£
Net rents received		40,000
Annual value of manor house		1,800
		41,800
Less repairs:		
Let property	6,000	
Manor house	25,000	
		31,000
Assessable/taxable		10,800

Maintenance funds for historic buildings

5.64 Under *TA 1988, s 27* an estate owner who transfers a property on an estate subject to a one estate election into a maintenance fund for historic buildings can continue to benefit from the one estate treatment of the settled property. The definition of income is widened to include all receipts of the estate. [*FA 1995, s 39(4), (5)* and *(6), 6 Sch*].

5.65 The deduction for disbursement and expenses is also brought into line with the Schedule D, Case I treatment of a Schedule A business. Excess maintenance expenditure of agricultural land may be deductible as a Schedule A loss under *TA 1988, s 379A*. Expenditure on maintaining any part of the estate within the maintenance fund can be deducted from income arising to the fund.

Rent a room relief

5.66 The rent a room relief available in respect of furnished lettings from a taxpayer's home under *F(No 2)A 1992, 10 Sch 2(1)*, which applied where the income was under Case VI, is preserved and applies to qualifying lettings within Schedule A. [*FA 1995, 6 Sch 38*].

Chargeable gains and reliefs

5.67 Although profits chargeable under Schedule A are taxed as a business, that business is nevertheless generally regarded as the holding of investments, rather than the carrying on of a trade, profession or vocation. Hence the various CGT reliefs for disposals of business assets, e.g. roll-over relief or reinvestment relief [*TCGA 1992, ss 152–153*], hold over relief on gifts [*TCGA 1992, s 165*] and retirement relief [*TCGA 1992, s 163*] are not available. The exception is for gains attributable to property used for furnished holiday lettings, as this activity is assimilated to a trade. [*FA 1995, 6 Sch 36; TCGA 1992, s 241(3)*].

5.68 In determining the gain arising on the disposal of leases with less than 50 years unexpired, the curved-line depreciation rules in *TCGA 1992, 8 Sch* exclude that proportion of the premium taxed under Schedule A as a receipt of a Schedule A business. There are like provisions in respect of Schedule A charges on the sale of land with a right to reconveyance, the assignment of a lease granted at an undervalue and certain deemed premiums; see 5.10 to 5.12. [*FA 1995, 6 Sch 37*].

Miscellaneous amendments

5.69 *FA 1995, 6 Sch 20–28* contains a number of amendments consequential upon Schedule A profits being computed in accordance with Schedule D, Case I rules, most of which have been dealt with already. Others include the following:

(*a*) Gifts to charities made from a Schedule A business are within the exemptions in *TA 1988, s 577(9)*. [*FA 1995, 6 Sch 22*].

(*b*) The owner of an historic home who has settled an associated maintenance fund is excluded from a double charge to tax both under Schedule A and as a settlor. [*FA 1995, 6 Sch 26; TA 1988, s 692(1)*].

(*c*) In a sale and leaseback transaction between associated persons the deduction for tax relief under *TA 1988, s 779(4)* is linked to the commercial rent by an amendment to the definition of relevant tax relief. [*FA 1995, 6 Sch 27; TA 1988, s 779(13)(a)*].

Chapter 6

Schedule D, Case III

Basis of charge

6.1 Shortly stated Schedule D, Case III charges tax in respect of:

(*a*) any interest of money whether yearly or otherwise, or any annuity or other annual payment, whether such payment is payable within or out of the United Kingdom, but not including any payment chargeable under Schedule A; and

(*b*) all discounts; and

(*c*) income, except income charged under Schedule C, from securities bearing interest payable out of the public revenue, prior to its abolition from 1996/97 by *FA 1996, 7 Sch 3* and *32*.

[*TA 1988, s 18(3)*].

The location of the source will usually determine whether it falls within Case III or within Cases IV or V.

Fiscal year basis

6.2 Under *TA 1988, s 64; FA 1994, s 206* income tax under Schedule D, Case III will be chargeable on the full amount of the income arising in the year of assessment without any deduction. The only exceptions will be income received by a partnership, dealt with in 12.12 below, and income falling within the transitional provisions.

Commencement date for new rules

6.3 The fiscal year basis applies to new sources arising on or after 6 April 1994 and for existing sources from 6 April 1997 (1997/98) provided that they continue beyond 5 April 1998 [*FA 1994, 20 Sch 4(1)*], with the transitional year being 1996/97.

Example 1

Mr Lebed opened a bank deposit account on 5 October 1994 with £100,000, on which interest was payable gross at 10 per cent p.a.

6.4 *Schedule D, Case III*

Interest was received as follows:

1994/95	$£100{,}000 \times 10\% \times \frac{6}{12} =$	£5,000
1995/96	£100,000 × 10%	£10,000
1996/97	£100,000 × 10%	£10,000
1997/98	£100,000 × 10%	£10,000

Assessable/taxable

1994/95	fiscal year basis	£5,000
1995/96	fiscal year basis	£10,000
1996/97	fiscal year basis	£10,000
1997/98	fiscal year basis	£10,000

New sources

6.4 Each lodgement is strictly a new source (*Hart v Sangster 1957 37 TC 231*) although this point is not normally taken by the Revenue. The Revenue will not continue their practice of assessing new accounts on a preceding year basis until 1996/97 merely because there is in existence an account dealt with on the preceding year basis, particularly if they consider that the taxpayer is trying to maximise transitional relief. New accounts from 6 April 1994 will be dealt with on a strict fiscal year basis under the new rules in all cases (see 24.27 *et seq*. below).

Cessation before 6 April 1998

6.5 If the source ceases prior to 6 April 1998 the transitional provisions do not apply and the old rules apply throughout. [*FA 1994, 20 Sch 5*].

Example 2

Mr Mackel closed his deposit account opened prior to 6 April 1994 on 31 December 1997. The interest received in 1997/98 was

$$£100{,}000 \times 10\% \times \frac{9}{12} = £7{,}500$$

Assessable/taxable

1994/95	actual basis	£5,000
1995/96	actual basis	£10,000
1996/97	preceding year basis	£10,000
1997/98	actual basis	£7,500

The taxpayer has the option to put 1996/97 on an actual basis under *TA 1988, s 66(1)(c)* (original enactment). The Revenue has the option to put 1996/97 on an actual basis under *TA 1988, s 67* (original enactment) under *FA 1994, 20 Sch 5*.

Transitional provisions – averaging

6.6 Other than as mentioned in 6.5 and 6.7 the transitional year 1996/97 is assessed on one-half of the aggregate of the full amount of the income arising in 1996/97 and the full amount of the income arising in the year 1995/96 (which under the old rules would have been assessed for 1996/97 on the preceding year basis of assessment). [*FA 1994, 20 Sch 4(1)(2)*].

Example 3

Mr Gribovsky had the following interest received, taxable under Schedule D, Case III.

1993/94		£1,000
1994/95		£2,000
1995/96		£4,000
1996/97		£8,000
1997/98		£9,000

Assessable/taxable

1994/95	preceding year basis	£1,000	
1995/96	preceding year basis	£2,000	
1996/97	transitional year	£6,000	(*a*)
1997/98	fiscal year basis	£9,000	

Note

(*a*) *FA 1994, 20 Sch 4(2)(a)*

income arising in 1996/97	£8,000
FA 1994, 20 Sch 4(2)(b) income arising in 1995/96	£4,000
aggregate	£12,000
50% thereof	£6,000

Transitional provisions where 1995/96 on actual basis

6.7 If the 1995/96 assessment is on the fiscal year basis, as a result of a taxpayer's election for the actual basis, under *TA 1988, s 66(1)(c)* the assessment for 1996/97 will also be made on an actual basis, not on the averaging basis. [*FA 1994, 20 Sch 4(3)*].

Example 4

Mr Petlyakov opened an account in 1993/94 and received the following deposit interest.

1993/94	£3,000
1994/95	£12,000
1995/96	£8,000
1996/97	£10,000
1997/98	£9,000
Total received	£42,000

Assessable/taxable

1993/94	actual basis	£3,000	
1994/95	actual basis	£12,000	
1995/96	preceding year	£12,000	
1996/97	transitional year	£9,000	(*a*)
1997/98	fiscal year basis	£9,000	
Total assessed		£45,000	

Notes

(*a*) Transitional period

1995/96 *FA 1994, 20 Sch 4(2)(a)*	£8,000
1996/97 *FA 1994, 20 Sch 4(2)(b)*	£10,000
	£18,000
50% thereof *FA 1994, 20 Sch 4(1)(2)*	£9,000

Mr Petlyakov elected to apply the actual basis for 1995/96 under *TA 1988, s 66(1)(c)* (original enactment).

Assessable/taxable

1993/94	actual basis	£3,000	
1994/95	actual basis	£12,000	
1995/96	actual basis	£8,000	
1996/97	fiscal year basis	£10,000	(*b*)
1997/98	fiscal year basis	£9,000	
Total assessed		£42,000	

Note

(*b*) *FA 1994, 20 Sch 4(3)*, 1996/97 assessed on a fiscal year basis as 1995/96 assessed on an actual basis.

Partnerships

6.8 Partnership untaxed investment income is not chargeable on a fiscal year basis but by reference to the basis period for Schedule D, Cases I or II under *TA 1988, s 111(7)(b); FA 1994, s 215; FA 1995, s 117*. The transitional provisions for such income are *TA 1988, s 111(4), (8); FA 1994, s 215; FA 1995, s 117*, see 12.23.

Chapter 7

Schedule D, Cases IV and V

General

7.1 Schedule D, Case IV charges tax in respect of income arising from securities out of the United Kingdom, except income charged under Schedule C prior to its abolition from 1996/97 by *FA 1996, 7 Sch 3* and *32*. Schedule D, Case V charges tax in respect of income arising from possessions out of the United Kingdom, not being income consisting of emoluments of any office or employment. [*TA 1988, s 18*]. The assessing provisions of *TA 1988, s 65* are modified to assess such income on a current fiscal year basis from 6 April 1994 for new sources, and from 6 April 1997 for sources in existence on or before 5 April 1994, and continuing beyond 5 April 1998. [*FA 1994, s 207(6) and 20 Sch 6(1)*].

Fiscal year basis

7.2 The alteration in the legislation is accomplished by deleting reference to 'the year preceding' in the existing legislation. [*FA 1994, s 207(1)(3)*]. The special rules for new sources of income and ceased sources in *TA 1988, ss 66, 67* no longer have effect [*FA 1994, s 207(4)*] and the provisions which preserve the arising basis for property etc. situated in the Republic of Ireland under *TA 1988, s 68* are amended to refer to the provisions of the main charging section in *TA 1988, s 65* only. [*FA 1994, s 207(5)*].

Example 1

Mr Belyayev, resident and domiciled in England, let out his holiday villa in Spain for the first time in the summer of 1994. He received the following net income as adjusted for tax purposes:

1994/95	£5,000
1995/96	£7,000
1996/97	£8,000
1997/98	£10,000

The profit chargeable to tax for each fiscal year is the net income as computed above.

Foreign trades and professions

7.3 A material change is made by *FA 1994, s 207(2)* which provides that income arising from a trade, profession or vocation, managed and controlled from outside the United Kingdom will remain chargeable on a UK resident under Schedule D, Case V, but the current year basis of assessment applicable to Schedule D, Cases I and II will apply. This means that the provisions relating to opening years, overlaps, change of accounting date, cessation, including deemed cessation on change of residence, and overlap relief will apply to such income, which will therefore be assessed by reference to basis periods and not the fiscal year. The rules as explained in Chapter 2 will therefore apply without amendment for a person assessed on an arising basis.

7.4 Income from a trade, profession or vocation carried on either solely or in partnership outside the UK by a UK ordinarily resident and domiciled individual is taxed on such an arising basis, regardless of remittances to the UK. The fact that the income is computed under Schedule D, Case I or II rules can cause considerable practical difficulties where overseas accounts are prepared locally and in accordance with the accounting and fiscal requirements of the source country. Losses and capital allowances may only be used against foreign income falling within *TA 1988, s 65*.

7.5 The remittance basis continues for non-UK domiciled individuals or not ordinarily resident British subjects or citizens of the Republic of Ireland. In order to qualify for the remittance basis the trade has to be carried on entirely outside the UK, because if the activities are from a single trade or profession carried out partly in the UK and partly abroad it will be taxable under Schedule D, Cases I or II (and not Case V) under *Davies v Braithwaite 1933 18 TC 198*. It is therefore often desirable to carry out overseas activities through an overseas partnership controlled and managed outside the UK under *TA 1988, s 112* or through an overseas employment.

Example 2

Mr Bolkhovitinov, resident and domiciled in England, was a partner in Borovkov-Florov a business managed and controlled outside the UK. The business made up its accounts to 31 December each year.

Profits (as adjusted for UK tax purposes) applicable to Mr Bolkhovitinov

y/e 31.12.94	£24,000
y/e 31.12.95	£30,000
y/e 31.12.96	£36,000
y/e 31.12.97	£42,000
y/e 31.12.98	£48,000

Assessable/taxable

1995/96 income arising in preceding year			
9/12 y/e 31.12.94	£18,000		
3/12 y/e 31.12.95	£7,500		
		£25,500	(*a*)
1996/97 transitional year		£33,396	(*b*)
1997/98 current year basis		£42,000	(*c*)
1998/99 current year basis		£48,000	(*d*)

Notes

(*a*) *TA 1988, s 66(1)(a)* (original enactment).

(*b*) Primary basis period 1996/97, y/e 31.12.96 [*FA 1994, 20 Sch 1(2)(a)*] £36,000

Relevant period under *FA 1994, 20 Sch 2(2)(b), 2(5)*

6.4.95 to 31.12.95

$\frac{270}{365} \times £30{,}000 =$ £22,192

Aggregate *FA 1994, 20 Sch 2(2)* £58,192

$£58{,}192 \times \frac{365}{270 + 366} =$ £33,396

(*c*) *TA 1988, s 60(3)(b); FA 1994, s 200*. Overlap period under *FA 1994, 20 Sch 2(4)*: part of basis period 1997/98, year ended 31.12.1997 which falls before 6 April 1997, i.e. 1.1.97 to 5.4.97, i.e. 95 days, overlap profits

$£42{,}000 \times \frac{95}{365} = £10{,}931$

(*d*) *TA 1988, s 60(3)(b); FA 1994, s 200.*

Determination of chargeable income

7.6 Income from abroad is assessed under Schedule D, Cases IV or V on the amount computed as if it were income arising in the UK, but subject to a deduction for any annual payments to a non-resident out of income which is not excluded by *TA 1988, s 347A(5)*. Interest used not to be deductible from rents from a foreign investment property, *Ockenden v Mackley* (*1982*) *STC 513*, but from 6 April 1994 interest was allowable under *TA 1988 s 353(1)* as amended by *FA 1994 s 81(1)* and from 6 April 1995 Schedule A treatment along Schedule D, Case I lines applies. *FA 1995, s 41*, see 5.29.

7.7 There is no express provision enabling expenses to be deducted in computing Schedule D, Case V income. The Revenue practice in the case of let property prior to *FA 1995, s 41* was to allow certain expenses such as rates, insurance premiums and agent's commissions. However, the Revenue maintained that in strictness only expenses incurred abroad were deductible. They argued that the Parliamentary debate on the *Finance Bill 1914*, which provided for income from overseas properties to be assessed on the arising rather than the remittance basis for the first time, shows that the intention of the original legislation was to liken the arising and remittance bases and it would therefore be unfair to give greater relief for income arising than income remitted. This view was disputed.

Remittance basis

7.8 Schedule D, Case IV or V income is taxed on an arising basis, except where the taxpayer is not domiciled in the UK or is a Commonwealth citizen or citizen of the Republic of Ireland and not ordinarily resident in the UK, in which case the income assessed is that remitted to the UK, if any (*Thomson v Moyse 1960 39 TC 291; Parkside Leasing v Smith 1985 STC 63; Walsh v Randall 1940 23 TC 55*). Income from foreign licences of UK patents is treated as foreign income for double taxation relief purposes (Extra-statutory concession B8).

Example 3

Mr Bratukhin, resident in the UK but domiciled abroad, let out his holiday villa in Spain for the first time in the summer of 1994. He received the following net income from the letting:

1994/95	£4,000
1995/96	£7,000
1996/97	£8,000
1997/98	£10,000

However, the rents were paid into his bank account in Jersey from which he remitted sums to the UK as follows:

1994/95	£1,000
1995/96	£3,000
1996/97	£10,000
1997/98	£2,000

The profits chargeable to tax for each fiscal year was the amount remitted to the UK in the fiscal year.

Partnerships

7.9 Partnership untaxed investment income is not chargeable on a fiscal year basis but by reference to the basis period for Schedule D, Cases I or II under *TA 1988, s 111(7)(b); FA 1994, s 215, FA 1995, s 117*. The transitional provisions for such income are in *TA 1988, s 111(4), (8); FA 1994, s 215; FA 1995, s 117* see 12.23. A trade controlled from the UK is charged under Schedule D, Case I, *Ogilvie v Kitton 1908 5 TC 338*, but if controlled abroad under Schedule D, Case V, *Colquhoun v Brooks 1889 2 TC 490*, see 12.17.

Planning remittances

7.10 If a non-UK domiciled individual is assessable on a remittance basis it is important to ensure that so far as possible remittances to the UK are out of capital, which means that foreign income should be paid into a separate account preferably with a different bank. Remittances from a mixed fund of income and capital are deemed to be remittances of income up to the amount of income in the fund (*Scottish Provident Institution v Allan 1901 4 TC 409 and 1903 TC 591 and 593*). However, chargeable gains are also assessed on a non-domiciled UK resident on a remittance basis under *TCGA 1992, s 12(1)* and therefore the proceeds arising on the sale at a profit of overseas investments should be paid into yet another account and not remitted unless necessary. Remittances proved not to be of income are not taxed under Schedule D (*Timbrell v Lord Aldenham's Executor 1947 28 TC 293*). Remittances from a mixed fund of capital and capital gains are deemed to be remitted pro rata, Inland Revenue Income Tax Manual 1567 and Capital Gains Tax Manual 25411.

7.11 Remittances within the same tax year but after the source has ceased are caught (*Joffe v Thain 1955 36 TC 199*). Remittances of income in a fiscal year following the cessation of the source are not taxable (*Kneen v Martin 1934 19 TC 33*), unless the remittances are of remuneration assessable under Schedule E, Case III, which are caught by *TA 1988, s 19(1)4A*.

Pensions

7.12 Foreign pensions or annuities are charged to tax (whether remitted to the UK or not) subject to a deduction of 10 per cent. Pensions granted in respect of Nazi persecution as a civil service or social security pension are brought within the total exemption enjoyed by annuities under *TA 1988, s 330*. The provisions apply to pensions charged under Schedule E under *TA 1988, s 19(1)(4)*. The remittance basis is maintained for non-UK domiciled pensioners.

Transitional provisions – averaging

7.13 Where income assessed under Schedule D, Case IV or V arose prior to 6 April 1994, and continues beyond 5 April 1998, the 1996/97 assessment will normally be on one-half of the aggregate of the income arising in 1996/97 and 1995/96. [*FA 1994, 20 Sch 6(1)(2)(a)*]. Under the old rules income arising in 1995/96 would, on a preceding year basis, have been assessed for 1996/97. Normal allowances and deductions are made from the appropriate source of income.

Example 4

Mr Dudakov, resident and domiciled in England, let out his holiday villa in Spain for many years. He received the following net income, as adjusted for tax purposes:

1993/94	£1,000
1994/95	£2,000
1995/96	£4,000
1996/97	£8,000
1997/98	£9,000

Assessable/taxable

1994/95	preceding year basis	£1,000	
1995/96	preceding year basis	£2,000	
1996/97	transitional year	£6,000	(*a*)
1997/98	fiscal year basis	£9,000	

Notes

(*a*) *FA 1994, 20 Sch 6(2)(a)(i)*

income arising in 1996/97	£8,000
FA 1994, 20 Sch 6(2)(a)(ii)	
income arising in 1995/96	£4,000
aggregate	£12,000
50% thereof	£6,000

This is precisely the same rule as applies for Schedule D, Case III (see 6.6 above).

7.14 Where the remittance basis applies, because, for example, the taxpayer is not domiciled in the United Kingdom, the charge for 1996/97 will under Schedule D, Case IV be one-half of the total of the remittances in 1995/96 and 1996/97 (so far as can be computed) without any other deduction. [*FA 1994, 20 Sch 6(2)(b)*]. Where the remittance basis applies to Schedule D, Case V income, the assessment for 1996/97 will be on one-half of the actual remittances in 1995/96 and 1996/97 with no other deduction.

[*FA 1994, 20 Sch 6(2)(c)*]. The reason for the slight difference in the wording between Schedule D, Cases IV and V in respect of remittances in the transitional period is not clear.

Example 5

Mr Chetverikov is a non-UK domiciled UK resident who had remitted to the UK income from his international trading partnership which is managed and controlled in the Bahamas.

Remittances received in the UK are:

1993/94	£1,000
1994/95	£2,000
1995/96	£4,000
1996/97	£8,000
1997/98	£9,000

Assessable/taxable

1994/95	preceding year basis	£1,000	
1995/96	preceding year basis	£2,000	
1996/97	transitional year	£6,000	(*a*)
1997/98	fiscal year basis	£9,000	

Notes

(*a*) *FA 1994, 20 Sch 6(2)(c)*

(i)	income remitted in 1996/97	£8,000
(ii)	income remitted in 1995/96	£4,000
	Aggregate	£12,000
	50% thereof	£6,000

Transitional provisions where 1995/96 on actual basis

7.15 If 1995/96 was assessed on the fiscal year basis as a result of the taxpayer's election under existing *TA 1988, s 66(1)(c)* the averaging provisions do not apply for 1996/97 which will also be assessed on a fiscal year basis. [*FA 1994, 20 Sch 6(3)*].

Example 6

Mr Ekonomov, resident and domiciled in England, first let his villa in Spain in the summer of 1993. He received the following income, as adjusted for tax purposes:

1993/94	£5,000
1994/95	£8,000
1995/96	£6,000
1996/97	£7,500
1997/98	£10,000

Assessable/taxable

1993/94	actual basis	£5,000	(*a*)
1994/95	actual basis	£8,000	(*b*)
1995/96	preceding year basis	£8,000	(*c*)
1996/97	transitional year	£6,750	(*d*)
1997/98	fiscal year basis	£10,000	(*e*)

Notes

(*a*) *TA 1988, s 66(1)(a)* (original enactment).

(*b*) *TA 1988, s 66(1)(b)* (original enactment).

(*c*) *TA 1988, s 65(1)* (original enactment).

(*d*) *FA 1994, 20 Sch 6(2)(a)*

Income arising in 1996/97	£7,500
FA 1994, 20 Sch 6(2)(a)(i)	
Income arising in 1995/96	£6,000
FA 1994, 20 Sch 6(2)(a)(ii)	
Aggregate	£13,500
50% thereof	£6,750

(*e*) *TA 1988, s 65(1); FA 1994, s 207(1)*.

Mr Ekonomov elects for 1995/96 to be on an actual basis under *TA 1988, s 66(1)(c)* (original enactment) and the income for that year therefore becomes £6,000.

This election causes the transitional year to be adjusted to the actual basis too, *FA 1994, 20 Sch 6(3)*, i.e. to £7,500. The total for 1995/96 and 1996/97 therefore becomes:

1995/96	£6,000
1996/97	£7,500
	£13,500

compared with:

1995/96	£8,000
1996/97	£6,750
	£14,750

so the election saves tax on the difference of £1,250.

Transitional overlap relief

7.16 Where income from an overseas trade, profession or vocation is assessed under Schedule D, Case V on a current year basis, as under Schedule D, Cases I and II, the tax is charged on the accounting period ending in the fiscal year and not on the fiscal year basis. The overlap provisions in *TA 1988, s 63A; FA 1994, s 205* apply to any transitional overlap arising on any part of the profits or gains for the basis period for 1997/98 which falls prior to 6 April 1997 as under Schedule D, Cases I and II under *FA 1994, 20 Sch 2(4)*. [*FA 1994, 20 Sch 6(4)*]. (See Chapter 2, 2.37–2.41 and 2.48.)

Cessation prior to 6 April 1998

7.17 If a source chargeable under Schedule D, Cases IV or V which commenced prior to 6 April 1994 ceases prior to 6 April 1998 the old rules continue to apply. [*FA 1994, 20 Sch 7*].

Example 7

Mr Konstantinov, resident and domiciled in England, had let his villa in Spain for many years until it was sold on 30 September 1997. He received the following income as adjusted for tax purposes:

1993/94		£6,000	
1994/95		£7,000	
1995/96		£8,000	
1996/97		£9,000	
1997/98		£5,000	
Assessable/taxable			
1994/95	preceding year	£6,000	(*a*)
1995/96	preceding year	£7,000	(*b*)
1996/97	preceding year	£8,000	(*c*)
1997/98	actual basis	£5,000	(*d*)

Notes

(*a*) *TA 1988, s 65(1)* (original enactment).

(*b*) *TA 1988, s 65(1)* (original enactment).

(*c*) *TA 1988, s 65(1)* (original enactment).

(*d*) *TA 1988, s 67(1)(b)* (original enactment).

The assessment for 1996/97 is adjusted to the income for that year on an actual basis of £9,000 under *TA 1988, s 67(1)(b)* (original enactment) because the new rules are disapplied by *FA 1994, 20 Sch 7*.

Income from Let Property Overseas

Background

7.18 Income from foreign property which is let is chargeable to income tax under Schedule D, Case V, unless, unusually, the nature and scale of the activities are such that the income is regarded as derived from a trade and chargeable under Schedule D, Case I. Previously such income was taxed on a preceding year basis. There were no statutory provisions stipulating the expenses which would be allowed in computing taxable income, but Revenue practice was to permit a deduction for current expenses incurred abroad such as repairs, insurance, real estate taxes, management and letting fees. Based on the Parliamentary debates on the *Finance Bill 1914*, which provided for income from foreign property to be assessed on the arising rather than the remittance basis for the first time, the Revenue argued that the intention of the original legislation was to liken the arising and remittance basis and it would be unfair to give greater relief for income arising than income remitted. Expenses in the UK were strictly not allowable (see 7.7).

Introduction to new provisions

7.19 Under the new provisions introduced by *FA 1995, s 41*, amending *TA 1988, s 65* and introducing a new *TA 1988, s 65A*, income derived from land, including residential caravans and houseboats, outside the UK is for income tax purposes generally to be determined in accordance with the new Schedule A rules, i.e. as a business computed under Schedule D, Case I principles and on a fiscal year basis; see 5.2. Hence the accruals basis is to apply and a deduction is available for interest. Moreover, income and expenses from different properties are to be pooled, albeit only from 1997/98. But the net income as so determined is to be kept separate from any Schedule A income, so that losses from the one source cannot be set against profits from the other.

7.20 The charge does not apply for corporation tax for the same reasons as set out in 5.1 in relation to Schedule A, or where the letting amounts to a trade. Likewise it does not apply to non-UK domiciled taxpayers who remain assessable only to the extent that foreign income is remitted to the UK. [*TA 1988, s 65(4)*]. In their case the new rules have no application and tax is payable by reference to any remittances of net rent. (SAT 1 (1995) 9.144 and 9.145(b)).

Timing for introduction of Schedule D, Case I computation principles

7.21 The Schedule D, Case I computation rules for determining profits, notably the application of the accruals basis rather than simply bringing in receipts and payments, apply from 1995/96. [*FA 1995, s 41(1)*]. Where this would result in some receipts and expenses entering into the computation for both 1994/95 and 1995/96, or alternatively not being taken into account for either year, the transitional provisions applicable for Schedule A set out at 5.47 *et seq.* are to be applied (SAT 1 (1995) 9.150).

Moreover, complete pooling of income and expenses from different properties is not to apply until 1997/98. This is to avoid the complications caused by the application of different rules from 1994/95 to 1996/97 for property held on 1 April 1994 and property acquired after that date, as outlined below. Until 1997/98 each property is treated as a distinct and separate business.

Timing for move to current year basis

7.22 Although Schedule D, Case I principles are to be applied from 1995/96, there is generally a longer phasing in for the change from the preceding year to the current year basis. Where the source of income was in existence before 1 April 1994, the preceding year basis is retained for 1995/96, and the transitional year will then be 1996/97. [*FA 1995, s 41(5)*]. Assuming that the strict fiscal year basis for the taxation of Schedule D, Case V income has been applied in the past, income will be computed under the Schedule D, Case I transitional basis period rules contained in *FA 1994, 20 Sch 6(2)*; see 7.13 *et seq*. Thus the measure of taxable income for 1995/96 will be half the aggregate income arising in 1995/96 and 1996/97. The current year basis will then apply for 1997/98 and subsequent years.

7.23 Where the source of income arose on or after 6 April 1994 the current year basis is to be applied throughout. In cases where the overseas property income ceases in 1995/96 the old rules are retained. [*FA 1995, s 41(9)*].

Each property a separate business until 1997/98

7.24 For the purposes of the above calculation rules, each overseas property is treated as a separate business for 1995/96 and 1996/97, and as if it were the only such business. [*FA 1995, s 41(6)*]. Accordingly, in the case of a taxpayer who only has one let overseas property, which was let before 1994 the position will merely be as outlined in 7.13 above; i.e. preceding year basis 1995/96, transitional rules 1996/97 and current year basis 1997/98. But if the taxpayer purchases a further overseas property to let in June 1995, the current year basis rules will apply immediately (i.e. in 1995/96) for that property. Hence he will be chargeable in respect of the income from the two properties on different bases until 1997/98.

Special transitional provisions for 1996/97 where accounts prepared on a non-statutory basis

7.25 Overseas letting income is strictly chargeable to tax on income arising in the previous fiscal year; i.e. tax for 1993/94 is assessed on the profits for the year ended 5 April 1994. But the Revenue have in many cases accepted chargeability based on profits shown in accounts made up for a twelve-month period ending in the preceding year. So where annual accounts are prepared, say, to 31 December, tax for 1993/94 is assessed on the profits for the year to 31 December 1992. In such cases, matters have to be placed on a proper current fiscal year basis for 1997/98 onwards.

7.26 Under Revenue guidelines this is to be accomplished by preparing accounts to cover the entire period from the end of the 1995/96 basis period to 5 April 1997 inclusive, and taking a twelve-month proportion for 1996/97. (See 5.55, 7.21 above).

Example 8

Mr Slutsky has been assessed in the past on profits shown in accounts drawn up to 30 June in the preceding year. Those accounts show the following profits:

Year to 30 June 1995 (12 months)	£22,000
Year to 30 June 1996 (12 months)	£26,000
1 July 1996 – 5 April 1997 (9 months)	£18,000
	£66,000

1996/97 assessment 12/33 × £66,000 = £24,000

7.27 Because this approach has no statutory basis, if it were considered unfair by the taxpayer the Commissioners on appeal would have to apply the strict statutory basis. Hence if there is a dispute between the taxpayer and his Inspector about the application of this approach, efforts should be made to reach a taxable figure which is regarded by both sides as fair. Otherwise the taxpayer's only recourse would be to the Revenue head office.

Interest

7.28 The decision in *Ockendon v Mackley (1982) STC 513* confirmed the Revenue's view that under the old rules interest paid on a loan to acquire an overseas investment property was not deductible in computing net income. The effect of applying Schedule D, Case I computation rules under the new provisions is that interest paid on a loan (or overdraft) to acquire an overseas property becomes an allowable expense. However, this is subject to the interest being 'wholly and exclusively' incurred for the purposes of the letting business. The Revenue have indicated that where the taxpayer occupies the property for part of the year, or the property is otherwise not available for letting for part of the year, there will be a restriction of relief by an apportionment on a time basis. There will likewise be an apportionment if part only of the property is let.

Travel costs

7.29 The special rules for travel connected with trades carried on abroad under *TA 1988, ss 80 and 81* are excluded from the new rules. [*FA 1995, s 41(2); TA 1988, s 65A(2)*]. However, relief will be available for travel costs if a taxpayer can show that the expenses were incurred wholly and exclusively for the purposes of the overseas letting business. Here the Revenue hold a sceptical view of the nature of an overseas property business, their thinking being that a let holiday flat is likely to have some private use. Their concern is that a business visit may well be extended into a holiday and that a deduction for travel costs is open to abuse. Unlike interest there is accordingly no provision for an apportionment of travel costs between business and private.

Lease premiums

7.30 A consequence of adopting the Schedule A rules for overseas properties is that, unlike the position under the old rules, premiums for leases of under 50 years are chargeable to income tax. The amount chargeable is computed in accordance with the rules for UK properties; see 5.10. [*FA 1995, s 41(4)* and *TA 1988, s 34*]. Since the new rules do not apply for corporation tax, this charge will not fall on UK resident companies granting short leases of overseas properties at a premium.

Furnished holiday lettings

7.31 Under *TA 1988, ss 503 and 504* furnished holiday lettings in the UK are treated as a trade, with various reliefs accordingly available, notably for losses and capital gains; see 5.50. The Revenue indicated that this legislation, introduced in 1984, was to ensure that property owners, who had in practice benefitted from trading treatment would not be adversely affected by a court decision (*Gittos v Barclay* (*1982*) *STC 390*) which held that property letting was not usually a trading activity. This was particularly the case with proprietors of furnished holiday lettings.

7.32 This favourable treatment is not accorded to foreign holiday letting businesses. [*FA 1995, s 41(2); TA 1988, s 65A(3)*]. The Revenue considered in 1984 that there were not sufficient grounds for extending trading treatment to landlords of overseas furnished holiday lettings, presumably on the basis that there was unlikely to be the same degree of activity involved in the management of the property and the arranging of the lettings, and this remains their position.

Capital allowances

7.33 Capital allowances will be available in respect of an overseas letting business just as for a UK Schedule A business; see 5.39 *et seq*. However, this will not be the case where for 1995/96 and 1996/97 the preceding year basis or the transitional provisions outlined in 7.13 apply. [*FA 1995, s 41(3)*].

Losses

7.34 Under the old rules there was no statutory relief for losses from overseas lettings. But ESC B25 permitted losses to be carried forward and set against future income, albeit only from the same overseas property. This remains the position for losses for all years of assessment up to 1996/97. Any remaining deficit on a particular property at the end of 1996/97 may be carried forward and set against net rental income from that property for 1997/98.

7.35 In 1997/98 pooling of income and expenses comes into effect as outlined in 7.24, which effectively permits sideways loss relief, i.e. the set off of losses from one property against the profits of another. Specific statutory relief for the carry forward of losses is introduced from 1998/99 onwards, when the Schedule A loss relief provisions contained in *TA 1988, s 379A* are introduced. [*FA 1995, s 41(8)*]. Under these provisions, any balance of loss in the current year arising after pooling the income and expenses of overseas let properties can be carried forward to the following year and so on. Additionally any unrelieved losses at 5 April 1998 including losses incurred on or after 6 April 1995 on properties where the lettings ceased before 5 April 1998 will be treated as available for carry forward to 1998/99 and subsequent years. The net result is that all losses will be carried forward to 1998/99 and beyond, whether by law or by concession. However, there is no other right of set off or carry forward of losses from overseas properties, whether against income from UK properties or other income generally.

Example 9

Mr Domrachyev, resident and domiciled in England had the following foreign property and income therefrom:

	Flat A	*Flat B*	*Flat C*	*Total*
	Acquired	*Acquired*	*Acquired*	
	1.4.92	*1.9.93*	*1.1.96*	
	£	£	£	
Net rents				
Year ended 5.4.94	5,000	2,000	–	
Year ended 5.4.95	6,000	4,000	–	
Year ended 5.4.96	7,000	4,500	1,000	
Year ended 5.4.97	8,000	5,500	6,250	
Year ended 5.4.98	9,000	6,500	7,250	

Schedule D, Case V assessments:

		Flat A	*Flat B*	*Flat C*	*Total*
		£	£	£	£
1994/95	previous year basis	5,000			
	actual year basis		4,000		
1995/96	previous year basis	6,000	4,000		
	current year basis			1,000	
1996/97	£7,000 + £8,000 ÷ 2	7,500			
£4,500 + £5,500 ÷ 2			5,000		
	Current year basis			6,250	
1997/98	Current year basis				
£9,000 + £6,500 + £7,250					22,750

Example 10

Mr Feniks, resident and domiciled in England had the following foreign property and results therefrom:

	Flat A	*Flat B*	*Flat C*	*Total*
	Acquired 1.4.92 Sold 31.12.95	*Acquired 1.9.93*	*Acquired 1.1.96*	
	£	£	£	£
Net rents				
Year ended 5.4.94	3,000	1,000	–	
Year ended 5.4.95	4,000	2,000	–	
Year ended 5.4.96	(2,500)	3,000	1,250	
Year ended 5.4.97	–	(1,500)	3,250	
Year ended 5.4.98	–	(4,500)	2,750	
Year ended 5.4.99		3,500	750	
Year ended 5.4.2000		(4,750)	3,750	
Year ended 5.4.2001		2,000	4,000	

Schedule D, Case V Assessments:

	Flat A	*Flat B*	*Flat C*	*Total*
1994/95 previous year basis	3,000			
actual		2,000		
1995/96 actual basis				
£4,000 × 3/12 – £2,500	NIL			
unrelieved loss £1,500				
previous year basis		2,000		
current year basis			1,250	
1996/97 average basis				
£nil + £1,500 ÷ 2		750		
current year basis			3,250	
1997/98 current year basis				
£2,750 – £4,500				
unrelieved loss £1,750				NIL

	Total
	£
1998/99 current year basis £3,500 + £750 – £1,500 – £1,750	1,000
1999/2000 current year basis £3,750 – £4,750 loss carried forward £1,000	NIL
2000/01 current year basis £2,000 + £4,000 – £1,000	5,000

7.36 In paragraph 9.160 of SAT 1 (1995) the Revenue observed that although all overseas let properties are to be regarded as a single business, the income from each property will have to be calculated specifically in order that, for the purposes of the source by source approach required for the computation of tax credit relief, the UK tax attributable to the income arising from a particular property can be identified *Yates v GCA International Ltd* (*1991*) *STC 157*. The new loss relief provisions present difficulties for the computation of UK tax on particular strands of foreign letting income and will require an ordering rule for the setting off of losses from 1998/99 onwards. Separate guidelines as to the principles are to be issued by the Revenue.

Chapter 8

Schedule D, Case VI

Fiscal year basis

8.1 Case VI is the sweep up charge which relates to tax in respect of any annual profits or gains not falling under any other case of Schedule D and not charged by virtue of Schedules A, C or E. *TA 1988, s 69; FA 1994, s 208* provides that income under Schedule D, Case VI shall be computed on the full amount of the profits or gains arising in the fiscal year. Previously there was an option for an averaging method that was little used in practice. There are no transitional provisions as Schedule D, Case VI income has always been assessed on a current year basis in theory

8.2 In practice, certain income assessable under Schedule D, Case VI, has been computed on a non-statutory preceding year basis on the income arising in the preceding fiscal year. In such cases the Revenue have confirmed that they will apply non-statutory transitional relief and assess 1996/97 on the appropriate proportion of the income arising in 1996/97 and 1995/96 which would have been assessed in 1996/97, had the *de facto* preceding year basis continued, generally following the Schedule D, Cases I and II provisions. Furnished lettings are assessed under Schedule A instead of Schedule D, Case VI from 6 April 1995.

Example 1

Mr Fedorov produced accounts for his income from casual commissions on a calendar year basis and by agreement with the Revenue was assessed on a preceding year basis.

Profits (as adjusted for tax purposes)

y/e 31.12.94	£40,000
y/e 31.12.95	£45,000
y/e 31.12.96	£50,000
period 1.1.97 to 5.4.97	£13,000
y/e 5.4.98	£53,000

Assessable/taxable

1995/96	preceding year basis	£40,000	(*a*)
1996/97	transitional year	£47,724	(*b*)
1997/98	fiscal year	£53,000	

Notes

(*a*) *TA 1988, s 69* (original enactment) non-statutory agreed basis.

(*b*) Extra statutory transitional relief.

1996/97 primary basis period		
y/e 5.4.97		
1.1.97 to 5.4.97		£13,000
y/e 31.12.96		
50,000 × 9/12		£37,500
		£50,500
Relevant period 1.1.95 to 5.4.96		
y/e 31.12.95	£45,000	
y/e 31.12.96		
£50,000 × 3/12	£12,500	
		£57,500
aggregate		£108,000
appropriate percentage $\frac{365}{366 + 460}$ =		£47,724

Partnerships

8.3 Partnership untaxed investment income is not chargeable on a fiscal year basis but by reference to the basis period for Schedule D, Cases I or II under *TA 1988, s 111(7)(b); FA 1994, s 215; FA 1995, s 117*. The transitional provisions for such income are in *TA 1988, s 111(4), (8); FA 1994, s 215; FA 1995, s 117*.

Transitional anti-avoidance

8.4 The Revenue have recognised that by assessing the income for 1996/97 on one-half of the total income for 1995/96 and 1996/97 a considerable incentive is given to taxpayers to accelerate income into the transitional period, only half of which will be taxed. The *Finance Act 1995* contains provisions to counter such avoidance, details of which are contained in Chapter 24.

Miscellaneous losses

8.5 Excess trading charges continue to be allowed as losses under *TA 1988, s 387*, as does excess trading interest under *TA 1988, s 390*, losses from trade carried on abroad under *TA 1988, s 391* and Schedule D, Case VI losses under *TA 1988, s 392*.

Chapter 9

Schedule E: Directors, Employees and Employers

Background

9.1 Since the publication in November 1992 of the Inland Revenue's second Consultative Document 'A Simpler System for Assessing Personal Tax' it has been integral to self-assessment that all who receive a tax return – including employees – are to be included within its ambit. Employees who are fully taxed under PAYE and have no other income are not obliged to notify the Revenue of their chargeability (or indeed to self-assess); see 16.7 and 18.9 below. But employees who receive a return will be obliged to complete and send it back to the Revenue by 30 September following the end of the tax year if the Revenue are to calculate their liability, or by 31 January if they are to self-assess (see 16.12 and 16.13).

9.2 Since employees were always to be within the self-assessing regime, it was evident that there would have to be legislation requiring employers to provide employees with information relating to benefits in kind and expenses payments, a feature absent from the former system. Questions then inevitably arose as to the extent of employers' reporting requirements, given the complexities of the charging provisions. Particular areas of difficulty related to the extent to which an employer should assume the responsibility for determining the taxable amount for each of his employees, and whether there should be any statutory information flow between employers and employees, for example in cases where the level of the charge depended on the actions of the employee, such as in respect of company cars, car fuel, and beneficial loans.

9.3 The various issues were canvassed in the Inland Revenue's Consultative Document 'Self-Assessment: What it will mean for Employers and Employees' issued in May 1994. This proposed that employers would be required to provide employees with P11Ds, or equivalent, by 6 July following the end of the tax year. To complete the form employers would have to: (*a*) assemble all the information regarding benefits in kind, (*b*) compute the cost of the benefit, and (*c*) determine the cash equivalent after deducting any amounts made good by the employee. The final stage in the benefits in kind calculation, i.e. taking into account any amounts deductible for business use as if the employee had incurred the cost, to arrive at the net taxable amount, was thought inappropriate for employers. Otherwise they would have to take a view as to the deductions, if any, due for the employee's business use. Furthermore, with only a figure for the net amount, employees would not have, as a matter of course, the underlying information on which to reach their own view of the cash equivalent and of any deductions that might be due.

9.4 On the question of the information flow between employer and employees, and the extent to which employees might be required to provide information to their employers, the imposition of statutory obligations on the employee was considered too regulatory. It was thought preferable to assume that existing arrangements between employer and employee would normally be sufficient to provide the information needed to calculate the cash equivalent. The Consultative Document accordingly proposed that in working out the amount chargeable to tax in respect of a benefit, the employer should not make any reductions or adjustments provided for in the statute unless he had that information. Another area dealt with related to benefits provided by third parties. The proposal here was that where a benefit was supplied by a third party to an employee under arrangements made or facilitated by the employer, the employer should be required to report the cash equivalent on form P11D.

9.5 The proposals put forward in the Consultative Document have been substantially implemented in *FA 1995* and proposed amendments to the PAYE regulations which are considered in this chapter. The new system takes effect for 1996/97 onwards, and will apply to some four and a half million individuals who are directors, employees or pensioners and are in receipt of a tax return. Employers will be required to provide employees, not only with details of wages and bonuses etc., but also with copies of the Form P11D, with details of benefits and calculations of the cash equivalents. Hence they will be required to assume a rather greater burden than before.

Wages, salaries, bonuses etc.

9.6 Under *TA 1988, s 19,* tax is chargeable under Schedule E on 'emoluments', which under *TA 1988, s 131* are defined to include 'all salaries, fees, wages, perquisites and profits whatsoever'. Emoluments paid to an employee fall within the PAYE procedure and no fundamental changes are needed under self-assessment. Information relating to salaries, fees and wages etc. is presently provided by the employer to the employee in the form of monthly payslips and at the end of the year on form P60. In principle, all that will be required will be to ensure that the employee receives the P60 well in time to complete his tax return.

9.7 The P60 generally shows the full pay and tax deducted during the year. However, there may be circumstances when this is not so, for example when there has been a breakdown in cumulation during the year (with the employee's code operated on a Week 1/Month 1 basis) and there has been a subsequent change of employment and the tax office has not instructed the new employer to restore a cumulative code before the end of the tax year. This will be remedied by a modified form P45 in four parts, so that on an employee leaving an employment he will receive notification as to total pay and tax to date. Then, in the event that the details on the P60 were confined to the current employment, the employee would simply need to add to this figure the information on the P45.

Expenses and expenses payments

General position

9.8 The position regarding the taxability of expenses may be summarised as follows.

(*a*) Payments by an employer to an employee to reimburse an expense incurred in the performance of the duties of the employment are not emoluments taxable under the general rule for Schedule E (although any profit element is so taxed).

(*b*) Expenses payments are chargeable as deemed emoluments where they are made to directors or employees earning over £8,500 per annum, except where a dispensation exists.

(*c*) Where an employer pays a personal bill of the employee, such as a home telephone bill (known as a 'pecuniary liability') the payment is taxable as part of the employee's income, although the employee may obtain a deduction of any amount which would have been deductible if the payment had been made out of his income from the employment as outlined in (*d*) below.

(*d*) Under *TA 1988, s 198* an employee is entitled to a deduction for travelling expenses necessarily incurred in the performance of his duties; or for other expenditure incurred wholly, exclusively and necessarily in the performance of those duties. It is well established that this section lays down a very strict test. In particular no relief is available for home to work travel.

(*e*) PAYE is generally applied to round sum allowances, but not to other expense payments, and not to payments to meet employees' pecuniary liabilities.

Travelling and subsistence

9.9 Generally a deduction is available for the expense of business journeys, travelling from one work place to another, but not from home to work. Costs of subsistence follow the same rules. The Schedule E deduction rules were devised in a more leisurely and simpler era, and have been subject to growing criticism in recent years. Whilst they are relatively straightforward where there is a stable place of work, problems can arise particularly for employees working more at home, or those with different work locations. The issue of tax relief for such 'triangular travel' is presently under review by the Revenue. The position of site-based employees is also a controversial one, although certain practices are adopted by agreement with the Revenue in some cases, such as construction site workers.

9.10 Under self-assessment, to enable an employee to make a claim for travel expenses reimbursed, where appropriate, he will need to know:

(*a*) if he has a 'normal place of work', and if so its location, since home to work travel costs are not deductible;

(*b*) if he has no normal place of work, whether he has a 'travelling appointment' (i.e. where travelling is an integral part of the job, for example a sales representative) so that expenses are deductible; and

(*c*) if he has no normal place of employment, and does not have a travelling appointment but works at different sites, the extent to which deductions can be claimed.

The Inland Revenue have published a consultative document on employees' travel and subsistence expenses. The document notes that the decision in *Elderkin v Hindmarsh (1988) STC 267* is widely perceived to be unfair and proposes to treat all travel and subsistence expenses, other than 'ordinary commuting', as allowable for tax purposes. 'Ordinary commuting' is defined as travel between home and 'a permanent workplace' and the proposal would therefore have the effect of reversing the decision in the *Elderkin* case. The document also proposes to make the tax treatment of triangular travel fairer by changing the allowable expense to any additional cost over his normal travel expenses incurred by the employee in travelling to or from home and the temporary workplace. Comments on the consultative document are invited by 30 September 1996.

9.11 Where an employee travels on business using his own car, he will be entitled to a deduction for expenses attributable to business use as described below. So far as subsistence is concerned, an area of potential difficulty is the extent to which the incidental element in overnight subsistence payments is taxable. This applies to such items as newspapers, telephone calls home and laundry etc. These are regarded by the Revenue as personal expenses, so the reimbursement for allowances made to employees are taxable. The position here has, however, been somewhat simplified by the exemption from tax for such amounts up to £5 per night for stays in the UK and £10 per night for stays abroad in *FA 1995, s 93*.

Motor mileage allowances

9.12 In cases where directors and employees earning £8,500 or more per annum use their own car on business car allowances or motor mileage allowances paid to them are chargeable to tax. Relief is given on the business proportion by reference to business miles, including capital allowances and qualifying loan interest. For other employees only the 'profit element' is taxable. There is no statutory definition of profit element, but in practice it is taken as the difference between the gross amount received, and the allowable expenditure and capital allowances.

9.13 An administrative arrangement for calculating the profit on motor allowances paid known as the fixed profit car scheme ('FPCS') is operated in certain cases. There is a published scale of tax-free mileage rates, linked to the size of the engine of the car and the number of business miles during the tax year; see 9.45. The tax on any profit element is calculated through the employee's PAYE coding, based upon an estimate of business miles in the previous year. If necessary an adjustment is made after the end of the year when the actual figures are returned. Any tax due is then collected or repaid as the case may be through an adjustment to the code or directly by tax assessment.

9.14 To simplify matters under self-assessment the same scale mileage rates can be used from 1996/97 for all employees who use their cars for business travel. Accordingly detailed records of costs will not need to be kept, merely details of business mileage and total allowances received. Employees can also use the mileage rate scale to support a tax deduction for allowable motoring expenses, whether or not they are paid allowances by their employers. Employees may still choose to be taxed on the strict statutory basis, but they will then need to keep full records.

Entertaining

9.15 There is a broad prohibition for entertaining costs, whether in calculating the employer's tax liability, or that of the employee. Generally, in trading concerns where an employee receives an allowance specifically earmarked for entertaining, the payment is disallowed in calculating the employer's tax liability. In such circumstances the employee can get tax relief on business entertaining under the Schedule E rules for expenditure incurred wholly, necessarily and exclusively in the performance of the duties of his employment. The position is similar for a reimbursement of expenditure incurred, or where the employer directly pays the particular entertaining bill. Hence the cost of the disallowance falls upon the employer rather than the employee. However, where the employee meets the expenditure from an inclusive salary or round sum allowance, the disallowance is made in calculating the employee's tax liability. He is not entitled to a deduction in such circumstances.

9.16 These principles are not changed under self-assessment, but provision is made for the supply of information to an employee, so that he can decide whether he is entitled to a deduction; see 9.33.

Benefits in kind

General position

9.17 The taxability of benefits in kind may be summarised as follows.

(*a*) There is a general Schedule E charge for goods, property and other assets transferred to employees which can be converted into cash by sale or exchange, tax being imposed by reference to the second-hand value.

(*b*) The charge has been considerably extended by legislation brought in to deal with items which are incapable of being converted into money; or where the measure of the taxable benefit is less than the commercial benefit, notably in the areas of vouchers/credit tokens, living accommodation; and other benefits applicable to directors and employees earning over £8,500 p.a.

(*c*) Benefits are generally taxable if provided by reason of the employment, whether by the employer or third parties. Also benefits provided for members of the employee's family or household are included.

(*d*) There are a number of exceptions under statute, for example canteens for staff, work place nurseries and some living accommodation.

(*e*) The determination of the taxable amount depends upon the nature of the benefit, being variously linked to cost, the price which the employee would pay and statutory figures.

(*f*) As regards deductibility for business use, in most cases the employee may deduct from the amount treated as income any amount which would have been deductible if he had incurred the cost out of income from the employment. Exceptions include company cars instead of mileage allowances, car fuel for private use, vans where the benefit is private use and mobile phones where the benefit is for the use thereof.

9.18 The general rule for calculating the cash equivalent (or taxable benefit) of a benefit in kind is that it equates with the actual cost of providing the benefit, less any contribution made by the employee. But there are special rules for some benefits, as now described.

Car, van and fuel benefits

9.19 The area is quite complicated, since there are various factors which go into the calculation of the benefit in kind for cars, for example list price, extras, the age of the car, the business mileage, the extent to which a car is available for the employee, whether it is a second car, and whether payments have been made by the employee for its use. Moreover, the employer will not necessarily know the business mileage, whether or not the car is a second car and whether there are periods of unavailability for the employee. Similar issues arise in relation to vans and fuel.

9.20 As explained in 9.30 below, the employer is to prepare the calculation of the benefit based on the information in his possession. For example, if the employer has no idea what the business mileage might be, the cash equivalent will be reported on the basis of under 2,500 business miles. But if the employer has information to show that it was between

2,500 and 18,000 miles, the cash equivalent will be reported as falling within that band. It will then be open to the employee to adjust the information on his return if he considers it appropriate, say if business mileage is in excess of 18,000 miles.

Beneficial loans

9.21 Where interest free loans or loans at less than a commercial rate ('beneficial loans') are provided for employees the benefit is taxable, although loans (or the aggregate of total loans) which at no time in the tax year exceed £5,000 are exempt, and tax relief may be available, for example on home loans. The rules for calculating the cash equivalent are contained in *TA 1988, s 160* and *Schedule 7, Part II*. The cash equivalent is the difference between interest at the 'official rate', broadly a variable commercial rate, and the amount of interest actually paid. The defined calculation method is generally the average of annual opening and closing balances of the loan, multiplied by the official rate of interest. Under self-assessment employers will have to work out the taxable value of the benefit and notify the employee and the Revenue accordingly.

9.22 The employee or the Revenue, but not the employer, can elect for an alternative method based on daily balances, which gives a more accurate result where the balance fluctuates widely. From 1996/97 onwards the time limit for the election is the second 31 January after the end of the year of assessment: e.g. 31 January 1999 for 1996/97. This applies to loans whenever made. [*FA 1996, s 107(2)* amending *TA 1988, 7 Sch 5*]. Employers are required to notify the Revenue of the maximum balances outstanding on the loan in the year. The Revenue are thus alerted to possible circumstances where the opening and closing balances are arranged to be at a much lower level than for the rest of the year.

9.23 The previous rules required loans, where the interest did not qualify for tax relief, to be aggregated. Loans where the interest did qualify were kept separate. For reasons of simplification, from 1996/97 loans are only to be aggregated where the lender so elects, by written notice to the Revenue within 92 days of the end of the relevant year of assessment. Moreover, an election for aggregation is only permissible in respect of loans to which the following conditions apply:

(*a*) the lender is a close company and the borrower is a director at any time during the year when any part of the loan is outstanding;

(*b*) the loan is obtained by reason of the borrower's employment;

(*c*) there is no time in the year when interest charged on the loan equals or exceeds the official rate;

(*d*) the loan is made in the same currency; and

(*e*) the loan is not a qualifying loan (i.e. it does not qualify for tax relief). [*FA 1996, s 107* and *TA 1988, s 160(1B), (1BA)*].

Living accommodation

9.24 Where living accommodation is provided by an employer to an employee there is a basic charge under *TA 1988, s 145* by reference to the greater of the rent paid by the employer for the premises or its annual value, the latter being taken from the rating list. Extra statutory concession A56 deals with property in Scotland, where there was a rating revaluation in 1985. Where the cost is over £75,000, under *TA 1988, s 146* the excess is regarded as giving rise to a loan by the employer to the employee, who is then charged by reference to the official interest rate on the notional loan. A deduction is permitted for business use or where rent is paid by the employee. An anti-avoidance measure has been introduced by *FA 1996, s 106* to counter arrangements for attracting a lower Schedule E charge by the offer of a cash alternative.

9.25 The employer will be obliged to report the measure of chargeable benefit. A Revenue Press Release – REV 38, 28 November 1995, introduced certain concessions relating to the charge. Where the same accommodation is provided to two or more employees, in principle a full charge could be made on both or all of them. The charge is to be limited to that which would be applicable if there were only one employee, with an appropriate apportionment between the employees. For property abroad, where the *TA 1988, s 145* charge is based upon the market rent, there is a waiver of the *s 146* charge. This is an area of the law which is presently under review and there may be changes to the basis of the Schedule E charge in due course.

Share option and acquisition schemes

General

9.26 There are many different kinds of share schemes for employees, which may essentially be divided into Revenue approved schemes, and other share option or share acquisition schemes. The tax consequences of each will vary, and are examined briefly below together with their ramifications under self-assessment. Various changes have been made by *FA 1996* relating to (*a*) savings-related share option schemes, (*b*) approved share option schemes, (*c*) profit sharing schemes and (*d*) employee share ownership trusts. [*FA 1996, ss 111–120*].

Approved share option schemes

9.27 These may be in quoted or unquoted shares, and can either be not related to savings or savings related. Since 28 November 1995 there has been a limitation to £30,000 on the value of shares over which an individual may hold an option. Whilst such schemes generally enjoy favourable Schedule E treatment, a charge can arise in certain circumstances, for example in the case of the first type of scheme on the exercise of an option where the conditions for a 'tax free' exercise are not met. Likewise a charge can arise on the second type of scheme on some early exercise options. In such cases the gain subject to income tax is the value of the shares at the date of exercise, less the price paid. Where quoted shares are involved the employee should have no problem in completing his return since the valuation will be a matter of public record. Where unquoted shares are concerned, and the shares are sold, the taxpayer will likewise have a value for computation (albeit one which the Revenue may be entitled to challenge).

9.28 But in the case of unquoted shares where there is no immediate sale, the employee will have to provide an estimate of the value, until that value is agreed with the Shares Valuation Division. In the absence of assistance from the company in arriving at the estimate, the employee may have to approach the Revenue for guidance. In a case where a significant number of employees need the same valuation, the Revenue seek at present to ensure there is only one negotiation, with the company or otherwise, so that not all employees are involved in negotiations. This system will continue under self-assessment, although it will not prevent any employee disputing an agreed valuation.

Unapproved schemes: options and shares acquired at less than their value

9.29 For share options, there may be a Schedule E charge on the grant if the option is capable of being exercised more than seven years later. This will likewise be the case if shares are actually purchased (without any option) at an undervalue. Otherwise, there will be a potential charge when the option is exercised. In the two former cases, the measure of the charge will be the value of the option, or the shares, as the case may be, on the date the option is granted or the shares are acquired, less anything paid for the option, or the shares. In the latter case the charge will generally be on the value of the shares at the date of exercising the option, less the amount paid for the shares. Similar considerations as to the determination of the taxable amount apply as set out in 9.28.

Employer reporting obligations

General

9.30 Employers' reporting obligations are contained in a substituted *TMA 1970, s 15*, which comes into effect as regards payments made or benefits provided on or after 6 April 1996. [*FA 1995, s 106(1)(2)*]. When requested by a notice from the Revenue an employer must prepare and deliver to the Revenue a return (i.e. P11D) in respect of all 'relevant payments' and benefits in kind provided to past and present employees for the years of assessment set out in the notice, giving names and home addresses where required. [Substituted *TMA 1970, s 15(1)(3)(4)*]. The time limit for information requests for past years of assessment is five years from 31 January following the end of the year. [Substituted *TMA 1970, s 15(2)*].

9.31 Amendments to Regulation 46 of the Income Tax (Employments) Regulations 1993 (SI 1993 No 774) (the 'PAYE Regulations') were announced on 12 May 1995 under the Income Tax (Employments) (Amendment No 4) Regulations 1995 which contains the detailed reporting provisions. These amendments come into effect on 6 April 1996. Further supplementary Regulations which have been issued in 1996 implement certain largely technical changes, without imposing any new obligations on employers or employees. They are consequential on the move from a Schedule E assessment to self-assessment and the cessation of the direct collection and assessment arrangements. They also implement certain changes relating to appeals and interest on tax.

9.32 Where the employer is a corporate body, the secretary is treated as the employer, so the P11D notice may be served on the secretary. Both the secretary and the body corporate are liable to penalties for failure to comply with their obligations. [Substituted *TMA 1970, s 15(12)*]. The Revenue have indicated that where they discover that P11D information is incomplete or contains errors they will usually invite the employer to give an explanation before considering penalty action, and that no penalty will arise if the error or omission was entirely innocent. The Revenue preference in any event is to arrange voluntary settlements with employers to collect any tax and NIC due. [SAT 3, paras 5.3–5.5]. This notwithstanding employers should be mindful that a penalty up to £3,000 may be exigible for each incorrect or incomplete P11D. [*TMA 1970, s 98(2)*]. The Revenue have indicated that the maximum penalty would only be pursued in the most exceptional circumstances. [SAT 3, para 5.16].

Parallel reporting to employees: P60, P11D, P45 and time limits

9.33 Employers have to give Form P60 (certificate of pay and tax deducted during year of assessment) to employees by 31 May following the end of the year of assessment; Regulation 39(1). The first deadline will be 31 May 1997. Moreover, employers have to give to their employees a copy of the Form P11D information provided to the Revenue: Regulation 46AA(1). There is no prescribed format for giving the information to employees, for example, it could be done by a photocopy or computer print out. The deadline is 6 July, one month later than at present. For those employees who have ceased employment between the end of the year of assessment and 6 July a copy of the return may be sent to the employee's last address: Regulation 46AA(2). There is no such automatic obligation in respect of employees who have left employment before 6 April. However, they are entitled to request their former employer to send the information on to them. Such request must be complied with by the later of 6 July following the end of the year of assessment and 30 days from receiving the request; Regulation 46AA(3).

9.34 Although generally Forms P60 and P11D will be sufficient to enable an employee to self-assess, the P60 may not give the requisite details where there have been changes in the employment in the year, or where PAYE has not been operated on a cumulative basis. From April 1996 Form P45 will have four parts instead of the previous three. Part 1 will continue to be sent by the employer to the tax office. Parts 1a, 2 and 3 will be given to the employee, who is to retain Part 1a, and give Parts 2 and 3 to his new employer.

Relevant payments

9.35 'Relevant payments' (for the purposes of P11D reporting) are any payments made to an employee in respect of his employment, including:

(*a*) payments in respect of expenses (including round sum allowances);

(*b*) payments made on his behalf and not repaid; and

(*c*) payments for services rendered in connection with a trade or business, whether rendered in the course of his employment or not. [Substituted *TMA 1970, s 15(6)*].

The employer must provide particulars of all such payments. Also included are emoluments other than money and removal expenses in excess of £8,000 within *TA 1988, 11A Sch*.

Benefits in kind

9.36 The framework of the existing reporting obligations remains. Particulars are required of any benefits provided for the employee or any other person by reason of his employment, chargeable under the following sections of *TA 1988: s 141* (vouchers), *s 142* (credit tokens), *s 143* (vouchers taxable under PAYE), *s 144A* (notional payments), *ss 145* and *146* (living accommodation), and *ss 154–165* (general charging provisions and certain specific items).

9.37 The obligation is no longer in respect of the particulars of the cost to the employer of providing the benefits but rather of the 'cash equivalent', being the amount chargeable to tax. [Substituted *TMA 1970, s 15(9)(a)* and Regulation 46(1)(d), (5)(6)]. In determining the amounts which are so chargeable to tax, no deductions or other adjustments are to be made unless the employer has the requisite information to justify making the deductions or adjustments. The employer is also specifically precluded from making a deduction where the employee remains responsible for making a business deduction claim. These provisions implement the proposals in the Consultative Document referred to in 9.3 *et seq*. It will of course be open to employees to claim further deductions (if appropriate) when they self-assess.

Third party payments and benefits

9.38 Particulars must be provided of any payments or benefits provided by third parties which have been arranged by the employer, including the name and business address of that third party. [Substituted *TMA 1970, s 15(5)(b), (9)(b)* and Regulation 46(8)]. This likewise implements the proposals in the Consultative Document. Should the employer not be able to obtain the information from the third party, he should complete form P11D to his best estimate and notify the Revenue. [SAT 3, para 2.21]. For these purposes 'arranged' includes guaranteed and in any way facilitated. [Substituted *TMA 1970, s 15(13)*]. Furthermore, in cases where the employer has not actually arranged the payment or benefit, but has knowledge that a third party has done so, he may be required to provide the Revenue with that person's name and business address. [*TMA 1970, s 15(5)(c), (9)(c)*].

9.39 The Revenue consider that an employer has arranged a benefit where he has played some active part in the expense or benefit being provided to the employee. This would be the case with benefits provided for an employee of one group company by another group member at the former's request, or reciprocal arrangements between different employers. There would be no arrangement where, as a matter of custom or practice in a particular industry or area of business, one employer provided free or cheap goods or services to employees of another employer, without that other's involvement. Furthermore, mere contact between an employer and a third party providing benefits does not mean that there has been an arrangement. In cases where an employer agrees with retailers to offer a small discount on goods to employees, although there might be an arrangement, there would be no P11D reporting requirement provided the retailer charged at least cost. [SAT 3, paras 2.11–2.19].

9.40 There is no responsibility on employers to provide particulars of benefits etc. which have nothing to do with them. However, under Regulation 46AB, third parties making payments or providing benefits will be required to provide the information to employees by 6 July, just as employers are required to do. The Revenue have said that third parties can choose when the information is given to employees, for example they can do so each time a payment or benefit is provided, or they can assemble the items into one notification after the end of the tax year. [SAT 3, para 4.6]. The third party will thus have to compute the amount chargeable to tax.

9.41 This is a novel obligation on the part of third parties, extending theoretically for example to tips given to waiters and taxi drivers; *Calvert v Wainwright 1947, 27 TC 475*. However, there is a 'de minimis' exclusion, in that small gifts to an employee costing in total £100 or less to the provider in the tax year are excluded, as are corporate hospitality benefits, tips and items included in a taxed award scheme. This exclusion from reporting does not affect the taxability of the benefit in the employees' hands. The information will not automatically have to be given to the Revenue as well, although the Revenue have powers to obtain it. In particular, where the Revenue use the P11D for up-to-date coding, on the basis that benefits normally continue from year to year, this is unlikely to apply to third party benefits.

Business entertaining

9.42 There is a new reporting requirement in relation to business entertaining expenditure. As set out in 9.15 employees of trading concerns obtain relief for qualifying expenses where there has been a disallowance for the employer, but not where the expenses are met from an inclusive salary or round sum allowance. In the case of employees of non-trading concerns, business entertaining expenses can be deducted if these have been incurred wholly, exclusively and necessarily in the performance of their duties. A dispensation may be granted where there is a matching expenses deduction against the payment received and no net tax liability.

9.43 Information will have to be supplied to the employee so that he can decide whether a deduction for tax purposes can be claimed from the amount on which he will be assessed. Accordingly Regulation 46(1)(c), (4) provides that the following particulars must be given to the employee:

(*a*) whether or not a trade, business, profession or vocation is being carried on by the employer; and, if so,

(*b*) the form in which the employee received the emoluments (whether by an allowance, reimbursement, payment made on behalf of the employee and not repaid, or otherwise); and

(*c*) whether the amount of the emolument has been or will be disallowed in the employer's tax computation under *TA 1988, s 577(1)(a)*.

Fixed profit car scheme

9.44 The background to fixed profit car schemes ('FPCS') is set out in 9.13. To claim tax relief on the statutory basis for motor expenses the employee has to provide details of total business and private miles in the year, expenditure on such items as fuel, insurance, maintenance and repairs, the cost of the car and capital allowances in previous years. Previously employees had to keep these records if the employer did not operate an FPCS, or if they thought that they might wish to opt out of it. The position becomes considerably simpler from 1996/97, with all employees having the right to use the FPCS scale, whether or not the employee operates the scheme.

9.45 In such cases the detail need not be shown on Form P11D or P9D, but a new Form FPCS2 can be used to give details to employees so that they can complete their tax returns. A new Regulation 46AA(1) and (4)(b) applies to employers operating an FPCS. An employer will be required to give to the employee the profit figure under the FPCS arrangements, and the business mileage for which payments were made, and the total miles of car travel and car mileage allowances. The FPCS rates for 1996/97 are:

	Up to 4,000 miles	*After 4,000 miles*
Up to 1000cc	27p	16p
1001–1500cc	34p	19p
1501–2000cc	43p	23p
Over 2000cc	61p	33p

(Inland Revenue Press Release 28 November 1995.)

Dispensations

9.46 Dispensations are bilateral arrangements between the Inspector and the employer to the effect that certain expense payments (and benefits in kind) need not be included on Form P11D. Dispensations do not reduce any tax liability, as they relate to expenses, and sometimes benefits, for which employees would be able to obtain a matching deduction. Employees are not involved, and there is no requirement on the part of the employer to inform them of arrangements made. However, the Revenue recommend that employees should be given particulars of any dispensation. [SAT 3, para 2.26]. The Revenue cannot volunteer information to employees because of the confidentiality of the agreement between the employer and the Revenue.

9.47 PAYE does not apply where there is a dispensation. The items need not be shown on Form P11D, and the employee need not show the items on his tax return. Examples are expenses paid in respect of specific claims for allowable items such as business travel, scale rate payments calculated only to reimburse entertaining expenditure at business occasions where the employer would not claim a deduction, allowable subscriptions, and mileage allowance at or below set levels. Where employees are not aware of the existence of a dispensation, they should enter the expenses or benefits on their tax return, even if they are not on the copy P11D received from their employer. [SAT 3, para 2.23].

Annual voluntary settlement

9.48 Prior to self-assessment an annual voluntary settlement ('AVS') involved an employer voluntarily settling an employee's tax liability by a single, usually annual, payment. These were typically to cover one-off benefits, such as Christmas parties and/or to save employees facing an unexpected tax charge. An AVS was not based upon statute, but derived from a contract between the employer and the Revenue. There was a dispensation from P11D reporting. Employers did not have to inform employees of their existence.

9.49 Normally the Inspector ascertained what proportion of employees were likely to be higher rate taxpayers and calculated a composite rate which was applied to the total of expenditure/benefits. The calculation of the tax was done so the benefits or expenditure were 'grossed up' at the composite rate, to take account of the fact that the employer was paying the employee's tax. There was no individual attribution of income and related tax, and no tax was repaid, even where it might be due.

9.50 The former AVS has been put on a statutory footing by *FA 1996, s 110*, which enables the PAYE Regulations to provide for such arrangements. At the time of writing the details of the new scheme remain to be announced but it is evident from the consultation process that its scope will be limited. AVS is not to be used for 'main line' benefits.

Employee responsibilities under self-assessment

9.51 Taking into account the general requirement to make a full return of income, the obligations which will fall upon employees under self-assessment will include the following.

(*a*) The reporting of expense payments received from employers which are taxable.

(*b*) The reporting of all benefits from employer and third parties, substantially based upon the P11D, to the extent that they are included thereon.

(*c*) The making of claims for available business deductions under *TA 1988, s 198*, or other applicable sections.

(*d*) The keeping of detailed records, in particular Forms P11D, 9D and P60; originals or photocopies of receipts and other documents, and data where these differ from Form P11D.

Record keeping for employers and employees

General

9.52 The statutory provisions imposing obligations on taxpayers to maintain records are set out in 19.3 etc. There are no separate specific record keeping provisions for employers and employees under self-assessment. However, the Revenue have provided a general guide to keeping records and a specific guide for the self-employed (SA/BK 4 and SA/BK 3 respectively). All individuals who let property are required to keep the same kind of records as the self-employed and should therefore refer to that guide. There is no specific guide to keeping records for employees. The following paragraphs review the position and summarise the kinds of records that will be required.

Employers

9.53 Regulation 55 of the PAYE Regulations and Regulation 41 of the Income Tax (Subcontractors in the Construction Industry) Regulations already impose certain record keeping requirements on employers. These are in addition to requirements under (*a*) the DSS Contribution Regulations, (*b*) *Companies Act 1985, s 221* (which requires a company to keep records that are sufficient to show and explain its transactions, contain entries from day to day of all sums received and expenses and show its assets and liabilities), and (*c*) the VAT legislation.

9.54 Regulation 55 specifies that an employer is to keep full records relating to emoluments and PAYE. These records must be retained for not less than three years after the end of the year to which they relate. The Revenue are not especially prescriptive about the kind of records that an employer must keep under this head, given that they will depend to some extent on the nature and size of the business, and whether the records are manual or computerised. However, in IR 71 the Revenue have indicated that 'any other records' referred to in Regulation 55 can include all records for wage earners, salaried employees, directors and executives; time sheets, clock cards and tachograph records; cash books and cheque stubs showing payments to employees; petty cash vouchers and records, and ledger records.

9.55 The above requirements are thus fairly comprehensive in any event, and if they are complied with they will satisfy an employer's obligation under self-assessment. Clearly the records will have to be such as to ensure that it can be demonstrated that the value of any chargeable benefits has been calculated correctly.

Employees

9.56 Prior to self-assessment, there were no statutory requirements imposed on employees to keep records. Under self-assessment employees will fall under the general rules outlined in 19.8 *et seq*. Hence they will have to keep all such records as may be requisite for the purposes of making a correct and complete return. These will have to be preserved until the first anniversary of 31 January following the year of assessment, or where a return is filed after that date, the quarter date following the first anniversary of the day on which the return is delivered.

9.57 In filing their tax returns they will no longer simply be able to enter 'per PAYE' or 'per P11D'. They will have to enter all amounts relating to pay and tax, and the cash equivalent of all benefits and expenses payments received. To enable them to do so, the records that in practice they will be required to maintain will include P60 and P11D copies; mileage details and other motoring records; foreign travel itineraries; receipted bills, vouchers and credit card statements for all travel and subsistence; other proof of payment records such as bank statements and cheque stubs; purchase and leasing agreements for assets used in the employment; tax award scheme certificates; and notification from third parties of benefits provided by them. In cases where an employee has presented receipted bills to his employer, he should keep a note to assist his own recollection. As indicated in 9.52 the Revenue have issued general guidance notes as to what records an employee should keep see 19.8 for further details.

Underpayments under PAYE

9.58 Under the old system the Inspector decided whether to collect the underpayment by coding out under PAYE in the following year, or by direct assessment. Under the new system this will be possible where the taxpayer chooses to submit his return by 30 September, as the Revenue will then be in a position to inform the taxpayer before 31 January whether the balance needs to be paid then, or whether it will be coded out.

9.59 In the case of self-assessment, the taxpayer will not automatically have all the relevant information to know his final liability, unless the Revenue have contacted him. The Revenue's preference is for dealing with underpayment by coding out wherever possible, up to a limit of £1,000.

Chapter 10

Capital Gains Tax

Introduction

10.1 No substantive changes to the CGT legislation have been implemented by self-assessment. The main amendments, which are contained in *FA 1996*, relate to (*a*) statutory provisions which previously gave the Revenue a degree of discretion, notably in relation to certain claims for relief, and (*b*) the procedure for claiming reliefs in cases where investment decisions may be taken in subsequent years of assessment.

Former discretionary powers of Revenue

10.2 It is the essence of self-assessment that a taxpayer should be able to file his tax return and self-assess without any reference to the Revenue. This has necessitated taking away from the Revenue many of their discretionary powers, a number of which related to CGT. For example, the exemption from CGT applicable to principal private residences contained in *TCGA 1992, s 222* extends to gardens or grounds, up to 0.5 of a hectare, inclusive of the site of the house. Under the old rules the 0.5 hectare could be increased if the Revenue were satisfied that the larger area was required for the reasonable enjoyment of the dwelling house as a residence, having regard to the latter's size and character. Under the new system it is no longer necessary to satisfy the Revenue that this is the case. The issue is left solely to the judgment of the taxpayer. These issues, together with the particular CGT provisions subject to the amendments in *FA 1996*, are further considered in 17.39. The potential for a discovery assessment, should the Revenue consider that the taxpayer's judgment is incorrect, is considered in Chapter 20.

10.3 Certain of these issues relate to liabilities of prior years. An instance in point is *TCGA 1992, s 49* which deals with contingent liabilities. In the first instance no account is to be taken, in determining the amount of the gain arising on the disposal of an asset, of any contingent liability assumed by the person making the disposal. Under the old rules a deduction was permitted if the Revenue were satisfied that a contingent liability had in fact crystallised. There is no longer any need so to satisfy the Revenue. The taxpayer may make a claim provided that the liability has become enforceable, and is being enforced, without reference to the

Revenue. Should this be the case, then the CGT liability arising on the original disposal is recomputed, and any additional liability discharged. [Amended *TCGA 1992, s 49; FA 1996, 20 Sch 49*].

10.4 An example would be the giving of warranties on a sale of shares, where the vendor was subsequently found to be in breach, and, say, an appropriate adjustment was made to the sale price of the shares. The vendor would accordingly be entitled to a corresponding discharge of his tax liability. Somewhat unfairly, in a case such as this, repayment supplement is not due to the taxpayer in respect of the overpaid tax, even though he may have an obligation to pay interest to the purchaser of the shares in respect of the excess consideration.

Payment of tax by instalments

10.5 There is provision for payment of tax by instalments where the consideration is payable by instalments: *TCGA 1992, s 280*. Under the old rules it was necessary for the taxpayer to be able to establish undue hardship. In practice the Revenue interpreted this requirement fairly leniently, so that in determining hardship the Revenue generally only looked at the instalments themselves, rather than the taxpayer's other available resources. But under the new rules there is no need for hardship. The ability to pay by instalments is solely at the taxpayer's option. [Amended *TCGA 1992, s 280; FA 1996, 20 Sch 65*]. Interest will, however, be payable on unpaid instalments from the original due date.

10.6 Tax which is payable on gifts of assets, such as land and shares in a family controlled or unquoted company, may also be paid by instalments over ten years under *TCGA 1992, s 281(5)*, subject to interest from the usual due date.

Business assets roll-over relief

10.7 Under the provisions of *TCGA 1992, s 152* gains arising on the disposal of certain qualifying business assets may be postponed if the consideration for the disposal is reinvested in replacement assets, either one year before or three years after the disposal. This poses a potential problem under self-assessment, because the owner of the business may well not have made the reinvestment before he has to file his return and self-assess. This is resolved by a new *TCGA, s 153A*, introduced by *FA 1996, s 141*, permitting roll-over relief to be obtained on a provisional basis in the first instance. The position is then finally determined at the end of the three-year reinvestment period in the light of the events actually taking place.

10.8 The person carrying on the trade may make a declaration in his return for the chargeable period in which the disposal takes place that the whole or part of the sale consideration will be applied in the acquisition of a new qualifying asset within the relevant three-year period, in which case relief will be given provisionally. [*TCGA 1992, s 153A(1)(2)*]. The declaration then ceases to have effect either if it is withdrawn by the 'relevant day', if the taxpayer no longer intends to make the reinvestment, or if it is superseded before then by a valid claim for relief. For CGT, the relevant day is the third anniversary of the normal filing date, i.e. 31 January following the year of assessment in which the disposal took place. For corporation tax, it is the fourth anniversary of the end of the accounting period in which the disposal took place. On the declaration ceasing to have effect all necessary adjustments are to be made to the person's assessment, with any repayment or discharge of tax, as the case may be. [*TCGA 1992, s 153A(3)(4)(5)*].

10.9 Although *TCGA, s 152(3)* gives the Revenue a discretion to extend the three-year period for reinvestment, there is no such discretion for extending the period within which a declaration is effective. Consequential amendments are made to the provisions regarding replacement of business assets by members of a group of companies, to permit the granting of provisional relief in cases where assets are only partly replaced. [*FA 1996, s 141(3)*].

Roll-over relief on compulsory acquisition of land

10.10 A form of roll-over relief is provided where land is compulsorily purchased. Parallel provisions to those outlined above in relation to business assets are also contained in *FA 1996, s 141*, permitting provisional claims for relief to be made. The taxpayer may make a similar declaration of intent to apply the whole or part of the sale proceeds of the compulsory disposal in the acquisition of a new qualifying asset within the time limits. The land acquired must not be a dwelling house, exempt from capital gains tax as a private residence, and hence excluded from relief under *TCGA 1992, s 248*. The declaration continues to have effect until it is withdrawn, superseded, or expires on the relevant day. [*TCGA 1992, s 247A(1)(2)* inserted by *FA 1996, s 141(6)*].

10.11 The time of disposal and acquisition of land acquired by a local authority under compulsory purchase powers in *TCGA 1992, s 246(1)* is amended so that the relevant date is the date on which the compensation is agreed, in all cases. [*FA 1996, s 141(4)*]. Under the previous rules the relevant date would have been the time on which the authority entered on the land, if earlier. This could have been problematical in that if agreement of the amount of compensation were delayed, there would have been no payment, and therefore the taxpayer would not have been in a position to reinvest.

Reinvestment relief

10.12 A wide form of reinvestment relief is provided by *TCGA 1992, s 164A et seq.*, in respect of capital gains of any kind realised by individuals and trustees, where the gain is reinvested in shares in qualifying trading companies within three years. As with business assets roll-over relief described above, the taxpayer may have to file his return and self-assess without either having made the actual reinvestment, or taken the final decision to do so. However, it has been decided that there should be no ability to make a provisional claim for relief on the lines of business assets relief in 10.8.

10.13 A number of reasons have been given by the Revenue for this, not all entirely convincing: (1) whilst business assets roll-over relief operates in the context of continuing businesses, and tax should not deplete the capital of the business where that capital remains in the business, the position is often otherwise for reinvestment relief, in that gains on the disposal of assets held purely as investments can qualify for relief; (2) for reinvestment relief only the chargeable gain has to be reinvested (not the sale proceeds); and (3) there was a concern that if provisional relief were available there could be a risk to the tax collectable generally on the disposal of all assets, with a possible serious disruption of Exchequer cash flow.

Allowable losses

10.14 Under *TCGA 1992, s 16* allowable losses can be carried forward indefinitely. Revenue practice in the past has been not to require details of such losses, or to agree the allowable amount, other than where relief has actually been claimed, on the basis that until then there has been no necessity to do so. This is rather unsatisfactory under self-assessment, where the taxpayer needs to know the quantum of a loss in order to enable him to self-assess accurately.

10.15 Under a new *TCGA 1992, s 16(2A)* a capital loss has to be notified to the Revenue as if it were a claim for relief under *TMA, ss 42 and 43*. These sections require claims to be submitted within 5 years 10 months of the end of the year of assessment in which the loss accrued for individuals and partners, and 6 years from the end of the accounting period for companies. A loss claimed under these provisions for 1996/97 onwards is relieved before previous losses brought forward. Consequently the Revenue only have to deal with losses quantified under the self-assessment provisions, unless it becomes necessary to quantify earlier losses in order to relieve them against gains. This is rather unsatisfactory in that the taxpayer will not know his capital loss availability for earlier years.

Premiums for leases

10.16 A capital sum paid by a tenant to obtain the variation, waiver or surrender of a lease, or the commutation of the rent payable under the lease, is treated as a taxable premium. [*TCGA 1992, 8 Sch 3*]. Certain of these sums were treated under the original provisions as received when the lease was granted, which accordingly required a recomputation of the gain accruing on the grant of the lease. To avoid the reopening of earlier years under self-assessment, these provisions have been modified. The position now is as follows for sums payable on or after 6 April 1996:

(*a*) Where the lease is surrendered, the property disposed of will be the landlord's leasehold interest, and the time of disposal will be when the premium is payable.

(*b*) Where the lease is varied, that will be treated as a part disposal of the landlord's freehold, or other interest out of which the lease was granted, and the time of disposal will again be when the premium is payable. Moreover, if the sum is payable in lieu of rent it is treated as paid in respect of the period of the lease which the rent covers. [Substituted *TCGA 1992, 8 Sch 3(4): FA 1996, s 142(4)*].

10.17 There is a modification where the landlord is himself a lessee under a short lease of under 50 years. The premium will be treated as paid in respect of the period to which the sublease relates. The sub-lessee is also treated as having incurred enhancement expenditure on any premium paid for the amendment of the terms of the sub-lease. [*TCGA 1992, 8 Sch 3(5); FA 1996, s 142(5)*].

Scheme of reconstruction: transfer to investment trust

10.18 Under a scheme of reconstruction or amalgamation within *TCGA 1992, s 139*, any assets transferred to implement the scheme are treated as disposed of for no gain/no loss. Where the transferee company becomes an investment trust, what would have been the gain or loss otherwise arising on the reconstruction is crystallised, since a gain accruing to an investment trust is not taxable. [*TCGA 1992, ss 100, 101*]. Under the previous rules that gain was treated as taking place at the time of the reconstruction. To avoid reopening assessments for earlier years, the provisions have been changed so that the gain is treated as accruing in the accounting period immediately before the transferee company becomes an investment trust. The new provisions apply for accounting periods ending on or after the appointed day under *FA 1994, s 199(3)*. [Inserted *TCGA 1992, s 101(1A): FA 1996, s 140*].

Chapter 11

Double Taxation Relief

Commencement – existing rules

11.1 Self-assessment does not require any change to the basic provisions for the relief of double taxation by crediting the foreign tax charged against the UK tax liability on the same income. The complication that arises under the old system is that under the commencement provisions, profits are doubly assessed until the preceding year basis of assessment is running, and *TA 1988, s 804* gives relief for the foreign tax on those profits, or the proportion of them, every time they are brought into assessment. This in turn results in the foreign tax for the opening period being credited more than once.

Cessation – existing rules

11.2 The converse of this is that on a cessation part of the profits, and therefore the double tax credit applicable thereto, falls out of assessment. On a cessation it is necessary to make an adjustment if, as a result of the opening and closing provisions, more double tax credit has been given than the foreign tax which was suffered. This is done by clawing back any excess relief by means of a charge under Schedule D, Case VI at the basic rate of an amount such that at the basic rate it equates with the excess foreign tax credit.

Commencement – new rules

11.3 The double relief is one of the complications not simplified under the self-assessment rules because there is still a double assessment on commencement in all cases other than where the accounting period ends with the end of the fiscal year. There can also be a double assessment on a change of accounting date resulting in a period of account of less than twelve months, in view of the requirement to tax at least twelve months profits in each fiscal year. Because the profits, to an extent, are doubly taxed it is necessary to give an additional double tax credit and *TA 1988, s 804(1)* is amended accordingly by *FA 1994, s 217*. Double taxation relief is therefore given against overlap profits notwithstanding the fact that relief has already been given in respect of the same overseas tax against the same profits in the first period common to the overlap period.

Excess relief

11.4 The withdrawal of excess credit applies where credit has been allowed in respect of an overlap profit, and overlap relief becomes available under *TA 1988, s 63A(1)* or *(3)* on a change of accounting date resulting in a period of in excess of twelve months, or on a cessation. [*TA 1988, s 804(5); FA 1994, s 217(2)*].

To ascertain the excess credit, it is first necessary to determine the difference between:

(*a*) the amount of double tax credit actually allowed as a result of giving credit twice on overlap profits [*substituted TA 1988, s 804(5A)(a)(i)*], and

(*b*) the amount of tax credit which would have been available had relief only been given once [*substituted TA 1988, s 804(5A)(a)(ii)*].

This difference must then be compared with;

(*c*) the credit which would have been allowed in the subsequent year of clawback had the profits not been restricted by overlap relief [*substituted TA 1988, s 804(5A)(b)*].

11.5 Where (*a*) minus (*b*) exceeds (*c*), there is an excess credit which is recovered by way of a Schedule D, Case VI charge at the basic rate, such that the tax due equals the excess credit. Where there has been an insufficient credit, i.e. where (*c*) exceeds (*a*) minus (*b*) it is given as a credit in the year of overlap relief in place of that otherwise available. [*TA 1988, s 804(5B); FA 1994, s 217(2)*].

Change of accounting date

11.6 Where the overlap profits are only partially relieved as a result of a change of accounting date, the proportion of the double tax credit in relation to each element of the overlap is treated as contributing proportionately to the adjustment required. The overlap profit references are introduced by *FA 1994, s 217(3)*.

Example 1

Mr Kalinin, domiciled and resident in the UK, started business in Canada on 1 August 1998 and produced accounts to 30 June 1999, i.e. for a period of less than twelve months ending in the fiscal year following that of commencement, and annually thereafter until 30 June 2001 when the business was sold. His other income absorbed his personal allowances and lower and basic rate bands except in 1998/99 when he was liable at the basic rate of (say) 25 per cent. The UK higher rate is assumed to be 40 per cent.

Profits (as adjusted for UK tax purposes)

1.8.98 to 30.6.99	£12,500	Canadian tax	£4,375
y/e 30.6.2000	£19,500	Canadian tax	£6,825
y/e 30.6.2001	£25,500	Canadian tax	£8,925
			£20,125

Taxable

1998/99 1.8.98 to 5.4.99		
8/11 × £12,500	£9,090	(*a*)
UK tax payable £9,090 @ 25%	£2,272	
Less credit for Canadian tax		
$£9{,}090 \times \frac{4{,}375}{12{,}500}$ limited to	£2,272	
UK tax payable	£Nil	
1999/00 1.8.98 to 31.7.99		
(£12,500 + 1/12 × £19,500)	£14,125	(*b*)
UK tax £14,125 @ 40%	£5,650	
Less credit for Canadian tax		
$£4{,}375 + \left(\frac{1}{12} \times £6{,}825\right)$	£4,944	
UK tax payable	£706	
2000/01 y/e 30.6.2000	£19,500	(*c*)
UK tax £19,500 @ 40%	£7,800	
Less credit for Canadian tax		
$£19{,}500 \times \frac{6{,}825}{19{,}500}$	£6,825	
UK tax payable	£975	
2001/02 y/e 30.6.2001	£25,500	(*d*)
Less overlap relief		
1.8.98 to 5.4.99 £9,090		
1.7.99 to 31.7.99 $\frac{£19{,}500}{12}$ = £1,625		
	£10,715	(*e*)
	£14,785	
UK tax £14,785 @ 40%	£5,914	
Less credit for Canadian tax		
£8,925 limited to	£5,914	
UK tax payable	£Nil	

Notes

(*a*) *TA 1988, s 61(1); FA 1994, s 201* commencement to 5 April.

(*b*) *TA 1988, s 61(2); FA 1994, s 201* first twelve months.

(*c*) *TA 1988, s 60(3)(a); FA 1994, s 200.*

(*d*) *TA 1988, s 60(3)(b); FA 1994, s 200.*

(*e*) *TA 1988, s 63A(3); FA 1994, s 205.*

Applying FA 1994, s 217(5A)
Credit available in opening years but for *TA 1988, s 804; FA 1994, s 217*

1998/99			£2,272
1999/00	$3/11 \times £12{,}500 \times \dfrac{4{,}375}{12{,}500}$	£1,194	
	$1/12 \times £19{,}500 \times \dfrac{6{,}825}{19{,}500} =$	£569	£1,763
*Balance of foreign tax unrelieved in 1998/99 (£3,181 − £2,272)			£909
2000/01	$11/12 \times £19{,}500 \times \dfrac{6{,}825}{19{,}500}$		£6,256
			£11,200

FA 1994, s 217(5A)(a)(ii)
Credit allowed

1998/99	£2,272
1999/00	£4,944
2000/01	£6,825
	£14,041

FA 1994, s 217(5A)(a)(i)

difference	£ 2,841

*The Inland Revenue has confirmed that, were it not for *s 804, TA 1988*, the foreign tax not relieved in 1998/99 would be eligible for credit in 1999/2000 even though some of the income has also been assessed for the earlier year.

Credit available y/e 30.6.2001 on assumption no overlap relief given.

Profits	£25,500
UK tax £25,500 @ 40%	£10,200
Less credit for Canadian tax	£8,925
Less difference as above	£2,841
Credit available *FA 1994, s 217(5B)(b)*	£6,084
UK tax payable – as before	£5,914
Less £6,084 credit as restricted	£5,914
Final UK tax payable	£NIL

The credit finally allowed of £14,041 as above plus £5,914 for 2001/02 i.e. £19,955 compares with the foreign tax suffered of £20,125, i.e. a shortfall of credit of £170.

Transitional provisions

Relief for Schedule D, Cases I and II

11.7 The transitional rules relating to double taxation relief apply where income first arose prior to 6 April 1994 and continues after 5 April 1998, unless there is a cessation in 1998/99. [*FA 1994, 20 Sch 10(1)*]. The credit for foreign tax in 1996/97 is one-half of the aggregate of the foreign tax paid on income arising in 1995/96 and 1996/97. [*FA 1994, 20 Sch 10(2)*]. This does not apply where Schedule D, Case I or II income for 1995/96 has been assessed on an actual basis, as this would have attracted its own foreign tax credit and there would be no double allowance. In 1996/97 the foreign tax paid in respect of the actual income for that year will be allowed as a credit in 1996/97, which will be assessed on an actual basis under *FA 1994, 20 Sch 2(3)*. [*FA 1994, 20 Sch 10(3)*].

11.8 The straightforward 50 per cent rule cannot apply where the aggregate period used in the transitional year 1996/97 is a shorter or longer period than two years because, for example, of a change of accounting date. In such circumstances the foreign tax credit for the two years 1995/96 and 1996/97 is reduced or increased proportionately by reference to the transitional period basis period under *FA 1994, 20 Sch 2(2)*. [*FA 1994, 20 Sch 10(4)*].

Example 2

Mr Sheremetyev, resident and domiciled in England, was a partner in a foreign partnership which made up its accounts to 30 September each year until 1997 when it made up accounts to 31 March. His UK income absorbed his personal allowances and lower and basic rate tax bands.

The profits as adjusted for UK tax purposes, applicable to Mr Sheremetyev, and the related foreign tax credit, were as follows:

	Profits	*FTC*
	£	£
y/e 30.9.94	40,000	11,000
y/e 30.9.95	38,000	12,000
y/e 30.9.96	45,000	15,000
1.10.96 to 31.3.97	25,000	7,000
y/e 31.3.98	50,000	14,000

Assessable/taxable

1995/96 y/e 30.9.94	£40,000
Tax payable at 40%	£16,000
Less foreign tax credit	£11,000
Tax due	£5,000

1996/97 primary basis period y/e 31.3.97	
1.10.96 to 31.3.97	£25,000
(FTC £7,000)	
½ y/e 30.9.96	£22,500
(FTC £7,500)	
relevant period 1.10.94 to 31.3.96	
y/e 30.9.95	£38,000
(FTC £12,000)	
½ y/e 30.9.96	£22,500
(FTC £7,500)	
Aggregate	£108,000
Appropriate fraction	
$£108,000 \times \dfrac{365}{365 + 365 + 183} =$	£43,176
Tax payable at 40%	£17,270
Less foreign tax credit (£7,000 + £7,500 + £12,000 + £7,500) =	
$£34,000 \times \dfrac{365}{365 + 365 + 183} =$	£13,593
Tax due	£3,677
1997/98 y/e 31.3.98	£50,000
Tax payable at 40%	£20,000
Less foreign tax credit	£14,000
Tax due	£6,000

Relief for Schedule D, Cases IV and V

11.9 Where the income is assessed under Schedule D, Case IV or V, by reference to the income arising in the fiscal year, the foreign tax credit is one-half of the foreign tax paid in the two years 1995/96 and 1996/97, i.e. the same basis on which the income is assessed. Where the income is assessed by reference to remittances, the foreign tax applicable to those remittances is credited and in the transitional year one-half of the foreign tax applicable to remittances in 1995/96 and 1996/97 is credited. [*FA 1994, 20 Sch 10(5)*]. The full credit for foreign tax paid in 1996/97 is available where 1995/96 is computed on an actual basis as a result of which the transitional averaging does not apply [*FA 1994, 20 Sch 10 (5A), FA 1995, s 122(4)(5)*] see 2.45.

11.10 Where the income is wholly or partly exempt from foreign withholding tax under a double taxation agreement, full relief should be available in the transitional period, see Inland Revenue Tax Bulletin No 16, April 1995, page 207 (Appendix F).

Cessation before 6 April 1998

11.11 If the source of income eligible for double tax credits commenced prior to 6 April 1994 and ceases prior to 6 April 1998 the Revenue may direct that the old rules should apply for 1996/97 under *FA 1994, 20 Sch 3(2), 7*. If the Revenue makes such a direction the tax credit would follow and any withdrawal of excess credit would be made under the old rules. [*FA 1994, 20 Sch 12(1)*].

Cessation in 1998/99

11.12 If the cessation takes place in 1998/99, the Revenue have the power to make a direction for 1996/97 to be assessed on an actual fiscal year basis under *FA 1994, 20 Sch 3(4)*. If they make such a direction the old rules continue to apply for calculating the withdrawal of excess relief, if any. [*FA 1994, 20 Sch 12(2)*].

Cessation after 5 April 1998

11.13 Where the business commenced prior to 6 April 1994 and continues after 5 April 1998, the double foreign tax credit will have been given under the old commencement provisions and the clawback will be charged under the new self-assessment rules. There are provisions in *FA 1994, 20 Sch 11* for calculating the excess relief to be recovered in such cases where a source of income ceases in 1998 or later; save when the Revenue make a direction to assess 1996/97 on an actual basis as set out in 11.12. The recovery provisions for excess relief are broadly similar to the new rules under substituted *TA 1988, s 804(5)(2)(5C)*. [*FA 1994, 20 Sch 11(2)(3)*]. It is necessary to compare:

(*a*) the tax credit actually allowed; with

(*b*) the aggregate of the credit which would have been allowed had there been no double allowance on commencement and as if the transitional credit had not been reduced.

[*FA 1994, 20 Sch 11(4)*].

11.14 The object of the calculation is to make sure that the credit that is actually allowed, taking into account the double allowance under the old commencement provisions, does not exceed the credit which falls out of assessment on the transitional provisions when only part of the credit is allowed. The transitional provisions do not appear to take account of the overlap relief on cessation, however, which could cause a loss of foreign tax credit in the final period.

11.15 The excess foreign tax credit as calculated is recovered by means of a Schedule D, Case VI charge of such an amount as at the basic rate equals the excess relief.

11.16 It is not clear that these provisions take the necessary account of any restriction in foreign tax credits arising as a result of overlap relief but do give a reasonably fair result in most cases.

Example 3

Mr Dubrovin, domiciled and resident in the UK, started business in Canada on 1 August 1993 and produced accounts to 30 June 1994, i.e. for a period of less than twelve months ending in the fiscal year following that of commencement, and annually thereafter until 30 June 2001 when the business was sold. His other income absorbed his personal allowances and lower and basic rate bands except in 1993/94 when he was liable at the basic rate of 25%. The UK higher rate is assumed to be 40%.

Profits (as adjusted for UK tax purposes)

1.8.93 to 30.6.94	£12,500	Canadian tax	£4,375
y/e 30.6.95	£14,000	Canadian tax	£4,900
y/e 30.6.96	£18,000	Canadian tax	£6,300
y/e 30.6.97	£16,000	Canadian tax	£5,600
y/e 30.6.98	£10,000	Canadian tax	£3,500
y/e 30.6.99	£15,000	Canadian tax	£5,250
y/e 30.6.2000	£19,500	Canadian tax	£6,825
y/e 30.6.2001	£25,500	Canadian tax	£8,925
	£130,500		£45,675

Taxable

1993/94 1.8.93 to 5.4.94	
8/11 × £12,500	£9,090 (*a*)
UK tax payable £9,090 @ 25%	£2,272
Less credit for Canadian tax	
£9,090 × $\frac{4,375}{12,500}$ limited to	£2,272
UK tax payable	£Nil
1994/95 1.8.93 to 31.7.94	
(£12,500 + 1/12 × £14,000)	£13,667 (*b*)
UK tax £13,667 @ 40%	£5,467
Less credit for Canadian tax	
£4,375 + $\left(\frac{1}{12} \times £4,900\right)$	£4,783
UK tax payable	£684
1995/96 1.8.93 to 31.7.94	
£12,500 + 1/12 × £14,000	£13,667 (*c*)

UK tax £13,667 @ 40%	£5,467
Less credit for Canadian tax	
$£4{,}375 + \left(\frac{1}{12} \times £4{,}900\right)$	£4,783
UK tax payable	£684
1996/97 transitional year	
primary basis period y/e 30.6.96	£18,000 (*d*)
relevant period y/e 30.6.95	£14,000 (*e*)
Aggregate	£32,000 (*f*)
Appropriate fraction	
$£32{,}000 \times \frac{365}{365 + 365}$	£16,000 (*g*)
UK tax £16,000 at 40%	£6,400
Less credit for Canadian tax	
$\frac{£4{,}900 + £6{,}300}{2}$	£5,600 (*h*)
UK tax payable	£800
1997/98 y/e 30.6.97	£16,000 (*i*)
UK tax £16,000 @ 40%	£6,400
Less credit for Canadian tax	
$£16{,}000 \times \frac{5{,}600}{16{,}000}$	£5,600
UK tax payable	£800
1988/99 y/e 30.6.98	£10,000 (*j*)
UK tax £10,000 @ 40%	£4,000
Less credit for Canadian tax	
$£10{,}000 \times \frac{3{,}500}{10{,}000}$	£3,500
UK tax payable	£500
1999/2000 y/e 30.6.99	£15,000 (*k*)
UK tax £15,000 @ 40%	£6,000
Less credit for Canadian tax	
$£15{,}000 \times \frac{5{,}250}{15{,}000}$	£5,250
UK tax payable	£750
2000/01 y/e 30.6.2000	£19,500
UK tax £19,500 @ 40%	£7,800

Less credit for Canadian tax	
$£19{,}400 \times \frac{6{,}825}{19{,}500}$	£6,825
UK tax payable	£975
2001/02 y/e 30.6.2001	£25,500 (*l*)
Less transitional overlap relief	£12,000 (*m*)
	£13,500
UK tax £13,500 @ 40%	£5,400
Less credit for Canadian tax	
£8,925 limited to	£5,400
UK tax payable	£Nil

Notes

(*a*) Original *TA 1988, s 61(1)* commencement to 5 April.

(*b*) Original *TA 1988, s 61(3)* first twelve months.

(*c*) Original *TA 1988, s 60(4)* first twelve months.

(*d*) *TA 1988, s 60(3)(b); FA 1994, s 200.*

(*e*) *FA 1994, 20 Sch 2(2)(b), (5).*

(*f*) *FA 1994, 20 Sch 2(2).*

(*g*) *FA 1994, 20 Sch 2(5).*

(*h*) *FA 1994, 20 Sch 10(2).*

(*i*) *TA 1988, s 60(3)(b); FA 1994, s 200.*

Transitional overlap relief

9/12 × y/e 30.6.97 falls before 5.4.97

9/12 × £16,000 — £12,000

(*j*) *TA 1988, s 60(3)(b); FA 1994, s 200.*

(*k*) *TA 1988, s 60(3)(b); FA 1994, s 200.*

Transitional charge applying *FA 1994, 20 Sch 11.*
Tax credit actually allowed:

	£
1993/94	2,272
1994/95	4,783
1995/96	4,783
1996/97	5,600
1997/98	5,600
1998/99	3,500

		£
1999/00		5,250
2000/01		6,825
2001/02		5,400
		£44,013

Credit allowable but for *TA 1988, s 804.*

1993/94 limited to UK tax			2,272
1994/95	$3/11 \times £12{,}500 \times \frac{4{,}375}{12{,}500} =$	1,194	
	$1/12 \times £14{,}000 \times \frac{4{,}900}{14{,}000} =$	408	
	Balance of foreign tax unrelieved 1993/94	909	
			2,511
1995/96	$3/11 \times £12{,}500 \times \frac{4{,}375}{12{,}500} =$	1,194	
	$1/12 \times £14{,}000 \times \frac{4{,}900}{14{,}000} =$	408	
		1,602	
		(but restricted to)	NIL
	(No tax credit allowed as all credit utilised in 1994/95 above)		
1996/97	y/e 30.6.96 } y/e 30.6.95 } $\frac{4{,}900 + 6{,}300}{2}$		5,600
1997/98	y/e 30.6.97		5,600
1998/99	y/e 30.6.98		3,500
1999/00	y/e 30.6.99		5,250
2000/01	y/e 30.6.00		6,825
2001/02	y/e 30.6.01 limited to UK tax		5,400
			£36,958

Credit allowed (*FA 1994, 20 Sch 11(3)(a)*)		44,013
Less (*a*) Credit available but for *FA 1994, s 804, 20 Sch 11(3)(b)(i)*	36,958	
(*b*) Difference that would have been allowed in 1996/97 and credit actually allowed (£11,200 − £5,600)	5,600	
FA 1994, 20 Sch 11(3)(b)(ii)		(42,558)
Recovery		£1,455
Schedule D, Case VI assessment £5,820 @ 25% =		£1,455

The excess credit allowed on commencement is the amount allowed in the years of commencement as defined by *TA 1988, s 804(8)* i.e. the first three fiscal years and any other years including the profit of those years. The same income is assessable for 1994/95 and 1995/96, although as all of the available tax credits have been given in 1994/95, nil tax credits are available for relief in 1995/96.

	£
1993/94	2,272
1994/95	4,783
1995/96	4,783
	£11,838

Less the amount available on assumption of no loss of credit in the transitional period

	£
1993/94	2,272
1994/95	2,511
1995/96	NIL
Plus amount under *FA 1994, 20 Sch 11(3)(b)(ii)*	5,600
That is	10,383
Difference	£1,455

The recovery of £1,455 effectively reduces the total amount of credit for foreign tax to £42,558 (i.e. £44,013 – £1,455). Out of the total profits earned and taxed abroad, £130,500, only £126,424 is actually assessed to tax.

In an ideal world one might say that all of these profits attract credit relief at the foreign tax rate of 35%, except the £9,090 profits assessed for 1993/94, where the relief must be restricted to 25%. Therefore:

Profits	TCR@	Relief
9,090	25%	2,272
117,334	35%	41,066
£126,424		£43,338

The credit actually allowed is £42,558, giving rise to a small shortfall of £780. It appears that this is an inevitable consequence given the complexity of the rules required to deal with the transition. As Donovan LJ said in *ICI v Caro 1960 39 TC 374*,

> '. . . in this particular field, . . . perfection in any system of double taxation relief must be almost impossible to achieve'.

11.17 Where income for 1996/97 has been charged on the basis of the actual income in the fiscal year there is no loss of credit except by reference to overlap relief causing the foreign tax credit to be restricted, which is ignored, so the excess credit is merely the amount doubly allowed on commencement. [*FA 1994, 20 Sch 11(5)*]. The clawback arises whether the excess credit was given under the old or new provisions. [*FA 1994, 20 Sch 11(6)*].

11.18 Where foreign tax is given as an expense under *TA 1988, s 811*, instead of as a credit, the transitional rules are applied to the profits as reduced. [*FA 1994, 20 Sch 13*].

Chapter 12

Partnerships

Introduction

12.1 There are fundamental changes to partnership taxation under self-assessment. Under the existing rules partnerships are assessed to tax as a single unit and the partnership profits are allocated among the partners in accordance with their profit sharing ratio in the year of assessment, not in accordance with the ratio in which they actually share the accounting profits forming the basis period for that assessment. Moreover the tax payable by the partnership is calculated as a joint and several liability of the partners. Under the new provisions each partner will be responsible for his own taxation in connection with his share of the partnership profit and there will be no joint liability. The suggestion in the Consultative Document that UK resident partners might be jointly liable for the payment of tax of non-resident partners has been included in *FA 1995, s 126(7)*, see 14.10.

12.2 The existence or otherwise of a partnership is governed by the *Partnership Act 1890, s 1*, which defines partnership as the relationship which subsists between persons carrying on business in common with a view to profits. The original version of *TA 1988, s 111* referred to a trade or profession carried on by two or more persons jointly whereas the new version refers to a trade or profession carried on by persons in partnership. The original wording suggested that a joint venture that is a business operation between two or more parties not constituting a full partnership might be assessed for taxation purposes as a partnership (*John Gardner and Bowring Hardy & Co Limited v IRC 1930 15 TC 602*). Whether or not a partnership exists for tax purposes is primarily a question of fact (*IRC v Williamson 1928 14 TC 335; Calder v Allanson 1935 19 TC 293*). The existence or otherwise of a partnership agreement is not itself conclusive, *Hawker v Compton 1922 8 TC 306; Dickenson v Gross 1927 11 TC 614; Fenston v Johnstone 1940 23 TC 29*. A partnership agreement can confirm the existence of a partnership already in being but cannot retrospectively create a partnership which did not exist at the time, *Ayrshire Pullman Motor Services & Ritchie v IRC 1929 14 TC 754; Waddington v O'Collaghan 1931 16 TC 187; Taylor v Chalklin 1944 26 TC 463*. Although there is no age limit for partnership, minor children were not accepted as genuine partners in *Alexander Bulloch & Co v IRC 1976 STC 514*.

Relevance of sharing profits and losses

12.3 Although an agreement to share profits implies a partnership, *Morden Rigg & R B Eskrigge & Co v Monks 1923 8 TC 450; George Hall and Son v Platt 1954 35 TC 440; John Gardner and Bowring Hardy & Co Ltd v IRS 1930 15 TC 602*, it is not conclusive, *Pratt v Strick 1932 17 TC 459* and could merely indicate a joint venture. The sharing of losses however, is highly indicative of a partnership, although again not conclusive, *Brown v Tapscott 1840 6 M&W 119; Bond v Pittard 1838 3 M&W 357*. The mere joint ownership of property is specifically excluded from being a partnership and the *Partnership Act 1890, s 2(1)* was confirmed in *McKie v Luck 1925 9 TC 511* although where the property is used for a business the totality of the arrangement may amount to a partnership, *Farrell v Sunderland SS Co Limited 1903 4 TC 605*. This distinction is recognised in relation to a Schedule A business by Tax Bulletin No 20, page 271 (Appendix F).

Salaried partners who do not have a proprietorial interest in the firm are assessed as employees under Schedule E or possibly as self-employed consultants under Schedule D, Case I or II, but not as a partner under the provisions dealt with in this chapter. However, it is possible for a salaried partner to have a proprietary interest in the firm even without providing any of the partnership capital, *Stekel v Ellice 1973 1 All ER 465*. A fixed salary as a first charge on profits implies a full partnership, *Marsh v Stacey 1963 107 Sol Jo 512*. Megarry J in *Stekel v Ellice 1973 1 All ER 465 at 473* stated:

> 'If then there is a plain contract of master and servant and the only qualification of that relationship is that the servant is being held out as being a partner, the name "salaried partner" seems perfectly apt for him and yet he will be no partner in relation to the members of the firm. At the other extreme there may be a full partnership deed under which all the partners, save one take a share of the profits with that one being paid a fixed salary, not dependent on profits. Again, "salaried partner" seems to be an apt description of that one I do not see why he should not be a true partner at all events if he is entitled to share in the profits and the winding up'.

A limited partner under the *Limited Partnerships Act 1907* is prohibited from taking part in the management of the firm by *LPA 1907, s 6*. However, a limited partner may well be and indeed would normally be a partner for tax purposes, although his losses and interest relief could be restricted under *TA 1988, ss 117* and *363(2)(a)* respectively.

Partners as notional sole traders

12.4 Once the new tax rules come into force (see 12.9) a partner who joins a firm will be treated as commencing a new trade or profession and his share of profits will be taxed on him personally under the commencement provisions, including an overlap. Conversely a partner who leaves the firm will be treated as ceasing to carry on the trade or profession and he will be entitled to overlap relief.

No separate taxable entity

12.5 New *TA 1988, s 111(1)* as introduced by *FA 1994, s 215(1)* and *FA 1995, s 117* provides that a partnership is not treated for tax purposes as an entity separate and distinct from the partners who carry it on. This radical change means partnerships will not be assessed in the partnership name under the new provisions; even where, as in Scotland, a partnership is a separate legal entity.

Partnership as deemed individual

12.6 Substituted *TA 1988, s 111(2)* provides that a partnership is to be treated as a UK resident individual for the purpose of computing the profits chargeable to tax where all the partners are subject to income tax as individuals or trustees. So even though a partnership is not a separate entity for tax purposes under the new provisions, it is effectively treated as such for determining the amount of chargeable profits.

Allocation of profits

12.7 Substituted *TA 1988, s 111(3)* provides that each partner is taxed as if he were carrying on a separate business, but the measure of profit is his share of the adjusted results of the partnership for the period. This means that usually the only difference between the accounting profit on which the partner's drawings are based and the taxable profit is that arising from the normal adjustments for tax purposes; i.e. disallowing depreciation, entertaining etc., and allowing capital allowances and other statutory deductions. The provisions of *TA 1988, s 277(2)* which allocated a partner's share by reference to his share in the fiscal year, and not in the accounting period which formed the basis for that assessment, are repealed by *FA 1994, s 215(3)(c)*.

Apportionment

12.8 The result of taxing each partner as if he were carrying on a separate business is that each one will be subject to tax on the opening year basis in the year in which he becomes a partner, or the business commences. His share of profit will then be taxed in accordance with the opening year provisions of *TA 1988, s 61(2); FA 1994, s 201*. Each partner will therefore have his own overlap profit and overlap period, calculated by reference to the date of his joining the partnership. Similarly, the cessation rules will be applied to the individual partner's share of the partnership profit on his ceasing to be a partner or if the business itself ceases. He will therefore be able to claim overlap relief under *TA 1988, s 63A* [*TA 1988, s 111(4)* substituted by *FA 1994, s 215(1)* and amended by *FA 1995, s 117(1)(2)*]. If the firm has a change of accounting date, any election to apply this date for tax purposes under *TA 1988, s 62A(3); FA 1994, s 203*, or subsequent appeal under *TA 1988, s 62A(6)* has, under *TA 1988, s 111(6)* as substituted by *FA 1994, s 215(1)* and amended by *FA 1995, s 117(1)(2)*, to be made on behalf of the partnership by a nominated partner. Such a change may result in individual partners having an addition to their overlap profits, or, on an extended accounting period, relief for overlap profits brought forward. A change of accounting date of the firm that is ineffective for tax purposes is treated as if the firm had retained the old accounting date for any new partner joining in order to bring him into line with the other partners for accounting date purposes, in respect of his own self-assessment. [*TA 1988, s 111(5)* as substituted by *FA 1994, s 215(1)* and amended by *FA 1995, s 117(1)(2)*].

Commencement date for new provisions

12.9 The new provisions come into force from 1997/98 in respect of partnerships carrying on a trade, profession or business on 5 April 1994. Partnerships commencing on or after 6 April 1994 are subject to the new rules from the start. If there is a change in partners after 5 April 1994 and the partners do not elect for continuation under *TA 1988, s 113(2)* there will be a deemed cessation and commencement and the new rules will therefore apply on the commencement. [*FA 1994, s 215(4)(5)*].

Example 1

Messrs Shishmaryev, Silvansky and Sukhoi were in partnership as solicitors sharing profits equally and preparing accounts, on a bills delivered basis, to 30 April each year. On 30 April 1994, Mr Sukhoi retired and Mr Kuznetsov joined. The goodwill passed under the partnership agreement to the new firm without payment and work in progress passed at a nominal £1, under *TA 1988, s 101*. There was no election for continuation under *TA 1988, s 113(2)*.

Profits (as adjusted for tax purposes, ignoring work in progress were):

y/e 30 April 1991	£150,000
y/e 30 April 1992	£140,000
y/e 30 April 1993	£120,000
y/e 30 April 1994	£100,000
y/e 30 April 1995	£140,000
y/e 30 April 1996	£180,000
y/e 30 April 1997	£200,000

Work in progress, on the basis of cost of professional staff time plus attributable overheads, was £120,000 at 30 April 1995, £145,000 at 30 April 1996, and £130,000 at 30 April 1997.

SP A27 requires work in progress to be taken into account in computing the profits of the new partnership commencing on 30 April 1994. The profit for the year ended 30 April 1995 of £140,000 has to be adjusted to £260,000 to reflect the closing work in progress of £120,000. The profit for the year ended 30 April 1996 has likewise to be adjusted to £205,000 to reflect the increase in work in progress (£145,000 – £120,000); and that for the year ended 30 April 1997 has to be adjusted to £185,000 to reflect the reduction in work in progress (£145,000 – £130,000).

Assessable/taxable

	Total	Sh	Si	Su	K
	£	£	£	£	£
(*a*) 1992/93 y/e 30.4.91	150,000	50,000	50,000	50,000	
(*b*) 1993/94 y/e 30.4.92	140,000	46,667	46,667	46,666	
(*c*) 1994/95 cessation 6.4.94 to 30.4.94 $\frac{25}{365} \times £100,000$	6,849	2,283	2,283	2,283	
(*d*) 1994/95 recommencement 1.5.94 to 5.4.95 $\frac{340}{365} \times £260,000$	242,191	80,730	80,730	–	80,731
(*e*) 1995/96 y/e 30.4.95	260,000	86,667	86,667		86,666
(*f*) 1996/97 y/e 30.4.96	205,000	68,333	68,333		68,334
(*g*) 1997/98 y/e 30.4.97	185,000	61,667	61,667		61,666
Total 1992/93 to 1997/98	1,189,040	396,347	396,347	98,949	297,397

Notes

(*a*) Preceding year basis, *TA 1988, s 60(3)* (original enactment).

(*b*) Preceding year basis, *TA 1988, s 60(3)* (original enactment).

Total for 1992/93 and 1993/94 £290,000.

Revenue option for actual basis under *TA 1988, s 63(1)(b)* (original enactment):

1992/93	$\frac{25}{365} \times £140,000$	£9,589	
	$\frac{340}{365} \times £120,000$	£111,780	£121,369
1993/94	$\frac{25}{365} \times £120,000$	£8,219	
	$\frac{340}{365} \times £100,000$	£93,151	£101,370
			£222,739

which is less than £290,000 originally assessed so there is no Revenue adjustment on cessation.

(*d*) Commencement to 5 April, substituted *TA 1988, s 61(1)*.

(*e*) Twelve months to first accounting date, substituted *TA 1988, s 60(3)(a)*. Overlap credit for £242,191 already assessed in 1994/95.

(*f*) Current year basis, substituted *TA 1988, s 60(3)(b)*.

(*g*) Current year basis, substituted *TA 1988, s 60(3)(b)*.

Had there been a continuation election on Mr Sukhoi's retirement and Mr Kuznetsov's arrival the position would have been markedly different. The absence of a cessation would have enabled the bills delivered basis to have been retained throughout.

Assessable/taxable

	Total	*Sh*	*Si*	*Su*	*K*
	£	£	£	£	£
(*a*) 1992/93 y/e 30.4.91	150,000	50,000	50,000	50,000	
(*b*) 1993/94 y/e 30.4.92	140,000	46,667	46,667	46,666	
(*c*) 1994/95 y/e 30.4.93	120,000	40,000	40,000	2,740	37,260
(*d*) 1995/96 y/e 30.4.94	100,000	33,333	33,333		33,334
(*e*) 1996/97 transitional year	160,000	53,333	53,333		53,334
(*f*) 1997/98 y/e 30.4.97	200,000	66,667	66,667		66,666
	870,000	290,000	290,000	99,406	190,594
As originally computed	1,189,040	396,347	396,347	98,949	297,397
Difference caused by failure to elect for continuation	319,040	106,347	106,347	(457)	106,803

Notes

(*a*) Preceding year basis, *TA 1988, s 60(3)* (original enactment).

(*b*) Preceding year basis, *TA 1988, s 60(3)* (original enactment).

(*c*) Preceding year basis, *TA 1988, s 60(3)* (original enactment).

Mr Sukhoi $\frac{25}{365} \times £40,000 =$ £2,740

Mr Kuznetsov $\frac{340}{365} \times £40,000 =$ £37,260

(*d*) Preceding year basis, *TA 1988, s 60(3)* (original enactment).

(*e*) Basis period 1996/97, *FA 1994, 20 Sch 1(2)*.

y/e 30.4.96	£180,000
Relevant period, *FA 1994, 20 Sch 2(5)*	
y/e 30.4.95	£140,000
Aggregate *FA 1994, 20 Sch 2(2)*	£320,000

Appropriate percentage, *FA 1994, 20 Sch 2(5)*

$£320,000 \times \frac{365}{365 + 365} =$ £160,000

(*f*) Current year basis, substituted *TA 1988, s 60(3)(b)*. Aggregate of partners' transitional overlap, *FA 1994, 20 Sch 2(4)*.

$\frac{340}{365} \times £200,000 =$ £186,301

The substantially increased taxable income arises from the combination of the work in progress adjustment increasing the profits of the commencement year, taxed nearly twice and the acceleration of increasing profits on moving to the current year basis in 1994/95 instead of 1997/98.

Equitable adjustments

12.10 The effect of the new rule is that the desirability of having an equitable adjustment in the partnership agreement to cater for the imbalance that can apply under the old rules between the profits in which the partner actually shares in a year and the assessment for that year (the latter being based on the profits of the basis period, but allocated in accordance with the profit sharing arrangements in the fiscal year) should no longer arise. However, an equitable adjustment might still be desirable if there are prior charges such as salaries to certain partners, and the total salaries exceed the adjusted profits.

Example 2

Messrs Semyenov, Sutugin and Goryelev were in partnership trading as 'Tri Druga'. Mr Semyenov and Mr Sutugin were entitled to 'salaries' of £30,000 each as a prior share of profits which were thereafter shared in the proportion 20, 20 and 60.

The profits, as adjusted for tax purposes, were:

y/e 30.6.98	£140,000
y/e 30.6.99	£ 40,000
y/e 30.6.2000	£180,000

Assessable/taxable

	Total £	*Se* £	*Su* £	*G* £
1998/99				
y/e 30.6.98				
Prior share	60,000	30,000	30,000	–
Profit/loss	80,000	16,000	16,000	48,000
	140,000	46,000	46,000	48,000
1999/2000				
y/e 30.6.99				
Prior share	60,000	30,000	30,000	–
Profit/loss	(20,000)	–	–	(20,000)
	40,000	30,000	30,000	(20,000)
G's notional loss shared equally		(10,000)	(10,000)	20,000
		£20,000	£20,000	–
2000/01				
y/e 30.6.2000				
Prior share	60,000	30,000	30,000	–
Profit/loss	120,000	24,000	24,000	72,000
	180,000	54,000	54,000	72,000

The loss shown in the accounts after the salaries of Mr Semyenov and Mr Sutugin in the year ended 30 June 1999, which is borne by Mr Goryelov, is not an allowable loss for tax purposes as the partnership shows an overall profit, which is allocated to those partners which share in it in their profit sharing ratio, i.e. Mr Semyenov and Mr Sutugin equally. They each receive £30,000 but pay tax on £20,000 while Mr Goryelov who suffers a loss of £20,000 obtains no relief for it. Equity would suggest that in these circumstances Messrs Semyenov and Sutugin should surrender their tax saved on £10,000 each to Mr Goryelov as an equitable adjustment under an appropriate clause in the partnership agreement.

Cessation provisions

12.11 Not only will each partner calculate his chargeable profits under the opening provisions of substituted *TA 1988, ss 60* and *61,* but on leaving the partnership he will fall within the cessation provisions of *TA 1988, s 63* and be eligible for overlap relief in respect of his partnership share under *TA 1988, s 63A; FA 1994, s 205*. Individual partners will of course also be affected by additional overlap or overlap relief arising on a change of accounting date under *TA 1988, s 62* and *62A*. [*FA 1994, ss 202, 203*].

Example 3

Mr Polikarpov and Mr Shavrov started business in partnership on 1 August 1998 sharing profits equally and produced accounts to 31 December 1999 and annually thereafter. On 1 July 2000 they were joined by Mr Michaelson and shared profits equally until 30 September 2001 when Mr Shavrov was tragically killed in an aircraft crash. The surviving partners continued to share profits equally.

Profits (as adjusted for tax purposes)

1.8.98 to 31.12.99	£43,000
y/e 31.12.2000	£45,000
y/e 31.12.2001	£57,000
y/e 31.12.2002	£48,000

Taxable	*Total* £	*P* £	*S* £	*M* £	
1998/99 1.8.98 to 5.4.99					
8/17 × £43,000	20,235	10,117	10,118	–	(*a*)
1999/00 1.1.99 to 31.12.99					
12/17 × £43,000	30,352	15,176	15,176	–	(*b*)
2000/01 y/e 31.12.2000					
1.1.00 to 30.6.00	22,500	11,250	11,250	–	(*c*)
1.7.00 to 31.12.00	22,500	7,500	7,500	7,500	(*d*)
1.1.01 to 5.4.01	4,750	–	–	4,750	(*e*)
	49,750	18,750	18,750	12,250	
2001/02 y/e 31.12.2001					
1.1.01 to 30.9.01	42,750	14,250	14,250	14,250	(*f*)
Less Overlap relief	(3,794)		(3,794)		(*g*)
1.10.01 to 31.12.01	14,250	7,125	–	7,125	(*h*)
	53,206	21,375	10,456	21,375	
2002/03 y/e 31.12.2002	48,000	24,000	–	24,000	(*i*)

Notes

(*a*) Substituted *TA 1988, s 61(1)* commencement to 5 April.

(*b*) Substituted *TA 1988, s 60(3)(a)* twelve months to first accounting date. Overlap period 1.1.99 to 5.4.99, overlap profits for P and S

$3/17 \times \frac{£43,000}{2} = £3,794$ each.

(*c*) Substituted *TA 1988, ss 60(3)(b), 111(3)(a)*.

(*d*) Substituted *TA 1988, ss 60(3)(b), 111(3)(a)*.

(*e*) Substituted *TA 1988, s 111(3)(b)* overlap period 1.1.01 to 5.4.01, overlap profits $3/12 \times \frac{£57{,}000}{3} = £4{,}750$.

(*f*) Substituted *TA 1988, ss 60(3)(b), 63, 111(3)(a)* period to date of cessation on death.

(*g*) Substituted *TA 1988, ss 63A(3), 111(3)(c)* overlap relief fully relieved on cessation (see (*b*) above).

(*h*) Substituted *TA 1988, ss 60(3)(b), 111(3)(a)* period to end of accounting period.

(*i*) Substituted *TA 1988, ss 60(3)(b), 111(3)(a)* accounting year ending in fiscal year apportioned to partners in profit sharing ratio.

Investment income

12.12 Each partner's share of taxed investment income received by a partnership in any fiscal year is brought into his individual self-assessment on the basis of the income arising in the fiscal year. Untaxed investment income, however, is assessed by reference to the partnership accounting period, as applied for Schedule D, Case I or II purposes. The income remains assessable under Schedule A or Schedule D, Cases III, IV, V or VI as appropriate, but is allocated to each partner as if it were income arising from a second deemed trade, which is segregated from the actual trading income, and is deemed to continue so long as the partner remains in the partnership, or until the partnership ceases to have any untaxed investment income. This avoids any complications that would arise on the cessation of any particular source of income as a result, for example, of the sale of an investment property or closure of an overseas bank account. This treatment also brings into play the opening year, change of accounting date and cessation provisions applicable to trades which are necessary as a result of taxing the income by reference to the partnership accounting period ending in the current fiscal year, applying a strict fiscal year basis [substituted *TA 1988, s 111(7)(8)*]. The post-cessation receipt provisions in *TA 1988, s 110(2)* are applied on the deemed cessation of a trade or deemed second trade by *FA 1995, s 117(3)* and losses of the deemed second trade are calculated according to the partnership basis period as applied for the calculation of actual trading losses by substituted *TA 1988, s 111(13)*. Overlap relief arising from the deemed second trade as a result of a basis period exceeding twelve months under substituted *TA 1988, s 62(2)(b); FA 1994, s 202*, or on cessation under *TA 1988, s 63A; FA 1994, s 205* may be set against total income under substituted *TA 1988, s 111(9)*. The treatment of a partnership as an individual resident in the UK under substituted *TA 1988, s 111(2)* does not apply for 1994/95 as a result of *FA 1995, s 117(4)*. This applies to property income assessable under Schedule A, interest and other income assessable under Schedule D, Case III, income from overseas securities under Schedule D, Cases IV and V and even sundry income under Schedule D, Case VI but not to dividends under Schedule F and taxed income which are taxable on a fiscal year basis. The fact that such income is assessed by reference to the accounting period should simplify each partner's self-assessment in respect of his partnership share and may be the precursor to the eventual abolition of the schedular system which has long ago outlived its usefulness.

Example 4

Zlokazov & Co was a partnership consisting of Mr Zlok and Mr Kazov sharing profits equally, which has the following income, as adjusted for tax purposes, which is assumed to accrue evenly throughout the period.

		Sch D Case I	*Sch A*	*Sch D Case III*	*Sch D Case V*
	£	£	£	£	£
y/e 30.4.94	113,000	80,000	20,000	5,000	8,000
y/e 30.4.95	130,000	90,000	24,000	6,000	10,000
y/e 30.4.96	141,000	100,000	25,000	4,000	12,000
y/e 30.4.97	129,000	85,000	22,000	2,000	20,000

Assessable/taxable

	Total	*Z*	*K*
	£	£	£
1995/96			
Schedule D, Case I – y/e 30.4.94	80,000	40,000	40,000
Schedule A – y/e 5.4.96			
$\frac{25}{365} \times £24,000$	1,644		
$\frac{340}{365} \times £25,000$	23,288		
	24,932	12,466	12,466
Schedule D, Case III – y/e 5.4.95 (PYB)			
$\frac{25}{365} \times £5,000$	343		
$\frac{340}{365} \times £6,000$	5,589		
	5,932	2,966	2,966

		Total	Z	K
		£	£	£
Schedule D, Case V – y/e 5.4.95 (PYB)				
$\frac{25}{365} \times £8{,}000$		548		
$\frac{340}{365} \times £10{,}000$		9,315		
		9,863	4,932	4,932
1996/97 transitional year				
Schedule D, Case I				
primary basis period y/e 30.4.96	£100,000			
relevant period y/e 30.4.95	£90,000			
Aggregate	£190,000			
Appropriate percentage				
$£190{,}000 \times \frac{365}{365 + 365} =$		95,000	47,500	47,500
Schedule A – y/e 5.4.97				
$\frac{25}{365} \times £25{,}000$		1,712		
$\frac{340}{365} \times £22{,}000$		20,493		
		22,205	11,103	11,102
Schedule D, Case III – y/e 5.4.96				
$\frac{25}{365} \times £6{,}000 =$	411			
$\frac{340}{365} \times £4{,}000 =$	£3,726			
y/e 5.4.97				
$\frac{25}{365} \times £4{,}000 =$	£274			
$\frac{340}{365} \times £2{,}000 =$	£1,863			
Aggregate	£6,274			
50% thereof		3,137	1,569	1,569

		Total £	*Z* £	*K* £
Schedule D, Case V – y/e 5.4.96				
$\frac{25}{365} \times$ £10,000 =	£ 685			
$\frac{340}{365} \times$ £12,000 =	£11,178			
y/e 5.4.97				
$\frac{25}{365} \times$ £12,000 =	£ 822			
$\frac{340}{365} \times$ £20,000 =	£18,630			
Aggregate	£31,315			
50% thereof		15,658	7,829	7,829
1997/98				
Schedule D, Case I – y/e 30.4.97		85,000	42,500	42,500
transitional overlap relief *FA 1994, 20 Sch 2(4)* £85,000 × $\frac{340}{365}$ =		79,178	39,589	39,589
Schedule A – y/e 30.4.97		22,000	11,000	11,000
Schedule D, Case III – y/e 30.4.97		2,000	1,000	1,000
Schedule D, Case V – y/e 30.4.97		20,000	10,000	10,000

Transitional overlap relief is given by *TA 1988, s 111(8); FA 1994, s 215(1); FA 1995, s 117(1)(2)*.

	£	£	£
Schedule A			
$\frac{340}{365} \times$ £22,000	20,493	10,246	10,247
Schedule D, Case III			
$\frac{340}{365} \times$ £2,000	1,863	932	931
Schedule D, Case V			
$\frac{340}{365} \times$ £20,000	18,630	9,315	9,315

Example 5

Mr Timareyev joined the firm of Omega & Co as a partner on 1 October 1998. The partnership made up accounts to 30 April each year and Mr Timareyev's share of profits as adjusted for tax purposes was as follows:

Year ended 30 April 1999	
Schedule D, Case I	£35,000
Schedule D, Case III	£15,000
Schedule D, Case V	£10,000
Schedule A	£12,000
Year ended 30 April 2000	
Schedule D, Case I	£80,000
Schedule D, Case III	£10,000
Schedule D, Case V	£20,000
Schedule A	£24,000

Assessable/taxable

1998/99	
1 October 1998 to 5 April 1999 (*a*)	
Schedule D, Case I 187/212 × £35,000	30,873
Schedule D, Case III (*b*) 187/212 × £15,000	13,231
Schedule D, Case V (*b*) 187/212 × £10,000	8,821
Schedule A (*b*) 187/212 × £12,000	10,585
	£63,510

Notes

(*a*) *TA 1988, s 61(1); FA 1994, s 201* commencement to 5 April.

(*b*) Other income included, *TA 1988, s 111(4); FA 1994, s 215*.

1999/2000	£	£
1 October 1998 to 30 September 1999 (*a*)		
Schedule D, Case 1		
1.10.98 to 30.4.99	35,000	
1.5.99 to 30.9.99 153/365 × £80,000	33,534	
		68,534
Schedule D, Case III		
1.10.98 to 30.4.99	15,000	
1.5.99 to 30.9.99 153/365 × £10,000	4,192	
		19,192
Schedule D, Case V		
1.10.98 to 30.4.99	10,000	
1.5.99 to 30.9.99 153/365 × £20,000	8,384	
		18,384

Schedule A		
1.10.98 to 30.4.99	12,000	
1.5.99 to 30.9.99 153/365 × £24,000	10,060	
		22,060
		£128,170

(*c*) *TA 1988, s 61(2)(a); FA 1994, s 201* applies because the period from commencement 1.10.98 to the accounting date is less than twelve months. The basis period is therefore twelve months from commencement.

(*d*) The period from commencement on 1.10.98 to 5.4.99 is taxed both in 1998/99 and 1999/00 and is therefore an overlap period relieved under *TA 1988, s 63A; FA 1994, s 205*, extended to other income by *FA 1995, s 117(2)* substituting *TA 1988, s 111(8)*. Overlap profits are:

	£
Schedule D, Case I	30,873
Schedule D, Case III	13,231
Schedule D, Case V	8,821
Schedule A	10,585
	£63,510

2000/01

Year ended 30 April 2000 (*a*)	£
Schedule D, Case I	80,000
Schedule D, Case III	10,000
Schedule D, Case V	20,000
Schedule A	24,000
	£134,000

(*e*) *TA 1988, s 60(3)(a); FA 1994, s 200* applies as 30.4.2000 is the first accounting date for Mr Timareyev which falls not less than twelve months after his commencement on 1.10.98.

(*f*) The period from 1.5.99 to 30.9.99 is taxed in both 1999/00 and 2000/01 and is therefore an overlap profit relievable under *TA 1988, s 63A; FA 1994, s 205*, resulting in overlap profits of:

Schedule D, Case I	33,534
Schedule D, Case III	4,192
Schedule D, Case V	8,384
Schedule A	10,060
	£56,170

Total overlap profits are:

		£
Schedule D, Case I	£30,873 + £33,534	64,407
Schedule D, Case III	£13,231 + £4,192	17,423
Schedule D, Case V	£8,821 + £8,384	17,205
Schedule A	£10,585 + £10,060	20,645
		£119,680

Non-trading businesses

12.13 If the partnership carries on a business but not a trade, the same rules apply as if it were carrying on a trade. This is presumably intended to cover income such as that from furnished holiday accommodation which is assessable under Schedule D, Case VI but under the rules of Schedule D, Case I, or other quasi-trading income. It is understood that this does not presage any move by the Revenue to extend the meaning of trade, but to permit joint investment activities which are carried on as a business to be treated as a partnership for tax purposes (as indeed it may need to be for VAT purposes in order to obtain VAT registration where appropriate so that input tax can be recovered). (See also 16.29 below.) It is unclear whether such a business has to use fiscal year accounting on the basis that the income is chargeable under Schedule D, Case VI, or whether as a partnership it can have any accounting date ending in the year and prepare accounts and computations accordingly. [Substituted *TA 1988, s 111(10)(11)*]. The latter would be consistent with assimilating partnership businesses to trades.

Joint investments

12.14 The partnership provisions would not extend to mere investments which were jointly owned and where there was no 'business' (*McKee v Luck 1925 9 TC 511*). There is no statutory definition of a partnership for tax purposes and therefore the definition in the *Partnership Act 1890, s 1* of the 'relation which subsists between persons carrying on a business in common with a view of profit', applies. The meaning of business has been considered in the context of VAT and the relevant principles were summarised in the case of *C & E Commissioners v Lord Fisher [1981] STC 238*. The following criteria were considered relevant in determining whether an activity constituted a business; whether:

(i) the activity was a serious undertaking earnestly pursued;

(ii) the activity was an occupation or function pursued with reasonable or recognisable continuity;

(iii) the activity had a measure of substance;

(iv) the activity was conducted in a regular manner and on sound and recognised business principles;

(v) the activity was predominantly concerned with making supplies for a consideration; and

(vi) the supplies were of a kind commonly made by those who sought to profit by them.

Corporate partners

12.15 Where a corporate partner is involved the provisions relating to partnerships involving companies in *TA 1988, ss 114* and *115* are amended by *FA 1994, s 215(2)* to apply to cases where the partnership is carrying on a profession or business as well as a trade, and to provide that in calculating the corporate partner's taxable profit it is necessary to compute the partnership results as if it were a corporation. However, to arrive at the individual partner's share of profits *TA 1988, s 114(3)*, as amended, provides that the individual's share of losses, profits and gains is arrived at on the basis that the partnership is an individual and ignoring the fact that any of the partners are companies. This enables the new provisions for individuals in substituted *TA 1988, s 111(2)* to apply, even where the partnership contains a company (see 12.6 above). See 4.26 for capital allowances and transitional overlap relief. Loss relief for a corporate limited partner may be restricted by *TA 1988, s 118*.

Deemed company

12.16 Where there is a mixture of partners therefore it is necessary to compute the profits under corporation tax rules to arrive at the corporate partner's share and to recompute the same profits under income tax rules in order to arrive at the individual partner's shares.

Foreign partnerships

12.17 The special rules where a partnership is managed and controlled from abroad in *TA 1988, s 112* are retained under self-assessment so that a non-resident partner is only liable to tax in the UK on his share of any profits of the partnership originating in the UK. The rules are amended by *FA 1995, s 125(1)(2)*, and the profits of the partnership are to be computed as if the partnership were an individual not resident in the UK. These provisions apply from 1997/98 and for 1995/96 and 1996/97 where the trade or profession carried on by the partnership was set up and commenced on or after 6 April 1994.

12.18 A non-UK domiciled but UK resident partner will be assessed to tax under Schedule D, Case V on remittances of income from the partnership, provided that the trade, profession or business is carried on wholly or partly outside the UK and control and management is also situated outside the UK. The remittance basis, as previously, also applies where the partner is a Commonwealth citizen or citizen of the Republic of Ireland not ordinarily resident in the UK.

12.19 The trade carried on by the partnership is not affected by the provisions of inserted *TA 1988, s 112(1B)* which provides that where a partner previously non-resident becomes resident in the UK or if previously resident ceases to be resident in the UK, his deemed trade as an individual partner is treated as having ceased and a new trade commenced. This is equivalent to the deemed cessation on change of residence which applies to individuals under *FA 1995, s 124* (see para 14.10). As for an actual sole trade, losses may continue to be carried forward and set against profits of the deemed trade under *TA 1988, s 385*, notwithstanding the change of residence, and the effect of the provisions is to ensure that a resident partner is taxable on his worldwide income (unless the remittance basis applies) and a non-resident partner only on income arising in the UK.

12.20 In *Padmore v IRC (1989) STC 493*, it was successfully argued that the share of profits of a UK resident partner in a foreign partnership protected by a double tax treaty was not subject to UK tax. This led to a change in the law in *F(No 2)A 1987, s 62* which became *TA 1988, s 112(4)(5)* and which continues to apply for self-assessment as a result of *FA 1995, s 125(3)*. The corporation tax profits of corporate partners are computed on the basis that resident companies are taxed on their share of the worldwide profits and non-resident companies on their share of the UK profits of a foreign partnership, as a result of amendments to *TA 1988, ss 114, 115* by *FA 1995, s 125(4)(5)*.

Example 6

Mr Danilov came to the UK on 1 January 1995 to start the UK branch of a US law firm which made up accounts for the calendar year. On 1 July 1996 he was joined by Mr Vlasov. Both remained partners of the US firm. The UK branch made profits of £50,000 in 1995, £200,000 in 1996 and £250,000 in 1997 and the US firm made profits of $15,000,000 worldwide, shared equally by the 50 partners.

Mr Danilov remitted overseas profits to the UK of £100,000 in December 1994, £20,000 in December 1995 and £30,000 in December 1996.

Mr Vlasov remitted overseas profits to the UK of £40,000 in June 1996 and £60,000 in December 1996.

Mr Danilov's assessable income was:

	£
1994/95	
Deemed UK resident from 1.1.95 – ESC A11	
Share of UK profits $\frac{£50,000}{50} \times 3/12$	250
Remittances of worldwide profits since 1.1.95	NIL
Personal allowances	(3,445)
Assessment	NIL

	£
1995/96	
Share of UK profits $\frac{£50,000}{50}$	1,000
Remittances of worldwide income	20,000
	21,000
Personal allowances	(3,525)
Assessment	£17,475

	£
1996/97	
Share of UK profits $\frac{£200,000}{50}$	4,000
Remittances of worldwide income	30,000
	34,000
Personal allowances	(3,765)
Self-assessment	£30,235

	£
1997/98	
Share of UK profits $\frac{£250,000}{50}$	5,000
Remittances	NIL
Personal allowances – say	(4,000)
Self-assessment	£1,000

Mr Vlasov's assessable income was:

	£
1996/97	
Deemed UK resident from 1.7.96 – ESC A11	
Share of UK profits $\frac{£200{,}000}{50} \times 6/12$	2,000
Plus 1.1.96 to 5.4.97 $\frac{£250{,}000}{50} \times 3/12$	1,250
Remittances since 1.7.96	60,000
	63,250
Personal allowances	(3,765)
Self-assessment	£59,485

	£
1997/98	
Share of UK profits $\frac{£250{,}000}{50}$	5,000
Remittances	NIL
Personal allowances – say	(4,000)
Self-assessment	£1,000

The US partners' share of UK profits were covered by personal allowances under the Anglo/US double taxation agreement SI 1980 No 568 Article 24(1), non-discrimination.

Partnership changes

12.21 Under the new rules, as each individual partner is taxed separately on his share of the partnership profits, and by reference to his joining and leaving the partnership, there is no requirement for the partnership itself to be deemed to cease on a change in partners, subject to any election for continuation. The partnership only remains relevant in the sense that there is a single partnership set of accounts and computations and a single partnership return and statement allocating the profits for the partners. The provisions of *TA 1988, s 113(2)* which allowed the partners to elect for continuation on a change of partners ceases to have effect. Instead, continuation treatment is automatic where there is at least one continuing partner. Accordingly the opening year and cessation provisions only apply to those individuals who are joining or leaving the firm. The consequences of such an election are no longer relevant and these provisions are repealed.

12.22 Until the new rules come into effect however, in most cases on the 6 April 1997 for existing businesses, it will be necessary to continue to make an election for continuation after a partnership change under *TA 1988, s 113(2)* within two years of the change. Failure to do so would not only give rise to a cessation, but would immediately put the continuing business on the new self-assessment rules because it would be deemed to commence on or after 6 April 1994 if the partnership change took place on or after that date. It is important to appreciate this in deciding whether or not to make the continuation election. (See 12.8 above.)

Farm profit averaging

12.23 Averaging claims under *TA 1988, s 96* will be made by individual partners and not by the firm. [*FA 1994, s 216(3)(a)*]. This will apply for the averaging of 1996/97 with 1997/98 and subsequent pairs of years. Farm profit averaging claims up to and including 1995/96 with 1996/97 will be done under the old rules at the partnership level. [*FA 1994, s 216(5)*]. If, however, the trade was set up and commenced on or after 6 April 1994, the averaging at the individual level applies from 1994/95 with 1995/96 or any subsequent pairs of years. For the treatment of capital allowances see 4.16 above.

Where a claim is made for farm profit averaging under *TA 1988, s 96*, it is treated as a claim for the later year of the two consecutive years being averaged under *TMA 1970, 1B Sch 3* (*FA 1996, s 128(2) and 17 Sch*). An averaging claim will be calculated as if the tax payable in the earlier year was recalculated and the amount of tax overpaid will be treated as an additional payment on account in the later year or if further tax is payable for the earlier year this is treated as an additional liability of the later year. If the later year then becomes the earlier year on a subsequent farm profit averaging claim, the second calculation of relief proceeds on the basis that the tax payable or repayable as a result of the first adjustment had not arisen. The purpose of this provision is to avoid reopening an earlier year but to give the same relief in terms of tax as would have been given, had the earlier year been reopened.

A farm profit averaging claim which affects the profits of an earlier year enables other claims for that year to be made, revoked or amended under *TA 1988, s 96(9)*, as substituted by *FA 1996, s 128(3)*. The difference in tax charged, or relieved, in the later period is the final amount after making all necessary adjustments. The calculation is made by reference to the earlier year, in terms of tax, and relief is given in the later year, which avoids changing the tax payable for the earlier year, *TMA 1970, 1B Sch 3; FA 1996, s 128(2) and 17 Sch*.

Losses

12.24 Prior to self-assessment, it was necessary to provide in loss relief claims for continuing partners to be treated as continuing and not eligible for terminal loss relief or relief for losses in the early years of a trade, but able to carry forward losses as if there had been no cessation, and to claim losses against total income on the same basis. These provisions are not required under the new rules and are deleted by *FA 1994, s 216(3)(b)–(g)*.

Terminal losses

12.25 There are consequential amendments to the terminal loss relief provisions in *FA 1994, s 216(4)*. A trade, profession or vocation shall be treated as discontinued, and a new one set up and commenced, only if:

(*a*) there is a cessation of the firm as a result of all the existing partners ceasing to be engaged in carrying on the trade, profession or vocation; or

(*b*) in the case of an individual partner, if he ceases to be a partner.

Transitional provisions

12.26 For an existing partnership the provisions in substituted *TA 1988, s 111* provide that the transitional rules applicable to an individual apply to the partnership, and the partnership itself continues to be assessed for years up to and including 1996/97. From 1997/98 each partner is dealt with on an individual basis by reference to his share of the partnership profits or losses shown by the partnership statement and has his own transitional overlap relief for his share of the partnership untaxed investment income through the deemed second trade as well as the trading income. The partnership assessment and payment provisions in 1996/97 are dealt with in detail in the Tax Bulletin Issue 21, page 286 and Issue 22, pages 293 *et seq*. (see Appendix F). The transitional rules for partnerships with ancillary letting income are explained in Tax Bulletin Issue 21, page 283 (see Appendix F).

Business Successions, Mergers and Demergers

12.27 Under the old rules a change in partners caused there to be a cessation under *TA 1988, s 113(1)* which could be subject to a continuation election under *TA 1988, s 113(2)*, original version, provided that at least one person was involved in carrying on the business both before and after the change, for example where a sole trader admitted a partner, a partner retired or joined, or a partnership was dissolved with one partner continuing to carry on the business as a sole trader. The continuation election was not possible where merely the assets of a business were acquired or where only part of a business was continued as a going concern. Under the current year rules there will still be a deemed cessation and recommencement whenever there is a complete change in the partners carrying on a business. A partial change in ownership on a partner joining or leaving does not give rise to a cessation for the continuing partners and the commencement and cessation rules apply to the individual partners joining or leaving.

On a merger of two or more businesses SP9/86 continues to apply under the current year basis (see SAT1, second edition, Chapter 8).

12.28 A merger can give rise to a situation where one business ceases and the other business is simply enlarged. This gives rise to a cessation of one business and continuation of the other. Where the merger creates an entirely new business there is a cessation of both businesses and commencement of a new business, *George Humphries & Co v Cook 1934 19 TC 121*. The third possibility is a continuation for tax purposes of both businesses. This may require the mixed basis period treatment where, for example, one part of the combined business is deemed to cease and the other to continue, or where one is on a preceding year and the other a current year basis. As soon as practicable the merged business will be assessed on a common basis. Under the old rules it could be up to five years following a merger until it was possible to assess all the profits as those of a single business.

12.29 Under the current year basis, if a new business is acquired by an existing business without taking on any of the previous proprietors, there is a cessation dealt with on the normal cessation basis under *TA 1988, s 63* as applied by *TA 1988, s 113(1)* with relief for any overlap profit under *TA 1988, s 63A*. The acquiring business is assessed on the basis that the profits arising from the original business are calculated on the normal continuing business basis, whereas the profits arising from the new business are segregated and taxed on a commencement basis before being aggregated to arrive at the final assessable profits. This segregation becomes unnecessary as soon as a common basis period applies to the two components. The profits of the combined business are apportioned on a just and reasonable basis, for example by reference to turnover.

Example 7

Mr Makarov, trading as ESKA, acquired the business assets of Mr Dosav on 1 June 1999.

Adjusted profits were as follows:

	Makarov	*Dosav*
	£	£
y/e 30.09.98	50,000	
y/e 31.10.98		25,000
y/e 30.09.99	60,000	
Period 01.11.98 to 31.05.99		17,000
y/e 30.09.2000	80,000	

Assessable/Taxable

Mr Dosav	
1998/99 y/e 31.10.98	25,000 (*a*)
1999/00 p/e 31.05.99	12,000 (*b*)
Mr Makarov	
1998/99 y/e 30.09.98	50,000 (*c*)
1999/00	73,698 (*d*)
2000/01	80,000 (*e*)

Notes

(*a*) *TA 1988, s 60(3)(b)*

(*b*) Cessation *TA 1988, ss 63, 113(1)*

p/e 31.05.99	17,000
less overlap relief, *TA 1988, s 63A* (say)	5,000
	£12,000

(*c*) *TA 1988, s 60(3)(b)*

(*d*) Turnover y/e 30.09.99

old ESKA	400,000
ex Dosav	100,000
	£500,000

y/e 30.09.99

$$\frac{£400{,}000}{£500{,}000} \times £60{,}000 = \quad £48{,}000$$

01.06.99 to 30.09.99

$$\frac{£100{,}000}{£500{,}000} \times £60{,}000 = \quad £12{,}000$$

01.10.99 to 05.04.00(*e*)

$$\frac{£300{,}000}{£900{,}000} \times £80{,}000 \times \frac{188}{366} = \quad £13{,}698$$

£73,698

(*e*) Turnover y/e 30.09.00

old ESKA	600,000
ex Dosav	300,000
	£900,000

$$£80{,}000 \times \frac{600{,}000}{900{,}000} \quad \textit{TA 1988, s 60(3)(b)} \quad £53{,}333$$

$$£80{,}000 \times \frac{300{,}000}{900{,}000} \quad \textit{TA 1988, s 60(3)(a)} \quad £26{,}667$$

£80,000

Overlap period 01.10.99 to 05.04.00
Overlap profit £13,698

12.30 On a complete merger each partner is assessed on his share of the profits from both businesses applying the change of accounting date rules where necessary.

Example 8

The two partners in Mikulin & Co merged with the three partners in Klimov & Co on 1 October 1999. Mikulin & Co made up accounts to 31 December and Klimov to 30 April. All profits were shared equally. Mikulin Klimov & Co makes up accounts to 30 April. There is no cessation; *TA 1988, s 113(2)* (new version), but a new changed accounting date to 30 April 2000 (*TA 1988, s 62)* for Mikulin & Co partners.

Adjusted profits for tax purposes:

Mikulin & Co	
y/e 31 December 1998	£150,000
1 January 1999 to 30 September 1999	£110,000
Klimov & Co	
y/e 30 April 1998	£200,000
y/e 30 April 1999	£180,000
1 May 1999 to 30 September 1999	£100,000
Mikulin Klimov & Co	
1 October 1999 to 30 April 2000	£240,000

Assessable/taxable

1998/99		
Mikulin partners y/e 31.12.98		
1/2 × £150,000 =	£75,000	each
Klimov partners y/e 30.04.98		
1/3 × £200,000 =	£66,667	each
1999/00		
Mikulin partners y/e 31.12.99		
1/2 × £110,000 =	£55,000	(*a*)
1/5 × £240,000 × 3/7	£20,571	(*b*)
	£75,571	each
Klimov partners y/e 30.04.99		
1/3 × £180,000 =	£60,000	(*a*) each
2000/01		
Mikulin partners y/e 30.04.2000 (*b*)		
1/2 × £110,000 × 5/9 =	£30,555	
1/5 × £240,000 =	£48,000	
	£78,555	each
Klimov partners y/e 30.04.2000 (*a*)		
1/3 × £100,000 =	£33,333	
1/5 × £240,000 =	£48,000	
	£81,333	each

Notes

(*a*) *TA 1988, s 60(3)(b)*.

(*b*) *TA 1988, s 62(2)* change of accounting date from 31 December 1999 to 30 April 2000. Overlap period 1 May 1999 to 31 December 1999, £30,555 + £20,571 (£48,000 × 3/7) = £51,126 each.

12.31 Where there has been a merger prior to 6 April 1994 and the mixed basis period treatment applies in 1995/96, because one of the merged firms elected for continuation and one did not, it is necessary to continue the apportionment of profits in 1996/97 and apply the normal transitional provisions to each component.

Example 9

Orlov & Co and Charomsky & Co merged on 01.01.1994. The new firm of Orlov Charomsky & Co made up accounts to 31 May each year. The Orlov & Co partners elected for continuation under *TA 1988, s 113(2)*, old version, but the Charomsky & Co Partners did not, necessitating the split accounts mixed basis period treatment.

The basis periods for Orlov Charomsky & Co are:

1993/94	Orlov component 3/12 × y/e 31.05.92 (*TA 1988, s 60(3)* old version)
	Charomsky component 01.01.94 to 05.04.94 (*TA 1988, s 61(1)* old version)
1994/95	Orlov component y/e 31.05.93 (*TA 1988, s 60(3)* old version)
	Charomsky component y/e 05.04.95 (*TA 1988, s 61(4)* old version)
1995/96	Orlov component y/e 31.5.94 (*TA 1988, s 60(3)* old version)
	Charomsky component y/e 05.04.96 (*TA 1988, s 61(4)* old version)
1996/97	Orlov component 12/24 × 24 months to 31.05.96 (*FA 1994, 20 Sch 2(2)*)
	Charomsky component y/e 05.04.97 (*FA 1994, 20 Sch 2(3)*)
1997/98	Assessed on partners individually
	Orlov component y/e 31.05.97 (*TA 1988, s 60(3)(b)*)
	Transitional overlap period 01.06.96 to 05.04.97 (*FA 1994, 20 Sch 2(4)*)

Charomsky component y/e 31.05.97
(*TA 1988, s 62(2)*)

Overlap period 01.06.96 to 05.04.97
(*TA 1988, s 63A*)

1998/99 Assessed on partners individually y/e 31.05.98
(*TA 1988, s 60(3)(b)*)

12.32 A similar situation can arise where there is a merger in the period from 6 April 1994 to 5 April 1997 where there is a continuation election under *TA 1988, s 113(2)*, original version, for one constituent in the merged firm. If there is no such election for the other constituent, that component will be dealt with on a current year basis and it will be necessary to keep the component parts separate because there will be a different transitional period fraction for each part.

Example 10

Ivchenko and Lyulka merged their businesses on 1 May 1996 having previously made up accounts to 31 December and 30 September respectively. The new accounting date is to be 30 April and continuation elections are made for both, under *TA 1988, s 113(2)*, old version. The basis periods for Ivchenko Lyulka & Co are:

1995/96 Ivchenko y/e 31.12.94
(*TA 1988, s 60(3)* old version)

Lyulka y/e 30.09.94
(*TA 1988, s 60(3)* old version)

1996/97 Ivchenko component

Basis period for 1996/97 y/e 30.04.96
(*FA 1994, 20 Sch 2(2)(a)*)

Relevant period 01.01.95 to 30.04.95
(*FA 1994, 20 Sch 2(2)(b)*)

Aggregate (*FA 1994, 20 Sch 2(2)*) 16 months

Appropriate percentage (*FA 1994, 20 Sch 2(5)*)
12/16 × 16 months profits

Lyulka component

Basis period for 1996/97 y/e 30.04.96
(*FA 1994, 20 Sch 2(2)(a)*)

Relevant period 01.10.94 to 30.04.95
(*FA 1994, 20 Sch 2(2)(b)*)

Aggregate (*FA 1994, 20 Sch 2(2)*) 19 months

Appropriate percentage (*FA 1994, 20 Sch 2(5)*)
12/19 × 19 months profits

12.33 *Partnerships*

1997/98	y/e 30.04.97 (*TA 1988, s 60(3)(b)*)

In 1995/96 1/12 is charged on Ivchenko and Lyulka individually and 11/12 on the firm of Ivchenko Lyulka, as the merger was on 1 May 1996.

Literary and artistic receipts

12.33 The literary and artistic spreading provisions in *TA 1988, ss 534, 535, 537, 537A and 538* (see 17.34) are disapplied for companies and partnerships by *TA 1988, s 534(6A), FA 1996, s 128(6)*, in respect of sums receivable on or after 6 April 1996.

Chapter 13

Companies

Introduction

13.1 Pay and File has implemented a streamlining of the corporation tax system with many of the hallmarks of self-assessment, notably a company's obligation to pay its estimate of the corporation tax liability nine months from the end of its accounting period. The form of the return (CT200) is such that the company or its agent can work through the computation and so determine its tax liability. But Pay and File is still partly a hybrid system, given that the Revenue are to make the actual tax assessment, usually once the profits have been agreed.

13.2 The general structure of Pay and File is not altered by self-assessment. There are also no changes to the basis of computing a company's tax liability. However, a number of changes have been made, particularly under *FA 1994*, to bring the position for companies in line with that for individuals and trustees, essentially relating to management and administration. These are to come into effect for accounting periods ending on or after the 'appointed day' under *FA 1994, s 199(3)*, which is a date yet to be announced but which is intended will be no later than 31 March 1998.

13.3 There are also a number of changes under *FA 1996* which are specifically referable to companies, dealing with such matters as accounting periods and advance corporation tax. Further changes are anticipated relating to such matters as transfer pricing and the Controlled Foreign Companies' legislation.

Outline of management and administration changes

13.4 The principal changes and provisions under *FA 1994* may be summarised as follows:

(i) A company will have to make a return of total income, including its share of any partnership profits allocated to it in the partnership statement. The corporation tax return will also have to include a self-assessment, this essentially being a change of form rather than substance. [*TMA 1970, ss 11, 11AA*].

(ii) For twelve months following the filing date a company will be entitled to amend its return and self-assessment. The Revenue will be entitled to correct any obvious errors or mistakes within nine months. [*TMA, s 11AA(2)*].

(iii) The Revenue may enquire into a company's return for twelve months after the filing date for a timeous return, and amend a self-assessment after an enquiry, if required. [*TMA 1970, ss 11AB, 28A*].

(iv) After the twelve-month period the figures in the return and self-assessment become final and cannot be reopened other than under a discovery assessment pursuant to an amended *TMA s 29*. [*FA 1994, s 191*].

(v) Where a company fails to file a return the Revenue will be able to make a determination, estimating the tax due. There is no appeal against such a determination, but it is automatically superseded by a completed return and self-assessment. [*TMA 1970, s 28C and D*].

(vi) The rules for payment of corporation tax remain the same, but they are now dealt with by *TMA 1970, s 59D* rather than *TMA 1988, s 10*, so that all rules for payment of tax are brought together within *TMA 1970*.

(vii) Companies involved in partnerships will be required to adhere to the rules for the making and keeping of documents applicable in respect of partnership returns, and the Revenue have the right to call for such documents. [*TMA 1970, ss 12B, 19*].

(viii) The procedures relating to claims have been amended, the general rule being that wherever possible any claim is to be included in a return or an amendment to a return. [*TMA 1970, s 42*].

(ix) Areas where previously the Revenue had a discretion or needed to be satisfied that certain conditions had been complied with, for example the car benefits provisions of *TA 1988, 6 Sch 2*, are brought on to an objective basis, with the taxpayer making the decision whether the conditions are satisfied or not; see Chapter 17.

13.5 These various issues are considered in further detail in the chapters that follow dealing with management and administration. The changes in *FA 1996* which are specific to companies are now examined.

Accounting for advance corporation tax ('ACT')

13.6 A company which makes qualifying distributions is required to make quarterly returns on form CT61 of franked payments and account for the ACT under *TA 1988, 13 Sch 1*. This is to continue under self-assessment but subject to certain amendments under *FA 1996, 23 Sch* for return periods ending on or after the appointed day under *FA 1994, s 199(3)*. Thereafter the return should also specify any estimated franked payments or estimated ACT. [Inserted *TA 1988, 13 Sch 2(b)(c)*].

13.7 In the case of qualifying distributions which are not payments, and payments whose nature is not clear, the main part of the ACT return does not require them to be shown. Also the company does not have to pay ACT on them at the time. But the company may nevertheless include estimated amounts in the return and pay ACT thereon. Where a company so pays an estimated amount of ACT it must give particulars of that distribution separately on the return form. [Substituted *TA 1988, 13 Sch 7(2), (3)*].

13.8 Should such an estimated amount not be included on the return or should a Revenue Officer consider it is incorrect, any ACT due is to be assessed on the company, and interest on unpaid tax is charged from the usual due date as if it had been correctly reported. The assessment is to be made without regard to franked investment income received. But in calculating the tax which is due, it is assumed that it is a franked payment which had been included in the relevant return. In computing the ACT liability for a subsequent period, any surplus franked investment income brought forward is reduced by any such deduction for franked investment income. [Substituted *TA 1988, 13 Sch 7 (3A), (4), (4A), (4B)*].

13.9 If a company becomes aware that it has made an omission or error in the CT61 return, including an estimate which is incorrect, it is required to file an amended return with the collector of taxes forthwith. The tax is then payable, or repayable as the case may be, with interest as if the original return had been correct. [Inserted *TA 1988, 13 Sch 7A*]. An Officer of the Board is empowered to make assessments to correct errors. [Amended *TA 1988, 13 Sch 8*].

Tax collection on company payments other than distributions

13.10 Certain amendments on the lines of those in 13.9 are made to *TA 1988, 16 Sch* by *FA 1996, 23 Sch 10–13* in respect of income tax on charges and other payments which are not distributions. If a company becomes aware that it has made an omission or error in a return it is required to submit an amended return to the collector. Tax is then payable, or repayable as the case may be, with interest as appropriate. [Inserted *TA 1988, 16 Sch 7A*]. An Officer of the Board may make an assessment to correct errors. [Amended *TA 1988, 16 Sch 8*].

Surrender of ACT

Introduction

13.11 *FA 1996, 25 Sch* brings in certain amendments to the provisions relating to the surrender of ACT contained in *TA 1988, s 240* without making any substantive changes to the amount of ACT which can be surrendered. It also establishes a formal procedure, notably in relation to the withdrawal of claims, in a new *TA 1988, 13A Sch*. The essence is to allow a subsidiary to take credit for the amount surrendered as soon as the claim is made. A company which has paid ACT in respect of dividends paid by it in an accounting period may surrender any available ACT to any company which was a subsidiary throughout that accounting period. A surrender takes effect as soon as it is made in accordance with *TA 1988, 13A Sch*. A claim to surrender more than the amount available will be of no effect. [*TA 1988, s 240(1), (1A), (1B)* substituted by *FA 1996, 25 Sch 1(1), (2) and (4)*]. The amount of ACT available for surrender is the amount paid on dividends in the accounting period, less (*a*) any amount repaid to the surrendering company, (*b*) any surplus ACT brought forward from an earlier period and (*c*) any amount already surrendered under a claim which has not been withdrawn. [*TA 1988, s 240(5D) and (5E)* substituted by *FA 1996, 25 Sch 1(3)*].

13.12 A claim for surrender may be withdrawn by the surrendering company, with the consent of the company to whom the ACT is surrendered; in which case the former status quo is restored with any necessary alterations. The withdrawal of a claim does not prevent the surrendering company from making a further claim for that accounting period or a surrender to the same company or different subsidiaries. [*TA 1988, s 240(5A), (5B), (5C)* substituted by *FA 1996, 25 Sch 1(3)*].

New procedure for ACT surrender claims under TA 1988, 13A Sch

General

13.13 For the purposes of the new provisions contained in *TA 1988, 13A Sch* a 'claim' is a claim falling within *TA 1988, s 240(1A)*, whilst 'relevant accounting period' is the accounting period referred to in *s 240(1)*, namely the period for which the claim is made. Surrenders to different subsidiaries or to the same subsidiary at different times are to be treated as separate claims. Where more than one claim is made at the same time, the claims are to be treated as made in the order in which the surrendering company elects or, in default of such an election, by a Revenue determination. [*TA 1988, 13A Sch 1 and 2*]. Given that the procedure only permits withdrawals, and not variations [*TA 1988, 13A Sch 10*] and that earlier claims will go to exhaust available ACT, claims will be dealt with in the order they are made. Hence if a number of claims are submitted in the wrong order, it seems that they will have to be withdrawn and resubmitted as appropriate.

13.14 A claim must specify the subsidiary to whom the surrender is made and the amount thereof and it must be made within six years of the end of the relevant accounting period of the surrendering company. [*TA 1988, 13A Sch 3 and 4*]. As the claim must actually be quantified, 'formula' claims will seemingly not be permitted. The claim must be made in a corporation tax return or amendment to such a return under

TMA 1970, s 11 wherever possible. A claim outside a return must be made in such form as the Revenue may determine, be accompanied by such supporting documentation as the Revenue may require and include a declaration to the effect that all the particulars are correct to the best belief of the claimant. [*TA 1988, 13A, Sch 5 and 6*].

Withdrawal of claims and amendments

13.15 Withdrawal of a claim must be made by notice to the Revenue in the required form specifying the surrendering company, the amount surrendered, the subsidiary to whom the surrender was made, the relevant accounting period of the surrendering company, and it must be accompanied by the consent of the subsidiary. Wherever possible the withdrawal must be made by an amendment to the return. [*TA 1988, 13A Sch 7*]. Where a claim is withdrawn and another substituted the withdrawal is treated as taking place before the subsequent claim. [*TA 1988, 13A Sch 8*].

13.16 A claim cannot be withdrawn more than the earlier of (i) six years after the end of the relevant accounting period of the surrendering company, and (ii) the date on which an assessment for the accounting period of the company to whom the surrender is made becomes final, if earlier. In this regard, in the absence of a Revenue enquiry and the making of a discovery assessment, the latter time limit will generally be that under the normal self-assessment rule, being twelve months after the filing date. However a claim may be withdrawn at any time within the first of the above six-year periods so long as (*a*) none of the ACT in the claim has been finally dealt with to the subsidiary's advantage, (*b*) the claim was made after the accounting period for the subsidiary had become final and (*c*) a further assessment has been made by the Revenue (i.e. where there has been a discovery assessment). For this purpose ACT has been finally dealt with if it has been set against any liability of the subsidiary to corporation tax which has become final or any of it has been repaid to the subsidiary. [*TA 1988, 13A Sch 9(5)*]. A claim to surrender cannot be amended; it can only be withdrawn and replaced by a new claim. [*TA 1988, 13A Sch 10*].

Claims made after set off of ACT against mainstream corporation tax – further self-assesments by the surrendering company

13.17 Where the claim is made to surrender ACT after it has already been set against the mainstream corporation tax liability of the surrendering company that company must make a further self-assessment and pay the additional corporation tax due as a result of the claim. The tax is treated as due nine months from the end of the accounting period. Such additional self-assessment may be enquired into by the Revenue in the normal way. [*TA 1988, 13A Sch 11*].

Example 1

Bark Ltd has a 100% subsidiary, Bite Ltd, with accounts drawn up to 31 December. Bark pays a dividend on 1 April 1999 on which the ACT is £20,000. It sets the whole of this ACT against its own mainstream corporation tax liability. Bite Ltd submits a self-assessment for the year to 31 December 1999 showing a nil corporation tax liability. Following a Revenue enquiry Bite's corporation tax liability is finally determined at £80,000. Bark then decides to surrender to Bite the whole of the ACT paid on 1 April 1999 and does so before the time limit of 31 December 2005. Bark will be obliged to submit a revised self-assessment for the year to 31 December 1999, and pay the additional tax. Interest will run from the normal due date of 30 September 2000. Bite may claim a repayment of the tax arising from the ACT set off, with repayment interest.

13.18 Similar provisions apply where the surrendering company has set ACT against the mainstream corporation tax liability of a subsequent accounting period and then makes a claim to surrender. An additional self-assessment is required and the tax is due nine months from the end of the later accounting period, i.e. as if the claim to set-off the brought forward ACT had not been made. Enquiries into such additional self-assessments may be made in the normal way. [*TA 1988, 13A Sch 12*].

Excess relief on surrender – further self-assessments by subsidiary

13.19 Where ACT has been set off against a subsidiary's liability which is in excess of the amount that should have been so deducted (i.e. where the parent purported to surrender more ACT than was available), whether in respect of surrendered ACT for the accounting period or brought forward, the subsidiary must within three months of becoming aware of the true facts submit a self-assessment of the amount of corporation tax which would have been due on the basis of the true facts. Tax is due nine months after the end of the accounting period as if it had been calculated correctly. The Revenue may enquire into such additional self-assessment in the normal way. ACT correctly treated is set against the subsidiary's liability before any ACT incorrectly dealt with. [*TA 1988, 13A Sch 13*].

Miscellaneous

13.20 The normal enquiry provisions apply to additional self-assessments to recover ACT which apply to any other self-assessments under *TMA 1970, s 28A*. [*TA 1988, 13A Sch 14*]. If, as a result of a withdrawal of a claim to surrender, the surrendering company has overpaid, it is entitled by notice to claim repayment. Similarly a subsidiary company which has overpaid tax as a result of a claim made after the corporation tax for that accounting period has been paid, may reclaim tax overpaid. [*TA 1988, 13A Sch 15*]. The ACT changes take effect from accounting periods ending after the appointed day, under *FA 1994, s 199(3)*. [*FA 1996, 25 Sch 3*]. Amendments are made to *TA 1988, s 239(5)* so that relief for ACT may be set against the corporation tax accounting period or future accounting periods, after the appointed day, without requiring any further claims. [*FA 1996, 25 Sch 4*]. The normal penalty provisions under *TMA 1970, s 98* apply to additional self-assessments under *TMA 1970, 13A Sch*. [*FA 1996, 25 Sch 5*].

Accounting periods

Introduction

13.21 Detailed rules are contained in *TA 1988, s 12* to determine the beginning and end of a company's accounting period for corporation tax purposes. But there can still be uncertainties in some cases, whether because of doubts as to, say, when a trade commenced or because of lack of information supplied to the Revenue. In *Kelsey v Stipplechoice 1995 STC 681* the Revenue were precluded from seeking to change the accounting period to which an assessment related. To provide for greater certainty under self-assessment there have been certain amendments introduced by *FA 1996, 24 Sch*. Whilst the *TA 1988, s 12* rules determining the beginning and end of an accounting period have not been altered, there has been a clarification of the Revenue's enquiry and amendment powers in cases of disputes over the true accounting period.

Power to enquire into return for wrong period

13.22 Under the new *TMA 1970, s 11AA(1)*, a corporation tax return must include a self-assessment of the corporation tax for the accounting period to which it relates. This is extended to cover a return for a period (*a*) which ends in or at the end of the period specified in the notice requiring the return; (*b*) which in the return is treated as an accounting period but (*c*) which is not, or may not be, an accounting period. The filing date is then the normal due date, as if it had been an accounting period under *TMA 1970, s 211(4)*. [*TMA 1970, s 11AA(5), (6)* inserted by *FA 1996, 24 Sch 3*]. The Revenue enquiry powers and their ability to call for documents apply to a return which is due, whether or not in respect of an accounting period, and even if it is a return for the wrong period. A return for a wrong period is one as just described (in new *TMA 1970, s 11AA(5)*) or one made for part of the period specified in the notice, which in the return is treated as not falling within an accounting period, but where there is an accounting period ending in or at the end of the period specified in the notice. [*TMA 1970, s 11AB(1)(d) and (4); s 19A(1)(d)* inserted by *FA 1996, 24 Sch 3–5*].

Amendment of return for wrong period

13.23 In an enquiry the Revenue may designate a period as the accounting period for which the return should have been made up, specifying the dates on which the period begins and ends. A duly amended return and self-assessment may then be required. [*TMA 1970, s 28AA* inserted by *FA 1996, 24 Sch 6*]. A notice designating an accounting period and the consequential amendments to a self-assessment may be appealed against in the usual way. If a further return is due, a notice under *TMA 1970, s 11* may require a return for the further period before the 'postponed final day', this being the later of the normal due date under *TMA 1970, s 11(4)* (i.e. the first anniversary of the end of the accounting period so determined) or the end of three months following the date of the notice, or thirty days after the date on which the accounting period is finally determined. [*TMA 1970, s 28AB* inserted by *FA 1996, 24 Sch 6*].

Determination of accounting dates

13.24 In the unusual case of a company making up accounts for different trades to different dates ending on or after the appointed day under *FA 1994, s 199(3)*, the company may determine the accounting date, save that the Revenue may determine a different date if the company's choice appears inappropriate. [*TMA 1988, s 12(1) and (5A)* as amended by *FA 1996, 24 Sch 11*].

Companies in liquidation

13.25 The provisions of *TA 1988, s 342* are amended to enable a liquidator to assume the date on which a company's affairs will be completely wound up, without the necessity of agreeing this in advance with the Revenue. [*TA 1988, s 342(5) and (6)* amended by *FA 1996, 24 Sch 12*].

Failure to deliver return

Determination of corporation tax where no return delivered

13.26 Provisions set out in *TMA 1970, s 28C* give the Revenue powers to make an initial determination of a person's tax liability in cases where a tax return is not submitted on time. The provisions in *TMA 1970, s 28C* apply to taxpayers generally, including companies. However, they have been specifically strengthened in respect of companies by a new *TMA 1970, s 28D to F* inserted by *FA 1996, 24 Sch 7*, notably where there may be more than one accounting period in the return period or where the accounting period is uncertain. Where a notice requiring a return has been served on a company, but the return has not been filed on time, the Revenue may make a determination of the tax for the 'relevant period'. If there is only one period ending within the period specified in the notice, that is the relevant period. If more than one accounting period ends within the notice period it will be each of them. If the Revenue have insufficient information, it will be the period they specify. A determination is initially treated as a self-assessment, but if the company subsequently files a return and a self-assessment, that will supersede the Revenue's determination. Moreover, if the company shows that the determination is for the wrong period, or that a self-assessment has been submitted, the determination has no effect. [*TMA 1970, s 28D*].

Determination of corporation tax where notice complied with in part

13.27 In cases where a return is filed for an accounting period, but there are other periods for which returns remain due, the Revenue may also make a determination. In the same way, the company may subsequently file a return for the missing period, which then supersedes the Revenue determination; or it may show that it has already delivered a return and self-assessment for the period, in which case the determination has no effect. [*TMA 1970, s 28E* inserted by *FA 1996, 24 Sch 7*].

Time limits, etc.

13.28 Such determinations have to be made within five years from the 'relevant day'. This is the final date for delivery of any return required by the section 11 notice, if this can be ascertained under *TMA 1970, s 11(4)*. Otherwise it is the later of thirty months from the end of the period specified in the notice, and the end of three months following the day on which the notice was served. In order to supersede a determination, an actual self-assessment must be made within five years of the relevant day or twelve months of the determination. Where proceedings are commenced to recover tax, these may be continued in the new figures where the determination has been superseded by the self-assessment. [*TMA 1970, s 28F* inserted by *FA 1996, 24 Sch 7*].

Records to be kept by companies

13.29 The general record keeping requirements for taxpayers contained in *TMA 1970, s 12B* are considered in Chapter 16. There are no specific provisions directed to companies. The Revenue have confirmed that a company which satisfies the record keeping requirements of *section 221* of the *Companies Act 1985* will be considered as having satisfied the self-assessment record keeping requirements, except that the records will have to be retained not just for three years but for the longer six-year period prescribed in *TMA 1970, s 12(B)*.

Controlled Foreign Companies

13.30 The Controlled Foreign Companies ('CFC') legislation, introduced in 1984, was designed to prevent UK tax avoidance by channelling income to subsidiaries resident in countries with low tax rates. It applies to corporate holders of a 10 per cent or greater interest in a CFC, being a company resident outside the UK, controlled from the UK, and paying tax at a rate of less than 75 per cent of the tax it would have paid had the company been UK resident. There is an exclusion from the charging provisions where the CFC is resident in a company within the Excluded Countries list. Otherwise, if the CFC is in a low tax jurisdiction there are certain exemptions, notably if it is publicly quoted, or pays a certain proportion of its profits back to the UK as dividends, i.e. it pursues an 'acceptable distribution policy' ('ADP'), or if tax avoidance was not a main reason for the company's existence.

13.31 If the CFC does not fall within these exclusions or exemptions, the Revenue may make a direction, imposing a tax charge on shareholders based on a proportion of the CFC's profits equivalent to the extent of the interest held. There is, however, no formal obligation on UK shareholder companies to notify the Revenue of potential chargeability on the CFC's profits, or indeed to report details of interests held or tax due within its return.

13.32 The Revenue consider that a system whereby there is no liability without a direction creates uncertainties and inequities. They also consider that if the CFC regime is not changed, to remove the necessity for a Revenue direction, it would result in the anomalous position that companies with shares in CFCs could not properly self-assess all their profits. Moreover, the certainty that is a central feature to self-assessment would be lacking. Thus if the Revenue do not open an enquiry within a year of the filing date, a company's tax liability becomes final in the absence of a discovery assessment. But under the present CFC provisions, Revenue enquiries could be commenced at any time within six years. The Revenue accordingly are of the view that there should be a fundamental change in the legislation, dispensing with the role of the Board in making a formal direction, and leaving any liability to be self-assessed.

13.33 The Revenue's proposals have been set out in a Consultative Document 'The Controlled Foreign Companies' Legislation' issued at the end of 1995. In essence the Revenue are proposing the abolition of the ADP exemption; replacing the existing CFC charge with one based on a proportion of the CFC's profits; and integrating the regime into self-assessment, reducing the need for Revenue intervention. In lieu of the Board's direction requirement, the operation of the legislation would be triggered by a set of objective conditions, and the Board would have no apportionment power. The 10 per cent lower limit for shareholdings would be lifted to 20 per cent.

13.34 The shareholders would then self-assess their liability calculated in respect of the profits of the CFC, but with a lower proportion of the CFC's profits than that taken as the basis under the present charge. When a dividend was in fact paid, the tax paid on the CFC self-assessment could be set against the Schedule D, Case V charge, taking into account the foreign tax suffered. So far as documentation is concerned, the proposals contemplate that the company tax return would include a statement of all 20 per cent interests in non-resident companies, other than those in the Excluded Countries list, with relevant details. In the absence of any exemption, the self-assessment would include the CFC charge.

13.35 A proportion of the CFC's profits would be treated as corporation tax profits received by the UK shareholder company in the accounting period in which the CFC's accounting period ends. So where the CFC had an accounting date of 31 December and the UK shareholder 31 March, the CFC's profits to, say, 31 December 1998 would form the basis for the UK company's self-assessment of its profits for the year to 31 March 1999. The tax would be payable, as would corporation tax, nine months after the UK company's year end, i.e. 1 January 2000 in this example. It seems that the relevant legislation to implement these proposals in their final form will be contained in *FA 1997*.

Transfer pricing

13.36 The transfer pricing legislation is contained in *TA 1988, s 770*, its objective being to ensure that transactions between companies under common control are taxed on an arm's length basis, particularly in respect of multi-nationals engaged in cross border transactions. The legislation is discretionary, in that it only applies to a transaction if the Board make a direction. There is no general requirement for a company to prepare its accounts or file its tax return in accordance with the arm's length principle.

13.37 Consistent with the general principle that a company will self-assess without reference to the Revenue, and will calculate its tax liability on an objective basis, it has been proposed by the Revenue that their present discretionary powers would be removed and the transfer pricing legislation made mandatory. UK members of multi-nationals would then be required to amend actual prices for inter group transactions as necessary for tax purposes. This proposal has met with considerable opposition from the consultative bodies and at the time of writing the issues are being further considered by the Revenue.

Chapter 14

Non-residents

Introduction

14.1 The tax treatment of non-residents has evolved over the years as a mixture of statute, case law, Revenue practice and concession. In essence, non-residents enjoying UK income from whatever source have been, and remain, subject to tax in the UK. With self-assessment the opportunity has been taken to remove or clarify certain areas of ambiguity, and to define more clearly the liabilities and reporting obligations of non-UK residents and their UK based representatives.

14.2 The new rules divide UK source income into three broad categories:

(1) earned income from trades, professions and employments;

(2) income from land; and

(3) other investment income, such as dividends and bank interest.

14.3 Non-resident individuals in receipt of income from the first two categories will be subject to income tax both at the basic and higher rate, subject to any reliefs available under the relevant double tax treaty. Payment of tax on income falling within these categories is enforced by imposing obligations, where necessary, on UK agents and tenants respectively. In the case of investment income falling within the third category, tax is limited to that, if any, deducted at source. For 1996/97 and subsequent years of assessment UK personal allowances are extended to all nationals of the European Economic Area. [*FA 1996, s 145*].

Income from trades, professions and vocations in the UK: Schedule D, Cases I and II

Background

14.4 The new rules do not change the basis on which tax is charged on non-residents carrying on a trade, profession or vocation. It is well established that the profits of a trade carried on wholly or partly in the UK are assessable under Schedule D, Case I, including trades carried on by non-residents; see, for example, *Ogilvie v Kitton (1908) 5 TC 338* and *Spiers v MacKinnon (1929) 14 TC 386*. It is likewise well established that the profits of a trade carried on wholly abroad are assessable under Schedule D, Case V, the charge being limited to UK residents; *Colquhoun v Brooks (1889) 2 TC 490*. In deciding the scope of trading activities assessable under Schedule D, Case I the cases have drawn a distinction between trading in the UK, for example, manufacture or sales taking place in the UK, and trading with the UK, for example, sales made outside the UK to UK customers. Essentially a person is regarded as trading in the UK if the economic activities from which the profits are derived are carried on in the UK; see, for example, *Firestone Tyre & Rubber Ltd v Llewellin (1957) 37 TC 111*. The test propounded in that case was where the activities were carried on from which the profits in substance arose.

14.5 In cases where a non-resident carries on a trade partly in the UK and partly outside, the charge is imposed only on the profits from the part of the trade carried on in the UK; *Pommery & Greno v Apthorpe (1886) 2 TC 189*. In order to arrive at the measure of taxable profits of trades in such cases the Revenue adopt the internationally accepted arm's length principle set out in Article 7(2) and (3) of the OECD model double tax convention, which is in any event explicitly required where a double tax agreement applies. Article 7(2) adopts a 'separate entity' approach, requiring the profits to be computed as if the activities carried on in the UK were carried on by a separate person dealing wholly independently and at arm's length with the non-resident. Article 7(3) allows actual expenditure incurred by the non-resident for the purposes of the UK business to be deducted, plus an appropriate mark-up for expenditure on trading stock and work-in-progress transferred to the UK business. The Revenue propose to set out their understanding of the relevant principles, both as regards trading in and with the UK, and the arm's length principles for determining profits, in an issue of their Tax Bulletin in due course.

UK representatives of non-residents

14.6 Subject to the terms of any double tax agreement, liability to tax arises on non-residents irrespective of whether or not they are trading through a branch or agency, or permanent establishment in the UK. However, so far as collection of tax is concerned, the Revenue generally have to look to UK agents of non-residents. Under the old system the Revenue had wide powers to assess any person acting for a non-resident, the broad effect being to make any person who acted for a non-resident answerable for the latter's tax affairs. This could impose a heavy burden on persons who acted for non-residents in a restricted capacity, and the old provisions were only invoked in practice in limited areas.

14.7 New rules are introduced from 1996/97 to replace those contained in *TMA 1970, ss 78–85*. They apply only where the non-resident is carrying on a trade in the UK through a branch or agency. The objective is to make the UK branch or agent jointly responsible with the non-resident for all tax matters. The rationale for this approach is that such branch or management is part of the business of the non-resident, so it is reasonable to place full responsibility on that branch or management in relation to tax. This is in contrast to independent agents, who are not wholly responsible for the non-resident's affairs, and those who do not carry on the regular agency of the non-resident. Their position, and that of brokers and investment managers, is dealt with in 14.15 *et seq*.

14.8 From 1996/97 (or 31 March 1996 in the case of companies) a branch or agency through which a non-resident carries on any trade, profession or vocation (whether solely or in partnership) is designated as the non-resident's 'UK representative' for income tax, corporation tax and CGT purposes in relation to the following:

(*a*) the income from the trade, profession or vocation arising directly or indirectly from the branch or agency;

(*b*) income from property or rights such as patents, copyrights, etc. which are used by or held by the branch or agency;

(*c*) capital gains on assets situated in the UK used for the purposes of a trade, profession or vocation or by the branch or agency within *TCGA 1992, s 10;*

(*d*) the chargeable profits of an overseas life insurance company, subject to tax under *TA 1988, 19 AC Sch 3*. [*FA 1995, s 126(1)(2)(9)*].

14.9 For these purposes a branch or agency is defined by reference to *TMA 1970, s 118(1)* as 'any factorship, agency, receivership, branch or management'. [*FA 1995, s 126(8)*]. The UK representative is treated as a separate and distinct person from the non-resident, which allows notices to be served on him and tax collected from him. Moreover, he remains the representative for the income or capital gains which he has received even though he ceases to be the branch or agent. [*FA 1995, s 126(3)(4)*].

Non-resident partners

14.10 Where the non-resident is carrying on the trade or profession through a branch or agency in the UK as a partner in a partnership, the trade or profession carried on through the branch or agency includes the deemed trade or profession arising from the non-resident's share in the partnership under *TA 1988, ss 111–114*. The partnership, as a deemed entity, is then the non-resident's UK representative. [*FA 1995, s 126(5)(6)*]. Where there is a UK resident partner, the partnership is treated as the branch or agent of each non-resident partner in respect of his share of partnership profit. [*FA 1995, s 126(7)*]. The effect is to make any partners present or resident in the UK jointly liable for tax on the non-resident's share of partnership profits, which overcomes the difficulty of collecting tax from a non-resident partner. It also has the effect of retaining the current liability of partners for the tax liabilities of non-resident partners, even though the joint liability will no longer apply under self-assessment for a UK-resident partner in respect of the tax liabilities of his partners, in view of substituted *TA 1988, s 111*.

Obligations imposed upon UK representatives

14.11 All the general reporting obligations and charging provisions contained in the various Tax Acts apply equally to non-residents and their UK representatives. Such obligations may be discharged either by the non-resident or his UK representative, and any acts or omissions of the UK representative are treated as acts or omissions of the non-resident. [*FA 1995, 23 Sch 1, 2*]. In order to make a non-resident's UK representative liable for the discharge of these obligations where the liability depends on the service of a notice, or other documents, or the receipt of a request or a demand, it is necessary to serve these on the representative, or to supply him with a copy. [*FA 1995, 23 Sch 3*]. This is the equivalent for self-assessment to the old rules under which the agent only became liable to tax where an assessment had been made on him.

Independent agents

14.12 The obligations to supply information to the Revenue are limited in the case of an independent agent, being a person acting on the non-resident's behalf in an independent capacity, i.e. where the relationship is at arm's length having regard to its legal, financial and commercial characteristics. [*FA 1995, 23 Sch 7; FA 1995, s 127(18)*]. Such an independent agent has to discharge his obligations only so far as is practicable to do so by acting to the best of his knowledge and belief, after having taken all reasonable steps to obtain the necessary information. The agent would therefore be exonerated where, for example, the non-resident withheld information. In such cases the non-resident would be obliged to supply the relevant additional information. Moreover, a non-resident is able to correct any error or mistake made by the independent agent which was not an act or omission of his own, one to which he consented, or one in which he connived.

14.13 Information for the purposes of these provisions includes anything contained in a return, self-assessment, account, statement or report that is required by the Revenue. [*FA 1995, 23 Sch 4(3)*]. An independent agent is entitled to be indemnified in respect of any tax obligation of the non-resident which he discharges, and to make an appropriate retention from any sums due to the non-resident, in like manner as a property agent under *FA 1995, s 40(1)*. [*FA 1995, 23 Sch 6*]. Moreover, an independent agent is not liable to any civil penalty or surcharge if the act or omission in question is not his, or one to which he did not give consent, or in which he did not connive, and in respect of which he is able to show that he cannot obtain indemnification. [*FA 1995, 23 Sch 5*].

Criminal offences

14.14 For the purposes of these provisions a person is not guilty of a criminal offence unless he committed the offence himself, or consented to, or connived in its commission. This will protect either the agent or the UK representative as appropriate, if criminal offences are committed by the other party.

Persons not treated as UK representatives – investment managers and brokers

General

14.15 The extensive obligations imposed on a UK branch or agent in trading cases are based on the premise that the branch or agent is in effect an arm of his overseas principal, and therefore should be responsible for his tax affairs. Agents who do not carry on the regular agency of the non-resident, notably brokers and investment managers, fall into a separate category, and are hence faced with considerably reduced obligations subject to certain conditions being satisfied.

14.16 In devising the self-assessment rules for agents of non-residents involved in financial trading transactions in the UK, a substantial degree of protection was accorded to agents in the investment management industry. This was in recognition of the importance to the UK economy of the London capital markets in particular and the wish to attract further investment management business to the UK. The expressed objective also was to ensure that non-residents engaged in such activities were not exposed to UK tax beyond the amount, if any, deducted at source on income from transactions carried out by investment managers or brokers in the normal course of their business.

14.17 The new provisions are in any event only relevant to those non-residents whose activities amount to trading in the UK. Thus UK-based agents generally do not need any protection where the transactions of the overseas resident give rise to capital gains, which are exempt from CGT in the hands of a person who is not resident and not ordinarily resident in the UK. This covers, for example, non-resident investors in venture capital funds, where the Revenue generally accept that there is no trading. But it might well not extend to, say, hedge funds which are likely to be regarded by the Revenue as engaged in a trade.

14.18 The general body of case law remains relevant in determining whether a person is an investor or a trader. In this regard the buying or selling of quoted shares and securities by an individual will generally be treated as an investment activity regardless of the timing and volume of the transactions, not least from the Revenue's point of view to avoid the generation of allowable trading losses; see for example, *Salt v Chamberlain (1979) 53 TC 143*. The position is likely to be otherwise in the case of the commodities; see for example, *Wisdom v Chamberlain (1968) 45 TC 92*.

14.19 There are certain general definitions which are applied for the purposes of the new rules. First, a branch or agency is defined as 'any factorship, agency, receivership, branch or management', *TMA 1970, s 118(1)*; and connected persons are defined by reference to *TA 1988, s 839*. [*FA 1995, s 127(17)*]. Secondly, an agent is deemed to carry out a transaction where he undertakes a transaction himself or gives instructions for it to be carried out by another person. Third, references to income arising from a business carried on through a branch or agency include income from property or rights used or held by the branch or agency. [*FA 1995, s 127(15)*]. The new provisions apply for income tax and CGT from 1996/97 and for corporation tax for accounting periods beginning after 31 March 1996. [*FA 1995, s 127(19)*].

Persons not regular agents of non-residents

14.20 The previous exception to the normal agency rules for those persons who do not carry on the regular agency of the non-resident is continued under the new rules. These provide that where the trading income in question, or capital gains from the trading business, arise from transactions carried out through a person who does not carry on a regular agency for the non-resident, that person is not to be treated as his UK representative. [*FA 1995, s 127(1)(a)*]. The Revenue regard the words 'regular agency' as having the same meaning as habitual agent in the OECD Model Tax Convention.

Brokers

14.21 A broker is not treated as the UK representative of a non-resident in respect of income or capital gains from business transactions carried out through him, provided that:

(*a*) at the time of the transaction the broker was carrying on the business of a broker;

(*b*) the transaction was carried out on behalf of the non-resident in the ordinary course of the broker's business;

(*c*) the remuneration received by the broker from the non-resident was not less than the customary charge for that class of business; and

(*d*) the broker is not otherwise the non-resident's UK representative. [*FA 1995, s 127(1)(b),(2)*].

14.22 A broker who provides other services is deemed to carry on a separate business for these purposes. [*FA 1995, s 127(14)*]. The Revenue have confirmed that the term broker is to have the same meaning as in *TMA 1970, s 82(1)*. The wording in (*a*) and (*b*) above reproduces the *section 82* definition of 'sales or transactions carried out on behalf of a non-resident through a broker in the ordinary course of his business as such'.

14.23 It was established in *Wilcock v Pinto 1924 9 TC 111* that the word 'broker' has a limited meaning, where Bankes L J stated at pages 129 and 130:

> 'As I understand that expression, it is used technically, and is used in reference to a class of persons who, by the custom of certain markets, are entitled and recognised as being entitled, to act for both purchaser and seller; and it is to that class of persons, as I understand it, that the expression "broker" is used, both in the cases in which reference has been made to that class of business, and in the statute'.

Investment managers

14.24 Under the previous provisions, an investment manager who acted for overseas based financial traders enjoyed exemption from liability as an agent under *TMA 1970, s 78(2)* for services rendered in the normal course of trade as an investment manager and for full remuneration provided that certain conditions were complied with. These provisions have now been revised to exclude investment managers from the definition of UK representatives, and hence from liability as agents to account to the Revenue for tax on gains made by non-resident financial traders, in cases where the investment manager is independent of the non-resident or otherwise acts on customary commercial terms.

14.25 Under the new legislation contained in *FA 1995, s 127(1)(c),(3)* which came into effect from 6 April 1995, an investment manager is not treated as a non-resident's UK representative in respect of income or capital gains from business transactions carried out through him, provided that:

(*a*) the investment manager is carrying on a business of providing investment management services;

(*b*) the investment transaction was carried out in the ordinary course of that business;

(*c*) the manager, when he acted on behalf of the non-resident in relation to the transaction, did so in an independent capacity;

(*d*) the remuneration received by the investment manager is not less than the customary charge for that class of business; and

(*e*) the investment manager is not otherwise the non-resident's UK representative. [*FA 1995, s 127(1)(c), (3)*].

14.26 For the purposes of condition (*b*) an investment transaction is defined to include transactions in shares, stocks, futures contracts, options contracts, securities dealing in a foreign currency, or such other transactions as may be specified by regulations which may be made by the Treasury. An option for a futures contract includes one where the only obligation is to make payment of a sum of money in full settlement as opposed to an obligation to transfer assets. [*FA 1995, s 127(12)(13)*].

14.27 For the purposes of condition (*c*) the relationship between the investment manager and the non-resident must have the same legal, financial and commercial characteristics as one between independent businesses dealing at arm's length. [*FA 1995, s 127(18)*]. Under a Revenue Press Release of 17 February 1995 it is stated that where the [other] conditions in *section 127(3)* set out above are satisfied, this 'independent relationship' will be satisfied if services for the non-resident and persons connected with the non-resident are not a 'substantial part' of the investment management business.

14.28 This condition is regarded as satisfied where no more than 70 per cent of the investment management business is with the non-resident and connected persons, either by reference to fees or some other measure where that would be more appropriate. An eighteen-month grace period is allowed from the start of a new investment management business to permit this 'substantial part' i.e. 70 per cent, test to be satisfied. Moreover the condition will not be regarded as breached where the investment manager intended to satisfy it but did not do so for reasons beyond his control, having taken reasonable steps to fulfil the intention.

14.29 If fee income exceeds 70 per cent, consideration will have to be given to whether the fee income is indeed a fair measure of the proportion of the business with the non-resident. Thus even if the 70 per cent level is exceeded the relationship might nevertheless be independent if, say, special deals have been reached on fees. Moreover, regardless of the normal 70 per cent rule, the relationship will still be considered to be independent where the investment management services are provided to a collective investment scheme which is quoted on a recognised stock exchange, or otherwise fully marketed, (seemingly meaning offered to the public) such as units in a unit trust or widely held. It is regarded as widely held if either no majority interest in the fund is held by five or fewer persons and persons connected with them or no interest of more than 20 per cent is held by one person and persons connected with him.

14.30 The Revenue Press Release further states that cases falling outside the above categories will have to be considered on their own facts to determine whether the independence requirement is satisfied and in this regard a subsidiary is not to be considered not independent of its parent company solely because of the parent's ownership of the share capital. It is to be hoped that even where the strict criteria are not satisfied there will be no charge to tax on the investment manager where the arrangements are commercial with no tax avoidance motive.

Participating investment managers – the 20 per cent rule

14.31 Further conditions must be satisfied for those investment managers that take a share in any overseas fund. The Revenue concern here was that by establishing a fund in a tax haven and investing in that fund, the manager might otherwise be able to avoid or defer UK tax on his share of any profits generated. Yet at the same time it was considered that it would be commercially desirable to allow financial groups to place seed money into offshore funds they were promoting and to permit cross holdings without exposing the fund to UK tax, or to have an incentive arrangement through a 'carried interest' in the capital of a managed fund, for example a performance fee structured as a special share in the fund. This has been accomplished by permitting investment up to a 20 per cent share in the fund without endangering the fund's tax status.

14.32 In such cases further conditions, in addition to those outlined in 14.25, need to be satisfied. Throughout a qualifying period (essentially not more than 5 years), the investment manager (and any connected persons) must intend that his share of profits or gains of the non-resident from transactions carried out through him should not exceed 20 per cent thereof. Professional fees paid to the investment manager, and connected persons, are to be netted off before the 20 per cent test is applied, provided they are allowable as deductions in arriving at taxable income. The requisite intention on the part of the investment manager must actually be fulfilled save to the extent that any failure is attributable to matters outside the control of the investment manager (and any connected persons) and does not result from a failure to take reasonable steps in mitigation. [*FA 1995, s 127(4)(5)*].

14.33 Hence there is a certain amount of flexibility if markets move in an unexpected way and the 20 per cent limit is temporarily breached. Moreover, where the 20 per cent rule is not satisfied but the other investment manager conditions in 14.25 are complied with, only that part of the income belonging to the investment manager will be subject to a tax charge. [*FA 1995, s 127(8)*].

14.34 For the purpose of determining what are the profits and gains in which the investment manager has a 20 per cent share, the profits or gains in question are those in which he has (or may acquire) a beneficial entitlement by virtue of an interest in reinvested securities, including rights to an immediate payment for a share in the profits and gains, and any other rights in relation to the non-resident which are attributable to those profits or gains. [*FA 1995, s 127(6)*]. An investment manager who provides other services is deemed to carry on a separate business for the purpose of these provisions. [*FA 1995, s 127(14)*].

Collective investment schemes

14.35 Where investment management services are provided to a collective investment scheme, as defined in the *Financial Services Act 1986*, which is financially transparent, the 20 per cent rule is applied by looking at the scheme as a whole, rather than by each participant separately. The rule is treated as satisfied by each participant in the scheme:

(*a*) where the scheme, if it were taxed as a separate entity would not be regarded as carrying on a trade in the UK, regardless of the level of beneficial entitlement; and

(*b*) where the scheme, if it were taxed as a separate entity, would be regarded as carrying on a trade, provided the 20 per cent rule is satisfied with regard to the beneficial entitlement of the investment manager (and connected persons) to the taxable income of the scheme. [*FA 1995, s 127(9)–(11)(17)*].

14.36 The provision in (*a*) – which excludes transparent schemes where the activities are investments rather than trading – is somewhat puzzling in that non-residents who invest, rather than carry on a trade, through a UK manager are generally not liable to tax in any event. For consideration of these provisions and some of the problems involved see two articles in Tax Journal, 16 February 1995, pages 16 and 17 and 23 March 1995, pages 10 and 11.

Non-resident members of Lloyd's

14.37 Where the non-resident is a member of Lloyd's, and the income arises from underwriting, the member's agent or the managing agent of the syndicate in question is excluded from being the non-resident's UK representative. [*FA 1995, s 127(1)(d)*]. This matches changes made to the taxation of Lloyd's underwriters in *FA 1994, ss 219–230*, which repealed the provisions relating to deduction of tax at source by members' agents and managing agents. Lloyd's terms are defined by reference to *FA 1993, ss 171–174* and *FA 1994, ss 219–230*. [*FA 1995, s 127(16)*].

Certain overseas funds in existence at 29 November 1994

14.38 There may be some overseas funds which qualified for exemption under the rules in *TMA 1970, ss 78(2)–(5), 82(1)*, but would not do so under the new rules. The Revenue intend to introduce 'grandfathering' arrangements in such cases and in the meantime Extra Statutory Concession B40 relating to UK investment managers acting for non-resident clients will continue to apply up to 5 April 1996 and in certain cases to 5 April 2005. (Inland Revenue Press Release 17 February 1995).

Schedule D, Case VI and Schedule E income

14.39 Non-residents generally remain subject to tax in respect of income falling within Schedule D, Case VI and Schedule E, but there are no specific provisions in the new legislation dealing with these sources of income.

Income from land in the UK: Schedule A

Background

14.40 Non-residents are subject to tax on income from property situated in the UK. In cases where the non-resident has an agent in the UK, the agent under the old system could be charged in the taxpayer's name. [*TMA 1970, Part VIII*]. He was obliged to notify chargeability and could be required to complete a tax return and pay the tax on behalf of the non-resident. This was unsatisfactory in that the agent was often not sufficiently well aware of his principal's affairs to enable him to complete a full return. In other cases, where the rent was paid directly by the tenant, the tenant was obliged to deduct tax at basic rate from the rent, and account for it to the Revenue. This was also rather unsatisfactory, particularly where there was no liability.

14.41 Under self-assessment, which came into operation from 6 April 1996, those non-resident landlords who can demonstrate compliance with their responsibilities under self-assessment will be permitted to receive rents without deduction at source. Otherwise tax at the basic rate will have to be deducted from net rental income, after certain permitted expenses, and paid to the Revenue.

14.42 The new provisions were enacted by *FA 1995, s 40*, inserting a new *TMA 1970, s 42A*, setting out the statutory framework and enabling the Board to issue regulations for the implementation of the new system. These regulations were duly issued in November 1995 as Statutory Instrument 1995 No 2902 'Taxation of Income from Land (Non-residents) Regulations 1995'. The Revenue have since issued detailed guidance notes for letting agents and tenants to what is described as the 'non-resident landlord's scheme' ('NRLS'). Those involved in such schemes should refer to these guidance notes. What follows is a summary of their provisions. The new provisions are administered by the Financial Intermediaries and Claims Office ('FICO') in Bootle. Another useful Revenue publication is booklet IR 50 entitled 'Taxation of Rents – A guide to property income – Schedule A for income tax 1995/96 and later years' issued in March 1996, is available free from any local tax office.

Non-resident landlords

Usual place of abode

14.43 Landlords are within the scheme if their usual place of abode is outside the UK, including individuals, companies and trustees. An individual is taken as having a usual place of abode outside the UK, if he usually lives outside the UK. Individuals temporarily living outside the UK for under six months are not included. The guidance notes do not provide any further guidance. But it is understood that the Revenue are prepared to give advice in particular cases.

14.44 A company with its main office or other place of business outside the UK, and a company incorporated outside the UK, is within the provisions. A company treated as UK resident for tax purposes is not within the provisions. Neither is a non-resident company with a UK branch chargeable to corporation tax, even if the rental income has nothing to do with the branch.

14.45 So far as trustees are concerned, they have a usual place of abode outside the UK, in accordance with the above rules for individuals and companies. If one or more of the trustees does not have a place of abode outside the UK, the trustees as a whole are outside the scheme.

Jointly-owned property

14.46 In the case of jointly-owned property, the share of any joint owner whose usual place of abode is abroad is within the scheme. The share of those in the UK is not within the scheme. For example, in a case where brother and sister own let property jointly, and the brother lives abroad his half share of the rent is within the NRLS scheme whilst that of his sister is not. Her half share should be paid without deduction, even where the entirety of the rent is paid to the brother. In such cases the UK owner may be a letting agent for the non-resident.

HM armed forces and other crown servants

14.47 The scheme applies to members of HM armed forces and other crown servants notwithstanding that their employment duties abroad are deemed to be performed in the UK for tax purposes.

Knowledge of landlord's status by letting agents and tenants

14.48 Should letting agents and tenants have reason to believe that a landlord may have a place of abode abroad, for example where he has an overseas address, they should satisfy themselves as to the position, consulting FICO if in difficulty. Unless they are satisfied that the Landlord does not have a usual place of abode outside the UK, they should deduct tax.

Landlords' ability to apply for rent to be paid gross

Application procedure

14.49 Landlords whose place of abode is outside the UK may apply to FICO for rent to be paid without any deduction of tax at source. There are standard forms for individuals (NRL 1), companies (NRL 2) and trustees (NRL 3). The application may be made at any time, for example those leaving the UK can apply before they go. Individuals who are already non-resident and who intend to let property in the UK, can apply before they start to let the property. It will be a requirement that:

(*a*) the person's tax affairs are up to date; or

(*b*) they have never had any UK tax obligations; or

(*c*) they do not expect to be liable to UK tax in the tax year in which the application is made.

14.50 Residential addresses should generally be provided, and if this is not done a brief explanation is required, for example where landlords live in a part of the world where they can only provide a 'care of' or 'PO Box' address. In cases where they have a residential address but this is not the correspondence address they should provide both. They should also provide details of any UK tax office and reference number. Where tax affairs have previously been dealt with via a letting agent or tenant, the latter's tax particulars should be given. These should assist in establishing that the non-resident landlord's tax affairs were up to date.

Approval of application

14.51 In cases where the application form is complete and correct, and FICO are satisfied that the non-resident landlord will comply with all his tax obligations, they will approve an application. FICO aim to deal with applications speedily. There will be an initial check, after which approval should normally be granted, followed by a later, detailed check. At that stage additional information may be required.

14.52 Notice of approval to receive rental income without deduction of tax will be sent to the non-resident landlord, with a copy to the non-resident landlord's accountant or tax adviser where they hold written authority, showing a reference number. A separate notice will be sent to the letting agents or tenants named on the application form authorising them to pay rental income to the non-resident landlord without deducting tax, again with a reference number. Such notices of approval will specify the date from which rental income should be paid without deducting tax, normally the first day of the quarter in which the notice is issued.

Refusal/withdrawal of approval

14.53 An application may be refused if FICO are not satisfied that the information provided in the application is correct; or they are not satisfied that the non-resident landlord will comply with his tax obligations. This will be by notice in writing. There is an initial right of appeal to FICO within 90 days of the date of the notice. There is then a further right of appeal to the General Commissioners or, if the landlord elects, the Special Commissioners.

14.54 An approval may be withdrawn if FICO cease to be satisfied that the information provided in the application is correct; or they are no longer satisfied that the non-resident landlord will comply with his tax obligations; or the non-resident landlord fails to supply information requested by FICO. A notice withdrawing approval will be issued by FICO stating the reason for the withdrawal and the date from which it is effective. The letting agent or tenant will also be notified of the date from which they should start deducting tax from rental income. The same appeals procedure applies as for refusals.

Changes of letting agent or tenant

14.55 Where a non-resident landlord changes letting agents, or tenants where there is no letting agent, it is not permissible to transfer a notice held by the old letting agent or tenant to the new letting agent or tenant. The landlord should write to FICO with details of the new letting agent or tenant, who will then send a notice to the new letting agent or tenant. New letting agents or tenants must deduct tax until they receive such a notice.

Deduction at source

14.56 In the absence of an authority to pay rent to an 'approved' non-resident landlord under the provisions outlined above, a letting agent or tenant must deduct basic rate tax from all property income, net of certain allowable expenses paid by the agent or tenant out of that income, and account quarterly for the tax to the Revenue. This will apply to payments made on or after 6 April 1996. No deduction is required where the rental income does not exceed £5,200 per annum in aggregate.

Letting Agents

Meaning of the term

14.57 A letting agent is a person whose usual place of abode is in the UK; who acts on behalf of a non-resident landlord in connection with the management or administration of his UK rental business; with power to receive income of that rental business, or control the direction of that income; and who is not an 'excluded person' as set out below. The category includes people acting in a professional capacity, such as estate agents, solicitors and accountants. Moreover, a friend or relative of the landlord may also be a letting agent for the purposes of the scheme, if they satisfy these criteria.

Excluded persons

14.58 An excluded person is one whose activity on behalf of the non-resident landlord is confined to the provision of legal advice or legal services. [Reg 4(1)]. The Revenue consider that solicitors who do no more than receive apportioned rental income in the course of a conveyance, or take legal proceedings for the recovery of arrears of rental income, are excluded persons. But solicitors who draw up a lease and collect the rent for the first period are not excluded persons. Whilst drawing up a lease would be the provision of a legal service, in collecting the rent the solicitor would be going beyond the provision of legal services and acting as a letting agent.

14.59 Banks and building societies who only provide an account into which rental income is paid and from which withdrawals are made are likewise not treated as letting agents. The same applies to other persons who merely receive income. For example, a tenant may pay rent into the bank account of a non-resident landlord's mother. If the mother simply receives the money into her bank account she is not a letting agent. But if she goes beyond this, for example, by asking the tenant for the rent if the tenant falls into arrears, she is a letting agent. Those who find tenants for non-resident landlords and who receive fees for that service but do not handle or control any rental income, or handle or control income only for short periods (described as 'tenant finders'), are outside the scheme; see 14.66.

Chains of letting agents

14.60 In cases where a non-resident landlord has more than one letting agent in the UK in respect of the same source of rental income this is referred to as a chain of letting agents. In such cases the last agent in the chain (being the agent who pays the income directly to the landlord) must generally operate the scheme. So if one letting agent collects rents and passes them on to a second letting agent the second letting agent must operate the scheme. However, the last letting agent in the chain and any other letting agent can jointly elect to transfer the responsibility for operating the scheme from the last letting agent to the other letting agent making the election. [Reg 4]. Such an election should be made in writing to FICO with the following information: the name and address of the elected agent; the name and address of the other letting agent; the name and address of the non-resident landlord or landlords; and the date from which the election is to take effect (not earlier than the first date of the quarter in which the election is made). An election may be made in respect of only part of a landlord's rental business by identifying the property to which the election relates. Such an election may be revoked subsequently.

Branches of letting agents

14.61 Letting agents with several branches may apply to FICO to register each branch as a separate letting agent on form NRL 5, but only if the branches deal with an average of five or more non-resident landlords each. 'Branches' means the units into which the letting agent divides his or her business, and includes areas, regions and other administration centres. [Reg 6(1)]. On the form letting agents must provide details of their name and head office address; their Tax Office and reference number; the name and address of each branch to be registered; the number of non-resident landlords dealt with by each branch; and a declaration that he does not act on behalf of any non-residents other than those whose business is managed by the branches listed on the form. [Reg 6(2)].

14.62 When approval has been granted each branch will be able to operate the scheme separately from the first day of the quarter following the quarter in which the approval is given and for any subsequent quarter. [Reg 6(3)]. Letting agents may revoke approval for branches to operate the scheme separately by giving notice in writing to FICO, which will take effect from the first day of the quarter following the quarter in which the revocation is made. [Reg 6(4)]. Where a branch closes or ceases to act for non-resident landlords FICO should be notified. Similarly, when a new branch opens or starts to act for non-resident landlords.

14.63 An application may be refused by FICO where they have reason to believe that the average number of non-residents per branch is less than five; or the letting agent is likely to fail to comply with the obligations imposed on him by the rules of the scheme; or the declaration on form NRL 5 is incorrect. [Reg 6(6)]. A refusal will be given by notice in writing to the letting agent, specifying the reasons. The letting agent may appeal against the refusal to FICO within 30 days of the date of the notice. If the appeal cannot be settled by agreement it will be referred to the General Commissioners or, if the letting agent elects, the Special Commissioners. [Reg 6(8)(9)].

14.64 There are like provisions enabling FICO to withdraw approval, with a similar procedure to be followed regarding written notice and the right of approval.

Notices from FICO to operate the scheme

14.65 A notice may be issued by FICO to a letting agent requiring the letting agent to operate the scheme. The notice will usually specify the landlord(s) in respect of whom the letting agent must operate the scheme, and the commencement date. A letting agent who receives such a notice must operate the scheme until the notice is withdrawn or until he ceases to act for the non-resident landlord(s), if earlier.

Tenant Finders

14.66 Some persons simply enter into arrangements with a non-resident landlord to find a tenant for the landlord's property. Having done so they may collect rent for a period, from which they recover the fee. The tenant subsequently pays rental income directly to the landlord. In such cases, the tenant finder does not have to operate the scheme in respect of the landlord provided the period for which rent is collected is no more than three months, and the tax which would be payable would be no more than £100.

Example 1

Mr Maltowski finds a tenant for a non-resident landlord at a rent of £600 per month. He collects two months' rent out of which he recovers his fee of £900. The tenant pays the rent direct to the landlord from the third month. If Mr Maltowski were required to operate the scheme, his tax calculation would be:

Rental income received	£1,200
Less fee (a deductible expense)	£900
	£300
Tax at 24%	£72

Since this is less than £100, the scheme does not have to be operated.

Example 2

Mr Robotov finds a tenant for a non-resident landlord at a rent of £2,000 a year. He collects six months' rent in advance out of which he recovers his fee of £500, also paying for insurance of £400. If he were required to operate the scheme, his tax calculation would be:

Rental income received	£1,000
Less deductible expenses	£900
	£100
Tax at 24%	£24

Notwithstanding that the tax is only £24 Mr Robotov must operate the scheme because he collects more than three months' rent.

14.67 In cases where tenant finders collect the initial rent but do not have to operate the scheme, the non-resident landlord will receive rental income gross for that period. Subsequently tenants paying the rent direct to the landlord may have to operate the scheme. The tenant finder should then notify the tenant of his obligations under the NRL scheme.

Registration

14.68 Letting agents who have to operate the scheme must register with FICO within 30 days of the date on which they are first required to operate the scheme, or by 5 May 1996, if later, giving their name and address; and their tax reference number and the name of their Tax Office.

They will then be allocated a registration number, and the appropriate forms and information will be issued to them by FICO.

Calculation of payment of tax by letting agents

Obligations and tax calculation

14.69 Unless they have been informed in writing by FICO that the landlord is approved to receive the rental income with no tax deducted letting agents must calculate the tax for each quarter beginning with the period from 6 April 1996 to 30 June 1996 and pay the tax due to the Inland Revenue within 30 days of the end of the quarter. Subsequent quarters end with the last day of September, December, March and June. [Reg 9]. Letting agents must not accept merely a non-resident landlord's statement that rental income may be paid without deduction of tax.

14.70 Tax should be calculated at the basic rate on rental income less expenses. Rental income actually received in the quarter is to be included, and also rental income which was income which the letting agent had the power to receive and was paid away in the quarter at his direction to another person without being received by him. Deductible expenses are those which the letting agent actually paid in the quarter, and also those paid away in the quarter at his direction by another person.

Example 3

Lettingco is due to collect rental income of £6,000 per quarter for a non-resident landlord. In a particular quarter they collect £3,000, and pay out £300 for gardening and cleaning.

Rental income received by Lettingco	£3,000
Less deductible expenses paid	£300
	£2,700
Tax due at 24%	£648

Example 4

Lettingco is due to collect rental income of £3,000 per quarter for another non-resident landlord. Lettingco authorises the tenant to pay £1,000 to a builder to repair the roof, this being a deductible expense. The rent paid to Lettingco is correspondingly reduced.

Rental income received by Lettingco	£2,000
Add rental income paid away at Lettingco's direction	£1,000
	£3,000
Less deductible expenses	£1,000
	£2,000
Tax due at 24%	£480

Example 5

As in previous example, save that instead of authorising the tenant to pay £1,000 to a builder for roof repairs, Lettingco authorises the tenant to pay £1,000 to a third party in settlement of a loan, which is not a deductible expense.

Rental income received by Lettingco	£2,000
Add rental income paid away at Lettingco's direction	£1,000
	£3,000
Tax at 24%	£720

Excess expenses

14.71 Where the deductible expenses for any quarter exceed the rental income to be taken into account for the quarter, the excess is first to be carried back and deducted from rental income of the same landlord for previous quarters in the same year to 31 March, taking later quarters before earlier quarters. Any balance is to be carried forward and deducted from rental income of the same landlord for subsequent quarters, taking earlier quarters before later quarters. This carry forward is not restricted to quarters within the same year to 31 March. [Reg 9(5)]. It should be stressed that any excess expenses paid in respect of one landlord cannot be deducted from the rental income of another landlord.

Example 6 – expenses carried back

Aceco, a letting agent, acts for a non-resident landlord. In the quarter to 30 September 1996 they receive rental income of £2,000 and pay deductible expenses of £500. In the quarter to 31 December 1996 they receive rental income of £2,000 and pay deductible expenses of £3,000.

Quarter to 31.12.96

Rental income received by Aceco	£2,000
Less deductible expenses paid	£3,000
Excess expenses	(£1,000)

The excess is to be carried back and set off against rental income received in the immediate preceding quarter being the quarter to 30 September 1996. The revised calculation for that quarter will then become:

Quarter to 30.9.96

Rental income received by Aceco	£2,000
Less deductible expenses paid	£500
Less excess expenses carried back from quarter to 31.12.96	£1,000
Revised net income on which basic rate tax is due	£500

Aceco will have paid tax of £360 for the quarter to 30 September 1996 (£2,000 – £500 at 24%). See paragraph 14.72 for the procedure to recover the repayable amount.

Example 7 – expenses carried forward

Aceco, a letting agent, receives £2,000 rental income for a non-resident landlord in the quarter to 30 June 1997 and pays £3,000 deductible expenses. In the quarter to 30 September 1997 they receive £500 and pay no expenses.

Quarter to 30.6.97

Rental income received by Aceco	£2,000
Less deductible expenses paid	£3,000
Excess expenses	(£1,000)

Aceco cannot carry back the excess expenses because carry back is restricted to earlier quarters in the same year to 31 March.

Quarter to 30.9.97

Rental income received by Aceco	£500
Less excess expenses brought forward	£1,000
Balance of excess expenses available to carry forward	(£500)

Repayable amounts

14.72 Excess expenses carried back to an earlier quarter will reduce the letting agent's tax liability in respect of that earlier quarter, this reduction being called a 'repayable amount'. This is recoverable by a set-off against the total tax due to the Inland Revenue in respect of the letting agent's other non-resident landlords for the same payment quarter as that in which the excess expenses arise. If the entirety cannot be recovered in this way, the letting agent may claim a repayment from the Revenue on the form NRLQ, which is to be completed for the quarter in which the excess expenses arise. [Reg 9(6)].

Example 8

	Landlord A	Landlord B
Quarter to 30.6.97		
Rental income	£1,000	£2,000
Less deductible expenses	£200	£1,000
	£800	£1,000
Tax at 24%	£192	£240
Tax payable	£432	
Quarter to 30.9.97		
Rental income	£1,000	£2,000
Less deductible expenses	£1,500	£1,400
	(£500)	£600
Tax at 24%	Nil	£144
Excess expenses	£500	

When the excess expenses of £500 are carried back to the quarter to 31.3.97 the letting agent's tax liability for that quarter will be reduced by £120 (£500 × 24%). This £120 can be set against the tax of £144 due for the quarter to 30.6.97, leaving £24 (£144 − £120) payable.

Example 9

	Landlord A	Landlord B
Quarter to 30.9.97		
Rental income	£1,000	£2,000
Less deductible expenses	£600	£1,000
	£400	£1,000
Tax at 24%	£96	£240
Tax payable	£336	
Quarter to 31.12.97		
Rental income	£1,000	£2,000
Less deductible expenses	£1,200	£1,950
	(£200)	£50
Tax at 24%	Nil	£12
Excess expenses	£200	

When the excess expenses of £200 are carried back to the quarter to 30.9.97 the letting agent's tax liability for that quarter will be reduced by

£48 (£200 × 24%). This £48 can be set against the £12 of tax due for the quarter to 31.12.97, leaving £36 repayable by the Revenue.

14.73 Tax due must be paid each quarter to the Inland Revenue with return form NRLQ. Letting agents who are not required to pay tax for any quarter do not need to complete a form for the quarter, unless specifically required by FICO. The following details must be shown on the return form: the quarter to which the return form relates; the total amount of tax due in respect of all their non-resident landlords for that quarter; or where there is no tax due in the quarter but the letting agent is due a repayment, the amount of the repayment claimed. The declaration on the form stating that the particulars given are, to the best of the letting agent's knowledge, correct and complete must also be signed. [Reg 10].

14.74 Letting agents acting for more than one non-resident landlord should calculate the tax due for each landlord separately, then add together the amounts due and subtract any repayable amount. Payment for the amount due with the completed return form should be sent to the Revenue Accounts Office at Cumbernauld. This must be sent in time to arrive no later than 30 days after the end of the quarter to which it relates. For example, form NRLQ for the quarter to 30 September 1996 must arrive at Accounts Office by 30 October 1996. Interest may be charged on late payment from the due date. [Reg 10(6)]. Where interest is so charged and that tax is subsequently repaid, the letting agent is not entitled to recover any of the interest. [Reg 10(7)].

Assessments to recover tax

14.75 Under the NRL scheme tax is payable by letting agents without the need for the Inland Revenue to make tax assessments. But, where FICO have reason to believe that an amount should have been paid but was not, or a quarterly return is incorrect, they can make an assessment. In these circumstances FICO will ask the letting agent's own Tax Office to make the assessment. [Reg 10(9)]. The letting agent has the right of appeal, which should be made in writing, either to FICO or to the Tax Office, within 30 days of the date of the assessment. If the appeal cannot be settled by agreement it will be heard by the General Commissioners, or if the letting agent elects, the Special Commissioners. Interest on assessed income may be charged tax from the date when the amount of tax became due until the date it is paid.

Annual returns

14.76 An annual return must be made by all letting agents who have to operate the NRL scheme by 5 July each year (beginning with 5 July 1997) in respect of the year to 31 March (beginning with the year to 31 March 1997). The following details must be shown separately for each non-resident landlord:

(*a*) the landlord's name and address;

(*b*) the amount of rental income for the year to 31 March before the deduction of expenses;

(*c*) if the letting agent is not authorised to pay rental income to the landlord with no tax deducted the deductible expenses for the year to 31 March, and the total of the tax shown as payable in the letting agent's quarterly returns for the year to 31 March; and

(*d*) if the letting agent is authorised to pay rental income to the landlord with no tax deducted, the landlord's approval reference number. [Reg 11].

14.77 The letting agent must also sign a declaration that the return is, to the best of his knowledge, correct and complete. Returns submitted on magnetic media conforming to Revenue guidelines will be acceptable. Penalties are exigible for failure to make a return, or for making an incorrect return.

Certificate to be provided by letting agents

14.78 Letting agents liable to pay tax in any year in respect of a non-resident landlord must provide the landlord with a certificate by 5 July following the end of the year to 31 March, the first by 5 July 1997. The certificate must show the non-resident landlord's name and address; the letting agent's name and address; the year ended 31 March to which the certificate relates; and the letting agent's total liability to tax for the particular year in respect of the landlord. The certificate must also contain a declaration by the letting agent that the particulars contained in the certificate are, to the best of his knowledge, correct and complete. [Reg 12].

14.79 Non-resident landlords should keep certificates. When they complete their UK Tax Return they can set off the tax shown on the certificate against their overall UK tax liability, subject to the letting agent actually deducting the tax shown. Landlords may be asked to provide the certificate to their Tax Office as evidence in support of their self-assessment.

Tenants of non-resident landlords

Tenants who must operate the scheme

14.80 Tenants of a non-resident landlord generally have to operate the scheme where they pay rent direct to a non-resident landlord; or where they pay rent to a person outside the UK; or where they pay rent to a person who is not a letting agent; or where they receive a notice from the Inland Revenue. Rent paid into a non-resident landlord's UK bank or building society account is treated as paid direct to the non-resident landlord.

14.81 FICO may issue a notice to a tenant requiring the tenant to operate the scheme. This will usually specify the landlord in respect of whom the scheme must be operated and the date of commencement. Tenants in receipt of such a notice must operate the scheme until the earlier of FICO withdrawing the notice or their ceasing to be a tenant of the non-resident landlord. [Reg 3(1)].

Tenants who do not have to operate the scheme

14.82 Tenants do not have to operate the scheme if they pay rent to a letting agent in the UK. They also do not have to operate the scheme if they pay rent of £5,200 or less per year, unless they receive a notice from FICO requiring them to do so. Where a tenant occupies property for part of the year, the figure of £5,200 is proportionately reduced. For example, a tenant who occupies property for six months in the year ended 31 March 1997 is not required to operate the scheme if he is due to pay £2,600 or less. But if the amount is greater than this the scheme must be operated. The limit of £5,200 applies in respect of each landlord. So, where a tenant has several non-resident landlords, he is required to operate the scheme only in respect of those landlords to whom he is due to pay more than £5,200 a year.

Notification

14.83 Tenants who have to operate the scheme should write to FICO providing their name and address, and the names and addresses of their non-resident landlords. FICO can then issue the appropriate forms and information in time for the tenant to complete returns and make payments of tax on time.

Tenant's obligations regarding calculation and payment of tax

14.84 Tenants should calculate the tax each quarter beginning with the period from 6 April 1996 to 30 June 1996. Subsequent quarters end with the last day of September, December, March or June. They must pay the tax due to the Inland Revenue within 30 days of the end of the quarter. They are not required to calculate or pay tax on the rental income of a non-resident landlord if FICO have told them in writing that the landlord is approved to receive the rental income gross. A mere statement from the non-resident landlord that rental income may be paid without deduction of tax will not suffice.

14.85 Tenants should calculate tax at the basic rate on rental income they pay to the landlord in the quarter, plus rental income they pay to third parties in the quarter which are not deductible expenses. [Reg 8]. A tenant who deducts insufficient tax will be able to recover tax from future rents. [*TMA 1970, s 42A (3)(b)*].

Example 10

Mr Steinowicki is due to pay rent of £2,000 per quarter to a non-resident landlord. In the quarter to 30 September 1996 he pays only £1,000. As the calculation is based on rental income paid, his calculation for the quarter to 30 September 1996 is:

Rental income paid	£1,000
Tax due at 24%	£240

Example 11

Mr Ostov pays rental income of £1,500 per quarter to a non-resident landlord. In the quarter to 30 June 1996 the landlord tells him to pay £400 to a third party in settlement of a loan (which is not a deductible expense) and to pay the landlord £1,100 for that quarter. Mr Ostov's calculation for the quarter to 30 June 1996 is:

Rental income paid to landlord	£1,100
Plus rental income paid away to third party at landlord's discretion	£400
	£1,500
Tax due at 24%	£360

Example 12

Mr Silver is due to pay rental income of £1,500 per quarter but pays a builder £200 for repairs. He pays £1,300 to the landlord. As the repairs are a deductible expense the calculation will be:

Rental income paid to landlord	£1,300
Tax due at 24%	£312

Quarterly returns and payment

14.86 The tax due must be paid each quarter to the Inland Revenue Accounts Office, Cumbernauld with return form NRLQ. Quarterly returns are due for the periods ending 30 June, 30 September, 31 December and 31 March. Tenants who are not required to make a payment for any quarter do not need to complete a quarterly return form for the quarter, unless they are required to do so by a notice in writing from FICO. The return form must give details of the quarter to which the return form relates and the total amount of tax due on rental income. The declaration on the form must also be signed by the tenant stating that the particulars given therein are, to the best of his knowledge, correct and complete. [Reg 10].

14.87 Tenants of more than one non-resident landlord should calculate the tax due for each landlord separately, adding together the amounts due and showing the total for the quarter on form NRLQ. The form and payment must be sent in time to arrive at Accounts Office no later than 30 days after the end of the quarter to which it relates. For example, the quarterly return form NRLQ for the quarter to 30 September 1996 must arrive at Accounts Office by 30 October 1996. Interest may be charged on late payment. [Reg 10(6)].

14.88 Although it is the tenant's responsibility to pay the tax without a tax assessment by the Revenue, FICO have the same powers to make an assessment on tenants as they have on letting agents as described in 14.75 and in the same circumstances. The same appeals procedure and liability to interest on late payment applies.

Annual returns

14.89 An annual return must be made by all tenants within the NRL scheme by 5 July each year (beginning with 5 July 1997) in respect of the year to the previous 31 March (beginning with the year to 31 March 1997). The following details must be shown separately for each non-resident landlord:

(*a*) the landlord's name and address;

(*b*) the total amount of rental income paid to the landlord and rental income paid away to third parties in the year;

(*c*) if the tenant is not authorised to pay rental income to the landlord with no tax deducted, the deductible expenses for the year to 31 March; and the total of the tax shown as payable in the tenant's quarterly returns for year to 31 March; and

(*d*) if the tenant is authorised to pay the landlord with no tax deducted, the landlord's approval reference number. [Reg 11].

14.90 The tenant must also complete the declaration that the return is, to the best of his knowledge, correct and complete. Where tenants have received notification from FICO that rental income may be paid to all their non-resident landlords with no tax deducted, they are not required to submit annual returns. Hence a person who is a tenant of only one non-resident landlord and who has authority to pay rental income gross is not required to submit annual returns. But a tenant of two non-resident landlords who has authority to pay rental income to only one with no tax deducted must submit a return with details for both non-resident landlords. [Reg 11(3)]. Penalties may be charged for failure to make a return or for making an incorrect return.

Certificate to be provided by tenants

14.91 Tenants liable to pay tax in any year in respect of a non-resident landlord must provide each landlord with a certificate by 5 July following the end of the year to 31 March, the first by 5 July 1997. The certificate must show the following information: the non-resident landlord's name and address; the year ended 31 March to which the certificate relates; and the tenant's total liability to tax for the year ended 31 March in respect of the landlord. The certificate must also contain a declaration by the tenant that the particulars contained in the certificate are, to the best of his knowledge, correct and complete. [Reg 12].

14.92 Non-resident landlords should keep certificates. When they complete their UK Tax Return they can set off the tax shown on the certificate against their overall UK tax liability subject to the letting agent actually deducting the tax shown. Landlords may be asked to provide the certificate to their Tax Office as evidence in support of their self-assessment.

Rental Income

Tax deduction calculation

14.93 Letting agents who have to operate the NRL scheme must calculate tax each quarter on the rental income received, less deductible expenses paid in the quarter. They should take into account all rental income they receive in the quarter, and rental income they do not receive in the quarter, but which is paid away to a third party (including the non-resident landlord) at the direction of the letting agent. Tenants must calculate tax each quarter on the rental income they have paid in the quarter. They should take into account all rental income they pay to the non-resident landlord in the quarter, and all rental income they pay to third parties in the quarter, unless the payments are deductible expenses.

14.94 Letting agents and tenants should take into account all rental income received or paid in the quarter notwithstanding that it relates to rent due for an earlier, or later, period. They should not calculate tax for a quarter on rental income which fell due in the quarter but was not paid in the quarter.

When rental income is received or paid

14.95 In the case of cheques for rent, letting agents are treated as receiving the income on the day the cheque is received and not on the day it is banked or cleared. But if the cheque is subsequently dishonoured it may be disregarded in calculating the tax due. Tenants paying rental income by cheque are treated as making the payment on the day they give the cheque to the landlord and not on the day the cheque is cashed or cleared.

But if the cheque is subsequently dishonoured it may likewise be disregarded in calculating the tax due.

Examples of rental income

14.96 Rental income includes a wide variety of receipts arising from land and property, as described in Chapter 5. In particular, rental income includes:

(*a*) income from furnished, unfurnished, commercial and domestic premises, and from any land;

(*b*) where property is let furnished, any separate sums from the tenant for the use of the furniture;

(*c*) rent charges, ground rents and feu duties;

(*d*) part of the premiums and other similar lump sums received on the grant of certain short leases, see 5.10;

(*e*) income arising from the grant of sporting rights, such as fishing and shooting permits;

(*f*) income arising from allowing waste to be buried or stored on land;

(*g*) income from letting others use land – for example, where a film crew pays to film inside a person's house or on their land;

(*h*) grants received from local authorities or others contributing to expenditure such as repairs to a let property;

(*i*) rental income received through enterprise investment schemes;

(*j*) income from caravans or houseboats where these are not moved around various locations;

(*k*) service charges received from tenants in respect of services ancillary to the occupation of property; and

(*l*) insurance recoveries under policies providing cover against non-payment of rent.

Income which is not rental income

14.97 There are certain receipts which arise out of the use of land which are not rental income, also as described in Chapter 5. These include:

(*a*) yearly interest;

(*b*) income from woodlands managed on a commercial basis; and

(*c*) income from the following types of concerns:

   (i) mines and quarries (including gravel pits, sandpits and brickfields);

(ii) ironworks, gasworks, salt springs or works, alum mines or works and waterworks and streams of water;

(iii) canals, inland navigations, docks, and drains or levels;

(iv) rights of markets and fairs, tolls, bridges and ferries;

(v) railways and other ways; and

(vi) lettings of tied premises by traders.

Deductible expenses

Test for deductibility

14.98 In determining tax due under the NRL scheme letting agents and tenants should take into account expenses they pay in a quarter which they can reasonably be satisfied are allowable expenses in computing the profits of the landlord's rental business. [Regs 8(2), 9(4)]. It is to be noted that the payment of the expenses must be made by the letting agent or tenant himself, or at his direction. Any payments made directly by the landlord are not deductible in computing the tax due to the Revenue by the letting agent or tenant. Moreover, a deduction is not available for expenses accrued in a quarter but not paid.

14.99 The test of reasonable satisfaction is considered by the Revenue to provide protection for letting agents and tenants in two ways:

(i) where they are uncertain whether an expense is an allowable expense they are justified under the rules in not deducting it when computing the tax due; and

(ii) where they can reasonably be satisfied that an expense is an allowable expense they can deduct the expense without fear of being penalised if it is later found that the expense is not in fact allowable.

14.100 Expenses are broadly allowable where they are incurred wholly and exclusively for the purposes of the rental business, and they are not of a capital nature. Expenditure on improvements and extensive alterations will be capital.

Examples of deductible expenses

14.101 The Revenue have said that the following expenses will normally be deductible:

(*a*) accountancy expenses (incurred in preparing rental business accounts but not for preparing personal tax returns);

(*b*) advertising costs of attracting new tenants;

(*c*) cleaning;

(*d*) costs of rent collection;

(*e*) Council Tax while the property is vacant but available for letting;

(*f*) gardening;

(*g*) ground rent;

(*h*) insurance against loss of rents;

(*i*) insurance claim fees;

(*j*) insurance on buildings and contents;

(*k*) interest paid on loans to buy land or property (but see 14.104 below);

(*l*) legal and professional fees;

(*m*) letting agents' fees;

(*n*) maintenance charges made by freeholders, or superior leaseholders, of leasehold property;

(*o*) maintenance contracts (e.g. Gas Board servicing);

(*p*) provision of services (e.g. gas, electricity, hot water);

(*q*) rates;

(*r*) rental warranty and legal expenses insurance;

(*s*) repairs which are not significant improvements to the property, including:

  (i) damp and rot treatment;

  (ii) mending broken windows, doors, furniture, cookers, lifts, etc;

  (iii) painting and decorating;

  (iv) replacing roof slates, flashing and gutters;

  (v) repointing; and

  (vi) stone cleaning;

(*t*) water rates.

14.102 A letting agent's own fees are deductible notwithstanding that they are retained by the agent from rent received, rather than paid out by him.

Interest paid on borrowings for the rental business

14.103 Interest paid directly by the landlord to a lender will not be taken into account in computing tax deductible by letting agents or tenants. This will therefore mean that a landlord will only be able to obtain a deduction for such interest if he satisfies the procedure laid down in 14.48 for payment of rent to be paid without deduction of tax or if he later files a tax return and self-assessment, in which case he may receive a repayment.

14.104 When the letting agent or tenant pays loan interest on behalf of a non-resident landlord the interest should rank as a deductible expense. However, in the case of mortgage interest, where the landlord claims mortgage interest relief (limited to interest on £30,000) rather than making a deduction in computing the profits of his rental business the position is as follows. Letting agents and tenants who pay the interest on behalf of the landlord should not deduct the interest if they have reason to believe that relief is given under MIRAS or the landlord is claiming mortgage interest relief.

Example 13

Mr Makarov, a non-resident, received rents from a property in the UK which were collected for him by an estate agent, who also paid out various disbursements such as advertising in connection with the property which was let furnished. Mr Makarov did not reply to any letters from the Inland Revenue and his agents were required to deduct tax under *TA 1988, s 42A*.

The situation in 1996/97 was as follows:

Rents collected by agent, monthly, in advance

	Accrued in year	
	£	£
1996		
April	1,000 × 25/30	833
May	1,200	1,200
June	1,050	1,050
July	1,150	1,150
August	1,225	1,225
September	1,025	1,025
October	1,175	1,175
November	1,200	1,200
December	1,375	1,375
1997		
January	1,175	1,175
February	1,125	1,125
March	1,150	1,150
April	1,075 × 5/30	179
		13,862
Less Agent's commission 15%	2,079	
Agent's disbursements	233	
		2,312
		£11,550

The agent deducted from payments made to Mr Makarov his commission and disbursements and tax at 24% on the balance. The tax withheld in respect of 1996/97 income was £11,550 × 24%		2,772

Mr Makarov had a salary from the UK for work in the UK as a director of a UK company of £40,000 per annum. He paid mortgage interest on the let property of £1,000 quarterly in arrears and sought advice on his correct tax liability under Schedule A, which was computed as:

	£	£
Gross rents		13,862
Less		
Wear and tear allowance 10%	1,386	
Agent's commission	2,079	
Agent's disbursements	233	
Mortgage interest	4,000	
Accountant's fees	250	
Assessable income		7,948
		£5,914
Tax due at 40%		2,366
Tax deducted by agent		2,772
Repayment due		406

Record keeping and audit

14.105 Sufficient records are to be kept by letting agents and tenants to be able to satisfy the Revenue that their obligations under the NRL scheme have been complied with. [Reg 15]. They should keep the following records, for each non-resident landlord separately: a record of rental income received by the letting agent or paid by the tenant; and copies of any correspondence with the landlord regarding his usual place of abode. Moreover, unless a letting agent is authorised to pay rental income with no tax deducted he should keep a record of expenses paid and invoices and receipts (or copies) to provide evidence of expenses paid.

14.106 A detailed audit procedure is set out in the Revenue guidance notes, containing their proposed practice on the conduct of audits, including sample reviewing and extrapolation to quantify any tax underpaid. Interest and penalties are exigible for default.

Investment income

14.107 Under the old system non-residents could be assessed to basic rate tax, and individuals also to higher rate tax, on UK source investment income such as dividends and interest income. In practice the imposition of tax was largely restricted to tax deducted at source, with relief under ESC B13 (which exempted interest paid gross from assessment), ESC B40 (which exempted income under the investment manager and broker provisions from assessment) and double tax agreements (which limited taxing rights to nil, or a reduced rate of withholding tax).

14.108 Under self-assessment, statutory effect is given to the old *de facto* position by restricting the tax charge on non-residents to any tax which is deducted at source in the cases of the following types of income (described as 'excluded income'):

(*a*) income from government securities;

(*b*) deposit interest and other income taxable under Schedule D, Case III;

(*c*) dividends taxable under Schedule F;

(*d*) income from certificates of deposit with financial institutions and banks taxable under Schedule D, Case VI under *TA 1988, s 56*;

(*e*) social security benefits (notably retirement pensions and unemployment benefit) taxable under Schedule E under *TA 1988, s 150* or *s 617* and incapacity benefits taxable under *FA 1994, s 139*;

(*f*) income received through a broker or investment manager that meets the requisite conditions for exemption in *FA 1995, s 127* (such as commodity dealing or trading in derivatives) other than underwriting profits of a Lloyd's name, currently excluded by ESC B40 (1992); and

(*g*) any other income that may be designated by the Treasury by Statutory Instrument. [*FA 1995, s 128(1)–(3)*].

14.109 It follows that normally a non-resident whose UK source income is wholly derived from investments will have no need to self-assess, except where a repayment is due. Excluded income taxed at source includes income where tax is deducted or treated as deducted, paid or treated as paid, or in respect of which there is a tax credit and the amount of tax is the amount deducted, paid or credited as appropriate. [*FA 1995, s 128(4)*]. For the purposes of computing the non-resident's tax liability on income which is generally chargeable to income tax (e.g. income from property, trading and employment), personal allowances given under a double tax agreement or to Commonwealth citizens or citizens of the Republic of Ireland and certain others under *TA 1988, s 278* are disregarded. [*FA 1995, s 128(1)(a)(ii)*]. Effectively, the personal allowances are set against the excluded investment income, although any balance of allowances in excess of this income can then be claimed against chargeable income assessed on a UK representative (income from a trade or profession) or under Schedule A. In essence ESC B13 is enacted.

14.110 A non-resident trust does not qualify for exemption for excluded income where there is a UK ordinarily resident individual or UK resident company as a relevant beneficiary. This mirrors exclusion in ESC B13 and for authorised unit trusts under SI 1994 No 2318. A relevant beneficiary is defined by reference to entitlement to income, current or prospective. [*FA 1995, s 128(5)(6)*].

14.111 These new provisions generally apply from 1995/96. But if the non-resident is trading in the UK through a branch or agency, such that the income would be taxed from 1996/97 on his UK representative as outlined in 14.11, these provisions also apply from 1996/97. Moreover, in the case of income within 14.108 (*a*) to (*d*) which arises from a transaction carried out by a broker or investment manager the provisions also apply from 1996/97 if the transaction is not in the ordinary course of business or for less than the normal remuneration.

Example 14

Mr Goryelov, a chartered surveyor, was a resident of Jersey and a non-resident of the UK and had the following UK income and allowances in 1995/96:

	£
Share of profits of UK partnership:	
y/e 30 June 1996	12,000
y/e 30 June 1995	10,000
Capital allowances:	
Written down value at 1 July 1994	15,000
Additions – y/e 30 June 1995	8,000
– y/e 30 June 1996	7,000
Profits on dealing in UK property through a UK firm of estate agents	16,000
Net rents before interest	4,000
Interest paid on loan to acquire let property	2,000
Dividends from UK companies	16,000
Tax credit thereon	4,000
Interest on UK debenture	3,000
Tax credit thereon	1,000
UK bank interest paid gross to non-resident	1,000
UK building society interest paid gross to non-resident	3,000
Personal allowances	4,000

		£
UK taxable income:		
Share of profits of UK partnership primary basis period, y/e 30.6.96 brought forward		12,000
FA 1994, 20 Sch 1(2)(a):		
Relevant period under *FA 1994, 20 Sch 2(2)(b), (5)* y/e 30.6.95		10,000
Aggregate, *FA 1994, 20 Sch 2(2)*		£22,000
$\frac{£22{,}000 \times 365}{366 + 365}$		£10,985
Less Capital allowances (*CAA 1990, s 160, FA 1994, s 211*)		
Written down value b/fwd	15,000	
Additions y/e 30.6.95 and 30.6.96	15,000	
		£30,000
Writing-down allowance 25%		£7,500
Assessable partnership income (£10,985 – £7,500)		3,485
Profit on dealing in UK property		3,485
UK estate agents are not regular agents within *FA 1995, s 127(1)(a)* and the profits are exempt from UK tax under the Anglo/Jersey double tax agreement as business profits under SI 1952 No 1216, para 3(2) and 2(1)(h)		Nil
Schedule A charge:		
FA 1995, s 40; TA 1988, s 42A		
Net rents	4,000	
Less Interest	2,000	
		2,000
Excluded income:		
FA 1995, s 128(1)(a)(i), 3(a)		
Dividends	16,000	
Tax credit	4,000	
Debenture interest	3,000	
Tax credit	1,000	
Bank interest	1,000	
Building society interest	3,000	
	28,000	

		£
Less Personal allowances *TA 1988, s 278(2); FA 1995, s 128 (1)(a)(ii)*	4,000	
No excess personal allowances	£24,000	
Not subject to any additional UK tax beyond that deducted at source		
Assessable UK income 1996/97		£5,485

Intellectual Property

14.112 The categories of excluded income outlined in 14.108 do not extend to intellectual property, for example royalties from a UK patent, trade mark or copyright. Moreover, it is understood that it is not presently planned for there to be any Treasury designation to this effect under the provisions referred to in 14.108(*g*). Royalties from a UK patent are in any event subject to deduction of tax at source at the basic rate under *TA 1988, s 349(1)(b)*. Copyright royalties are similarly subject to deduction at source under *TA 1988, s 536*, unless the royalty owner is the author whose usual place of abode is abroad and the Hansard Statement of 10 November 1969, vol 791, col 31 applies. There are like provisions for public lending right under *TA 1988, s 537*. There is, however, no withholding tax on royalties paid for the licensing of trade marks or know-how, although the sale of know-how is a trading receipt.

14.113 In so far as royalties accrue to the originator of the patent, trade marks or copyright, they are likely to be derived from a trade or profession carried on by him. The exploitation of the patents etc., might indicate that the trade or profession was being carried on partly in the UK, in which case it would be taxable. If the trading took place through a branch or agency, the UK representative would be jointly liable with the non-resident under *FA 1995, s 126* and *Schedule 23*. If the trading or profession was carried out wholly abroad there would be no UK income tax liability.

14.114 Where the royalties constituted investment income, say in the hands of the assignee of a copyright, because the income would not be within the category of excluded income the royalties would be subject to both basic and higher rate tax in the hands of an individual.

Trust income

Interest in possession trusts

14.115 A beneficiary with an interest in possession in trust property, i.e. where he is entitled as of right to any income arising, is treated as receiving the income from its original sources (less trust management expenses); *Williams v Singer (1920) 7 TC 387* and *Archer-Shee v Baker (1927) 11 TC 749*. Accordingly a non-resident beneficiary in receipt of excluded income from which basic rate tax has been deducted (see 14.108) will have no further tax liability. Where the income is not excluded income (e.g. income from property) the trustees will generally be liable to tax at the basic rate, and the beneficiary will be liable to higher rate tax if appropriate.

14.116 In computing the beneficiary's higher rate tax liability, a deduction is available for management expenses of the trustees. Given that non-resident beneficiaries are generally only subject to higher rate tax on UK property or trading income, if relief were given for the entirety of the trustee's expenses against such income there could be an excess of relief. There are accordingly restrictions contained in a new *TA 1988, s 689A* and *689B*, introduced by *FA 1996, 6 Sch 16*.

14.117 There is first of all a partial disallowance of trust management expenses which are attributable to income which before distribution is income of a beneficiary rather than the trustees, and where the beneficiary is not liable to tax on the whole of the income because of his non-resident status, or deemed non-resident status under a double tax agreement. [*TA 1988, s 689A(1)*]. This envisages the case of a non-resident beneficiary with an interest in possession in a trust with both UK and foreign source income. A proportion of the management expenses which is equal to the proportion of the income not bearing UK tax is disregarded in computing the beneficiary's taxable income. [*TA 1988, s 689A(2)*]. Excluded income under *FA 1995, s 128* (see 14.108) is treated as having borne tax for this purpose. [*TA 1988, s 689A(5)*]. In computing the disallowable proportion income tax and foreign tax of a similar character chargeable on the trustees is excluded from both total income and untaxed income. [*TA 1988, s 689A(3)* and *(4)*].

14.118 Having ascertained in this manner the proportion of the trustees' total management expense which may be set-off against the beneficiary's income in determining his higher rate tax liability, the new *TA 1988, s 689B* prescribes the order of set-off as follows:

(*a*) First, against qualifying distributions of UK companies in respect of which the trustees are not entitled to a tax credit by reason of their residence status, under *TA 1988, s 233 (1A)*, foreign income dividends and stock dividends within *TA 1988, s 246D(4)* and *249(6)*; and amounts assessable in respect of released or written off loans from close companies under *TA 1988, s 412(1)(a)*.

(*b*) Secondly, against investment income within the scope of the new *TA 1988, s 1A* (broadly interest etc., chargeable under Schedule D, Case III, distributions chargeable under Schedule F and equivalent foreign income chargeable under Schedule D, Cases IV and V, but excluding any income within the first category above). This is subject to the provisions expressly disallowing a proportion of expenses equivalent to the proportion of any trust income not bearing tax because of the non-resident status of the trustees or the beneficiary; *TA 1988, s 686 (2A)* and *689A*.

(*c*) Finally, against any income outside the above categories.

Discretionary and accumulation and maintenance trusts

14.119 Under the old system non-resident trustees of discretionary and accumulation and maintenance trusts were liable to basic and additional rate income tax on UK source income under *TA 1988, s 686* following *IRC v Regent Trust Co Ltd (1980) STC 140*. This remains the position where there is a 'relevant beneficiary' of the trust who is either an individual ordinarily resident in the UK or a company resident in the UK. [*FA 1995, s 128(5)*]. A relevant beneficiary is defined as one who is, or will or may become, entitled under the trust to receive the whole or any part of any income under the trust, or a person to or for whose benefit the whole or any part of the trust income may be paid or applied in exercise of any discretion of the trustees. For these purposes income which has been accumulated and applied as capital is included. [*FA 1995, s 128(6)*]. Whilst this definition is extremely wide, it may not apply to settlements where no actual beneficiaries fall within the definition, but the trust contains a power for beneficiaries to be added. In parallel cases the Revenue apparently interpret such provisions as only relating to persons actually within the class of beneficiaries as it exists at the time.

14.120 UK resident beneficiaries in receipt of income from such trusts would be potentially taxable at the higher rates, but with the benefit of the credit mechanism under Extra-Statutory Concession B18 provided the trustees have complied with their obligations. Non-resident beneficiaries would be regarded as taxable not by reference to the original income sources, but under Schedule D, Case III. This is automatically excluded income, so there would be no further tax liability.

14.121 Where there are no relevant beneficiaries of the trust, the trustees will not be subject to the additional rate of tax on UK source excluded income.

Change of residence

14.122 Under self-assessment a UK resident will normally be taxable on his worldwide income, but a non-resident only on income arising in the UK. It is therefore provided by *TA 1988, s 110A* [inserted by *FA 1995, s 124*] that where there is a change of residence, i.e. when a non-resident becomes resident in the UK or a resident ceases to be resident in the UK, there will be a deemed cessation for tax purposes of any trade, profession or vocation carried on by an individual where that trade etc. is carried on wholly or partly outside the UK other than in partnership. Parallel provisions for partnerships are dealt with in paragraph 12.19. The deemed cessation takes place in 1997/98, or later years, on a change of residence or in 1995/96 or 1996/97 where the current year basis of assessment applies, as a result of the trade, profession or vocation commencing on or after 6 April 1994. The deemed cessation gives rise to the same consequences as an actual cessation including overlap relief and terminal loss relief, and the recommencement is treated as the commencement of a new trade which would allow relief for losses in the first four years of trading under *TA 1988, s 381*. Unlike the rules for a deemed cessation and commencement on a partnership change under the preceding year basis of assessment, where losses in the first four years of the deemed new trade were prohibited by *TA 1988, s 381(6)*, there is no such restriction on change of residence. However, losses up to the date of change may be carried forward and set against profits of the deemed new trade under *TA 1988, s 385*, under *TA 1988, s 110A(1)*.

14.123 Where a non-UK domiciled non-resident becomes resident in the UK without acquiring a UK domicile, he will be assessed to tax on the remittance basis under Schedule D, Case V. If a trade remains carried on wholly abroad, for example through an agent with a power of attorney, the income would be assessable under Schedule D, Case V [*Trustees of Ferguson Deceased v Donovan (1927) IR 489*], whereas the assessment would be under Schedule D, Case I if the business were controlled from the UK [*Ogilvie v Kitton (1908) 5 TC 338*]. Under Schedule D, Case V, remittances from a continuing source are assessed as income in the UK even though the income may have arisen in an earlier year [*Back v Whitlock (1932) 16 TC 723; Carter v Sharon (1936) 20 TC 229*]. However, remittances of income from a source that has ceased would not be taxable as income under the remittance basis following *Kneen v Martin (1934) 19 TC 33*, unless the income were assessable under Schedule E where *TA 1988, s 19(4A)* would apply to assess the income to tax, as income for the last year of assessment in which the office or employment was held. It follows therefore that income from a Schedule D, Case V trade that arose prior to the deemed cessation could be remitted tax-free to the UK in the fiscal year following that in which the change of residence took place as there will be no source of income in that year even though the business in the commercial sense continued.

14.124 A taxpayer is resident for a complete fiscal year if he is resident for any part of it [*Neubergh v IRC (1958) STC 181; Gubay v Kington (1984) STC 99*]. The deemed cessation and commencement would therefore be effective from 6 April in the year in which a non-resident became UK resident or on 5 April following the change of residence if a UK resident became non-resident. However, under Extra Statutory Concession A11, a fiscal year is split for tax purposes so that a non-resident becoming resident is deemed to be resident in the UK only from the day of arrival and a resident ceasing to be resident is treated as non-resident from the day following the day of departure, provided that the various conditions in the Concession and IR20 regarding residence are satisfied. The conditions of ESC A11 were revised during 1996 so that split-year treatment will now be available to individuals intending to stay in the UK for at least two years whether or not for employment reasons. Unless, therefore, the taxpayer elects for the strict legal position, the deemed cessation would take place at the time of the change of residence even if part way through the fiscal year. Whether or not to insist upon the statutory treatment could depend on such matters as loss relief claims under *TA 1988, s 380*, or the stock values applicable on the change under *TA 1988, s 100* as amended by *FA 1995, s 140*.

Example 15

Mr Chkalov left the UK to become non-resident on 30 September 1997, retaining a branch in the UK.

He made up the accounts of his import and export business to 31 December each year. His adjusted profits were:

Year ended 31 December		
1993	£20,000	
1994	£25,000	
1995	£30,000	
1996	£35,000	
1997 (UK branch profit from 1.10.97 £6,000)	£40,000	
1998 (UK branch profits £20,000)	£60,000	
Assessable/taxable		
1994/95 preceding year basis	£20,000	(*a*)
1995/96 actual year basis	£31,250	(*b*)
1996/97 actual year basis	£36,250	(*c*)
1997/98 actual year basis	£31,205	(*d*)
1998/99 current year basis	£20,000	(*e*)

Notes

(*a*) *TA 1998, s 60(3)* original version.

(*b*) £25,000 on preceding year basis under *TA 1988, s 60(3)* original version displaced by *FA 1994, 20 Sch 3(2)* see (*d*).

(*c*) Primary basis period for 1996/97 under *TA 1988, s 60(3)(b)*;

FA 1994, s 200 y/e 31.12.96	£35,000
Relevant period under *FA 1994, 20 Sch 2(2)(b), (5)* i.e. 1.1.95 to 31.12.95	£30,000
Aggregate, *FA 1994, 20 Sch 2(2)*	£65,000

Appropriate percentage under *FA 1994, 20 Sch 2(5)*

$$£65{,}000 \times \frac{365}{366 + 365} = \qquad \underline{£32{,}456}$$

Displaced by *FA 1994, 20 Sch 3(2)* see (*d*).

(*d*) Deemed cessation 30 September 1997

Final period 1.1.97 to 30.9.97, *TA 1988, s 63; FA 1994, s 204* 9/12 × £40,000	30,000
Less transitional overlap relief period 1.1.97 to 5.4.97 95/365 × £40,000	10,411
	£19,589

This is subject to a Revenue direction on a deemed cessation period to 6 April 1998 under *FA 1994, 20 Sch 3(2)*, to compute profits under the old rules.

1994/95 preceding year basis, y/e 31.12.1993 *TA 1988, s 60(3)* original version	£20,000
1995/96 preceding year basis, y/e 31.12.1994 *TA 1988, s 60(3)* original version	£25,000
1996/97 preceding year basis, y/e 31.12.1995 *TA 1988, s 60(3)* original version	£30,000
1997/98 actual 6/12 × £40,000 *TA 1988, s 63(1)(a)* original version	£20,000
	£95,000

The Revenue have a further option to compute 1995/96 and 1996/97 on an actual fiscal year basis under *TA 1988, s 63(1)(b)* original version:

	£	£
1995/96 actual basis		
3/12 × £35,000, y/e 31.12.1996	8,750	
9/12 × £30,000, y/e 31.12.1995	22,500	
		31,250
1996/97 actual basis		
3/12 × £40,000 y/e 31.12.1997	10,000	
9/12 × £35,000 y/e 31.12.1996	26,250	
		36,250
		£67,500

Compared with £55,000 (£25,000 + £30,000) on normal old rule cessation basis, so Revenue option exercised:

	Old Basis	*New Basis*
Assessable	£	£
1995/96	31,250	25,000
1996/97	36,250	32,456
1997/98	20,000	19,589
	£87,500	£77,045

Revenue direction made to apply old basis, final period 1997/98 to deemed cessation £20,000 1995/96 and 1996/97 old basis applied. Deemed commencement—limited to UK source income from UK branch.

Commencement 1 October 1997, *TA 1988, s 61(1)*; *FA 1994, s 201*	£
1.10.97 to 31.12.97	6,000
1.1.98 to 5.4.98 95/365 × £20,000	5,205
	11,205
Plus assessable to cessation	20,000
	£31,205

(*e*) Year ended 31 December 1998, *TA 1988, s 60(3)(a); FA 1994, s 200*	£20,000

Limited to income arising in UK through UK branch.

The period from 1.1.98 to 5.4.98 is taxable both in 1997/98 and 1998/99 and is therefore an overlap period relievable under *TA 1988, s 63A; FA 1994, s 205*, resulting in overlap profits of £5,205 (95/365 × £20,000).

Example 16

Mr Agitov, who is not domiciled in the UK, became UK resident on 5 October 1998 by arriving here with the intention of staying for five years.

He is entitled to substantial rental income in the UK which amounts to £10,000 net in the year ended 5 April 1999 and £5,000 net in the year ended 5 April 1998, after loss relief for that year (see Chapter 4).

He is a partner in a firm managed and controlled in the UK which trades internationally and which made a loss in the year ended 31 December 1998 of which Mr Agitov's share was £16,000 and his share of transitional overlap relief was £5,000. His share of the loss for 1999 was anticipated at £12,000.

He is also the agent in Hong Kong of a US manufacturer which is run by a manager under a power of attorney from Mr Agitov, which made a profit of £10,000 in the year ended 31 January 1999. He had remitted £1,000 to the UK in December 1998 from this source.

Mr Agitov takes advantage of Extra Statutory Concession A11 and is deemed to have become resident on 5 October 1998.

His self-assessment for 1998/99 is:

	£	£
Schedule A		10,000
Partnership income, Schedule D, Case I—deemed cessation on 5 October 1998 *TA 1988, s 112(1B); FA 1995, s 117*		
Loss 9/12 × £16,000	(12,000)	
Transitional overlap relief	(5,000)	
Loss available for relief	(17,000)	NIL
Deemed commencement 6 October 1998 *TA 1988, s 61(1), FA 1994, s 201*		
Loss 3/12 × £16,000	(4,000)	
Loss 3/12 × £12,000	(3,000)	
Loss available for relief	(7,000)	NIL
Agency profits remitted—Schedule D, Case V (since 5 October 1998)		1,000
Total income		11,000
Less loss relief *TA 1988, s 380(1)(a), FA 1994, s 209(1)*		(11,000)
Assessable 1998/99		NIL
Schedule A income 1997/98		5,000
Loss relief available against Schedule A income 1997/98, *TA 1988, s 380(1)(b), FA 1994, s 209(1)* £17,000 − £11,000 = £6,000 limited to available income		(5,000)
		NIL
Terminal loss, year ended 5 October 1998 *TA 1988, s 388*		
1.1.98 to 5.10.98	17,000	
6.10.97 to 31.12.97	NIL	(loss relieved)
	17,000	
Less relieved in 1998/99 and 1997/98	16,000	
Available for carry forward under *TA 1988, s 385*	£1,000	
Loss in 1998/99 unused		£7,000

Available for carry back to 1995/96 *et seq*. under *TA 1988, s 381, FA 1994, s 209(2)* or carry forward under *TA 1988, s 385, FA 1994, s 209(4)(5)*

In 1999/2000 Mr Agitov could remit profits from Hong Kong earned up to 5 October 1998, the date of the deemed cessation, without incurring a UK tax charge as the source was deemed to have ceased on 5 October 1998.

Had ESC A11 not applied, Mr Agitov would have been deemed to have been UK resident throughout 1998/99 and his self-assessment would have been:

	£	£
Schedule A		10,000
Partnership income—commencement 6 April 1998		
Loss 9/12 × £16,000 to 31.12.98	12,000	
3/12 × £12,000 to 6.4.99	3,000	
	£15,000	
Remittance		1,000
		11,000
Less loss relief *TA 1988, s 380(1)(a), FA 1994, s 209(1)*		11,000
Assessable 1998/99		NIL
Loss relief available to carry back under *TA 1988, s 381; FA 1994, s 209(2)* to 1995/96 *et seq.*, £15,000 less relieved £11,000		4,000

or carry forward under *TA 1988, s 385* against future partnership profits.

Terminal loss relief under *TA 1988, s 388* for 1997/98 on deemed cessation

	£
5 April 1988	
Loss 3/12 × £16,000 to 31.12.98	4,000
9/12 × 31.12.97 relieved 1997/98	NIL
Transitional overlap relief *FA 1994, 20 Sch 2(4)*	5,000
	£9,000
Available 1997/98, limited to available income	£5,000
Carried back to 1996/97 and then 1995/96 or carry forward under *TA 1988, s 385* against future partnership profits	£4,000

Chapter 15

Settlements and Estates in the Course of Administration

Introduction

15.1 Self-assessment has not implemented any fundamental changes in the taxation of income and gains of settlements. Trustees are generally liable to income tax at the basic rate (or in the case of dividend income) at the lower rate, and at the rate applicable to trusts in the case of discretionary and 'accumulation and maintenance' settlements. They are also liable to CGT in respect of income and gains accruing to them. Beneficiaries in receipt of trust income are potentially liable to higher rate tax. As regards estate income, there has been a simplification to facilitate self-assessment. Personal representatives remain liable to basic rate tax on income and gains, and lower rate tax on dividends. But residuary beneficiaries are assessable on estate income in the year in which it is paid to them, rather than spread over the period of administration.

15.2 The management provisions under self-assessment for trustees and personal representatives are in line with those for individuals. They both have an obligation to notify the Revenue of taxability, to file returns, and they may self-assess. Personal representatives are also now given a specific reporting obligation to legatees.

Settlements

General tax position of trustees

15.3 So far as income tax is concerned, there are no express charging provisions applicable to settlement trustees, other than in the case of trustees for minors and incapacitated persons. But it is well established that trustees are generally assessable in respect of trust income; see for example *Reid's Trustees v IRC 1929 14 TC 512*. Their personal circumstances are not relevant to any question of personal reliefs or higher rate tax, these being linked to the total income of individuals. Accordingly trustees are subject to income tax at the basic rate on trust income, or in the case of shares in UK companies and other savings income at the lower rate. Moreover, income of 'accumulation and maintenance' or discretionary trusts is subject to the rate applicable to trusts, being the sum of the basic and the rate applicable to trusts, presently 34 per cent.

15.4 Settlement trustees are likewise chargeable to CGT on chargeable gains accruing to them from the disposal of trust assets. The rate of CGT depends on the circumstance of each trust, in particular whether a beneficiary has an interest in possession therein, or whether it is an 'accumulation and maintenance' or discretionary trust.

Management provisions applicable to trustees

15.5 Under self-assessment trustees will continue to have the obligation to notify the Revenue of chargeability and to file returns (see 16.6 and 16.11 below). They will also have the ability to self-assess (see 8.5). The general provisions regarding Revenue audit and collection of tax outlined in later chapters will also apply. Trustees will also have to issue form R185 certificates to beneficiaries, with details of income paid to the beneficiaries, and the tax paid or treated as paid.

15.6 Under *FA 1989, s 151*, income arising to trustees of a settlement may be assessed on and charged on and in the name of any one or more of the trustees. There are like provisions for CGT from 1996/97. However, an assessment under *TCGA 1992, s 80* on a trust ceasing to be resident in the UK will not be made on a former trustee who can show that there was no proposal that the trustees might cease to be UK resident at the time he resigned. [*FA 1995, s 114* substituting a new *TCGA 1992, s 65(1)(3)*].

15.7 The various provisions in *TMA 1970* referring to 'trustees' (for example the notification, reporting and self-assessing provisions) are amended with effect from 1996/97 to refer to 'relevant trustees'. These are defined in relation to income as persons who are trustees when the income arises, or who subsequently become trustees, and in relation to chargeable gains as the persons who are trustees in the year of assessment in which the chargeable gain arises, or who subsequently become trustees. [*FA 1995, s 103(1)–(4)*].

15.8 Moreover, new rules are introduced for the assessment and collection of tax on trust income and gains where there is more than one trustee. Anything done by, or in relation to, any one or more relevant trustees is treated as being done by, or to, all the relevant trustees. This means that any trustee will be able to make a return and self-assessment. He will then be treated as satisfying the tax obligations of the other trustees. The converse is that where a penalty is imposed for any error, failure or omission the amount may be recovered from any one or more of the trustees, albeit only once. [*FA 1995, s 103(5)* inserting a new *TMA 1970, s 107A*]. It is understood that where money to pay tax has been extracted from trust funds by a fraudulent trustee, and the trust fund has not benefited, the Revenue's normal practice is to recover tax, interest and penalties from that trustee. They would look to other trustees only if they had not taken appropriate action to recover the trust funds.

Trustees for minors and incapacitated persons

15.9 A person who is legally incapacitated may be assessed and charged to tax through his trustee or guardian. [*TMA 1970, s 72(1)*]. 'Incapacitated person' means an infant, person of unsound mind, lunatic, idiot or insane person. [*TMA 1970, s 118(1)*]. The powers contained in *TMA 1970, ss 7, 8* (see 16.5 and 16.11 below) relating to the notification of chargeability and the submission of personal tax returns are sufficiently wide to cover the case of persons who are in receipt of income which is not their own but in respect of which they are assessable.

Taxation of beneficiaries

15.10 While income of a trust in the first instance bears tax in the trustees' hands as outlined above, whether by deduction at source or direct assessment, it will in certain cases form part of the total income of the beneficiaries. Such cases include those where:

(i) a beneficiary has a vested interest in income, regardless of whether he has actually received it;

(ii) amounts in the nature of income are paid or applied to a beneficiary who is not entitled as of right to that income, for example, income payments out of discretionary trusts; and

(iii) other payments are made to a beneficiary which have the character of income in his hands, albeit that they are derived from capital (*Brodie's Trustees v IRC 1933 17 TC 432*).

Interest in possession trusts

15.11 Beneficiaries of interest in possession trusts fall within 15.10(i), being entitled to any income as it arises, with the source of the income generally being regarded as the property itself, rather than the trust fund: *Baker v Archer-Shee 1927 11 TC 749*. This contrasts with beneficiaries of discretionary trusts, where the source of income is the trust, and income payments from the trust are taxable under Schedule D, Case III. So far as interest in possession settlements are concerned, the precise status of the life tenant of the interest in possession trust is particularly relevant in relation to Schedule A income.

15.12 Whether it is the trustees or the life tenant who are to be treated as carrying on the Schedule A business can have different tax consequences in some cases. Thus the new Schedule A rules set out in Chapter 5 permit a pooling of income and expenses, so it is necessary to establish whether the income and expenses relating to a particular property fall within the life tenant's or the trustees' pool. The issue is also relevant to the carry forward of unrelieved losses from 1994/95 to 1995/96.

15.13 The application of the *Baker v Archer-Shee* principle would suggest that the Schedule A business should be treated as carried on by the life tenant. It seems that the Revenue accept this in cases where the land is held in a strict settlement within the *Settled Land Act 1925*, or where the trustees have delegated their powers of liaising and management etc to the beneficiary under the *Law of Property Act 1925, s 29(1)*. But otherwise it will normally be the trustees carrying on the business, support for this proposition being provided by *Fry v Shiely's Trustees 1914, s 6 TC 583* and *McDougall v Smith 1918 7 TC 134*.

15.14 The point also arises where the life tenant is also the settlor, in the context of *TA 1988, s 660C* and whether this section operates to prevent the set-off of Schedule D, Case VI income against personal Schedule A losses, or vice versa. It is understood that the Revenue's view is as follows. If it is a strict settlement or where there has been a delegation of liaising and management powers by the trustees, the settlor will be able to set his personal property losses against trust property profits and vice versa. Although the Schedule A profit from the trust will remain assessable under Schedule D, Case VI, the correct approach will be first of all to measure the amount of income so treated as part of the settlor's income in accordance with the rules relating to the particular type of income involved.

15.15 However, if the trustees are carrying on the Schedule A business, the life tenant cannot utilise trust losses against his personal Schedule A income (although neither can a non-settlor life tenant). Thus *s 660C(2)* is not in point since the subsection is only concerned with reliefs/deductions to which the settlor is entitled. If there are two separate businesses and the trust business makes a loss, that is a relief to which only the trustees, and not the settlor, are entitled.

Non-resident trustees or beneficiaries

15.16 The tax position of non-resident trustees and beneficiaries is considered in full at 14.115 *et seq*.

Reporting and self-assessing by beneficiaries

15.17 In all cases where a beneficiary is in receipt of taxable income that beneficiary, as well as the trustees, will have a reporting obligation under self-assessment. This should pose no problem where trust income is actually paid to the beneficiary on a timely basis, and where he has received form R185 from the trustees. But the position is rather more difficult in cases where income has arisen to which the beneficiary is entitled, but which he has not actually received, and indeed which he may not know about.

15.18 There may even be cases where the beneficiary's precise entitlement is unclear as a matter of law, for example in the case of a demerger where there is doubt whether the shares in the demerged company constitute income or capital in the trustees' hands. Likewise there may be cases of the kind described in 15.10(iii) above where the source of the payment is capital, but where case law may suggest that it nevertheless constitutes income in the beneficiary's hands.

15.19 It may be that a beneficiary will have to use estimates in those cases where he is unsure of the position, adopting the procedure outlined in 11.28 *et seq*. Moreover, in cases where he has received payments which are from a capital source, but which may have the quality of recurrence in his hands, or where it is uncertain whether a receipt in the trustees' hands is capital or income in, say, the case of a demerger, the beneficiary may perhaps avail himself of any post-transaction rulings provisions. But beneficiaries must be mindful of their possible exposure to surcharges, interest and penalties if they are in default.

Personal representatives

General position

15.20 On a person's death, his property vests in his personal representatives, whose responsibility is to administer the estate by getting in the property, discharging the deceased's debts, and distributing the residue to the persons entitled under the Will or intestacy. They are liable for any tax chargeable on the deceased, albeit to the extent of assets of the deceased, out of which they may recover any payments made. [*TMA 1970, s 74*]. The Revenue have confirmed that under self-assessment they will continue to issue a tax return before the end of the year to which it relates, to agree liabilities quickly and to give early written confirmation if they do not intend to enquire into the return, if requested to do so by the personal representatives or trustees of a deceased person. (See Inland Revenue Press Release of 4 April 1996, Appendix C).

15.21 Moreover, during the administration period, the income of the estate is at common law that of the personal representatives, in their representative capacity, rather than that of the beneficiaries. Accordingly, income other than that received under deduction of tax is in the first place assessable on them. Personal representatives are not entitled to any personal reliefs, but other statutory reliefs and deductions may be available, for example loss relief for trading losses. Under *FA 1989, s 151*, the assessment may be raised in the name of one or more of the personal representatives.

15.22 Personal representatives will also be liable to CGT in respect of chargeable gains accruing on disposals of assets (other than to legatees, where there is no chargeable gain and the personal representatives' acquisition is treated as if it had been the legatee's acquisition). [*TCGA 1992, s 62(4)*]. The CGT may be assessed and charged on and in the name of any one or more of the 'relevant personal representatives', being the personal representatives in the year of assessment in which the chargeable gains accrue and any subsequent personal representatives. [*FA 1995, s 114* substituting a new *TCGA 1992, s 65(1)(4)*].

Reporting and self-assessing by personal representatives

15.23 The notification and reporting obligations of individuals outlined in the following chapter extend to personal representatives, as 'persons chargeable to income tax and CGT' within *TMA 1970, ss 7, 8*. Accordingly they may self-assess. Personal representatives also fall within the scope of *TMA 1970, s 13* which enables the Revenue to require returns from a person in receipt of money or value, profits or gains, belonging to another. There are further specific reporting provisions relating to personal representatives contained in *TA 1988, s 700(4)* which enable an Inspector to require a personal representative to furnish him within a period of not less than 28 days with such particulars as he considers necessary for determining the income tax liability arising from estates in the course of administration.

15.24 Personal representatives will also have a reporting obligation to beneficiaries of the estate if a request in writing is put to them. In the case of beneficiaries with an absolute or limited interest in residue, or those who have received income in the exercise of a discretion, the personal representatives have to provide them with a written statement setting out the amounts paid or treated as paid as income for any year of assessment. The statement must also set out the amount of tax at the applicable rate which that income is deemed to have borne, distinguishing between tax at the basic rate and tax at the lower rate on dividends and savings income. The purpose of course is to ensure that the beneficiaries have full information to enable them to self-assess. [*FA 1995, 18 Sch 6* inserting a new *TA 1988, s 700(5)(6)*].

Position of legatees

15.25 During the course of administration of an estate, the income is in the first place assessable on the personal representatives, but the income will in due course be taken into account in determining the total income of the persons ultimately entitled to it. The relevant legislation is contained in *TA 1988, ss 695–702*, and distinguishes between those persons who have a 'limited interest' and those who have an 'absolute interest'. A limited interest is one where, if the administration of the estate had been completed and the residue had been ascertained, the legatee would be entitled to receive all or part of the income only and not capital. [*TA 1988, s 701(3)*]. An example would be a life interest. An absolute interest is one where in such circumstances the legatee would be entitled to both income and capital. [*TA 1988, s 701(2)*]. Legatees have the general obligation to report income and the right to self-assess.

The old rules

Limited interests

15.26 Although a legatee may not demand income or capital, as the case may be, until the administration of the estate is complete, it is usual for the personal representatives to make interim distributions. Under the old system a legatee with a limited interest was provisionally taxed on the grossed up equivalent of any payments made in a particular year of assessment during the administration period. On completion of the administration the payments were then re-allocated as though they had been spread evenly over the period of administration, grossed up at the basic or lower rate, as appropriate, for each year of assessment. There were provisions for consequential adjustments to the beneficiary's tax liabilities over the years in question, up or down.

Absolute interests

15.27 The position with legatees with absolute interests is more complicated because of their capital entitlement. Thus it cannot be assumed that all payments received are income. Indeed many payments during the administration period may well be capital in nature. Under the old system, which applies to cases where the administration was completed before 5 April 1995, the position was as follows. A legatee with an absolute interest was provisionally taxed as for legatees with limited interests, namely by reference to the grossed up equivalent of income distributions in a year of assessment. But on completion of the administration the readjustment was made by reallocating the income to the years in which it actually arose.

The new rules

15.28 Under self-assessment the former spreading rules for both limited and absolute interests have been much simplified. Essentially income from estates has been placed so far as is possible on a receipts basis. This facilitates self-assessment, and an early finality for each year of assessment. Moreover, it also gives rise to planning opportunities on the part of personal representatives. Thus by carefully structuring payments made to beneficiaries over a period of years they can maximise the utilisation of the lower rate bands. Conversely, if payments are deferred for a period of years, with a large payment made at the completion of the administration representing the income of several years, there can be a significant higher rate liability. There is no top slicing relief for this bunching effect.

Limited interests

15.29 Where the administration of the estate is still continuing on 6 April 1995, a person with a limited interest is still taxed on the grossed up equivalent of any actual payments made as income distributions. On completion of the administration, any amount which remains payable to a beneficiary is deemed to have been paid as income for the year of assessment in which the administration period ends. Where an interest ceased, for example on the death of a beneficiary before the end of the administration period, any final payment is deemed to be paid for the last year of assessment in which the limited interest existed, for example the year of the beneficiary's death. [Substituted *TA 1988, s 695(3); FA 1995, 18 Sch 2(1)*].

Example 1

Mr Kostin died on 5 October 1994 and left the residue of his estate to his widow for life and after her death to their children. The administration of the estate was completed on 5 January 1996.

Gross and net income of the residue and the tax liability of the personal representatives and payments to the widow, after the trustees' expenses chargeable to income, were as follows:

Income of residue

	Gross	*Tax*	*Net*	*Payments to Widow*
1994/95	£		£	£
Interest	1,000	25%	750	600
Dividends	1,000	20%	800	500
Net rents	2,000	25%	1,500	1,200
	4,000		3,050	2,300
1995/96				
Interest	800	25%	600	300
Dividends	500	20%	400	400
Net Rents	3,200	25%	2,400	1,500
	4,500		3,400	2,200
1996/97				
Final payment to widow				£400

As the administration was completed after 5 April 1995, it is not necessary to allocate the residuary income over the period of administration and the widow's taxable income is as follows:

	Gross	*Tax*	*Net*
1994/95	£		£
Dividends	625	20%	500
Taxed income	2,400	25%	1,800
	3,025		2,300
1995/96			
Dividends	500	20%	400
Taxed income (including final distribution)	2,933	25%	2,200
	3,433		2,600

Absolute interests

15.30 As with limited interests, where an estate is in administration on or after 6 April 1995 the system is put on a receipts basis as follows. Any payment made on or after that date is deemed to be income of the year of assessment in which it is actually paid, grossed up at the applicable rate. [Substituted *TA 1988, s 696(3)(4)*]. Where any payment brings the total of the payments above the cumulative income to which the beneficiary would be entitled on an arising basis the excess is to be excluded. This cumulative income is referred to as the 'aggregated income entitlement', and in the case of UK source income is to be ascertained after deducting income tax at the applicable rate for the year in which it arises. [*TA 1988* inserted *s 696(3A)(3B)*].

15.31 If on completion of the administration the total amount paid out during the course of the administration is less than the aggregate income entitlement for the year of assessment in which the administration is completed (i.e. less than the full amount of cumulated income has then been distributed) the balance is treated as paid immediately before the end of the administration period. [*TA 1988* substituted *s 696(5)*]. As with limited interests therefore, there is this bunching effect for the final 'balloon' income payment.

15.32 These provisions only apply to payments made on or after 6 April 1995. Payments made, or deemed to be made, prior to that date are taxable under the original provisions of *TA 1988, s 696(3)* i.e. as income for 1994/95 or any previous year. They are treated as paid in respect of the beneficiary's absolute interest in residue in that year (even if actually paid later) in calculating the payments made during the administration period under the amended rules. [*FA 1995, 18 Sch 3(3)(4)*].

15.33 For the purposes of determining the tax liability of a person with an absolute interest, the residuary income for any year of assessment is generally taken as the aggregate income of the estate of that year less any interest, annuity or annual payments charged on residue, and the personal representatives' management expenses of the estate properly chargeable to income, and less any specific entitlement of another person to a share of the income. [*TA 1988, s 697(1)*]. If these deductions exceed the income the deficit may be carried forward and treated as a deduction in the following year. [Inserted *TA 1988, s 697(1A)* enacting ESC A13]. [*FA 1995, Sch 18(4)*].

15.34 Moreover, where the net benefits received by the beneficiary are less than the aggregated residuary income, for example where debts are discovered at a late stage in the administration which are payable out of residue, the deficiency is deducted in the year of completion of the administration, and carried back to previous years if necessary. [Substituted *ICTA 1988, s 697(2)*]. This allocation to later years in priority to earlier years, rather than pro rata over the administration period as under the old rules, will reduce the number of years potentially subject to revision. The provisions in 15.33 relating to the computation of residuary income apply from 1995/96 onwards, and the provisions in this paragraph 15.34 relating to a deficiency in benefits apply to estates where the administration is completed on or after 6 April 1995.

Example 2

Mr Shvetsov died on 1 September 1994 and bequeathed the residue of his estate to his son, Andrei, absolutely. The administration was completed on 12 February 1996. The residuary income of the estate, the tax thereon and the payments in respect of Andrei's interest were as follows:

Income of residue

	Gross	*Tax*	*Net*	*Payments to Andrei*
1994/95	£		£	£
Interest	1,000	25%	750	600
Dividends	1,000	20%	800	500
Net Rents	2,000	25%	1,500	1,200
	4,000		3,050	2,300
1995/96				
Interest	800	25%	600	300
Dividends	500	20%	400	400
Net rents	3,200	25%	2,400	1,500
	4,500		3,400	2,200

February 1996
Assets transferred to Andrei £300,000

The payments during the administration period are treated as Andrei's income as follows:

Payment 1994/95		*Gross*	*Tax*	*Net*
		£		£
1994/95				
500	Dividends	625	20%	500
1,800	Other income	2,400	25%	1,800
2,300		3,025		2,300
1995/96				
400	Dividends	375	20%	300
1,800	Other income	600	25%	450
2,200		4,000		3,050

Payment 1995/96		*Gross*	*Tax*	*Net*
		£		£
	Dividends	125	20%	100
	Other income (balance not allocated to 1994/95)	1,800	25%	1,350
		1,925		1,450
£300,000	Apportionment of final distribution			
	Dividends	375		300
	Other income	2,200		1,650
		4,500		3,400

Successive interests in residue

15.35 Provisions are introduced to cover the case of successive interests, such as those which arise as the result of the assignment or disclaimer of an interest, but not those arising as the result of a death of a beneficiary. In the case of limited interests, successive interests are deemed the single interest of the beneficiary to whom the income is paid unless another beneficiary has or has had an interest deemed to be included within the deemed single interest and is entitled to receive the payment. Where an absolute interest follows a limited interest, that absolute interest is deemed always to have existed, and as if the payment to the limited interest beneficiary had been paid to the absolute interest beneficiary. Hence each beneficiary is taxed on what he receives. [Substituted *TA 1988, s 698(1A)(1B)*].

15.36 Where there are successive absolute interests, the change in beneficiary is ignored for the purposes of calculating the aggregated income entitlement in 15.34 above. The effect is that the first residuary legatee is assessed on the grossed up equivalent of the income actually paid to him, and any adjustment required on the completion of the administration is treated as the income of the subsequent beneficiary. So each beneficiary is again taxed on what he actually receives. [*FA 1995, 18 Sch 5(2)*].

Chapter 16

Notices and Returns, Electronic Lodgement

Introduction

16.1 The machinery for the administration and collection of tax is contained in *TMA 1970*, which consolidated the provisions in earlier legislation. This book is concerned to explain the changes made under self-assessment, rather than to provide a detailed explanation of the entire system. For this readers are referred to Tolley's *Taxes Management Provisions*. But a brief overview may be helpful prior to a consideration of the changes made by *FA 1994*, *FA 1995* and *FA 1996*.

16.2 Taxes are under the care and management of the Commissioners of Inland Revenue. [*TMA 1970, s 1(1)*]. Referred to as 'the Board', they consist of a Chairman, two Deputy Chairmen and presently four other senior civil servants. The representative of the Revenue who generally deals with the taxpayer or his agent is the local district inspector, officially 'HM Inspector of Taxes' and his staff. Their principal functions under the previous system were to examine tax returns and the accounts of businesses, compute the profits for tax purposes, and then raise and subsequently agree the tax assessments with the taxpayer or his agent. Tax is collected by a separate Collector of Taxes, also a Revenue Official.

16.3 Later Chapters in this book look more closely at the rules relating to the assessment of tax, particularly the new system of self-assessment, the rights of appeal which remain open to taxpayers, the provisions for payment of tax, and the sanctions of the Revenue against non-compliance. This Chapter examines the machinery for information gathering in the light of *FA 1994*, *FA 1995* and *FA 1996*.

16.4 In this regard there are a series of existing provisions in *TMA 1970* which enable Inspectors to obtain information about taxpayers, notably the right of an Inspector to require the taxpayer to make a return of his income, profits and gains. The previous system relating to information collection and the requirement of taxpayers to submit tax returns is substantially retained under self-assessment. But a number of changes have been made to reflect the general principle of self-assessment. The new legislation generally adopts the neutral expression 'Officer of the Board', in lieu of 'Inspector of Taxes'.

Notification of liability to income tax and CGT

16.5 The provisions regarding notification of chargeability to tax are contained in *TMA 1970, s 7*. Their purpose is to ensure that every person who is chargeable to income tax or CGT is duly 'logged in' with the Revenue, so that he can be sent a tax return. These provisions are slightly amended as from 1995/96 to reflect the new system. [*FA 1994, 19 Sch 1(2)*]. They came into force earlier than the other self-assessment provisions to ensure that the Revenue were informed of all taxpayers likely to be affected by the new rules.

16.6 Every person who is chargeable to income tax or capital gains tax, and has not received a tax return, must notify the Revenue within six months of the end of the year of assessment, i.e. by 5 October, commencing 5 October 1996. [*TMA 1970, s 7(1) (2)*]. This compares with twelve months under the previous system, and is the principal change. These notification provisions specifically extend to 'relevant trustees' of a settlement. In relation to income tax these are defined as persons who are trustees when the income arises, and any persons who subsequently become trustees. In relation to chargeable gains they are the persons who are trustees in the year of assessment in which chargeable gains accrue and any persons who subsequently become trustees. [*FA 1995, s 103;* substituted *TMA 1970, s 7(9)*].

16.7 However there is no reporting obligation if the person has no chargeable gains and all his income falls into one or more of the following categories:

(*a*) it is chargeable under Schedule E and has been taxed or taken into account under PAYE (including benefits in kind);

(*b*) it has already been assessed or taken into account in computing his tax liability; or

(*c*) basic or lower rate income tax has been deducted (or treated as deducted) or the income consists of dividends from UK resident companies, and the person is not liable to higher rate tax.

[*TMA 1970, s 7(3)–(7)*].

16.8 If a person fails to comply with his reporting obligation, he is liable to a penalty of up to the tax which is due and unpaid by the following 31 January [*substituted TMA, s 7(8)*] and see 22.27 below, which is the same penalty as at present. It is to be noted that there is no penalty provided that tax is paid on time even if a taxpayer has been dilatory in notifying the Revenue as to his liability. Otherwise there is a significant potential cost for those who are behind in notifying the Revenue.

Example 1

Mr Blank only notified the Revenue in January 2000 that he had taxable income in 1998/99. He made a payment in January 2000 of £10,000 but the actual tax liability was £15,000. The balance of £5,000 was only paid in March 2000 after the return had been sent to him and the correct amount of tax calculated. He is potentially liable for a penalty of up to £5,000.

16.9 The reason given by the Revenue for the reduction in the notification period from twelve months to six months was that otherwise notification at the end of the permitted period could lead to returns being issued for two years, followed by estimated assessments if the returns were not submitted properly. This was an example of the wasteful procedures that self-assessment should avoid. Moreover, there could be an advantage in delaying notification to the last possible moment. For example, a twelve-month period would mean that notification for chargeability in 1997/98 would only have to be made by April 1999. The return for 1997/98 would then need to be submitted and the tax paid within three months (see 21.14 below) which would be July 1999 at the earliest. This would be at least six months after the normal final payment date of 31 January 1999, and would be unfair on those who notified the Revenue earlier. Nevertheless the six-month period is quite short and can be a trap for those uninitiated in the tax system, notably non-resident individuals taking up UK residence, or for example taxpayers within PAYE who find themselves in receipt of additional non-Schedule E income.

Procedure for giving notices

16.10 The procedure for making claims under self-assessment was modified by amendments to *TMA 1970, s 42* (see Chapter 17) and for claims not included in returns by *TMA 1970, 1A Sch*. However, these provisions also applied to notices, in error, and *FA 1996, s 130* restores the status quo ante in respect of notices which taxpayers are required to give to the Revenue. This means that notices will not have to be included in returns but may be given to the Revenue on an ad hoc basis within the appropriate time limit, for example the notice of an accounting change to have effect for tax purposes under *TA 1988, s 62A(3)*. Corresponding changes have been made for notices required to be made by partnerships.

Tax returns of individuals and trustees

16.11 The provisions in *TMA 1970, ss 8, 8A*, relating to the submission of tax returns by individuals and relevant trustees (see 16.6) of a settlement, are amended with effect from 1996/97 by *FA 1994, s 178* and *FA 1996, s 121* to reflect the principle of self-assessment, although the information requirements are essentially the same. The returns (and any self-assessments) are to reflect the amount payable by way of income tax after (*a*) taking into account reliefs, allowances or repayments of tax, (*b*) giving credit for tax deducted at source (or treated as so deducted or paid such as deductions under the sub-contractors provisions in *TA 1988, ss 559–567* inclusive) and any tax credit for ACT on a company distribution. Appropriate information as regards such reliefs, allowances and tax deductions is to be included. [*TMA 1970, ss 8(1)(1A)(5), 8A(1)(1A)(5)*].

16.12 Where a tax return is sent by the Revenue to an individual or trustee, this must be completed and sent back to the Revenue together with any accounts, statements and documents as may reasonably be required. [*TMA 1970, ss 8(1), 8 A(1)*]. The requirement for 'documents' is a new one, and may perhaps be linked with the new requirement to keep records and the Revenue's enquiry powers (see Chapter 19). The reporting obligations are also applicable to personal representatives (see 15.23).

Filing deadline – self-assessment

16.13 The general rule under the new provisions is that the return has to be filed by 31 January following the end of the year of assessment. [*TMA 1970, ss (1A)(a), 8A(1A)(a)*]. But this deadline only applies to taxpayers who self-assess. In their case the return must also include the self-assessment (see 18.5). [*TMA 1970, s 9(1); FA 1994, s 179*]. Moreover, where the tax return is only sent to the taxpayer after 31 October following the end of the year of assessment, the time limit for filing (and self-assessment) is three months from the issue of the return. [*TMA 1970, ss 8(1A)(b), 8A(1A)(6)*]. There are penalties for late filing (see 22.22). It is understood that there will be a Revenue practice statement dealing with these issues, and that there may be a 14-day period of grace before a penalty is imposed.

Example 2

Mr Green is sent a tax return on 1 July 1998 in respect of 1997/98. Assuming he wishes to self-assess the deadline for filing is 31 January 1999. However, if the return had been issued on 1 December 1998, the deadline for filing would be 28 February 1999.

Filing deadline – Revenue assessment

16.14 Where a taxpayer does not want to self-assess, but prefers to leave it to the Revenue, generally the return has to be sent back to the Revenue by 30 September following the end of the year of assessment.

[*TMA 1970, s 9(2)*]. This is earlier than the previous filing date of 31 October, and the date has been brought forward to assist the Revenue in calculating the person's tax liability. In the consultation process the Revenue indicated that since the annual coding exercise was concentrated in October, November and December returns would be needed by the end of September if the information was to be taken into account in the coding.

16.15 However, if the return is only sent to the taxpayer after 31 July he is still permitted to require the Revenue to make the assessment if he sends back the return within two months.

Example 3

Mr White is sent a tax return on 1 July 1999 in respect of 1998/99. If he does not wish to self-assess the return must be filed by 30 September 1999. If the return is only sent to him on 1 September 1999 he must send the return back to the Revenue by 31 October 1999 for them to make the assessment.

16.16 Where the taxpayer is a partner in a profession, trade or business, the return is to include his share of any income or loss as reported in the partnership statement referred to in 12.26 and made under *TMA 1970, s 12AB; FA 1994, s 185*. [*TMA 1970, s 8(1B)(1C); FA 1994, s 178(1)*].

Form of return

16.17 The tax return will be substantially amended, reflecting the move to the current year basis and self-assessment. There has been an extensive consultation process regarding the form of the return, to assist the Revenue in the final design. There is to be a relatively short summary form, with accompanying modules to contain the details of particular sources of income. There will also be an electronic lodgement service, particulars of which are set out in 16.65 *et seq*.

16.18 The form of self-assessment return has developed over the years since self-assessment was first promulgated but the basic concept of a core return plus supplementary pages (originally known as schedules) remains. The latest drafts at the time of writing consist of an eight page core return plus additional pages known as employment pages, share option pages, self-employment (sole trader) pages, partner pages, UK land and property pages, foreign income and gains and tax credit relief pages, trusts, settlements and estates pages, capital gains pages and non-residents and non-domicile pages.

Core return

16.19 The core of the return makes it clear that the return should reach the Revenue by 30 September following the end of the tax year if the taxpayer wants the Revenue to calculate the tax due or to include any tax owed up to £1,000 in the following year's tax code, or 31 January following the end of the fiscal year if the taxpayer is prepared to calculate the tax himself. The core return is coded SA 100 and begins with a checklist to make sure the taxpayer has any supplementary pages necessary for the completion of the return. The supplementary pages have to be completed before the core return can be completed. It is envisaged that taxpayers will be sent the appropriate supplementary papers relevant to their known income and that there will be extended returns containing, for example, core return plus employment pages, core return plus self-employment pages and probably other combinations to cover the most common cases but it will always be the taxpayer's responsibility to request such additional pages as may be required.

16.20 The return then requests particulars of interest and dividends, pension retirement annuity or social security benefits, sundry income such as alimony, gains on life insurance policies etc., other income such as casual earnings, post-cessation receipts, accrued income etc. This is followed by claims for pension contributions, loan interest, alimony, venture capital or enterprise investment scheme investments, charitable covenants and gift aid payments, post-cessation expenses etc. Page six deals with personal allowances including blind person's allowance, additional personal allowance, widow's bereavement allowance etc. The taxpayer is then asked whether he wishes to calculate his own tax in which case he is referred to the ten page tax calculation guide consisting of a four page tax calculation working sheet and guidance on filling up the boxes. The return includes a claim for repayment of overpaid tax and asks for personal details such as a daytime telephone number, date of birth and marital status. Under self-assessment both the return of income and the claim for allowances relate to the same year and there is therefore a section dealing with anticipated changes in the coming year. There is a white space for additional information where the taxpayer is expected to indicate estimates or provisional figures, claims relating to different years etc.

Return guides and help sheets

16.21 In addition to the core return and tax calculation guide (SA 151) the taxpayer receives a tax return guide covering the core income. It seems that where the taxpayer receives a composite return consisting of the core return plus supplementary pages he would also receive a tax return guide containing notes on the completion of the supplementary pages.

16.22 As well as the guide for each set of supplementary pages the Revenue intend to publish help sheets in connection with the core return covering topics such as calculating age-related allowances (2 pages) or widow's independent pensions (1 page) relief for loans not in MIRAS (2 pages), pension payments (8 pages) as well as various aspects of income such as vouchers, credit cards and tokens (2 pages), employees' living accommodation (3 pages), car benefits and car fuel benefits (4 pages), motor mileage and car allowances (2 pages), lump sum and compensation payments (2 pages), foreign earnings deduction (2 pages), capital allowances and balancing charges (8 pages), exemptions and extra statutory concessions for employees (4 pages), P45s, P60s, payslips and coding notices (2 pages), mobile telephones (1 page), assets provided for private use (2 pages), payments in kind (1 page), shares as benefits (2 pages), shares acquired, post acquisition charges (2 pages), more than one business (2 pages), new businesses (6 pages), basis period (3 pages), rent a room (3 pages), farmers (3 pages), turnover allowable expenses and taxable profit or loss (3 pages), capital allowances and balancing charges (2 pages), losses (2 pages), cessation (2 pages), standard accounts information (7 pages), transitional rules for 1996/97 (4 pages), capital gains tax rebasing (8 pages), husband and wife divorce and separation under capital gains tax (2 pages), death, personal representatives and legatees (8 pages), private residence relief (4 pages), shares and capital gains tax (4 pages), share reorganisations and company takeovers and capital gains tax (4 pages) income tax, losses on new shares in unlisted trading companies (2 pages), employees' share schemes and capital gains tax (4 pages) partnerships and capital gains tax (4 pages), retirement relief (6 pages), business asset roll-over relief (3 pages), reinvestment relief (4 pages), land and leases and capital gains tax (4 pages), chattels (2 pages), trusts and capital gains (4 pages), gifts and hold-over relief (4 pages), debts and capital gains tax (6 pages), trusts and settlements, income treated as the settlor's (4 pages), restriction of tax credit relief where overlap relief allowed, capital allowances and balancing charges, land and property in the UK and agricultural land and land managed as one estate. These help sheets supplement the Revenue guides for Inland Revenue officers and tax practitioners SAT 1, 'The new current year basis of assessment', SAT 2, 'Self Assessment: The legal framework' and SAT 3, 'Self Assessment: What it will Mean for Employers'. The amount of guidance is indeed formidable, although the extent to which it will be comprehensible is perhaps open to doubt.

Employment income

16.23 The employment income pages (2 pages per employment) require details of the employer, income from employment, benefits and expenses, lump sum and compensation payments, expenses claimed for an earnings deduction and foreign tax not claimed as a credit. There are 8 pages of notes on completing the employment income pages.

16.24 The introduction of self-assessment requires that the employee be given a copy of his form P11D (or P9D) being a return of expenses, payments and benefits not covered by a dispensation. This information is needed to complete the employment supplementary pages of the employee's tax return.

16.25 The new P11D requires details of the employer and employee, assets transferred to the employee, payments made on his behalf, vouchers and credit card payments, accommodation provided, mileage allowance, particulars of cars and car fuel, interest free and low interest loans, mobile telephones, private medical treatment or insurance, qualifying vocational expenses, services supplied, assets placed at the employee's disposal, share-related benefits, other items such as subscriptions and professional fees and payments made to or on behalf of the employee. There are separate working sheets for living accommodation, car benefit and car fuel benefits, vans available for private use, relocation expenses payments and benefits, interest free and low interest loans, car and mileage allowances and the P9D for employees paid at a rate of less than £8,500 per annum.

16.26 The share schemes and share related benefits pages (SA 102) (2 pages), request details of share options under approved savings-related share option schemes, approved discretionary share option schemes, other share options and shares acquired at undervalue. These pages are accompanied by 5 pages of notes.

Self-employment income

16.27 The self-employment income schedule requires 1 schedule for each business and consists of 4 pages (SA 103). This requires details of the name and address and description of the business, the accounting date, abridged particulars where the annual turnover is below £15,000 and standard accounts information. The standard accounts information particulars are a bone of contention between the Revenue and taxpayers' representatives on the Self-Assessment Consultative Committee as the Revenue are convinced that this information is essential for their computer assisted risk assessment in helping to determine which taxpayers' affairs will be subject to formal enquiry. The taxpayers' representatives, however, do not consider that the allocation of income and expenses under the headings required by the standard accounts information are appropriate to more than a minority of businesses and any computerised analysis of such information is likely to be a very unreliable method of risk assessment. They also object to the increased work involved in reanalysing the commercial accounts to fit with the standard accounts information headings. They also consider that the requirement to summarise the balance sheet under standard accounts information headings only where a balance sheet is available to be contrary to the taxpayer's charter as well as giving rise to difficulties as to precisely what constitutes a balance sheet as opposed to spreadsheet figures.

Standard Accounts Information

16.28 The standardised accounts information required is set out in Appendix G. The help sheet entitled 'Information from your Accounts' dealing with the standard accounts information is essential reading to supplement the 10 pages of SA 103 notes if the taxpayer is to have any hope of completing the standard accounts information in the form required by the Revenue.

Partnership income

16.29 SA 104 requires income from a partnership and in its unabridged form requires partnership details including the partnership reference number, trade or profession, basis period, losses, class 4 national insurance, UK savings income, income from foreign savings and dividends, other untaxed UK income, other untaxed foreign income, income from offshore funds, income from UK land and property, furnished lettings, overlap relief, taxed income for the fiscal year, tax credits for the fiscal year. This is accompanied by 8 pages of notes on income from partnerships. There is an abridged partnership return and income from partnership form which will apply to the majority of partners.

Income from land

16.30 SA 105 requires income from land and property in the UK on 2 pages and includes particulars from rent-a-room claims, furnished holiday lettings, property business, income and expenditure and is accompanied by 8 pages of notes.

Foreign income

16.31 Foreign income and gains and tax credit relief extends to 4 pages (SA 106) covering foreign income from dividends, foreign income from interest, pensions, social security benefits and property, other income and foreign tax credits and income from property abroad which requires a separate sheet for each property. The notes for foreign income extend to 19 pages.

Trust income

16.32 SA 107 requests income from trusts, settlements and the estates of deceased persons and is a single page form with a mere 2 pages of notes.

Chargeable gains

16.33 The capital gains form (SA 108) requests details of chargeable gains and allowable losses and includes a permanent record of allowable losses and sheets as required for the various assets covered. As is to be expected, for a complex area such as capital gains tax 20 pages of notes are required to explain the form.

Residence and domicile

16.34 SA 109 covers non-residence and non-domicile in 3 pages, requesting reasons for the claimant to be not resident, not ordinarily resident, or not domiciled and whether the claim is for split year treatment or under a double taxation agreement. This is covered by some 15 pages of notes.

Special cases

16.35 Special forms are available for income and expenses of ministers of religion (SA 101(M)) and Lloyd's Underwriters (SA 103(L)). In each case the supplementary pages are explained by 8 and 13 pages of notes respectively.

It must be emphasised that the description of the tax returns supplementary pages, notes and help sheets are all subject to revision for the final version which will be issued in April 1997.

Tax returns of companies

16.36 The obligation of a company to complete a tax return is contained in *TMA 1970, s 11* as amended by *FA 1994, s 181*, which has already been amended under Pay and File for accounting periods ending after 30 September 1993. The return may call for such information, accounts and reports relevant to the application of the *Corporation Tax Acts* to the company as are stipulated in the notice. [*TMA 1970, s 11(1A)*]. Although it is intended that the self-assessment regime will extend to companies in the relatively near future, it is unlikely that major changes to the existing pay and file returns will be required for self-assessment when it is introduced following the appointed day under *FA 1994, s 199(3)*. The Corporation Tax (pay and file) return form (CT 200 1996) has been revised to take account of the new provisions relating to the taxation of profits and losses on loan relationships, and the amendments made to the taxation of foreign exchange profits and losses on certain financial instruments introduced by *FA 1996*. The new form CT 200 (1996) is expected to be issued automatically to companies from September 1996. The previous version of the return may continue to be used by companies not involved in such transactions, and by any company for accounting periods ending on or before 31 March 1996.

16.37 There is an addition to *TMA 1970, s 11* of new *subsections 2A* and *2B* which apply to a company carrying on a profession, trade or business in partnership with another person or persons. The company must include in the return its share of any income, loss or charge for the period concerned as shown in the partnership statement prepared by the partnership. This reflects the general changes relating to partnerships and reporting, discussed next.

Tax returns of partnerships

16.38 The provisions regarding partnership tax returns are presently contained in *TMA 1970, s 9*. For 1996/97 and subsequent years these provisions are replaced by a new *TMA 1970, s 12AA* by *FA 1994, s 184*, which reflects the significant changes in partnership taxation set out in Chapter 12, in particular the changes from a joint partnership assessment to a separate assessment for each partner. The changes and information requirements in the legislation are quite extensive. The legislation, however, really only provides a framework, which the Revenue have indicated will be expanded by practice procedures in due course.

16.39 Where a profession, trade or business is carried on by two or more persons in partnership, a Revenue Officer will be empowered to serve a notice either on the partners as a body [*TMA 1970, s 12AA(2)*] or on a particular partner [*TMA 1970, s 12AA(3)*] requiring a return to be made. The partnership return (and partnership statement; see Chapter 12) is to reflect the amount payable by way of income tax after claims, reliefs, allowances and deductions as for individuals and trustees. In the case of a notice on the partners as a body this may be given to such person 'as is identified in accordance with rules given with the notice'. These provisions are amended by *FA 1996, s 123* to provide for a successor to the partner so identified. Where the partner responsible for dealing with tax matters ceases to be available to do so, a successor may be nominated by a majority of the partners and if they fail to do so the Revenue may nominate a successor partner. To be eligible as a successor partner, the partner must have been a partner at any time during the period to which the return was made or is required, or a personal representative of such a partner. A nomination of a successor cannot be retrospective. The selected person must deliver the return to the Revenue, together with such accounts, statements and documents, relating to the information contained in the return as are required. [*TMA 1970, s 12AA(1)–(3)*].

16.40 It can be noted that the Revenue will not need to nominate a partner if the partnership return is not addressed to a particular partner. In practice, the Revenue will presumably continue to send partnership returns and statements to the precedent acting partner, until notified otherwise. Although there is reference to the partner to whom the notice is delivered being no longer available, there is no definition of what is meant by this term and it appears that the Revenue will accept that any relevant partner may be appointed a successor partner on the grounds that the previous incumbent has either ceased to be a partner or has ceased to be authorised to act as the relevant partner for completing partnership returns and statements.

16.41 Because the partnership return and statement will include details of taxed income by reference to the fiscal year and other income by reference to the accounting year ending in the fiscal year, the legislation required amendment to cater for this point. References to the person required to complete the partnership tax return and statement are amended to include his successor. The new definition of successor is inserted into the interpretation provisions in *TMA 1970, s 118*.

16.42 The notice may require different information, accounts and statements for different periods, or in relation to different descriptions of sources of income. [*TMA 1970, s 12AA(8)*]. Hence all income (not just trading income) is covered. Moreover, the provisions reflect the fact that the partnership period of account may not coincide with the normal basis period for a particular class of income. The return may also require different information, accounts and statements in relation to different descriptions of partnerships. [*TMA 1970, s 12AA(9)*]. The return must also include a 'partnership statement', as explained in 16.47 below.

16.43 If there have been any disposals of partnership property in the period, the return is to contain the details that would be required for a capital gains tax computation if the partnership were chargeable. Details of all acquisitions of partnership property are also to be given. [*TMA 1970, s 12AA(7)*]. However, the Revenue have intimated that information about a reallocation of property within the firm would not fall within this subsection.

16.44 The return is to include a declaration of the names, residence (which, in the case of a company means its registered office and in the case of individuals is to be their address) and tax references of anyone who has been a partner in any part of the period to which the return relates. The purpose of requiring this information is that:

(*a*) an automatic cross check of arithmetic can be made to see that individual partner's returns are consistent with the partnership return;

(*b*) any formal notices relevant to the partnership, can if necessary, be issued to individual partners if the notice is relevant to their personal tax liability; and

(*c*) when final figures are agreed at the end of an audit, notice of conclusion of the review and amended computations of individual liability to tax can be issued automatically to all partners.

The person making the return also has to make a declaration to the best of his knowledge that it is correct and complete. [*TMA 1970, s 12AA(6)*].

16.45 Where at least one of the partners is an individual, the filing date for the return (as specified in the notice) is to be no later than 31 January following the end of the year of assessment, or if notice is served on the partners after 31 October no later than three months from the date of issue of the return. [*TMA 1970, s 12AA(4)*]. Where at least one of the partners is a company, the filing date is no later than one year after the period in respect of which the return is issued, except that if the notice is served more than nine months after the end of that period the filing date is no later than three months from the issue of the return. [*TMA 1970,* *s 12AA(5)*]. In the event that the partnership consists of at least one individual and one company the filing date is the latest of the above dates.

16.46 It is to be noted that the requirement to submit a return extends to a 'business' carried on in partnership. This is wider than the current requirements which do not extend to a business which is not a trade. It seems that this is aimed at joint commercial activities falling short of a trade. The Revenue have intimated that not every form of joint ownership will necessarily constitute a business, and that they have not sought to prejudge the issue. Rather they are content to let joint owners file as partners in a business should they wish (see 7.11).

Partnership statement

16.47 As part of the mechanism for self-assessment, a partnership return delivered to the Revenue under the above provisions must now include what is described as a 'partnership statement'. This is a statement of:

(i) the income or loss from each source which has accrued to or has been sustained by the partnership for each period of account ending in the period covered by the tax return, taking into account any relief or allowance for which a claim under *TMA 1970, s 42(7)* has been included in the return (see Chapter 17 *et seq.*);

(ii) the income tax deducted, or treated as deducted, from any partnership income, or treated as paid on such income for the period;

(iii) each tax credit accruing to the partnership for the period; and

(iv) any charges on income for the period.

The statement must also set out the share of each partner in such income, loss, tax credit or charge so that he can self-assess [substituted *TMA 1970, s 12AB(1); FA 1995, s 104*]. In relation to changes in accounting date it is understood that the requirements for a valid change in *TA 1988, s 62A; FA 1994, s 203* apply on the level of the partnership, and not the individual partner; see 2.25 above.

Partnership return

16.48 The full partnership return SA 800 extends to some 13 pages including the partnership statement. There is an abridged 8 page return and statement which applies where the only income for the return period was trading or professional income or taxed interest. The full return which is accompanied by a 30 page partnership return guide requires supplementary pages for foreign income, income from land and property in the UK, capital gains and an additional return if there is a corporate or non-resident partner as the partnership's taxable income will be calculated separately, in such cases, for the purposes of corporation tax for the corporate partner and UK income tax for the non-resident partner. Apart from these points the partnership return is not unlike the self-employed sole trader's supplementary sheets in that it requires details of the business, standard accounts information under the same headings as the sole trader (unless the turnover is below £15,000 or above £15,000,000). It also requires details of savings, investments and other income for the accounting period ending in the fiscal year and taxed income for the fiscal year as well as details of other partnership income and allocates the income by source among the partners in the partnership statement. A partnership of more than 3 partners will require additional partnership statement sheets for this purpose. The particulars of foreign income from a partnership extend to 3 pages with 7 pages of notes. Partnership income from land and property in the UK requires 2 supplementary pages accompanied by 8 pages of notes and the partnership capital gains particulars extend to 2 pages with 4 pages of notes.

Trustees and personal representatives

16.49 The tax return for trustees and personal representatives (SA 900) extends to 6 pages with supplementary pages for self-employment by a trustee as sole trader, partnership income, income from land and property in the UK, foreign income and gains and tax credit relief, capital gains, non-residence, details of trustees and personal representatives, capital transactions, deductions, discretionary payments, computation of tax pool and charges and reliefs. As usual the supplementary pages must be completed first and the return requires details of the total income less reliefs, double taxation relief, capital gains liability, income from UK banks and building societies, dividends from UK companies, calculation of tax, overpayments and repayment claims and details of the trustees and personal representatives. A 26 page tax return guide is available to assist the completion of the return and there are notes to cover the various supplementary pages, some of which have not yet been revealed, even in draft form.

Return trials

16.50 The clarity and ease of completion of tax returns under self-assessment is likely to be a key to the success of the whole project. The Revenue have consulted extensively on the form of the return and have had dummy runs at Leicester for 1994/95 and 1995/96 and London Provincial 9 in Southampton for 1995/96. Only time will tell whether the British public will be prepared to plough through the voluminous paperwork needed to complete their own returns or whether they will seek professional advice or bring the whole system grinding to a halt through the sheer complexity of the UK tax system.

Estimates in Accounts

16.51 In *Dunk v Havant Commissioners (1976) STC 460* the taxpayer appealed against the award of penalties for the non-submission of tax returns. The taxpayer argued that under *TMA 1970, s 8* he was required to make a return which to the best of his knowledge, was correct and complete. The taxpayer could not afford professional help and had lost certain documents and therefore argued that if he were to make a return it could not be correct and complete and therefore he would be liable for penalties for an incorrect return.

16.52 This did not impress Goulding J, who stated:

> 'what the taxpayer has to declare is that the return is to the best of his knowledge, correct and complete. If . . . a taxpayer finds particular circumstances that make the best of his knowledge more than usually unreliable it is open to him to put against his figure for a particular item of income some such words as "estimated, see accompanying memorandum" or something of that kind and explain the circumstances. If he has done his best and of course he is under a duty to use all proper sources of knowledge he will not in my view be guilty of making a false statement providing, as I say, he puts in a genuine estimate and if necessary explains that it is not very reliable'.

On the basis of this decision the Revenue suggested that where records have been lost or destroyed or there are insufficient records or information to reach a reliable judgment on the apportionment of an expense, estimates to the best of the taxpayer's knowledge and belief would be accepted, provided that the circumstances were explained to the Revenue.

16.53 However, most business accounts contain estimates of some kind or another and it is not necessary to inform the Revenue that the accounts include such estimates provided that they are reasonably reliable estimates.

16.54 Such estimates fall into various categories such as recurrent payments where details of a particular payment such as a quarter's electricity charge is missing and has been estimated with a reasonable degree of accuracy. Secondly there may be cash payments where detailed records have not been kept such as the purchase of trade journals, taxi fares or tips. Thirdly the private proportion of business expenses with a private element are usually estimated on the basis of a roughly calculated apportionment based on estimated mileage, number of available rooms in a house partly used for business purposes, the estimated private usage of telephone equipment etc. Finally there may be unidentified receipts which are assumed to be business receipts in the absence of evidence to the contrary and such working assumption is acceptable to the Revenue without specific notification.

16.55 Revenue advice on record keeping is referred to below and the Revenue distinguish, quite properly, between records which are less than perfect but which enable accounts to be prepared with a reasonable degree of accuracy and records that are wholly inadequate such that the figures are little better than guesses, in which case the Revenue should be informed of the reason for the inadequacy and the steps being taken to prevent its recurrence.

Provisional estimates

16.56 In certain cases information to prepare a complete and proper return is not available at the time by which the return has to be delivered, but the information is expected to become available in due course. This might include for example, dividends declared by overseas companies, distributions from foreign trusts or income from overseas estates in the course of administration. In such cases it is perfectly proper for the taxpayer to indicate the source of income and a provisional estimate of the likely income expected to arise. This figure will be used for self-assessment purposes and the taxpayer will not be liable for penalties for an incorrect return provided that the reason for the provisional figure is explained and the correct figure is notified to the Revenue as soon as it becomes available. At this point an additional assessment or repayment will be made together with an interest adjustment as appropriate.

Valuations

16.57 A third and quite distinct area requiring judgement in the preparation of figures used in a tax return relates to a valuation which will often be required for capital gains tax computations. Valuation of land and shares in unquoted companies is an art rather than a science and an area where there is room for a difference of professional opinion even among experts as to the open market value of such assets in hypothetical circumstances. Valuations may also be required for accounts purposes in the valuation of stock at the lower of cost or net realisable value. In many cases stock adjustments will not require specific notification to the Revenue as they would fall within the definition of estimates used in preparing accounts which are reasonably reliable.

16.58 In the case of specialist valuations where the taxpayer is unlikely to have the requisite specialist knowledge, it may be necessary to obtain a professional valuation from a surveyor or valuer in the case of land or an accountant or share and business valuer in the case of unquoted shares, but the size of the transaction and the amount of tax at stake would also be relevant. It would be unreasonable for the Revenue to expect a taxpayer to go to the trouble and expense of obtaining a professional valuation for shares worth a few hundred pounds or where a used car is given to an employee or furniture provided together with living accommodation.

16.59 Provided that the taxpayer has taken proper care in the preparation of his return he will not be penalised for a valuation that is subsequently agreed by a negotiation with the District Valuer or the Shares Valuation Division of the Inland Revenue in a different figure. Tax would be payable by reference to the finally agreed figure and any interest adjustment made. If, on the other hand, the taxpayer merely put a wild guess as the basis of his valuation without taking professional advice or without supplying the valuer with the information necessary to make a proper valuation the Revenue could well regard the return as being made negligently and seek penalties if the tax under-declared was material.

16.60 In straightforward cases it may be possible to submit details of disposals requiring valuations to the Revenue prior to filing and ideally to agree the figures to be submitted before the final filing date for the return. Even where it is not possible to agree figures by this time, the dialogue with the Revenue valuation department will have commenced leading to a speedier resolution of an acceptable valuation with the subsequent reduction in any interest adjustment.

16.61 In the absence of a pre-filing agreed valuation it is probable that in all cases involving a material valuation the Revenue will have to open enquiry proceedings even where the valuation is the only point in dispute.

Companies – judgmental matters

16.62 There are two areas where under the existing law the Revenue is required to make a direction before bringing anti-avoidance provisions into play, first of all in connection with controlled foreign companies under *TA 1988, s 747(1)* and under the transfer pricing provisions of *TA 1988, s 770*.

16.63 The Revenue have suggested that a direction in such circumstances is inappropriate under self-assessment and the taxpayer should be required to judge whether he could avoid a controlled foreign company direction on the ground that a reduction in UK tax was not a main purpose of the transaction under *TA 1988, s 748(3)(a)* or that their transactions had taken place at an arm's length price under the transfer pricing rules. Not surprisingly, taxpayers regard this as an unreasonable requirement and hope to retain the existing direction provisions.

Returns of deceased persons

16.64 The Revenue have confirmed that under self-assessment they will continue to issue a tax return before the end of the tax year to which it relates, to agree liabilities quickly and to give early written confirmation if they do not intend to enquire into the return, if requested to do so by the personal representatives or trustees of a deceased person. [Inland Revenue Press Release of 4 April 1996 (see Appendix C)].

Electronic lodgement of tax returns

Introduction

16.65 Following initial research in 1993 the Revenue decided that it was advantageous and feasible to offer an electronic lodgement service ('ELS') for tax returns and a consultative document was issued in February 1994. This proposed that approved accountants and other agents could prepare electronic returns using software which had been approved to meet the ELS specifications. The electronic transfer would take place using standard electronic mail facilities to a central Revenue computer. Floppy disks would not be accepted for a number of administrative reasons, not the least of which was their capability of transmitting viruses.

16.66 'Proof of concept' trials took place between November 1994 and March 1995 which seemingly met with varying degrees of success. While confirming the overall viability of the proposed ELS system, these trials identified problem areas. The Revenue have accordingly undertaken a further evaluation exercise (a test service was introduced in April 1996) and another consultative document was issued in November 1995. The Revenue have confirmed that development of ELS remains on schedule for live release in April 1997 and, following a survey of accountants' attitudes to ELS, have introduced a pre-registration scheme for those accountants who want to keep up to date with its development. (Inland Revenue Press Release of 15 May 1996). In the meantime, the statutory framework for ELS has been introduced by *FA 1995, s 153*, inserting a new *TMA 1970, s 115A* and *3A Sch* which is now considered.

General provisions relating to ELS

16.67 Subject to certain conditions being complied with as outlined below, a taxpayer's obligation to file his tax return will be fulfilled if that return is transmitted electronically to the Revenue. In such cases the usual requirement that the return contain a signed declaration by the taxpayer is not applicable. Supporting documents, including any accounts, statements or reports, which must be filed with the return may also be filed electronically, subject to approval by the Revenue and the same conditions being complied with or may be sent by post within one month of the return being filed electronically, Revenue Press Release of 31 May 1996. The return and documents will be regarded as duly filed when the last of the specified conditions are complied with. [*TMA 1970, 3A Sch 1, 2, 3*].

16.68 In those cases where electronic lodgement is accepted by the taxpayer, the Revenue have all the powers that they would have had if the information had been contained in a return delivered by post. Likewise, the usual rights of the taxpayer to amend his return and to make an error or mistake claim are preserved. [*TMA 1970, 3A Sch 10*].

16.69 In any proceedings, including those before the General or Special Commissioners or any tribunal having jurisdiction under the Tax Acts, an authenticated hard copy (see 16.70 (*c*)) is to be treated as if it were a tax return duly delivered. If there is no such authenticated hard copy, a hard copy certified by a Revenue officer as a true copy of the information transmitted is to be treated as such. A hard copy means a printed out version of the information. [*TMA 1970, 3A Sch 11*].

One of the main advantages of ELS, apart from speed and the elimination of transcription errors, is that the Revenue will be able to send information, such as copies of taxpayers' statements to the agent, electronically.

Conditions for ELS

16.70 A number of conditions must be complied with to permit electronic filing, as follows.

(*a*) The transmission must be made by a person approved by the Revenue. A person seeking approval to transmit will be given notice of whether approval has been granted or refused. If approval is refused or later withdrawn, the notice shall state the grounds for this. Any person who is refused approval, or whose approval is withdrawn has the right of appeal to the Special Commissioners. If an appeal is to be made, notice must be given to the Board within 30 days of the appellant being notified of the refusal or withdrawal. The Special Commissioners shall not allow the appeal unless they consider the refusal or withdrawal of approval to be unreasonable. If the appeal is allowed, approval will be effective from a date specified by the Special Commissioners. [*TMA 1970, 3A Sch 4*].

(*b*) The transmission must comply with any requirements laid down by the Revenue relating to the hardware or software, or the type thereof. [*TMA 1970, 3A Sch 5*].

(*c*) The transmission has to signify that before it was made, an authenticated hard copy was made under arrangements designed to ensure that the information contained in the hard copy is that actually transmitted. Such authentication is implemented by an appropriate declaration by the taxpayer endorsed on the hard copy, or by the taxpayer's signature on the hard copy. [*TMA 1970, 3A Sch 6, 8, 9*].

(*d*) The Revenue must have accepted the information transmitted as suitable for electronic lodgement in accordance with their selected procedures. [*TMA 1970, 3A Sch 7*].

Further developments

16.71 The Revenue have announced that they intend to produce an electronic version of the self-assessment tax return. The floppy disk, which will be available free to taxpayers in April 1997, will enable returns to be produced using a personal computer. The return can then be printed out, signed, and sent back to the Revenue. (Inland Revenue Press Release, 3 April 1996.)

Post- and pre-transaction rulings

16.72 As part of the self-assessment regime it is proposed that a post-transaction, pre-return, rulings system ('post transaction rulings') be introduced. This would be a formal procedure enabling a taxpayer to ascertain the Revenue's view of the consequences of a particular transaction which he had carried out. This would be intended to supplement, and not supplant, informal advice given to taxpayers already by Revenue staff, and would be particularly appropriate in the case of complex transactions.

16.73 From the taxpayer's perspective this would provide some certainty as to his tax liability, since he should be able to establish the tax consequences of a transaction before the filing date, and it would also assist him in complying with his obligations. So far as the Revenue are concerned, voluntary compliance with the tax laws should thereby be encouraged. Such systems operate in the USA and Australia, where self-assessment applies.

16.74 The Revenue's proposals were set out in a consultative document 'Post transaction rulings' issued in May 1994. If these proposals were adopted the system would be non-statutory, with the details set out in a statement of practice. Subject to full disclosure by the taxpayer, the Revenue would be bound by any favourable ruling. Although there would be no right of appeal as such against an adverse ruling, a taxpayer would not be bound thereby, but would be entitled to pay tax on his view of the consequences of the transaction if this differed from the views of the Revenue. He would also have the right of appeal should the Revenue seek to enquire into his return and amend his assessment, which it is to be assumed they would normally do.

16.75 In terms of the information which would have to be supplied to the Revenue to obtain a ruling, in the consultative document the Revenue envisaged that this would have to include:

(*a*) the name and tax reference of the taxpayer;

(*b*) full particulars of the transaction or event in question;

(*c*) a statement of the issue(s) to be considered;

(*d*) copies of all relevant documents, with the relevant passages identified;

(*e*) a statement that to the best of the taxpayer's knowledge and belief the facts as stated were correct and all relevant facts had been disclosed;

(*f*) a statement of the specific point(s) of difficulty giving rise to the ruling request;

(*g*) a statement of the ruling requested or suggested as appropriate by the applicant;

(*h*) particulars of sections of the Taxes Acts considered to be relevant;

(*i*) particulars of any case law, statements of practice, extra statutory concessions etc. considered to be relevant;

(*j*) particulars of any previous discussions or correspondence about the tax treatment of the transaction, or of any similar transaction between the taxpayer and any Revenue office; and, where the taxpayer or his advisers were aware of correspondence on the transaction between any other person and any Revenue office, particulars of that correspondence;

(*k*) a statement of the applicant's opinion of the tax consequences of the transaction, along with reasons to the extent that they were capable of being supplied.

16.76 The Revenue indicated that in practice they would interpret the last four of these requirements flexibly and in the light of all the circumstances of the case. Most unrepresented taxpayers, for example, could not reasonably be expected to quote relevant statute or case law, statements of practice etc. The Revenue expected, however, that in most such cases an approach to the tax office for informal help and advice would be likely to be a more appropriate as well as a more practical course than a formal ruling application.

16.77 No ruling would normally be given:

(*a*) if the facts and documents supplied were, in the Revenue's view, insufficient to allow a properly evaluated decision to be made. The Revenue would normally explain what further information or clarification was required;

(*b*) where the tax involved or (e.g. in the case of loss-making concerns) potentially involved was below a *de minimis* threshold;

(*c*) on asset valuations, which do not in themselves involve the interpretation of tax law;

(*d*) in response to frivolous or vexatious applications not involving genuine points of doubt or difficulty for the taxpayer;

(*e*) in respect of transactions which, in the Revenue's view, may have been undertaken wholly or mainly with the purpose of avoiding tax;

(*f*) if, in respect of the transaction and suggested tax treatment set out in the application, it had been open to the taxpayer to apply for a statutory clearance (whether he did so or not) before carrying out the transaction;

(*g*) in relation to the tax consequences of the making of any settlement within *TA 1988, Part XV*;

(*h*) in any case where in the Revenue's view it would not be possible, without unreasonable diversion of resources, to resolve the issue within an appropriate time.

16.78 The consultative document invited comments on the proposals, and these were duly submitted by the principal taxpayer representative bodies. The principles of post-transaction rulings were generally welcomed, but concerns were expressed as to a number of aspects of the proposals, notably the form of the application and the information requirements.

16.79 These matters are now under consideration by the Revenue, together with a pilot scheme. As a quite separate matter the Revenue are proposing to publish a further consultative document on a comprehensive ruling system, incorporating pre-transaction rulings.

Chapter 17

Claims, Elections and Revisions

Background

17.1 Under the old system, the *Taxes Act* provided for a multitude of claims, elections and notices, with different sets of rules and varying time limits. The objective was to grant the taxpayer a degree of choice in relation to the particular issues involved, and formal notification to the Revenue was required. Claims needed Revenue acceptance to be valid, whilst elections simply required unilateral action by the taxpayer, generally by the service of a written notice on the Inspector.

17.2 As regards claims, it was often necessary for the taxpayer to establish to the Revenue's satisfaction that particular conditions had been complied with, necessitating an investigation by the Inspector into the facts, and then the exercise of a judgment. It is an integral part of self-assessment that a taxpayer should be able to file his tax return and determine his own tax liability without reference to the Revenue. Hence there is a radical change to the basis of the system in respect of claims. The essence of the new system is that the taxpayer alone needs to be satisfied that the conditions to enable a claim for relief have been met, and he will then pay tax on this basis. Hence a significant judgmental role will be transferred to the taxpayer.

17.3 The matter is somewhat complicated by the time frame relating to claims. Most will relate to the income and gains of the particular year covered by the return, and can generally be dealt with simply by inclusion in the return. But some claims will relate to income and gains of future years, and these will be made in advance. Other claims allow a carry back to earlier years, for example in respect of trading losses, permitting a revision of the tax paid. The latter presented a particular conundrum to the Revenue, as once a self-assessment has been made for a year, and the deadline for a Revenue enquiry has passed, that year is generally to be regarded as final. The Revenue are extremely loath to re-open such a closed year. The legislation dealing with such claims to carry back relief has in fact now been changed three times, with the latest version set out in *FA 1996* and occupying a new Schedule in *TMA 1970*.

New Provisions for claims and elections

17.4 The provisions for making claims are contained in substituted *TMA 1970, s 42; FA 1994, 19 Sch 13, FA 1995, s 107* and *FA 1996,* *ss 128(1), 130(3)*. These come into effect for individuals and partnerships from 6 April 1996, and for companies for accounting periods ending on or after 'the appointed day' as determined by the Treasury: *FA 1995, s 103(7)*. They apply in all cases where relief is given, or any other thing is to be done on the making of a claim or election, unless specifically provided to the contrary. [*TMA 1970, s 42(1)(10)*]. The general rule is that all claims are to be made by inclusion in the return wherever possible, or an amendment to a return. This reflects the move to self-assessing as an integral part of the return procedure, and that income and gains, relief and allowances are all brought together to arrive at net taxable income and gains. Notices will not have to be included in returns, but may be given to the Revenue on an ad hoc basis within the applicable time limit. An example would be the notice of an accounting change to have effect for tax purposes under *TA 1988, s 62A(3)*. The position is likewise for notices required to be made by partnerships.

17.5 Claims are to be quantified at the time when they are made, except where a claim is to be reflected in a PAYE code number. [*TMA 1970, s 42(1A)(2)*]. The latter should enable capital losses to be claimed in the year that they arise, and then subsequently utilised without any further claim. This will hopefully enable taxpayers to agree capital losses carried forward, which they have hitherto been unable to do until a claim has been made for the loss to be set against a profit.

17.6 A provisional claim in an estimated amount may not be made. However, in cases where, for example, it is clear that a claim will be appropriate but the amount cannot precisely be determined the Revenue will accept the taxpayer's best estimate, which will have to be revised to the final figure as soon as available. An example will be where a loss has been established but the exact amount cannot be finalised before the return is filed. Moreover, the Revenue will also accept that in cases where a claim is for an allowance that is fixed, such as a personal allowance, that will be treated as a quantified claim even the claimant does not know the amount due: see SAT 2 (1995) paras 6.14–6.15.

17.7 A claim may be made on behalf of an incapacitated person by his trustee, guardian, tutor or curator. Moreover, a person who is charged to tax on the profits of another under *TMA 1970, Pt VIII, ss 78–85* (persons responsible for tax payable by non-residents) may make a claim for relief by discharge or repayment of that tax. [*TMA 1970, s 42(8)*].

Claims to be included and quantified in tax return

17.8 The form of the return will reflect the fact that claims and elections are to be made with the return if at all possible. Certain reliefs will be claimed merely by a deduction of the relevant amount such as personal allowances. Others will be claimed by adoption of a particular treatment such as the use of a 'tick box' in the return, or by set-off of trade losses.

Others again will be in a formal claim either on the return or as a separate claim to be submitted with the return. In some circumstances it will be impossible or inappropriate for a claim to be made as part of a return, and the procedure set out in 17.13 *et seq*. will then apply. This separation between the two procedures does not depend on the type of claim, but purely on whether a claim in the return is appropriate or possible.

17.9 The amended legislation specifically provides that where a taxpayer has been sent a tax return a claim has to be made by being included in the relevant return, or an amended return as the case may be, if it could be made by being so included. [*TMA 1970, s 42(2)(5)*]. In the case of companies, this does not extend to a claim for payment of a tax credit which will continue to be made on Form CT61. [*TMA 1970, s 42(4)*]. An exception arises here where the company is exempt from corporation tax (or is only chargeable to corporation tax in respect of its trading income) and the company claiming the tax credit is not an insurance company carrying on a pension business [inserted by *TMA 1970 (4A); FA 1995, s 107(6)*]. Another exception is where the claim relates to Schedule E and is dealt with by an adjustment to a PAYE coding. A further exception is a claim to carry back losses and other reliefs, where the procedure is dealt with below.

17.10 When a tax return can be amended, such as under the repairs procedure outlined in 18.19 below (generally twelve months from the filing date) any claims which would generally be included in a tax return and which are made subsequent to the filing date are to be made by an amendment to the return and the self-assessment. The same applies to an amendment of a return following the resolution of a Revenue enquiry (see 20.20 and 20.30 *et seq*.).

Partnership claims expressly to be included in the return

17.11 In the case of partnerships where a return form has been sent to a particular partner, a claim under any of the following *sections* is specifically to be included in the return. (In other cases it is to be made by any person nominated by the partners for the purpose.) [*TMA 1970, s 42(6)*]. *TA 1988, s 84* (gift to educational establishment), *s 91B* (waste disposal: preparation expenditure), *s 101(2)* (value of stock-in-trade on discontinuance), *s 120(2)* (rent for electric line wayleaves), *s 401* (pre-trading expenditure), *s 471* (exchange of securities), *s 472* (securities issued in connection with nationalisation), *s 484* (savings banks), *s 504* (letting of furnished holiday accommodation), *s 531* (know-how), *ss 534 and 535* (copyrights), *s 537A* (payments for designs), *s 538* (painters, sculptors and other artists), *ss 570 and 571(4)* (industry rationalisation schemes), *s 579(4)* (statutory redundancy provisions), *s 723(3)* (foreign securities: delayed remittances), *s 810* (capital allowances and to secure double tax relief), *5 Sch 2, 6 and 11*, (herd basis). *FA 1989, s 43(5)* (Schedule E emoluments and computation of Schedule D liability). *CAA 1990, s 1* (enterprise zones), *s 11* (long lease of industrial building), *s 17* (mining structures), *ss 22 and 23* (first year allowances), *ss 24 and 25* (writing-down allowance), *ss 30, 31, 33 and 33A* (ships), *s 37* (short life assets), *ss 48 and 49* (leased plant and machinery), *ss 53 and 55* (fixtures), *s 68(5) and (9)* (films, tapes and discs), *ss 77 and 78* (successions), *ss 124A and 129(2)* (agricultural buildings), *s 140(3)* (allowance in taxing trade), *s 141* (other income tax allowances) and *s 158* (connected persons). *F(No 2)A 1992, ss 41 and 42* (expenditure on films).

Claims not in tax return

17.12 A new *TMA 1970, 1A Sch* inserted by *FA 1994, 19 Sch 35* sets out the procedure which is to apply for the making of a claim where the claim is not included on the taxpayer's return, and does not relate to a matter dealt with by a PAYE adjustment. [*TMA 1970, s 42(11)*]. This procedure therefore applies, for example, to cases where a retrospective claim is made within the two- (or six-) year period which may be allowed to enable an adjustment to be made to a prior year's liability.

17.13 A claim is to be made to a Revenue Officer, except where there is a specific provision requiring the claim to be made to the Board, and it has to be in the prescribed form. [*TMA 1970, 1A Sch 2(1)(3)*]. There has to be a declaration to the effect that all the particulars given are correctly stated to the best of the information and belief of the person making the claim. [*TMA 1980, 1A Sch 2(4)*]. The form of claim may require:

(*a*) a statement of the tax which is to be discharged or repaid to give effect to the claim;

(*b*) such information as the Revenue may reasonably require to determine whether the claim is correct, and also the delivery of such accounts, statements and documents as are reasonably required to substantiate the claim; and

(*c*) any particulars of assets acquired as may be required in a tax return containing information about chargeable gains.

[*TMA 1970, 1A Sch 2(5)* as amended by *FA 1995, 20 Sch 1*].

17.14 No claim requiring the repayment of tax is to be made unless the claimant has documentary proof of payment. [*TMA 1970, 1A Sch 2(2)*]. In the case of a claim by or on behalf of a non-UK resident, or a person claiming to be not resident, not ordinarily resident, or not domiciled in the UK, a statement or declaration in support of the claim may be required by way of affidavit. [*TMA 1970, 1A Sch 2(6)*].

Claims for medical insurance and vocational training relief

17.15 The normal procedure for making claims in *TMA 1970, s 42*, including claims not included in returns under *TMA 1970, Sch 1A*, is dis-applied to claims for repayment of tax deducted at source by companies providing medical insurance under *FA 1989, s 54* and educational institutions providing vocational training relief under *FA 1991, s 32*. Instead, regulations will be made laying down the repayment rules and enabling the insurers and educational institutions to claim repayment of tax deducted at source by payers under provisions similar to those currently existing, under the Private Medical Insurance (Tax Relief) Regulations 1989, SI 1989 No 2387 and the Vocational Training (Tax Relief) Regulations 1992, SI 1992 No 746. [*FA 1996, s 129*]. Currently, monthly repayments are provided for under both sections.

Giving effect to a claim

17.16 The Revenue are required to give effect to a claim as soon as is practicable after the claim is made, which will generally be by way of a discharge or repayment of tax. In the case of a partnership claim, they are likewise required to give effect to the claim as respects each partner, by a discharge or repayment of tax. In the case of claims relating to income tax under Schedule E that would normally be dealt with under PAYE, these may continue to be dealt with by revising the taxpayer's PAYE coding. The Revenue are also given power to give effect to claims or amendments on a provisional basis as they consider appropriate, pending finalisation of any Revenue enquiries. [*TMA 1970, 1A Sch 4(1)(2)* as amended by *FA 1995, 20 Sch 4*].

17.17 Where a claim results in an entitlement to a tax repayment, this will generally be made automatically subject only to certain security checks instituted by the Revenue. In cases where risk is perceived to be involved, such as claims by non-residents, the Revenue may verify the claim before any tax repayment is made. The Revenue will also have the right to audit the claim, with essentially the same rights as under their normal enquiry procedures.

Time limits for claims

17.18 The time limit for making claims has in many cases been two years from the end of the year of assessment in which the event giving rise to the claim happens, although the time limit for making certain claims has been six years from the end of the year of assessment, which also tied in with the time limit for assessments. These time limits remain unchanged under self-assessment for corporation tax purposes, but for income tax purposes they are aligned to the usual time limits for individuals or partnerships, being 31 January following the end of the year of assessment or the final date for making amendments to a return (normally one year ten months after the end of the year of assessment) or the ordinary time limit for making an indate assessment, normally five years ten months after the end of the year of assessment. The new provisions apply from 1996/97 for income tax and from the appointed day under *FA 1994, s 199(3)* for corporation tax; *FA 1996, s 135 and 21 Sch*.

17.19. So far as capital allowances are concerned, under the self-assessment transitional rules, the old capital allowances provisions apply for the transitional year 1996/97 and the new current year basis of assessment rules apply for 1997/98 onwards. It is therefore provided that for 1996/97 the two-year period that would normally apply is amended to one year ten months for trades, professions or vocations set up and commenced before 6 April 1994. This also applies to notification of expenditure on plant and machinery under *FA 1994, s 118*. [*FA 1996, s 135(3)(4)*].

17.20. The detailed time limits are as follows:

Taxes Act 1988

(*a*) *s 62A* (Change of basis period – conditions for such a change) – return date.

(*b*) *s 84* (Gifts to educational establishments) – 1 year 10 months.

(*c*) *s 101* (Valuation of work in progress at discontinuance of profession or vocation) – 1 year 10 months.

(*d*) *s 257BB* (Transfer of relief under *Section 257A* – Married Couple's Allowance – where relief exceeds income) – 5 years 10 months.

(*e*) *s 257D* (Transitional relief: husband with excess allowances) – 5 years 10 months.

(*f*) *s 265* (Blind person's allowance) – 5 years 10 months.

(*g*) *s 306* (Enterprise Investment Scheme – claims) – 5 years 10 months.

(*h*) *s 356B* (Relief for payments of interest – residence basis: married couples) – 1 year 10 months.

(*i*) *s 356C* (Relief for payments of interest – substitution of security: supplemental) – 1 year 10 months.

(*j*) *s 381* (Further relief for individuals for losses in early years of trade) – 1 year 10 months.

(*k*) *s 392* (Case VI losses) – 5 years 10 months.

(*l*) *s 471* (Exchange of securities in connection with conversion operations, nationalisations etc.) – 1 year 10 months.

(*m*) *s 472* (Distribution of securities in connection with nationalisation etc.) – 1 year 10 months.

(*n*) *s 504* (Letting of furnished holiday accommodation treated as a trade: supplementary provisions) – 1 year 10 months.

(*o*) *s 524* (Taxation of receipts from sale of patent rights) – 1 year 10 months.

(*p*) *s 585* (Relief from tax on delayed remittances) – 5 years 10 months.

(*q*) *s 619* (Retirement annuities – exemption from tax in respect of qualifying premiums) – 10 months: This is an important change for many taxpayers allowing further time to elect to carry back premiums.

(*r*) *s 641* (Personal pension schemes – carry back of contributions) – 10 months: This is an important change for many taxpayers allowing further time to elect to carry back premiums.

(*s*) *s 691* (Maintenance funds for historic buildings – certain income not to be income of settlor) – 1 year 10 months.

(*t*) *s 700* (Estate of deceased persons in course of administration – adjustments and information) – 3 years 10 months: The additional time of 10 months to raise assessments or allow claims following completion of the estate should be noted.

(*u*) *s 781* (Assets leased to traders and others) – 5 years 10 months.

(*v*) *s 804* (Double taxation relief – relief against income tax in respect of income arising in years of commencement) – 5 years 10 months.

(*w*) *s 806* (Double taxation relief – time limit for claims etc.) – 5 years 10 months.

(*x*) *Sch 11, para 12* (Relief as respects tax on payments on retirement or removal from office or employment) – 5 years 10 months.

Finance Act 1988

(*a*) *s 38* (Maintenance payments under existing obligations: elections for new rules) – 1 year 10 months.

Capital Allowance Act 1990

(*a*) *s 25* (Machinery and plant – allowances and charges general provisions – qualifying expenditure) – 1 year 10 months.

(*b*) *s 30* (Ships – first-year allowances) – 1 year 10 months.

(*c*) *s 31* (Ships – writing-down allowances) – 1 year 10 months.

(*d*) *s 33* (Ships: exclusion of *CAA 1990, s 31*) – 1 year 10 months.

(*e*) *s 37* (Short-life assets – election for certain machinery or plant to be treated as short-life assets) – 1 year 10 months.

(*f*) *s 53* (Fixtures expenditure incurred by equipment lessor) – 1 year 10 months.

(*g*) *s 68* (Exclusions of certain expenditure relating to films, tapes and discs) – 1 year 10 months.

(*h*) *s 129* (Agriculture – balancing events) – 1 year 10 months.

(*i*) *s 141* (Supplementary provisions – other income tax allowances) – 1 year 10 months.

Taxation of Chargeable Gains Act 1992

(*a*) *s 35* (Computation of gains: general provisions – asset held on 31 March 1982) (including assets held on 6 April 1965)) – 1 year 10 months.

(*b*) *s 161* (Appropriations to and from stock) – 1 year 10 months.

(*c*) *s 242* (Small part disposals) – 1 year 10 months.

(*d*) *s 243* (Part disposal to authority with compulsory powers) – 1 year 10 months (previously 6 years).

(*e*) *s 244* (Part disposal; consideration exceeding allowable expenditure) – 1 year 10 months (previously 6 years).

(*f*) *s 253* (Debts – relief for loans to traders) – 5 years 10 months.

(*g*) *s 279* (Foreign assets: delayed remittances) – 5 years 10 months.

(*h*) *Sch 2* (Assets held on 6 April 1965) – 1 year 10 months.

(*i*) *Sch 4* (Deferred charges on gains before 31 March 1982) – 1 year 10 months.

(*j*) *Sch 6* (Retirement relief etc) – 1 year 10 months.

Finance (No 2) Act 1992

(*a*) *S 41* (Films – relief for preliminary expenditure) – 1 year 10 months.

(*b*) *s 42* (Films – relief for production or acquisition expenditure) – 1 year 10 months.

(*c*) *ch 10* (Furnished accommodation) – 1 year 10 months.

Finance Act 1994

(*a*) *s 118* (Expenditure on machinery or plant: notification) – 1 year 10 months.

Amendments to claims/repairs

17.21 As with the 'repairs' procedure relating to a taxpayer's return and self-assessment outlined in 18.19, the Revenue may repair a claim. They can do so at any time within nine months from the date on which the claim is made, correcting any obvious errors or mistakes, whether errors of principle, arithmetical mistakes or otherwise. [*TMA 1970, 1A Sch 3(1)(a)*]. The taxpayer may likewise amend his claim within twelve months from the day on which the claim is made by the appropriate notice on a Revenue Officer. [*TMA 1970, 1A Sch 3(1)(b)*]. However, where the Revenue initiate a formal enquiry into the claim no amendment of the claim may be made thereafter until the enquiry is completed. [*TMA 1970,*

1A Sch 3(2)]. This follows the similar prohibition on repairs to a return as explained in 18.24.

Error or mistake claims – individuals, trustees and companies

17.22 Under the previous system a taxpayer who considered that an assessment was excessive by reason of an error or mistake in a return, could make a claim for a repayment of tax within six years after the end of the year of assessment or, if the assessment was to corporation tax, six years after the end of the accounting period to which the assessment related. This ability to make a repayment claim is retained under self-assessment and applies also when the taxpayer has made a self-assessment. The time limit for such a claim becomes five years from 31 January following the year of assessment to which the return relates for income tax and CGT, and remains at six years after the end of the accounting period to which the return relates for corporation tax. [*TMA 1970, s 33(1)* as amended by *FA 1994, 19 Sch 8*].

17.23 On receiving the claim the Board are to enquire into the matter, and give by way of repayment such relief as is reasonable and just. [*TMA 1970, s 33(2)*]. However, there is no relief where the return was made on the basis of or in accordance with the practice generally prevailing at the time when it was made, or where the error or mistake was in a claim which was included in the return. [*TMA 1970, s 33(2A); FA 1994, 19 Sch 8*].

17.24 Where a taxpayer discovers that he has made an error or mistake in a claim, he may make an appropriate supplementary claim provided that the time limit for making the original claim has not expired [*TMA 1970, s 42(9); FA 1994, 19 Sch 13*].

Error or mistake claims – partnerships

17.25 Bearing in mind that partnerships are to submit a partnership statement as well as a partnership return the rules have to be amended to deal with errors or mistakes in a partnership statement. This is done by a new *TMA 1970, s 33A*, as inserted by *FA 1994, 10 Sch 9* which follows the format of the revised *TMA 1970, s 33*. Any partner ('the representative partner') or his successor may within five years from the filing date make a claim for relief. [*TMA 1970, s 33A(2)(10)*]. The Board are then to enquire into the matter, and make any amendment to the partnership statement to give such relief as is reasonable or just. [*TMA 1970, s 33A(3)*]. Where this is done they are to give notice to each partner so that his self-assessment can be amended. [*TMA 1970, s 33A(4); FA 1994, 19 Sch 13*].

17.26 The Board are to have regard to all the relevant circumstances of the case and are to consider whether the granting of relief would result in the exclusion from the charge to tax of any part of the profits of any of the partners. They may take into consideration a partner's liability in respect of chargeable periods other than that to which the claim relates. [*TMA 1970, s 33A(6)*]. No relief is permitted where the partnership statement was made on the basis of or in accordance with, the practice generally prevailing when the statement was made. [*TMA 1970, s 33A(5)*].

17.27 There is a right of appeal to the Special Commissioners against the Board's decision. They are to hear and determine the appeal in accordance with the principles laid down for the Board to follow in determining the claim. [*TMA 1970, s 33A(7)*]. If either the Board or the representative partner then subsequently require a case to be stated under *TMA 1970, s 56* (necessary to pursue a further appeal to the High Court) that case stated can only be in respect of a point of law arising in connection with the computation of the partnership profits. [*TMA 1970, s 33A(8)*].

Procedure for carry back of reliefs

17.28 Where a claim for relief involves two or more years, there is a special procedure contained in a new *TMA 1970, s 42(11A) and 1B Sch*. [*FA 1996, s 128(1) and 17 Sch*]. For these purposes a claim includes an election or notice, and the amount in which a person is chargeable to tax is calculated after taking into account such claims. [*TMA 1970, 1B Sch 1(1)*].

Loss relief

17.29 So far as relief for losses is concerned the position is as follows. Where a claim is made for the carry back of losses it is treated as a claim for the later year. But the amount of the claim is calculated as the difference between the amount actually charged to tax in the earlier year, and what the tax would have been had the relief been given in that year. [*TMA 1970, 1B Sch 2(1)–(4)*]. The relief given is calculated in terms of tax, being treated as an additional payment on account in the later year, or repaid, or set off. [*TMA 1970, 1B Sch 2(6)*]. Whilst such a procedure has the advantage of avoiding the re-opening of prior years, it does have the adverse effect for the taxpayer of inflating the interim payments due in respect of the later years.

17.30 Where such a carry-back claim has already been made, a further claim to carry back another loss to the same year proceeds on the basis that the tax repayable in respect of the first claim had actually been made in the earlier rather than the later year. [*TMA 1970, 1B Sch 2(5)*]. This ensures that, in terms of tax, relief is given for the correct amount as if the claims had actually both been relieved in the earlier year. So far as capital losses are concerned, where these arise in the year of death and are carried back for the preceding three years under *TCGA 1992 s 62(2)*, this is treated as done pursuant to a claim for these purposes. [*TMA 1970, 1B Sch 2, para 2(7)*].

Relief for fluctuating profits of farming

17.31 Where a claim is made for farm profit averaging under *TA 1988, s 96*, it is treated as a claim for the later year of the two consecutive years being averaged. An averaging claim will be calculated as if the tax payable in the earlier year was recalculated and the amount of tax overpaid will be treated as an additional payment on account in the later year or, if further tax is payable for the earlier year, this is treated as an additional liability of the later year. If the later year then becomes the earlier year on a subsequent farm profit averaging claim, the second calculation of relief proceeds on the basis that the tax payable or repayable as a result of the first adjustment has not arisen. [*TMA 1970, 1B Sch 3*]. Again the purpose of the provision is to avoid re-opening an earlier year but to give the same relief in terms of tax as would have been given, had the earlier year been re-opened.

17.32 A claim may be made within one year ten months of the second of the two years to be averaged. A claim which affects the profits of an earlier year enables other claims for that year to be made, revoked or amended also in this period under *TA 1988, s 96(9)*, as substituted by *FA 1996, s 128(3) and (4)*. The difference in tax charged, or relieved, in the later period is the final amount after making all necessary adjustments. The calculation is made by reference to the earlier year, in terms of tax, and relief is given in the later year, which avoids changing the tax payable for the earlier year. [*TMA 1970, 1B Sch 4*].

Carry back of post-cessation etc. receipts

17.33 Post cessation receipts received within six years following discontinuance may be carried back and treated as receipts of the day on which the discontinuance took place under *TA 1988, s 103*. Similar rules apply on a change of basis under *TA 1988, s 104* from a conventional (cash) basis to an earnings basis. The year of discontinuance is referred to as the earlier year. Tax due for the year of receipt (the later year) is calculated as if the tax payable for the earlier year had been adjusted. The post-cessation expenses that had already been relieved under *TA 1988, s 105* cannot be relieved again in this computation. [*TMA 1970, IB Sch 5*].

Spreading of certain payments by authors, designers etc.

17.34 *TA 1988, ss 534, 537A and 538* allow authors, designers and artists to spread sums received from the sale of their works over the period of creation subject to a maximum of three years. This involves carrying back part of the receipt in the payment year and subjecting it to tax as if it were received twelve or twenty-four months prior to the actual date of receipt. For self-assessment, in order to avoid re-opening earlier years, the receipt is subject to tax in the year of payment but the tax is calculated as if it had been spread backwards, and the tax payable for earlier years is not disturbed.

Where there are associated claims, the additional tax is payable on the assumption that any earlier claims had been given effect to in the years to which they were theoretically spread back, in order to calculate the tax due for the year of payment. [*TMA 1970, IB Sch 6*].

17.35 The rules in *TA 1988, s 534* are changed for the backward spreading of copyright payments received in the first two years after publication. A claim must be made by 31 January following one year after the end of the year of assessment and would therefore affect that year and the two previous years. It is treated as a timeous claim for those earlier years. This is a considerable reduction from the previous claim period of up to seven years ten months after 5 April following publication, but is arguably in line with the normal self-assessment provisions. Similar alterations are made to the time limit for an election for the carry back of post cessation receipts, with appropriate amendments to cater for self-assessment. Corresponding changes are made to the provisions allowing the backward spreading of designs under *TA 1988, s 537A* and for painters, sculptors and other artists under *TA 1988, s 538*. In spite of the backward spreading, the income is still regarded as that of the year of assessment in which it would normally fall were it not for the application of the spreading provisions, but the tax is calculated as if the earlier years were adjusted. [*FA 1996, s 128(5)*].

17.36 The forward spreading provisions in *TA 1988, s 535* are also amended to delete the personal representative's ability to elect for re-spreading on death or cessation. [*FA 1996, s 128(7)*]. This election is thought to be an unnecessary complication under self-assessment. For forward spreading to apply a claim has to be made by 31 January following one year after the end of the year of assessment for the relevant year in which the copyright is sold, being the normal time limit for self-assessment.

17.37 Partnerships and companies are taken out of these literary and artistic spreading provisions. [*FA 1996, s 128(6)*]. Seemingly the Revenue considered that they were inappropriate for companies, on the basis that a company cannot be an author, designer or artist. Moreover, so far as partnerships are concerned, the Revenue apparently have no record of a partnership claiming under these spreading provisions. The Revenue considered that the removal of these reliefs from companies and partnerships would simplify the tax legislation.

Consequential amendments in cases where Revenue previously had a discretion

17.38 As set out in 17.2, in the context of claims the introduction of self-assessment inevitably has to remove the former discretionary powers of the Revenue that existed in many cases. This is implemented by a series of specific changes to many charging sections of the various Taxes Acts, these being contained in *FA 1996, 20 Sch*. The changes take place for income tax and CGT purposes from 1996/97, and for corporation tax purposes for accounting periods commencing after the 'appointed day' designated by the Treasury. [*FA 1996, s 134*].

17.39 The position under the amendments is that a taxpayer is simply required to self assess on the basis that the particular condition for any relief or treatment exists, and he will only be called upon to prove it if the Revenue make an investigation under their enquiry powers. The position will be essentially the same in the context of judgmental issues. Here the taxpayer will have to be satisfied that on an objective appraisal of all the facts the relief is available, for example in the case of a taxpayer claiming that he is not domiciled in the UK, and thereby qualifying for remittance basis treatment. It is in such judgmental areas that inevitably problems are likely to arise, whether on an enquiry by the Revenue or on a later discovery. In doubtful cases it will be advisable for the taxpayer to draw to the Revenue's attention any questionable matters on his tax return.

17.40 The following sets out in summary form the sections which are amended by *FA 1996, 20 Sch* to reflect the above changes.

Taxes Act 1988

(1) *s 24(2)*: lease premiums, presumption that any sums paid are by way of premium unless the contrary can be shown.

(2) *s 38(4)*: in ascertaining the duration of a lease the assumptions as to any benefits conferred apply unless it can be shown that the benefits were not conferred for the purposes of securing a tax advantage.

(3) *s 65(4)*: no longer necessary to satisfy the Revenue as to non-UK domiciled status in order to claim the remittance basis for Schedule D, Cases IV and V.

(4) *s 74(1)(j)*: no longer necessary to prove a debt to be bad in order to claim relief.

(5) *s 109A(4)*: for allowable post-cessation expenditure, wording recast to give relief for debts at cessation which subsequently prove to be bad where there is a relevant arrangement or compromise.

(6) *s 132(1)*: emoluments for a period of absence from an office or employment treated as emoluments for duties performed in the UK unless they would have been emoluments for duties performed outside the UK but for that absence: no longer necessary to show this.

(7) *s 145*: living accommodation provided for an employee deemed to be provided by reason of his employment unless provided in the normal course of his domestic, family or personal relationships or by a local authority on normal council house terms: no longer necessary to show this to be the case.

(8) *s 159*: no longer necessary to satisfy the Inspector that a car is a pool car, and meets the relevant requirements.

(9) *s 161*: no longer necessary to show in advance the exceptions from the beneficial loan charge.

(10) *s 168*: no longer necessary to show that sums are paid or a car or van provided in the normal course of domestic, family or personal relationships.

(11) *s 186(10)*: the Board's opinion on approved profit-sharing schemes no longer needed.

(12) *s 231(3A)*: the restriction of tax credits for certain recipients of qualifying distributions no longer requires the Inspector to consider the anti-avoidance provisions.

(13) *s 257*: no longer necessary to prove old age to obtain age allowance.

(14) *s 257A*: no longer necessary to prove that a taxpayer has a wife living with him in order to claim married couple's allowance.

(15) *s 257E*: no longer necessary to prove in advance entitlement to transitional age relief.

(16) *s 257F*: no longer necessary to provide proof in advance to qualify for transitional relief for separated couples.

(17) *s 259*: no longer necessary to prove in advance that the taxpayer has a resident qualifying child, in order to claim additional personal allowance.

(18) *s 261A*: no longer necessary to prove a resident qualifying child in the year of separation in order to claim additional relief.

(19) *s 265*: no longer necessary to prove that a taxpayer is a registered blind person in order to claim the allowance.

(20) *s 274(4)*: the war insurance premium element of life insurance premiums qualifying for relief is ignored without the necessity for the Inspector to consider them attributable to those risks.

(21) *s 278(2)*: no longer necessary to satisfy the Revenue that a person is a Commonwealth citizen to claim personal reliefs.

(22) *s 306(2)*: a claim for relief under the Enterprise Investment Scheme does not have to be accompanied by an appropriate certificate from the company, so long as one has been issued.

(23) *s 311(4)*: in order to claim relief for an approved fund, the company must have issued a certificate to the managers, and the managers to the claimant, but this does not need to be sent to the Revenue.

(24) *s 381(4)*: loss relief in the early years of a trade: no longer necessary to show that the trade was carried on on a commercial basis.

(25) *s 384*: restrictions on the right to set off losses: no longer necessary to show the trade was carried on on a commercial basis with a view to the realisation of profits.

(26) *s 393A*: corporation tax losses can be carried back to an earlier accounting period without having to show in advance that the trade was carried on on a commercial basis with a view to the realisation of gain.

(27) *s 397(3)*: farming losses are not restricted where the taxpayer could not reasonably have expected the activities to become profitable until later.

(28) *s 488*: relief to a cooperative housing association no longer requires advance proof.

(29) *s 489*: eligibility to claim relief for a self-builder society no longer requires advance proof.

(30) *s 503(6)*: the apportionment where letting relates only in part to holiday accommodation will be applicable in the appropriate circumstances without satisfying the Inspector.

(31) *s 570(2)*: the scheme for rationalising industry may be claimed in the appropriate circumstances.

(32) *s 582(2)(b)*: the Board no longer has to be satisfied to give relief for cases where retention of funding bonds is impracticable.

(33) *s 584*: the provisions giving relief for unremittable overseas income are recast to bring in an objective test of when income is unremittable.

(34) *s 585*: a claim for delayed remittances may be made in appropriate circumstances without showing in advance that the conditions are satisfied.

(35) *s 717(9)*: the accrued income scheme is modified to substitute an objective, just and reasonable test for what was previously the Inspector's decision.

(36) *s 731(3)*: the provisions relating to the purchase and sale of securities are recast on an objective basis, rather than there being a requirement to show to the satisfaction of the Board that the relevant provisions do not apply in respect of dealers in securities under *s 732*, persons entitled to exemptions under *s 733*, and persons other than dealers in securities under *s 734*.

(37) *s 769*: under the rules for ascertaining the change of ownership of a company leading to the disallowance of trading losses, it is no longer necessary to show in advance that a gift is unsolicited.

(38) *s 812*: the provisions relating to the withdrawal of tax credit for certain non-resident companies connected with the unitary states is recast to make the various tests objective, rather than having to prove them to the satisfaction of the Board. *Section 812* only comes into effect if a Treasury order to this effect has been approved by a resolution of the House of Commons, which has not yet happened.

(39) *s 815A*: the provisions on the transfer of a non-UK trade within the mergers directive is recast to avoid the necessity of producing an appropriate certificate.

(40) *Sch 6, para 2*: the business mileage provisions are recast in an objective form, i.e. where the employee is required by the nature of his employment to use and does use the company car for business travel.

(41) *Sch 7*: the exception for the benefit of a loan not obtained by reason of employment does not have to be so shown.

(42) *Sch 12(2)*: claim for foreign earnings deduction no longer requires proportion to be shown to be reasonable in advance.

(43) *Sch 21*: rationalisation and redundancy schemes no longer require a chargeable person to show damage.

Capital Allowances Act 1990

(1) *s 29(3)*: capital allowances are available where a letting relates partly to holiday accommodation in appropriate circumstances without having to appear to the Inspector to be just and reasonable.

Taxation of Chargeable Gains Act 1992

(1) *s 30(4)*: the value shifting anti-avoidance provisions do not apply where there is no tax avoidance purpose for the obtaining of benefits without it having to be shown to that effect.

(2) *ss 30(5)(6), 32(4)(b) and 33(7)(8)*: the just and reasonable adjustments required in the value shifting benefit provisions apply on an objective basis.

(3) *s 48*: the reduction for consideration proving to be irrecoverable is amended from a subjective to an objective basis.

(4) *s 49*: if a contingent liability becomes enforceable a consequential adjustment may be made on an appropriate claim.

(5) *s 52(4)*: the just and reasonable apportionment required in computations, where necessary, is put on an objective footing.

(6) *s 116(13)*: in the case of reorganisations, conversions and reconstructions within *s 116* any cash element is chargeable unless it may be ignored as being small. This is now arrived at on an objective basis. Although there is no statutory definition of small, in June 1965 the CCAB published a press release confirming that the Revenue will normally regard one amount as small in comparison with another if the first amount does not exceed 5 per cent of the second. The Revenue manual at paragraph CG 53857 confirms that in the Revenue's view small means 5 per cent or less of the market value of the old assets.

(7) *s 122*: a capital distribution treated as a part disposal is deducted from the cost of the shares, if small. This is now put on an objective basis. Again there is no statutory definition of small, but the Revenue manual at paragraph CG 57801 confirms that small means 5 per cent or less of the value of the shares.

(8) *s 133*: a small premium on the conversion of securities may be deducted from cost rather than treated as a part disposal on an objective basis. The Revenue manual paragraph CG 55031 confirms that in the Revenue's view small means 5 per cent or less of the market value of the converted securities before the conversion. Also see CG 57836.

(9) *ss 150(10)(a) and 150A(9)(a)*: under the Business Expansion Scheme and Enterprise Investment Scheme relief may be reduced on an objective just and equitable basis on a reorganisation.

(10) *s 164F(8)(a)*: the charge on the failure of the conditions for roll-over relief on reinvestment does not apply on a *bona fide* winding up, as objectively determined.

(11) *s 164FG*: multiple claims for reductions under the roll-over and reinvestment provisions are treated as separate claims, in such sequence as the claimant elects, the Board no longer having a determination in default of elections.

(12) *s 176(4)(6)*: the disallowance of losses arising out of depreciatory transactions within a group are to be calculated on an objective, just and reasonable basis.

(13) *s 181(1)(b)*: relief for a *bona fide* merger is given on an objective basis.

(14) *s 222(5)*: main residence relief is recast to provide for land in excess of 0.5 of a hectare on an objective basis, not such larger area as the Commissioners may determine. Determination of an individual's main residence by an Inspector is no longer needed.

(15) *s 224(2)*: the just and reasonable test for changes occurring during the period of ownership for main residence relief is put on an objective basis.

(16) *s 226(5)*: the private residence relief for dependent relatives in occupation prior to 6 April 1988 no longer requires the claimant to show that a spouse's claim would not be precluded or has been relinquished.

(17) *s 241(7)*: the apportionment provisions in relation to accommodation only partly let as holiday accommodation are put on an objective basis.

(18) *s 271*: the requirement to show that the Revenue are satisfied that investments are held on behalf of an exempt approved pension fund or an approved superannuation fund no longer applies.

(19) *s 279*: the requirements for relief for delayed remittance of foreign gains are put on an objective basis.

(20) *s 280*: where consideration is payable by instalments it will now be possible for the taxpayer to elect to pay the tax by instalments without having to show hardship. The instalments will be such as the Board may allow over a period not exceeding eight years. The Revenue manual at CG 14912 states that the tax instalments should be limited to fifty per cent of each instalment of future consideration as it becomes receivable. The total period for paying the tax should not exceed eight years, the period for paying the tax should not end later than the date on which the last instalments of consideration is receivable, and where practicable the agreed instalment should be payable at not less than six-monthly intervals. CG 14920 states 'for the purposes of charging interest on late paid tax the collector uses a series of reckonable dates determined by reference to the date on which the agreed instalments of tax become payable.'

(21) *Sch 6, para 3*: the retirement relief provision allowing early retirement on the grounds of ill health only requires the production of evidence of ill health if the Revenue raise the enquiry.

(22) *Sch 8, para 10(2)*: in the curved line depreciation provisions for leases of less than fifty years as wasting assets, the presumption of sums being paid by way of premium is excluded where other sufficient consideration for the payment can be shown to have been given.

Finance Act 1993

(1) *s 144*: the irrecoverable debt provisions for exchange gains and losses are put on an objective basis.

(2) *s 145*: similarly, the requirement for the Inspector's satisfaction or opinion is removed from the decision as to the recoverability of the outstanding amount of an exchange debt.

(3) *Sch 15, para 3(4)*: for the purpose of the alternative calculations for exchange gains and losses the meaning of unremittable income is put on an objective basis.

Finance Act 1994

(1) *s 163*: the definition of an irrecoverable payment, for interest rate and currency contracts, is recast on an objective basis.

Record Keeping

17.41 A taxpayer is required to keep and preserve the records required to make a claim, which must be kept until the later of the date on which a formal enquiry into the claim is completed, or the date on which it becomes impossible for any such enquiry to be opened. A penalty up to £3,000 may be charged for failure to comply with the record keeping requirements. [*TMA 1970, 1A Sch 2A*].

Revenue powers of enquiry into claims

17.42 The Revenue are given the same powers to enquire into claims and call for documents as apply to enquiries into tax returns, whether the claim is contained in a self-assessment or otherwise, and whether or not the claim gives rise to an immediate discharge or repayment of tax. The time limit for opening enquiries is the quarter day following the first anniversary of the day on which the claim or amendment was made, or if it relates to a year of assessment, the first anniversary of 31 January following the end of that year. Where the claim or amendment relates to a period other than a year of assessment, the time limit is twelve months after the end of that period. [*TMA 1970, 1A Sch 5,6; FA 1995, 20 Sch 5; FA 1996, s 19 and 19 Sch*].

17.43 The rules are essentially the same as for enquiries into a self-assessment or the return itself as described in 20.27 to 20.32, with the same procedure for completing the enquiry, the ability of the taxpayer to apply to the Commissioners for a notice that the enquiry is complete, and for amendments to the claim by the Revenue, and the ability of the taxpayer to appeal to the Commissioners against any such amendment.

Crown option

17.44 The Inland Revenue has power to determine, in the case of a financial trader whether the investment income should be assessed under Schedule D, Cases III, IV or V or under Cases I or II. Similarly in the case of a life insurance company, the Revenue may determine whether the company's profits should be assessed under Schedule D, Case I or on the basis of the income less management expenses (normally known as the I–E basis). This right to determination which the Revenue have is normally known as the Crown option, and arises from case law such as *Clerical Medical and General Life Assurance Society v Carter (1889) 2 TC 437*, *Revell v Edinburgh Life Insurance (Company (1906) 5 TC 221*, *Liverpool and London and Globe Insurance Company v Bennett (1913) 6 TC 327* and *Gresham Assurance Society v Attorney General (1916) 7 TC 36*. The existence of the Crown option is confirmed by *TMA 1970, s 28A(7A)(d) and TMA 1970, s 28B(6A)(d)* is introduced by *FA 1996, 19 Sch 4 and 5*. To enable the Revenue to determine which of the alternative bases should be applied, the power to call for documents provisions in *TMA 1970, s 19A* are extended to enable the Revenue to call for these documents which would enable them to apply the Crown option correctly.

17.45 Where there is a Crown option, the alternative chosen by the Revenue must be applied for the purposes of self-assessment and any enquiries and amendments relating thereto. The provisions enabling a partnership statement to be amended are duly modified to provide for the application of the Crown option. [*FA 1996, 19 Sch 5*]. There is no right of appeal against the exercise of the Crown option, as the choice is entirely at the discretion of the Revenue. [*FA 1996, 19 Sch 6*].

Carry-back of personal pension contributions

17.46 For years before 1996/97, claims to carry-back contributions had to be made before 6 July following the end of the tax year in which the premium was paid, and were given effect by adjusting the tax liability of the earlier year. Under self-assessment, claims must be made by 31 January following the tax year in which the premium is paid. The tax saving resulting from the carry-back claim is worked out by reference to the tax position of the earlier year, but the legislation provides that the claim is treated as relating to the later year, and affects the tax liability of that later year. This treatment strictly applies to a payment carried back from 1996/97 to 1995/96. The Revenue have, however, announced that the previous treatment will apply for one more year and such payments will be taken into account in calculating the provisional half-yearly payments on account to be made for 1996/97. (Inland Revenue Press Release of 21 March 1996).

Chapter 18

Assessments and Time Limits

Introduction

18.1 Under the old system, the process which generally followed that of information gathering was that of assessing the taxpayer to tax. This covered the process from the examination of the completed tax returns to the issue of notices of assessment, stating the income, profits or gains which had been assessed, and the amount of tax payable. Except for certain specific cases where the power of assessment was reserved to the Board, assessments were made by an Inspector based upon the information in the return. [*TMA 1970, s 29(1)(a)*]. In cases where no return had been made by a taxpayer, or where the Inspector was dissatisfied with the return, he could make an assessment to the best of his judgment. [*TMA 1970, s 29(1)(b)*].

18.2 Notice of the assessment had to be served on the person assessed and had to state the date on which it was issued and the time within which an appeal could be made. [*TMA 1970, s 29(5)*]. Once it had been served it could not be altered except by express provision. [*TMA 1970, s 29(6)*]. The taxpayer had the right of appeal against the assessment within 30 days of the notice. [*TMA 1970, s 31(1)*]. The issue might then subsequently be resolved by agreement with the Inspector. [*TMA 1970, s 54(1)*]. Otherwise, the appeal was to be determined by the General or Special Commissioners under the provisions outlined in Chapter 23. If there was no appeal the assessment generally became final.

18.3 The basis of the new system under self-assessment is for the taxpayer to assess his own tax liability. Hence most of the old assessment machinery is no longer appropriate. The changes to this machinery, and the instances where parts of the existing system are retained, are examined in this chapter.

Self-assessment for individuals and trustees

18.4 The radical change under self-assessment is the move away from assessment by the Inspector in every case. From 1996/97 the taxpayer is permitted, and indeed encouraged, to make his own assessment to income tax and CGT, based upon the information provided in his tax return. This right to self-assess also extends to trustees. As part of this self-assessment procedure, the old system with each source of income the subject of a separate assessment, is abolished. Income is still calculated by reference to the existing sources of income, e.g. Schedule D, Cases I, II and III etc., but there is a single tax assessment, incorporating all sources of income and CGT. The various strands of income are aggregated to give a total figure upon which the tax liability is based.

18.5 Unless the taxpayer files his return early, generally by 30 September following the end of the year of assessment, so leaving the Revenue time to calculate the tax due, he is required to include a self-assessment with his tax return. The filing date will at the latest therefore be 31 January following the end of the year of assessment, unless the return is sent to the taxpayer after 31 October when the deadline is three months from the sending of the return; see 16.13. Based on the information included in the return, the self-assessment, which will create a legal charge to tax, must show (a) the amounts chargeable to income tax and CGT, net of reliefs or allowances and (b) the amount of income tax actually payable, taking into account any tax deducted at source and the tax credit on dividends. In so far as the self-assessment indicates an overpayment of income tax, it is not repayable to the extent that it relates to income which has notionally suffered tax at the basic rate, such as a non-qualifying distribution, a foreign income dividend, a stock dividend, a release of a loan to a participator, a non-qualifying insurance policy or a repayment to an employee out of a pension fund surplus. [Substituted *TMA 1970, s 9(1), FA 1996, ss 121(4) and 122(1)*].

18.6 There are no specific provisions in the legislation requiring the Revenue to acknowledge receipt of a return and self-assessment. However, there will be a series of taxpayer statements issued to taxpayers throughout the year, generally reminders as to the payment of tax and interest and receipts, the principal one of which will be sent to taxpayers in February. This will show the amount of the self-assessment as calculated, recording receipt of the balancing payment for the previous year of assessment and the first interim payment for the current year (see Chapter 21).

18.7 In the event that the taxpayer does not wish to self-assess, he may instead leave it to the Revenue to make the assessment, but the tax return must then generally be submitted by 30 September following the end of the year of assessment (see 18.11). Where a taxpayer does self-assess, any reference in *TA 1988* and *TCGA 1992* to a person being assessed to tax, or being charged to tax by an assessment, is to be construed as a reference to self-assessment. [*FA 1994, s 197*].

18.8 In cases where there has been a self-assessment the Revenue have twelve months within which they have the right to enquire into the assessment, i.e. audit the return and the self-assessment. Otherwise, and subject to any 'repairs' made to the return by the taxpayer or the Revenue under the procedure described later in this chapter and the possibility of 'discovery' by the Revenue in cases of fraud, neglect, or mistake, the self-assessment becomes final and the Revenue are precluded from reopening it.

Self-assessment for employees

18.9 No self-assessment (or Revenue assessment) need be made in the case of individuals whose income has been fully taxed under PAYE. This will also include individuals with small amounts of other income which is taxed under the PAYE system. But an assessment will be required if the net tax deducted in the year in question is not the same as it would have been if:

(*a*) all the relevant circumstances had been known to all parties throughout the year (i.e. that the code number was correct); and

(*b*) cumulative PAYE tables had been used.

[*TA 1988, s 205(1)(2)* substituted by *FA 1995, s 111(1)*].

18.10 These provisions do not prevent an assessment or self-assessment being made for the year of assessment. Furthermore, within five years and seven months of the end of the fiscal year the taxpayer can demand a return so that he can self-assess, giving him three months to complete the return within the normal five-year and ten-month time limit. [*TA 1988, s 205(3)(4)* substituted by *FA 1995, s 111(1)*].

Revenue assessment where return but no self-assessment filed

18.11 As indicated in 18.7 self-assessment is not compulsory. The taxpayer is permitted to leave all the relevant calculations and the making of the assessment to the Revenue, as under the old system. However, the tax return must then be submitted to the Revenue by 30 September following the end of the year of assessment or, if the return is issued after 31 July, within two months of its issue. [*TMA 1970, s 9(2); FA 1994, 179*].

18.12 Where a tax return has been filed by 30 September (or the two-month extended deadline) and it does not include a self-assessment the Revenue must make an assessment on the taxpayer on the basis of the information in the return. Where the return is filed out of time and without any self-assessment the Revenue may make an assessment, although they are not then obliged to base it on the return figures. In either case the taxpayer is to be sent a copy of the assessment, which is treated for all purposes as a self-assessment. [*TMA 1970, s 9(3); FA 1994, s 179*].

18.13 The legislation contemplates that the Revenue will make the assessment without any verification or checking of the underlying information, which is different from the present system where the underlying data in a return, particularly any accounts, may be scrutinised. The Revenue can subsequently open an enquiry into that information should they wish.

Revenue determination where no return filed

18.14 Special provisions deal with cases where the taxpayer has been sent a return, but fails to submit it by the filing date. In such cases the Revenue may make a determination to the best of their information and belief of the amounts chargeable to income tax and CGT, and the actual amount of income tax payable taking into account reliefs, allowances, tax deducted at source and tax credits. [*TMA 1970, s 28C(1)(1A); FA 1994, s 190* and *FA 1996, s 125(1)*]. This is to be served on the taxpayer, and is to state the date of issue. [*TMA 1970, s 28C(2)*]. There are corresponding provisions for companies. [*TMA 1970, s 28D,* inserted by *FA 1996, s 138, 24 Sch 7*].

18.15 The determination may be superseded by a later self-assessment, whether an actual self-assessment or a 'deemed' self-assessment made by the Revenue, and based upon information provided in a return submitted subsequently. Until then it is to count as a self-assessment. [*TMA 1970, s 28C(3)*]. References in *TA 1988* and *TCGA 1992* to a person being assessed to tax, or charged to tax by an assessment, include such determination. [*FA 1994, s 197(1)(b)*]. However, such a determination is not a self-assessment, and it is automatically displaced by the submission of an outstanding return. For payment or repayment purposes, the tax shown as payable in the return is substituted for that shown in the determination, but the due dates remain the same. [*TMA 1970, s 59B(5A)* inserted by *FA 1996, s 125(4)*]. For the time limits applicable to such determinations and subsequent self-assessment see 18.38.

18.16 Where recovery proceedings have been commenced following such a determination, and before they are concluded the taxpayer makes a self-assessment, the proceedings may be continued as though they were for tax due according to the self-assessment but unpaid. [*TMA 1970, s 28C(4)*]. This is to avoid the necessity of recovery proceedings having to be recommenced.

Procedure where assessment made by Revenue

18.17 Minor changes are made to the assessing procedure which applies where the Revenue make an assessment. The present provisions in *TMA 1970, s 29* are to be replaced by a new *TMA 1970, s 30A* as inserted by *FA 1994, 19 Sch 5*. All assessments which are not self-assessments are to be made by an officer of the Board except for those which in law can only be made by the Board. [*TMA 1970, s 30A(1)*]. Notice of assessment is to be served on the taxpayer, stating the date of issue and the time limit for appealing. [*TMA 1970, s 30A(3)*].

18.18 Notwithstanding that the taxpayer may have income chargeable under more than one Schedule (and might therefore receive several assessments representing the different sources of income) a single assessment covering all sources of income may be made. [*TMA 1970, s 30A(2)*]. Notice having been so served, the assessment is not to be altered, except expressly in accordance with the provisions of the *Taxes Acts*, e.g. by an amended self-assessment or by an appeal to the Commissioners. [*TMA 1970, s 30A(4)*]. These provisions generally take effect for 1996/97, although for partnerships in existence at 5 April 1994 they take effect from 1997/98. [*FA 1994, 19 Sch 5(2)*].

Amendments to self-assessments/repairs

18.19 An important feature of the new system is the ability of a taxpayer to amend his return and self-assessment within twelve months of the filing date, colloquially described as 'repairing' the return. [*TMA 1970, s 9(4)(b)*]. This could cover cases, for example, where a taxpayer, having filed his return, subsequently realises he has made a mistake in the computation, or where the self-assessment was initially based on an estimate, and a final figure has since become available. Where the taxpayer repairs his return in these circumstances, although interest will run on any additional tax which is payable, the Revenue will not generally seek to exact penalties.

18.20 Moreover, certain mistakes in a self-assessment (for example an arithmetic error) may also be picked up by the Revenue without any detailed audit or verification of the self-assessment, say, by computer scanner or by a Revenue Officer giving it a cursory check. Where there have been any 'obvious' errors or mistakes (whether errors of principle, arithmetical mistakes or otherwise) the Revenue may within nine months from the date the return is filed, correct them by an appropriate amendment to the self-assessment. [*TMA 1970, s 9(4)(a)*]. As with amendments by the taxpayer, it seems in such cases that the Revenue would not seek to exact penalties, but that such an amendment would be part of the 'customer service' procedure to ensure the smooth and effective working of the new system.

18.21 As to the meaning of an 'obvious' error or mistake, this might be thought as somewhat loose terminology in a taxing statute. The Revenue's view is that it covers mistakes which are self-evident, such as the transposition of figures, arithmetical mistakes and other matters which are obvious in the every day sense of the word. In practice it may well be evident in most cases that a particular error falls within this description.

18.22 It is not clear how the Revenue will deal with cases where they have information in their possession which casts doubt on the correctness of a self-assessment. An obvious example is when a taxpayer's declaration of bank interest does not correspond with the information received by the Revenue from the bank. Where the amounts are relatively small it would appear to be reasonable for the matter to be dealt with by suggesting to the taxpayer that a repair be made, rather than by opening a formal enquiry into the person's tax return.

18.23 There is no specific right of appeal as such against a Revenue repair to a taxpayer's self-assessment. But if a taxpayer disagrees with the Revenue that a repair was appropriate, the Revenue accept that he may simply amend his return and self-assessment as he sees fit, substituting his own figures. This would then supersede the Revenue's repair. If the Revenue disputed what had been done they could open a formal enquiry into the return. (Otherwise, given that a Revenue repair can only be made to 'correct' an error or mistake, it would in an extreme case be open to an aggrieved taxpayer to seek judicial review if the Revenue refused to accept that their repair could be superseded, on the basis that the Revenue amendment was simply not a correction.)

18.24 No amendment of a self-assessment can be made once the Revenue announce their intention to make a formal enquiry into a taxpayer's return, until the enquiry is concluded. [*TMA 1970, s 9(5)*]. This precludes, for example, a series of repairs during the course of an audit. The reason is to prevent the situation of a taxpayer making amendments to which the Revenue have to give immediate effect, with a view to disrupting the Revenue enquiry.

18.25 But the Revenue have intimated that it would be expected that the taxpayer would notify them during the enquiry period if he became aware of any mistakes in the return. Thus amendments would be notified informally. The cooperation of the taxpayer in this way would then be a factor in his favour in determining penalties, in the event that the return and the self-assessment were found to be incomplete or incorrect. Moreover, further payments of tax could be made to stop interest running if the taxpayer considered that these were due.

18.26 Similar provisions to the above apply to enable repairs to be made to partnership statements within the same time periods and on the same grounds. [*TMA 1970, s 12AB(2)(3)*]. Where a statement is so amended (whether by the Revenue or the partner making the return) the Revenue Officer is required to give notice to the various partners to amend their own self-assessments accordingly. [*TMA 1970, s 12AB(4)*]. There is a similar prohibition on repairs once an enquiry has begun. [*TMA 1970, s 12AB(4)*].

Self-assessment for companies

18.27 The self-assessment provisions relating to individuals and trustees are reflected in similar provisions for companies, contained in a new *TMA 1970, s 11AA* as inserted by *FA 1994, s 182*. The difference is that it is compulsory for the return to include a self-assessment of the corporation tax for which the company is chargeable for the particular period. The self-assessment is specifically to take into account any relief, allowance or repayment of tax, a claim for which is included in the return. [*TMA 1970, s 11AA(1)*]. Given that the current form of Pay and File return already amounts to a self-assessment, this is no real change.

18.28 However, a new feature is that when there are any obvious errors or mistakes in the self-assessment there is a 'repairs' procedure on the lines of that for individuals and partners described in 18.19 to 18.26. The Revenue are permitted within nine months from delivery of the return to amend the company's self-assessment. [*TMA 1970, s 11AA(2)(a)*]. The company may also submit an amended self-assessment at any time within twelve months of the filing date. [*TMA 1970, s 11AA(2)(b)*]. No amendment can be made once the Revenue have given notice of their intention to enquire into the return until the enquiry is concluded. [*TMA 1970, s 11AA(3)*].

Time limits for Revenue assessment or determination

18.29 The time limits for the making of assessments by the Revenue are amended. The previous normal time limit of six years from the end of the year of assessment becomes five years from 31 January following the end of the year for income tax and CGT. [*TMA 1970, s 34(1)(a)*]. It remains at six years after the end of the accounting period for corporation tax. [*TMA 1970, s 34(1)(b)*].

18.30 In the case of fraudulent or negligent conduct, the time limit becomes 20 years from 31 January following the end of the year of assessment for income tax and CGT, and 21 years after the end of the accounting period for corporation tax. [*TMA 1970, s 36(1)*]. Moreover, in the case of a partnership, the assessment can be made not only on the person in default, but also on any partner or partners of his. [*TMA 1970, s 36(2)*].

18.31 In the case of assessments on personal representatives, the time limit is three years from 31 January following the end of the year of assessment in which the deceased died. [*TMA 1970, s 40(1)*]. When there has been fraud or neglect on the part of the deceased, the six years of assessment before the deceased's death may be reopened, again within three years after 31 January following the end of year of assessment in which he died. [*TMA 1970, s 40(2)*].

18.32 Where no tax return has been delivered, so that the Revenue are empowered to make a determination of the tax liability, there is a time limit of five years from the filing date. Moreover no self-assessment can supersede such a determination unless made within twelve months of it. [*TMA 1970, s 28C(5)*].

Assessment to recover overpayment of tax

18.33 In circumstances where tax has been repaid to a taxpayer and the Revenue consider that this ought not to have been done, they may raise an assessment on the taxpayer to recover the tax overpaid. [*TMA 1970, s 30(1)*]. The assessment and appeals procedure set out in the amended *TMA 1970, s 29* relating to discovery by the Revenue (see 12.51) is then to apply.

18.34 The usual six-year time limit for such an assessment in *TMA 1970, s 34* is amended by *FA 1994, 19 Sch 10* permitting the Revenue to raise an assessment to recover the tax before the later of:

(*a*) the end of the chargeable period following that in which the tax was repaid; and

(*b*) if there has been a Revenue enquiry into the taxpayer's return, or an amendment to it, the end of the enquiry period.

[*TMA 1970, s 30(5)*].

Time limits: special cases

Farm profits averaging

18.35 There is an amendment to the prescribed time limits for claims relating to farm profit averaging and the relief for fluctuating profits. Where the first of the two years of assessment to which the claim relates is 1996/97 or any subsequent year, a claim is to be made twelve months from 31 January after the end of the second of the years of assessment to which the claim relates. Any further claim must be made before 31 January following the end of the year of assessment following that in which the adjustment is made. [*TA 1988, s 96(8)* as amended].

Copyrights and designs

18.36 There is an amendment to the spreading relief for payments from copyright sales. A claim is to be made within seven years from 31 January following the year of assessment in which the work was first published. [*TA 1988, s 534(5)* as amended]. There is a like amendment in relation to payment for the sales of designs. [*TA 1988, s 537A(5)* as amended].

Herd basis

18.37 There are a number of minor changes relating to the making of elections for the herd basis to apply under *TA 1988, 5 Sch*. Given the specialist nature of the matter, these are not analysed in detail here, but the principal change is that the time limit for an election for individuals and partnerships becomes twelve months after 31 January in the following year of assessment. The time limit for companies remains at two years after the end of the accounting period.

Chapter 19

Record-keeping

Background

19.1 Extensive provisions have been introduced laying down particulars as to the records which a taxpayer is now required to maintain. Previously (and unlike VAT) there was no general obligation on the part of the taxpayer to retain records for tax purposes. Some form of record-keeping was indirectly imposed by the ability of the Revenue to raise an estimated assessment of a substantial amount where there was no return, or where they doubted the veracity of the information in a taxpayer's return and accounts. If the taxpayer disputed the assessment, and could not resolve the matter by agreement with the Inspector, his only remedy would be to appeal to the Commissioners. On appeal the onus would be on the taxpayer to provide evidence to satisfy the Commissioners that the assessment was excessive. [*TMA 1970, s 50(6)*]. The most obvious form of evidence would be documentary evidence, specifically records of business transactions. It would, however, be open to the taxpayer to convince the Commissioners of the merits of his case by his own oral testimony and by other forms of evidence other than that contained in the primary documents relating to his trade, profession or vocation.

19.2 The Revenue considered that in the new self-assessment system, enforcement of data retention by means of estimated assessments and setting down cases for appeal was quite inappropriate. Moreover, given that greater responsibility was placed on the taxpayer to determine his own tax liability, checks and balances should be provided by detailed powers of audit. Linked with this was the view that obligations should be imposed upon the taxpayer to maintain full documentary evidence to support the figures used in self-assessment. The Revenue also considered that a simpler procedure for obtaining information than that contained in *TMA 1970, s 20* should be implemented.

Records to be maintained

19.3 The new provisions are to be found in *TMA 1970, s 12B* as inserted by *FA 1994, 19 Sch 3*. Any person who may be required to deliver a tax return under *TMA 1970, ss 8, 8A, 11* or *12AA* (individuals, trustees, companies and partnerships) must keep certain records for the period set out in 19.16 (generally five years from the filing date for those in business, with six years for companies). The records are all those which may be required for the purpose of enabling the taxpayer to make and deliver a correct and complete tax return. [*TMA 1970, s 12B(1)(a)*]. Appropriate records are also to be kept to substantiate any claims which the taxpayer may wish to make under the procedure outlined in 17.4 *et seq*. [*TMA 1970, 1A Sch 2A(1)(a)* inserted by *FA 1995, 20 Sch 2*].

19.4 In the case of a person carrying on a trade, profession or business these records are specifically to include records of all amounts received and expended in the course of the trade, profession or business and the matters in respect of which the receipts and expenditure took place. Furthermore, if the trade involves dealing in goods, the records must also be of all sales and purchases of goods made in the course of the trade. All supporting documents (including accounts, books, deeds, contracts, vouchers and receipts) relating to these various items must be retained. [*TMA 1970, ss 12B(3)(6)*].

19.5 The duty to preserve records may be discharged by the preservation of the information contained in them, and a copy of any document is to be admissible in any proceedings before the Commissioners. [*TMA 1970, s 12B(4)*]. See Tax Bulletin Issue 21, page 283, (Appendix F). The latter differs from the previous position where, strictly speaking, any documents used in proceedings before the Commissioners had to be proved in accordance with the law of evidence. However, where the documents show tax as having been deducted or creditable, the originals have to be kept, from 6 April 1996, or for companies from the appointed day under *FA 1994, s 199(3); TMA 1970, s 12B(4A); FA 1996, s 124(1)–(3)*. These include dividend vouchers under *TA 1988, s 234*, annual payment certificates under *TA 1988, s 352*, subcontractors' certificates under *TA 1988, s 566* and overseas income certificates to which a tax credit applies under *TA 1988, s 788(5)*. Original documents are also required for making a claim outside a tax return. [*TMA 1970, 1A Sch 2A*]. The revised provisions take effect from Royal Assent, 29 April 1996. It appears that electronic payment of dividends in an essentially voucherless system might become possible in the near future and the question of verification of tax deducted in such cases will no doubt have to be addressed.

19.6 Where the original records cannot be produced as required, penalties may nonetheless be avoided if any facts which the Revenue reasonably require to be proved are proved by other documentary evidence such as bank statements, duplicate vouchers, share certificates etc. [*TMA 1970, s 12B(5B); FA 1996, s 124(5)*].

19.7 It will be seen that these provisions impose a comprehensive obligation on the part of taxpayers engaged in a trade, profession or business. Virtually all records of the business and all transactions therein, even down to the smallest petty cash document, are apparently to be retained. The Revenue have issued two booklets, SA/BK4 'A general guide to keeping records' and SA/BK3 'A guide to keeping records for the self-employed' (which also applies to owners of let property) indicating what records they would expect to see. There is a sanction against taxpayers who fail to comply with their obligations, taking the form of a penalty up to £3,000. [*TMA 1970, s 12B(5)*]. It will remain to be seen in practice how strictly the Revenue seek to apply these provisions and exact penalties in cases of default, although they have indicated that they will apply the same standards of mitigation in respect of the gravity of the offence as in any other case.

A general guide to keeping records – employees

19.8 Booklet SA/BK4 suggests that wage and salary slips do not have to be kept but it may be sensible to keep them. The annual form P60 given to employees is an important document and should be retained. Forms P45 issued when an employee leaves a job now contain an extra part (1A) which the employee should retain. Similar changes have been made to form P160 given when an employee retires.

19.9 Under self-assessment, employees will be entitled to a copy of the form P11D or information in connection with expenses and benefits in kind, shown on this form. Under self-assessment it will be necessary to return actual figures for expenses and benefits less amounts claimed as tax deductible. It will no longer be sufficient simply to refer to the P11D on the return form. The copy P11D is therefore an important document to the employee and should be retained. Particulars of participation in share incentive schemes and other benefits should also be retained. It is not necessary but may be helpful to retain PAYE coding notices.

19.10 Booklet SA/BK4 also suggests the retention of tax deduction certificates although it does not emphasise the statutory requirement to do, so having been published prior to the Finance Act 1996, which introduced these provisions. Suggestions are also made for the retention of records relating to capital gains or allowable losses. Booklet SA/BK4 also sets out suggestions for the likely records needed to support tax return entries for foreign income and gains, personal allowances and other deductions or reliefs including deeds of covenant, pension plan certificates, retirement annuity premium certificates, certificates of allowable interest paid etc.

19.11 It is also suggested that employees should keep a record of expenses reimbursed by employers even though the original vouchers will have been given to the employer to support the expenses claim. The Revenue do not expect photocopies but seem to expect employees to keep a personal record of the expenses they incur. They also recommend a log to support car mileage claims showing dates, trips made and business miles travelled and details of any motoring costs incurred. This is, to an extent, a policy of perfection in that the statutory requirement is merely for taxpayers to keep records in order to deliver a correct and complete return, and there is no requirement for those not in business to create records merely for this purpose, although it may be sensible to do so.

A guide to keeping records for the self-employed

19.12 Booklet SA/BK3 which is aimed at the self-employed but also applies to owners of let property, expands on the areas applicable to those running a business to emphasise the necessity to retain all bank and building society statements, stock records, (with the suggestion that a physical stocktaking exercise should be carried out at the year end), particulars of money introduced into the business and personal drawings, as well as wages and PAYE records for employees, and payments to subcontractors. The booklet is aimed very much at the small self-employed business with suggested basic records including a cashbook and petty cashbook.

19.13 Common points of difficulty are dealt with in the booklet such as goods taken for own consumption, bartering, cash payments not backed by vouchers, where it is suggested that a contemporaneous note be made of the expenditure, and the allocation of expenditure such as car expenses between business and private purposes, where a mileage log is suggested. Retailers are recommended to keep till rolls or other forms of electronic record of sales as well as the usual invoices, cashbooks etc. Similar guidance is given for labour only sub-contractors in the construction industry and manufacturing businesses.

19.14 By and large, most well organised businesses will already be retaining all the records they need for self-assessment and most taxpayers would, in the past, have kept details of investment income and purchases and sales of investments which would be adequate under self-assessment. The main change will probably be for employees who will be expected to keep records to back up claims for expenses or reductions in benefits under self-assessment where previously expenses have merely been returned to the Inland Revenue as 'per P11D' which will not be permissible under self-assessment. It is understood that Inspectors will be expected to take a sensible and pragmatic approach to record keeping and penalties for failure to keep adequate records will, at least in the early years of self-assessment, have to be approved by head office.

19.15 It is also to be noted that the obligation to retain detailed records is imposed not just upon those engaged in a trade or profession, but also those engaged in a business. The latter would include persons who, although not actually carrying on a trade, within the precise meaning of the term as interpreted by case law, were nevertheless involved in quasi-trading activities. A business could include, for example, an investment activity carried on in a businesslike manner. *Prima facie* it would also extend to certain forms of property letting, but the legislation specifically provides that a person engaged in the letting of property is to be treated as carrying on a trade [*TMA 1970, s 12B(6)(a)*] for the purpose of record-keeping. Vocations are apparently excluded from these detailed provisions regarding data retention, but the extension of the obligations to persons engaged in a business may in appropriate cases bring in persons carrying on a vocation, where the vocation is carried on in a businesslike way.

Period for retention of records

19.16 In the case of an individual carrying on a trade, profession or business alone or in partnership and for owners of let property all relevant records have to be preserved until the fifth anniversary of the 31 January following the end of the year of assessment. In the case of a company all records have to be preserved until the sixth anniversary of the end of the accounting period in question. In any other case records have to be kept until the first anniversary of the 31 January following the end of the year of assessment (i.e. 22 months). [*TMA 1970, s 12B(2); FA 1995, s 105*]. As the legislation is drafted those carrying on a trade, profession or business and owners of let property have to retain non-trading records (e.g. details of investment income) for the full five-year period.

19.17 In all cases where enquiries are being made into the taxpayer's return the records must be kept until the enquiries are completed. Moreover, if the time limit for enquiries expires after the dates in 19.16 the records have to be kept until the expiry of the time limit. [*TMA 1970, s 12B(1)(b), (2)*, as amended by *FA 1995, s 105(1)(2)*]. Furthermore, where a taxpayer is required to submit a return after the time limits in 19.16 (perhaps as a result of Revenue enquiries) any records that he has retained must be preserved until any Revenue enquiries have been completed, or until the time limit for making such enquiries has expired. [*TMA 1970, s 12B(2A)* inserted by *FA 1995, s 105(3)*].

19.18 In relation to records relating to claims, the information has to be kept until the latest of the day on which any Revenue enquiries into the claim, or any amendment of it, are completed, and the day on which the Revenue no longer have power to make such enquiries. Revenue enquiries are completed when so confirmed by the Revenue by notice under *TMA 1970, 1A Sch 7(4)*.

Chapter 20

Finality and Certainty, Revenue Powers of Enquiry; Discovery

Finality and certainty

20.1 The issues of finality and certainty are most important features of any tax system. In particular the taxpayer should be reasonably sure that, given full disclosure on his part, once his liability for a particular year has been determined, the matter cannot be reopened and reviewed at a later date.

20.2 The method of achieving this under the former system was for a review by the Inspector of every single case, aimed at satisfying himself as to the taxpayer's liability. The procedures involved, namely the submission by the taxpayer of his return, together with any accompanying accounts and other data, followed by subsequent requests by the Inspector for further information if required, correspondence, and negotiations in some cases, generally ensured that any controversial issues had been explored. The usual result was a tax assessment being agreed and becoming final. The matter could only be opened subsequently if there had been fraud or neglect by the taxpayer, or if the Revenue's discovery powers could be invoked.

20.3 The matter becomes more complicated in a system based upon self-assessment, where it is contemplated that in the vast majority of cases a taxpayer will calculate his own liability and the matter will not be reviewed by the Revenue. A balance has to be struck between giving reasonable certainty to taxpayers and the need to ensure that individual taxpayers do not benefit to the detriment of the general body of taxpayers, either by deliberately or carelessly underdeclaring their taxable income, or by taking an unjustifiably 'liberal' interpretation of the law, for example claiming a deduction for expenditure which on any reasonable view is unlikely to be allowable.

20.4 The approach which has been taken in the new system to resolve these issues may be summarised as follows.

(*a*) For a given period, which is generally twelve months after the filing date for returns and the making of a self-assessment, the Revenue have complete freedom to audit a taxpayer's return and self-assessment.

(*b*) Once that period has elapsed, a taxpayer's liability becomes final and conclusive, subject to the ability of the Revenue to reopen the matter in cases of fraud or neglect, or where they 'discover' an error or mistake.

20.5 The Revenue's powers of enquiry are considered in 20.7 *et seq*. The rights given to the Revenue in connection therewith, for example to require the taxpayer to produce data, are much greater than those previously available to an Inspector carrying out his normal review of a taxpayer's affairs. But this is perhaps an inevitable outcome of a self-assessment system.

20.6 The Revenue's powers of discovery are considered in 20.37 *et seq*. They generally allow the Revenue to open a matter only if there has not been full disclosure by the taxpayer. Inevitably there may be some doubt as to the proper treatment of certain items in the taxpayer's computation, and questions then arise as to the extent to which these must be drawn to the Revenue's attention. This has led to the introduction of a post-transaction rulings system as outlined in 16.72 *et seq*. Taking advantage of the ability to obtain such a ruling may in certain instances be the only safe way in which a taxpayer can be assured of finality and certainty in difficult cases.

Revenue enquiry/audit

Revenue powers of enquiry

20.7 The ability and freedom of the individual taxpayer to self-assess his liability is balanced by giving to the Revenue detailed powers of enquiry and investigation into his return and his self-assessment. There are like powers to enable the Revenue to enquire into partnership returns. It has been decided that the usual period within which such an enquiry can be commenced is one year from the filing date, namely 31 January for individuals and trustees. No justification is required for opening an enquiry. In some cases returns may be selected for enquiry because computer checks indicate an apparent inconsistency. There will also be an element of random selection.

20.8 The Revenue considered that a year from the filing date would give them sufficient time to amass and assimilate other information received about taxpayers' returns from third parties, such as employers, contractors and financial institutions, as well as a reasonable period within which to decide whether to raise an enquiry within their normal work programme. They have stated that they are not prepared to give any taxpayers an earlier assurance or clearance that they would not be audited, as this would be unfair on others who could not be given such an assurance. The nature of any particular enquiry will depend upon the particular case, and could range from a straightforward computational question to a full investigation.

20.9 A Revenue Code of Practice for enquiry work is to be issued together with information for taxpayers who are selected for enquiry. There is to be a short version which would be issued to taxpayers in cases where the enquiries were expected (*a*) to be brief and straightforward, (*b*) not to involve extensive records examination and (*c*) not to involve questions of culpability. There is also a right of taxpayers to ask the Commissioners to close enquiries when these are unreasonably prolonged (see 20.23). The Revenue envisage that failure to follow up notice of enquiries within a reasonable period would be a justifiable cause of complaint under the Code.

Individuals and trustees

20.10 To implement the new powers of enquiry, there is a new *TMA 1970, s 19A* dealing with individuals and trustees. A formal notice in writing must be served on the taxpayer within specified time limits. [*TMA 1970, s 19A(1)* as inserted by *FA 1994, s 187*]. Where the taxpayer has a professional adviser acting for him, he will also be notified. In the case of a tax return, or any amendment to it, delivered before the filing date (31 January) the time limit is twelve months from that date. In the case of a return or amendment delivered after the filing date, the time limit is the quarter day following the anniversary of the date of delivery of the return or the amendment. [*TMA 1970, s 19A(2)*]. For these purposes the quarter days are 31 January, 30 April, 31 July and 31 October. So if a return for 1997/98 is submitted to the Revenue on 15 March 1999 the Officer can serve a notice of enquiry on the taxpayer up to 30 April 2000. There is a like provision for companies in *TMA 1970, s 11AB*, and for partnerships in *TMA 1970, s 12AC*. [*FA 1994, ss 183, 186*].

20.11 Where the return and self-assessment are delivered to the Revenue before the filing date, but an amendment is made after the filing date, enquiries can only be raised by the Revenue after the first anniversary of the filing date in respect of items that were the subject of the amendment. Once a return or amendment has been the subject of an enquiry, there can be no further enquiry. [*TMA 1970, s 9A(3)*]. Where an enquiry has been opened, the ability of the taxpayer to amend his return or self-assessment is frozen. However, the Revenue would expect the taxpayer to inform them of any 'repairs' (see 18.25) he considered appropriate and these would be taken into account at the end of the enquiry, notably in determining any penalties.

Partnerships

20.12 Essentially the same provisions apply to enable the Revenue to enquire into partnership statements or amendments to such statements, with the same time limits applying. [*TMA 1970, s 12AC*]. Notice is to be given to the person who delivered the return or his successor. For this purpose, 'successor', in a case where the person who delivered the return is no longer a partner or is otherwise not available, means a partner nominated by the majority of the remaining partners. [*TMA 1970, s 12AC(6)*]. It is understood that the Revenue will in practice notify individual partners of the opening of their enquiries. The opening of an enquiry into a partnership return automatically extends to the partners' personal returns.

Companies

20.13 Under new *TMA 1970, s 11AB* the Revenue are given matching powers to enquire into a company's tax return or any amendments to it. The time limit is also twelve months from the filing date if the return was delivered on time, otherwise it is the quarter day following the first anniversary of the date of delivery of the return. [*TMA 1970, s 11AB(2)*].

Production of documents

20.14 The investigating officer may require the taxpayer (on not less than 30 days notice) to produce such documents, accounts or particulars as are in his possession or power as the officer may reasonably require for the purpose of determining whether a return is correct or complete or any amendment to it is correct. [*TMA 1970, s 19A(2)(a)*]. The officer may also require the taxpayer to furnish him with such accounts or particulars as he may reasonably require. [*TMA 1970, s 19A(2)(b)*]. The purpose of this is to obtain information not in existence at the time the return was submitted, for example to obtain written answers to questions. There are penalties for failure to comply (see 22.38). This power to require information ties in with the new obligations imposed on taxpayers with regard to the preservation of records (see Chapter 19). Inevitably questions will arise as to what is 'reasonable' in any particular case, for example, whether reasonableness relates to materiality (such as a request for petty cash dockets) or to other criteria. These issues are to be covered in the Revenue's Code of Practice on enquiries.

20.15 It is in order for the taxpayer to supply photographic or other facsimile copies of documents, but the Revenue can require (on not less than 30 days notice) to see the originals and take copies or make extracts. [*TMA 1970, s 19A(3)(4)*]. The Revenue already have powers of investigation under *TMA 1970, s 20*, but these are subject to particular safeguards. They evidently considered that they required almost an unfettered right to examine prime records, and that the existing *section 20* powers were too cumbersome for general use in policing self-assessment. But the Revenue did not apparently consider that a right of entry into the taxpayer's premises was required, although a 'field audit' might in practice be the simplest way of confirming the taxpayer's accounts with the original books of accounts, invoices and other original documents.

20.16 A taxpayer is not obliged to produce documents, or furnish accounts or particulars which relate to the conduct of any pending appeal by him. [*TMA 1970, s 19A(5)*]. The value to a taxpayer or the relevance of this is debatable since under self-assessment it is unlikely that an appeal will be pending.

Right of appeal against notice to produce documents

20.17 A taxpayer has the right of appeal to the Commissioners against a notice to produce documents, or furnish accounts or particulars. The same appeals procedure then applies as if it were an appeal against an assessment to tax. [*TMA 1970, s 19A(6)(7)(8)*]. The Commissioners are empowered to confirm the notice if it appears to them that the production of the documents etc. was reasonably required, otherwise they are to set it aside. [*TMA 1970, s 19A(9)*]. How this ties in with the limitation on the obligation to produce documents when an appeal is pending or documents containing legal advice is not clear. There is no further right of appeal by way of case stated. [*TMA 1970, s 19A(11)*]. It would seem that an aggrieved taxpayer's only remedy would then be by way of judicial review. This right of appeal does provide some element of balance, and is an assurance for the taxpayer against possible abuse of their powers by the Revenue.

Assessment of tax after opening of enquiry

20.18 Where an enquiry into a taxpayer's return has been opened, if it appears to the Revenue Officer that the tax paid under the self-assessment was too low, and that unless there was an immediate amendment to the assessment there was likely to be a loss of tax to the Crown, he is entitled to amend the assessment by notice served on the taxpayer. [*TMA 1970, s 28A(2); FA 1994, s 188*].

20.19 The purpose of this power is to enable the Revenue to move quickly, well before the enquiries are completed, to try and forestall the loss of tax by, for example, a taxpayer skipping the jurisdiction or contriving a bankruptcy. The taxpayer has the right of appeal against such an amended assessment, as shown by the procedures as set out in 23.4 below. But the appeal is not to be heard until the enquiries are completed. So the taxpayer's only interim remedy to expedite the matter is to apply to the Commissioners to direct the Officer to bring the enquiries to an end (see 20.23).

Conclusion of enquiry and amendment of assessment – individuals, trustees and companies

20.20 Having completed his enquiries, the Revenue Officer is obliged to issue a notice to the taxpayer, informing him he has done so and stating his conclusions as to the proper amount of tax. [*TMA 1970, s 28A(5)*]. The taxpayer is then allowed 30 days to amend his self-assessment to make good any deficiency or eliminate any excess. [*TMA 1970, s 28A(3)*]. The taxpayer thus has the opportunity to amend his assessment upwards or downwards to accord with the views of the Revenue Officer (or indeed to some other level which the taxpayer considers appropriate).

20.21 Amendment by agreement between the Revenue and the taxpayer is the clearly desired course, as it would result in the enquiry coming to an end without the necessity for any further consideration of the matter. Furthermore, in the event that during the enquiry it became evident that additional tax was due it would be to the benefit of the taxpayer to make further payments on account in order to prevent further interest running. It is contemplated that the agreement would follow a negotiation process, effectively resulting in an arbitrated figure.

20.22 In the event that the taxpayer does not amend his self-assessment to the Officer's satisfaction within the 30-day period, the Officer is permitted, within the next 30 days, to amend the assessment to what he considers is the appropriate figure. The taxpayer has a right of appeal against such amendment (see 23.4). This effectively preserves a system similar to the present in cases where agreement cannot be reached between the taxpayer and the Inspector.

Direction to bring enquiry to an end

20.23 At any time during the enquiry period the taxpayer is entitled to apply to the Commissioners to direct the Officer to bring the enquiries to an end. The issue is then heard and determined in the same way as an appeal, and the Commissioners are to give such a direction unless they are satisfied that the Officer has reasonable grounds for continuing his enquiries. [*TMA 1970, s 28A(6)(7)*]. There is thus some protection against the Revenue prolonging their enquiries beyond a reasonable period.

Conclusion of enquiry and amendment of assessment – partnerships

20.24 *TMA 1970, s 28B* as inserted by *FA 1994, s 189* contains the provisions which apply where the Revenue have made an enquiry into a partnership statement. These largely mirror the provisions relating to enquiries made into the tax returns of individuals, trustees and companies outlined above. Thus, having completed his enquiries the Officer is to inform the taxpayer (which includes a reference to any predecessor or successor of his) [*TMA 1970, s 28B(8)*] that he has completed those enquiries, stating his conclusions as to the proper amount of tax. [*TMA 1970, s 28B(5)*].

20.25 The taxpayer is then allowed 30 days to amend the partnership statement to make good any deficiency of tax or eliminate any excess. [*TMA 1970, s 28B(2)*]. Should the taxpayer not do so the Officer is permitted, within the next 30 days, to amend the assessment as appropriate. [*TMA 1970, s 28B(3)*]. In either case the Officer is to give notice to the various partners to amend their self-assessment to give effect to the amendments of the partnership statement. [*TMA 1970, s 28B(4)*].

20.26 The taxpayer has the right of appeal to the Commissioners against such Revenue amendment to the partnership statement (see 23.4). Moreover, at any time in the enquiry period, the taxpayer has like powers to apply to the Commissioners to direct the Officer to bring the enquiries to an end as those set out in 20.23.

Revenue enquiry into claims

General position

20.27 In the same way as the Revenue are empowered to enquire into a taxpayer's return and self-assessment (which will include any claim made in the return) there are like powers to enquire into a claim made by a taxpayer other than in his return, or any amendment made to such a claim. [*TMA 1970, 1A Sch 5(1)* as inserted by *FA 1994, 19 Sch 35*]. A formal notice in writing must be served on the taxpayer, or in the case of a partnership claim, any successor, within specified time limits. The time limit is the period ending with the quarter day following the first anniversary of the day on which the claim or amendment was made. [*TMA 1970, 1A Sch 5(2)*]. Once such an enquiry has been made into a claim there cannot be a further enquiry. [*TMA 1970, 1A Sch 5(3)*].

20.28 Where an enquiry has been opened, the Revenue may require the taxpayer (on not less than 30 days' notice) to produce such documents as are in his possession or power and are reasonably required for the purpose of determining whether the claim or amendment is incorrect. There are like powers to request accounts or particulars. [*TMA 1970, 1A Sch 6(2)*]. All the provisions which apply in a case of a Revenue enquiry into a taxpayers return, as outlined in 20.10 *et seq.* above, are to apply. [*TMA 1970, 1A Sch 6(3)*].

20.29 The Revenue have intimated that such enquiry will require the same sort of dialogue between the Inspector and the taxpayer as is seen at the moment. In the progression towards agreement it is anticipated that points would be agreed along the way and that the Inspector's conclusions at the end of the enquiry would summarise the agreed positions and the Inspector's position in any items in dispute. As set out below there would then be 30 days for the taxpayer to deal with the mechanics of any amendments, such as additional or amended claims, in line with the procedure relating to enquiries into tax returns.

Conclusion of enquiry and amendment of claim

20.30 As with Revenue enquiries into a taxpayer's return, once the enquiries have been completed the Revenue Officer must inform the taxpayer and state his conclusions as to the amount which should have been in the claim. [*TMA 1970, 1A Sch 7(4)*]. The taxpayer is then allowed 30 days to amend his claim to eliminate or make good any excess or deficiency, or to give effect to any amendments to the claim which he has notified to the Officer. [*TMA 1970, 1A Sch 7(2)*].

20.31 The taxpayer thus has the opportunity to amend the claim, so as to reflect the conclusions of the Revenue Officer. Should he not do so the Officer is permitted, within the next 30 days, to amend the claim as appropriate. [*TMA 1970, 1A Sch 7(3)*]. The taxpayer has the right of appeal against such amendment by the Revenue Officer [*TMA 1970, 1A Sch 9*] (see 23.6). After a claim has been so amended, effect is to be given to the amendment within 30 days either by way of an assessment on the taxpayer, or by a discharge of tax, or a repayment of tax as the case may be. [*TMA 1970, 1A Sch 8(1)*]. Like provisions are included for partners. [*TMA 1970, 1A Sch 8(2)*].

20.32 As with the like provisions relating to enquiries into a taxpayer's return, at any time during the enquiry period the taxpayer may apply to the Commissioners to direct the Officer to bring the enquiries to an end. The provisions set out in 20.23 are to apply as regards the handling of the matter thereafter. [*TMA 1970, 1A Sch 7(5)*].

Discovery

Previous position and background

20.33 The previous rules relating to discovery developed from two apparently contradictory provisions in *TMA 1970*, and were a continuing source of controversy. They were contained in a combination of statute and case law, Revenue practice and concession. Outside the fields of fraud and neglect, *TMA 1970, s 29(3)* gave the Inspector an ostensibly untrammelled right to raise a further assessment, within six years of the end of the year of assessment in question, if he 'discovered' that the original assessment was incorrect. But where an assessment had been determined by agreement under *TMA 1970, s 54*, following an appeal by the taxpayer, the determination was treated as final and conclusive under *TMA 1970, s 46(2)*. Where there was new evidence, the matter could be reopened. But where there was merely a change of mind by the Inspector (or his successor) there was a limitation on the right to make further assessments.

20.34 The issues were considered in two leading cases. The first, *Cenlon Finance Co Ltd v Ellwood 1962 40 TC 176* held, in a case where the Inspector had explicitly agreed the point in issue, that a further assessment was not possible on a point which had been agreed in the course of determining the first appeal. The second case, which found its way to the House of Lords, *Olin Energy Systems Ltd v Scorer [1985] STC 218* concerned a company's computation in which the point at issue was identified, but was not explicitly addressed by the Inspector, and which was technically incorrect. Losses which had arisen from one trade were carried forward and set against the profits of another trade in the following year. This was not in fact permissible under the relevant corporation tax provisions. It was held that the matter could not be reopened, since it was reasonable to accept that the Inspector had *implicitly* considered and accepted the position put forward by the company in the computation.

20.35 After considerable debate the Revenue issued a Statement of Practice, SP 8/91, which set out their interpretation of the position where there had been an appeal by the taxpayer against an assessment which was determined by a *TMA 1970, s 54* agreement. The stance taken by the Revenue, in cases where there had been no *explicit* agreement, was to accept that discovery could not be made if:

(*a*) the point was fundamental to the basis of computation of the taxpayer's liability; and

(*b*) it was so clearly and fully described in the accounts or computations that its significance was clearly apparent and the Inspector was put on notice of the point.

20.36 By concession the Revenue took the same line in cases where there had been no formal appeal and determination. Moreover, in cases where the point was not fundamental, they did not seek to raise a further assessment if the position taken by the original Inspector was a tenable one.

Discovery under self-assessment

Disclosure by taxpayer

20.37 As outlined above, apart from fraud or neglect, the ability under the previous system to make a discovery assessment was essentially linked to two questions:

(*a*) whether there had been full disclosure by the taxpayer; and

(*b*) whether the Inspector had agreed the point at issue, which must be fundamental, either explicitly or implicitly.

20.38 In self-assessment, the second question is no longer relevant because there is no requirement for the Inspector to be satisfied as to the information in a taxpayer's return and agree upon a particular point, so that he can raise the requisite assessment. The issue accordingly becomes one of full disclosure by the taxpayer only.

Codification of old rules

20.39 Given this narrowing down of the position, and the fact that the problem becomes somewhat simpler, the Revenue have chosen to codify the law in appropriate statutory provisions. Their expressed intention has been to follow the tests which they consider emerge from the judgments in the *Olin* case. In particular, for a taxpayer to avoid any possibility of a discovery assessment being raised at a later date, the disclosure of a particular point has to be sufficiently full and clear to put an ordinarily competent Inspector on notice of precisely what issues need to be considered and the stance taken on them. The Revenue have issued a paper concerning the operation of the discovery and disclosure rules under self-assessment. The paper addresses the concerns that have been expressed about the circumstances in which the Revenue will make assessments on the discovery of profits that have not been assessed or were inadequately assessed, or where excessive relief has been given. For the full text of the paper see Inland Revenue Press Release 31 May 1996 (Appendix C).

New statutory provisions

20.40 The position for 1996/97 and subsequent years (and in the case of companies for accounting periods ending on or after 1 April 1996, at the earliest, probably 1 April 1988) is set out in substituted *TMA 1970, s 29*, as follows. If the Revenue discover that any profits which should have been assessed to tax have not been assessed to tax, or that an assessment has been insufficient, or excess relief has been given, they may make the appropriate assessment to make good the loss of tax only if one of two alternative conditions is satisfied. [*TMA 1970, s 29(1)*].

20.41 The first alternative condition is that the loss of tax is the result of fraudulent or negligent conduct by the taxpayer, or any person acting on his behalf. [*TMA 1970, s 29(4)*]. 'Fraudulent or negligent' conduct would extend to a failure to observe the standards to be expected of a reasonable man in the circumstances. An arithmetical error, a double deduction, or such other obvious error would possibly amount to negligence.

20.42 The second alternative condition (and the one relevant to the issues raised in 20.38 to 20.40) is that when a Revenue Officer ceased to be entitled to enquire into a return or, in the event of any enquiry, informed the taxpayer that he had completed his enquiries, he could not reasonably have been expected to be aware of the tax deficiency on the basis of the information made available to him. [*TMA 1970, s 25(5)*]. For the purposes of this second condition information is treated as made available to the Officer if:

(*a*) It is contained in the taxpayer's tax return, or in any accounts, statements or documents accompanying the return (which includes any amended return and accompanying documents). For this purpose the return is that for the chargeable period in question and the two immediately preceding periods. [*TMA 1970, ss 29(6)(a), (7)(a)(i)*].

(*b*) It is contained in any claim made by the taxpayer, or in any accounts, statements or documents accompanying the return. [*TMA 1970, s 29(6)(b)*].

(*c*) It is contained in any documents, accounts or particulars which are produced during the course of any Revenue enquiry. [*TMA 1970, s 29(6)(c)*].

(*d*) It is information the existence and relevance of which could reasonably be expected to be inferred by the Revenue Officer from the information in (*a*)–(*c*), or which is notified in writing by the taxpayer to the Revenue. [*TMA 1970, s 29(6)(d)*].

20.43 Provided that the information submitted to the Revenue is sufficiently comprehensive, and either any controversial point is specifically raised, or its relevance can clearly be inferred, under these new rules discovery will not be possible. Although the test of 'reasonableness' in the opening words of the second alternative condition is ostensibly linked to the particular Officer concerned with the taxpayer, it would seem that an objective standard of reasonableness is appropriate. So, for example, the degree of reasonableness does not depend on the grade and experience of the actual Officer concerned. It seems that this is the view of the Revenue and that the hypothetical Officer will be the 'ordinarily competent' Officer. Questions will inevitably arise as to whether the information, or the form in which it was presented, were indeed sufficient to satisfy this 'reasonableness' test or the 'inference' and 'relevance' tests set out in 20.42(*d*).

20.44 A further point is that a taxpayer is not protected from the kind of case where, for example, the information given should have put the Officer on enquiry, but he actually decided not to make such an enquiry. An example could be a practice of calculating work-in-progress which might not strictly be correct, but which had been agreed with the Officer's predecessor as satisfactory, possibly on the basis that it was straightforward, applied consistently, and saved time in calculations. If such approach was applied in future periods, but the accounts and return did not fully describe the particular method, it would appear that the successor Officer would not be precluded from reopening the case.

Information submitted on past returns

20.45 There is a limited extent to which information given to the Revenue in past periods is to be assumed to be known to them in the current period (see 20.42(*a*)) which only brings in the two prior returns). In this regard, even a permanent note on the taxpayer's file would not suffice. The Revenue have observed that it cannot be assumed that a Revenue Officer will always make systematic permanent notes regarding a particular taxpayer. It would seem that some form of cross-referencing to past periods might be in order, but to be sure any potentially controversial areas would have to be dealt with explicitly, at least once every three years.

Filing of business accounts

20.46 The issue of disclosure can arise acutely in relation to the preparation and submission of business accounts and computations. For example, changes of business or accounting practice may have occurred during a period and there may be scope for different interpretations as to the correct tax position, notably whether the adoption of a particular accounting practice is also appropriate for tax purposes. So far as tax returns and business accounts are concerned, there is no formal requirement for businesses to submit anything other than the standard accounting information (SAI) referred to in 16.28, other than for the larger partnerships with turnover exceeding £15m where formal business accounts will be required.

20.47 The Revenue's view is that most taxpayers will need to do little more than supply this information, identifying any possible areas of concern in the 'white space' on the return. In this regard the majority of income tax cases involve reasonably straightforward accounts, with some 95 per cent returning profits or losses below £50,000, and the Revenue estimating that up to 99 per cent have turnover below £1m. In these cases the Revenue consider that the SAI and white space should normally enable a complete and fair picture of the business to be presented.

20.48 In large or more complex cases the position may well be otherwise. A full picture of the business may only be provided if full business accounts are submitted in addition to the SAI. The question then arises whether the mere inclusion of such accounts, and any other documentation considered to be relevant, would protect the taxpayer against a later discovery assessment. Provided the relevant issues could be reasonably identified from these documents (for example, by a note to the accounts regarding a change in accounting policy) then the requirements of *TMA 1970, s 29* referred to in 20.42 would seem to be satisfied, without any further flagging of the point.

20.49 However, the Revenue take a more restrictive view. They consider that where voluminous material is sent in with the return, it would be unreasonable to expect Revenue Officers to examine that material in detail if there is no obvious reason why it has been sent. Their recommendation is that there should be a brief indication of the relevance of the material. So even if detailed accounts were included, a change of accounting policy relating to say, stock valuation, should be highlighted. Moreover, if a capital gain was reported on the tax return, and the sale agreement was included, its relevance would need to be explained.

20.50 Whether or not the Revenue's restrictive interpretation of the law is correct (and there must be some considerable doubt about it given the express reference to accounts or documents accompanying the return being treated as made available to the Revenue, (see 20.42(*a*)), the prudent course would be to submit full accounts and highlight any potentially controversial areas in anything other than cases of the smaller business.

Discretionary and judgemental issues

20.51 As described in 17.38 the move to self-assessment has radically changed the procedure, relating to reliefs in particular, where a person's tax position previously depended on the Revenue either formally accepting a state of affairs or exercising their discretion in favour of the taxpayer in a particular way. Generally specific claims had to be made. *FA 1996, s 134* and *20 Sch* have amended seventy-one different provisions in the Taxation Acts to transfer the complete onus in deciding the issue to the taxpayer. To avoid the risk of discovery assessments being made by the Revenue at a later date, where advantage has been taken of reliefs in particular, in circumstances where entitlement may be open to question, the issue should be highlighted in the return.

Valuations

20.52 In cases where liability is determined by reference to valuations, for example, a CGT computation where 31 March 1982 value was relevant, it seems that if a professional valuation has been included in the return, which is within a reasonable range, the matter cannot be reopened under a discovery assessment after the twelve-month period has elapsed (see 20.4). This assumes that the information given to the valuer is sufficiently comprehensive.

Error and prevailing practice

20.53 Finally, where a tax return has been filed and the tax shortfall results from an error or mistake as to the basis on which the liability should have been computed, the shortfall is not recoverable if the return was made on the basis of, or in accordance with, the practice generally prevailing at the time when it was made. [*TMA 1970, s 29(2)*]. An objection by a taxpayer to the making of a discovery assessment is to be made by an appeal against the assessment. [*TMA 1970, s 29(8)*]. The usual appeal procedures set out in Chapter 23 then apply.

Discovery and partnership statements

20.54 There are similar discovery provisions relating to partnership statements on the same lines as those described above. Subject to one of two alternative conditions, if the Revenue discover that any profits which should have been included in the partnership statement have not been included, or that the profits therein are insufficient, or that any relief given is excessive, they may by notice given to the representative partner (or his successor) amend the statement accordingly. [*TMA 1970,* *s 30B(1)(4); FA 1994, 19 Sch 6*]. The Revenue Officer is then, by notice given to each of the relevant partners (being persons who were partners at any time in the period in respect of which the partnership statement was made) [*TMA 1970, s 30B(9)*], required to make the appropriate amendments to their self-assessments. [*TMA 1970, s 30B(2)*].

20.55 The first alternative condition is that the incorrect partnership statement is attributable to fraudulent or negligent conduct of the representative partner or a person acting on his behalf, or a relevant partner or a person acting on his behalf. [*TMA 1970, s 30B(5)*].

20.56 The second alternative condition is that when a Revenue Officer ceased to be entitled to enquire into the representative partner's return (or, in the event of an enquiry, informed him that he had completed his enquiries), the Officer could not reasonably have been expected to be aware of the tax deficiency on the basis of the information made available to him. [*TMA 1970, s 30B(6)*]. In determining the extent of the information which is regarded as made available to the Revenue Officer, the corresponding provisions relating to individuals set out in 20.42 are to apply with appropriate amendments. [*TMA 1970, s 30B(7)*].

20.57 There is provision for appeal against a notice of amendment to a partnership statement served by the Revenue. [*TMA 1970, s 30B(8)*]. Moreover, as with individuals, where the tax deficiency in the partnership statement results from an error or mistake as to the basis of which the statement should have been made, the deficiency is not recoverable if the statement was made on the basis of, or in accordance with, the practice generally prevailing at the time when it was made. [*TMA 1970, s 30B(3)*].

Chapter 21

Payment of Tax

Background

21.1 The old system for the payment of tax had become far too complex. An individual with different sources of income and capital gains had several separate payment dates, and indeed more if assessments were issued after the normal due date. All the paperwork involved, with separate assessments and payment slips, posed an enormous administrative burden on the Revenue and led to errors. In devising the new system there were two evident objectives. First, the existing arrangement had to be streamlined and simplified. Secondly, exchequer cash flow had to be preserved in the transition from the preceding year to the current year basis.

New system in outline

21.2 Under the new system income tax is to be payable in three instalments. Payment is not linked to any assessment system. It will have to be made automatically by the taxpayer, although there will be a system of statements issued by the Revenue in advance of the due date. The first two instalments are payments on account, due on 31 January in the year of assessment and 31 July in the next year of assessment. The general rule is that each payment on account is 50 per cent of the income tax and Class 4 NIC liability of the preceding year of assessment, less any tax deducted at source. The third and final payment discharges the balance of the taxpayer's income tax liability, and the whole of any CGT. It is due on 31 January following the end of the year of assessment.

Example 1

Mr Andrew was assessed to income tax of £24,000 for 1997/98, of which £6,000 was deducted at source. The interim payments for 1998/99 will be £9,000 each, due on 31 January 1999 and 31 July 1999. (To each of these will have to be added 50% of the previous year's Class 4 NIC liability.) His self-assessment for 1998/99 in due course indicates a total income tax liability of £32,000. The final payment for 1998/99 will be £8,000 due by 31 January 2000, assuming again £6,000 deducted at source.

Payments on account – interim payments

21.3 The system of payments on account (called 'interim payments') is to operate in all cases of a continuing trade, profession or vocation, where (*a*) the person concerned is assessed to tax for the preceding year, and (*b*) the amount so assessed exceeds the income tax deducted at source. Each interim payment is generally to be 50 per cent of the preceding year's income tax and Class 4 NIC liability, net of any tax deducted at source. [*TMA 1970, s 59A(1)(2)*]. There will be no interim payments in respect of CGT.

21.4 In the event that an assessment (including a self-assessment) for the preceding year is raised or amended after the due date for either payment, the amount due is deemed to have been 50 per cent of the amount determined on the basis of the assessment so raised or amended. Moreover, where for the year preceding the year of assessment, an assessment has been made following a Revenue discovery that tax has been lost, the tax charged in that assessment is to be included in the calculation of the payment on account. Any variation in the Revenue assessment is to be reflected in the payment due. [*TMA 1970, s 59A(4A)(4B)* inserted by *FA 1995, s 108(3)* and *FA 1996, 18 Sch 2*]. Thus a payment on account will be due whether or not a taxpayer has made a self-assessment for the preceding year. The position will be likewise if an assessment is later amended, say as the result of a Revenue enquiry. Any amount which is underpaid as a result will fall due for payment at that time. Likewise any amount overpaid can be reclaimed. [*TMA 1970, s 59A(5)* as amended by *FA 1995, s 108(4)*].

21.5 Tax deducted at source means:

(i) the aggregate of:

- (*a*) income tax deducted or treated as deducted from any income, or treated as paid on any income in respect of the year;
- (*b*) tax credits attaching to dividends; and
- (*c*) any PAYE deducted in the year, and any PAYE in respect of the year but to be deducted in subsequent years;

(ii) less:

- (*a*) any PAYE deductions made in the year but which relate to previous years. [*TMA 1970, s 59A(8)* substituted by *FA 1995, s 108(5)*].

21.6 Even where the assessed amount exceeds the tax deducted at source there will not automatically be an obligation to make a payment on account. Thus regulations are to be issued in due course establishing minimum limits below which interim payments will not be required. The limits have not yet been announced, but it is envisaged there will be two alternatives, an absolute minimum level and a percentage of total income not taxed at source. [*TMA 1970, s 59A(1)(c)(d)*]. So a taxpayer may be excused from making payments on account if a significant proportion of his tax liability is met by deduction at source. The intention will be to set the limits at a level such that most employees, pensioners, and others who receive the bulk of their income under deduction of tax or who have relatively small outstanding tax liabilities, will not have to make payments on account.

21.7 In other cases, in particular where the year of assessment is the year in which a trade is commenced there will be no interim payments, all the tax being due under the final payment procedure. Moreover, the interim payments may be eliminated or reduced in certain cases, for example, where a trade has ceased or where profits are falling. If the taxpayer believes that he will not be assessed to tax for a particular year of assessment, or that the amount assessed will not exceed the tax deducted at source, he may submit a claim to this effect before 31 January following the year of assessment, giving the reasons for his belief. Interim payments will then not be required [*TMA 1970, s 59A(3)*], and all necessary and consequential adjustments are to be made; whether by repayment of tax, or otherwise. [*TMA 1970, s 59A(5)*]. The Revenue have no power to reject such claims, but after processing, the claim will be reviewed for possible fraud or neglect.

21.8 For recovery purposes any amount payable on account by way of interim payment is treated as income tax. [*TMA 1970, s 59A(7)*]. Moreover, the Revenue are empowered to direct at any time prior to 31 January following the year of assessment that payments on account are not required, and to make any necessary adjustments to give effect to that direction. [*TMA 1970, s 59A(9)* inserted by *FA 1995, s 108(5)*].

Example 2 (continuing)

Mr Brown is a property developer and is considering the interim payments for 1998/99. His profits for the year to 31 December 1997 were £60,000 (being the profits assessable for 1997/98). He has no other sources of income and his actual tax liability for 1997/98 is £18,000. His management accounts prepared towards the end of the following year to 31 December 1998 indicate that a loss will be likely. Accordingly he submits a claim that there should be no interim payments for 1998/99, the first of which in the amount of £9,000 would otherwise fall due on 31 January 1999.

21.9 If the taxpayer believes that he will have some tax liability for a particular year, but the difference between the tax deducted at source and his anticipated total liability will be less than the equivalent difference for the previous year, he may submit a claim for the interim payment to be calculated by reference to his estimate of the difference in the current year. The claim must again be made by 31 January of the following year and must state the reasons. [*TMA 1970, s 59A(4)*]. Likewise any appropriate adjustments or repayments are to be made to give effect to the claim.

Example 2

Continuing the previous example, assume that Mr Brown's management accounts for the year to 31 December 1998 indicated a profit of £40,000, rather than a loss. The anticipated tax liability on this figure would be say £10,000. The claim would then be for interim payments of £5,000 each, rather than £9,000.

21.10 This example illustrates the difficulty in which a taxpayer might find himself when his accounting year end is close to the end of the year of assessment. Indeed when the year end falls after 31 January in the year of assessment he will not know what his profits are yet he will still be obliged to make an interim payment before the year end. The legislation does not specifically provide for any amended claims to be made if circumstances change between the due dates for the interim payments. It is understood, however, that the Revenue's intention is for the second interim payment to be amended, upwards or downwards, to reflect any underpayment or overpayment of the first interim payment, in recognition of the fact that self-assessment is a taxpayer driven system.

21.11 Where an incorrect statement is made in such a claim, whether fraudulently or negligently, the taxpayer will be liable to a penalty. The maximum is the difference between the correct amount and the actual interim payment made. [*TMA 1970, s 59A(6)*]. The severity of the potential penalty highlights the dilemma of the taxpayer who believes that his profits are falling, but does not know his precise position. However, the Revenue have stated that the intention of this penalty is to prevent gross or persistent abuse of the provisions, and that a penalty would be applied in cases either of large reductions made without foundation or where the taxpayer year on year claims to pay less tax than he should. The Revenue will not seek to apply hindsight or penalise someone who acted in good faith but got his sums wrong.

Final payment

21.12 The balance of the taxpayer's liability, calculated under the self-assessment to be submitted by the taxpayer by 31 January (or by the Revenue where the return is submitted by 30 September) is then normally also due on 31 January. This also includes the whole of any CGT liability for the year in question. Thus CGT is not subject to payment by instalments, and is not taken into account in computing any of the interim payments of income tax. The amount payable reflects any tax which has been deducted at source and tax credits on dividends. In the event that the assessment indicates that tax has been overpaid, this is then repayable. [*TMA 1970, s 59B(1)(4)* as inserted by *FA 1994, s 193*].

21.13 In the case of tax deducted under the PAYE procedure, the tax deduction from the final payment is to reflect the liability of the year in question, rather than the actual year of payment. Take the case of an employee paid at the end of each calendar month. PAYE for 1 to 5 April 1999 will be accounted for on 30 April 1999, i.e. in the following year of assessment 1999/2000. An appropriate adjustment would be required in determining the final payment on 31 January 2000 for 1998/99, giving credit for the tax paid in April 1999 (and where appropriate making a compensating adjustment for any overpayment in April 1998). The position is similar for tax credits attaching to dividends. [*TMA 1970, s 59B(2)*].

21.14 In cases where the taxpayer has notified the Revenue of his chargeability to income tax within six months of the end of the year of assessment [as required by *TMA 1970, s 7*], but was not sent a tax return until after 31 October, the final payment is not due (or repayment is not to be made as the case may be) until three months after the day on which the return was issued. [*TMA 1970, s 59B(3)*]. So take the case where a person (not previously chargeable to tax) commences a trade in 1997/98 and notifies the Revenue in August 1998 that he has done so. If he is not issued a return until 15 December 1998 he is not required to pay any tax until 15 March 1999.

Payment after amendment of self-assessment/discovery

21.15 Where a self-assessment is amended, special rules apply. Such an amendment may be made by the taxpayer or the Revenue under the 'repairs' procedure (see 18.19) or after a Revenue enquiry has been carried out (see 20.22) or under the 'discovery' procedure in the case of partnership statements (see 20.54). If the amended self-assessment is made more than 30 days before the normal due date for the final payment, or the extended due date as set out above, the tax consequential to the amendment is payable (or repayable) on that due date. Otherwise it is payable, or repayable, within 30 days of notice of the amendment. [*TMA 1970, s 59B(5)*].

21.16 In a case where the Revenue make a discovery assessment under the revised procedures set out in *TMA 1970, s 29*, tax is due within 30 days of the issue of the discovery assessment. [*TMA 1970, s 59B(6)*]. But these rules relating to amended self-assessments and discovery assessments do not displace the right of the taxpayer to postpone tax under *TMA 1970, s 55* where there is an appeal.

Corporation tax

21.17 The basic rule that corporation tax is payable nine months after the company's accounting period is not changed. [*TMA 1970, s 59(1)*]. In particular there are to be no interim payments on account. However, certain specific provisions are introduced regarding overpayments of tax. If tax has been paid which the company considers is excessive because of a change in circumstances since the tax was paid, a claim can be made for the recovery of the excess at any time before the corporation tax assessment for the period has become final. [*TMA 1970, s 59D(2)* as inserted by *FA 1994, s 195*]. Such a claim can only be made after the due date and must spell out the reasons why it is justified. [*TMA 1970, s 59D(3)*].

21.18 In any case where a company has appealed against an assessment, and it has not been finally determined, the company may apply to the Commissioners for a repayment of tax pending determination of the actual liability if it believes that there has been an overpayment of tax due to changed circumstances. [*TMA 1970, s 59D(4)*]. An application for repayment, whether to the Revenue Officer or to the Commissioners, is to be determined in the same way as an appeal. [*TMA 1970, s 59D(5)*]. An application for repayment may be combined with a postponement application under *TMA 1970, s 55*. [*TMA 1970, s 59D(6)*].

21.19 It is understood that in cases where tax paid in excess of a company's liability on Form CT 200 is left with the Revenue 'on deposit' to cover any extra tax liability which may arise (so performing a similar function to certificates of deposit, a facility now withdrawn for companies) a Revenue Officer will not repay the extra tax, in the absence of the company's formal request, until such time as the assessment for the period has been fully determined.

Interim payments in 1996/97

21.20 Payments on account for the transitional year 1996/97 (due on 31 January 1997 and 31 July 1997) will be required where an assessment was raised for 1995/96 under the old assessment procedure in *TMA 1970, s 29*, and the assessed amount exceeds the amount of tax deducted at source in 1995/96. The matter becomes somewhat complicated because the tax for 1995/96 may have been charged in a number of separate instalments. Depending on the source of income some of these may have required payment in two instalments on 1 January 1996 and 1 July 1996 (Schedule D, Cases I and II), others in a single instalment on 1 January 1996 (Schedule A and Schedule D, Cases III to VI). Moreover, any higher rate tax on taxed income and CGT would have been payable on 1 December 1996.

21.21 The normal interim payment rules in 21.3 are amended for 1996/97 only, effectively continuing the one instalment/two instalment treatment for 1996/97 but doing so by allocating the tax due (based upon the 1995/96 actual tax liability) between the two interim payments on 31 January 1997 and 31 July 1997 respectively. The provisions are contained in *FA 1995, 21 Sch 2,* amending *TMA 1970, s 59A* purely for 1996/97. The drafting of these provisions is rather complicated, but their effect is to allocate the tax between the two interim payments in the following way:

(i) Schedule D, Cases I and II (and Class 4 NIC): 50 per cent each, including higher rate tax;

(ii) Schedule A: 100 per cent on 31 January 1997, including higher rate tax;

(iii) Schedule D, Cases III to VI: 100 per cent on 31 January 1997, but not including higher rate tax or income where basic or lower rate tax is deducted at source.

21.22 It will be noted that the higher rate tax liability on income sources which are taxed by deduction at source will be excluded from interim payments for 1996/97, but not for future years. This means that for higher rate taxpayers there could be a substantial tax bill on 31 January 1998; consisting of (*a*) 100 per cent of the higher rate liability on taxed sources for 1996/97 and (*b*) 50 per cent of the 1996/97 tax bill, net of tax deducted at source, this representing the first instalment for 1997/98.

Simplified example

Mr Jacobs' 1995/96 income and tax liability (excluding Class 4 NIC) may be summarised as follows:

Source	*Amount*	*Total Tax liability*
	£	£
Schedule A	12,000	4,800
Schedule D, Case I	40,000	10,785
Bank interest (£2,500 deducted at source)	10,000	4,000
UK dividends (£1,600 ACT)	8,000	3,200
	70,000	22,785

Interim payments required

Source	*31 January 1997*	*31 July 1997*
	£	£
Schedule A	4,800	–
Schedule D, Case I	5,393	5,392
Bank Interest	–	–
Dividends	–	–
	10,193	5,392

The balance of the actual 1996/97 liability will be due for payment on 31 January 1998.

Fully worked example

Facts as for Mr Jacobs above

1995/96 income and tax

	Total	*Sch A*	*Case I*	*Interest*	*Sch F*
	£	£	£	£	£
Income	70,000	12,000	40,000	10,000	8,000
Personal allowances	(3,525)		(3,525)		
Income after allowances	66,475	12,000	36,475	10,000	8,000
Tax calculation					
20% (£3,200)	640		640		
25% (next £21,100)	5,275		5,275		
40% (balance £42,175)	16,870	4,800	4,870	4,000	3,200
Total tax	22,785	4,800	10,785	4,000	3,200
Less: Deducted at source	(4,100)	–	–	(2,500)	(1,600)
Tax due	18,685	4,800	10,785	1,500	1,600

Normally the two interim payments would each be 50 per cent of the difference between the total tax liability for the preceding year (known as the 'assessed amount'), namely £22,785, and the tax deducted at source of £4,100; i.e. 50% × (£22,785 – £4,100) = £9,342 each. But because 1996/97 is the transitional year a different calculation is required. The first stage is to recompute the assessed amount. The assessed amount means:

(i) the difference between the amount assessed and the sum of:

   (*a*) any income tax (in excess of the basic rate) charged on income from which tax has been deducted or is treated as having been deducted at source (except under PAYE); and

   (*b*) any income tax (in excess of the basic rate) chargeable under Schedule F attributable to the difference between that rate and the lower rate. [*FA 1995, 21 Sch 2(3)* amending *TMA 1970, s 59A(1)(b)*].

The assessed amount for 1996/97 thus becomes:

	£
Amount before recalculation	22,785
Less higher rate tax on bank interest taxed at source (£4,000 – £2,500)	(1,500)
higher rate on Schedule F income (£3,200 – £1,600)	(1,600)
	£19,685

The next step is to compute the 'relevant amount'. This is taken as the difference between the assessed amount (£19,685) and the amount of any income tax deducted at source (£4,100), less any income tax chargeable under Schedule E and not deducted under PAYE or the subject of a direct assessment under Regulation 103 of the PAYE Regulations (nil). The relevant amount is thus £19,685 – £4,100 = £15,585. [*FA 1995, 21 Sch 2(4)* amending *TMA 1970, s 59A(1)(c)*].

The first interim payment is then the aggregate of (*a*) such part of the relevant amount as represents tax charged on income within Schedule A and Schedule D, Cases III–VI, and (*b*) 50 per cent of the balance of the relevant amount i.e. that relating to Schedule D Cases I and II (and Class 4 National Insurance Contributions). [*FA 1995, 21 Sch 2(5)* amending *TMA 1970, s 59A(2)*]. Part of the relevant amount represents tax charged at the basic and higher rates under Schedule A (£4,800) and the balance is £10,785 (which represents tax relating to Schedule D, Case I). The second interim payment consists of the rest of the relevant amount.

Hence:

(i) the first interim payment is £4,800 + (50% × £10,785) = £10,193 (due 31 January 1997);

(ii) the second interim payment is 50% × £10,785 = £5,392 (due 31 July 1997).

21.23 As with the normal payment on account rules in 21.6, an interim payment will not be required if the relevant amount is either less than a *de minimis* figure to be announced in due course, or is less in percentage terms than a particular percentage of the assessed amount, also to be announced. Moreover, if the taxpayer considers that he will not have a tax liability for 1996/97 or that the liability will not exceed the tax deducted at source, he may make a claim on the lines of 21.9, in which case the payments on account will be waived. [*TMA 1970, s 59A(3)*].

21.24 A similar claim to pay a reduced rate can be made if the taxpayer considers that he will have some tax to pay for 1996/97, but that it will be less than the amount under the above formula based on the 1995/96 assessment. The amount payable on 31 January 1997 will then be his estimate of the tax applicable to income charged under Schedule A and Schedule D, Cases III–VI, and 50 per cent of the tax charged under Schedule D, Cases I and II. The second instalment due on 31 July 1997 will then be the balance of the tax under Schedule D, Cases I and II. [*FA 1995, 21 Sch 2(6)* amending *TMA 1970, s 59A(4)*].

21.25 Where the assessment for 1995/96 is amended, the payments on account for 1996/97 are recalculated on the amended figures. If necessary, further interim payments are to be made. Conversely, if appropriate, repayments of interim payments are to be made. [*FA 1995, 21 Sch 2(7)* amending *TMA 1970, s 59A(4A)*].

Tax payments – effective payment dates

Payment by cheque

21.26 A new *TMA 1970, s 70A* is introduced by *FA 1994, 19 Sch 22*, to clarify the date on which payment by cheque is made. For the purpose of *TMA 1970* and for the repayment supplement, where any payment to the Revenue is made by cheque, and the cheque is paid on its first presentation to the bank on which it is drawn, the payment is treated as made on the day it was received by the Revenue. This applies in respect of cheques received on or after 6 April 1996. If the cheque is handed in, the date of receipt will be the date of handing in. If posted, the payment date will be the date of receipt by the Revenue. If it is received by post following a day when the office has been closed, the payment date will be the day the office was first closed. If postdated, the payment date will be the date of the cheque.

Payment by electronic funds transfer

21.27 Electronic fund transfers may be made by BACS (Bankers' Automated Clearing Services) and CHAPS (Clearing House Automated Payment System). BACS is a system through which Bank-sponsored organisations make payments into accounts at any bank branch in the UK. CHAPS provides same-day settlements for high value inter-bank payments and is used by the twelve settlement banks and the Bank of England. Revenue practice is that payments made through electronic funds transfer by CHAPS and BACS are given payment dates of one working day immediately before the day value is received, as announced in an Inland Revenue Press Release of 1 April 1993. A working day is a Bank of England working day. This rule is to continue to apply for all payments of tax by electronic funds transfer.

Payment by Bank Giro

21.28 Under this system money can be paid into any bank to the credit of an account holder recognised for the acceptance of payment by Bank Giro. In order to encourage payment by this method, it is understood that the Revenue will treat the payment as received three working days prior to the date of processing at the Accounts Offices. This will apply to both Bank Giro on tape and clerical Bank Giro.

Payments by Girobank

21.29 This is a similar system to Bank Giro except that payments are made through Girobank. Taxpayers with a Girobank account can pay by Girobank Transfer by notifying payment details to Girobank direct. Payment by cash or cheque at a PO counter (Transcash) are also dealt with via Girobank. It is understood that the Revenue will likewise treat the payment as received three working days prior to date of processing at the Accounts Offices.

Subcontractors in the construction industry

21.30 Subcontractors in the construction industry might be particularly affected by the interim payment provisions. It would seem rather unrealistic for a subcontractor to make interim payments on the basis of preceding year's income, with a credit for the tax deducted at the time of payment in the current year, given that his income would be subject to deduction of tax at source. In fact the Revenue are according no special treatment to subcontractors as such. But where all or substantially all of their income is subject to deduction of tax at source they may well be excluded from the need to make interim payments because of the *de minimis* proportionate test applicable to those whose income is predominantly taxed at source set out in 21.6.

Chapter 22

Surcharges, Interest, Penalties and Repayment Supplement

Surcharges on late payment

22.1 A novel feature of the self-assessment system is the imposition of an automatic 5 per cent surcharge on late payment of CGT or the final income tax instalment. It is not imposed on late interim payments. The surcharge is aimed at achieving a high degree of voluntary compliance, keeping the costs of running the tax system as low as possible, yet without over-penalising defaulters. The amount of surcharge originally proposed was 10 per cent of the tax paid late, but this was reduced to an initial 5 per cent in the light of objections about its steepness and its arbitrary automatic imposition for payment made even one day after the due date. The surcharge will also be payable on any Class 4 NICs unpaid as if they were income tax charged under Schedule D, Cases I or II.

22.2 The surcharge applies when payment is 28 days in arrears, i.e. 28 days from the due date, generally 31 January following the year of assessment (see 21.10 and 21.12 above). If any tax still remains unpaid six months later there is a further 5 per cent surcharge. [*TMA 1970, s 59C(1)(2)(3)*]. The surcharge generally applies for 1996/97 or subsequent years. It is also applied to any income tax or CGT assessment for 1995/96 or earlier years where the assessment is made on or after 6 April 1998. [*FA 1995, s 109(2)*]. It is understood that where a taxpayer has not self-assessed, but has filed his return by 30 September to enable the Revenue to make the assessment, and the Revenue are late in assessing, the trigger date for the surcharge will be 30 days after issue of the tax bill, if this is later than 31 January. In the Standing Committee debates on the 1994 Finance Bill the Financial Secretary gave an assurance that if a taxpayer paid tax late as a result of a *bona fide* mistake in his self-assessment, interest would be payable but not a surcharge, provided that the taxpayer volunteered the information and paid promptly.

Example 1

Mr Green's final liability for 1998/99 is £40,000. Tax deducted at source was £5,000 and interim payments totalling £20,000 were made in the correct amounts. The balancing payment of £15,000 would thus fall due on 31 January 2000. If this was only paid on 15 March 2000 in addition to interest there would be a surcharge of £15,000 × 5% = £750. Assume that the only amount paid then was £5,000. There would then be a further surcharge of £10,000 × 5% = £500 on 1 August 2000.

22.3 In a case where the tax due in a self-assessment is increased following an amendment, whether by the taxpayer or the Revenue, the due date for any additional tax is 30 days after the amendment. The surcharge is accordingly only payable on any of the additional tax that is unpaid 28 days after that due date. So where an estimate is included in a self-assessment, which is later amended when the final figure is known, there will be no surcharge provided the additional tax is paid within 58 days of the amendment.

22.4 Notice of any surcharge is to be served formally on the taxpayer, stating the day on which it is issued and the time within which an appeal may be brought. The taxpayer has a right of appeal to the Commissioners against a surcharge within 30 days of its imposition, which is then dealt with as though it were an appeal against an assessment. [*TMA 1970, s 59C(5)(7)(8)*]. If a taxpayer has a reasonable excuse for not paying the tax the Commissioners may set aside the surcharge, otherwise they are to confirm it. They have no power to reduce it. Inability to pay is not a reasonable excuse for this purpose. [*TMA 1970, s 59C(9)(10)*]. The proposed Revenue practice regarding reasonable excuse is set out below. So far as trustees are concerned the surcharge is generally recoverable from any one or more of the 'relevant trustees' (see 15.7). [*TMA 1970, s 107A* as inserted by *FA 1995, s 103*].

22.5 Where a tax-geared penalty is imposed on the taxpayer under *TMA 1970, s 7* (failure to notify Revenue of chargeability), *s 93(5)* (failure to complete a return), *s 95* (fraud or neglect), or *s 95A* (incorrect partnership return) he is excused from surcharges. [*TMA 1970, s 59C(4)* as amended by *FA 1995, s 109(1)*]. The rationale is that the penalty is likely to be rather greater than any surcharge, and the amount will reflect the fact that payment is in arrears. A surcharge which is more than 30 days in arrears itself carries interest. [*TMA 1970, s 59C(6)*]. The Board have the discretion to mitigate any surcharge, or stay or compound any proceedings for the recovery of any surcharge. [*TMA 1970, s 59C(11)*]. This power can be exercised after judgement has been given in the Revenue's favour for non-payment.

Reasonable excuse against imposition of surcharge

22.6 The Revenue will be providing guidance as to the principles they will apply in determining whether they will accept a reasonable excuse claim against a surcharge, without the necessity of taking an appeal to the Commissioners. It is understood that these principles will be on the following lines:

(i) appropriate arrangements to pay the tax will be the norm, given that taxpayers generally have ample notice of payment dates;

(ii) the taxpayer must have been prevented from paying by an exceptional event out of his control;

(iii) it might be necessary to consider the taxpayer's general ability to manage his business and private affairs at the time; and

(iv) the reasonable excuse must continue right up until the time the tax is paid.

22.7 The following are the kinds of case where a reasonable excuse might be accepted:

(i) circumstances in which the taxpayer can demonstrate that a cheque discharging the tax was sent to the Revenue, but was lost or received late because of circumstances beyond the taxpayer's control, such as industrial dispute, fire or flood at the post office sorting office. But if the cheque were lost a replacement cheque would have to be issued as soon as the taxpayer realised that the cheque had not been received.

(ii) an illness which was so serious that it prevented a taxpayer from making the payment or any arrangements for the payment, e.g. coma, major heart attack, stroke;

(iii) bereavement of a close relative or companion, although payment would have to be made within a reasonable time;

(iv) cheque dishonoured solely because of bank error or unexpected action by the bank, provided payment made within a reasonable time; and

(v) misleading advice from the Revenue.

22.8 The following are the kinds of case where an excuse will be rejected:

(i) 'cheque lost in the post', in the absence of clear evidence;

(ii) illnesses that are not life-threatening or similar, for example a broken leg;

(iii) loss of records due, for example, to flood or fire particularly where the return had been submitted. Where the return had not been submitted the Revenue would expect to have been notified of the loss and arrangements made for a reasonably calculated final payment;

(iv) loss or unavailability of key personnel;

(v) insufficiency of funds, save in some limited cases where the insufficiency arises directly from circumstances beyond the taxpayer's control;

(vi) cheque dishonoured because of insufficiency of funds;

(vii) cheque incorrectly made out;

(viii) computer problems.

Interest on unpaid tax

22.9 A substituted *TMA 1970, s 86; FA 1995, s 110* sets out the new rules regarding interest on overdue tax or NIC. Any arrears carry interest from the 'relevant' date until the date of payment at the rate specified in *FA 1989, s 178*. The fact that the date of payment may be a non-business day is disregarded. [*TMA 1970, s 86(3)* substituted by *FA 1995, s 110*]. With regard to trustees, interest is generally recoverable from any one or more of the 'relevant trustees' (see 16.16). [*TMA 1970, s 107A* as inserted by *FA 1995, s 103*]. The rate of interest will be that set by regulations made under *FA 1989, s 178*.

22.10 Interest automatically arises on late payment, irrespective of any reason why payment has not been made by the due date. It is regarded simply as 'commercial restitution' for the payment being late. An interest charge could arise on any of the following:

- an interim payment;
- a final payment;
- any tax due following an amendment to a self-assessment, whether made by the taxpayer or the Revenue;
- any tax payable on a discovery assessment by the Revenue; and
- any tax payable following a postponement (in relation to a discovery assessment or Revenue amendments pursuant to an enquiry).

22.11 The relevant date for interim payments is the date on which each payment falls due, namely 31 January in the year of assessment and 31 July in the next year of assessment respectively (see 21.12). The relevant date for interest on the final payment is generally the following 31 January, again being the due date for that final payment. [*TMA 1970, s 86(2)* substituted by *FA 1995, s 110*]. However, in cases where the taxpayer duly notified the Revenue of his chargeability to tax under the provisions of *TMA 1970, s 7* within six months from the end of the year of assessment, and was only sent a tax return after 31 October in the year of assessment, the relevant date for the final payment is the end of the three-month period within which the return has to be submitted (see 21.10 and 21.12). [*TMA 1970, s 86(2)* substituted by *FA 1995, s 110*].

22.12 Tax which has been postponed under an appeal or tax which is charged under an amended self-assessment or discovery generally carries interest from the annual filing date of 31 January, even though the due date for payment of the additional tax may be later; see 22.3. As with surcharges, if the taxpayer has opted for Revenue assessment and the assessment is late, the trigger date for interest will be 30 days after issue of the tax bill (see 22.2).

22.13 So far as interim payments are concerned, interest will be due on the difference between what is actually paid and what should have been paid. Thus, if an interim payment of £4,000 should have been paid on 31 July 1998, but only £3,000 is paid, interest is charged on the balance of £1,000 from 1 August 1998 until paid. The point should also be made that even in cases where the tax liability for the current year exceeds that of the previous year, so that the interim payments (being based on the previous year's liability) are less than the actual tax liability, there is no interest charge on the excess.

22.14 Where a taxpayer has made a claim to reduce his interim payments (see 21.7 and 21.9) and it transpires that these are less than they should have been, interest is charged. The principle is that the charge is based on the lesser of the actual underpayment of tax for the year (i.e. determined by reference to the actual tax liability) and what the tax would have been on the preceding year basis. The amount underpaid in respect of an interim payment, on which interest is then charged, is calculated by deducting the payment from the lesser of:

(*a*) the aggregate of that interim payment and 50 per cent of the final tax payment, excluding CGT; and

(*b*) what the interim payment would have been under 21.2 if based on the preceding year's liability. [*TMA 1970, s 86(4)(5)(6)* substituted by *FA 1995, s 110*].

Example 2

Mr Robert's tax liability for 1997/98 was £15,000, none of which represented tax deducted at source. For 1998/99 he estimates that his tax liability will be reduced to £10,000. Therefore, instead of making interim payments of £7,500 each (by reference to the 1997/98 liability) he claims that the payments should be reduced to £5,000 each, and duly makes the payments on this basis. It transpires that his actual tax liability is £12,000, so he makes the final payment of £2,000 on 31 January 2000.

Applying the method of calculation prescribed in 22.14, (*a*) in the calculation is the aggregate of the actual interim payment (£5,000) and 50 per cent of the final payment (£1,000), namely £6,000; while (*b*) is the amount of the interim payment based on the preceding year's tax liability, namely £7,500. The lesser amount is £6,000. So the underpayment, on which interest is payable until the date of the final payment, is £6,000 – £5,000 = £1,000.

In the event that Mr Robert's tax liability for 1998/99 had turned out to be £20,000, so that the final payment was £10,000, the lesser amount in the calculation would have been £7,500, i.e. the amount calculated by reference to the preceding year. So the underpayment on each interim payment, liable to interest, would have been £2,500.

22.15 In the event that interim payments are made late, thus incurring an interest charge, there will be a partial remission of interest if there is an eventual repayment of tax. Each interim payment is deemed to be reduced by 50 per cent of the final repayment in so far as this relates to income tax in calculating the interest charge. To the extent that this does not affect the interest remittable with regard to one of the interim payments, the overpayment may be allocated to the other interim payment. In effect interest on the overpayment element of the interim payment is remitted. [*TMA 1970, s 86(7)(8)(9)* as substituted by *FA 1995, s 110*].

22.16 The new interest rules will generally apply for 1996/97 and subsequent years. However, they will also apply to any income tax or CGT assessment made on or after 6 April 1998 relating to 1995/96 or earlier. Interest then generally runs from 31 January following the end of the year of assessment. [*FA 1995, s 110(2)(3)*]. For partnerships whose trades, professions or businesses commenced before 6 April 1994, the provisions only apply from 1997/98 onwards. [*FA 1995, s 110(4)* inserted by *FA 1996, s 131(1)*].

Miscellaneous interest charges

22.17 Provision is made by *FA 1996, s 132* and *Schedule 18* for interest to be charged in certain other cases of overdue tax and where tax relief has been granted, which is later clawed back. There are also certain consequential amendments to existing provisions with regard to the date from which interest becomes payable. These include:

(i) withdrawal of relief in respect of enterprise investment and business expansion schemes;

(ii) excess relief under MIRAS;

(iii) life insurance premium relief;

(iv) excessive medical insurance relief;

(v) vocational training relief; and

(vi) interest on CGT on gifts paid by instalments.

Penalties

Introduction

22.18 The penalty regime was subject to substantial changes and consolidation in *FA 1989* in the light of the deliberations of the Keith Committee. The pre self-assessment provisions and the historical background are examined in depth in Tolley's *Interest and Penalty Provisions*, to which the reader is referred for a detailed review. It is an area of considerable importance, with a steady increase in the number of investigations, and a substantial and growing yield from such compliance and investigation work. See also Tolley's *Tax Compliance and Investigations*.

22.19 The power to impose penalties of one kind or another, and the accompanying provisions relating to penalty determinations and proceedings are contained in over 30 *sections* of *TMA 1970*. Penalties are generally to be determined by a Revenue Officer under *TMA 1970, s 100*, with the taxpayer having the right of appeal to the Commissioners under *TMA 1970, s 100B*. But in certain cases the Officer has to apply to the Commissioners for the imposition of a penalty, notably for daily penalties. The rest of this chapter reviews the principal penalties under self-assessment and the changes which have been made. So far as trustees are concerned, penalties are generally recoverable from any one or more of the 'relevant trustees' (see 16.6) but only once. [*TMA 1970, s 107A* as inserted by *FA 1995, s 103*].

Failure to notify Revenue of chargeability

22.20 From 1995/96 where a person who is chargeable to income tax or CGT, but who is not on the records of the Revenue and hence has not received a tax return, fails to notify the Revenue as to his chargeability within six months of the end of the year of assessment as required by *TMA 1970, s 7(1)* (see 16.6) he is liable to a penalty. (Under the old rules the notification period was 12 months). [*TMA 1970, s 7(8)*]. The penalty is not to exceed the tax to which he is assessed, whether under a self-assessment or a Revenue assessment [under *TMA 1970, s 9 or 29*] for the period. Moreover, the imposition of the penalty is subject to the tax itself not having been paid before 31 January following the end of the year of assessment. This is the same penalty as under the present system, although the notification period has been shortened from twelve to six months.

22.21 There is no reporting obligation where the person's income is fully taxed at source, whether under PAYE in respect of Schedule E income, or in respect of other income which has been taxed by deduction at source and there is no higher rate tax liability. The Revenue's views concerning the new rules are set out in Statement of Practice SP 1/96 issued on 1 February 1996. So far as employees are concerned, the Revenue will generally accept that employees in receipt of a P11D can assume that any items included on it which have not been taken into account as chargeable benefits in kind for Schedule E purposes will be taken into account in an amended PAYE coding, so there will be no requirement to notify the Revenue of chargeability in respect of those items. This will not be the case if the employee is aware that the P11D has not been submitted to the Revenue. A reporting obligation also remains if there are items not shown in the P11D, or if the P11D is incorrect or incomplete, or if the employee has not received a P11D and has received chargeable benefits.

Failure to make a return by individuals or trustees

22.22 There are significant changes to the penalty provisions for failure to complete and deliver a tax return by the required filing date (generally 31 January following the end of the year of assessment (see 16.13)). Under the old system there was a penalty up to £300. Under the new system there is an automatic flat rate penalty of £100. [*TMA 1970, s 93(1)(2)* as inserted by *FA 1994, 19 Sch 25*]. There is a further automatic penalty also of £100 if the failure continues after six months from the filing date. [*TMA 1970, s 93(4)*]. But this second penalty is not exigible if an application is made to the Commissioners for daily penalties under the provisions set out in 22.30. It is understood that in practice there will be a 14-day period of grace before a penalty is imposed.

22.23 If the taxpayer establishes that his actual tax would have been less, these fixed £100 penalties are to be reduced to the amount of tax. [*TMA 1970, s 93(7)*]. So if a taxpayer's actual liability turns out to be only £50, the penalties are likewise limited to £50 in total. On an appeal to the Commissioners against the imposition of these flat rate penalties, they can be set aside if it appears to the Commissioners that the taxpayer had a reasonable excuse for not delivering the return. Otherwise, the Commissioners are to confirm the penalties. [*TMA 1970, s 93(8)*].

22.24 As with surcharges, the Revenue will be providing guidance as to the principles they will apply in determining whether a reasonable excuse claim will be accepted, without requiring an appeal to the Commissioners. It is understood that these will be on similar lines to those set out in 22.6–22.8, the general principles being as follows:

(i) the taxpayer must have been prevented from making the return by an exceptional event outside his control;

(ii) where appropriate the Revenue will consider the position in the light of the taxpayer's ability to manage the rest of his private or business affairs at the time of the event giving rise to the appeal;

(iii) the taxpayer must have had a reasonable excuse throughout the period of default. Appeals will not be considered until the return is delivered, when the period of default can be established;

(iv) where an acceptable reasonable excuse ceases, there will be no penalty provided the return is submitted without unreasonable delay thereafter.

22.25 An excuse might be accepted in the following kinds of case:

(i) where the return was delayed or lost in the post through unforeseen delays, such as industrial disputes, fire or flood at the post office sorting office. Details of the place and posting would be required;

(ii) a very serious illness preventing the taxpayer from having control over his affairs, for example, coma, heart attack or stroke. The timing of the illness would of course be relevant;

(iii) a very serious illness or bereavement of a close relative or partner;

(iv) loss of records due to fire, flood or criminal activity.

22.26 An excuse is likely to be rejected in the following kinds of case:

(i) illnesses that are not so serious, for example, a broken leg;

(ii) where certain information is unavailable. Where the taxpayer genuinely cannot obtain certain details he should include an estimate in his return, with an explanation;

(iii) unavailability of key personnel;

(iv) computer failure, unless arising from the breakdown of a software package at a critical time close to the filing date. In relation to electronic lodgement, a loss in transmission is unlikely to be a reasonable excuse as a Revenue acknowledgement will normally follow within 24 hours of the transmission;

(v) difficulty in completing the return;

(vi) pressure of work;

(vii) failure of agent;

(viii) failure of the Revenue to issue any reminder.

22.27 If the failure to deliver the return continues after the anniversary of the filing date, and the taxpayer would have been liable to tax had the return been duly submitted, he is liable to a further penalty of up to the amount of tax. [*TMA 1970, s 93(5)*]. This penalty, the same as under the present system, is to be imposed by a Revenue Officer, and is subject to the normal right of appeal by the taxpayer rather than limited to grounds of limited excuse.

22.28 A Revenue Officer can also apply to the General or Special Commissioners for the imposition of daily penalties, a feature of the present system. The Revenue is to use this sanction where the tax at risk is believed to be high and therefore the fixed penalties are an insufficient deterrent. On such an application the Commissioners can direct that the taxpayer is liable to a further penalty or penalties up to £60 for each day on which the failure to deliver the return continues. [*TMA 1970, s 93(3)*]. No such penalty is to be imposed after the failure has been remedied. [*TMA 1970, s 93(6)*].

Failure to make partnership return

22.29 Similar penalties to those set out above in relation to individuals and trustees are imposed in respect of partnerships. The provisions apply where a representative partner has been required by notice to deliver a partnership return and has failed to comply. [*TMA 1970, s 93A(1) as inserted by FA 1994, 19 Sch 26*]. Each person who was a partner at any time during the period in respect of which the return was required (defined as a 'relevant' partner) is liable to an automatic penalty of £100. [*TMA 1970, s 93A(2)(8)*]. There is a further automatic penalty, also of £100, on each relevant partner after a default longer than six months. [*TMA 1970, s 93A(4)*]. Again, this second penalty is not exigible if the Revenue Officer applies for daily penalties. Unlike the position applicable to individuals, there is no provision for these fixed penalties to be restricted where the tax due on the partnership profits is minimal.

22.30 A Revenue Officer can apply to the General or Special Commissioners for further daily penalties. The Commissioners can then direct that each relevant partner is liable to a further penalty or penalties up to £60 for each day on which the failure continues after the day on which the representative partner is notified of the direction. No such penalty is to be imposed after the failure has been remedied. [*TMA 1970, s 93A(3)(5)*].

22.31 Where more than one partner appeals against the imposition of any of these penalties the appeals are to be treated as a single, composite appeal by the representative partner. On an appeal against the £100 flat rate penalties the Commissioners can set them aside if it appears to them that the representative partner had a reasonable excuse for not delivering the return. Otherwise they are to confirm the determination. [*TMA 1970, s 93A(6)(7)*].

22.32 It is to be stressed that the fixed and daily penalties apply to each partner and not the partnership as a whole. Hence in a large partnership the total penalties can be significant. It is also to be noted that there is no procedure to impose tax-related penalties for failure to deliver a return, the partnership return not forming the basis of an assessment.

Failure to make return – European economic interest groupings

22.33 The existing provisions in *TMA 1970, s 98B*, regarding EEIG's are amended by *FA 1994, 19 Sch 30*. Where an EEIG or a member fails to deliver a tax return or other required documents the EEIG or member thereof will be liable to a penalty of up to £300 multiplied by the then number of members. [*TMA 1970, s 98B(2A)*]. An application can also be made by a Revenue Officer to the General or Special Commissioners for further daily penalties of £60 per day multiplied by the number of members at the end of each day. [*TMA 1970, s 98B(2B)*]. Under the present provisions the penalties are £300 and £60 respectively, regardless of the number of members.

Incorrect returns by individuals or trustees

22.34 Penalty provisions for failure to deliver a correct return are contained in *TMA 1970, s 95* as amended by *FA 1994, 19 Sch 27*. No fundamental changes have been made to these provisions, which apply where an individual or trustee fraudulently or negligently:

(*a*) delivers an incorrect tax return; or

(*b*) makes any incorrect return, statement or declaration in connection with any claims for any allowance, deduction or relief in respect of income tax or CGT; or

(*c*) submits any incorrect accounts in connection with the ascertainment of his liability to income tax or CGT.

The penalty is of an amount up to the difference between the tax actually payable, and that which was shown as due.

22.35 Where any of the above returns, statements, declarations etc. have not been made fraudulently or negligently, and it comes to the person's notice (or the notice of his personal representatives if he has died) that they were incorrect, the error must be remedied without unreasonable delay. Otherwise the returns etc. are to be treated as made negligently. [*TMA 1970, s 97*]. This provision remains unaltered.

Incorrect partnership return

22.36 New penalty provisions are included as *TMA 1970, s 95A* [*as introduced by FA 1994, 19 Sch 28*] dealing with incorrect partnership returns or accounts. They apply where a partner (the representative partner) fraudulently or negligently:

(*a*) delivers an incorrect return; or

(*b*) makes any incorrect statement or declaration in connection with the return; or

(*c*) submits incorrect accounts in connection with the return.

22.37 These provisions also apply where the making of the incorrect return etc. is attributable to the fraudulent or negligent conduct of another partner who was a partner at any time during the period in respect of which the return was made. [*TMA 1970, s 95A(1)(4)*]. In either case each partner is then liable to a penalty up to the difference between the tax actually payable (including corporation tax) and the amount shown as payable. In determining each penalty regard is to be had only to the fraudulent or negligent conduct mentioned in the *section*. [*TMA 1970, s 95A(2)*]. Where two or more partners wish to appeal they have to do so via an appeal brought by the representative partner. The appeal is then treated as a composite appeal against the determination of each penalty. [*TMA 1970, s 95A(3)*].

Failure to produce documents

22.38 New provisions are included as *TMA 1970, s 97AA* [as introduced by *FA 1994, 19 Sch 29*] for failure to provide documents requested during a Revenue enquiry under the new *section 19A* (see 20.14 above). Where a person fails to comply with a notice to provide the documents or other information he is liable to an initial penalty of £50.

22.39 If the failure continues, a Revenue Officer may directly impose a further penalty of up to £30 per day for each day on which the failure continues under the determination provisions of *TMA 1970, s 100*. [*TMA 1970, s 97AA(1)(b), (2)(a)*]. In the alternative, the Officer may commence penalty proceedings before the General or Special Commissioners, in which case the Commissioners may, if satisfied, impose a penalty of up to £150 per day. [*TMA 1970, s 97AA(2)(b)*]. In either event no penalty is to be imposed after the failure has been remedied.

Failure to retain and preserve records

22.40 The new *TMA 1970, s 12* imposes an obligation on a taxpayer to retain and preserve his records (see 19.3 above). Generally these have to be kept for five years after 31 January following the end of the year of assessment for individuals, and six years after the end of the accounting period for companies. A penalty of up to £3,000 is exigible for any taxpayer who fails so to do. [*TMA 1970, s 12B(5); FA 1994, 19 Sch 3*]. A penalty of up to the same amount may be imposed for failure to keep proper records to substantiate claims, albeit only if a claim is in fact made. [*TMA 1970, 1A Sch 2A(4)* inserted by *FA 1995, 20 Sch 2*].

22.41 It is understood that in cases where tax-geared penalties are due because of the understatement of income or gains the Revenue will not normally seek additional penalties for record-keeping failures. The position might be otherwise where the offence was particularly serious, such as a deliberate destruction of records during an enquiry.

Claim to reduce interim payments – fraud or neglect

22.42 A taxpayer subject to income tax may make a claim to make either nil or reduced interim payments (see 21.6 and 21.7 above). If in doing so he fraudulently or negligently makes any incorrect statement he is liable to a penalty up to an amount equal to the difference between what he should have paid and what he did pay.

Time limit for tax-related penalties

22.43 At present a penalty determination must generally be made or proceedings commenced within six years of the date on which the penalty was incurred, or at any later time within three years of the final determination of the tax liability. [*TMA 1970, s 103(1)*]. This is not altered. However, in the case of a deceased taxpayer the later date is not permissible under self-assessment if the tax was charged in an assessment made later than six years after 31 January following the year for which it is charged. [*TMA 1970, s 103(2)*].

Repayment supplement – income tax

22.44 Where a taxpayer has overpaid tax, so that a tax repayment is made to him, he is entitled to a repayment supplement under *TA 1988, s 824* if the repayment is made after a certain period, effectively representing interest on the overpayment. The repayment supplement is calculated as simple interest on the amount of tax repaid but is itself completely free of tax. [*TA 1988, s 824(8)*].

22.45 Under the old rules entitlement to the supplement generally only ran from the later of the end of the year of assessment following that for which the repayment was made and the end of the year in which the overpayment was made. So if the year of assessment was 1992/93 and the tax was paid on, say, 1 October 1993, repayment supplement would run from 5 April 1994. But if the tax was paid on 1 October 1994, repayment supplement would run from 5 April 1995.

22.46 The provisions in *TA 1988, s 824* are substantially amended by *FA 1994, 19 Sch 41* under self-assessment from 1996/97 (and from 1997/98 for partnerships commencing before 6 April 1994) particularly regarding the dates used for calculation of the supplement. Repayment supplement will apply to repayments of any of the following:

(*a*) interim payments on account of income tax;

(*b*) income tax paid by an individual;

(*c*) surcharges on late payment of tax; and

(*d*) any penalties imposed.

The Revenue are shortly to draw up guidelines concerning the timing of subcontractors' SC 60 tax repayments under self-assessment. [See HC Written Answer, Vol 278 cols 512, 513 of 6 June 1996].

22.47 The repayment supplement on such amounts will be equal to interest at the rate specified from time to time under *FA 1989, s 178* for the period between the 'relevant time' and the date on which the order for repayment is issued. [*TA 1988, s 824(1)* as amended]. For payments of income tax the relevant time is the later of the date on which the payments were due (namely 31 January in the year of assessment and the following 31 July for interim payments, and generally the following 31 January for the final payment) and the date of payment. So under the new system there is a substantial acceleration of the date from which repayment supplement runs on overpaid tax. If the repayment was of a surcharge or penalty the relevant time is the later of 30 days from the date when the penalty or surcharge was imposed or repaid, and the date when it was actually paid. [*TA 1988, s 824(3)* as amended].

22.48 The previous requirement that the taxpayer had to be UK-resident is removed. This follows the judgment of the European Court in *R v CIR ex parte Commerzbank AG* [*1993*] *STC 605* where it was held that the restriction of repayments to residents of the UK was an unlawful discrimination against residents of other member states of the European Community.

22.49 Under the present *TA 1988, s 824(5)* where there is an overpayment of Schedule E tax for several years, the Revenue are empowered to make regulations to attribute repayments of Schedule E tax to particular years. This power under *TA 1988, s 824(5)* is to be abolished, reflecting the new regulations which will be given to the Revenue to make regulations on repayment supplement for Schedule E, using the payment date as the starting point for the calculation of a supplement. These regulations have at the time of writing not been published.

Repayment supplement – CGT

22.50 The rules for repayment supplement for CGT in *TCGA 1992, s 283* are brought into line with the new income tax rules set out above. [*FA 1994, 19 Sch 46*]. It will no longer be a requirement for the taxpayer to be UK-resident. Moreover, repayment supplement is to run from 31 January in the year following that to which the repayment relates, or the date on which the tax is paid if later, until the date on which the repayment is made.

Chapter 23

Appeals: Collection and Recovery

Introduction

23.1 Under the previous system, once an assessment in respect of a particular income source or capital gain had been raised the taxpayer had a general right of appeal under *TMA 1970, s 31* against the assessment. After a notice of appeal had been lodged, unless the taxpayer and the Inspector determined the matter by agreement under *TMA 1970, s 54*, the assessment had to be determined by proceedings before the General or Special Commissioners.

23.2 The General Commissioners are laymen who have local jurisdiction. They are persons of standing in their area who provide their services without remuneration. In England and Wales they are appointed by the Lord Chancellor, in Scotland by the Secretary of State. They are assisted by a clerk, who can advise them on legal issues. The Special Commissioners are remunerated, and are appointed by the Lord Chancellor from persons with relevant legal experience of tax matters, gained either in private practice or within the Revenue.

23.3 Certain appeals, generally involving technical matters, had to be heard by the Special Commissioners. But generally the appeals were to be heard by the General Commissioners, subject to the right of the taxpayer to elect to bring the appeal before the Special Commissioners instead. For more details on the role of the Commissioners, the conduct of appeals before them, and the rights of appeal to the High Court against their determinations, see Tolley's *Taxes Management Provisions*. Also of interest will be Tolley's *Tax Appeals to the Commissioners*.

Appeals under self-assessment

23.4 With a system of self-assessment, the taxpayer no longer needs a general right of appeal against an assessment to tax as was provided by *TMA 1970, s 31* in its previous form. However, there are still cases where a right of appeal is required, in particular where the taxpayer does not self-assess, and the assessment is raised by the Revenue. The provisions of *TMA 1970, s 31(1)* have been amended accordingly by *FA 1994, 19 Sch 7*, preserving the taxpayer's rights of appeal in the following cases:

(*a*) Where a self-assessment is amended by a Revenue Officer under *TMA 1970, s 28A(2)*, which permits an immediate assessment to be raised after a Revenue enquiry has been opened, with a view to avoiding a loss of tax (see 20.18). But the appeal is not to be heard until the enquiry has been completed. [*TMA 1970, s 31(1A)*].

(*b*) Where a self-assessment is amended by a Revenue Officer under *TMA 1970, s 28A(4)* after a Revenue enquiry has been completed (see 20.22).

(*c*) Where a partnership statement is amended under *TMA 1970, s 28B(3)* as the result of a Revenue enquiry (see 20.25) or under *TMA 1970, s 30B(1)* as the result of a 'discovery' by the Revenue (see 20.24).

(*d*) In all other cases where a tax assessment is made which is not a self-assessment. This covers such cases as:

- (i) assessments by the Revenue where there has been no self-assessment (see 18.12); and
- (ii) a 'discovery' assessment by the Revenue (see 20.40).

The notice of appeal is to be given to the Officer by whom the notice of amendment or assessment was given, within 30 days of the issue of notice of amendment or assessment. [*TMA 1970, s 31(1)(2)*].

Appeals against amendments to claims

23.5 The procedure relating to claims for relief, and the review of such claims by the Revenue, has been substantially changed under self-assessment as outlined in Chapter 17. The procedure permits the Revenue to enquire into a claim made otherwise than in a tax return under the provisions of *TMA 1970, 1A Sch*, in the same way that they have the right of enquiry into a tax return and a claim made therein. There are like powers given to the Revenue to amend claims made under *TMA 1970, 1A Sch* if they consider it appropriate (see 20.31).

23.6 Where a Revenue Officer amends such a claim under *TMA 1970, 1A Sch 7(3)* the claimant taxpayer has the right of appeal by written notice to the Officer within 30 days of the amendment. [*TMA 1970, 1A Sch 9(3)*]. This time limit is extended to three months where the issues arising include:

(*a*) any question under *TA 1988, s 278* (personal reliefs for non-residents);

(*b*) any question of residence, ordinary residence or domicile; or

(*c*) the question whether a fund is one to which *TA 1988, s 615(3)* applies (pension funds for service abroad).

[*TMA 1970, 1A Sch 9(2)*].

The Commissioners may then vary the amendment appealed against, whether or not it is to the advantage of the appellant. [*TMA 1970, 1A Sch 9(3)*]. Due effect is then to be given to such variation, either by an assessment on a claimant, or by a repayment of tax. [*TMA 1970, 1A Sch 9(4)*].

Appeals against surcharge and penalties

23.7 As set out in 22.1 above there is a 5 per cent surcharge for late payment of CGT and the final income tax instalment. There is a limited right of appeal against the surcharge, namely on the grounds of reasonable excuse, as set out in 22.4.

23.8 As regards penalties, although there has been some change to the provisions relating to penalties as outlined in 22.18 *et seq.* there has not been any fundamental change to the system itself. The taxpayer's existing right of appeal to the Commissioners under *TMA 1970, s 100B* generally remains. Flat rate penalties for failure to make a return can be set aside by the Commissioners if there has been a reasonable excuse (see 22.23 and 22.31).

Whether appeal heard by General or Special Commissioners

23.9 Under the previous system, taxpayers generally had a choice as to whether their appeals against assessments were heard by the General or Special Commissioners, although certain appeals had to go to the Special Commissioners. Moreover, appeals against capital gains tax assessments involving a question of the value of land had to be referred to the Lands Tribunal on that point. Under this system different tribunals could hear different assessments relating to the same year of assessment. But because self-assessment brings together all of a taxpayer's income and gains, reliefs and allowances, and results in a single figure of tax due, changes were required.

23.10 In devising the self-assessment appeals system the Revenue wished to maintain the principle of the taxpayer's choice between the General or Special Commissioners, but with the requirement that certain important or difficult decisions should only be heard by the Special Commissioners or the Lands Tribunal. The essence is that the appeal should initially be to either the General or the Special Commissioners as the principal tribunal. That tribunal would then be responsible for establishing the questions which needed to be addressed, referring particular questions to other tribunals as appropriate, and eventually determining the final taxable amount, and the tax due. In the majority of cases the principal tribunal would itself decide the majority of the issues. Consideration is being given by the Revenue to an appropriate amendment of the procedural rules, notably the Regulations applicable to proceedings before the Special and General Commissioners, being SI 1994 Nos 1811 and 1812 respectively.

23.11 In the meantime certain substantial changes have been implemented in *FA 1996, 22 Sch 7*, which set out a list of those questions which must be referred to the Special Commissioners and the Lands Tribunal, even though the overall appeal may be to the General Commissioners. Moreover, an appeal against an assessment made by the Board, or under *TA 1998, s 350* (recovery of tax on annual payments) must be determined by the Special Commissioners in any event. [Amended *TMA 1970, s 31(3); FA 1996, 22 Sch 4*].

Questions to be determined by Special Commissioners

23.12 Under a new *TMA 1970, s 46B* certain questions arising in respect of any of the following appeals must be determined by the Special Commissioners:

(*a*) an appeal against a Revenue amendment to a self-assessment under *TMA 1970, s 28A(2)* or *(4)*;

(*b*) an appeal disallowing a claim or election under *TMA 1970, s 28A(4A)*;

(*c*) an appeal against an amendment to a partnership statement under *TMA 1970, s 28B(3)* or *30B(1)*;

(*d*) an assessment which is not a self-assessment;

(*e*) an amendment to a claim or election not in a return under *TMA 1970, 1A Sch 9(3)*; and

(*f*) an appeal against the disallowance of a claim or election under *TMA 1970, 1A Sch 7(3A)*.

23.13 These questions, which are only to be determined by the Special Commissioners, are those relating to:

(i) the valuation of shares or securities in an unquoted company;

(ii) the taxation of chargeable gains, whether under capital gains tax or corporation tax, or in relation to a claim under *TCGA 1992*;

(iii) the settlement provisions, under *TA 1988, Part XV Chapter 1A* or *1B*;

(iv) the administration of estates, under *TA 1988, Part XVI*;

(v) the transfer of assets abroad, under *TA 1988, ss 740* and *743(1)*;

(vi) a controlled foreign company, under *TA 1988, s 747(4)(a)*; and

(vii) the territorial sea and designated areas, under *TA 1988, s 830* or *TCGA 1992, s 276*.

Jurisdiction of Special Commissioners over certain claims included in returns

23.14 Under a new *TMA 1970, s 46C*, in the case of appeals against an amendment to a self-assessment under *TMA 1970, s 28A(2)* or *(4)* or an amendment to a partnership assessment under *TMA 1970, s 28B(3)* or *30B(1)*, questions relating to the following must be determined by the Special Commissioners:

(i) a claim made to the Board;

(ii) a claim for management expenses for owners of mineral rights under *TA 1988, s 121*;

(iii) a claim for exemption for certain friendly societies under *TA 1988, ss 459* and *460*;

(iv) a claim for exemption for certain trade unions and employers' associations under *TA 1988, s 467*;

(v) a claim for spreading provisions in respect of patent royalties, copyright royalties, or receipts of painters, sculptors and other artists under *TA 1988, ss 527, 534* and *538*; or in respect of deduction of tax at source from copyright royalties where the author's usual place of abode is abroad under *TA 1988, s 536*; and

(vi) a claim for double taxation relief under *TA 1988, Part XVIII Chapter 1*.

Questions to be determined by the Lands Tribunal

23.15 Under a new *TMA 1970, s 46D* in respect of all appeals set out in 23.12 disputes in connection with the value of any land or lease of land for chargeable gains purposes must be determined by the relevant Lands Tribunal, but only in so far as it relates to that value.

Jurisdication on claims not included in returns

23.16 In the following specific cases appeals relating to claims not included in the return must be to the Special Commissioners:

(i) an appeal against a claim to the Board;

(ii) an appeal in connection with the administration of estates under *TA 1988, Part XVI*;

(iii) an appeal in connection with the matters listed in 23.14 (ii) to (vi). [*TMA 1970, 1A Sch 10; FA 1996, 22 Sch 9*].

23.17 Apart from the above specific cases an appeal on a claim is to be to the General Commissioners. This is subject to the taxpayer's right to elect for the appeal to be heard before the Special Commissioners, but this in turn may be overturned by the General Commissioners. [*TMA 1970, 1A Sch 11; FA 1996, 22 Sch 9*].

Rules for assigning proceedings to General Commissioners

Introductory

23.18 A substituted *TMA 1970, Sch 3* contains the rules for determining which body of General Commissioners hears a taxpayer's appeal. These rules come into effect for proceedings relating to 1996/97 and subsequent years of assessment, and so far as companies are concerned, for accounting periods ending on or after the appointed day under *FA 1994, s 199*. For these purposes the 'relevant place' determines the division of the General Commissioners. [*TMA 1970, 3A Sch 1, 12*].

General rule for income and capital gains tax proceedings

23.19 Except where the proceedings are commenced by the Board, the taxpayer may elect for the hearing to take place at the division of the General Commissioners appropriate to his last known place of residence, place of business or place of employment. Where he fails to make an election the Revenue may specify the appropriate division. In the case of a taxpayer's election, his place of residence is defined as his usual place of residence. Where the Board commences the proceedings, it is his usual place of residence or, if that is unknown, his last known place of residence. A taxpayer's place of business is that place where his trade, profession, vocation or business with which the proceedings are concerned is carried on; or if carried on at more than one place, the head office or place where it is mainly carried on. For partnerships it is the place where the partnership business is carried on, or mainly carried on. These provisions do not apply to PAYE or corporation tax appeals. They also do not apply for partnership appeals, save in relation to determining the partnership place of business. [*TMA 1970, 3 Sch 2, 7*].

PAYE appeals

23.20 If the right of appeal is given by the PAYE regulations, the place where the appeal is heard is determined by the regulations, unless the taxpayer elects for his place of residence, place of business or place of employment. [*TMA 1970, 3 Sch 3*].

Corporation tax etc.

23.21 Company appeals in connection with corporation tax, income tax of non-resident companies, or loans to participators under *TA 1988, ss 419* and *420* may at the company's election be heard by the division of General Commissioners for the place where the company's business is carried on, or where its head office is situated, or where it resides, being its place of effective management. However, if the Board institute the appeal, or the company fails to elect, the Board chooses the appropriate divisions for one of these places. [*TMA 1970, 3 Sch 4*].

Procedure for making elections etc.

23.22 The taxpayer should make the election to determine the appropriate division of General Commissioners by a notice in writing served on the Revenue. The time limit is when the taxpayer gives notice of appeal, or if the proceedings are not an appeal, when the taxpayer otherwise commences the proceedings, or later if the Revenue allow it. The election is irrevocable. An election by the Revenue has to be notified in writing to the taxpayer. [*TMA 1970, 3 Sch 5, 6*].

Directions by the Board

23.23 Notwithstanding the normal rules set out above the Revenue may direct which is to be the appropriate division in cases where there is no relevant place within 23.19 or where it would be outside the UK. The taxpayer must be notified accordingly, and such a direction is ineffective if the taxpayer objects in writing within 30 days. [*TMA 1970, 3 Sch 8, 9*].

Other provisions

23.24 These general rules apply subject to the specific rules in various sections which have their own rules for determining the appropriate appeals procedure, i.e. by agreement between the parties under *TMA 1970, s 44(2)*, under regulations introduced by the Lord Chancellor under *TMA 1970, s 46A* (currently the Special Commissioners (Jurisdiction and Procedure) Regulations, SI 1994 No 1811 and the General Commissioners Jurisdiction and Procedure Regulations, SI 1994 No 1812), and under regulations made by the Board under *TMA 1970, s 57* (currently the Capital Gains Tax Regulations, SI 1967 No 149). Other provisions which have their own rules are *TA 1988, s 102(1)*, in connection with the valuation of stock or work in progress at discontinuance; *TA 1988, s 113(5)*, elections for partnership continuation for pre-6 April 1994 partnerships prior to 1997/98; *TA 1988, s 343(10)*, apportionments for company reconstructions without change of ownership; *TA 1988, s 783(9)*, apportionments in connection with leased assets; and *CAA 1990, s 151*, procedure on apportionments. [*TMA 1970, 3 Sch 10*].

Appeals relating to Revenue enquiries

23.25 Where the Revenue call for documents under *TMA 1970, s 19A* and the taxpayer appeals, the Commissioners' determination of the appeal is final and conclusive. [Substituted *TMA 1970, s 19A 11; FA 1996,*

22 Sch 2]. Where the Revenue are enquiring into a taxpayer's self-assessment, the taxpayer may apply to the Commissioners to bring the enquiries to an end by requiring the Revenue to give a notice of any proposed amendment. Such appeal is to be heard in the same way as an appeal against an amended self-assessment made at the end of the Inspector's enquiries under *TMA 1970, s 28A(2)* or *(4)* so that the Commissioners shall give the direction applied for unless they are satisfied that the Inspector has reasonable grounds for not giving the notice. [Substituted *TMA 1970, s 28A(6), (6A); FA 1996, 22 Sch 3*].

Procedure on appeal

23.26 The procedure for appeals to the Commissioners is contained in *TMA 1970, s 50*. The basic provisions have not been changed. The appellant is to be given notice of the day for hearing the appeal. [*TMA 1970, s 50(1)*]. A Revenue Officer may attend every appeal, and is entitled to be present during the entire hearing and to give reasons in support of the assessment. [*TMA 1970, s 50(3)*]. The Commissioners are empowered to postpone the appeal for absence, sickness or other reasonable cause. [*TMA 1970, s 50(4)*]. The taxpayer may be represented by a barrister, solicitor or accountant.

23.27 There are then some consequential amendments in *TMA 1970, s 50(6)(7)* made by *FA 1994, 19 Sch 17*, reflecting the procedure for assessments under self-assessment, notably the right of the Revenue to amend self-assessments and partnership statements. The Commissioners are directed to make the appropriate adjustments to any assessments, or any amendment to a self-assessment, whether upwards or downwards as the case may be, or to hold that the assessment etc. should stand good.

Postponement of tax pending appeal

23.28 Provisions are contained in *TMA 1970, s 55* dealing with the postponement of tax pending an appeal by the taxpayer to the Commissioners. For a summary of these provisions and the procedure see Tolley's *Taxes Management Provisions* (6.37–6.43). *TMA 1970, s 55(1)* is amended by *FA 1994, 19 Sch 18* to ensure that these rules for postponement of tax and the collection of tax which has not been postponed apply to appeals to the Commissioners under self-assessment.

Error or mistake in partnership statement

23.29 An appeal against a determination of the Special Commissioners to refuse an error or mistake claim in a partnership return or statement under *TMA 1970, s 33A* can only be on a point of law.

Collection and recovery

23.30 The proceedings relating to the collection and recovery of tax are presently contained in *TMA 1970, ss 60–70*, which are described in Tolley's *Taxes Management Provisions*. The first of these deals with the Collector's powers to distrain upon the goods and chattels of a taxpayer in default, and the Revenue's prior claims over other creditors, and the separate recovery and priority procedures in Scotland. These provisions are unchanged under self-assessment.

23.31 Under *TMA 1970, s 65* small amounts of tax can be recovered summarily in the Magistrates Court. *TMA 1970, s 65(1)* is amended by *FA 1994, 19 Sch 19* to increase the amount which can be so collected from £1,000 to £2,000, which will include interim payments. Proceedings are to be brought within twelve months from the time of default. [*TMA 1970, s 65(3)*]. The provisions in *TMA 1970, s 66* regarding recovery in the county courts remain unchanged.

23.32 At present, interest which is due on unpaid tax is treated as tax for recovery purposes under *TMA 1970, s 69*. Under amended *TMA 1970, s 69*, penalties and surcharges will also be regarded as tax. [*FA 1994, 19 Sch 20*]. A certificate from a Collector that such interest, penalties and surcharges are payable is sufficient evidence of that fact for recovery purposes. [*TMA 1970, s 70(2)*].

Chapter 24

Tax Planning and Anti-Avoidance

New businesses – choice of accounting date

24.1 Where a new business is being set up after 6 April 1994, the date to which accounts are prepared will obviously affect the basis period and therefore the assessable profits for the fiscal year. An accounting period ending on 5 April is the simplest under the new rules and will avoid any overlap on commencement and hence any overlap relief on cessation. Accounts will be made up for the fiscal year and the profits as adjusted for tax purposes will be those taxed.

24.2 Attractive as this may appear it may not be the best solution. The self-assessment rules require the return and accounts to be submitted by 31 January following the end of the fiscal year, or if the Revenue are to compute the tax payable, by 30 September following the fiscal year. In the latter case this would give less than six months for the preparation and agreement of the accounts. If the accounting date year end is 30 April and self-assessment is being applied, there will be 21 months from the end of the year to allow for the filing date of the accounts.

24.3 There is also the question of a timing delay in that the longer the period between earning the profits and the payment of the tax on them, the easier it may be to meet the tax charge. If, therefore, as under the existing rules, an accounting date is chosen early in the fiscal year, and the profits for the first twelve months are kept to an absolute minimum, the overlap profits over the overlap period which are doubly taxed will be kept to a minimum. If inflation were to return at a material level, it would obviously increase the advantage of the delay between the end of the accounting period and the payment of tax.

Minimising profits in initial period

24.4 Legitimate means of keeping profits as low as possible in the opening period would include renting rather than buying premises and leasing rather than buying equipment, if it makes economic sense to lease short term. However because capital allowances are given as an expense under self-assessment, the advantage of leasing equipment is not nearly so marked as under the old rules where capital allowances were given once only for expenditure on plant and machinery, but lease payments (treated as a trading expense) were effectively allowed up to three times in the opening period.

24.5 Techniques used under the old system such as engaging potential partners as employees in the first period in order that their salaries should be a deduction from profits, do not achieve quite the advantage that they did under the old system. Although this would reduce the base line profit for the equity partners in the opening period, when the employee became a partner he would himself have an overlap resulting from his share of profits in the year in which he joined the partnership.

Change of accounting date

24.6 Whether a change of accounting date would be beneficial in 1993/94, 1994/95 or 1995/96 under the existing rules, or whether there should be a change of accounting date in the transitional year of assessment 1996/97, or under the new rules in 1997/98 or later, will depend on the figures in each case. It is impossible to generalise.

24.7 Under the existing rules, if the profits of a period omitted on the change of accounting date were relatively low, or the profits of the period coming in twice were relatively high, the Revenue would gain: conversely, if the profits of a period omitted were relatively high, or the profits of the period coming in twice were relatively low, the taxpayer would gain. The averaging provisions set out in IR 26 (Appendix D) are designed to prevent this happening to any material extent, although a slight advantage may be possible under the existing rules.

24.8 Under the transitional rules, a change of accounting date to a date later in the fiscal year, or even to 5 April, would maximise the profits falling out of assessment on averaging. It would however result in loss of overlap relief on cessation as the period from the end of the accounting period to 5 April would be reduced. Conversely, if the accounting date in the transitional period were brought forward, the profits falling out on averaging would be reduced, but the transitional overlap would be increased.

24.9 As explained in Chapter 2, a change of accounting date under the new rules to a date earlier in the fiscal year results in a further overlap and the change to a date later in the fiscal year involves the profits of in excess of twelve months being charged, subject to possible overlap relief.

Change of accounting date under existing law

24.10 The preceding year basis of assessment can only be applied where the business consistently makes up profits to the same date in each year. It is normally permissible to make up accounts on a 52- or 53-week accounting period provided that the year end remains within four days either side of a particular date.

24.11 If no accounts for a suitable period are available, the Revenue decide what period of twelve months ending on a date within the year preceding the year of assessment shall be deemed to be the 'year' the profits or gains of which are to be taken to be the profits or gains of the 'year preceding the year of assessment' under *TA 1988, s 60(4)* as originally enacted. The Revenue apply an averaging procedure on a change of accounting date. On such a change the profits of the twelve-month period ending on the new accounting date form the basis of the assessment on the normal preceding year basis. If the new accounting date is later than the old accounting date, some profits will fall out of assessment and if it is earlier some profits will be assessed twice. The averaging procedure then applied is as explained below. The Revenue procedure has been approved in *CIR v Helical Bar Ltd 1972 48 TC 221*.

Averaging procedure

24.12 First, it is necessary to adjust the profits for the year to the new accounting date, making any necessary apportionments on a time basis. It is then necessary to compute adjusted profits for the previous twelve months (the corresponding period). The assessments originally based on the profits included in these computations should be examined. If the earliest of those years of assessment cannot be based on the original accounting date on the normal preceding year basis, it is necessary to go back a further year and introduce another corresponding period. The total period of the accounts affected is compared with the total period of the fiscal years affected and the profits are expanded or contracted proportionately to arrive at the total notional adjusted profits. From this is deducted the assessments which are final leaving an adjusted figure for the intermediate period. If the intermediate period figure falls between the corresponding period figure and the original unadjusted assessment for that fiscal year, the intermediate figure will be substituted provided that the difference is at least 10 per cent of the average profits or £1,000, whichever is lower.

24.13 This change of accounting date computation can best be illustrated by an example and further details will be found in the Revenue leaflet IR 26, reproduced in Appendix D. This averaging basis is not used by the Revenue where it would produce an unfair result, for example, where the intermediate figure does not fall between the original and corresponding figures or where the profits of the business are seasonal or where some of the periods involved were loss-making, or during the opening or closing years of a business.

The capital allowances basis periods will be recalculated in accordance with *CAA 1990, s 160* only if the taxpayer so requires. By unpublished concession, the Revenue only adjust the capital allowances basis periods if the taxpayer so insists.

Example 1

On 30 April 1994 Mr Yermolayev changed his accounting date. The results were:

		£
30 April 1994	– 4 months	10,000
31 December 1993	– 12 months	28,000
31 December 1992	– 12 months	24,000
	28 months	£62,000

Accounts will be made up to 30 April in future:

	£
Assessment 1995/96	
Year ended 30.4.94	
4 months to 30.4.94	10,000
8/12 × £28,000 (y/e 31.12.93)	18,667
	£28,667
Assessment 1994/95	
Year ended 30.4.93	
4/12 × £28,000 (y/e 31.12.93)	9,333
8/12 × £24,000 (y/e 31.12.92)	16,000
	£25,333
Original assessment 1994/95	
Year ended 31.12.93	£28,000
Original assessment 1993/94	
Year ended 31.12.92	£24,000

Fiscal years originally based on these profits 1993/94, 1994/95 and 1995/96
3 years = 36 months
Average profits

	£	£
$\frac{36 \text{ months}}{28 \text{ months}}$ × £62,000		79,714
Less Assessed 1995/96	28,667	
1993/94	24,000	52,667
Intermediate period		£27,047

This £27,047 falls between the original assessment (£28,000) and the corresponding period assessment (£25,333), but is within £1,000 of the original assessment. As the difference is also less than 10 per cent of the average profits for the current (1995/96 £28,667) and preceding years' assessments (1994/95 £28,000) i.e. £2,833, the average basis for 1994/95 is not used and the original assessment of £28,000 remains.

24.14 The old change of accounting date rules give rise to a problem where no accounts are made up to a date in 1994/95, for example, if a change of accounting date occurs in 1995/96 and the accounting date is changed from 31 December 1994 to make up accounts to 30 April 1995, the assessment for 1994/95 would, under the old rules of IR26, have been the year ended 31 December 1993 and the assessment for 1996/97 the year ended 30 April 1995, with 1995/96 being the intermediate period calculated on an annualised averaging basis.

However, because 1996/97 is the transitional year it seems to be that 1995/96 would continue to be based on the profits for the year ended 31 December 1994 and assuming accounts are made up to 30 April in future the transitional period would be the 16 months ended on 30 April 1996.

If, however, the business did not prepare accounts to 31 December 1994, but produces a 16 month account to 30 April 1995, 1994/95 is assessed on the profits for the year ended 31 December 1993, but it is not clear what profits would be assessed for 1995/96.

24.15 The Revenue's solution is that where it is necessary to carry out a change of accounting date calculation to determine a basis period for 1995/96 (or earlier) the calculations should proceed using existing practice as if the transitional rules for 1996/97 did not exist, Inland Revenue Tax Bulletin No 18, August 1995, page 242 (see Appendix F). Any figure or basis period for 1996/97 should be ignored. Instead the transitional basis period for 1996/97 will commence immediately after whatever basis period is used for 1995/96, in the normal way.

As previously, there may be circumstances in a particular case that merit special consideration (for example, a seasonal business). Such cases will be reviewed by the taxpayer's local office, and, if necessary referred to the Revenue's Business Profits Division (Period of Accounts) for guidance.

There is, under the old rules, a precedent for this type of approach. Where there is a change of accounting date within two years of the year of assessment in which a business ceases, the averaging calculations are made as if the business had not ceased. Of course, any figures generated for the year of cessation itself must be ignored.

Example 2

The accounts of a business have been made up annually to 31 December for years up to and including 31 December 1993. The next account is for the 16 months to 30 April 1995, and it is intended that subsequent accounts will be made up annually to 30 April.

The trading profits are as follows:

	£
12 months to 31 December 1992	15,000
12 months to 31 December 1993	50,000
16 months to 30 April 1995	70,000
40	135,000

The 1994/95 assessment has been made on £50,000, the profit of the year to 31 December 1993.

The basis of assessment for each of the years 1995/96 and 1996/97 requires to be determined under *TA 1988, s 60(4)* (original version). In accordance with IR26, paragraph 3 the years to 30 April 1994, and 30 April 1995, will be taken as the basis years and the assessments will be:

		£
1995/96	(8/12) × £50,000 =	33,333
	(4/16) × £70,000 =	17,500
		50,833
1996/97	(12/16) × £70,000 =	52,500

The following review is made to see whether the 1994/95 assessment of £50,000 should be revised.

(i) *'Aggregate profit'*

The profit for the relevant accounting periods is £135,000 for the 40 months to 30 April 1995.

The relevant years are 1993/94, 1994/95, 1995/96 and 1996/97, a period of 48 months.

The aggregate profit is therefore the profit for 48 months at the rate of £135,000 for 40 months, i.e.

48/40 × £135,000 = £162,000

(ii) Sum of assessments for 'relevant years' without revision under *TA 1988, s 60(5)* (old version)

	'Relevant Years'	Assessments £
	1993/94	15,000
	1994/95	50,000
	1995/96	50,833
	1996/97	52,500
Sum of assessments for 'relevant years'		168,333

Since the difference between (i) £162,000 and (ii) £168,333 is greater than £1,000 (see IR26, paragraph 8) the calculation proceeds as follows:

(iii) Sum of assessments for 'relevant years' after revision under *TA 1988, s 60(5)*.

'Relevant years'		Assessments £
1993/94		15,000
1994/95	(8/12) × £15,000 = £10,000	
	(4/12) × £50,000 = £16,667	26,667
1995/96		50,833
1996/97		52,500
Sum of assessments for 'relevant years'		145,000

The figure at (i) £162,000 is intermediate between (ii) £168,333 and (iii) £145,000. The assessment for 1994/95 is therefore revised to such an amount that the total of the assessments for the relevant years equal the figure at (i) as follows:

	£	£
Figure at (i)		162,000
Assessed 1993/94	15,000	
Assessed 1995/96	50,833	
Assessed 1996/97	52,500	118,333
Balance to be assessed for 1994/95		43,667

The assessment for 1994/95 is therefore revised to £43,667.

The basis period for 1995/96 is the year ended 30 April 1994 (£50,833). The transitional year basis period is the period from 1 May 1994 to 30 April 1996 i.e. basis period for 1996/97 under *TA 1988, s 60(3)(b)* (*FA 1994, 20 Sch 2(2)(a)*) the year ended 30 April 1996 (say) £65,000

	£
Relevant period, i.e. 1 May 1994 to 30 April 1995 (*FA 1994, 20 Sch 2(2)(b)*)	
12/16 × £70,000 =	£52,500
Aggregated	£117,500
Appropriate percentage under *FA 1994, 20 Sch 2(5)*	
$£117{,}500 \times \dfrac{365}{365 + 365}$	£58,750

The position becomes slightly more complicated where the IR26 averaging does not work.

Example 3

The accounts of a business have been made up annually to 31 December for years up to and including 31 December 1993. The next account is for the 16 months to 30 April 1995, and it is intended that subsequent accounts will be made up annually to 30 April.

The trading profits are as follows:

	£
12 months to 31 December 1992	15,000
12 months to 31 December 1993	20,000
16 months to 30 April 1995	60,000
40	95,000

The 1994/95 assessment has been made on £20,000, the profit of the year to 31 December 1993.

The basis of assessment for each of the years 1995/96 and 1996/97 requires to be determined under *TA 1988, s 60(4)* (original version). In accordance with IR26, paragraph 3 the years to 30 April 1994, and 30 April 1995, will be taken as the basis years and the assessments will be:

		£
1995/96	(8/12) × £20,000 =	13,333
	(4/16) × £60,000 =	15,000
		28,333
1996/97	(12/16) × £60,000 =	45,000

The following review is made to see whether the 1994/95 assessment of £20,000 should be revised.

(i) *'Aggregate profit'*

The profit for the relevant accounting periods is £95,000 for the 40 months to 30 April 1995.

The relevant years are 1993/94, 1994/95, 1995/96 and 1996/97 a period of 48 months.

The aggregate profit is therefore the profit for 48 months at the rate of £95,000 for 40 months, i.e.

48/40 × £95,000 = £114,000

(ii) Sum of assessments for 'relevant years' without revision under *TA 1988, s 60(5)* (old version)

	'Relevant Years'	Assessments £
	1993/94	15,000
	1994/95	20,000
	1995/96	28,333
	1996/97	45,000
Sum of assessments for 'relevant years'		108,333

Since the difference between (i) £114,000 and (ii) £108,333 is greater than £1,000 (see IR26, paragraph 8) the calculation proceeds as follows:

(iii) Sum of assessments for 'relevant years' after revision under *TA 1988, s 60(5)*.

'Relevant years'		Assessments £
1993/94		15,000
1994/95	(8/12) × £15,000 = £10,000	
	(4/12) × £20,000 = £6,667	16,667
1995/96		28,333
1996/97		45,000
Sum of assessments for 'relevant years'		105,000

The figure at (i) £114,000 is not intermediate between (ii) £108,333 and (iii) £105,000. The assessment for 1994/95 is therefore not revised and the Revenue seek a basis period for 1995/96 which produces a profit of £34,000 to bring the total up to £114,000, less any losses used in aggregation. This basis period must be 12 months long and end in 1994/95. The desired basis period is found by extrapolation to be the year ended 23 July 1994. The profit for this period is as follows:

161/365 × £20,000 (£8,822) + 204/485 × £60,000 (£25,237) = £34,059

The overall result is as follows:

Period	Profits
	£
1993/94	15,000
1994/95	20,000
1995/96	34,059
1996/97	45,000
Total	£114,059

The profit for the year ended 30 April 1996 was £65,000.

The basis period for 1996/97 under *TA 1988, s 60(3)(b); FA 1994, s 200, 20 Sch 2(2)(a)* (accounting year to 30 April 1996 ending in current fiscal year)	£65,000
Relevant period under *FA 1994, 20 Sch 2(2)(b)* i.e. 24 July 1994 to 30 April 1995	
$\frac{281}{485} \times £60,000$	£34,763
Aggregate, *FA 1994, 20 Sch 2(2)*	£99,763
Approprite percentage under *FA 1994, 20 Sch 2(5)*	
$£99,763 \times \frac{365}{365 + 281}$	£56,368

The period 1 May 1994 to 23 July 1994 is not brought into the transitional averaging period, nor is it averaged down.

Final position:

Profits	£
y/e 31/12/92	15,000
y/e 31/12/93	20,000
16 months to 30/4/95	60,000
y/e 30/4/96	65,000
	£160,000

Assessed	£
1993/94	15,000
1994/95	20,000
1995/96	34,059
1996/97	56,368
	£125,427

It is arguable that another way of dealing with the problem would be to assess 12/28ths of the profits for the period from 1 January 1994 to 30

April 1996 in each of 1995/96 and 1996/97 i.e. £53,571 in each year which, on these figures, would be less favourable to the taxpayer:

	£
1993/94	15,000
1994/95	20,000
1995/96	53,571
1996/97	53,571
	£142,142

Transitional year planning and anti-avoidance

24.16 The Revenue are well aware that the averaging of profits in the transitional year 1996/97 gives the taxpayer the incentive to maximise the profit for the basis period concerned, as normally only half this profit would be charged to tax. Similarly, the transitional overlap relief would encourage the maximisation of the profit for the 1997/98 basis period because that part of the basis period which falls before 6 April 1997 is ultimately relieved from tax by way of overlap relief. Detailed anti-avoidance measures are contained in *FA 1995*, but to give taxpayers some forewarning of the provisions the Revenue issued a Press Release on 31 March 1994 (Appendix C). In order to discourage attempts at avoidance, the result of falling foul of the anti-avoidance measures will put the taxpayer in a materially worse position than he would have been had he not attempted to take undue advantage of the transitional measures.

Transitional averaging anti-avoidance

24.17 The anti-avoidance measures relating to trades, professions or vocations taxed under Schedule D, Cases I, II or V apply where one or more triggering events apply. These are:

(*a*) A 'relevant change' being an accounting change or change of business practice other than a change made exclusively for *bona fide* commercial reasons, or where the obtaining of a tax advantage is not the main benefit that could reasonably be expected to arise from the making of the change. [*FA 1995, 22 Sch 14(1)*]. A change of business practice means any change in an established practice of a trade, profession or vocation as to timing of the supply of goods or services, the invoicing of customers or clients, the collection of outstanding debts, the obtaining of goods or services, the incurring of business expenses and the settlement of outstanding debts; or as to obtaining or making payments in advance or payments on account. [*FA 1995, 22 Sch 14(3)*]. An accounting change means any change of accounting date, or modification of an accounting policy, or substitution of one policy for another, other than a change of accounting date which brings the end of the basis period for 1996/97 closer to 5 April 1997. [*FA 1995, 22 Sch 14(2)*]. Accounting policies are defined similarly to Statement of Standard Accounting Practice No 2 (Appendix B) which states 'accounting policies are the specific accounting bases judged by business enterprises to be most appropriate to their circumstances and adopted by them for the purpose of preparing their financial accounts'.

(*b*) A 'relevant transaction' being any self-cancelling transaction or transaction with a connected person other than one entered into exclusively for *bona fide* commercial reasons, or where the obtaining of a tax advantage is not the main benefit that could reasonably be expected to arise from entering into transaction. [*FA 1995, 22 Sch 15*]. Connected persons are defined by reference to *TA 1988, s 839* but with some extensions. [*FA 1995, 22 Sch 17*]. A connected person is a spouse, brother or brother-in-law, sister or sister-in-law, parent or parent-in-law, grandparent or grandparent-in-law, son or son-in-law, daughter or daughter-in-law, grandson or grandson-in-law, granddaughter or granddaughter-in-law. In addition, a trustee of a settlement is connected with a settlor, or with a company connected with a settlement under *TA 1988, s 681*. A partner is connected with his other partners and their spouses or relatives. Partners are also connected with (i) an individual if he controls the partnership (ii) a company if the company controls the partnership and (iii) other partnerships if the same person controls both. Companies are connected if they are under common control and two or more persons acting together to exercise control of a company are connected with each other.

(*c*) An agreement by which the person carrying on the trade, profession or vocation agrees to sell or transfer trading stock or work in progress is a self-cancelling transaction, if there is an agreement to buy back or reacquire the trading stock or work in progress, or where there is an option duly exercised under which the trading stock or work in progress is reacquired. Trading stock is defined by reference to *TA 1988, s 100* i.e. property of any description whether real or personal which is sold in the ordinary course of a trade, or would be so sold if it were mature or its manufacture, preparation or construction were complete, or materials used in the manufacture, preparation or construction of any such property including work in progress. Work in progress in relation to a profession or vocation is defined as services performed in the ordinary course of the profession or vocation the performance of which is wholly or partly completed at the time of the sale or transfer and which would have been charged for on completion if the transfer had not been effected and any articles produced or material used in the performance of such services, which effectively repeats the definition in *TA 1988, s 101*. [*FA 1995, 22 Sch 16*]. Obtaining a tax advantage is not regarded as a *bona fide* commercial reason [*FA 1995, 22 Sch 21(2)*]. Tax advantage is not defined but in the view of the Inland Revenue it has a very wide meaning and includes a timing advantage or an increase in a loss.

Change in business practice and accounting change

24.18 These would encompass any major change in the procedure followed for the issue of bills to customers, which would include arrangements for payments on account, procedures for the collection of debts, or procedures for the payment of bills for business expenses including salaries or bonuses. This would be particularly relevant for businesses preparing accounts on a conventional basis such as cash receipts and payments, or bills delivered. The Inland Revenue booklet published on 29 November 1994 entitled 'Self Assessment – Transition to the Current Year Basis – Anti-avoidance Provisions' states at paras 3.14–3.24 as follows.

'Change in business practice

Expenses as well as receipts

3.14 The legislation refers to amounts included in the profits or gains of the periods in question. It is important to note that the profit shifting envisaged does not refer only to the movement of receipts from one period to another. As the definition of "change of business practice" at paragraph 13(3) of the draft legislation makes clear, the rules target equally situations where expenses are shifted to increase profits.

Established business practices

3.15 The rules refer to a change occurring in an **established** business practice.

3.16 Whether a practice is established or not is ultimately a question of fact, but expenditure of a largely discretionary nature (such as routine decoration arising **broadly** every, say, 5–7 years) would not normally be included in this category. However, where there was, say, a regular annual routine maintenance task necessitated by the specific nature of the trade (Health and Safety Regulations applying to a food processing plant for example) bringing forward or deferring the related expenditure, exceptionally, to the (respectively) previous or following year would be likely to constitute a change in an established practice.

Timing is crucial

3.17 The rules target specifically changes which impact on the timing of recognition of profits so changes in practices which are not, in themselves, directly timing oriented, will normally be outside the rules. An example would be a change from a policy of leasing to purchasing capital assets.

3.18 On the other hand, a farmer (for example) departing from his established practice and delaying the sale of his crops in order to gain a tax advantage by shifting the proceeds into the transitional basis period would be in a trigger situation.

Accounting change

3.19 "Accounting change" includes both a change of accounting policy and a modification of an existing policy.

3.20 An example of a change of accounting policy would be a change in the time at which profits from long term contracts are recognised (for example from recognition on completion to recognition over the life of the contract).

3.21 An example of a modification of an existing policy would be a change in the basis of valuation of trading stock at the account end (involving perhaps a re-appraisal of what overhead costs are to be included in calculating the cost of the stock).

3.22 The accounting change trigger can include any change of accounting date other than (a statutorily prescribed exception) one which brings the end of the basis period for the year 1996/97 closer to 5 April 1997.

3.23 Also within the trigger situations would be a change, for a professional partnership, from a cash to, for example, an earnings basis of assessment.

3.24 Not all accounting changes, however, have an effect on the accounting **policy** of a business. An example would be a change, based on practical experience, in measuring the useful life of leased assets with the result that the expenditure passing through the profit and loss account is reduced. This would not be considered a change of accounting policy but merely a re-appraisal of the basic facts to which an accounting policy was applied.'

24.19 If the triggering event is not within the escape provisions, 1.25 times the profits so identified will be charged to tax as additional profits in 1996/97, which will not qualify for any averaging reduction; see 24.26 (*FA 1995, 22 Sch 1(2)*). The taxpayer is therefore in a worse position than if the profits had not been shifted into the transitional basis period because half (or the appropriate proportion) of the profits shifted into the transitional period are already taxed under the averaging provisions.

Escape provisions

24.20 There are basically four ways of avoiding a penalty under the transitional anti-avoidance rules. These are the *de minimis* test, the motive test, the benefit test and the declaration of guilt. A relevant change or a change of business practice, or relevant transaction, or relevant arrangement passes the motive test if the change is made, the transaction is entered into or the arrangements are made exclusively for *bona fide* commercial reasons. This motive test is likely to be difficult to pass in practice where there are any mixed motives, such that it could not be said that the *bona fide* commercial reasons were exclusive given that the obtaining of a tax advantage is not to be regarded as a *bona fide* commercial reason. The main benefit test applies where it is shown that the obtaining of a tax advantage is not the main benefit that could be reasonably expected to arise from making the accounting change, or change of business practice, or entering into the transaction or arrangement. In most commercial situations, it should be possible to show that although a benefit might be the obtaining of a tax advantage it was not the main benefit and this is reinforced by *FA 1995, s 123* which brings in the anti-avoidance provisions of *FA 1995, 22 Sch* 'for preventing the exploitation of the transitional provisions'. If there is no attempt to exploit the transitional provisions *Schedule 22* should not be in point.

24.21 Where the taxpayer accepts that the anti-avoidance provisions are likely to bite, he can avoid the penalty element by declaring on his original return that there is an increase of profits or gains of the transitional period, an increase of profits or gains of the transitional overlap period, or an increase of Schedule D, Case III, IV or V profits or gains in the transitional overlap period. In this case, *FA 1995, 22 Sch 13(1)* provides that the anti-avoidance provisions will be applied without the penalty multiplier of 1.25 times the tax at stake. Similarly, where the return as originally made states that there has been an increase in profits or gains taxable under Schedule D, Cases III, IV or V in 1995/96 and 1996/97, including interest, the transitional provisions are applied to the tainted income at 50 per cent instead of the penalty rate of 62.5 per cent, under *FA 1995, 22 Sch 13(2)*. The effect of these provisions is that the transitional anti-avoidance rules will claw back the tax that would have been saved as a result of the triggering event. Where the position is in doubt, the Revenue have confirmed informally that the penalty element can be avoided by bringing the triggering event to the notice of the Revenue with the original return if submitted on time and putting forward the reasons why the *de minimis*, motive or main benefit test should prevent the anti-avoidance provisions applying. There will then be no penalty even if it is ultimately agreed that the anti-avoidance provisions do bite and the tax sought to be saved is recovered.

De minimis provisions

24.22 The transitional anti-avoidance provisions do not apply where:

(*a*) the increased profit in 1996/97, or the increase in the transitional overlap credit is less than £Z (*FA 1995, 22 Sch 1(3)(a)*); or

(*b*) the profit diverted as a result of the triggering event, is less than Y per cent of the base line profit. The base line profit is the profit that would have arisen had the triggering event not taken place (*FA 1995, 22 Sch 1(3)(b)*); or

(*c*) the turnover is less than £X per annum during the 1996/97 basis period, or the 1997/98 transitional overlap period (*FA 1995, 22 Sch 1(3)(c)*).

Turnover is defined by *FA 1995, 22 Sch 21(1)* as the amount derived from the provision of goods or services in the normal course of a trade, profession or vocation, after deduction of trade discounts and Value Added Tax.

24.23 It appears that the *de minimis* amounts and percentages i.e. X, Y and Z above, will only be announced immediately prior to the issue of the tax returns for the year. Presumably, therefore, the 1996/97 figures will not be announced until April 1997 and the 1997/98 figures until April 1998. The intention is to discourage taxpayers from activities which would divert profits into the transitional period in order to try and obtain a tax advantage. Accordingly they will not be told the 'safe harbour' rules until it is too late to take any action.

24.24 This probably means that the *de minimis* figures will be fairly high unless in due course it appears to the Revenue that taxpayers generally have been shunting excessive profits into the transitional period. This could have the negative effect of the imposition of low *de minimis* figures, thereby allowing the Revenue to collect substantial additional tax under this penalty element in the anti-avoidance provisions. The *de minimis* exemptions will be fixed by Statutory Instrument under the enabling powers in *FA 1995, 22 Sch 1(3)(a)*.

Partnerships

24.25 The *de minimis* provisions for partnerships are applied as if X and Z were multiplied by the average number of partners throughout the basis period for 1996/97, subject to averaging. In the case of the transitional overlap, the turnover of the whole firm is divided among the partners.

Transitional averaging – Schedule D, Cases I and II

24.26 The effect of transitional averaging in 1996/97 is that the effective rate of taxation on profits falling in the transitional period is only a proportion of the normal rate, depending on the length of the transitional averaging period and in most cases will be one-half of the normal rate which on current rates would give an effective tax charge of 20 per cent. There is obviously an incentive for taxpayers to shift profits into the transitional averaging period which could be done by increasing the income in the period or reducing the expenses. If this is achieved as a result of a triggering event (see 24.17 *et seq*. above), the anti-avoidance provisions in *FA 1995, 22 Sch 1* apply. Obviously if 1995/96 is assessed on an actual basis, so would 1996/97 under the transitional provisions of *FA 1994, 20 Sch 2(3)* and the anti-avoidance provisions would have no relevance.

The benefit of the amount diverted into the transitional averaging period is computed by taking the complementary percentage of the amount diverted and assessing this to tax in 1996/97, in addition to the average profits calculated under *FA 1994, 20 Sch 2*. The penalty element to discourage taxpayers from attempting such manoeuvres is achieved by charging to tax 1.25 times the complementary percentage of the amount diverted. To compute the complementary percentage, it is first necessary to compute the appropriate percentage which is 365 divided by the number of days in the transitional period, i.e. the basis period for 1996/97 and the relevant period under *FA 1994, 20 Sch 2(5)*. The complementary percentage is the difference between 100 per cent and the appropriate percentage. In the normal case of annual accounts both the appropriate percentage and complementary percentage would be 50 per cent.

Example 3

Mr Komta has been in business for many years and produces accounts for each year to 30 April.

Profits (as adjusted for tax purposes)

y/e 30.4.94	£20,000
y/e 30.4.95	£40,000
y/e 30.4.96	£60,000
y/e 30.4.97	£55,000

Assessable/taxable

1995/96	Preceding year basis	£20,000	(*a*)
1996/97	Transitional year	£56,250	(*b*)
1997/98	Current year basis	£55,000	(*c*)
	Total	£131,250	

Notes

(*a*) *TA 1988, s 60(3)* original version.

(*b*) Primary basis period for 1996/97 under *TA 1988, s 60(3)(b)*;

FA 1994, s 200, y/e 30.4.96	£60,000
Relevant period under *FA 1994, 20 Sch 2(2)(b), (5)* i.e. 1.5.94 to 30.4.95	£40,000
Aggregate *FA 1994, 20 Sch 2(2)*	£100,000

However, it transpires that profits of £10,000 were artificially shifted from the year ended 30 April 1994 to the year ended 30 April 1995. Mr Komta is unable to demonstrate any *bona fide* commercial reason for this shift. The Revenue therefore impose the anti-avoidance provisions.

Appropriate percentage *FA 1995, 22 Sch 1(4)*	$\frac{365}{365 + 365} = 50\%$
Complementary percentage *FA 1995, 22 Sch 1(4)*	$100 - 50 = 50\%$

Aggregate

FA 1995, 22 Sch 1(2)(a)	
50% × £60,000	£30,000
50% × £40,000	£20,000
FA 1995, 22 Sch 1(2)(b)	
1.25 × 50% × £10,000	£6,250
	£56,250

Transitional overlap period under *FA 1994, 20 Sch 2(4)*: part of basis period for 1997/98, year ending 30 April 1997, which falls after 30 April 1996 and before 6 April 1997, i.e. 1.5.96 to 5.4.97, i.e. 340 days overlap profits

£55,000 × 340/365 = £51,233

(*c*) *TA 1988, s 60(3)(b); FA 1994, s 200*

Had no shift of profits taken place the profits (as adjusted for tax purposes) would have been:

y/e 30.4.94	£30,000
y/e 30.4.95	£30,000
y/e 30.4.96	£60,000
y/e 30.4.97	£55,000

Assessable/taxable

1995/96	Preceding year basis	£30,000	(*d*)
1996/97	Transitional year	£45,000	(*e*)
1997/98	Current year basis	£55,000	(*f*)
	Total	£130,000	

Notes

(*d*) *TA 1988, s 60(3)* original version.

(*e*)

Primary basis for 1996/97 under *TA 1988, s 60(3)(b)*; *FA 1994, s 200*, y/e 30.4.96	£60,000
Relevant period under *FA 1994, 20 Sch 2(2)(b),(5)* i.e. 1.5.94 to 30.4.95	£30,000
Aggregate *FA 1994, 20 Sch 2(2)*	£90,000

Appropriate percentage under *FA 1994, 20 Sch 2(5)*

$$£90,000 \times \frac{365}{365 + 365} = £45,000$$

(*f*) *TA 1988, s 60(3)(b): FA 1994, s 200.*

The unjustified shift of profits into the transitional period results in additional profits being charged of £1,250 (£131,250 − £130,000), i.e. a penalty of tax on one-quarter of £5,000 which is the amount that would have escaped tax on averaging £10,000 (£10,000 × 365/730).

Example 4

Mr Kolyesnikov has been in business for many years and produced accounts each year to 31 December until 1996 when he produced accounts for the 15 months to 31 March 1997.

Profits (as adjusted for tax purposes)

y/e 31.12.94	£20,000
y/e 31.12.95	£40,000
p/e 31.3.97	£60,000
y/e 31.3.98	£55,000

Assessable/taxable

1995/96	Preceding year basis	£20,000	(*a*)
1996/97	Transitional year	£51,448	(*b*)
1997/98	Current year basis	£55,000	(*c*)
	Total	£126,448	

Notes

(*a*) *TA 1988, s 60(3)* original version.

(*b*) Primary basis period for 1996/97 under *TA 1988, s 60(3)(b)*; *FA 1994, s 200*, p/e 31.3.97 (12/15 × £60,000) £48,000

Relevant period under *FA 1994, 20 Sch 2(2)(b), (5)* i.e. 1.1.95 to 31.3.96

y/e 31.12.95	£40,000
1.1.96 to 31.3.96 (3/15 × £60,000)	£12,000
Aggregate *FA 1994, 20 Sch 2(2)*	£100,000

Appropriate percentage under *FA 1994, 20 Sch 2(5)*:

$$£100,000 \times \frac{365}{365 + 365 + 90} = £44,512$$

However, it transpires that profits of £10,000 were artificially shifted from the year ended 31 December 1994 to the year ended 31 December 1995. Mr Kolyesnikov is unable to demonstrate any *bona fide* commercial reason for this shift. The Revenue therefore impose the anti-avoidance provisions.

Appropriate percentage *FA 1995, 22 Sch 1(4)* $\frac{365}{365 + 365 + 90} \times 100 = 44.512\%$

Aggregate

FA 1995, 22 Sch 1(2)(a)

44.512% × £48,000	£21,366
44.512% × £40,000	£17,805
44.512% × £12,000	£5,341

FA 1995, 22 Sch 1(2)(b)

1.25 × 55.488% × £10,000	£6,936
	£51,448

Transitional overlap period under *FA 1994, 20 Sch 2(4)*: part of basis period for 1997/98, year ending 31 March 1998, which falls after 31 March 1997 and before 6 April 1997, i.e. 1 April 1997 to 5 April 1997, i.e. five days overlap profits

£55,000 × 5/365 = £753

(*c*) *TA 1988, s 60(3)(b)*; *FA 1994, s 200*

Had no shift of profits taken place the profits (as adjusted for tax purposes) would have been:

y/e 31.12.94	£30,000
y/e 31.12.95	£30,000
y/e 31.3.97	£60,000
y/e 31.3.98	£55,000

Assessable/taxable		
1995/96	Preceding year basis	£30,000 (*d*)
1996/97	Transitional year	£40,061 (*e*)
1997/98	Current year basis	£55,000 (*f*)
	Total	£125,061

(*d*) *TA 1988, s 60(3)* original version.

(*e*) Primary basis for 1996/97 under *TA 1988, s 60(3)(b)*;

FA 1994, s 200, p/e 31.3.97 (12/15 × £60,000)	£48,000
Relevant period under *FA 1994, 20 Sch 2(2)(b),(5)*	
i.e. 1.1.95 to 31.3.96	
y/e 31.12.95	£30,000
1.1.96 to 31.3.96 (3/15 × £60,000)	£12,000
Aggregate *FA 1994, 20 Sch 2(2)*	£90,000

Appropriate percentage under *FA 1994, 20 Sch 2(5)*

$$£90{,}000 \times \frac{365}{365 + 365 + 90} = £40{,}061$$

(*f*) *TA 1988, s 60(3)(b); FA 1994, s 200.*

The unjustified shift of profits into the transitional period results in additional profits being charged of £1,387 (£126,448 – £125,061), i.e. a penalty of tax on one-quarter of £5,548 on the amount shifted of £10,000, which is the amount that would have escaped charge on averaging, $£10{,}000 - \left(£10{,}000 \times \frac{365}{365 + 365 + 90}\right)$.

Privatisation of interest – transitional averaging

24.27 The Revenue are also well aware that a partner could obtain an advantage by procuring the repayment of partnership borrowings and substituting personal loans to provide capital for the firm, rather appropriately described as 'privatisation'. Interest on a partnership borrowing would be relieved as a trading expense and under the averaging provisions normally only half of this expense would be so relieved. On the other hand if the partners were to borrow personally, the interest would be claimed under *TA 1988, s 353* as payable in respect of a loan to the partnership and there would be no loss of interest relief.

24.28 To counter this, *FA 1995, 22 Sch 2* is introduced to remove the intended benefit. This applies where there is (*a*) a transitional period dealt with under the averaging provisions, and (*b*) a claim by the partners individually for tax relief on interest borrowed personally and on-lent to the partnership, such that the interest may be claimed as a charge on income of the individual partners under *TA 1988, s 353*. The anti-avoidance provisions do not apply where the money raised by the partners individually is used wholly or mainly for *bona fide* commercial reasons, or otherwise than to reduce the borrowings of the partnership for any period falling wholly or partly within the transitional period (a relevant period). [*FA 1995, 22 Sch 2(6)*].

24.29 The attempted avoidance is countered by restricting the interest claimable as a charge under *TA 1988, s 353* to the appropriate percentage of the interest paid. The appropriate percentage is the percentage of the profits in the transitional period charged to tax as a result of the averaging provisions in *FA 1994, 20 Sch 2* and is defined in *FA 1995, 22 Sch 2(6)*. The effect is to give the same relief for interest as if the borrowing had been retained within the partnership and claimed as a trading expense, with only the appropriate proportion being allowed because of transitional averaging. There is no penalty element in this anti-avoidance provision and it does not apply where the loan was made before 1 April 1994 or the amount of interest involved is below a *de minimis* limit, which will be fixed by regulations expected immediately prior to 5 April 1997. *FA 1995, 22 Sch 2(5)* prevents a series of loans being used to circumvent the anti-avoidance restrictions.

Example 5

Captain Lak is a partner in Kuichyeisky & Co which draws up accounts to 30 April each year. On 1 May 1994 he borrows £100,000 and introduces it to the partnership to reduce the partnership overdraft. In each of the years 1994/95 to 1996/97 he claims relief under *TA 1988, s 353* for interest paid of £10,000, the interest being payable quarterly in advance.

Captain Lak is unable to provide evidence that the refinancing was undertaken for *bona fide* commercial reasons. His relief under *TA 1988, s 353* is therefore reduced as follows:

'Appropriate percentage' *FA 1995, 22 Sch 1(4)*	$\frac{365}{\text{No of days in transitional period (730)}}$
'Relevant period' *FA 1995, 22 Sch 2(a)*	Any period falling within the transitional period
Transitional period	Basis period for 1996/97 (year ended 30 April 1996) and the relevant period (defined by *FA 1994, 20 Sch 2(5)*) (year ended 30 April 1995)

Therefore relief for interest paid in 1994/95 and 1995/96 (i.e. the years in which the interest for the transitional period is actually paid) is restricted to:

£10,000 × 365/730 = £5,000 for each year

Transitional overlap

24.30 Under the preceding year basis of assessment, the early years' profits were normally charged to tax between two and three times depending on the precise accounting date. The object of the transitional relief is to try, so far as possible, to ensure that the profits of a business are charged to tax for a similar period to the period in which the business had been carried on. Ignoring the effect of possible changes in accounting date, the transitional averaging provisions in *FA 1994, 20 Sch 2* effectively give relief for one year of the multiple charge on commencement under the preceding year basis, and the transitional overlap relief given by *FA 1994, 20 Sch 2(4)* grants relief for the remainder of the multiple charge on commencement. As overlap profits of an overlap period, these profits, for the period from the end of the basis period for 1996/97 to 5 April 1997, will be relieved in full on cessation or in part on a change of accounting date. The Revenue perceive this as an opportunity for taxpayers to divert profits into the basis period for 1997/98 in order to maximise the transitional overlap relief and *FA 1995, 22 Sch 3* is designed to discourage taxpayers from attempting to exploit these rules. The anti-avoidance provisions only apply where there is a transitional overlap period eligible for relief under *FA 1994, 20 Sch 2(4)* and where profits have been diverted into the transitional overlap period as a result of a relevant change, or a relevant transaction that is an accounting change or change of business practice, or a connected party or self-cancelling transaction as defined by *FA 1995, 22 Sch 14–17*. There is a penalty element of tax on 25 per cent of the amount by which the taxpayer sought to increase the transitional overlap relief, which is achieved by reducing the overlap relief by 1.25 times the profits diverted into the transitional overlap relief period. It would appear that this anti-avoidance provision can reduce the transitional overlap relief to zero, but would not impose a charge to tax if the overlap profit is less than 1.25 times the amount diverted into the overlap relief period.

24.31 The motive and main benefit escape routes apply through the definition of relevant change or relevant transaction and there will be *de minimis* limits introduced by regulation, expected to be published just before 5 April 1997, which are applied by *FA 1995, 22 Sch 3(3)* introducing, with amendments, the *de minimis* provisions within *FA 1995, 22 Sch 1(3)*. The *de minimis* limits will therefore be applied by reference to an aggregate amount of transitional overlap profit, the proportion of the amount diverted to the overlap profit and the appropriate percentage of turnover for the transitional overlap period. The appropriate percentage is defined by *FA 1995, 22 Sch 3(4)* in the same way as for transitional averaging anti-avoidance as 365 divided by the number of days in the transitional overlap period, which itself is defined as the period beginning immediately after the end of the basis period for 1996/97, or for a partnership the basis period of the partnership for that year, and ending with 5 April 1997.

Example 6

Mr Maksimov is a sole trader and his self-assessments for 1997/98 and 1998/99 are as follows:

1997/98 – y/e 30.4.97	£40,000
1998/99 – y/e 30.4.98	£20,000

His transitional overlap profits are £37,260 (340/365 × £40,000). However, it transpires that profits of £15,000 were shifted from the year ended 30 April 1998 into the year ended 30 April 1997, falling foul of the anti-avoidance provisions. The transitional overlap profits are therefore restricted as follows:

Transitional overlap profit (*FA 1994, 20 Sch 2(4)*)	£37,260
Less 1.25 times aggregate of amounts falling within *FA 1995, 22 Sch 3(1)(b)* 340/365 × £15,000 × 1.25 =	£(17,466)
Revised transitional overlap relief	£19,794

The unjustified shift of profits into the transitional overlap period results in an additional reduction in overlap relief of £3,493 (£17,466 – (£15,000 × 340/365)), i.e. a penalty of tax on one-quarter of £13,973 (15,000 × 340/365) which is the amount by which the transitional overlap relief was artificially inflated.

These anti-avoidance rules could eliminate a claim for transitional overlap relief but would not impose a charge to tax on a negative figure.

Retiring partners

24.32 Where the Revenue identify a potential for the avoidance of tax, they approach the problem of combating such practices with considerable enthusiasm. It is perceived that it might be possible to avoid the effects of restricting the transitional overlap relief by arranging for a partner to retire in 1996/97 and avoid part of the impact of the transitional overlap relief anti-avoidance rules by manipulating profit-sharing ratios. The partner who retired prior to 1997/98 would not be within the charge to tax for 1997/98 in view of *FA 1994, s 215(4)* and would therefore escape the anti-avoidance charge and penalty were it not provided, as it is, by *FA 1995, 22 Sch 4* that a partner retiring in 1996/97 is chargeable on any restriction in transitional overlap relief that would have applied had he not retired.

Example 7

Messrs Alexandrovich, Victor and Pissarenko have for many years traded in partnership. Alexandrovich leaves the partnership on 31 December 1996. Accounts are made up annually to 30 June and profits are shared as follows:

Year ended	*30.6.94*	*30.6.95*	*30.6.96*	*30.6.97* Time apportioned (1.7.96 to 31.12.96)	*30.6.97* Time apportioned (1.1.97 to 30.6.97)	*30.6.98*
Profit sharing ratios	33:33:33	33:33:33	33:33:33	50:25:25	50:50	50:50
Profits adjusted for tax purposes	£100,000	£200,000	£300,000	£250,000	£250,000	£100,000
A	33,333	66,667	100,000	125,000	–	–
V	33,334	66,666	100,000	62,500	125,000	50,000
P	33,333	66,667	100,000	62,500	125,000	50,000
	£100,000	£200,000	£300,000	£250,000	£250,000	£100,000

A continuation election (*a*) is made in respect of Alexandrovich's departure from the partnership and each partner is assessed to tax as follows:

1995/96	*Total*	*A*	*V*	*P*
y/e 30.6.94 preceding year basis (*b*)				
Profit sharing ratio				
(6.4.95 to 30.6.95) 33:33:33 3/12	25,000	8,333	8,333	8,334
(1.7.95 to 5.4.96) 33:33:33 9/12	75,000	25,000	25,000	25,000
	£100,000	£33,333	£33,333	£33,334
1996/97				
Transitional year (*c*)				
Profit sharing ratio				
(6.4.96 to 30.6.96) 33:33:33 3/12	62,500	20,834	20,833	20,833
(1.7.96 to 31.12.96) 50:25:25 6/12	125,000	62,500	31,250	31,250
(1.1.97 to 5.4.97) 50:50 3/12	62,500	–	31,250	31,250
	£250,000	£83,334	£83,333	£83,333
Anti-avoidance adjustment (*f*)		23,438		
		£106,772		

1997/98	*Total*	*V*	*P*
y/e 30.6.97 current year basis (*d*)			
Profit sharing ratio			
(1.7.96 to 31.12.96) 50:25:25 6/12	125,000	62,500	62,500
(1.1.97 to 30.6.97) 50:50 6/12	250,000	125,000	125,000
	£375,000	£187,500	£187,500
Transitional overlap relief (*e*) 9/12		140,625	140,625
Less anti-avoidance adjustment (*f*)		(35,156)	(35,156)
Revised overlap relief		£105,469	£105,469

Notes

(*a*) *TA 1988, s 113(2).*

(*b*) *TA 1988, s 60(3)* original version.

(*c*) Primary basis period for 1996/97 under *TA 1988, s 60(3)(b), FA 1994, s 200*, y/e 30.6.96 — £300,000

Relevant period under *FA 1994, 20 Sch 2(2)(b), (5)* i.e. 1.7.94 to 30.6.95 — £200,000

Aggregate *FA 1994, 20 Sch 2(2)* — £500,000

Appropriate percentage under *FA 1994, 20 Sch 2(5)*

$$£500,000 \times \frac{365}{365 + 365} = £250,000$$

(*d*) Profit for year ended 30.6.97 = £500,000. Share of Victor and Pissarenko computed in accordance with current year basis under *TA 1988, ss 60(3)(b), 111(3)(a)*. Alexandrovich retires on 31 December 1996 and therefore is not assessable in 1997/98.

(*e*) *FA 1994, 20 Sch 2(4)*.

(*f*) It transpires that profits of £100,000 were shifted from the year ended 30 June 1998 into the year ended 30 June 1997, falling foul of the anti-avoidance provisions. The transitional overlap profts are therefore restricted as follows:

Transitional overlap profit assuming Alexandrovich had not retired:

	Total	*A*	*V*	*P*
Profit y/e 30.6.97	£500,000	£125,000	£187,500	£187,500
Transitional overlap profit 9/12 (*FA 1994, 20 Sch 2(4)*)	£375,000	£93,750	£140,625	£140,625
Less 1.25 times aggregate of amounts falling within *FA 1995, 22 Sch 3(1)(b)* 9/12 × £100,000 × 1.25 in deemed profit-sharing proportion	£93,750	£23,438	£35,156	£35,156
A's share is charged for 1996/97 under *FA 1995, 22 Sch 4*				

The unjustified shift of profits into the transitional overlap period results in an additional reduction in overlap relief of £18,750 (£93,750 – (£100,000 × 9/12)), i.e. a penalty of tax on one-quarter of £75,000 (£100,000 × 9/12) which is the amount by which the transitional overlap relief was artificially inflated.

Example 8

Doctors Savelyeva, Likoshin and Nevdachin practice in partnership until Dr Savelyeva's retirement on 31 March 1997. Accounts are made up annually to 30 April and profits are shared as follows:

Year ended	*30.4.94*	*30.4.95*	*30.4.96*	*30.4.97* Time apportioned (1.5.96 to 31.3.97)	(1.4.97 to 30.4.97)	*30.4.98*
Profit sharing ratios	33:33:33	33:33:33	33:33:33	90:5:5	50:50	50:50
Profits adjusted for tax purposes	£300,000	£100,000	£600,000	£366,667	£33,333	£200,000
S	100,000	33,334	200,000	330,000	–	–
L	100,000	33,333	200,000	18,334	16,666	100,000
N	100,000	33,333	200,000	18,333	16,667	100,000
	£300,000	£100,000	£600,000	£366,667	£33,333	£200,000

A continuation election (*a*) is made in respect of Dr S's retirement and each partner is assessed to tax as follows:

	Total	*S*	*L*	*N*
1995/96				
y/e 30.4.94 preceding year basis (*b*)				
Profit sharing ratio				
(6.4.95 to 30.4.95) 33:33:33 1/12	25,000	8,333	8,333	8,334
(1.5.95 to 5.4.96) 33:33:33 11/12	275,000	91,667	91,667	91,666
	£300,000	£100,000	£100,000	£100,000
1996/97				
Transitional year (*c*)				
Profit sharing ratio				
(6.4.96 to 30.4.96) 33:33:33 25/365	23,972	7,990	7,991	7,991
(1.5.96 to 31.3.97) 90:5:5 335/365	321,234	289,110	16,062	16,062
(1.4.97 to 5.4.97) 50:50 5/365	4,794	–	2,397	2,397
	£350,000	£297,100	£26,450	£26,450
Anti-avoidance adjustment (*f*)		115,274		
		£412,374		
1997/98		*Total*		
y/e 30.4.97 current year basis (*d*)				
Profit sharing ratio				
(1.5.96 to 31.3.97) 90:5:5 11/12		36,666	18,333	18,333
(1.4.97 to 30.6.97) 50:50 1/12		33,334	16,667	16,667
		£70,000	£35,000	£35,000

Transitional overlap relief (*e*) 340/365	32,603	32,603
Less anti-avoidance adjustment (*f*)	(12,226)	(12,226)
Revised overlap relief	£20,377	£20,377

Notes

(*a*) *TA 1988, s 113(2)*.

(*b*) *TA 1988, s 60(3)* original version.

(*c*)

Primary basis period for 1996/97 under *TA 1988, s 60(3)(b), FA 1994, s 200*, y/e 30.4.96	£600,000
Relevant period under *FA 1994, 20 Sch 2(2)(b), (5)* i.e. 1.5.94 to 30.4.95	£100,000
Aggregate *FA 1994, 20 Sch 2(2)*	£700,000

Appropriate percentage under *FA 1994, 20 Sch 2(5)*

$$£700,000 \times \frac{365}{365 + 365} = £350,000$$

(*d*) Profit for year ended 30.4.97 = £400,000. Share of Likoshin and Nevdachin computed in accordance with current year basis under *TA 1988, ss 60(3)(b), 113(3)(a)*. Savelyeva retires on 31 March 1997 and therefore is not assessable in 1997/98.

(*e*) *FA 1994, 20 Sch 2(4)*.

(*f*) It transpires that profits of £120,000 were shifted from the year ended 30 April 1998 into the year ended 30 April 1997, falling foul of the anti-avoidance provisions. The transitional overlap profits are therefore restricted as follows:

Transitional overlap profit assuming Savelyeva had not retired:

	Total	*S*	*L*	*N*
Profit y/e 30.4.97	£400,000	£330,000	£35,000	£35,000
Transitional overlap profit 340/365	£372,603	£307,397	£32,603	£32,603
Less 1.25 times aggregate of amounts falling within *FA 1995, 22 Sch 3(1)(b)* 340/365 × £120,000 × 1.25 in deemed profit sharing proportion	£139,726	£115,274	£12,226	£12,226
S's share charged for 1996/97 under *FA 1995, 22 Sch 4*				

The unjustified shift of profits into the transitional overlap period results in an additional reduction in overlap relief of £27,945

(£139,726 – (£120,000 × 340/365)), i.e. a penalty of tax on one quarter of £111,781 (£120,000 × 340/365) which is the amount by which the transitional overlap relief was artificially inflated.

Privatisation of interest – transitional overlap

24.33 Just as the privatisation of partnership interest could be used to reduce the effective loss of relief for part of the interest as a result of transitional averaging so it could be used to increase the profit falling within the transitional overlap period under *FA 1994, 20 Sch 20(4)* by substituting relief for the individual partners, as a charge on income under *TA 1988, s 353*, rather than the interest being relieved as a trading expense in computing the partnership profits under *TA 1988, s 74*. *FA 1995, 22 Sch 5* counters this device by providing that the transitional overlap profit is to be reduced to the figure which it would have been had the firm continued to pay the interest, rather than the borrowing being diverted to the individual partners and claimed as a charge on income. There is no penalty element in this anti-avoidance measure.

Example 9

Messrs Tomsk, Trapeznikov and Kvasnikov have for many years traded in partnership together. Tomsk makes a loan to the partnership on 1 May 1996 of £100,000 to reduce partnership borrowings. He pays interest on that loan of £10,000 each year (the interest that the partnership would otherwise have paid) and claims the appropriate relief under *TA 1988, s 353* for 1997/98 and 1998/99. Tomsk's share of the partnership profits for the year ended 30 April 1998 is £60,000 and his transitional overlap profits amount to £55,000. However, this arrangement falls foul of the anti-avoidance provisions and Tomsk's transitional overlap relief is adjusted as follows:

Transitional overlap profits (*FA 1994, 20 Sch 2(4)*)	£55,000
Amounts not included in overlap profit as a result of Tomsk's loan to the partnership *FA 1995, 22 Sch 5(2)* 11/12 × £10,000 =	(9,167)
Revised overlap relief c/fwd	£45,833

24.34 The anti-avoidance rules do not apply where the loans were taken out for *bona fide* commercial reasons or for a purpose other than the reduction of the partnership's borrowings for the relevant period [*FA 1995, 20 Sch 5(2)*] or where the loan was made before 1 April 1994, or is within *de minimis* limits to be published by regulations in due course; in all probability immediately prior to 5 April 1997. [*FA 1995, 22 Sch 5(4)*].

The transitional overlap period is defined as the period from the end of the basis period for 1996/97 to 5 April 1997 and the transitional overlap profit is the profit for that period under *FA 1994, 20 Sch 2(4); FA 1995, 22 Sch 5*. Relevant period means a period the whole or part of which falls within the transitional overlap period.

Transitional averaging Schedule D, Case V

24.35 It is clearly as potentially beneficial for a taxpayer carrying on a trade, profession or vocation outside the United Kingdom assessed to tax under Schedule D, Case V to increase profits in the transitional averaging period by increasing income or reducing expenses in that period as it is for a UK business charged under Schedule D, Cases I or II. The corresponding anti-avoidance provisions are in *FA 1995, 22 Sch 6* and apply where transitional averaging under Schedule D, Case V is given by *FA 1994, 20 Sch 6(2)(a)* where the profits in 1995/96 and 1996/97, which will be subject to the transitional averaging, have been increased by a relevant accounting change or change of business practice, or a self-cancelling or connected person transaction within *FA 1995, 22 Sch 14–17* (paras 24.17 *et seq.*). The attempted avoidance would be countered by assessing 50 per cent of the profits diverted into the transitional averaging period in addition to the normal transitional assessment on 50 per cent of those profits. The penalty element of 25 per cent of the tax sought to be saved is arrived at by charging to tax 62.5 per cent of the profits diverted into the transitional period in addition to 50 per cent of the profits of the transitional period under *FA 1994, 20 Sch 6(2)(a)*. This penalty element can be avoided in the same way as other transitional anti-avoidance penalties by the appropriate declaration on submitting the original tax return as explained in paragraph 24.20.

24.36 The Revenue do not regard the acceleration of remittances into the transitional averaging basis periods of 1995/96 and 1996/97 as exploitation of the transitional provisions, even though the effect is that only 50 per cent of the remittances in this period are chargeable to tax as a result of transitional averaging. There are therefore no anti-avoidance provisions to prevent any bunching of remittances.

Example 10

Ivanov, resident and domiciled in the UK, is a partner in a partnership managed and controlled outside the UK and he is assessed under Schedule D, Case V. His partnership profits, as adjusted for UK tax purposes are as follows:

Year ended 5 April 1995	£5,000
Year ended 5 April 1996	£15,000
Year ended 5 April 1997	£10,000

It transpires that profits totalling £5,000 were shifted from the year ended 5 April 1995 to the year ended 5 April 1996. Ivanov is unable to show that the shift in profits does not fall within the anti-avoidance provisions. The provisions of *FA 1995, 22 Sch 6* are therefore applied in calculating Ivanov's assessments:

1995/96 *TA 1988, s 65*			
Year ended 5 April 1995			£5,000
1996/97 *FA 1994, 20 Sch 6(2)*			
Year ended 5 April 1996	£15,000		
Year ended 5 April 1997	£10,000		
	£25,000	× 50% =	£12,500
Plus amount falling within *FA 1995, 22 Sch 6(1)(b)*	£5,000	× 62.5% =	£3,125
Assessable 1996/97			£15,625

Assessments for 1995/96 and 1996/97 thus total £20,625. Had no profits been shifted then the assessments would only have totalled £20,000 as follows:

1995/96 *TA 1988, s 65*			
Year ended 5 April 1995			£10,000
1996/97 *FA 1994, 20 Sch 6(2)*			
Year ended 5 April 1996	£10,000		
Year ended 5 April 1997	£10,000		
	£20,000	× 50% =	£10,000
			£20,000

The unjustified shift of profits into the transitional period results in additional profits being charged of £625 (£20,625 – £20,000), i.e. a penalty of tax on one quarter of the amount that would have escaped tax on averaging (£5,000 × 50%).

24.37 The usual defences of the motive and benefit test are contained within the definition of relevant change and relevant transaction in *FA 1995, 22 Sch 14–17* and the *de minimis* provisions to be introduced by regulations are introduced by *FA 1995, 22 Sch 6(3)*. These will apply where the amount diverted is less than a *de minimis* percentage of the aggregate income for 1995/96 and 1996/97, or is less than the *de minimis* percentage of turnover for those years. It is anticipated that the *de minimis* levels will not be published until immediately prior to 5 April 1997.

Transitional overlap anti-avoidance – Schedule D, Case V

24.38 Where income from a trade, profession or vocation carried on overseas has been assessed under Schedule D, Case V on a non-statutory basis by reference to the accounting year ending in the preceding fiscal year instead of the income of the preceding fiscal year itself, transitional overlap relief is given by *FA 1994 20 Sch 6(4)* in the same way as for a trade, profession or vocation within Schedule D, Cases I or II. It is therefore necessary to introduce a corresponding anti-avoidance provision to prevent the exploitation of the transitional overlap period by artificially increasing the profits of this period which would ultimately fall out of assessment on a cessation or partially on a change of accounting date. The rules, which are set out in *FA 1995, 22 Sch 7*, are similar to those applicable to Schedule D, Cases I and II in *FA 1995, 22 Sch 3* and apply where there has been a relevant accounting change or change in business practice, or a self-cancelling or connected person relevant transaction within *FA 1995, 22 Sch 14–17* (see paras 24.17 *et seq.*). The 25 per cent penalty on the tax sought to be saved is achieved by reducing the transitional overlap profit by 1.25 times the amount diverted.

Example 11

Palmen, a UK resident and domiciled individual is a partner in a partnership managed and controlled abroad and he is assessed under Schedule D, Case V. He receives a share of partnership profits as follows:

1997/98 – year ended 30 April 1997	£20,000
1998/99 – year ended 30 April 1998	£10,000

(Transitional overlap relief 11/12 × 20,000 = £18,333, *FA 1994, 20 Sch 6(4)*).

However it transpires that profits totalling £5,000 were shifted from the year ended 30 April 1998 to the year ended 30 April 1997 thus falling foul of the anti-avoidance provisions. Palmen's transitional overlap profit is adjusted as follows:

Transitional overlap profit	£18,333
Less 1.25 times the aggregate of the amounts falling in *FA 1995, 22 Sch 7(1)(b)* 11/12 × 5,000 = £4,583 × 1.25 =	£5,729
Revised transitional overlap relief	£12,604

Had there been no such profit shift the transitional overlap would have been £13,750 (11/12 × £15,000).

The unjustified shift of profits into the transitional period results in additional profits being charged of £1,146 (£13,750 − £12,604) i.e. a penalty of tax on one-quarter of £4,583 (11/12 × £5,000) which is the amount by which the transitional overlap relief was artificially inflated.

24.39 The definition of relevant change and relevant transaction bring in the motive test and benefit test potential escape routes from the anti-avoidance provisions, and the *de minimis* regulations will be by reference to an absolute amount or a proportion of the transitional overlap profit, or a proportion of the transitional overlap period as fixed by regulations expected immediately prior to 5 April 1997 under *FA 1995, 22 Sch 1(3)* as applied to Schedule D, Case V by *FA 1995, 22 Sch 7(3)*. The appropriate percentage of turnover is defined as 365 divided by the number of days in the transitional overlap period which in turn is defined as the period beginning immediately after the end of the basis period for 1996/97, or the basis period of a partnership for that year, and in either case ending with 5 April 1997. [*FA 1995, 22 Sch 7(4)*].

Retiring partners – Schedule D, Case V

24.40 As with a UK business assessed under Schedule D, Case I or II, the Revenue are concerned about the possible avoidance of the transitional overlap anti-avoidance provisions for a Schedule D, Case V business where a partner retires in the transitional overlap period, i.e. before 6 April 1997, and is therefore assessed under the old cessation rules in *TA 1988, s 67* under *FA 1994, 20 Sch 6(1)*. *FA 1995, 22 Sch 8* sets out the equivalent penalty provisions for Schedule D, Cases IV or V to *FA 1995, 22 Sch 4* which applies for Schedule D, Cases I or II. A partner retiring in 1996/97 is still assessed to his share of the anti-avoidance charge and penalty as if he had not retired.

Example 12

Pavel was a UK resident and English domiciled partner of a foreign partnership managed and controlled abroad which makes up accounts annually to 6 April in each year.

He was entitled to one-third of the profits of £300,000 for the year ended 6 April 1997. He retired on 5 April 1997 and was assessed under the old cessation rules in *TA 1988, s 67*.

The Revenue make the enquiries which reveal that £60,000 had been shifted from the year ended 6 April 1998 to fall in the year ended 6 April 1997 by switching from one acceptable accounting policy to another, which is a change in accounting policy.

The transitional relief penalty reduction would have been 1.25 × (1/3 × 364/365 × £60,000).

Pavel is therefore assessed on £24,931 in 1996/97 in addition to the normal cessation charge.

Interest received

24.41 Interest received from a new source starting on or after 6 April 1994 is on a current year basis under Schedule D, Cases III, IV or V. So it is not possible to set up new accounts specifically designed to avoid the transitional rules, which average the interest arising in 1995/96 and 1996/97 to form the basis of the transitional year assessment in 1996/97. If the Revenue identify any accounts designed to take advantage of the new rules set up prior to 5 April 1994, they will, as new accounts, be assessed on the actual interest arising in 1993/94 and 1994/95. The object is to prevent the creation of accounts with artificial interest arrangements which will concentrate income into the transitional period reduced by averaging.

Existing accounts

24.42 The strict legal situation is that any new deposit in an existing account charged on a preceding year basis is a new source of income (*Hart v Sangster 1957 37 TC 231*). In practice, the Revenue have not treated additional deposits as a new source, but have taxed new accounts on a preceding year basis where there was already in existence a preceding year basis source. From 6 April 1994, any new source of income will be charged on a current year basis under the new provisions even where there are existing 'preceding year basis' sources.

24.43 Where a taxpayer has accounts where the interest is paid gross and which are assessed on a preceding year basis, and accounts where the interest is subject to the deduction of tax and dealt with on a current year basis, the Revenue reserve the right to assess any new deposit to an existing account as if it were a new source on the current year basis, to prevent taxpayers obtaining a transitional year averaging advantage by moving funds from an account dealt with on a current year basis to an account dealt with on a preceding year basis.

24.44 There is obviously a temptation for banks to alter the terms of interest payable on existing accounts to concentrate the interest into the fiscal years 1995/96 and 1996/97 in order to maximise the amount subject to averaging. The anti-avoidance provisions outlined in 24.47 effectively enable the Revenue to reallocate interest on a day-to-day basis to prevent such bunching.

24.45 It would also be possible to achieve the same effect by adjusting the rate at which interest is paid while leaving unchanged the normal dates of payment of interest, i.e. increasing the interest received in the transitional period subject to averaging and reducing the interest payable that is fully taxed in 1994/95 or 1997/98. In such cases the interest will effectively be recalculated on the average rate of interest for the whole period of the deposit and tax recalculated accordingly also as outlined in 24.47. *FA 1995, 22 Sch 9* provides for *de minimis* limits below which such anti-avoidance provisions will not be used, but the safe harbour levels will be fixed by Statutory Instrument immediately after the end of the relevant fiscal year.

Relevant arrangements – interest

24.46 Relevant arrangements are defined by *FA 1995, 22 Sch 18* as any arrangements under which interest arises at irregular intervals during the years 1994/95 to 1997/98 or where there are artificial variations in the rate of interest applicable during those years; unless the obtaining of a tax advantage is not the main benefit that could reasonably be expected to arise from the making of the arrangements. Any variations in the rate of interest are artificial unless they are based on variations in a variable rate of interest, the values of which are regularly published. The Revenue in their publication of 29 November 1994 'Self-assessment – transition to the current year basis anti-avoidance provisions' at para 3.26 confirmed that 'savings products offered by, for example, building societies, providing increasing amounts of interest in successive years, would not be caught by the rules provided the savings arrangements had not been entered into with a view to exploiting the transitional arrangements'.

Increase of interest arising in 1995/96 and 1996/97

24.47 Where, as a result of these relevant arrangements, additional interest arises in 1995/96 and 1996/97, only 50 per cent of the income will be chargeable to tax in view of the averaging provisions in *FA 1994, 20 Sch 4(2)* or *6(2)*. A charge of 50 per cent of the interest applicable to the relevant arrangements would recover this tax sought to be avoided, but this is increased to 62.5 per cent in order to introduce the 25 per cent penalty on the amount diverted. [*FA 1995, 22 Sch 9*]. This penalty can be avoided by declaration as explained in 24.19.

Example 13

Ivensen receives untaxed interest assessable under Schedule D, Case III as follows:

Year ended 5 April 1995	£10,000
Year ended 5 April 1996	£8,000
Year ended 5 April 1997	£4,000

His assessments for 1995/96 and 1996/97 would therefore be as follows:

1995/96 Preceding year,	
TA 1988, s 64 (original version)	
Year ended 5 April 1995	£10,000

1996/97 Transitional year, *FA 1994, 20 Sch 4(2)*			
Year ended 5 April 1996	£8,000		
Year ended 5 April 1997	£4,000		
	12,000 × 50%	=	£6,000

However, it transpires that the receipt of interest due in the year ended 5 April 1995 totalling £6,000 was delayed until the year ended 5 April 1996, thus falling within the anti-avoidance provisions. Ivensen's 1996/97 assessment is therefore adjusted as follows:

FA 1995 22 Sch 9(2) 50% of the amounts in *FA 1994, 20 Sch 4(2)*			
Year ended 5 April 1996	£8,000		
Year ended 5 April 1997	£4,000		
	£12,000 × 50%	=	£6,000
Plus			
Amounts falling within *FA 1995, 22 Sch 9(1)(b)*	£6,000 × 62.5%	=	£3,750
Revised assessment 1996/97			£9,750

Had there been no delay in the payment of interest, Ivensen's assessments for 1995/96 and 1996/97 would have been as follows:

1995/96 *TA 1988, s 64* (original version)			
Year ended 5 April 1995			£16,000
1996/97 *FA 1994, 20 Sch 4(2)*			
Year ended 5 April 1996	£2,000		
Year ended 5 April 1997	£4,000		
	£6,000 × 50%	=	£3,000
Total assessments			£19,000

However, as a result of the anti-avoidance provisions an extra £750 is assessed:

1995/96	£10,000
1996/97	£9,750
	£19,750

The shift of interest into the transitional period results in an additional amount being charged of £750 (£19,750 – £19,000), i.e. a penalty of tax on one quarter of the amount that would have escaped tax on averaging (£6,000 × 50%).

Schedule D, Cases III (excluding interest) IV and V

24.48 Non-trading income and income other than interest assessable under Schedule D, Cases III, IV and V is also brought within a transitional averaging arrangement giving similar opportunities for exploitation. Anti-avoidance measures adopting a similar approach to that applied for interest are introduced where there are 'relevant arrangements' by *FA 1995, 22 Sch 10*.

Relevant arrangements – non-interest

24.49 *FA 1995, 22 Sch 19* defines relevant arrangements for non-interest investment income taxable under Schedule D, Cases III, IV or V as any arrangements under which income arises at irregular intervals during the years 1994/95 to 1997/98, unless the arrangements are made exclusively for *bona fide* commercial reasons or the obtaining of a tax advantage is not the main benefit that could reasonably be expected to arise from the making of the arrangement. With the same caveats, *FA 1995, 22 Sch 20* defines a relevant transaction as any transaction with a connected person as defined by *TA 1988, s 839*.

Increase in income arising in 1995/96 and 1996/97

24.50 Where there are relevant arrangements or transactions, *FA 1995, 22 Sch 10* provides that the benefit of transitional averaging under *FA 1994, 20 Sch 4(2)* or *6(2)* is removed from the income diverted into 1995/96 and 1996/97 as a result of such relevant arrangements or transactions. As 50 per cent of the total income has already been taxed under the transitional provisions, a charge of 50 per cent of the amount diverted would remove the benefit which the taxpayer sought to achieve, but the actual charge is increased by a 25 per cent penalty loading to 62.5 per cent of the amount diverted.

Example 14

Pavlov, a UK resident and domiciled individual receives dividends assessable under Schedule D, Case V from an overseas company, as follows:

Year ended 5 April 1995	£5,000
Year ended 5 April 1996	£20,000
Year ended 5 April 1997	£10,000

He calculates that his assessments are as follows:

1995/96 Preceding year, *TA 1988, s 65*	
Year ended 5 April 1995	£5,000

1996/97 Transitional year, *FA 1994, 20 Sch 6(2)*			
Year ended 5 April 1996	£20,000		
Year ended 5 April 1997	£10,000		
	30,000 × 50%	=	£15,000

However, it transpires that the payment of overseas dividends totalling £10,000 due in the year ended 5 April 1995 was delayed until the year ended 5 April 1996, falling within the anti-avoidance provisions. The Revenue therefore seek to amend Pavlov's assessments as follows:

FA 1995, 22 Sch 10(2) 50% of the amounts in *FA 1994, 20 Sch 6(2)(a)*			
Year ended 5 April 1996	£20,000		
Year ended 5 April 1997	£10,000		
	£30,000 × 50%	=	£15,000
Plus Amounts falling within *FA 1995, 22 Sch 10(1)(b)*	£10,000 × 62.5%	=	£6,250
Revised assessment 1996/97			£21,250

Had there been no delay in the payment of dividends, Pavlov's assessments for 1995/96 and 1996/97 would have been as follows:

1995/96 *TA 1988, s 65*			
Year ended 5 April 1995			£15,000
1996/97 *FA 1994, 20 Sch 6(2)*			
Year ended 5 April 1996	£10,000		
Year ended 5 April 1997	£10,000		
	£20,000 × 50%	=	£10,000
Total assessments			£25,000

However, as a result of the anti-avoidance provisions an extra £1,250 is assessed:

1995/96	£5,000
1996/97	£21,250
	£26,250

The shift of dividends into the transitional period results in an additional amount being charged of £1,250 (£26,250 – £25,000), i.e. a penalty of tax on one quarter of the amount that would have escaped tax on averaging (£10,000 × 50%).

Remittances

24.51 As with trading income from abroad, the Revenue do not regard the concentration of remittances into the transitional averaging basis years of 1995/96 and 1996/97 as exploitation of the transitional rules and there are no anti-avoidance provisions to prevent bunching or remittances, where the remittance basis applies, into this period.

Schedule D, Case VI

24.52 Miscellaneous income assessed under Schedule D, Case VI is often in practice assessed on a preceding year basis, in particular furnished lettings. Transitional relief will be given on the non-statutory basis by way of averaging in a similar manner to trades under Schedule D, Cases I and II. But for anti-avoidance purposes the Revenue will rely on the powers in *TA 1988, s 69* which allow them to fix the basis period.

Time limits

24.53 *FA 1995, 22 Sch 11* provides that nothing in *TMA 1970, s 29* (discovery provisions), or *TMA 1970, s 30B* (partnership statements) will prevent an assessment for 1996/97 being made under the transitional anti-avoidance provisions whether or not an assessment or partnership statement has been made for 1997/98 and is still capable of being amended.

Advance notice

24.54 The Revenue are required by *FA 1995, 22 Sch 12* to give a notice quantifying the aggregate profits diverted into the transitional overlap period, or the aggregate interest paid in respect of the transitional overlap period as a result of the diversion of profits into the transitional overlap period for Schedule D, Cases I or II, Case V or following the privatisation of partnership interest.

24.55 *FA 1995, 22 Sch 12* requires a notice reducing transitional overlap relief to be given at a time when an assessment for 1998/99 is still capable of being amended or where no such assessment has been made. An appeal may be brought against such a notice within 30 days as if it were an appeal against an assessment and the Commissioners may confirm or set aside the notice as appropriate subject to appeal to the court.

Deterrence

24.56 The whole approach of the anti-avoidance measures is not merely to recover tax lost by the Revenue as a result of artificially shifting profits into the transitional averaging period, or the transitional overlap period. It is to deter taxpayers from attempting such manoeuvres by making the anti-avoidance provisions penal in their effect, so that the taxpayer is worse off if caught by the anti-avoidance provisions than he would have been had no attempt been made to divert profits in order to maximise the transitional relief.

Appendix A

Hunt the Basis Period

Fiscal year in which business commences or is deemed to commence on or after 6 April 1994

Figure A

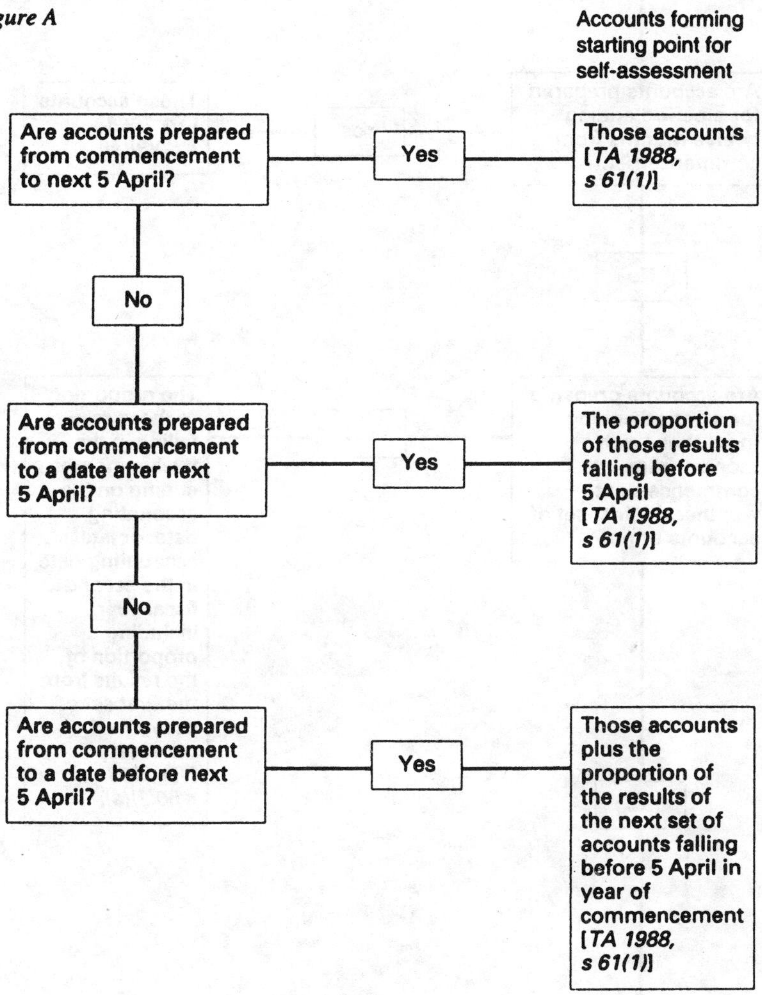

Second fiscal year—year following year of commencement

Figure B

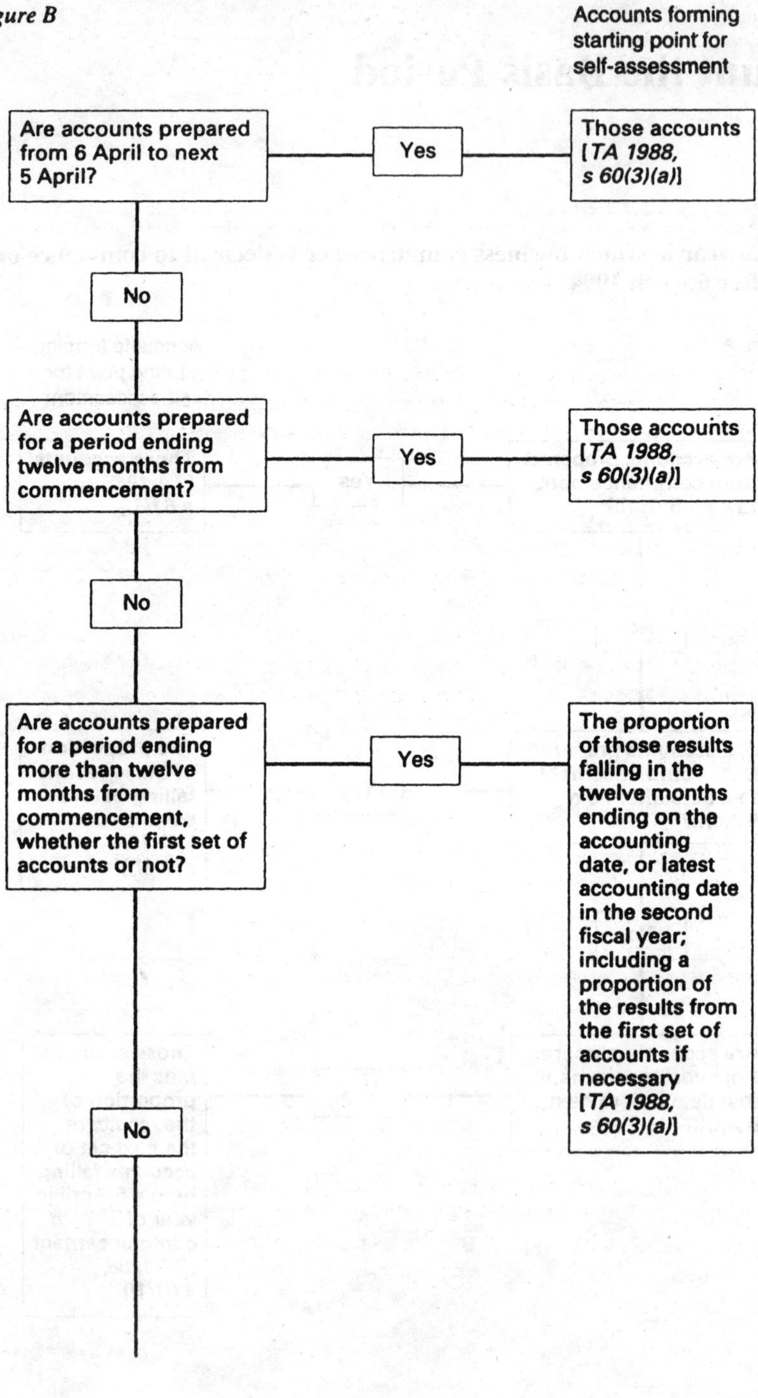

Figure B – contd.

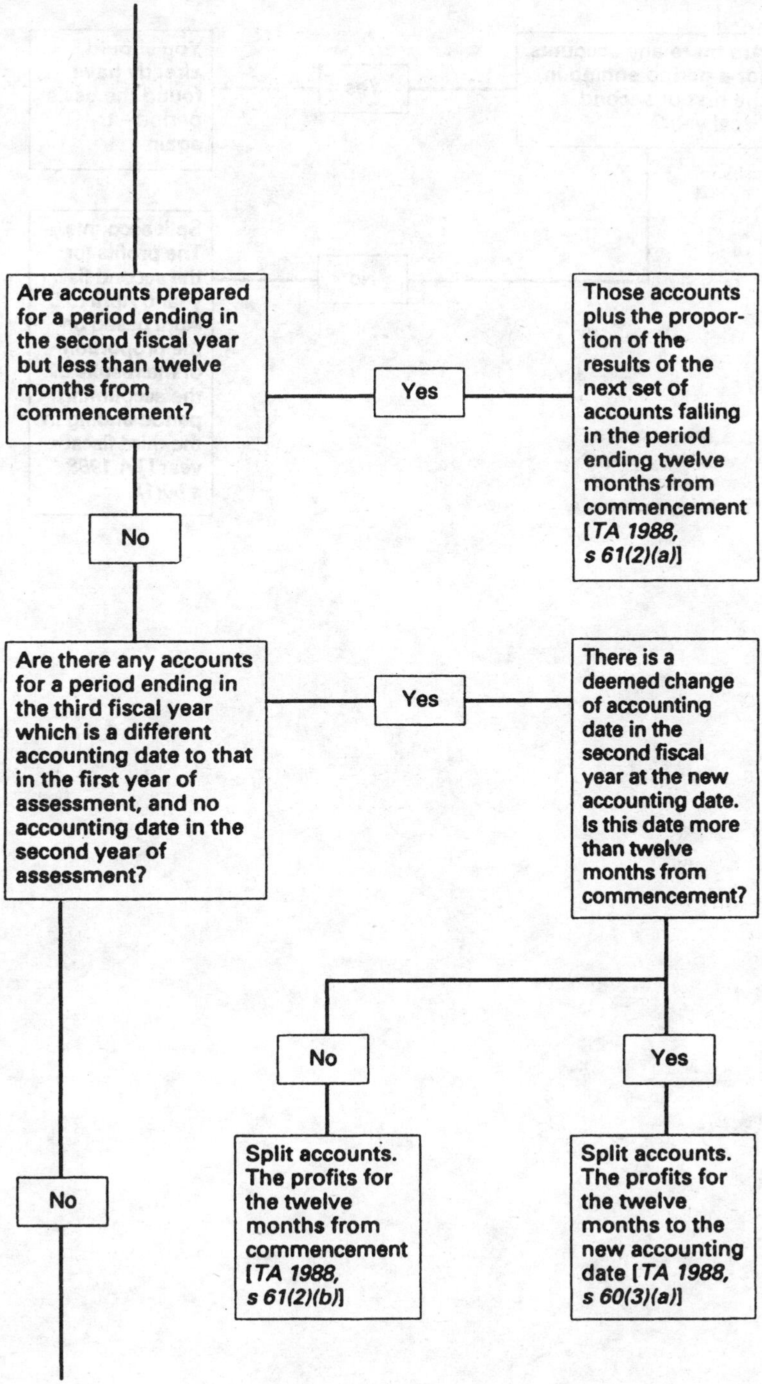

Figure B – contd.

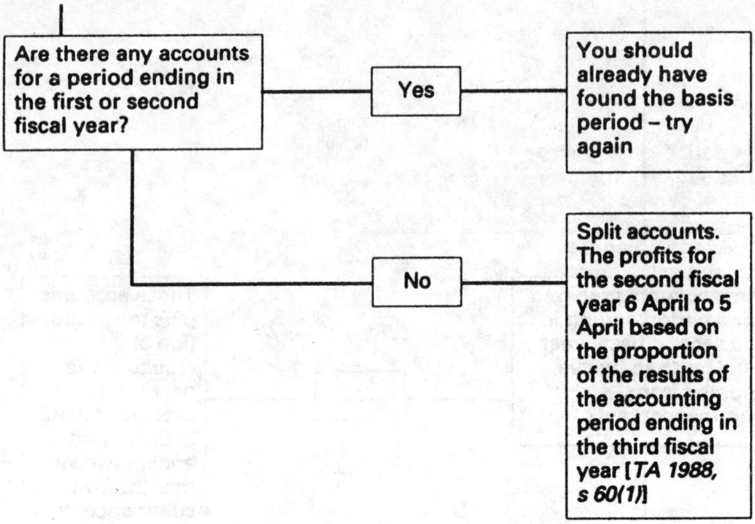

Third fiscal year in which business commenced

Figure C

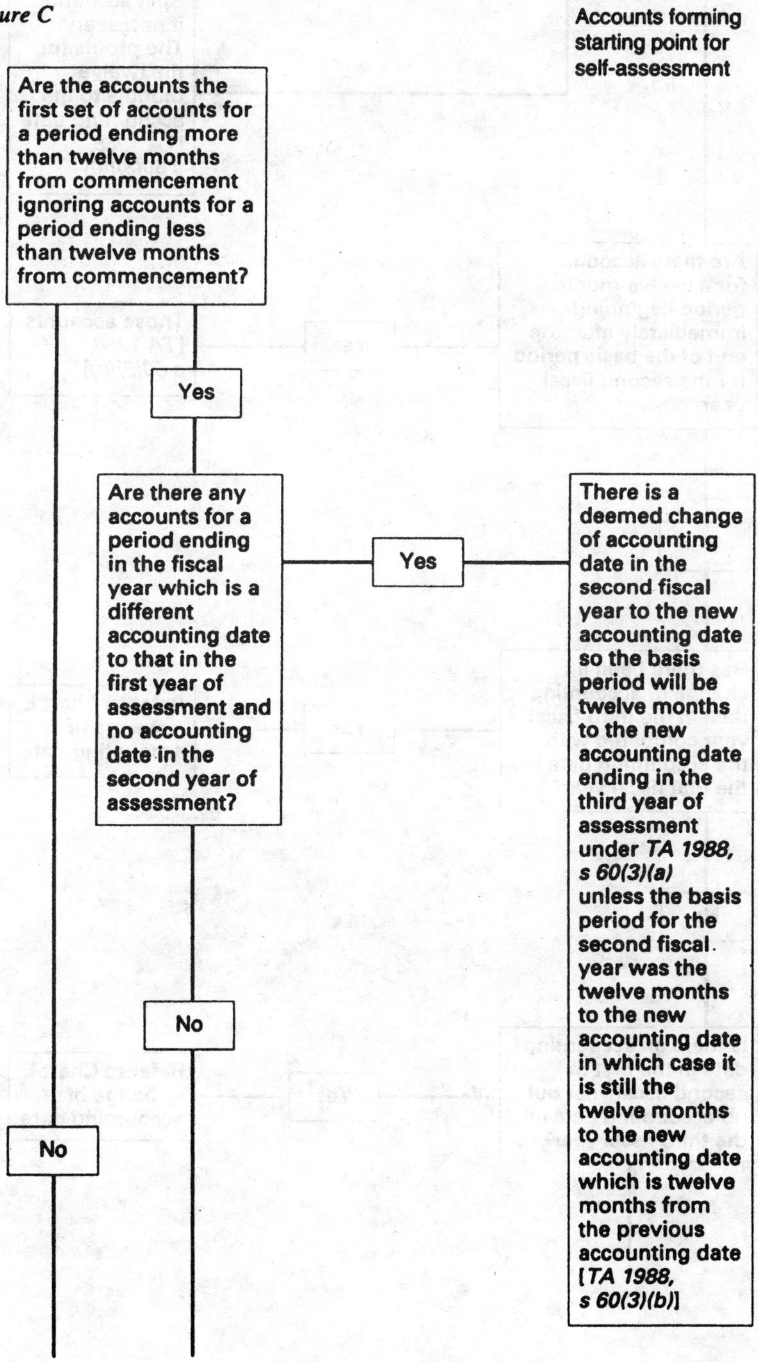

Figure C – contd.

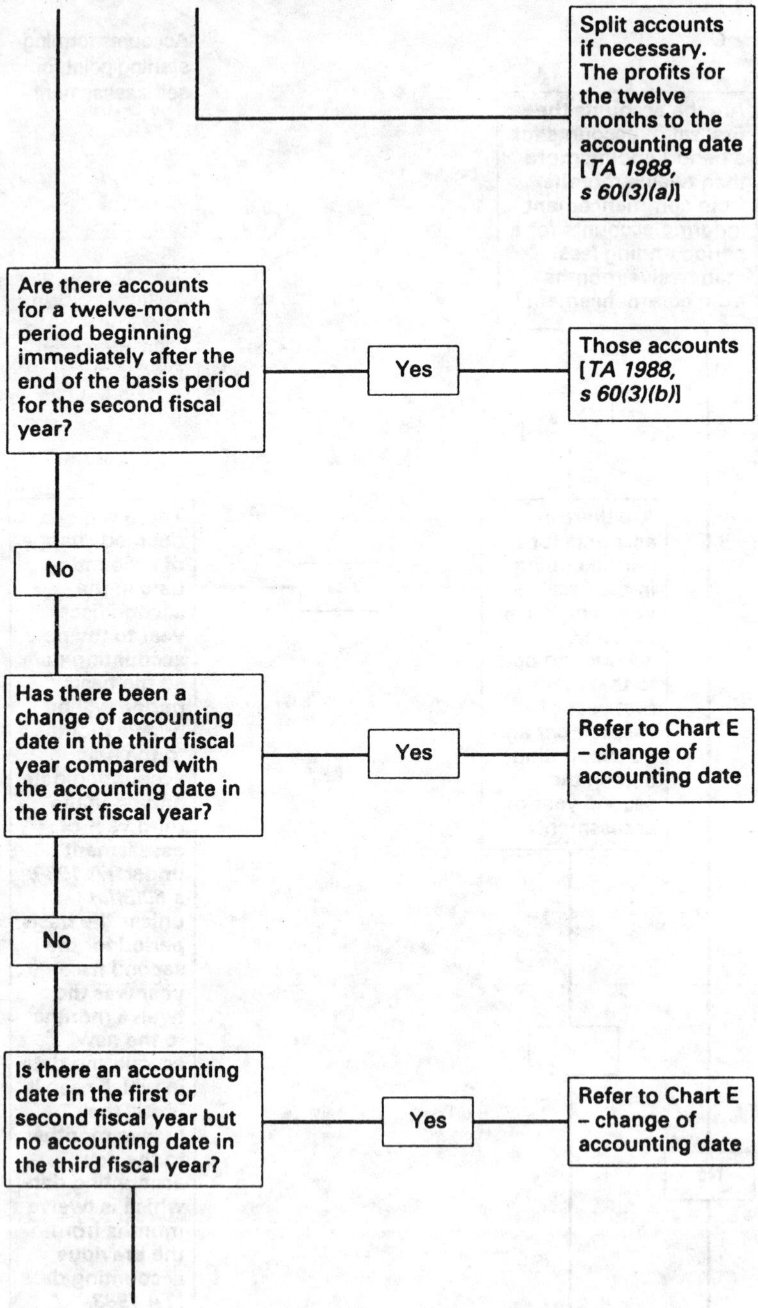

Figure C – contd.

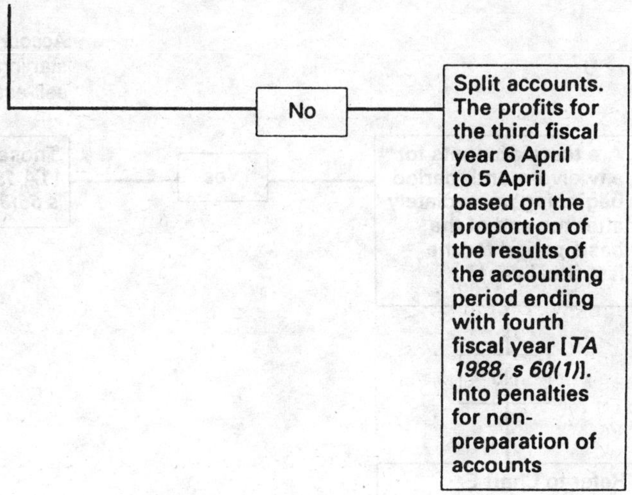

Fourth and subsequent fiscal years

Figure D

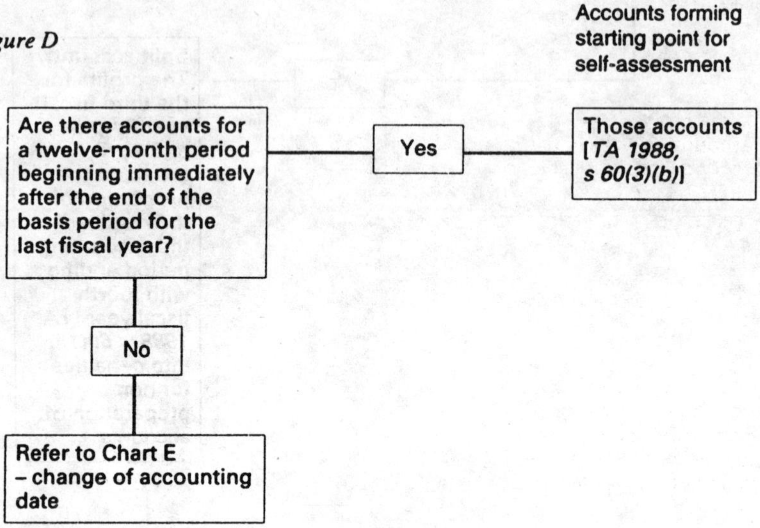

Change of accounting date (change of basis period)

Figure E

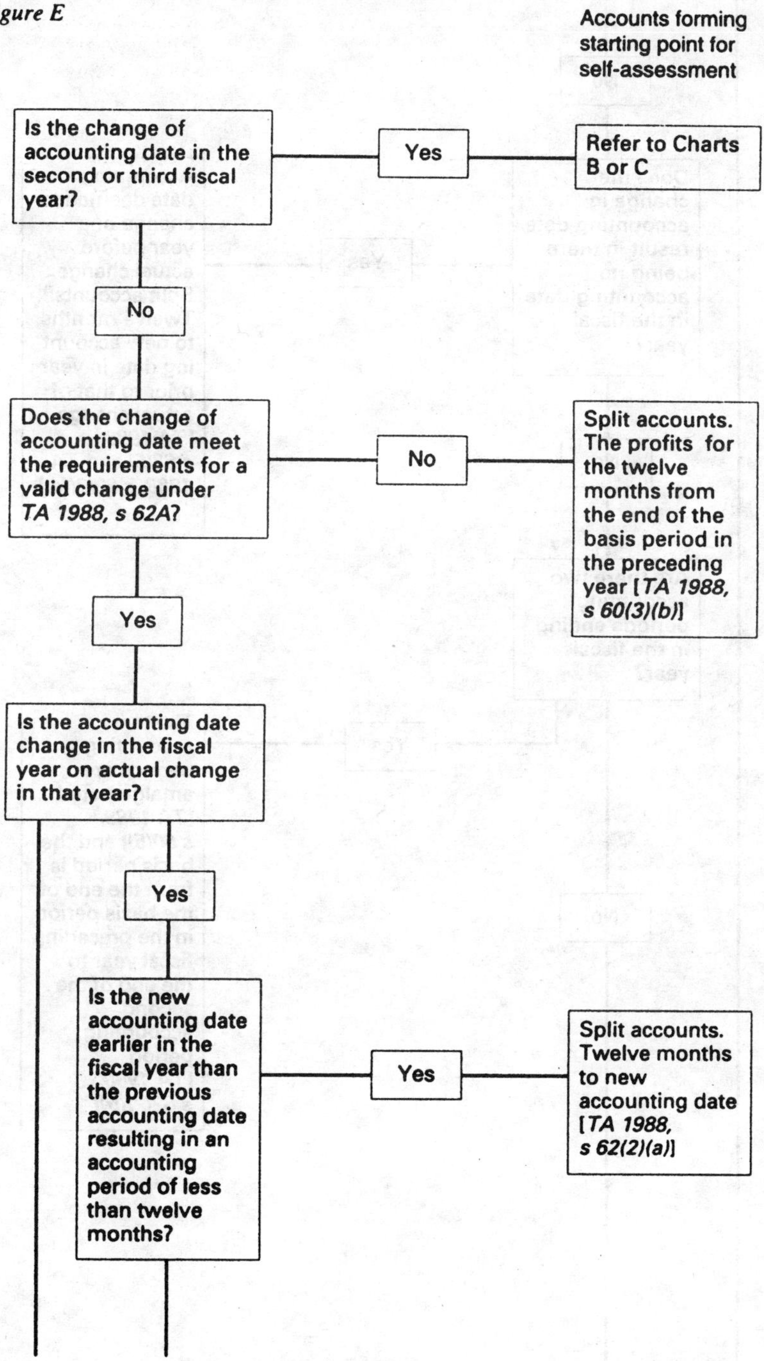

Figure E – contd.

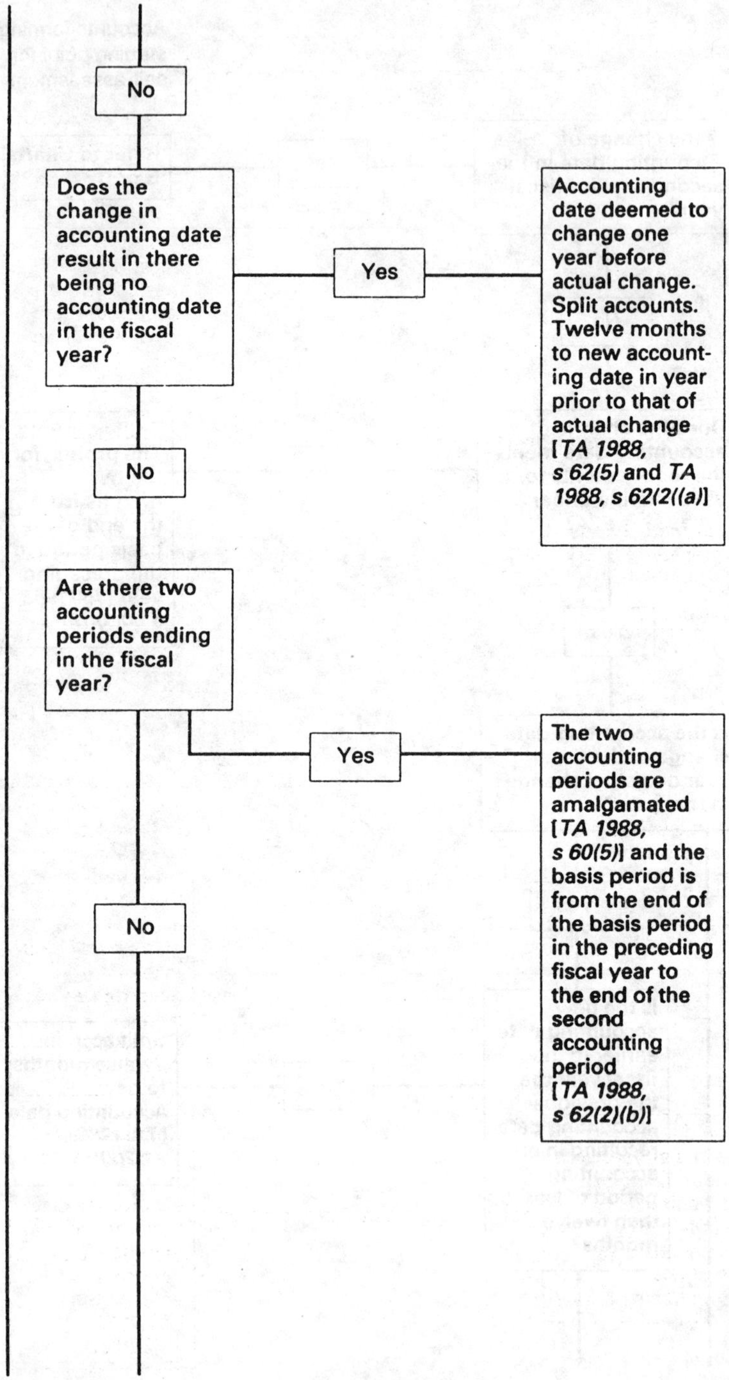

Figure E – contd.

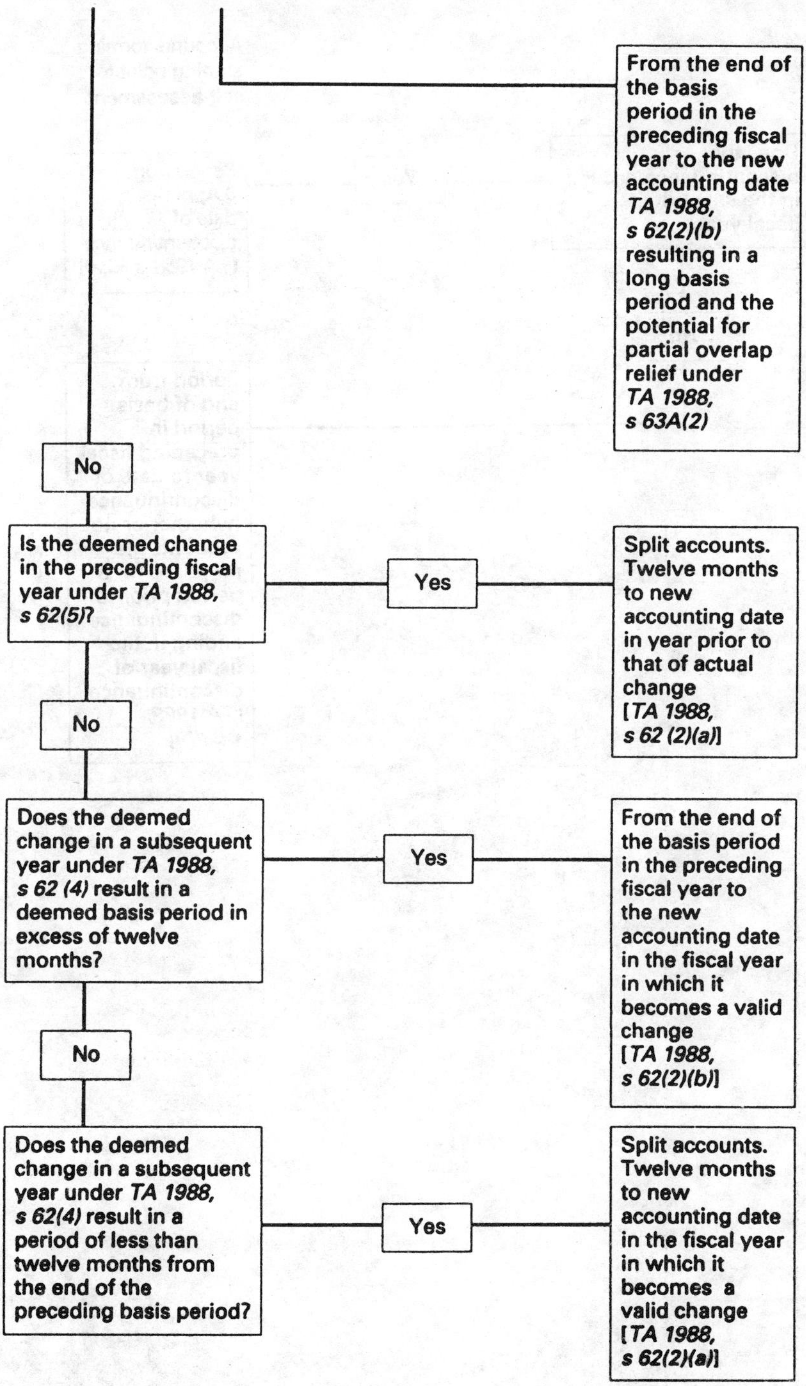

Discontinuance

Figure F

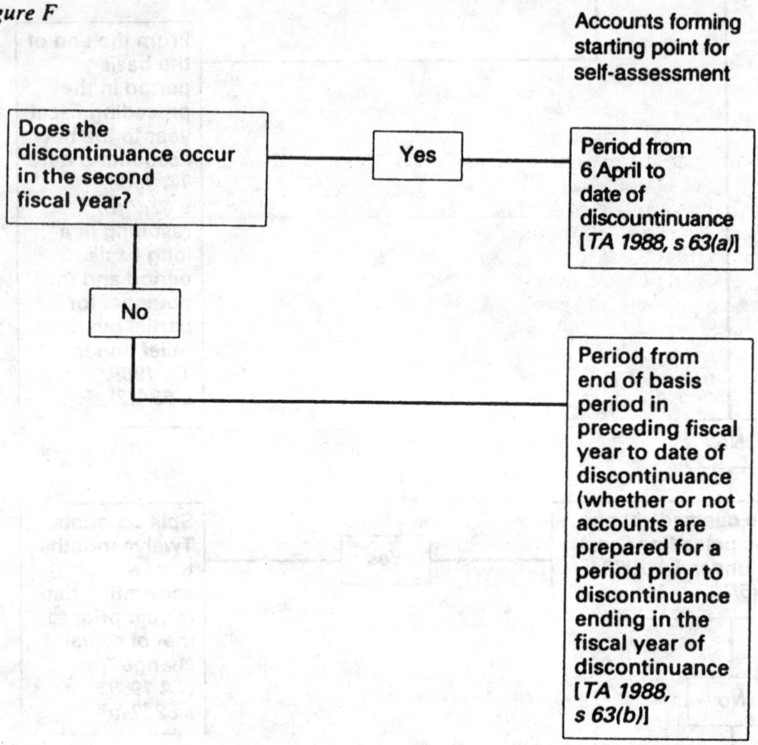

Transition—from old system to new. Basis period for 1996/97

Figure G

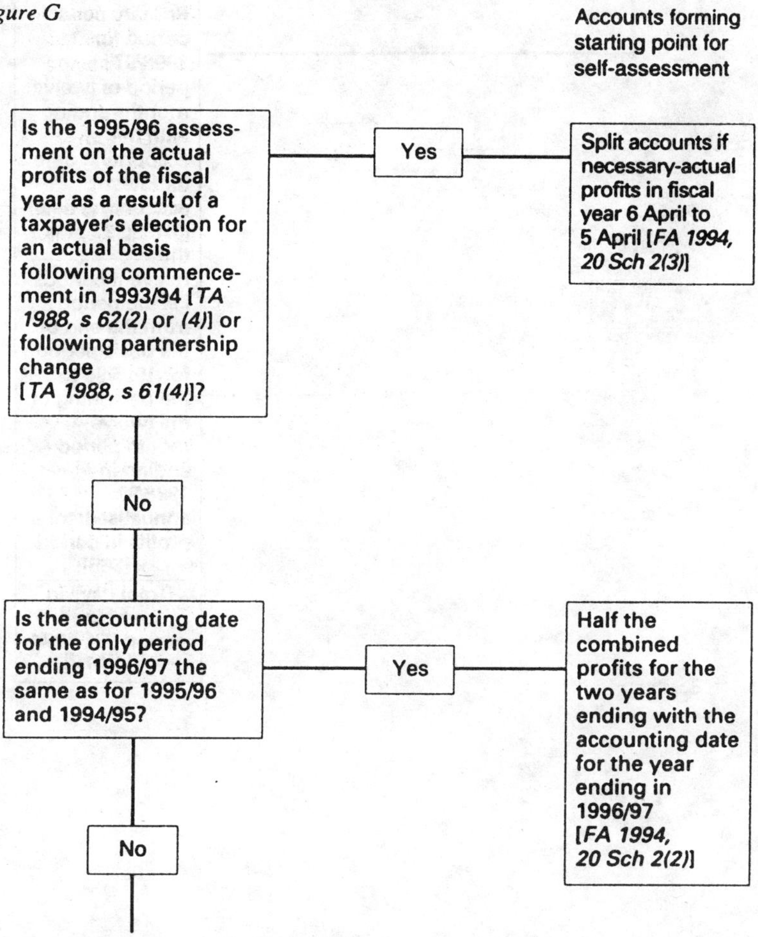

Figure G – contd.

Primary basis period for 1996/97 i.e. the period of twelve months ending with the accounting date (or latest accounting date) in 1996/97 plus the relevant period, i.e. the period from the end of the basis period for 1995/96 to the beginning of the twelve-month period ending in 1996/97, annualised; total profits in period x [365]

Total days in combined period [*FA 1994, 20 Sch 2*]

Transitional overlap

Figure H

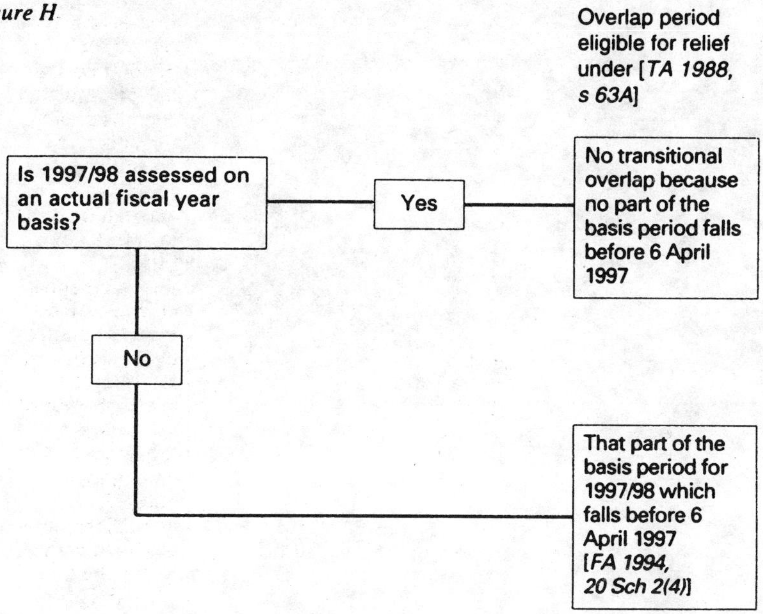

Appendix B

SSAP2 – Disclosure of Accounting Policies

Statement of Standard Accounting Practice (SSAP) No 2 'Disclosure of Accounting Policies' was issued by the Institute of Chartered Accountants in England and Wales and other governing bodies of the Accounting Standards Committee in November 1971.

It is fundamental to the understanding and interpretation of financial accounts that those who use them should be aware of the main assumptions on which they are based. The purpose of the statement which follows is to assist such understanding by promoting improvements in the quality of information disclosed. It seeks to achieve this by establishing as standard accounting practice the disclosure in financial accounts of clear explanations of the accounting policies followed in so far as these are significant for the purpose of giving a true and fair view. The statement does not seek to establish accounting standards for individual items; these will be dealt with in separate statements of standard accounting practice issued from time to time.

Part I – Explanatory Note

Fundamental accounting concepts, accounting bases and accounting policies

1 In accounting usage terms such as 'accounting principles,' 'practices,' 'rules,' 'conventions,' 'methods' or 'procedures' have often been treated as interchangeable.* For the purpose of this statement it is convenient to distinguish between fundamental accounting concepts, accounting bases and accounting polices.

2 Fundamental accounting concepts are hence defined as broad basic assumptions which underlie the periodic financial accounts of business enterprises. It is expedient to single out for special mention four in particular:

(*a*) the 'going concern' concept;

(*b*) the 'accruals' concept;

(*c*) the 'consistency' concept; and

(*d*) the 'prudence' concept.**

The use of these concepts is not necessarily self-evident from an examination of accounts, but they have such general acceptance that they call for no explanation in published accounts and their observance is presumed unless stated otherwise. They are practical rules rather than theoretical ideals and are capable of variation and evolution as accounting thought and practice develop, but their present generally accepted meanings are restated in paragraph 14 below.

* In this series 'accounting practices' has been adopted as a generic term to encompass all aspects of financial accounting methods and presentation.

** It is emphasised that it is not the purpose of this statement to develop a basic theory of accounting. An exhaustive theoretical approach would take an entirely different form and would include, for instance, many more propositions than the four fundamental concepts referred to here. It is, however, expedient to recognise them as working assumptions having general acceptance at the present time.

3 Accounting bases are the methods which have been developed for expressing or applying fundamental accounting concepts to financial transactions and items. By their nature accounting bases are more diverse and numerous than fundamental concepts, since they have evolved in response to the variety and complexity of types of business and business transactions, and for this reason there may justifiably exist more than on recognised accounting basis for dealing with particular items.

4 Accounting policies are the specific accounting bases judged by business enterprises to be most appropriate to their circumstances and adopted by them for the purpose of preparing their financial accounts.

Particular problems in application of the fundamental concepts

5 The main difficulty in applying the fundamental accounting concepts arises from the fact that many business transactions have financial effects spreading over a number of years. Decisions have to be made on the extent to which expenditure incurred in one year can reasonably be expected to produce benefits in the form of revenue in other years and should therefore be carried forward in whole or in part; that is, should be dealt with in the closing balance sheet, as distinct from being dealt with as an expense of the current year in the profit and loss account because the benefit has been exhausted in that year.

6 In some cases revenue is received for goods or services the production or supply of which will involve some later expenditure. In this case a decision must be made regarding how much of the revenue should be carried forward, to be dealt with in subsequent profit and loss accounts when the relevant costs are incurred.

7 All such decisions require consideration of future events of uncertain financial effect, and to this extent an element of commercial judgement is unavoidable in the assessment.

8 Examples of matters which give rise to particular difficulty are: the future benefits to be derived from stocks and all types of work in progress at the end of the year; the future benefits to be derived from fixed assets, and the period of years over which these will be fruitful; the extent to which expenditure on research and development can be expected to produce future benefits.

Purpose and limitations of accounting bases

9 In the course of practice there have developed a variety of accounting bases designed to provide consistent, fair and as nearly as possible objective solutions to these problems in particular circumstances; for instance bases for calculating such items as depreciation, the amounts at which stocks and work in progress are to be stated, and deferred taxation.

10 Accounting bases provide an orderly and consistent framework for periodic reporting of a concern's results and financial position, but they do not, and are not intended to, substitute for the exercise of commercial judgement in the preparation of financial reports. Where a choice of acceptable accounting bases is available judgement must be exercised in choosing those which are appropriate to the circumstances and are best suited to present fairly the concern's results and financial position; the bases thus adopted then become the concern's accounting policies. The significance of accounting bases is that they provide limits to the area subject to the exercise of judgement, and a check against arbitrary, excessive or unjustifiable adjustments where no other objective yardstick is available. By definition it is not possible to develop generalised rules for the exercise of judgement, though practical working rules may be evolved on a pragmatic basis for limited use in particular circumstances. Broadly, the longer a concern's normal business cycle – the period between initiation of business transactions and their completion – the greater the area subject to judgement and its effect on periodic financial accounts, and the less its susceptibility to close regulation by accounting bases. These limitations to the regulating powers of accounting bases must be recognised.

Significance of disclosure of accounting policies

11 In circumstances where more than one accounting basis is acceptable in principle, the accounting policy followed can significantly affect a concern's reported results and financial position and the view presented can be properly appreciated only if the policies followed in dealing with material items are also explained. For this reason adequate disclosure of the accounting policies is essential to the fair presentation of financial accounts. As accounting standards become established through publication of statements of standard accounting practice, the choice of accounting bases regarded as generally available will diminish, but it has to be recognised that the complexity and diversity of business renders total and rigid uniformity of bases impracticable.

12 The items with which this statement is mainly concerned are those which are subject to the exercise of judgement as to how far they should be dealt with in the profit and loss account for the period under review or how far all or part should be carried forward in the balance sheet as attributable to the operations of future periods. The determination of the annual profit or loss of nearly every business substantially depends on a systematic approach to a few material items of this type. For the better appreciation of the view they give, annual accounts should include a clear explanation of the accounting policies followed for dealing with these few key items (some examples of which are given in paragraph 13 below). The intention and spirit of this statement are that management should identify those items of the type described which are judged material or critical for the purpose of determining and fully appreciating the company's profit or loss and its financial position, and should make clear the accounting policies followed for dealing with them.

Examples of matters for which different accounting bases are recognised

13 Significant matters for which different accounting bases are recognised and which may have a material effect on reported results and financial position include:

- depreciation of fixed assets
- treatment and amortisation of intangibles such as research
- and development expenditure, patents and trademarks
- stocks and work in progress
- long-term contracts
- deferred taxation
- hire-purchase or instalment transactions
- leasing and rental transactions
- conversion of foreign currencies
- repairs and renewals
- consolidation policies
- property development transactions
- warranties for products or services.

This list is not exhaustive, and may vary according to the nature of the operations conducted.

Part 2 – Definition of Terms

14 Fundamental accounting concepts are the broad basic assumptions which underlie the periodic financial accounts of business enterprises. At the present time the four following fundamental concepts (the relative importance of which will vary according to the circumstances of the particular case) are regarded as having general acceptability.

(*a*) The 'going concern'concept: the enterprise will continue in operational existence for the foreseeable future. This means in particular that the profit and loss account and balance sheet assume no intention or necessity to liquidate or curtail significantly the scale of operation.

(*b*) The 'accruals' concept; revenue and costs are accrued (that is, recognised as they are earned or incurred, not as money is received or paid), matched with one another so far as their relationship can be established or justifiably assumed, and dealt with in the profit and loss account of the period to which they relate; provided that where the accruals concept is inconsistent with the 'prudence' concept (paragraph (*d*) below), the latter prevails. The accruals concept implies that the profit and loss account reflects changes in the amount of net assets that arise out of the transactions of the relevant period (other than distributions or subscriptions of capital and unrealised surpluses arising on revaluation of fixed assets). Revenue and profits dealt with in the profit and loss account are matched with associated costs and expenses by including in the same account the costs incurred in earning them (so far as these are material and identifiable).

(*c*) The 'consistency' concept: there is consistency of accounting treatment of like items within each accounting period and from one period to the next.

(*d*) The concept of 'prudence': revenue and profits are not anticipated but are recognised by inclusion in the profit and loss account only when realised in the form either of cash or of other assets the ultimate cash realisation of which can be assessed with reasonable certainty; provision is made for all known liabilities (expenses and losses) whether the amount of these is known with certainty or is a best estimate in the light of the information available.

15 Accounting bases are the methods developed for applying fundamental accounting concepts to financial transactions and items, for the purpose of financial accounts, and in particular:

(*a*) for determining the accounting period in which revenue and costs should be recognised in the profit and loss account; and

(*b*) for determining the amounts at which material items should be stated in the balance sheet.

16 Accounting policies are the specific accounting bases selected and consistently followed by a business enterprise as being, in the opinion of the management, appropriate to its circumstances and best suited to present fairly its results and financial position.

Part 3 – Standard Accounting Practice

Disclosure of adoption of concepts which differ from those generally accepted

17 If accounts are prepared on the basis of assumptions which differ in material respects from any of the generally accepted fundamental concepts defined above, the facts should be explained. In the absence of a clear statement to the contrary, there is a presumption that the four fundamental concepts have been observed.

Disclosure of accounting policies

18 The accounting policies (as defined above) followed for dealing with items which are judged material or critical in determining profit or loss for the year and in stating the financial position should be disclosed by way of note to the accounts. The explanations should be clear, fair, and as brief as possible.

Date from which effective

19 The accounting practices set out in this statement should be adopted as soon as possible and regarded as standard in respect of reports relating to accounting periods starting on or after 1 January 1972.

Appendix C

Inland Revenue Press Releases

Disclosure and discovery under self assessment. IRPR 31.5.96

The Inland Revenue have today issued a paper about the operation of the discovery and disclosure rules under self assessment. This follows discussions with representatives of accountants, tax advisers, businesses and other professional bodies. The paper addresses the concerns that have been expressed about the circumstances in which the Inland Revenue will make assessments on the discovery of profits that have not been assessed or were inadequately assessed, or where excessive relief has been given.

It makes it clear that where a taxpayer has made a self assessment for the relevant chargeable period, the Inland Revenue may raise an assessment if there would otherwise be a loss of tax resulting from the taxpayer's failure to make a complete disclosure of all the relevant facts relating to his liability to tax.

The statement also makes it clear that while the new self assessment return has been designed to enable the vast majority of taxpayers fully to disclose their liability without the need to submit accounts or computations, the Inland Revenue will accept any additional information sent in with the return.

The paper is reproduced as an annex to this Press Release.

ANNEX

Discovery and Disclosure under Self Assessment

Introduction

1. The introduction of self assessment (SA) and the Electronic Lodgement Service (ELS) heralds a new approach to the handling of tax returns, with more realistic filing dates and streamlined procedures. In particular, the new return has been designed to enable full disclosure to be made without the need to send in accounts or computations in most cases. But concerns have been expressed that reliance on the SA return, without additional information, such as accounts, might expose taxpayers to a greater risk of 'discovery' assessments under (new) Section 29 Taxes Management Act 1970 (TMA). This paper addresses the concerns that have been raised during the Inland Revenue's discussions with representative bodies.

Appendix C

Discovery

2. New Section 29 TMA introduced by Section 191 Finance Act 1994 is designed to reproduce the current mix of law, practice, and concession on discovery set out in the Inland Revenue's Statement of Practice 8 of 1991 as it applies for self assessment.

3. The foundation of the principle of discovery is that the Inland Revenue should be able to recover tax which has been under-assessed (or over-relieved) where there is fraudulent or negligent conduct or where the Inland Revenue officer could not be reasonably expected to be aware of the under-assessment (or excessive relief) from the information provided in or with the tax return.

Disclosure

4. This paper is concerned only with the second of these two aspects, the concept of 'disclosure'. Where all relevant facts are disclosed to the Inland Revenue, taxpayers can be certain (except in the case of fraud or neglect) they have gained finality at the end of the enquiry period.

5. Section 29 sets out the ways in which information is made available for the purpose of making a disclosure. These include providing details in the return or claim, or in any material accompanying the return or claim, for the year in question or the two preceding years. In addition, it is open to the taxpayer or agent to write to the Inland Revenue explaining the existence and relevance of any particular material for the purposes of making an adequate disclosure.

A change of opinion on information that has previously been made available to the Inland Revenue will not be grounds for a discovery assessment.

The self assessment return and standard accounts information

6. Additional information takes more time to process and store, costs which all taxpayers bear by extension. The new return is designed to enable full disclosure to be made without the need to send in accounts or computations in most cases. Taxpayers and practitioners are entitled to send in additional material if they consider that it adds information of relevance to the tax liability which cannot be contained within the return. The Inland Revenue will accept any additional information sent in with the return; see paragraph 13 (accompanying documents) below.

7. The self assessment return requires comprehensive information regarding each taxpayer's affairs. With the exception of partnerships whose annual turnover exceeds £15 million (see paragraph 10 below), separate accounts and computations are not required to be submitted with the return. Instead specific details, including standard accounts information (SAI), are required within the return.

8. The majority of income tax cases involve reasonably straightforward accounts. In these cases the fully completed return and SAI will enable a full and fair picture of the taxpayer's affairs including any business to be presented. In otherwise straightforward cases there may be the odd point of difficulty which needs further explanation. Such aspects may be dealt with by providing extra information within the areas provided on the return.

9. In some of the larger or more complex cases the SAI details and the space provided in the return for additional information may not by themselves provide a means of adequate disclosure. The submission of further information, including perhaps the submission of accounts, may be considered appropriate by the taxpayer or agent. Such cases would include, for example, large partnerships with substantial turnovers or cases where, although not large, the business is complex – perhaps because it is a highly specialised trade, or where accounts or computations are required for a proper understanding of the figures.

10. The SAI will have to be completed in order for the return to be accepted, even where the accounts are submitted. To leave this information to the discretion of the taxpayer would seriously undermine its value to the Inland Revenue. The only exception is for the very largest partnerships (i.e. annual turnover over £15 million) where taxpayers are required to submit accounts and computations as well as the return instead of completing SAI. This difference in treatment is justified because the Inland Revenue are likely, anyway, to require to see the accounts and computations of these large cases every year, on account of their size and inherent complexity. Tax returns will be considered to be incomplete where, at the filing date, the SAI boxes have not been completed or, in cases where partnership turnover exceeds £15 million per annum, the accounts have not been submitted.

The submission of additional material

11. Taxpayers and agents should be aware that the submission of accounts and computations or other documents may not provide protection against a discovery assessment beyond that arising from the submission of the return alone. The information contained in the additional material may have been fully covered within the return or, alternatively, there may be so much material that the Inland Revenue officer 'could not have been reasonably expected, on the basis of the information made available to him before that time, to be aware' (new section 29(5) TMA 1970) of the particular point of liability, unless the taxpayer or agent had explained its relevance. Where voluminous information beyond the accounts and computations is sent with the return, therefore, it is recommended that there should be a brief indication of the relevance of the material.

Electronic Lodgement Service

12. The Electronic Lodgement Service (ELS) will accommodate all the information which may be given on the self assessment return, including any additional details in the 'white space'. Furthermore, recent developments in the design of the ELS system mean that the service will be able to cope with substantial amounts of additional information such as accounts or computations should their submission be considered appropriate by the taxpayer or accountant.

Accompanying documents

13. The Section 29 definition of disclosures includes information in 'any accounts, statements or documents accompanying the return'. The Inland Revenue consider that any material sent in support of a return 'accompanies' the return for that purpose. Although advised that, in strictness, statutory time-limits for filing a return apply equally to any documents intended to accompany it, the Inland Revenue will accept that any documents submitted within one month of the return 'accompany' it for the purpose of making a disclosure within section 29 TMA if the return indicates that such documents have been, or are to be, submitted. Where documents have been sent outside that time limit, the Inland Revenue will consider sympathetically any request for them to be treated as supporting the return in question for that purpose.

Conclusion

14. It is in everyone's interests that the new self assessment system enables taxpayers to disclose their affairs fully. The Inland Revenue believe that this can be achieved through the return and SAI, explanations in the space provided in the return for additional information, or the submission of accounts or computations where appropriate. The self assessment return and the guidance notes will help taxpayers to be aware of matters which should be disclosed and, where there are doubts, taxpayers can consult their tax adviser or the Inland Revenue.

Bovine Spongiform Encephalopathy (BSE) and Farm Stocktaking Valuations. IRPR 29.4.96

Following discussions, the Inland Revenue today clarified the approach which applies to the valuation of livestock for stock taking against the background of BSE. The need to value stock at the end of March 1996 can be avoided by many taxpayers by the submission of a two year account covering the whole of the self assessment transition period. In cases where a valuation is required the normal rules will continue to apply subject to a modification of the way in which market value is computed for cull cows, male calves born to dairy cows and beef cattle.

The Financial Secretary to the Treasury, Michael Jack, MP, said: 'At this very difficult time for farmers, I hope that this Inland Revenue announcement will be helpful in removing one area of uncertainty, namely the approach to be adopted on stock valuations in the BSE crisis. This approach has been agreed after contact with interested parties and is to be welcomed.'.

DETAILS

1. In calculating taxable profits from farming, like those from other businesses, it is necessary to value trading stock at the annual date to which the accounts of the business are drawn up. This press release explains how the Inland Revenue will approach the valuation of cattle in farm accounts at a date when markets are affected by public concern over BSE.

2. Methods of valuation of farm stock for income tax and corporation tax purposes acceptable to the Inland Revenue are set out in Business Economic Note 19 (BEN 19). This note was issued in March 1993 following consultation between the Inland Revenue and bodies representing farmers, landowners, agricultural valuers, accountants and chartered surveyors.

3. Many livestock farmers account to Lady Day (25 March) or 31 March and some to dates in April and May. In view of the limited and unsettled market in cattle following public concern over BSE, farmers and their professional advisers have been uncertain as to how to value cattle at these year ends.

4. In many cases the recent market conditions will affect valuations at the end of the first of the two years which form the self assessment (SA) transition period. Farmers may prefer to prepare a two year account for the whole of their SA transition period thus saving the need to value animals for income tax purposes at a time when the market is unsettled. The Inland Revenue welcome this practice. However if a farmer wishes to claim a loss for one of the years forming the basis of the SA transition period then a separate account for that year will be needed.

5. Until now the Inland Revenue have responded to queries from those who wish to prepare accounts by suggesting that they categorise and count the animals at the year end but await further guidance on how to value them. Following contact with representative bodies, the Inland Revenue are now able to give further guidance.

6. Notwithstanding the market disruption caused by developments regarding BSE, the principles agreed between the Inland Revenue and representative bodies and set out in BEN 19 will continue to apply to the valuation of livestock for stock taking.

7. The main principle of stock valuation for income tax purpose, which is reflected in BEN 19, is that the valuation should reflect the cost of production or, if it is lower, the net realisable value of the stock.

8. Where the farmer's records are not adequate to compute the cost of animals which are home bred or substantially home reared a percentage of market value can be used to arrive at a deemed cost of production. For cattle the percentage is 60 per cent. Deemed cost should not be used for purchased animals if it is less than the original purchase price plus, if the animal was immature when purchased, the costs of rearing from the date of purchase to the valuation date or, if earlier, to maturity.

9. Public concern over BSE has considerably disrupted the normal markets for barren (or cull) cows, bull calves born to dairy cows and beef cattle. For animals in these categories there may be insufficient evidence to arrive at market value in the normal way because there was no market or only a very limited market at the valuation date. In such cases the Inland Revenue will accept that market value for the purposes of valuations in accordance with BEN 19 may be taken as either

- the compensation subsequently paid on the slaughter of the animal, adjusted where necessary to reflect a change in weight between the accounting date and the date of slaughter or the compensation which would have been payable under the arrangements announced by the Government on April 16, by reference to the estimated weight of the animal at the accounting date, or
- the latest normal market value before 20 March 1996 less
  - 30 per cent for cull cows
  - 40 per cent for bull calves born to dairy cows
  - 20 per cent for beef cattle.

10. A farmer may choose whether to estimate market value by using compensation value or the latest normal market value modified in accordance with the previous paragraph for animals in these categories but the same basis should be used for all the animals in any one of the three categories mentioned. Where deemed cost is used it will be 60 per cent of this figure.

11. This arrangement may be applied for valuations at normal stocktaking dates between 20 March 1996 and 31 May 1996, both dates inclusive.

12. Some people have suggested that stocktaking valuations of cattle at dates late in March 1996 at nil or nominal amounts can be used for tax purposes. This is not the Inland Revenue's view. Such figures would only be appropriate if at those dates there was evidence that sellers were not simply holding their animals back from market but rather were willing to dispose of them for at most nominal consideration. The Inland Revenue has not seen any evidence of such behaviour by sellers.

13. Farmers remain at liberty, however, to value animals at net realisable value where there is no reasonable expectation that the eventual sale of the stock will cover its costs. Guidance on the calculation of net realisable value is to be found in Business Economic Note 19. Where under BEN 19 open market value at the valuation date may be used in

arriving at net realisable value, farmers may use the method described above to work out for this purpose the open market value of barren cows, bull calves and beef cattle.

Self Assessment: Early Settlement of a Deceased Taxpayer's Tax Affairs or Those of a Trust or Estate Following Cessation.
IRPR 4.4.96

The Inland Revenue have always been prepared, when asked to do so by the Personal Representatives or Trustees of a deceased person, to issue a tax return before the end of the tax year to which it relates and to agree liabilities quickly. They have done this to minimise delays in winding up an estate and distributing estate or trust property.

The time limit for enquiring into tax returns under self assessment, however, means that Personal Representatives may not know for some time whether the deceased's tax affairs can be regarded as settled. That could result in delays winding up an estate.

To help Personal Representatives settle the affairs of the deceased as quickly as possible, the Inland Revenue have today announced that, under self assessment they will, on request, issue a tax return before the end of the tax year in which death occurred and give early written confirmation if they do not intend to enquire into that return. Personal Representatives can also request such confirmation at any time before the expiry of the normal enquiry time limit.

A similar situation may arise where the administration of a deceased person's estate is completed or a trust is wound up during a tax year. The Inland Revenue will, on request, adopt the same approach to the tax affairs of Personal Representatives and Trustees.

DETAILS

1. Self assessment comes in for the tax year 1996–97 onwards for around 9 million taxpayers.

2. If one of those taxpayers dies after 5 April 1996 and the Inland Revenue needs to send a tax return to the deceased's Personal Representatives, covering the period to the date of death, they will usually do this *after* the end of the tax year in which death occurred.

3. Under self assessment, however, the Inland Revenue can enquire into a tax return up to 12 months after the fixed filing date – that is up to 12 months after 31 January following the end of a year of assessment.

4. This could mean that if a taxpayer died in, say, early April 1996 the Personal Representatives of the deceased could not be sure, until after 31 January 1999, whether the Inland Revenue were going to enquire into the return for the period to the date of death.

5. Representations have been made that this could delay the winding up of estates.

6. To help Personal Representatives settle the tax affairs of the deceased quickly the Inland Revenue will, on request, issue a tax return *before* the end of the tax year in which death occurred; and whether issued before or after the end of that tax year, they will also give early written confirmation if they do not intend to enquire into that return.

7. This confirmation would not preclude, in exceptional circumstances, the Inland Revenue enquiring into the tax return at a later date if they discovered that the return had been incomplete or incorrect.

8. But, in the vast majority of cases, receipt of this written confirmation will signify the end of the Inland Revenue's interest in the Income and Capital Gains tax affairs of the deceased and, where that is the only open matter, will enable the deceased's Personal Representatives to finalise the estate.

9. Where administration of a deceased person's estate is completed or a trust is wound up in a tax year, the Personal Representatives or Trustees will similarly be able to request the issue of a tax return before the end of the tax year. And confirmation that the Inland Revenue does not intend to enquire into that return will be given on the same basis. This will enable Personal Representatives and Trustees to finalise tax liabilities and distribute estate or trust property.

Obligation to Notify Chargeability to Income Tax and Capital Gains Tax for Tax Years 1995–96 Onwards. IRPR 1.2.96

The Inland Revenue have today published a Statement of Practice (SP 1/96) which explains how the new rules on notifying chargeability to income tax or capital gains tax apply to certain employees.

A copy of the statement is attached as an annex to this Press Release.

DETAILS

1. Under the new rules for notifying chargeability which started on 6 April 1995 employees who do not receive a tax return have six months from the end of the tax year on 5 April to notify the Inland Revenue of any taxable employment income that is not being dealt with under PAYE. (The same rules also apply in respect of other sources of income and to other people who do not receive tax returns.)

2. The new time limit expires on 5 October in any tax year. That is generally before the Inland Revenue send out annual notices of PAYE coding containing adjustments for such matters as new expenses or benefits for the tax year just ended (usually the following January or February)

or make assessments. Employees will not therefore know for sure by 5 October that the Inland Revenue have taken account of information about expenses and benefits received for the first time.

3. To create certainty for those affected by the new limit, and remove the need for them to notify the Inland Revenue just in case, today's statement makes it clear that employees who receive a copy of P11D information from their employers can assume that the Inland Revenue know about any items on the P11D and that they will be taken into account for PAYE, provided that the employees are satisfied that the information is correct and complete and that they have no reason to believe that the P11D information has not been passed to the Inland Revenue.

SP1/96 Notification of Chargeability to Income Tax and Capital Gains Tax for Tax Years 1995–96 Onwards

Introduction

This statement sets out the Inland Revenue's views on the changes to the obligation to notify chargeability to income tax and capital gains tax for tax years 1995–96 onwards, which were introduced by Finance Act 1994. The changes affect all taxpayers, but have a particular impact on directors, employees and other persons, such as those receiving pensions, who have income chargeable to tax under Schedule E. That is why the statement concentrates mainly on that area.

Background

Present position – general

1. The obligation to notify chargeability to income tax to the Inland Revenue applies to a person for any tax year for which he or she has not been required to complete a tax return by the Inland Revenue within 12 months after the end of the tax year. (There is a similar obligation for capital gains tax.) A tax year begins on the 6 April and ends on 5 April.

2. Shortly after the end of any tax year the Inland Revenue send returns to those known or likely to have income or gains which have not been taxed in full. Those who receive returns have no separate obligation to notify chargeability. But there will be some people who have not received a return who have income or gains which have not been taxed in full. Such individuals are required to notify chargeability.

3. The present obligation to notify chargeability to income tax is under Section 7 Taxes Management Act 1970 which requires individuals who have not received tax returns within 12 months from the end of the tax year to notify the Revenue within that time that they are chargeable to income tax and specify each separate source of income. The requirement does not apply to certain sources, for example where a source only produces taxed income and there is no higher rate liability. The obligation to

notify liability to capital gains tax is under Section 11A Taxes Management Act 1970. Where there is a failure to notify chargeability to income or capital gains tax, a penalty not exceeding the amount of tax due can be sought. But the penalty may be reduced in any particular case.

Present position – income from employments etc

4. The Inland Revenue send tax returns to employees and pensioners on a selective basis. This is because most obtain the benefit of all the reliefs due to them and pay tax on all of their income automatically, through the PAYE system and the taxation of interest and dividends at source and through MIRAS.

5. Section 7 Taxes Management Act 1970 provides that employees and pensioners who do not receive a tax return do not have to notify a source such as a specific employment for a particular tax year if they know all the income from it has been taken into account in making deductions through PAYE. Income includes items such as benefits in kind and expenses payments, as well as wages or salaries. Thus, for example, an employee who receives benefits in any tax year which are taken into account in the code number for that year which is operated in respect of the wages or salary will not have to notify the source. And there is no requirement to notify sources such as national insurance benefits and minor amounts of Schedule D income which are effectively taxed through the PAYE system by being taken into account in setting the PAYE code.

6. By the end of the 12 month period after any tax year persons within the PAYE system whose income is wholly or mainly within Schedule E and who have not received returns should normally know whether or not they need to notify chargeability. This is because any changes in circumstances affecting their liability for the year just ended which they or their employers have notified to the Inland Revenue should be reflected in an assessment and/or in changes to their current and future PAYE code numbers. If for instance a person gets a new and continuing benefit in a tax year the employer should report it to the Inland Revenue by 6 June after the end of the tax year (on Form P11D) and the Revenue will usually issue an assessment. The current code number will be revised and, if the Revenue decide to collect the additional tax due for the year just ended through PAYE, the taxpayer will normally be aware of this also as he/she will receive a code number for the following year showing how the extra tax will be collected; the taxpayer will therefore know there is no need to notify chargeability in respect of income from the employment.

Finance Act 1994 – changes

General

7. Under self assessment, for tax year 1996–97 onwards, taxpayers who are sent returns at the normal time, shortly after the end of the tax

year, will be required to file those returns by the following 31 January and, at the same time, to pay the balance of any income tax due for the year (unless the additional tax liability is to be collected through PAYE by a coding adjustment).

8. Because of the new time limits for filing returns and paying tax, taxpayers will be required to notify chargeability no later than six months after the end of the tax year (that is by 5 October). This will allow a taxpayer who has not received a tax return to ask for one, if there is a need to notify chargeability, and to complete it and send it back to the Revenue (with any payment needed) by the following 31 January. (The new time limit is introduced by Paragraph 1 Schedule 19 Finance Act 1994 which substitutes a new Section 7 Taxes Management Act 1970.) If a taxpayer wants the Revenue to calculate the tax liability, a return issued on or before 31 July after the end of the tax year has to be filed by 30 September. However a taxpayer can still require the Revenue to calculate the tax liability when a return is issued after 31 July, provided the return is filed by two months from the date of issue.

9. In self assessment penalties for failure to notify chargeability will be based on the amount of tax that was unpaid at 31 January following the end of the tax year, which is the due date for the balance of tax due. This means that a person who does not notify chargeability within the six months period can reduce or eliminate any penalty by paying some or all the tax due by 31 January. And, as at present, where tax is due any penalties chargeable because of a failure to notify chargeability are mitigable by reference to the amount of tax unpaid, the nature of the disclosure and the level of co-operation given to the Inland Revenue during the course of any resulting enquiry.

10. As now, people with income that is not taxed under Schedule E, or with capital gains, will need to notify their chargeability to tax. There is likely to be little cause for doubt in their case whether they should notify chargeability. People setting up in business or newly receiving income other than from employment or making capital gains will know by the end of the tax year that they should complete a return for that year. If they do not receive one, they have six months to notify the Inland Revenue of the position and ask for a return. It is not necessary for them to have worked out the amount of the income or gain by that time.

Directors, employees, pensioners etc

11. The change in the time limit for notifying chargeability to six months will have a particular impact on those with income chargeable to tax under Schedule E. Paragraph 6 above explained how, within the current twelve month period after any tax year, a taxpayer will normally be aware if liability on an untaxed item such as a new and continuing benefit will be dealt with through PAYE. But the change to a new six month limit means that within that period a taxpayer will not generally be in a position to know for certain whether the Revenue is aware of any changes in his

circumstances for the tax year just ended or if his code number will be revised to take account of such changes. Any change to the current code number may have been made before 6 October after the end of the tax year, but the issue of a code change for the following year, to collect tax for the year just ended through PAYE, will not. However, the new Section 7(5) provides that an employee is relieved of an obligation to notify chargeability if income from a source has been or 'will be' taxed through PAYE.

12. The PAYE regulations have been changed to give effect to the proposals in the Inland Revenue consultative document: Self Assessment: what it will mean for employers and employees, published in May 1994. (The changes are in the Income Tax (Employments) (Amendment No. 4) Regulations 1995 (SI 1995/1284) which come into force on 6 April 1996). Under the revised regulations those employees who are in employment on the last day of a tax year should be provided by the employer, by the following 6 July, with a copy of the information about expenses payments and benefits which is supplied to the Inland Revenue on form P11D or equivalent. (Employees who left an employment during the course of a tax year can obtain a copy of the P11D information from the employer on request.)

13. Subject to paragraphs 14 and 15 below, the Inland Revenue will accept that employees who receive such a copy of the information on a P11D can assume any items on it which are not already taken into account for PAYE 'will be' taken into account for PAYE, so that there is no need to notify chargeability because of them.

14. In assuming that chargeability need not be notified in respect of items on the P11D, employees will need to be satisfied the information on the P11D is correct and complete. There may be circumstances where employees are aware that, even though they have a copy of P11D information, the actual P11Ds have not been submitted to the Inland Revenue; in such a case employees are not relieved of any obligation to notify chargeability.

15. There is still an obligation to notify chargeability in respect of any items not shown in the copy of the P11D information. And employees who have not received a copy of the P11D information from their employers, even though they believe a P11D was due, are not relieved of any obligation to notify chargeability. Employees cannot assume they are relieved of any obligation to notify chargeability because information may be supplied by employers to the Inland Revenue on returns other than the P11D, for example those in relation to share schemes.

16. In considering whether it was reasonable for an employee to consider that a notification of chargeability was not needed, the Inland Revenue will take into account broadly the same factors as now, that is, where there has been an apparent failure, the Revenue will consider whether any explanation given by the employee is a 'reasonable excuse' (Section 118 Taxes Management Act 1970), so that, in effect, there has been no failure.

17. Although, as explained at paragraph 7 above, the first full year of self-assessment is tax year 1996–97, the new Section 7 applies from tax year 1995–96. Thus the time limit for notifying chargeability for 1995–96 is 5 October 1996. The requirement for employers to provide employees with a copy of the information provided to the Revenue only comes into effect for 1996–97 and later years. Some employees may not receive such information for 1995–96. The Inland Revenue will therefore take the absence of any such information into account as a mitigating factor in looking at any case where there is a failure to notify chargeability on P11D items by an employee for 1995–96.

Schedule A transitional proposals. IRPR 10.2.95

This year's Finance Bill includes proposals for a new income tax regime for taxing income from property under Schedule A. The new rules will apply from the start of the tax year 1995/96. The Inland Revenue have published guidance notes to their Inspectors regarding the principles to be adopted in seeking agreement with individual taxpayers on a reasonable approach to moving from the existing statutory basis or from various non-statutory practices to the new statutory Schedule A basis.

DETAILS

1. Clause 33 and Schedule 6 to the Finance Bill make changes to the income tax rules which apply to the taxation of income from property. The proposals do not, however, contain transitional provisions covering the change from the existing system to the new one. This is because the present rules have been widely adapted in practice by agreement between taxpayers and their Inspectors. Attempting to legislate for the transition would involve describing all the existing practices and dealing with them one by one.

2. Instead, the Inland Revenue have decided to publish the principles they intend to adopt to arrive at a fair and reasonable result. If any taxpayer does not accept the proposed approach, he or she can be taxed on the formal statutory basis. Disagreements can also be independently reviewed.

3. The guidelines attached to this Press Release have been the subject of widespread consultation with various bodies representing the property sector and with other professional bodies. At the end of the guidance is a list of the bodies which have endorsed the approach.

Schedule A transitional proposals

Introduction

1. This paper is concerned with Income Tax payers who have liabilities under Schedule A in respect of income from property, or under Case VI of Schedule D in respect of furnished lettings. It provides guidance to

Inspectors, which has been made public, on how to deal with the transition from present practices to the proposed new scheme which will operate from 1995/96 *et seq*. It has been discussed with various representative bodies listed at the end of the document who endorse the approach recommended.

2. The present rules of Schedule A have been widely adapted in practice by agreement between taxpayers and their Inspectors. These adaptations typically result in computations which taxpayers and their Inspectors agree give a reasonable measure of the income arising from property, but those computations are not in accordance with law. For 1996/97 and subsequent years taxpayers will have to self assess their total income, including their income from property and this will increase the need for certainty about how income should be computed. The proposed new system is simpler and easier to operate. It adopts many features of the existing informal practices.

3. The proposed timetable is that the new rules should first be applied for 1995/96, the final year of Revenue assessment. Returns of 1995/96 income, made under the new rules, will be examined and agreed by the Revenue before an assessment is finalised. Whenever possible agreement should be reached well before 31 January 1998 which is the filing date for the 1996/97 return. This will enable taxpayers to self assess with confidence for 1996/97 under the new rules. If the new rules are to apply for 1995/96 then any transitional problems have to be dealt with in assessing 1994/95.

Transitional issues

4. There are two main problems that need to be dealt with in transition. First, there are variations in the way receipts and payments are taken into account and set off against each other in order to arrive at a measure of profit for a period. Second, some taxpayers use a basis period rather than computing income for the fiscal year ended 5 April. For 1995/96 income from property will be computed by reference to the rules that apply for Case I of Schedule D. And the basis of assessment will be the income of the fiscal year 1995/96. The 1994/95 assessment needs to bridge the gap between the existing statutory basis, or the non statutory practice that has been adopted in the particular case, and the new rules that will apply for 1995/96. In addition there may be problems to be addressed on how we give relief for capital allowances and for interest in 1994/95 assessments.

5. As in many cases the existing practice is non statutory any attempt to legislate for transition would first need to describe all the existing practices and then deal with the transition for each one. This would need lengthy and complicated legislation and because of the wide spread of practices, and incomplete knowledge of them at the centre, there is a danger that even long and detailed legislation would not be comprehensive. The intention therefore of this note is to give guidance to Inspectors

regarding the principles to be adopted in seeking agreement with taxpayers case by case on a reasonable basis for transition. The contents of this note have been subject to consultation with representative bodies and those listed below have endorsed the principles proposed.

6. Any non statutory basis must be predicated on an existing trust between taxpayers and their Inspector that they will both act in good faith to ensure that a fair measure of income will be taxed taking one year with another. The guidance on transitional issues builds on and relies on that trust.

7. Taxpayers with income from property or from furnished lettings that first arises in 1994/95 will be invited to apply the new computation rules for 1994/95 to avoid any need for transitional adjustments.

Basis of Computation

8. The present statutory basis of computing Schedule A profit requires that we take account of receipts to which a person is entitled in the chargeable period (S 15(1)2 and S 25(1) ICTA) and allow the deduction of payments that have been made in that period (S 25(2)ICTA). Under the new rules Schedule A income is to be computed as it would be if it arose from a trade chargeable to tax under Case I of Schedule D.

9. For Case I of Schedule D the profits are computed by starting with accounts produced in accordance with correct commercial accounting practice and adjusting the profits shown by such accounts to take account of tax law, whether in the form of specific statute or principles developed by the courts from the basic charging provisions. In accounting for a commercial transaction, or set of transactions, there may be more than one generally acceptable practice. Each of these will be acceptable for Case I purposes unless they violate tax law. Figures prepared on a receipts and payments basis, or cash basis, will in principle be outside the circle of what amounts to generally acceptable commercial accountancy. In practice, however, for a small, simple business, the difference between the profit struck by such a method and the profit on the normal accruals basis is unlikely to be material.

10. Where the strict legal basis of the existing Schedule A rules has been applied three options may be considered with taxpayers and agreement reached on the most suitable option for each case. If neither (*a*) nor (*b*) below is agreed then, in the absence of statutory provision for transition, (*c*) is the correct legal result.

a. If the Schedule A source ends in 1995/96 the new rules do not apply; that is, the computation is still made on the old rules. If it is clear that the source is likely to come to an end soon after 1995/96 then the existing Schedule A rules may be continued until the source ceases on the basis that those rules may be adopted as an acceptable Case I basis.

b. A special transitional computation may be produced. This computation should start with the profit computed for 1994/95 according to the existing rules and adjust that profit, by adding any receipts or deducting any payments that would otherwise fall through a gap between the 1994/95 computation and the accounts to be produced for 1995/96, and by deducting any receipts or adding back any expenses from the 1994/95 computation that will also be included in the accounts for 1995/96.

c. Otherwise it will be appropriate to compute the 1994/95 income on the Schedule A statutory basis and the 1995/96 income according to the rules of Case I, Schedule D without any intervening adjustment.

11. Where taxpayers who are landlords in a small way have departed for the purposes of Schedule A from the statutory basis of computing profit they may well have adopted an accounting basis that would often in practice be acceptable for Case I purposes for a trade of comparable turnover. For example taxpayers with a single property giving rise to small amounts of income will commonly have adopted a cash basis for computing their income giving a result close to what would have been struck if debtors, creditors, accruals, prepayments etc. had been taken into account. And in complex cases they may well have employed an accountant to produce accounts that will already conform to correct commercial accounting practice. Inspectors should therefore bear in mind that an existing basis of computing the net income of a period for Schedule A purposes may well be acceptable without amendment for the new Schedule A.

12. If a non statutory basis has been adopted which, contrary to the comments in paragraph 11 above would not be acceptable for the purposes of Case I of Schedule D, then the same three options listed in paragraph 10 above should be considered subject to para 13 below.

13. Where the taxpayer's existing practice uses the profits of an accounting period not ending on 31 March or 5 April as the basis period it is likely that they will be using a method to compute profits for Schedule A that is acceptable for Case 1 of Schedule D. If exceptionally this situation does not arise it will usually be the case that taxing an average profit as described in paragraph 16 below will be sufficient and no other change should be needed. In particular the method described in paragraph 10(*b*) above will not usually be suitable. Although all cases will need to be considered on their merits method 10(*c*) above is likely to be the most appropriate.

14. Problems should not arise with the computation of profits from furnished lettings which have been taxed under Case VI of Schedule D. It has long been our view that the correct basis of computation of Case VI income is to follow, so far as is possible, the rules that would apply for Case I of Schedule D. Existing bases of computing income from furnished lettings should therefore be continued. And the present practice of allowing a notional expense deduction of 10% of the relevant receipts as an

alternative to a renewals allowance should also be continued. Relevant receipts are gross receipts less adjustments described in Statement of Practice A19.

Basis Periods

15. Different issues arise with respect to basis periods for furnished lettings taxed under Case VI of Schedule D and income from property taxed under Schedule A. For 1995/96 et seq. under the new rules of Schedule A both will be taxed by reference to the income of the fiscal year.

Furnished Lettings Basis Periods

16. S 69 ICTA (before amendment by FA 1994) gives the Inspector a wide statutory discretion (subject to appeal to the Commissioners) to select a twelve month period the profits of which should be taxed for a particular year of assessment. Inspectors have agreed varying practices with taxpayers who have income from furnished lettings but these will usually involve treating profits of an accounting year ended in the year of assessment or in the previous year as being the profits of the year of assessment. The preferred option for 1994/95 furnished lettings is to follow so far as possible the principles of the transitional rules adopted for 1996/97 for Case I of Schedule D. That is to ask the taxpayer to produce an account, or accounts, that cover the whole of the period from the end of the 1993/94 basis period to 5/4/95 inclusive and if that period is Y months long to tax a fraction 12/Y of those profits.

17. If for example the taxpayer was taxed for 1993/94 on the profits of the 12 months to 5/4/93 (a PY fiscal basis) then for 1994/95 the assessment should be on 12/24 of the profit for the two years ended 5/4/95. There is existing statutory approval for this in S69 as arithmetically it gives the same result as if the Inspector chose to tax the profits of the 12 months ended 5/10/94. Similarly if the taxpayer would normally have been taxed for 1994/95 on the 12 months to 5/10/94 then taxing him for 1994/95 on 12/18 of the profit of the 18 months to 5/4/95 is arithmetically the same as if the Inspector chose to tax the profits of the 12 months ended 5/2/95.

Existing Schedule A Basis Periods

18. Under the existing rules of Schedule A the assessment should be on the profits of the fiscal year. This rule is generally followed but it is known that there are a small number of cases where agreement has been made to tax by reference to an accounting period ended in the year of assessment and an even smaller number where agreement has been reached to tax by reference to an accounting period based in the previous year. Such agreements are more likely in cases where the income arising

is similar from one year to the next so that the agreement does not materially affect the profits chargeable.

19. Here too the preferred option is for the taxpayer to produce an account for the period from the end of the 1993/94 basis period through to 5/4/95 and if this period is Y months long to be assessed on the proportion 12/Y of those profits.

Disagreement over Method of Computation or Basis Periods

20. Any existing arrangement between a taxpayer and his Inspector that assessments should be based on a PY or some other accounting basis must have implicitly recognised that over the lifetime of a business there would be the possibility of a mismatch between the total profits earned and those that are taxed. This mismatch would necessarily mean that more or less than the true profits would be taxed. Agreements have been reached in the expectation that they would continue to apply for a reasonable length of time and would not be withdrawn arbitrarily but it cannot be supposed that they could never be changed. In particular it is reasonable that arrangements should be modified by the Inspector when there is a statutory change in the basis of assessment. The proposals in paragraphs 15 to 19 above are thought to be fair both to the taxpayer and to the Revenue.

21. If there is a disagreement between the taxpayer and the Inspector over the application of the above proposals to a particular case the Inspector should first consider carefully whether they give a fair result. If the figures over the lifetime of the business from commencement to 5/4/95 are available, and it is clear that the proposals above give a result that is unfair to the taxpayer, then in furnished lettings cases the Inspector should use the discretion under S 69 to select the 12 months, out of the period from the end of the 1993/94 basis period to 5/4/95, that gives the fairest result. In Schedule A cases an attempt should be made to agree a similar approach with the taxpayer.

22. Where no agreement is possible the Inspector should determine the Case VI basis period under S 69 to correspond to the fairest possible result and assess Schedule A by reference to the profits of the fiscal year 1994/95. In both instances this should be by apportionment of profits of different accounting periods if necessary.

23. As these transitional problems will often arise outside the statutory framework the Commissioners on appeal will only be able to apply the strict statutory basis. Every effort should be made to reach an agreement with the taxpayer but where this cannot be done he or she should be reminded of the right to ask for the decision to be reviewed by the Officer in Charge of the office or unit concerned when they are not satisfied. More information about how to make a formal complaint, if the Officer in Charge cannot settle the matter, is set out in leaflet IR120 'You and the Inland Revenue'. That leaflet includes information about the

Revenue Adjudicator and the Parliamentary Ombudsman and it should be offered to taxpayers who ask for it or are dissatisfied with the decision of the Officer in Charge in cases of dispute.

Other Transitional Issues

Capital Allowances

24. Where assessments have been based on a period other than the fiscal year capital allowances may similarly have been based on a non fiscal basis. Where this happens allowances for 1994/95 should be based on the balance of qualifying expenditure brought forward at the end of the 1993/94 computation. This should be adjusted to take account of additions and disposals in the whole of the period through to 5/4/95 and one year's writing down allowance given.

Interest

25. At present interest that is within the qualifying conditions in S 355(1)(b) ICTA is relieved under S 353 ICTA. Relief is given for a year of assessment by reference to the amount of interest paid in the year. Under the new rules of Schedule A interest will be one component of the computation of Schedule A income and will be allowed if it would be within the normal rules of Case I of Schedule D. The most important test in this context will be whether or not it is laid out wholly and exclusively for the purpose of the business (S 74(1)(a) as adopted for Schedule A).

26. Whether or not any transitional issue arises for interest will depend on the basis on which accounts are produced for 1995/96 and subsequent years. If accounts are produced on a receipts and payments basis, so that the 1995/96 accounts will include interest paid in that year, and interest relief for 1994/95 was given by reference to interest paid in that year, no gap will arise in the pattern of relief for interest.

27. If accounts are produced on an accruals basis they will, in the normal case of a continuing business, include a full year's interest and give a valid measure of income for the year taking account of interest. As in paragraph 10c above there may be no need to make any further adjustment.

28. Where however a switch from an interest paid basis (under S 353) to an interest accrued basis (using accounts produced in accordance with normal accounting practice) will result over the lifetime of a business, or of a loan, in relief being given for less interest than is paid, it will often be fair to give some further relief. If further relief is to be given it should be by way of a deduction of a further amount in arriving at the amount chargeable for 1995/96. In considering whether it is fair to give further relief the Inspector should have regard to all relevant information including details of amounts that may have fallen out of charge to tax as a result of a change in the accounting basis on which profits are computed

or as a result of a change in basis periods. The principle should be that if rents and expenses are taken fully into account over the lifetime of the business full relief ought also to be given for all the interest. But if rent or expenses fall out of relief on transition the overall effect taking account of interest as well should be considered.

Conclusion

29. The hope is to produce a system that is simpler for taxpayers to self assess from 1996/97 by moving 1995/96 onto a new statutory basis. The Revenue's immediate aim is to assess 1994/95 on a basis that will get people up to date by assessing profits up to 5/4/95. Taxpayers should, wherever possible, move immediately to a basis of computation and a basis period that give a fair measure of income under the new scheme taking one year with another. If 1994/95 has already been agreed and is not capable of further amendment transitional adjustments should all be made in the 1995/96 assessment.

30. Transitional issues should be settled wherever possible by agreement. The use of basis periods in the past means that something other than a perfect match between profits made and profits assessed was always likely. Transition necessarily involves some approximations so a perfect match should not be expected in all cases. Where however it can be seen that an unfair result would be achieved by applying an immediate change in the means of computing profit or in the change of a basis period Inspectors should agree adjustments which so far as possible give a fair result.

Organisations that have endorsed the Guidance

Association of Residential Letting Agents

British Property Federation

Chartered Institute of Taxation

Country Landowners' Association

Federation of Small Businesses

Institute of Chartered Accountants in England and Wales

Institute of Chartered Accountants of Scotland

National Farmers Union

Royal Institution of Chartered Surveyors

Scottish Landowners' Federation

Appendix D

Change of Accounting Date

Revenue leaflet IR 26 is reproduced below (with dates in examples updated). References are to sections as originally enacted.

1. This leaflet sets out briefly the practice of the Board of Inland Revenue in cases where a trader permanently changes his accounting date.

Statutory provisions

2. The relevant statutory provisions are contained in *TA 1988, s 60*. The effect of these provisions is briefly as follows.

(i) In the normal case where there is only one account ending in the year preceding the year of assessment and that account is for a period of one year, the assessment is to be based on the profit of that account. [*TA 1988, s 60(3)*].

(ii) In other cases, the Board of Inland Revenue are to decide what period of 12 months ending on a date in the preceding income tax year is to be the basis year. [*TA 1988, s 60(4)*]. There is no appeal against that decision.

(iii) Where the Board have determined the basis year for any income tax year under (ii), they may direct that the assessment for the preceding income tax year is to be adjusted to the profits of the corresponding period, i.e. the year ending on the same date in the previous year [*TA 1988, s 60(5)*]; an appeal against the Board's decision to make or not to make any such direction lies to the General or Special Commissioners, who are empowered to grant 'such relief, if any, as is just'.

Board's normal practice

3. Under *TA 1988, s 60(4)* the Board normally decide that the assessment is to be based on the profits of the period of 12 months ending on the new accounts date in the preceding income tax year, i.e. the date to which the trader proposes to make up his accounts in future.

4. The question then arises whether there is to be any adjustment of the assessment for the preceding income tax year under *TA 1988, s 60(5)* to the profits of the 'corresponding' period. Such an adjustment may increase or decrease the liability, according to the trend of profits.

5. The considerations which the Board have in mind in determining this question are as follows. Where there is a permanent change of accounting date then, whether or not revision under *TA 1988, s 60(5)* is ordered, one of two things must, in the ordinary course, happen:

(*a*) If the new date is later in the income tax year than the old, the profits of some period will not come into assessment at all.

(*b*) If the new date is earlier in the income tax year than the old, the profits of some period will come into assessment twice.

If the profits of the period omitted were relatively low, or the profits of the period coming in twice were relatively high, the Revenue would gain: conversely, if the profits of the period omitted were relatively high, or the profits coming in twice were relatively low, the taxpayer would gain. The Board attempt to secure that the profits to be assessed twice, or to be omitted from assessment, as the case may be, are 'average' profits. As a rule this object can be secured neither by straightforward revision nor by non-revision, but only by taking for the year to which *TA 1988, s 60(5)* applies some figure intermediate between the revised and unrevised figures, and it is the Board's normal practice to propose, subject to the concurrence of the Commissioners of Income Tax having jurisdiction in the particular case, the adoption of such an intermediate figure. That intermediate figure is computed by reference to a consideration of:

(i) the profits of all the accounting periods of which any part enters into either the basis year (or, in some cases, years) under *TA 1988, s 60(4)* or the 'corresponding period' under *TA 1988, s 60(5)* (referred to subsequently as the 'relevant accounting periods'), and

(ii) the number of years for which the assessments are based in whole or in part on any of the profits of the 'relevant accounting periods' are expanded or reduced on a time basis so as to give a proportionate figure (referred to subsequently as the 'aggregate profit') for the 'relevant years', and the assessment for the year to which *TA 1988, s 60(5)* applies is adjusted, up or down as the case may be, so that the total of the assessments for all the 'relevant years' is precisely equal to the 'aggregate profit'.

The working of this practice can best be illustrated by an example – see *Example 1*.

Right of appeal

6. It is open to the taxpayer, if he does not accept the Board's proposal to appeal to the General or Special Commissioners against any direction by the Board that may be made under *TA 1988, s 60(5)* or against a decision not to issue a direction, and the Commissioners are empowered on appeal to give such relief, if any, as is just. The Board's proposal represents the solution which they consider would be likely to commend itself to the Commissioners and where it is accepted there is in effect an agreed recommendation as to what is thought to be just.

Special cases

7. The practice outlined above is suitable for the majority of cases. There are, however, certain classes of case which are incapable of solution along these lines for which modifications are necessary, e.g.:

(*a*) cases where the 'aggregate profit' is not intermediate between the sum of the assessments for the 'relevant years' without revision under *TA 1988, s 60(5)* and the sum of the assessments for those years after revision under that section;

(*b*) cases where there is a marked seasonal fluctuation in the rate of profit (e.g. in the case of the seaside hotel);

(*c*) cases where in some or all of the periods concerned losses were incurred;

(*d*) cases where any one of the years concerned is affected by the commencement or cessation provisions.

The modifications that are introduced to deal with these special types of case cannot be described in detail within the limits of this leaflet, but the general method followed throughout is that of equating the average rate of assessments over the years affected to the average rate of profits in the accounting periods that form the basis of those assessments. In cases falling within head (*a*) it may be necessary in order to secure this result to depart from the general rule mentioned in paragraph 3 and to determine a basis year under *TA 1988, s 60(4)* which, when regard is had to the profits of that year and existing assessments, will enable effect to be given to the 'average' adjustment. Again in cases falling within head (*b*) it may be necessary to modify the 'average' adjustment so that the assessments reflect a true annual rate of profit and not a rate that is inflated or depressed by seasonal results.

Small differences

8. Where the 'average' computation brings out an 'aggregate profit' which exceeds, or falls short of, the sum of the unrevised assessment for the preceding year and the assessments for the other 'relevant years' by a relatively small amount, it is not the Board's normal practice to take any action by way of 'average' adjustment. For this purpose, the Board would normally regard as relatively small a difference that was less than 10 per cent of the average of the current and preceding years' assessments and also less than £1,000 – see *Example 2*.

Example 1: Normal practice – paragraphs 3–5

The accounts of a business have been made up annually to 30 September for years up to and including 30 September 1991. The next account is for the nine months to 30 June 1992, and it is intended that subsequent accounts will be made up annually to 30 June.

The trading profits are as follows:

	£
12 months to 30 September 1990	36,000
12 months to 30 September 1991	18,000
9 months to 30 June 1992	12,000
33	66,000

The 1992–93 assessment has been made on £18,000, the profit of the year to 30 September 1991.
The 1993–94 assessment based on the year to 30 June 1992, under *TA 1988, s 60(4)* will be

	£
(3/12) × £18,000	4,500
	12,000
	16,500

The following review is made to see whether the 1992–93 assessment of £18,000 should be revised.

(i) *'Aggregate profit'*
The profit for the 'relevant accounting periods' is £66,000 for the 33 months to 30 June 1992.
The relevant years are 1991–92, 1992–93 and 1993–94, a period of 36 months.
The aggregate profit is therefore the profit for 36 months at the rate of £66,000 for 33 months, i.e.
(36/33) × £66,000 = £72,000

(ii) *Sum of assessments for 'relevant years' without revision under s 115(3).*

	'Relevant Years'	*Assessments* £
	1991–92	36,000
	1992–93	18,000
	1993–94	16,500
Sum of assessments for 'relevant years'		70,500

Since the difference between (i) £72,000 and (ii) £70,500 is greater than £1,000 (see paragraph 8) the calculation proceeds as follows:

(iii) *Sum of assessments for 'relevant years' after revision under TA 1988, s 60(5).*

'Relevant years'		*Assessments*
		£
1991–92		36,000
1992–93	(3/12) × £36,000 = £9,000	
	(9/12) × £18,000 = £13,500	22,500
1993–94		16,500
Sum of assessments for 'relevant years'		75,000

The figure at (i) £72,000 is intermediate between (ii) £70,500 and (iii) £75,000. The assessment for 1992–93 is therefore revised to such an amount that the total of the assessments for the relevant years equal the figure at (i) as follows:

		£
Figure at (i)		72,000
Assessed 1991–92	£36,000	
Assessed 1993–94	£16,500	52,500
Balance to be assessed for 1992–93		19,500

The assessment for 1992–93 is therefore revised to £19,500 by means of a further assessment of £1,500 (£19,500–£18,000).

Example 2: Small difference – paragraph 8

The accounts of a business have been made up annually to 31 March for years up to and including 31 March 1991. The next account is for the 18 months to 30 September 1992, and it is intended that subsequent accounts will be made up annually to 30 September.

The trading profits are as follows:	£
12 months to 31 March 1990	2,400
12 months to 31 March 1991	3,000
18 months to 30 September 1992	6,000
42	11,400

The 1991–92 assessment has been made on £3,000, the profit of the year to 31 March 1991.

The basis of assessment for each of the years 1992–93 and 1993–94 requires to be determined under *TA 1988, s 60(4)*. In accordance with paragraph 3 the years to 30 September 1991, and 30 September 1992, will be taken as the basis years and the assessments will be

		£
1992–93	(6/12) × £3,000 =	1,500
	(6/18) × £6,000 =	2,000
		3,500
1993–94	(12/18) × £6,000 =	4,000

The following review is made to see whether the 1991–92 assessment of £3,000 should be revised.

(i) *'Aggregate profit'*
The profit for the relevant accounting periods is £11,400 for the 42 months to 30 September 1992.
The relevant years are 1990–91, 1991–92, 1992–93 and 1993–94 a period of 48 months.
The aggregate profit is therefore the profit for 48 months at the rate of £11,400 for 42 months, i.e.
(48/42) × £11,400 = £13,028

(ii) *Sum of assessments for 'relevant years' without revision under TA 1988, s 60(5)*

	'Relevant Years'	Assessments £
	1990–91	2,400
	1991–92	3,000
	1992–93	3,500
	1993–94	4,000
Sum of assessments for 'relevant years'		12,900

The difference between (i) £13,028 and (ii) £12,900 is £128. This is less than £1,000 and 10 per cent of mean of £3,500 for 1992–93 and £3,000 for 1991–92 i.e. 10 per cent of ½ of (£3,500 + £3,000) = £325.

The case accordingly falls within paragraph 8 and no action is therefore necessary under *TA 1988, s 60(5)*.

Appendix E

Effect of New Rules on Partnership Agreements

Removal of joint and several liability

A fundamental change is that partnerships will not be assessed jointly in the partnership name [substituted *TA 1988, s 111*]. Rather, each partner will be separately assessable. The consequences for partnerships and partnership agreements can be summarised as follows.

(*a*) There will no longer be a requirement for tax reserves to be made with a view to protecting the partners as a body. In this regard, it has been usual for a provision in partnership agreements that profits are not to be drawn out unless and until there is a surplus available after providing for all amounts of tax which it is anticipated may become payable. Nevertheless, a retention may still be thought desirable, as a means of forced saving to ensure that each partner can discharge his tax liabilities in due course, and does not cause embarrassment to his fellow partners.

(*b*) There will be no need for a partner to indemnify the other partners jointly and severally for his proportion of any tax payable by the partnership.

(*c*) Since tax will no longer be a partnership debt, on the retirement of a partner any provision that the continuing partners will take over all the partnership liabilities will not extend to any tax liability of the retiring partner.

Financial reporting and partnership returns

With the new filing deadlines under self-assessment, namely 30 September for assessment by the Revenue and 31 January for self-assessment, it will be necessary for each partner to be in receipt of the appropriate financial information to enable him to file his own return on a timely basis. The legislation also imposes upon the partnership certain reporting requirements relating to the partnership return and the partnership statement. These will also need to be complied with to avoid penalties (see 16.38 *et seq.*).

Various points arise in connection with the drafting of the partnership agreement.

(*a*) A fairly standard clause in a partnership agreement requires a partnership accountant to prepare accounts for the firm for the financial year. It will be advisable for such clause specifically to provide that the accounts are prepared well before the 30 September initial deadline for Revenue assessment.

(*b*) The partnership agreement should likewise provide for the preparation of the partnership return and the partnership statement in the form required by *TMA 1970, s 12AA* and *12AB*, also well before 30 September if possible. Otherwise, if these are only made available to the partners and filed shortly before the 31 January second deadline, each partner will be forced to self-assess. Provision should be made in the partnership agreement for the filing of such return and partnership statement in any event by the 31 January deadline (see 16.45).

(*c*) There should be further provision in the partnership agreement to ensure that any requisite claims for relief are made, a number of which have to be included in the partnership return (see 17.11).

These latter aspects are perhaps most appropriately dealt with under a separate clause relating to the precedent partner, dealt with below.

Record-keeping

It is again a usual term of a partnership agreement that proper books of account are kept by the partnership, showing all receipts and payments on behalf of the firm. But now that *TMA 1970, s 12B* contains specific provisions relating to data retention by businesses, both as regards the precise data to be retained and the period for keeping records, it would be advisable as an *aide-mémoire* for the relevant book and record-keeping provisions in the partnership agreement to mirror the requirements of *section 12B* (see 16.38 *et seq.*). There should also be provision for keeping records of acquisitions and disposals of partnerships assets, this being a specific requirement of *TMA 1970, s 12AA(7)* (see 16.43).

The relevant clause might take the following form:

> 'Proper books of accounts and records shall be kept of all matters transactions and things that are usually entered in such accounts by those engaged in a business similar to the partnership business (including details of acquisitions and disposals of chargeable assets) and such accounts together with all letters, bills, vouchers, papers and other documents relating to the partnership business (including for the avoidance of doubt all such records as are specified in *TMA 1970, s 12B*) shall be kept in a place agreed upon the partners for at least [6] years and shall be open at all times to inspection by any of the partners.'

Change of partners

On a change of partners there will no longer be a cessation, subject to the possibility of making a continuation election. Instead, provided that there is at least one person engaged in the trade, profession or vocation after the change, there is an automatic continuation. Accordingly:

(*a*) There will be no necessity for the usual provision whereby an outgoing partner is required to join with the continuing partners or any new partner in making the continuation election.

(*b*) There will likewise be no necessity for any indemnity to be given to the outgoing partner or his estate in respect of any additional tax which he would not have suffered if he had not joined in such continuation election.

Precedent partner

Given the obligations imposed upon the partnership as a body, and in default on individual partners, to supply the Revenue with information, it would be advisable for the partnership agreement to provide for the appointment of a precedent partner who had the specific authority and obligation to deal with the making of the partnership return and partnership statement.

A clause on the following lines might be appropriate:

(i) The partners shall [on or before . . . [date] and in every subsequent [third] year] elect one of their number to be the precedent partner of the firm for the purposes of the provisions of the *Taxes Management Act 1970* ('TMA') to take office on [1 January] of the following year for the term of [three] years.

(ii) If during his term of office the precedent partner shall resign his appointment by notice in writing to the other partners or be removed from office then the other partners shall as soon as possible after any such event elect a successor who shall immediately take office for the remainder of the term of office of the partner who has been replaced.

(iii) The precedent partner shall ensure that the partnership return and statement is prepared and that a copy thereof is delivered to each partner by [31 August] in any financial year and is duly filed with the Inland Revenue in accordance with *TMA 1970, ss 12AA* and *12AB* and the precedent partner will further ensure that all claims for relief required by *TMA 1970, s 42(6)* and all such other matters as are appropriate to such return are included in the return.

Appendix E

Equitable adjustments

Most partnership agreements are silent about the imbalance that can arise under the existing preceding year system as a result of the tax for a year of assessment being calculated by reference to profits of the preceding year, but allocated in accordance with the profit-sharing arrangements of the current year. However, sometimes there are equitable adjustment clauses. These will generally no longer be required under self-assessment. One exception perhaps is where there are prior salaries to certain partners which exceed the profits of the period (see *Example 2* in 12.10).

A clause on the following lines might be appropriate to cover such a possibility:

(i) [Name] shall [in addition to the share of profits to which he is entitled under Clause . . .] be paid by way of salary as a prior charge the sum of £. . . per annum which shall be treated as an expense of the partnership in computing the partnership profits.

(ii) In the event that the payment of the said salary results in any of the other partners incurring a loss for the financial year which in computing the income of [name] for tax purposes results in a corresponding reduction in his taxable income, an amount equal to the consequent reduction in his tax liability shall be paid by [name] to the other partner or partners pro-rata to their profit-sharing ratio.

Appendix F

Tax Bulletin: main articles on self-assessment

The information published in Tax Bulletin is reported because it may be of interest to tax practitioners. You can expect that interpretations of the law contained in the Bulletin will normally be applied in relevant cases, but this is subject to a number of qualifications.

Particular cases may turn on their own facts, or context, and because every possible situation cannot be covered there may be circumstances in which the interpretation given here will not apply.

There may also be circumstances in which the Board would find it necessary to argue for a different interpretation in appeal proceedings.

'Revenue decisions' report conclusions that were reached on the facts of individual cases, but do not necessarily include all the detailed facts which may have been relevant to the decision. They provide an indication of the approach the Revenue has adopted in the past, but have not been drafted as generally applicable statements of the Revenue's position. It cannot be assumed therefore, that interpretations of the law contained or implicit in these decisions will necessarily be applied in other cases.

The Board's view of the law may change in the future. Readers will be notified of any changes in future editions.

Nothing in this Bulletin affects a taxpayer's right of appeal on any point.

To find out more, contact: Ms Nahid Shariff, Room 435, 22 Kingsway, London WC2B 6NR. Telephone 0171–438 7842.

To receive Tax Bulletin only (the subscription for 1996 is £20.00) send a cheque made payable to 'Inland Revenue' to: Inland Revenue, Finance Division, Barrington Road, Worthing, West Sussex, BN12 4XH.

Appendix F

Issue 10, February 1994

Page 111. Self-assessment and simplification of personal tax

GETTING UP TO DATE

. . .

TRANSITION TO THE CURRENT YEAR BASIS [2.42 *et seq.*]

This article explains how the transition from the 'preceding year' (PY) basis to the 'current year' (CY) basis will be achieved. It illustrates the positions where businesses cease in or near the transitional year; and where losses are incurred in the transitional basis period. It also covers the accelerated introduction of the 'current year' basis for businesses/ sources which commence on or after 6 April 1994, and introduces details of what the changes mean for partnerships. The latter topic will be developed in later articles. The article is based on the legislation contained in Finance Bill 1994, which is not due to receive Royal Assent until May 1994. Readers are advised that the validity of the comments made is subject to any amendments which may be made to this legislation during its passage through Parliament. In addition attention is drawn to paragraph 35 of the Press Release accompanying publication of the Finance Bill on 11 January, which refers to legislation to be brought forward in Finance Bill 1995 to deal with attempts to take unfair advantage of the transitional provisions.

Who will be affected by the transition?
All taxpayers who receive income taxed under Schedule D on the 'preceding year' basis may be affected, not just those taxed under Cases I and II. In general, where the preceding year basis applies for 1995–96, 1996–97 will be a 'transitional year', although cessation by 5 April 1999 may subsequently revise the basis period for that year.

What basis period will apply?
The basis period for 1996–97 *i.e.* the transitional basis period will be the 12 month average of the profits for the period between the end of the 1995–96 PY basis period and the start of the 1997–98 CY basis period. If there is no change of accounting date this simply means half the profits for the 2 years to the accounting date in 1996–97. Where the accounting date is changed so that the period to be averaged is not 24 months, this simply changes the fraction to be applied to the profits of the period. For other sources of income, assessed on the fiscal year basis, the period averaged will be from 6 April 1995 to 5 April 1997.

Note: in these examples 5 April and 31 March are treated as interchangeable. Taxpayers who make up accounts to either date should be regarded as on the fiscal year basis.

EXAMPLE 1
In a long-standing business accounts are made up to 30 June annually. Basis periods will be as follows:

1995–96 Year ended 30 June 1994
1996–97 12/24 × 2 years ended 30 June 1996
1997–98 Year ended 30 June 1997.

EXAMPLE 2

The same business changes its accounting date to 30 September during 1996.

1995–96 As before
1996–97 12/27 × period 1 July 1994 to 30 September 1996
1997–98 Year ended 30 September 1997.

Cessations in 1996–97

Where the business ceases in 1996–97, the existing rules will continue to apply.

EXAMPLE 3

A long standing business, making up accounts annually to 30 June, ceases trading on 30 June 1996. Basis periods will be as follows:

1994–95 Year ended 30 June 1993
1995–96 Year ended 30 June 1994
1996–97 Period from 6 April 1996 to 30 June 1996.

It will be possible for 1994–95 and 1995–96 to be adjusted to actual basis under TA 1988, s. 63.

Cessations in 1997–98 or 1998–99

Where the business ceases in 1997–98 or 1998–99, the basis period for 1996–97 (and, for cessations in 1997–98, 1995–96 also) may be adjusted to the actual basis.

EXAMPLE 4

As in Example 3, but the business ceases trading on 30 April 1997.

1995–96 Year ended 30 June 1994
1996–97 12/24 × 2 years to 30 June 1996
1997–98 Period from 1 July 1996 to cessation on 30 April 1997. (Transitional relief relating to the period 1 July 1996 to 5 April 1997 will be given here. Transitional relief is covered later in this article.)

Here the Revenue will have a right, akin to the existing s. 63 provision, to direct that the new rules be disapplied if the old rules would lead to higher aggregate profits being charged to tax for 1995–96 and 1996–97. 1997–98 will be unaffected by this direction. [*Note*. This is incorrect, see 2.50.]

EXAMPLE 5

As before but the business ceases trading on 30 April 1998.

1996–97 12/24 × 2 years ended 30 June 1996
1997–98 Year ended 30 June 1997
1998–99 Period 1 July 1997 to 30 April 1998. (Transitional relief due here exactly as for 1997–98 in Example 4)

Here the Revenue's right to make a direction disapplying the new rules extends only to 1996–97 if the old rules would result in a higher assessment for that year. [*Note*. This is incorrect, see 2.51.]

Other situations

It may be that although a business or source began before 6 April 1994, it is not assessed on a PY basis for 1995–96. This could be because:

- an election has been made under TA 1988, s. 62 (2) or (4) for the income to be assessed for 1995–96 on an actual basis; or
- after a partnership change the first 4 years of assessment of the new partnership (including 1995–96) are on the actual basis under TA 1988, s. 61 (4).

In these cases the basis period for 1996–97 will be the 12 months to 5 April 1997.

EXAMPLE 6

A business commences on 1 May 1993 making up accounts annually to 30 April. It makes an election under s. 62 (2) during 1996–97. The basis periods are:

1993–94 Period 1 May 1993 to 5 April 1994
1994–95 Year ended 5 April 1995
1995–96 Year ended 5 April 1996
1996–97 Year ended 5 April 1997
1997–98 Year ended 30 April 1997. (Again, transitional relief will be due in respect of the period from 1 May 1996 to 5 April 1997 – see below.)

A similar situation arises in relation to income under Case III, IV or V where an election has been made under s. 66 (1) (c) so that income is assessed for 1995–96 on the actual basis. The basis period for 1996–97 will simply be the fiscal year.

Transitional relief

The existing commencement rules for Schedule D income involves taking certain periods into account more than once for the purposes of determining amounts to be taxed in early years. For sources taxed by reference to a fiscal year and for businesses adopting 5 April as an accounting date the period is one year, counted twice exactly. For businesses using a different accounting date the period will be one year, counted between two and three times. The nearer the date is to 6 April, the larger the factor.

EXAMPLE 7

A new business commences on 1 October 1992, making up first accounts to 30 September 1993. The basis periods are:

1992–93 1 October 1992 to 5 April 1993
1993–94 1 October 1992 to 30 September 1993
1994–95 1 October 1992 to 30 September 1993

Here the first accounting period has been used twice fully as well as to the extent of 6 months in the first year. If the first accounting period had run from 1 July to 30 June, it would have been counted twice fully plus 9 months in the first year.

EXAMPLE 8
The business in Example 7 ceases on 30 September 1999:

Year	*Basis Period*	*Period of trading*	*Period taxed*
1992–93	1 October 1992–5 April 1993		6 months
1993–94	1 October 1992–30 September 1993	12 months	12 months
1994–95	1 October 1992–30 September 1993		12 months
1995–96	1 October 1993–30 September 1994	12 months	12 months
1996–97	1 October 1994–30 September 1996 × 12/24	24 months	12 months
Subtotal		*48 months*	*54 months*
1997–98	1 October 1996–30 September 1997	12 months	12 months
1998–99	1 October 1997–30 September 1998	12 months	12 months
1999–00	1 October 1998–30 September 1999	12 months	12 months
Total		*84 months*	*90 months*
Relief		*6 months*	*84 months*

This double counting is usually unwound on cessation, where the basis period rules ensure that the periods taxed exactly match the period of trading. But for businesses continuing through the transition to the new system, these cessation provisions no longer exist. By taking two years' results to make one year's tax assessment in the transitional year part of this unwinding is achieved. But the number of months assessed would still exceed the months traded by the extent to which the accounting period ending in 1996–97 precedes 5 April 1997. This manifests itself in the basis period for the first CY year of assessment. Where 5 April accounting is not used, part of the basis period for 1997–98 will relate to pre-CY times. Relief is to be given equal to the amount of profits attributable to the period falling before CY but also forming part of the first basis period under CY. This relief will also complete the unwinding made necessary by the PY commencement provisions. (See Example 8.)

This relief is utilisable against:

(*a*) years where a change of accounting date results in a period longer than 12 months being assessed – here the relief given is proportionate to the extension over 12 months; *i.e.* if the relief represents 6 months, and the accounting period is later extended from 30 September to 31 December, so that the basis period is 15 months long, relief of 3/6ths of the total relief is due; otherwise,

(*b*) the year of cessation.

Losses

The rules shown above apply where the business makes profits. Losses incurred during the transitional basis period will be relievable in full. Where more than one period of account is prepared for the transitional basis period, one of which shows a loss, while the other shows a profit, the loss will be counted as NIL for the purposes of working out the assessable amount for 1996–97 (though the entire length of the basis period will be taken into account in the fraction applied to the profit figure).

EXAMPLE 9
Basis period for 1996–97 is 1 July 1994 to 30 June 1996.
Results are:

- year ending 30 June 1995
  Profit £20,000;
- year ending 30 June 1996
  Loss (£30,000).

The assessment for 1996–97 will be: £20,000 × 12/24 = £10,000.

Loss relief will be available by reference to the current rules.

New businesses/sources
Where businesses commence or sources of income first arise after 5 April 1994, there will be no transition, instead the current year basis will apply immediately. In situations where an unchanging accounting date is adopted this means that the first year will be taxed on profits to 5 April, and each subsequent year will be taxed on profits in accounts ending in the year of assessment. It will be observed that this is simplest where the accounting date chosen is 5 April, *i.e.* it matches the tax year. Where a different date is chosen and is not changed, part or all of the first year's basis period may also enter into the second year's basis period. Without more, this would disturb the principle that profits taxed equal profits earned. So relief, called 'overlap relief' will be available to restore the situation. It will be allowed in the same manner as transitional relief. Overlap relief can also arise as a result of some changes of accounting date – these will be the subject of a separate article.

Partnerships
The new system will involve major changes to the way partnerships are taxed. The basic change is that whereas currently partnership profits are assessed on and collected from the partnerships themselves, under the new system each partner will be responsible for tax on his or her own share of the partnership profits. Partners will have their own basis periods, just as if they were sole traders carrying on a business, the profits of which equated to the partner's share of partnership profits. And those shares will be allocated on the basis of the profit sharing ratios in the basis period rather than in the fiscal year.

This means that when a new partner joins a partnership the first assessment will not be based on profits earned before he or she joined. It also means that each partner will have an individual entitlement to transitional or overlap relief which can be given when that partner leaves the partnership regardless of whether the partnership continues or not. (See Example 10.)

Another change refers to the consequences of a partnership change. Currently any change in the composition of a partnership is treated as a cessation of one business immediately followed by commencement of a new one, unless an election for continuation treatment is submitted under TA 1988, s. 113 (2). This procedure will be amended in respect of changes on or after 6 April 1997, when continuation treatment will be standard without the need for an election. Where there is a change in partnership composition between 6 April 1994 and 5 April 1997, if no election is submitted, a new business is still treated as having commenced immediately after the change. But the CY basis period rules as outlined in the previous section will apply straight away to the new business.

EXAMPLE 10
On 1 May 1999, A joins an established partnership, formerly run only by B and C, which makes up its accounts to 30 June each year. B and C both have 9 months transitional relief available. C leaves the partnership on 30 April 2002. Basis periods will be as follows:

Year	*A*	*B*	*C*
1997–98	N/A	y/e 30 June 1997	y/e 30 June 1997
1998–99	N/A	y/e 30 June 1998	y/e 30 June 1998
1999–2000	period 1 May 1999 to 5 April 2000	y/e 30 June 1999	y/e 30 June 1999
2000–01	y/e 30 June 2000[1]	y/e 30 June 2000	y/e 30 June 2000
2001–02	y/e 30 June 2001	y/e 30 June 2001	y/e 30 June 2001
2002–03	y/e 30 June 2002	y/e 30 June 2002	period 1 July 2001 to 30 April 2002 (less transitional relief)[2]

[1] Of the 11 months assessed in 1992–2000, 9 months are also assessed in 2000–01, and these become available for later overlap relief.

[2] Transitional relief is due in respect of the period 1 July 1996 to 5 April 1997 *i.e.* 9 months. When C leaves the partnership, this is given against his profits for 2002–03. The relief due to B is still stored up for future utilisation.

NEW STYLE RETURN FORM

The return form is perhaps the single most important element of a self-assessment system. We announced in a Press Release dated 30 November 1993 that we would be consulting on the design of the new tax return. This article summarises the work done so far, and our plans for future consultation.

We estimate that in April 1997, or shortly thereafter, about 9 million people, half of whom are professionally represented, will be sent a return form. They are the 4 million or so taxpayers whose main source of income is from self-employment or investments, and around 5 million directors, employees and pensioners.

It is of course important that the return form should be so designed that taxpayers can fill it in accurately without necessarily having to seek help from the Inland Revenue or from professional advisers. This is equally the case whether they wish to file their return by 30 September so that the assessment can be calculated by the Inland Revenue or to file it by

31 January along with their own calculation. So we want to make the return form as clear as possible in order to help taxpayers to fill it in correctly first time.

If most taxpayers find the return easy to complete accurately, this will help us to target assistance towards those who need help and to speed up the processing of returns when we get them back. Good design of the return form should help us to provide good customer service.

We have already begun work on designing first drafts of what the return could look like. We approached the task by looking at how other countries with self-assessment systems design their returns – there are wide variations – and by re-examining our own approach in the light of the research which we undertook before and after last year's forms were introduced.

Because of the importance of the return form, we intend to have the fullest possible consultations with interested parties on its development. We have more than two years within which to consult before the form needs to be signed off for production.

In this first period of development we have consulted tax professionals, people in business and a small focus group of taxpayers, staff and agents. This first round of consultations has been an extremely useful sounding board for the different ways in which the form could be designed.

These consultations are now at an end and we hope to have evaluated the comments by the end of March. It is our intention thereafter to have wider consultations.

Taxpayers will be able, if they wish, to file their return forms electronically rather than on paper. We plan during 1994 to run a trial of electronic filing for the corporation tax return form. At the same time we shall discuss our proposals with accountants and software houses.

At this stage, no decisions have been taken about the design of the return. This remains wide open. We shall be interested in hearing other ideas of how different models of the return might best suit the needs of taxpayers as well as those of the Inland Revenue.

Anyone who wishes to comment is invited to write to: Tom Hudson, Room 650, South West Wing, Bush House, Strand, London WC2B 4RD.

Issue 11, May 1994

Page 124. Self-assessment

PARTNERSHIPS AND THE CURRENT YEAR BASIS OF ASSESSMENT

The main changes introduced in the Finance Act 1994 will apply to partners just as they apply to other taxpayers who make returns. But there will also be some changes particular to partnerships. Issue 10 of *Tax Bulletin* touched briefly on how the change to the 'current year' (CY) basis of assessment will affect partnerships in the context of the computational rules for the transitional year. Apart from that, we have received a number of questions on how the new rules will apply in the less straightforward types of situation, and this article seeks to cover some of these areas.

New partnerships commencing after 5 April 1994

As with sole traders, where a new partnership commences after 5 April 1994, the CY basis rules apply immediately. These include personal basis periods and overlaps for each partner as well as the end of the option of continuation or cessation and commencement treatment on a change of partners. (See Example 1.) The continuation election option remains for any partnership that was in existence on 5 April 1994 but if the partners do not elect for continuation on any change after that date it becomes a new partnership from the date of that change.

EXAMPLE 1

On 1 July 1994 A and B go into business in partnership for the first time. Their annual accounting date is 30 June. On 1 October 1994, C joins. Basis periods etc. will be

Basis Period	*Partners A and B*	*Partner C*
1994–95	1 July 1994 to 5 April 1995	1 October 1994 to 5 April 1995
1995–96	1 July 1994 to 30 June 1995	1 October 1994 to 30 September 1995
1996–97	1 July 1995 to 30 June 1996	1 July 1995 to 30 June 1996
Overlap profit	9 months	9 months
(for later relief)	–1 July 1994 to 5 April 1995	–1 October 1994 to 5 April 1995 plus 1 July 1995 to 30 September 1995

Assuming the business does not as a question of fact cease, the computation of partnership profits and the basis periods of A and B are not affected by the arrival of a new partner. There is no question, for tax purposes, of the partnership ceasing or commencing just because there is a change in partners.

Continuation treatment where the partnership existed at 5 April 1994

EXAMPLE 2

If, in Example 1, the business had been carried on by A, B and D since 1988 (say) and D leaves on 30 June 1994 the position is slightly different in that a continuation election is still competent. If one is submitted:

- all the existing rules continue to apply, so the CY basis of assessment does not come into immediate effect; and
- a further continuation election is competent when C joins the partnership on 1 October 1994 and, assuming one is made on that occasion, on any subsequent partnership change up to 5 April 1997. If one is made then, or in respect of any change in partnership composition short of total cessation of the business, the 'preceding year' (PY) basis and transitional year basis period rules will apply just as for sole traders; and
- joint liability for the partnership tax will also continue up to and including 1996–97.

But if, at either of the changes in Example 2, a valid continuation election is not made:

- there is a deemed cessation and recommencement;
- the old style cessation rules will apply to the ceasing partnership;
- the CY basis will apply immediately to the new partnership (as in Example 1 – TA 1988, s.61(4), being 'old' rules, is overridden); and
- the new partnership will continue for tax purposes until the business ceases in fact, notwithstanding any subsequent changes in composition.

Clearly therefore it will be important to give early attention to the question of whether or not to submit a continuation election in respect of partnership changes during 1994–95, 1995–96 and 1996–97.

Partners joining 'continuing' partnerships between 6 April 1994 and 5 April 1997

A mechanism is needed to work out the personal basis period for 1997–98 of a partner who joins a continuing partnership during the three years ended 5 April 1997. This is straightforward in most cases because the same pattern is followed as for a sole trade which has the same start and cessation dates as the partnership. In most cases a partner's first CY basis period will be the same as the partnership's 12 month accounting period ending in 1997–98.

But where partners newly join in 1996–97 they may not have been in the partnership for as long as 12 months by the firm's accounting date in 1997–98. 1996–97 will be assessed on the partnership on its transitional basis period. For 1997–98 it is necessary to look at the notional trade which will determine the partner's basis periods after 1997–98 and ask what the basis periods of that trade would have been *if it had* been put straight on to the CY basis from the time the partner joined the partnership.

EXAMPLE 3

Partnership PQ has been running for many years accounting to 30 April annually. On 1 October 1996, R joins the partnership. This has the following consequences:

1996–97 1 May 1994 to 30 April 1996 × 12/24 – partnership assessment.
1997–98 1 May 1996 to 30 April 1997 – basis period for both P and Q.

In addition they will later be due transitional relief in respect of the profits for the period 1 May 1996 to 5 April 1997.

1997–98 R is treated as if his notional trade had begun on 1 October 1996. If it had, the basis periods under the new rules would be:

1996–97 1 October 1996 to 5 April 1997
1997–98 1 October 1996 to 30 September 1997
1998–99 1 May 1997 to 30 April 1998

For 1997–98 and 1998–99 these are also the actual basis periods for R. For 1996–97 the real basis period was the transitional basis period. That does not change. R's share of the partnership profits assessed for that year would be determined in the normal way as his allocation of profits on the fiscal year basis to 5 April 1997. But it is necessary to determine the notional basis period for 1996–97 so that the basis periods for later years can be properly calculated, and in particular that a full 12 months can be assessed for the second year.

The precise amount of profit potentially available as transitional and overlap relief also needs to be calculated. In this example, the period from 1 October 1996 to 5 April 1997 will be subject to transitional relief, and that from 1 May 1997 to 30 September 1997 to overlap relief. Although the mechanics of computation and method of giving effect to transitional and overlap relief are identical, the distinction is important because transitional relief is subject to the proposed anti-avoidance provisions announced in the Press Release of 31 March 1994.

EXAMPLE 4
If, in Example 3, partner R had joined one year earlier on 1 October 1995, the outcome would be the same for the 1996–97 transitional basis period on the partnership. The notional details for R personally are:

1995–96 1 October 1995 to 5 April 1996
1996–97 1 October 1995 to 30 September 1996
1997–98 1 May 1996 to 30 April 1997 (Transitional relief 1 May 1996–5 April 1997)

The notional periods for 1995–96 and 1996–97 are ignored as those years were assessed on the partnership. But for 1997–98 the notional basis period becomes the actual basis period.

Partnership cessations during 1997–98 and 1998–99
The article in Issue 10 of *Tax Bulletin* described the 'direction' which can be issued by the Revenue in respect of 1995–96 and 1996–97 where the business ceases in the year ended 5 April 1998 (or 1996–97 only for cessations in the year ended 5 April 1999). Such a direction will only be possible where the business fully ceases, *i.e.* the business ceases to exist, or the business continues but there is a complete change in the persons carrying it on.

EXAMPLE 5
Partnership WXYZ has been in business for many years with results for the most recent periods as follows:

Year ended 30 April 1994	£100,000
Year ended 30 April 1995	£120,000
Year ended 30 April 1996	£150,000
Year ended 30 April 1997	£180,000
Period ended 31 October 1997	£75,000

On 31 October 1997 the business closed down. Original assessments would be:

1995–96 £100,000 (Preceding year basis to 30 April 1994)
1996–97 £135,000 (Average of two years to 30 April 1996)
1997–98 £180,000 (CY) (£165,000 transitional relief arises in respect of the period from 1 May 1996 to 5 April 1997).

On cessation:

1997–98		£180,000
		75,000
		255,000
less transitional relief		*165,000*
		(£90,000)
1996–97		
Actual	£180,000 × 11/12 =	£165,000
	£150,000 × 1/12 =	12,500
		£177,500
1995–96		
Actual	£150,000 × 11/12 =	£137,500
	£120,000 × 1/12 =	10,000
		£147,000

£147,500		£100,000
177,500		135,000
£325,000	*is greater than*	£235,000

so a direction can be issued to apply the old computational rules throughout. Practically, this means revising 1995–96 and 1996–97 assessments to the fiscal year basis.

EXAMPLE 6

The figures are the same except that cessation takes place one year later and closing results are:

Year ended 30 April 1998	£150,000
Period ended 31 October 1998	£80,000

Assessments would be:

1996–97 £135,000 (averaged under the transitional rules, as in Example 5)
1997–98 £180,000 (as in Example 5)
1998–99 £230,000 (the basis period for all partners is 1 May 1997 to 31 October 1998, thus £150,000 plus £80,000)
less *£165,000 transitional relief*

Because of the cessation in 1998–99 the amount assessed for 1996–97 is reviewed. As above, actual earnings in that year are £177,500.

As this sum is greater than the amount assessed (£135,000) a direction can be issued to increase the assessment.

Contrast with Example 5 – for a cessation in 1997–98 both 1995–96 and 1996–97 are reviewable in the normal way. But the 1998–99 cessation does not open up 1997–98 for review because the CY basis operates for that year. The above example is of course equally applicable to individual taxpayers. Where a partner leaves in the two years to 5 April 1999 but the partnership continues, no adjustments to 1995–96 or 1996–97 are made either to the partnership or the retiring partner. (See Example 7.)

EXAMPLE 7

A long-standing partnership ABCDE accounts annually to 30 April. Partner E leaves on 31 December 1997. The basis periods and assessments are as follows.

Taxpayer	*1996–97*	*1997–98*	*Transitional/Overlap Profits*
Partnership	1 May 1994 to 30 April 1996 × 12/24	None	None
A,B,C and D (individually)	None	1 May 1996 to 30 April 1997	1 May 1996 to 5 April 1997
E	None	1 May 1996 to 31 December 1997 (less transitional relief)	1 May 1996 to 5 April 1997 – *given immediately**

* Effectively tax is due for 1997–98 on the profits from 6 April 1997 to 31 December 1997. This of course is just as it would be at present.

Subsidiary income

Many partnerships also receive income which is not trading or professional income, *e.g.* interest on bank deposits. The strict position presently is that such income is removed from the partnership accounts and assessed on the partners separately under, *e.g.* Case III on a fiscal PY basis. Treating the income separately from other income, and by reference to different basis periods, overlooks the underlying reality, that the income belongs to the partnership. In practice it is in fact often aggregated with the mainstream income. The new system will reflect that reality. Thus, for trading and professional partnerships only, the same basis period rules will apply to partnership Case III to VI income and Schedule A income as apply to trading or professional income.

This will be straightforward once the new rules are firmly established. But it does have implications for the transition and for new partners. Example 8 shows how the new rules apply in the same way on joining a partnership as for trading or professional income, as well as confirming how this change fits with transitional relief.

EXAMPLE 8

A long-running professional partnership, LM, makes up accounts to 30 April each year. It also receives bank interest (untaxed) on partnership funds. A new partner, N, joins on 1 May 1997.

Basis periods will be:

1996–97 (Interest arising in the 2 years to 5 April 1997) ÷ 2 ('old' rules apply)

1997–98 For L and M, the year to 30 April 1997.

Transitional relief arises for the period 1 May 1996 to 5 April 1997.

N's assessment will relate to the basis period 1 May 1997 to 5 April 1998.

1998–99 Interest arising in the year to 30 April 1998.

This applies to the new partner as well. Overlap profit arises to him for the period 1 May 1997 to 5 April 1998.

Future articles

It is planned in coming editions of *Tax Bulletin* to illustrate, amongst other things, how the new filing/payment and Revenue enquiry rules will affect partnerships, as well as covering the administrative (as opposed to computational) transitional arrangements.

Issue 12, August 1994

Page 146. Self assessment: new procedures for taxing partnerships

FA 1994 introduced new rules which change the way partnerships are taxed. Previous Tax Bulletin articles have dealt with the computational aspects of the changes. In this article we outline the administrative framework which will apply generally from 1996–97. We also explain the slightly different position for 1994–95 and 1995–96 for partnerships which commence or are deemed to commence in those years.

A technical guide to the new computation rules – The New Current Year Basis of Assessment (SAT 1) – has just been published. If you do not have a copy please contact your local tax office. Details of the changes made by FA 1994 to the Taxes Management Act will be given in a technical guide (SAT 2) to be published and distributed to practitioners shortly.

1996–97 and later years

Under the new self assessment provisions each partner will be required to self assess his or her total income. This means that partners will have to include their share of the partnership's profits in their total income. Composite Case I and II partnership assessments will not be made after 1996–97. For 1996–97 only, partners will be separately assessable on their share of partnership profits but, for partnerships in existence at 5 April 1994 a composite partnership assessment may also be made.

One reason for this is to deal with payments on account for 1996–97. For individuals these payments on account ('interim payments') will be based on their tax situation for the previous year. But partners have no such situation for the previous year, except in relation to non-partnership income because partnership profits were assessed on the partnership. So payments on account for partnerships will be put in place by way of assessment, estimated if necessary, with the 'old' rights of appeal. Any tax due is paid by the partnership.

When the partner comes to self assess for 1996–97 his or her share of the partnership income will be included and the overall tax liability computed will include tax on his or her share of transitional profits. But a credit will be due equal to the amount of tax already paid by the partnership in respect of that partner's share. In other words, the partner will be treated as if partnership profits were received under deduction of tax. This is not necessary for later years as the amount shown on the partner's self assessment for 1996–97, including tax on partnership income, will form the basis for the interim payments for 1997–98.

But dealing with partners separately would be unnecessarily cumbersome if each partner had to submit full accounts of the partnership in support of his or her return etc. So there are special rules in FA 1994 which mean that accounts, enquiries (and appeals where necessary), will be dealt with centrally. The partnership's 'representative partner' will have responsibility for filing the 'partnership statement'. The statement will contain full details of the partnership income and the allocation between the partners, as well as information to enable the return to be linked with each partner's tax record.

What is different about 1994–95 and 1995–96?

PARTNERSHIPS IN EXISTENCE AT 5 APRIL 1994

For a partnership which exists at 5 April 1994 and which has no changes in composition between 6 April 1994 and 5 April 1997 inclusive, nothing will change, and 1996–97 will be dealt with as above. Where there are changes in partnership composition, again nothing changes where the change generates a s. 113 (2) election. Composite Case I and II assessments for the years 1994–95 to 1996–97 are to be made on its trading and professional profits *up to the date of any change in membership for which a s. 113 (2) election could be but is not made.* For subsequent periods separate assessments are to be made on the individual partners.

Where, in a particular year of assessment, there is a change in membership and a continuation election is made a new partner is for tax purposes allocated a share of the partnership's assessable profit according to his entitlement in that fiscal year. This share is part of the composite assessment. *There is no question of the new partner being individually assessed under the new rules whilst the remaining partners continue to be assessed under the old (and transitional) rules.*

The old Taxes Management Act rules relating to the issue of partnership returns (TMA 1970, s. 9) and the handling of appeals will continue to apply to composite partnership assessments.

Appendix F

PARTNERSHIPS COMMENCING, OR DEEMED TO COMMENCE, ON OR AFTER 6 APRIL 1994

The new rules by which partners are to be separately assessed on their share of the partnership profits apply to partnership businesses which commence on or after 6 April 1994. They also apply to the period subsequent to a change in the membership of a partnership for which a s. 113 (2) election could be made but is not.

You will find examples of how these rules work in Tax Bulletin Issue 11 and the booklet SAT 1.

The new Taxes Management Act rules for partnership returns and partnership statements do not come into effect until 1996–97. There is no special legislative provision for dealing with returns for 'new' partnerships for 1994–95 and 1995–96, and this article describes how we propose in practice to deal with this situation.

The rest of this article refers only to partnership businesses which commence, or are deemed to commence, on or after 6 April 1994.

THE LEGAL POSITION

There are no special interest provisions to handle the change over from partnership to individual assessments in 1994–95 and 1995–96. If an estimated assessment is made on the wrong basis it may need to be discharged and new assessments made on the individual partners. As soon as the possibility emerges that a continuation election may not be made the inspector will consider whether to make assessments on the individual partners as alternatives to the partnership assessment.

PARTNERSHIP RETURNS

For these new partnerships the Taxes Acts provide no specific authority to require a partnership to make a return for 1994–95 and 1995–96. Existing TMA 1970, s. 9, provides for a return to be issued 'for the purposes of making assessment to income tax in the partnership name'. The new power to issue a partnership return (FA 1994, s.184) does not take effect until 1996–97 (FA 1994, s.199).

Because a partnership has two years after a partnership change to decide whether a continuation election is to be made, it will not be clear for some time after a change under which rules a partnership should be taxed.

We propose therefore to issue partnership returns to all partnerships, both old and new, for 1994–95 and 1995–96. Old partnerships will be required to complete the return but new partnerships will only be *requested* to do so. The return will contain guidance to partnerships enabling them to decide whether they are required or only requested to complete the return.

PERSONAL RETURNS

Although a new partnership cannot be required to complete a partnership return the Revenue will still be able to obtain details of a partnership's income. A personal return can be issued to each partner under s. 8 and we will, where necessary look to these as the statutory means of obtaining information about partnership income. The statutory position is that each partner is required to make a return of income for the purpose of making an assessment and this will include his share of the partnership profits.

ASSESSMENTS AND APPEALS

Each partner will have a personal assessment with an individual right of appeal. But it will be to the mutual advantage of the Revenue, taxpayers and Commissioners if points at issue are only subject to appeal proceedings once. Any disputes relating to the partnership income, or the allocation between the partners, could affect all the partners even though the appeal is against only one partner's assessment. We consider it desirable for all partners to receive equal treatment and for all appeals to be resolved in the same way and we therefore intend that no appeals on these aspects will be determined without reference to the relevant assessments on all the other partners.

Where only some of the partners appeal against their assessments on their share of partnership income, we propose to invite those partners who have not appealed to do so. In such circumstances we will be prepared to accept a late appeal. For this purpose we propose to deal with and agree a partnership's affairs centrally. We will however take care to continue to treat the appeals against the individual partners' assessments separately, but in parallel, by the issue of similar letters, notices and determinations in each case.

There is presently no mechanism for Commissioners to hear such appeals together, other than where all the parties agree. But the new Procedural Rules for the General and Special Commissioners [S.I.s 1994 Nos. 1811, 1812] include provisions whereby Commissioners can direct that appeals should be heard together where they are satisfied that they involve a common issue. We envisage that appeals against these assessments would come within that category.

A PRACTICAL APPROACH

So far as possible we would hope to deal with partnerships that commence on or after 6 April 1994 in the same way as we will do for 1996–97 and later years. We would therefore ask practitioners to submit a single copy of the partnership accounts and computations to the inspector on behalf of all partners. Any necessary enquiries would then be dealt with by the inspector in correspondence with a single partner or agent, and agreement reached as to the amount of partnership income and its allocation between the partners.

If it becomes necessary to take any issue on these questions to the Commissioners we will seek to join appeals, so that all partners' appeals are heard together.

Appendix F

Issue 14, December 1994

Page 174. Self assessment: payments on account

Under the present rules, income tax payments against assessments are concentrated around January and July. Tax under Cases I and II of Schedule D, which is payable in two instalments, is due on 1 January in the tax year and 1 July immediately after. Tax under Schedule D Cases III to VI and Schedule A is due on 1 January in the tax year, and income tax on taxed income and capital gains tax is due on 1 December after the tax year.

Under self assessment, where all income and capital gains will be brought together on one overall bill for a year, these different payment dates for different sources will end. However, it will still be important to maintain the flow of tax to the Exchequer on broadly the same timetable, and to avoid generating an unnecessary peaking of demands on taxpayers. To achieve this, the new system will involve making payments on account. The timing and level of these will try to ensure that money reaches the Exchequer at broadly the same times as it does currently, without either overcharging taxpayers or underpaying the Exchequer. The payments on account will need to become due automatically in most cases, but be flexible enough to respond to changing circumstances. The process will incorporate safeguards against possible abuse.

The normal situation
Two payments on account will be required annually, on 31 January in a year of assessment and 31 July after that year of assessment. Initially each payment will be equal to half of the income tax liability for the previous year (after taking account of tax deducted at source in that year). If, year on year, income tax liability increases by a moderate amount (perhaps because a business is steadily developing), this would mean that a substantial amount of the tax liability for the year is paid by way of payment on account, leaving only the increase over the previous year's liability and any capital gains tax for the year to be paid by way of balancing payment on 31 January after the year of assessment. (**Note** – capital gains tax will not be subject to payments on account.)

So taxpayers will be asked to make payments on two occasions in the year. On 31 January each year, the balancing payment for the tax year most recently ended will be due, together with the first payment on account for the current tax year. Then on 31 July that calendar year a further payment on account will be due in the same amount. Any balancing payment due for that year would be due on the following 31 January together with the first payment on account for the next year, and so on. This is illustrated in Example 1.

EXAMPLE 1
Income tax liability for 1997–98 is £1,200. Assume no payments on account are made during the year to 31 January 1999 – the filing and

payment date for 1997–98. So £1,200 will be due on that date.

Payment on account for 1998–99 will be based on 1997–98 figures. So they will each be £600. If the final liability for 1998–99 is £1,600, the balancing payment for 1998–99 will be:

Total liability			£1,600
Paid on account 31.1.99	£600		
Paid on account 31.7.99	600		1,200
Balancing payment			400
Payment on account for 1999–2000:			
Total liability for 1998–99	£1,600 × 50%	=	800
Total due on 31.1.2000			£1,200
Due on 31.7.2000			£800

Where no tax is suffered at source, and no claim is made to reduce the payments on account (see below) the balancing payment will always be the amount by which the tax liability for the year is greater than the previous year's tax liability.

Claims to reduce payments on account

It may be that profits do not increase steadily year by year. If there is a fall in income during a year, payments on account made on the basis of the preceding year's liability might exceed the current year's liability, so that a repayment would be due on 31 January following the year of assessment. Where this is reasonably foreseeable taxpayers can claim that payments on account should be lower than half of the preceding year's liability on the basis that the lower amount is a more realistic estimate of the tax which will be due for the year. A penalty can be imposed where such a claim is made fraudulently or negligently.

Payments on account for 1996–97

As, under self assessment, all income is combined in one assessment, tax which is at present paid in one annual instalment will be spread between both payments on account in the future. To smooth the transition from the old tax payment calendar to the new, there will be special rules for 1996–97.

For 1996–97 only, the payments on account in respect of trading and professional income will be split equally between 31 January 1997 and 31 July 1997, but a single payment on account in respect of tax on Schedule A, and Cases III–VI of Schedule D will be due on 31 January 1997. Again this will be computed on the basis of the 1995–96 figures, and will be reducible on a claim. No payment on account will be required for 1996–97 in respect of tax on taxed income (the full liability from this source will be due with the balancing payment on 31 January 1998). Example 2 [below] may help to explain the transitional rules for 1996–97.

EXAMPLE 2

Income tax liability for 1995–96 is as follows:

Case I	£10,000	
Schedule A	£3,000	
Case III (untaxed)	£1,000	
Dividends	£4,000	(out of which £2,000 has been deducted at source)

The payments on account for 1996–97 will be based on:

31.1.97	All the Cases III to VI of Schedule D and Schedule A for 1995–96 (£3,000 + £1,000)	£4,000
	Half the Case I/II and Class 4 NIC for 1995–96	5,000
		£9,000
31.7.97	Half the Case I/II and Class 4 NIC for 1995–96	£5,000

No payment on account is due for 1996–97 in respect of the dividend income.

As explained above, it is possible to make a claim to reduce or cancel the payment on account for 1996–97 just as for later years.

Because 1996–97 is the first year of self assessment there will not have been any self assessment for the previous year (1995–96) upon which the payments on account can be based. Instead, all the income tax assessments for 1995–96 will be aggregated to calculate the payments on account due for 1996–97. It will be possible to make a claim to reduce this payment on account just as for later years. However, whereas in later years the figure will be identifiable from a person's self assessment return, this is not the case for 1996–97 payments on account. The Inland Revenue will tell people what these should be in time for the first payment on account for 1996–97 due by 31 January 1997.

Partnerships

1996–97 payments on account due from partnerships are computed differently. This subject was covered in Issue 12 [p. 146] of Tax Bulletin. To recap, a partnership assessment will be issued for 1996–97 as usual. The partnership will pay the tax (due on 1 January and 1 July 1997) on this assessment which will be subject to appeal and postponement as normal. But, 1996–97 is the first year of self assessment and so each partner will be required to file a self assessment return reflecting his or her share of the partnership profits. In so doing each partner's share of the 1996–97 tax paid by the partnership will be credited on the personal self assessments as if the income had been received under deduction of tax. So partners will not be expected to make payments on account for 1996–97 in respect of their partnership income. They may of course be liable to make payments on account in respect of income received in their personal capacity *i.e.* unconnected with the partnership.

De minimis amounts

Where the payments on account would be below certain limits, no payments will be required. There are two limits:

Absolute limit
This will make it unnecessary to make small payments.

Proportionate limit
This will exclude from the payment on account regime people whose tax is predominantly collected by deduction at source, especially PAYE taxpayers.

The precise levels of these limits will be announced in good time before any payments on account are due.

The tax return
The Inland Revenue will notify taxpayers of the expected level of their payments on account for 1996–97 sometime during the Autumn of 1996, well in advance of 31 January 1997 when the first payment will be due.

Taxpayers who complete self assessment tax returns will have the option of calculating the tax bill based on the entries they make. The form itself will guide them through this. It will also set out the calculation required to arrive at the payments on account for the next year. So the 1997–98 tax return, which will cover all 1997–98 tax liabilities, will also contain guidance on the calculation of the 1998–99 payments on account.

Alternatively, taxpayers who do not wish to take this option may ask the Inland Revenue to do all the calculations for them, including the calculation of payments on account.

In addition, the taxpayer statements which the Inland Revenue will use to give taxpayers information about their 'account' will contain reminders of payments which are expected (based on the information held at the time) at appropriate times during the year.

Surcharge
Surcharge does not apply to payments on account which are made late, (though late payments will attract **interest**). Surcharge can only apply in respect of the balancing payment, *i.e.* the full tax liability for a year, less amounts deducted at source/tax credits and less the payments on account already made for the year, and then only to any part not paid by 28 February after the tax year.

Issue 15, February 1995

Page 199. Self assessment and technical guidance

Last year we published two technical guides for practitioners on aspects of the Self Assessment system. The first one called 'The new current year basis of assessment' described the new basis of assessment for Schedule D Cases I to VI and the second 'Self Assessment the legal framework' described the 'process now – check later' system for the assessment and collection of tax. These two guides known as SAT1 and SAT2 contain the technical guidance issued to our own staff on the new legislation. In line with Open Government principles we published the guides for general use. Districts issued a free copy to each tax practice in their area and further copies are available on paper or disk for £3 a copy from the Inland Revenue Library, New Wing, Somerset House, Strand WC2R 1LB.

The current Finance Bill contains further legislation for Self Assessment. The main topics dealt with are:

- Reform of Schedule A for income tax;
- Provision of information by employers to their employees;
- Taxation of non-residents under self assessment;
- Income from overseas property;
- Treatment of partnerships including foreign partnerships and non-resident partners;
- Transitional period anti-avoidance provisions.

And there are a number of other miscellaneous changes to facilitate self assessment.

We intend to publish new editions of SAT1 and SAT2 following Royal Assent to Finance Act 1995. Districts will again issue a free copy to each tax practice in their area. These new editions will replace the existing publications. They will clarify any existing items that have given rise to misunderstandings and will explain the 1995 legislative changes for self assessment. Any guidance on changes involving non-residents trading through investment managers in the U.K., for which the audience is more specialised, would be published separately. And we are still considering what is best for PAYE where the audience is much bigger than for SAT1 and SAT2.

The Finance Bill does not deal with transitional issues for Schedule A. This is because a diverse range of non-statutory practices has developed under the existing rules. We think it is best to deal with any transitional issues by discussion between taxpayers and their inspector on a case by case basis. We are in detailed discussion with a number of representative bodies about the best way to do this. The guidance we offer inspectors will be included in SAT1 but we are hoping to be able to publish these notes earlier. The intention wherever possible is to deal with Schedule A transitional issues in settling the 1994–95 liability. This would allow taxpayers to gain experience of assessment under the new rules for 1995–96 before they have to self assess for 1996–97.

Issue 16, April 1995

Page 205. Self assessment electronic lodgement system

This year's Finance Bill introduces new provisions to establish an electronic lodgement service (ELS). ELS is being set up to enable the information in respect of certain tax returns to be transmitted to the Inland Revenue by electronic means. We intend to make the service available initially to accept the self assessment returns issued from April 1997 onwards. We will be looking at the potential to develop the system to handle other returns and documents later.

ELS will enable approved persons (filers) to make use of the latest communications technology to do away with the need to send paper returns. Transmitting returns by ELS will also be much quicker than by post, and will provide agent and taxpayer alike with the certain knowledge that the information has been properly received by the Revenue. In addition, the technology will provide tight security, giving taxpayers the confidence that unauthorised persons will not be able to gain access to information transmitted in this way.

In order to use the system, filers will need enhanced tax return software to enable information on their computer system to be transmitted electronically to the Inland Revenue computer system via a Secure Messaging Gateway. The transmission process will include checks to identify particular errors in the return information and to ensure that they are corrected before the information is accepted on the Inland Revenue's computer system. Once the information is accepted, an automatic acknowledgement will be sent to assure the filer that the return has been successfully lodged.

The legislation provides that the statutory requirement to deliver a return to the Inland Revenue will be deemed to be fulfilled where the relevant information is transmitted electronically and certain conditions are met. These are that –

- the person filing the information is approved to do so,
- the manner of transmission meets the Inland Revenue requirements,
- a hard copy of the information is authenticated by the taxpayer, and
- the formal acceptance of the information is issued by the Inland Revenue.

In response to concerns about the effect on a potential filer of the Revenue's refusal to grant approval, the Government have accepted the need for an appeals procedure. This has now been provided by amendment to the Finance Bill legislation. The Revenue are keen for the system to be widely available, and it is likely that the vast majority of those applying for approval would be successful.

A further amendment to the Finance Bill has removed the requirement for the hard copy to be made shortly before the information is transmitted. Instead, the manner of transmission will include a requirement to supply the date on which the taxpayer authenticated the hard copy.

A trial of the system has been carried out since November last year, and is due to be evaluated shortly. The early results from an interim evaluation report prepared jointly by the Revenue and participants in the trial are encouraging, and demonstrate the viability of the proposed approach to ELS. The results of the trial will be published in due course.

Although the trial was conducted using the corporation tax return, ELS will not be made available for the live transmission of these returns for the foreseeable future. This is because the Revenue cannot dispense with the need for company accounts to be submitted, in view of their greater complexity compared to income tax accounts, and at present there is no information technology support to transmit such data. Those involved in consultations on the project have made it clear that unless all the information associated with a return can be transmitted electronically they would have little use for the system.

There are benefits to be gained by the taxpayer and agent in filing electronically, including the greater certainty of lodgement of the return and improvements in the overall efficiency of their operations. We will continue to look at additional ways of making the system attractive to potential users, for example by providing a two-way flow of information, as well as allowing more prompt processing of repayments. But the option of filing returns by paper in the traditional way will of course remain.

We will continue to consult on the development of ELS and will provide in due course further details on the requirements and procedures which are expected to be incorporated into the ELS system.

Page 206. Self assessment: Issues relevant to 1994–95 income tax returns and associated assessments

Over the past 12 months we have published a number of articles on self assessment. We have also published comprehensive technical guides to the new legislation: SAT1 '*The new current year basis of assessment*' and SAT2 '*Self Assessment: the legal framework*'. But the first real test of the new rules and procedures will arise during the completion and processing of 1994–95 tax returns and the associated accounts.

This article highlights those parts of the self assessment provisions which can have effect in 1994–95 and 1995–96 for income tax purposes and directs you to the relevant guidance that has been published.

Revised versions of both SAT1 and SAT2 will be published in May/June 1995. These new editions will include material relating to the current Finance Bill, for example, the new Schedule A rules and the provisions countering exploitation of the rules for the transition from the preceding year to the current year basis of assessment.

ASPECTS OF SELF ASSESSMENT RELEVANT TO INCOME TAX RETURNS FOR 1994–95 AND 1995–96

The new computational rules for Cases I to VI of Schedule D apply

- from 1994–95 for all new businesses set up and commenced on or after 6 April 1994;
- from 1994–95 for any existing businesses treated as set up and commenced on or after 6 April 1994 by virtue of TA 1988, s. 113(1);

- from 1994–95 for all new sources of income arising on or after 6 April 1994. [The new rules will apply to all new sources of income, without exception, even though the taxpayer may have sources of income of the same class in existence at 5 April 1994.]

The new rules for Schedule A (including furnished lettings currently within Case VI) apply, for income tax purposes, to all taxpayers from 1995–96 onwards.

For 1994–95 and 1995–96 you will need to be familiar with the new rules for:

- *Case I/II basis periods (SAT1, Chapter 1)*
- *Overlap profit (SAT1, Chapter 1)*
- *Capital allowances (SAT1, Chapter 3)*
- *Losses (SAT1, Chapter 4)*
- *Case III/VI basis periods (SAT1, Chapter 2)*
- *Partnerships (SAT1, Chapter 5; Tax Bulletin 11, p. 124; Tax Bulletin 12, p. 146)*
- *Double Taxation Relief (SAT1, Chapter 7)*
- *Schedule A*
  Full details of these rules will appear in the revised SAT1. In the meantime you should note the procedures for dealing with the transition to the new rules which were attached to the Press Release issued on 10 February 1995 entitled Schedule A transitional proposals.
- *Anti-avoidance rules*
  The Finance Bill 1995 contains special rules to counteract tax avoidance through the exploitation of the rules for the transition from the preceding year to the current year basis of assessment. The main effect will be on the profits included in the 1996–97 return, but there may be some implications for other years.
  For example, a change of accounting date made in 1994–95 **may** bring a taxpayer within the general scope of the rules. This is because a change to the basis period for 1995–96 will, in turn, change the basis period for 1996–97.
  Normally, however, a change of accounting date in 1994–95 will only bring the taxpayer within the anti-avoidance rules **if it moves the taxpayer's accounting date away from 5 April 1995**. For example, a change from 5 April 1995 to 30 April 1994 would be caught. Even so this does not mean that the anti-avoidance rules will definitely apply because one of the statutory let outs may apply. This point cannot be resolved until the profits for 1996–97 and/or 1997–98 are known.
  Full details of the anti-avoidance rules will be given in the revised SATI.

ASPECTS OF SELF ASSESSMENT NOT RELEVANT IN 1994–95 AND 1995–96

None of the changes to the rules for

- SA returns and self-assessment;

- the new enquiry procedures;
- the payment and collection of tax;

apply until 1996–97. Therefore, for example, even if a 1994–95 or 1995–96 assessment is based on the new computational rules the **existing rules** for the payment of tax apply. Similarly the existing rules for interest and penalties will apply to the tax charged in that assessment.

However, you should note that:

- there is a new rule requiring a taxpayer to keep and preserve the business records on which a return is based (*TMA 1970, s. 12B (1), SAT2 Chapter 2*). This rule may apply to periods in 1994–95 and 1995–96 because the basis period for 1996–97 can commence as early as 7 April 1994. We shall be issuing guidance on this in the summer.
- the new rule for failure to notify chargeability first applies in respect of 1995–96 (*TMA 1970, s. 7 SAT2 Chapter 2*).

Page 207. United Kingdom/Germany Double Taxation Convention: withholding tax on certain income: arrangements for 1995–96 and 1996–97 [11.10]

Taxpayers who normally receive German income (for example royalties) without deduction of withholding tax may recently have received notification of a proposed change of practice from the German tax authorities. The proposal was that any income paid between 6 April 1995 and 5 April 1997 would be subject to withholding tax on one half of the sums paid, and was intended to reflect the changes to U.K. tax law which will apply in 1996–97 to allow a transition to the new current year basis of assessment.

Following discussions between the Inland Revenue's International Division and the German tax authorities it has now been agreed that all such income should continue to be exempted from tax in Germany under the Double Taxation Convention. The following is the text of a letter which is being issued by the Inland Revenue to those taxpayers who have already been in contact with us on this issue.

UNITED KINGDOM/GERMANY DOUBLE TAXATION CONVENTION: WITHHOLDING TAX ON CERTAIN INCOME

Introduction

1. Thank you for your enquiry on this subject. Discussions between the U.K. and German authorities have now taken place, and, as a result, the German tax authorities have decided to cancel the amendments to its notices of exemption which were set out in recent letters from the Bundesamt fur Finanzen.

Background: changes in the United Kingdom

2. As you may know, the rules for assessing U.K. tax on certain income are due to change. Under the new system, income tax will be charged not by reference to the income which a taxpayer received in the preceding year (the old system), but by reference to the income received in the current year.

3. The U.K. tax year 1996–97 will be a transitional year from the old (preceding year) to the new (current year) rules for assessing tax on the income in question. Where a business started, or income such as interest first arose from a particular source, before 6 April 1994, the general rule is that income tax will be charged for the 1996–97 tax year on a percentage (typically, but not always, half) of the income of a period longer than the twelve months of that particular tax year. In 1997–98 and subsequent years, the new (current year) rules will apply.

The United Kingdom/Germany Double Taxation Convention
4. Under the Double Taxation Conventions between the U.K. and Germany various forms of German income – including payments of interest, royalties and certain pensions – are exempt from tax in Germany, provided that they are subject to tax in the U.K.

5. When this condition is met, the Bundesamt fur Finanzen in Germany generally issues a notice of exemption (Freistellungsbescheid) which authorises the payer of the income to pay it gross, without deducting German tax.

Proposed amendments to notices of exemption
6. When the authorities in Germany considered the transitional arrangements for 1996–97 in the U.K. (see paragraph 3 above), they concluded that the result was that not all the income taken into account in calculating U.K. tax for that year would in fact be subject to tax in the U.K. It therefore appeared to them that, under the terms of the United Kingdom/Germany Double Taxation Convention, German tax ought to be deducted from half the income. That view was reflected in the recent letter sent out by the Bundesamt fur Finanzen.

Discussions between the U.K. and Germany
7. Representatives of the Inland Revenue have discussed this issue with members of the Bundesministerium der Finanzen and the Bundesamt fur Finanzen, under a procedure in the Double Taxation Convention which provides for the taxation authorities of the U.K. and Germany to resolve by mutual agreement any difficulties or doubts about the application of the Convention.

Result of the discussions
8. As a result of these discussions, the U.K. and Germany have agreed that the income in question is, in fact, subject to tax in the U.K. and that it should therefore continue to be exempted from tax in Germany under the Double Taxation Convention.

9. The Bundesamt fur Finanzen is making arrangements to cancel the amendments to its notices of exemption. The notices of exemption will therefore continue to apply as before. You should expect to receive written confirmation of this from the Bundesamt fur Finanzen in due course.

Conclusion

10. We hope that this note explains clearly the background to this issue; and that you will find the results of our discussions with the German tax authorities reassuring. If you have any further questions, please contact: Mrs Suzanne Darken, International Division, Room G17, Strand Bridge House, 138–142 Strand, LONDON WC2R 1HH, Telephone: 0171 438 6118 (International: +44 171 438 6118)

11. The contents of this note have been agreed with the tax authorities in Germany.

Issue 17, June 1995

Page 221. Mortgage interest relief: letting a private residence – new rules from 6 April 1995 [5.31]

Tax Bulletin Issue 14 (December 1994) explained the rules which apply from 6 April 1994 for giving relief on interest paid on a loan to purchase a private residence which is also commercially let. This article explains the new rules which apply from 6 April 1995 and reiterates the main points on the 1994–95 rules for the benefit of those who did not see Issue 14.

The most common circumstances in which a private residence is also let are where the borrower is living in job-related accommodation or is temporarily absent by reason of employment (see Extra-Statutory Concession A27).

New rules from 6 April 1995

From 6 April 1995, the rules for calculating income from property under Schedule A and furnished lettings under Schedule D Case VI have changed. Profits from these sources of income are assessable under the new Schedule A rules introduced by Section 39 Finance Act (FA) 1995 and are calculated in much the same way as trading profits under Schedule D Case I.

Accordingly, interest paid is no longer allowable as a deduction or set off against letting income under Section 353 Income and Corporation Taxes Act (ICTA) 1988. Instead, interest payable in respect of a Schedule A business is allowable as a deduction in calculating the profits of the business, under the same rules as apply for other expenses incurred for the purposes of the business.

Section 355(1)(b) ICTA 1988 has been repealed and a borrower who is eligible for mortgage interest relief in respect of a property which is let may choose each year whether to:

- claim mortgage interest relief (restricted to interest on the qualifying maximum of £30,000 and to the rate of 15%); or
- make a deduction in computing the profits of the Schedule A business.

Loans eligible for MIRAS

For loans **eligible** for relief under the MIRAS arrangements, relief **must** be given under MIRAS **unless** the borrower elects to make a deduction in computing Schedule A profits.

This applies whether or not the loan was actually in MIRAS in 1994–95. Where a loan was outside of MIRAS at 5 April 1995, Tax Offices will ask borrowers whether they intend to elect to make a deduction in computing Schedule A profits, before putting the loan into MIRAS. (In most cases, it will only be possible to put the loan into MIRAS from 6 April 1996 and relief for 1995–96 will be given in the borrower's code number or assessment.)

Where a loan was in MIRAS at 5 April 1995, no action need be taken unless the borrower wishes to elect to make a deduction in computing the profits of the Schedule A business.

An election must be made in writing within 22 months of the end of the tax year in which it is first to have effect (for example, an election having effect from 1996–97 can be made at any time up to 6 February 1999). This is to coincide with the date a Self Assessment return will become final. There is no specific form for an election. Once made, the election is irrevocable and the loan must remain outside the MIRAS arrangements until the Schedule A business ceases.

Even where an election has been made, and consequently the loan cannot be dealt with under the MIRAS arrangements, the borrower may still choose each year whether to claim mortgage interest relief outside MIRAS or make a deduction in computing the profits of the Schedule A business.

Joint borrowers

For loans not eligible for relief under the MIRAS arrangements, each borrower can choose each year whether to claim mortgage interest relief or make a deduction in computing the profits of the Schedule A business.

For loans eligible for relief under the MIRAS arrangements, an election by any one borrower will require the whole loan to be taken out of MIRAS. Any borrower who does not make an election will be given relief as an income tax reduction.

Rules for 1994–95

Interest paid by a borrower who let his or her main residence is eligible for relief under either:

- Section 355(1)(a) ICTA 1988 (main residence) or Section 356(1) (job-related accommodation) as an income tax reduction against general income, **or**
- Section 355(1)(b) ICTA 1988 (let property) against letting income.

Section 353(1C) ICTA 1988 provides that, where a borrower had dual eligibility, relief is given as a deduction or set off against letting income, **unless** an election is made for relief to be given as an income tax reduction (restricted to interest on the qualifying maximum of £30,000 at 20%).

Elections

An election must be made in writing by 5 April 1996. It may only take effect from:

- 6 April 1994, or if later,
- the date when dual eligibility first occurred.

Once made, an election will remain in force until the earliest of:

- 5 April 1995,
- the date the letting ceases, or
- the date the conditions in Section 355(1)(a) ICTA 1988 or Section 356(1) cease to apply.

An election may be withdrawn at any time up to 5 April 1996. No specific form is required for making or withdrawing an election. The election should be sent to the borrower's tax office together with a certificate of interest paid.

Loans eligible for MIRAS

Where a borrower has dual eligibility and his or her loan was in MIRAS for 1994–95, the tax office will withdraw the relief obtained under MIRAS unless the borrower makes an election by 5 April 1996. If no election is made, or if an election is withdrawn, relief will be given against letting income and any excess MIRAS relief will be recovered in the Schedule A (or Schedule D Case VI for furnished lettings) assessment or in an assessment under Regulation 19(4) SI 1982 No 1236.

Relief for any period covered by an election but for which the loan was not in MIRAS will be given in the borrower's code number or assessment, or, if the borrower is not a taxpayer, by payment from Financial Intermediaries and Claims Office (FICO) (under Section 375(8) ICTA 1988).

Joint borrowers

Each borrower can make or withdraw an election and receive relief accordingly.

Transitional Provisions for 1995–96

Where a source of letting income ceases in 1995–96, the letting income for that year is assessable under the 'old' Schedule A or Schedule D Case VI rules as appropriate and any excess interest over income from 1994–95 can be set against that income.

In all other cases, any excess interest over income from 1994–95 is carried forward to 1995–96 or a subsequent year as a loss under the new Schedule A rules.

Page 225. Self-assessment: transitional arrangements – submission of accounts

In 1996–97, transitional arrangements will apply to allow self-employed taxpayers to move from the preceding year (PY) basis of assessment to the new current year (CY) basis. These arrangements mean that accounts for periods ending in 1995–96 will not, by themselves, provide a basis for calculating 1996–97 business income. This article considers the implications of these arrangements for the 1995–96 tax return.

1995–96 will be the last year in which income can be taxed on a PY basis. Therefore, the last accounts required as the basis for a PY assessment are those ending in the tax year 1994–95. These accounts will form part of the taxpayer's return of income for the tax year 1994–95, normally issued in April 1995.

For 1996–97, all income will be taxed by reference to a basis period ending in that year. In any case where a PY basis of assessment is used in 1995–96, the profits assessed in 1996–97 will be a percentage of the profits of a transitional basis period. The transitional basis period is the aggregate of:

- a notional CY basis period for the year, identified as the 12 months to the date to which accounts are made up in 1996–97, and
- the period beginning immediately after the end of the basis period for 1995–96 and ending immediately before the beginning of the period given above.

More detailed guidance and examples can be found in the Inland Revenue booklet (SAT1) entitled 'The new current year basis of assessment'.

Taxpayers will be required to include the income of the transitional basis period in the Self Assessment tax return issued in April 1997.

1995–96 tax return – normally issued in April 1996

Generally, the only circumstances in which taxpayers with a Case I or II business will be required to send in accounts for periods ending in 1995–96 with their 1995–96 tax returns are where:

- the income is assessable for 1995–96 on a CY basis, or
- a claim is made to offset losses suffered in a period ending in 1995–96 against other income for 1995–96, or earlier years.

The CY basis will apply to 1995–96 business income in the following cases:

- businesses that commenced, or are deemed to commence following a change in ownership under Section 113(1) Income and Corporation Taxes Act (ICTA) 1988, after 5 April 1994;
- businesses which cease during 1995–96;
- where a claim is made under Section 62(2) or 62(4) ICTA 1988 for 1995–96 to be assessed on an actual basis of assessment;
- where, following a partnership change, Section 61(4) ICTA 1988 applies and 1995–96 is to be assessed on an actual basis of assessment.

The notes which accompany the tax return issued for 1995–96 will set out the limited circumstances in which the Inland Revenue will require accounts. Any other accounts submitted (even though not required) will be acknowledged. But the figures in those accounts cannot be agreed by the Inland Revenue, for two reasons:

- first, they will form only part of the 1996–97 basis period, and
- second, 1996–97 will be the first year of Self Assessment.

Under Self Assessment, the Inland Revenue will not have to agree returns on receipt but will have at least a year to decide whether to make enquiries into them.

1996–1997 tax return – normally issued in April 1997

Self-employed taxpayers whose 1995–96 assessment was made on a PY basis, will be required to provide information relating to their transitional basis period (see above) in order to calculate their 1996–97 income.

In the case of a business drawing up accounts to a regular annual accounting date, this will mean providing details for two successive 12 month periods in the one return. The profits assessable for 1996–97 will be the 12 month average profits of the two periods. But there is no requirement for separate accounts to be prepared for each period. It is entirely a matter for taxpayers to decide whether to have a single account prepared for the whole transitional basis period, or to draw up separate accounts for each component period. For example, there may be benefits to having separate accounts made up where a loss is incurred.

It is intended that information from either the single account or each set of accounts prepared will be required in a standardised form, as will computations in respect of the two year period as a whole. The accounts themselves and other supporting documents will not be required for submission with the return, but may be asked for at a later date. The design of the return incorporating this approach is currently being tested in the Leicester area.

Inland Revenue confirmation of income or earnings

Self-employed taxpayers sometimes ask the Inland Revenue to confirm figures of business profits that have been agreed for assessment to support applications for mortgage advances and educational grants, for example. Subject to certain caveats, Inspectors have usually been able to do so.

We will continue to respond to such requests under Self Assessment, but will only be able to confirm that a certain figure has been returned, not that it has been agreed.

Further details of these arrangements were given in the Inland Revenue Press Release of 24 April 1995.

Launch of public information campaign for self assessment

A campaign to inform taxpayers about Self Assessment was launched on 8 June. Spearheaded by TV and press advertising, the first phase of the campaign will run until mid-July. Subsequent phases are planned for the Autumn and New Year.

The TV advertisements aim to raise general awareness of Self Assessment while the press advertisements specifically target self-employed people and those who need to bring their tax affairs up-to-date. All advertisements carry a telephone number – 0345 161514 – that people may call to request further information. Booklets and a video are available for self-employed taxpayers.

The TV advertising features a cartoon 'taxman' animated by the Oscar-winning film company, Snowden Fine, and a voice-over by Sir Alec Guinness. The humour of the cartoon character, carried across onto press advertisements, booklets and posters, aims to attract attention and get information across on the difficult subject of tax and Self Assessment.

From 8 June, to coincide with the launch of the campaign, tax agents, solicitors and financial advisers will receive a Self Assessment information pack that includes sample copies of the booklets for taxpayers.

Issue 18, August 1995

Page 237. Non-residents trading in the UK: The arm's length principle

The rules for taxing non-residents were revised in FA 1995, s 40, FA 1995, s 124 to FA 1995, s 129 and FA 1995, 23 Sch. The new rules simplify the procedures for taxing non-residents and align them with Self Assessment. The main effect is to codify the present practices by replacing the present patchwork of statutory rules, administrative procedures and extra statutory concessions with clear simple rules. The amount of tax charged is left broadly unchanged.

The new rules clarify the way in which non-residents will be taxed under Self Assessment and the extent of the tax charge. Non-residents are taxed in the UK on the shoreline principle, that is on income arising in or connected with the UK. The new rules divide this into three broad categories which can loosely be described as:

- income from property in the UK,
- investment income (most types of income from investments in the UK other than land) and,
- earned income (income from an employment, trade, profession or vocation in the UK and any income not included in the previous categories).

Income from property will continue to be taxed in full either through deduction at source, with a final settling up with the non-resident through Self Assessment where necessary, or, where the non-resident chooses by agreement with the Inland Revenue, wholly through Self Assessment.

Earned income will also continue to be taxed in full. Income from employment will normally be taxed through PAYE, with a final settling up with the non-resident through Self Assessment where necessary. Income from a trade, profession or vocation will normally be taxed through Self Assessment by the non-resident or, where the trade is carried on through a branch or agency, by the branch or agent.

Investment income will continue to be taxed principally through deduction at source. The new rules limit the tax chargeable on investment income to the tax, if any, deducted at source. There will therefore normally be no need for non-residents whose UK income is wholly investment income to self assess, except where a repayment is due.

In the case of a non-resident trust where all the existing and potential beneficiaries are not ordinarily resident (or not resident in the case of corporate beneficiaries), there will be no charge at the rate applicable to trusts under ICTA 1988, s 686 in respect of income falling within FA 1995, s 128(2) and (3).

These rules are in line with the agreed principles of international taxation as set out in the OECD model tax convention (MTC), which are also followed in double taxation agreements (DTAs) between the UK and other countries. The main difference is that there is no requirement, except where a DTA applies, for the non-resident to have a fixed presence in the UK before earned income may be taxed.

The new rules leave the provisions for charging tax on the income of non-residents from carrying on a trade, profession or vocation unchanged. The main rule is in paragraph (a)(iii) of Schedule D in ICTA 1988, s 18(1) which limits the charge to trades, professions and vocations exercised within the UK.

Two main principles were established in early tax cases. First, trades carried on wholly or partly in the UK, including trades carried on by non-residents, are chargeable under Case I of Schedule D. Trades carried on wholly outside the UK are chargeable under Case V of Schedule D, which is limited by paragraph (a) to UK residents (Colquhoun v Brooks 2 TC 490, San Paulo (Brazilian) Railway Co v Carter 3 TC 407). Second, trades carried on by non-residents are chargeable only where the non-resident trades in the UK, which means broadly that economic activities are carried on in the UK that give rise to trading profits (e.g. sales or manufacture). Trading by non-residents with the UK, as opposed to in the UK, (e.g. purchases or delivery) is not chargeable, (Erichsen v Last 1 TC 351 and 4 TC 422, Pommery and Greno v Apthorpe 2 TC 182, Werle v Colquhoun 2 TC 402, Grainger & Son v Gough 3 TC 311 and 462, Smidth & Co v Greenwood 8 TC 193, Firestone Tyre & Rubber Ltd v Lewellin 37 TC 111).

These principles are well understood. They are also in line with principles in the MTC which exempt trading functions of a resident of the other state from charge if they are solely of a preparatory or auxiliary nature.

It is also well understood that, where a non-resident carries on a trade partly in the UK and partly outside the UK, the charge is limited to the profits from the part of the trade carried on in the UK.

It is perhaps less obvious how the profits from the part of the trade carried on in the UK should be measured. They are required to be measured on the arm's length principle set out in the MTC where a DTA applies which includes the relevant provisions. It is considered that it also follows from the main rule in Schedule D that the same principle applies even if there is no treaty.

There is support for this principle in the early tax cases on non-residents trading in the UK. For example, in Pommery and Greno v Apthorpe at 2 TC 189, Denman J said, with regard to the profits chargeable in the UK from merchanting champagne produced in France, that:

> 'It may be that there may be some difficulty in some respects as to the manner of calculating the amount of expenditure to be put against the profits, whether it would be a proper course to look at the goods sent over to England and then to consider what profit they make, putting a fair valuation on them as they arrive, and as the money is transmitted, or whether it would be necessary in such a case to look more minutely into the profits and losses upon the whole trade carried on partly in France and partly in England. I do not think it is necessary at all at this stage of the case to decide that. That is a matter of quantum, a matter for the consideration of persons skilled in dealing with such matters as assessing profits of trade:–

> This can be seen as an early description of the arm's length principle and as a recognition of the need to develop methods to apply that principle in practice. Such methods were developed in the OECD 1979 Report on "Transfer Pricing and Multinational Enterprises" and have been reaffirmed and clarified in the recently published 1995 revision of that report by OECD "Transfer Pricing Guidelines for Multinational Enterprises and Tax Administrations".'

The new rules in FA 1995 were developed in consultation with the Self Assessment Consultative Committee (SACC). We asked the Committee whether the application of the arm's length principle to the measure of trading profits should be made explicit in the statute. The Committee decided this was neither necessary nor desirable. They considered that it is well established that the arm's length principle applies as a matter of law and that this is accepted by taxpayers, tax advisers and the Inland Revenue as the correct basis for taxing non-residents in the UK.

The Committee also pointed to the lack of recent cases on the taxation of non-residents trading in the UK as confirmation of the principle. They were concerned that a new provision to put that beyond doubt could create uncertainty or have unforeseen consequences through the inevitable differences between the wording which would be used in the statute and that used in the MTC. They suggested that it would be better to confirm that the arm's length principle applies automatically through an article in Tax Bulletin.

The new rules in FA 1995 replace the whole of the existing rules in TMA 1970, Part VIII. The rules which are still relevant, that is those in TMA 1970, s 78, 82(1) and 83–85, reappear in the new rules with any necessary modifications. The rules which are no longer relevant, that is those in TMA 1970, s 79, 80, 81 and 82(2), do not reappear. Nothing of significance is lost as a result. The rules which have disappeared did not affect the measure of charge on the non-resident. But they were also otiose as they were no more than a reflection of the arm's length principle. In particular, the double foreigner provision in TMA 1970, s 82(2) was of no effect. In the cases which would have fallen within the subsection, the arm's length principle would have left no profits to tax in the UK once the arm's length fee payable to the agent had been deducted, leaving nothing for the subsection to bite on.

Sir George Young Bt MP, the former Financial Secretary to the Treasury, also reaffirmed that 'the arm's length principle applies generally to the measure of profits brought into charge on a non-resident' when these sections were debated in the Standing Committee on the Finance Bill.

To summarise, it is generally agreed by taxpayers, tax advisers and the Inland Revenue that the arm's length principle, as set out in the MTC and explained in OECD publications, applies to the measure of profits chargeable on a non-resident in respect of trading in the UK as a matter of law, irrespective of whether a DTA applies.

The following bodies are represented on SACC – Chartered Association of Certified Accountants, Chartered Institute of Taxation, Confederation of British Industry, Federation of Small Businesses, Institute of Chartered Accountants of England and Wales, Institute of Chartered Accountants of Scotland, Institute of Directors, Law Society, Law Society of Scotland. This article was agreed with the members of the Committee.

Page 241. Income from UK property: Basis periods: partnerships with ancillary letting income

Background

Finance Act 1995 introduced new rules for calculating taxable income from UK property. These rules apply for income tax purposes only and take effect for the 1995–96 year of assessment onwards. For any individual or partnership, income from furnished lettings formerly within Case VI of Schedule D and income formerly within the old Schedule A rules are treated as arising from a single rental business. The taxable profits from that business are computed broadly in the same way as profits from a trade.

The new rules are much simpler than those they replace in a number of respects. For example, there is now no need to identify different types of lease and to segregate expenditure accordingly. As a result it should be possible to do without much of the considerable body of non-statutory practice which grew up around the old Schedule A and furnished lettings rules. This will enable letting profits to be self assessed to income tax more easily and with greater certainty than would otherwise have been possible.

Basis periods – new schedule A

Like the old Schedule A, the new rules provide that the income arising during a year of assessment is taxable in that year (the 'fiscal year' basis). But in practice, under the old rules the income for a period of account ending at some point in the year of assessment could be regarded as the income arising in the year of assessment itself.

There will be no equivalent practice under the new Schedule A and in general, individuals will be required to return their Schedule A profits on a fiscal year basis. (The way the transition to the new rules is to be made is the subject of our Press Release of 10 February 1995.)

Partnerships

There is, however, one statutory exception to the use of the fiscal year basis. This applies to partnerships for years to which the rules introduced to facilitate Self Assessment apply. Under those rules, the members of a partnership carrying on a trade or profession are assessed to tax on their share of all partnership income (other than income which has suffered tax by deduction at source) on the accounts basis. The effect of the rule is that a partner's share of income within Schedule A will be assessed using the same basis period as that for trading or professional income.

Where the trade or profession commenced after 5 April 1994, partnerships' income is immediately taxed under the new Self Assessment rules described above. But if the partnership's trade or profession commenced prior to 6 April 1994 these rules will not normally apply until 1997–98.

In strictness, therefore, under the new rules, any Schedule A income of established partnerships should be calculated on a fiscal year basis for 1995–96 and 1996–97 but on an accounts year basis subsequently. In the case of a partnership whose ancillary Schedule A income was taxed on an accounts basis up to 1994–95, this would involve a switch to the fiscal year basis in 1995–96 and then a switch back to the accounts basis in 1997–98.

To avoid temporary changes of this nature we are prepared to allow the Schedule A or furnished lettings income of trading and professional partnerships assessed on a current year accounts basis for 1994–95 to be taxed on the same basis for 1995–96 and 1996–97.

[ICTA 1988, s 111, FA 1995, s 39, Press Release of 10 February 1995].

Page 242. Changes of accounting date in advance of transition to current year assessing [2.24 and 24.15]

This article summarises our views on the practice to be adopted when considering a case in which a basis period for 1995–96 (or earlier) must be determined by reference to an account ending in 1995–96.

Board's policy for changes of accounting date

Under the preceding year basis of assessment, the Board's general policy at a change of accounting date is to secure that the profits to be assessed twice, or to be omitted from assessment, are 'average profits'. In this context 'average profits' means an average calculated by reference to both the number of months in the accounting periods used in the averaging calculations and the number of months in the relevant years of assessment.

The fine detail of the averaging calculations used in different circumstances need not concern us here. But the general principles are:

– the 'aggregate profit' is calculated. This is the profit of the relevant accounting periods grossed up (or reduced down) in proportion to the number of months in the relevant years of assessment. [For example, if a 13 month account were to form the basis of assessment for 2 years, the 'aggregate profit' would be 24/13 of the profit in that accounting period.]

- then (subject to a de minimis test) basis periods are adopted that ensure that the profits assessed in the 'relevant years' total the 'aggregate profit'. The key to this process is the ability to generate (and vary) overlaps and/or gaps between the basis periods for adjacent years. In this way the total profit assessed in the relevant years can be increased, or if the case demands, reduced.

The flexibility needed to manipulate basis periods in this way is provided by combinations of ICTA 1988, s 60(5) (assessment of the 'corresponding period') and the Board's discretionary power in ICTA 1988, s 60(4).

Changes of accounting date in advance of the transition to current year assessing

Many taxpayers are making, or considering, changes of accounting date in advance of the transition to current year assessment. For many of these taxpayers, the averaging calculations will generate a basis period for 1995–96 without any reference to 1996–97 as a 'relevant year'.

However, there will be other cases in which the averaging calculations would normally include 1996–97 as a relevant year. And in some of these cases the 'aggregate profit' could only be assessed by the use of ICTA 1988, s 60(4) to generate overlaps (or gaps) between the basis periods for 1995–96 and 1996–97.

But the reality is that the basis period for 1996–97 will be determined by the transitional rules in FA 1994, 20 Sch and will begin immediately after the end of the basis period for 1995–96 without a gap or overlap.

Existing practice will apply to determine a basis period for 1995–96 or earlier

It has been decided that the existing practice should be used, unchanged, as the means of determining basis periods for years up to and including 1995–96.

In particular, where it is necessary to carry out a change of accounting date calculation to determine a basis period for 1995–96 (or earlier) the calculations should proceed using existing practice as if the transitional rules for 1996–97 did not exist. But any figure or basis period for 1996–97 should subsequently be ignored. Instead, the transitional basis period for 1996–97 will commence immediately after whatever basis period is used for 1995–96, in the normal way.

As now, there may be circumstances in a particular case that merit special consideration (for example, a seasonal business) and such cases will be reviewed by the taxpayer's local office.

Example
Consider a business for which accounts are made up to 31.12. every year including 31.12.93. The accounting date is then changed to 30.4.95 (and

there is no account ending in 1994–95). An accounting date of 30.4 is retained in subsequent years.

Applying existing practice as if 1996–97 were a normal PY year (i.e. ignoring the transitional rules for 1996–97), the averaging calculations might generate basis periods as follows (other combinations are possible, but the same principle will apply):

1994–95 – 12 mths to 31.12.93
ICTA 1988, s 60(3) (original basis period retained)

1995–96 – 12 mths to 31.7.94
ICTA 1988, s 60(4) (12 mths to an accounting date intermediate between the old date and the new date)

1996–97 – 12 mths to 30.4.95
ICTA 1988, s 60(4) (12 months to the new accounting date)

The basis periods and profit figures for 1994–95 and 1995–96 remain as calculated. But the basis period for 1996–97 must be replaced by a transitional basis period given by FA 1994, 20 Sch. And the profit assessed will be the 'appropriate percentage' of that period.

The transitional basis period is the period between the end of the basis period used for 1995–96 and the accounting date used in 1996–97. This period is the 21 months 1.8.94 to 30.4.96, and the appropriate percentage is 57%.

[ICTA 1988, s 60, FA 1994, 20 Sch].

Page 245. Excessive assessments: The practice known as 'equitable liability'

Most people keep their tax affairs up to date and pay their tax at the right time. If people have genuine difficulties in meeting their payments they should let us know as soon as possible. The more we are kept informed, the more we are likely to be able to help.

If a taxpayer receives an assessment and does not think it is right, he or she can appeal against it and has thirty days from the date on which the notice of assessment was issued to do so. Inspectors will accept appeals once that time limit has passed if they are satisfied that there was a reasonable excuse for not making the appeal within the time limit and the application to admit the appeal late was made without unreasonable delay thereafter. If the Inspector does not think these requirements have been met, the application must be referred to the Appeal Commissioners for a decision. The Appeal Commissioners are completely independent of the Inland Revenue and their decision on this matter is final.

Otherwise, an assessment is final and conclusive and the Inland Revenue is able to take recovery proceedings – through to bankruptcy if necessary – for the full amount. There is no legal right to adjustment of the liability.

However, where the taxpayer has exhausted all other possible remedies, the Inland Revenue may, depending on the circumstances of the particular case, be prepared not to pursue its legal right to recovery for the full amount where it would be unconscionable to insist on collecting the full amount of tax assessed and legally due.

This practice is known as 'equitable liability' and was originally introduced to protect other creditors in a bankruptcy at a time when, prior to the 1986 Insolvency Act in particular, the Inland Revenue's preferential rights were wider. Crown preference meant that, if the Inland Revenue maintained an 'excessive' claim for a sum above that which would be due if based on the true profits, other creditors would be at a disadvantage. The term 'equitable liability' therefore reflects the original principle of fairness to other creditors.

It has become increasingly apparent to us that, while many practitioners know of this practice, some do not. To remedy this apparent unfairness, the Chairman of the Board of Inland Revenue confirmed in evidence to the Select Committee on the Parliamentary Commissioner for Administration that we would publish an explanation of the practice in an article in Tax Bulletin.

The Inland Revenue may be prepared to consider applying 'equitable liability' where, in the circumstances of the particular case and in the light of all the evidence, it is clearly demonstrated that:

- the liability assessed is greater than the amount which would have been charged had the returns, and necessary supporting documentation, been submitted at the proper time, and
- acceptable evidence is provided of what the correct liability should have been.

In such cases the Inland Revenue may be prepared to accept a reduced sum based on the evidence provided, and not to pursue its right of recovery for the full amount.

This treatment will depend on the circumstances of the particular case, and is conditional on the taxpayer's affairs being brought fully up to date. The Inland Revenue would expect full payment to be made of the reduced sum. Furthermore, it would be most unusual for such treatment to be applied more than once in favour of the same taxpayer.

In determining the revised liability, the Inland Revenue will have regard to all the relevant circumstances of the case. Acceptable evidence of the reduced liability must be produced. It will not be sufficient to seek to replace the assessment merely with the taxpayer's or the accountant's estimate of the liability.

Cases are dealt with in the Inland Revenue's Enforcement Offices in Worthing and Belfast and Enforcement Section in Edinburgh, but Inspectors in local offices will be involved in considering the quantum of any claims for reduction of liability and the acceptability of the supporting evidence.

Position under self assessment

Self Assessment will change the way in which liability is established and will remove the Inland Revenue's reliance on estimated assessments. The liability that taxpayers declare on their returns should normally reflect their proper liability and there should be no need for the Inland Revenue to review those cases in the way described above.

However, where a taxpayer has not submitted his or her return, the Inland Revenue can determine the taxpayer's likely tax liability so that the tax can be pursued. There is no right of appeal against such determinations, and the tax determined is legally enforceable. Taxpayers can displace the determination with their own self assessment at any time up to the fifth anniversary of the statutory filing date for the year of assessment in question (or one year after the determination was issued, if later).

It is unlikely therefore, that the point will often be reached where a determination can no longer be displaced. Where exceptionally that does occur and the conditions of the practice described are fulfilled, then the Inland Revenue will be prepared to consider extending their practice to meet this situation.

Page 246. Vouchers for claim to repayment by or on behalf of individual taxpayers

Readers will be aware that the Revenue asks for vouchers – certificates of tax credit or tax deducted – to be produced in support of claims to repayment of tax and that the relevant legislation is at TMA 1970, s 42(7). We have been asked if our requirements have changed since the introduction of the lower rate band.

There are three requirements:

- when the person is not liable to tax for the repayment year, all vouchers should be forwarded. This requirement has not changed;
- when any repayment computation includes interest from bank, building society or other licensed deposit takers, all vouchers from this source should be forwarded regardless of whether or not the tax on that particular item of income is repayable. These vouchers are issued under ICTA 1988, s 352 and this requirement has not changed;
- in other cases, we have always asked for vouchers to cover the amount of income which is being relieved from tax by repayment. This requirement has not changed. What has changed is the amount of income which can be wholly or partly relieved from tax. Until 1991–92, it was only necessary to produce vouchers for income equal to the unused personal allowances of the person concerned and in practice these would show tax equal to the repayment due.

For 1992–93, in addition to the tax repayment on account of personal allowances, another £2,000 of income can be partly relieved of tax – i.e. at the difference between 25% and 20%. If, for instance, an individual had £1,500 of unused lower rate band, it would be necessary to produce vouchers for income of £1,500 to enable repayment of £75 to be made.

For 1993–94 and later years, there is a further factor to be taken into account. Some income may be received under deduction of tax at the basic rate but dividends and other qualifying distributions will only carry tax credit at the lower rate. This means that vouchers for income taxed at basic rate should be produced in preference to those carrying tax credit at the lower rate. Tax credit is only available at the lower rate and there will of course, be no entitlement to repayment in respect of the lower rate band, if only vouchers for tax credit are available.

Issue 20, December 1995

Page 261. Taxation of the property income of non-resident landlords

ICTA 1988, s 42A, introduced by FA 1995, s 40, provides for a new scheme for taxing the income of a Schedule A business carried on by a person whose usual place of abode is outside the UK (a 'non-resident landlord'). The detail of the scheme is set out in Statutory Instruments (SI 1995 No 2902 'The Taxation of Income from Land (Non-resident) Regulations 1995' which became law on 1 December 1995. The new scheme applies to rents and other income of a Schedule A business paid on or after 6 April 1996.

The new scheme replaces the present arrangements in ICTA 1988, s 43 and TMA 1970, s 78, which apply to income of a Schedule A business paid before 6 April 1996. The changes are necessary because the present arrangements do not fit well with Self Assessment.

How the new scheme works

From 6 April 1996, letting agents or, where there is no letting agent, tenants of a non-resident landlord must:

- deduct tax at the basic rate from the landlord's UK rental income; and
- pay the tax quarterly to the Inland Revenue.

But non-resident landlords can apply to the Inland Revenue for approval to receive their rental income with no tax deducted.

Letting agents or, where there is no letting agent, tenants, will also be required to submit annual information returns providing details of income, expenses and tax deducted for each non-resident landlord.

The scheme will be administered by the Inland Revenue's Financial Intermediaries and Claims Office (FICO). Further information can be obtained from FICO and the address and telephone numbers are given at the end of this article. The Inland Revenue have also published a leaflet,

IR140 'Non-resident landlords, their agents and tenants' which explains the scheme. It can be obtained from any Tax Office or Tax Enquiry Centre or from FICO.

Who are letting agents?

Letting agents are persons in the UK who act in connection with the management or administration of all or part of a Schedule A business. This is a wide definition and includes friends and relatives of the non-resident landlord as well as professionals such as estate agents, who collect rents for him. But it excludes, for example, banks and building societies who do no more than provide accounts into which Schedule A income is paid and from which withdrawals for expenses are made.

Letting agents are required to operate the scheme only if they handle or control UK rental income on behalf of a non-resident landlord. This excludes, for example, accountants who do no more than prepare accounts and tax computations, and agents who do no more than find a tenant in return for a fee (without collecting any rents).

The Regulations also specifically exclude as letting agents persons who do no more than provide legal advice or legal services. This covers, for example, solicitors who take proceedings to recover arrears of rent or who receive apportioned rents in the course of a conveyance. But the exclusion does not cover solicitors who draw up a lease and collect the First payment of rent on behalf of the landlord. That is because, in collecting rents, the solicitor is going beyond the provision of legal advice or services.

There may, exceptionally, be two or more letting agents acting in respect of the same part of a Schedule A business. In such a case it is the agent who pays the income directly to the landlord (or to his overseas agent) who must operate the scheme. But letting agents may jointly elect that responsibility for operating the scheme be transferred from one of them to the other.

The tax calculation – letting agents

Letting agents must calculate tax quarterly in respect of non-resident landlords for whom they act, unless they have written authority from the Inland Revenue to pay the income with no tax deducted. For each landlord, separately, they will have to calculate tax at the basic rate on:

- Schedule A income they have received in the quarter, plus
- other Schedule A income paid away by the tenant in the quarter at the letting agent's direction; less
- expenses paid in the quarter by the letting agent (or paid at his direction) which the letting agent can reasonably be satisfied are allowable expenses of the non-resident landlord's Schedule A business.

If expenses paid in the quarter exceed income received in that quarter in respect of a non-resident landlord, the letting agent can carry back the surplus expenses to earlier quarters in the same year ended 31 March, taking later quarters before earlier ones. Any surplus which cannot be used in this way can be carried forward to future quarters, including quarters in a later year. But surplus expenses for one landlord cannot be set against the income of another landlord.

Letting agents must then add together all tax due for their non-resident landlords for the quarter and show this Figure on the quarterly return which they must submit to the Inland Revenue, with payment of the tax, within 30 days of the end of the quarter.

If a repayable amount rises as a result of the carry back of surplus expenses, the letting agent will set this off against tax due for the quarter in respect of other non-resident landlords, thereby reducing his liability for that quarter. Any repayable amount that cannot be set off in this way can be claimed on the quarterly return and the Inland Revenue will repay the tax to the letting agent.

Example: Agent's calculation

	Non-resident landlord 1	**Non-resident landlord 2**
Quarter 1		
Income	£1,000	£2,000
Expenses	£800	£1,000
	£200	£1,000
Tax (@ 25%)	£50	£250
Tax payable		£300
Quarter 2		
Income	£1,000	£2,000
Expenses	£1,500	£1,400
	−£500	£600
Tax (@ 25%)	NIL	£150
Surplus expenses carried back	£200	
Tax repayable	£50	
Tax payable		£100
Surplus expenses carried forward	£300	

In Quarter 2 the agent has £500 surplus expenses in respect of landlord 1. Only £200 can be carried back to Quarter 1. This gives a repayable amount of £50 which can be set against the tax otherwise due, £150. This gives tax payable of £100.

The tax calculation – tenants

Where there is no letting agent, the tenant must operate the scheme. However, unless they receive a notice from the Inland Revenue requiring them to operate the scheme, tenants paying rent of £100 per week or less are excluded from the scheme.

Tenants calculate tax at the basic rate on:

- Schedule A income they paid in the quarter to the non-resident landlord; plus
- Schedule A income they paid to a third party in the quarter, not being a payment they can reasonably be satisfied is an allowable expense of the landlord's Schedule A business.

Tenants must show the tax due on the quarterly return which they must submit, with payment of tax, within 30 days of the end of the quarter. As tenants calculate tax on amounts paid, the carry back of surplus expenses does not arise.

Income within the scheme

The scheme applies to all income of a non-resident's Schedule A business which is:

- received by, or within the control of, a letting agent; or
- where there is no letting agent, paid by a tenant.

It includes all annual profits or gains arising from any land in the UK including income from the letting or licensing of any furnished or unfurnished property and any premiums chargeable as income, rent charges, ground rents, wayleaves and feu duties.

Expenses within the scheme

The scheme provides for the deduction of all expenses which the letting agent or tenant can reasonably be satisfied are allowable in computing the profits of the non-resident's Schedule A business and which are:

- paid by, or at the direction of, the letting agent; or
- paid by the tenant, where there is no letting agent.

The Regulations provide that letting agents and tenants can deduct expenses if they can reasonably be satisfied that they are allowable deductions. Early in 1996 the Inland Revenue will publish guidance notes for letting agents and tenants which will include a section on allowable deductions. Provided letting agents and tenants follow this guidance, the Inland Revenue will not penalise them for deducting an expense which later turns out not to be deductible. Where letting agents or tenants are unable to satisfy themselves whether an expense is deductible, perhaps because they do not have sufficient information about the purpose of the expenditure, they should not deduct it.

Payment without deduction of tax

Non-resident landlords who wish to receive their Schedule A income with no tax deducted can apply to FICO for approval. They can obtain forms from the address below. They can apply on the basis that:

- their UK tax affairs are up to date; or
- they have never had any UK tax obligations; or
- they do not expect to be liable to UK income tax; and
- they undertake to comply with all their UK tax obligations. In particular this means that they must complete all tax returns sent to them and pay all tax due, on time.

A landlord's UK tax affairs are up to date if he or she has paid all tax due and submitted all tax returns issued (other than tax for which the due date for payment has not passed and returns for which the filing date has not passed).

When FICO approves an application they will write to the landlord and the letting agent(s) and/or tenant(s) named on the application form, telling them that the landlord is entitled to receive rental income with no tax deducted. Letting agents and tenants who receive such a notice should stop deducting tax from the date shown in the notice. But they should only do so when they get a notice from the Inland Revenue: they must not stop deducting tax simply because the landlord tells them to do so.

When FICO refuses an application, or withdraws approval, they will tell the landlord the reason why. The landlord may appeal to the General or Special Commissioners. If approval is withdrawn, FICO will tell agents and tenants to start deducting tax.

Self assessment

Landlords who suffer deduction of tax can set the tax off against their UK tax liability through their self-assessment. Letting agents and tenants who deduct tax must provide the landlord with a certificate showing the amount of tax deducted for each year ended 31 March, by 5 July after the end of that year. In the landlord's self-assessment, tax deducted for the year ended 31 March will be set off against his or her tax liability for the year ended 5 April.

Payments on account under Self Assessment will be calculated by reference to a 'relevant amount' of the income tax assessed for the previous year. The relevant amount is the amount by which the total income tax assessed exceeds the credits for tax deducted at source. Tax 'deducted at source' includes tax deducted by letting agents and tenants under this scheme (TMA 1970, s 59A).

But, where a year in which tax was not deducted follows a year in which it was deducted, landlords must compute their payments on account for the second year as if tax had not been deducted in the first year.

For example, in year 1 a landlord has income of £10,000 and tax deducted £2,500. In year 2 he has approval to receive Schedule A income with no tax deducted. In year 2 he will calculate payments on account as if he had received the £10,000 in year 1 with no tax deducted.

Further Information

If you have any technical enquiries you can contact:

Paul Blackwell
FICO (FIT)
St John's House
Merton Road
BOOTLE
Merseyside L69 9BB
Telephone: 0151–472 6159
Minicom: 0151–472 6112
Fax: 0151–472 6006.

If you require application forms for non-resident landlords to receive Schedule A income with no tax deducted, or copies of leaflet IR140 'Non-resident landlords, their agents and tenants' you can contact:

FICO (Non-residents)
St John's House
Merton Road
Bootle
Merseyside L69 9BB
Telephone: 0151–472 6208/6209
Minicom: 0151–572 6112
Fax: 0151–472 6067.

Page 268. Schedule A: Transitional proposals [5.2 and 5.48 *et seq*.]

From 6 April 1995, new rules apply where profits from land and property in the UK are charged to income tax. These rules are to be found in FA 1995, s 39 and FA 1995, 6 Sch.

The key changes which apply for the tax year 1995–96 and later years are that:

- profits for tax purposes must be calculated for the tax year itself – this is the year to 5 April. It is no longer possible to use a different basis period (with the exception of certain trading partnerships with ancillary Schedule A income – see Tax Bulletin: Issue 18, page 241); and
- the starting point for the calculation of the Schedule A income is the profit computed in accordance with normal commercial accountancy principles.

We have been asked to:

- provide examples of situations where transitional adjustments are necessary; and
- explain the action to be taken where a transitional adjustment is to be made in the 1995–96 assessment (because 1994–95 has already been agreed).

Transitional adjustments

As part of the process of moving onto the new rules, a special one-off transitional adjustment may be needed. An Inland Revenue Press Release dealing with Schedule A transitional proposals was issued on 10 February 1995 and that guidance has now been incorporated in the Revenue guide SAT1 (1995) 'Notes on the new current year basis of assessment'.

An adjustment may be needed for two reasons:

– first, receipts or expenses may be double counted or omitted entirely because of the change from a 'cash basis' or 'entitlement' basis to accruals basis in 1995–96;
– second, there may be a gap between the basis periods for 1994–95 and 1995–96 which is not taxed and the profits or losses of the period are untypically high or low.

In some cases, both situations may apply.

In small cases, or cases where profits are much the same from year to year, either no adjustment will be due under transition or the adjustment will be small.

The transitional adjustment cannot be calculated by taking only the items which work in a taxpayer's favour, everything must be brought in. Tax Offices may make further enquiries where the computations put forward for 1994–95 or 1995–96 appear to be materially unreasonable; for example, where untypically high profits fall out of charge in the gap period. There may be special circumstances to be taken into account.

When to make the adjustment

As stated in our previous guidance, any adjustment should be made in 1994–95. This should still be the aim but it may not be possible if that year was settled early. In that case the adjustment should be calculated in the same way but made in 1995–96.

Situations where adjustments commonly needed

It is only possible to cover here the more common situations giving rise to a transitional adjustment. The examples have been simplified to illustrate the principles.

Receipts or expenses double counted or omitted

Receipts and expenses are taken into account in arriving at the taxable profit in different ways under the old and new rules and this means items could be **counted twice or omitted altogether**.

Double counting or omissions may arise as follows:

– receipts could be taxed twice, both under the old rules as income of 1994–95 and under the new rules for 1995–96;
– receipts could fall out of account altogether. In practice, this is unlikely unless rents are due substantially in arrear (which is not common in commercial situations);

- expenses could be deductible under the old rules for 1994–95 and under the new rules for 1995–96, this would give a double taxation;
- expenses could fall out of account under both the old and new rules. Hence the expenses are not deducted at all.

The general aim is to correct any double counting and omissions and to ensure that the profits or losses of any gap period (which drops out of charge) are average amounts.

The following examples show how the need for a transitional adjustment arises where the old Schedule A basis applied and how to compute a fair measure of relief. But similar principles may apply where furnished letting under Case VI of Schedule D has been dealt with in the past on a fiscal year cash basis. For simplicity, these examples make apportionments to the nearest month. But if the taxpayer prefers these can, of course, be dealt with on a daily basis (which is the strictly correct approach). A daily basis should also be used if the figures are substantial and a strict computation would produce a materially different result.

Example 1

A house is let unfurnished from 1 July 1993 onwards. The following rent is charged:

- £4,000 for each half year payable half yearly in advance from 1 July 1993
- £6,000 for each half year payable half yearly in advance from 1 January 1995
- £8,000 for each half year payable half yearly in advance from 1 January 1996.

Accounts have been prepared each year to 5 April and the profit shown in those accounts is charged for that tax year.

The assessments will be as follows:

1994–95

The assessment is based on rents to which the taxpayer was entitled in that year

1 July 1994	£4,000
1 January 1995	£6,000
TOTAL	£10,000

1995–96

The assessment is based on the amount earned in that year

6 April 1995 to 30 June 1995: 3/6 × £6,000 =	£3,000
1 July 1995 to 31 December 1995:	£6,000
1 January 1995 to 5 April 1996: 3/6 × £8,000 =	£4,000
TOTAL	£13,000

Note: the date the rent was due and the date the rent was paid do not affect the calculation of the rent earned.

Transitional adjustment

Of the 6 months rent of £6,000 due on 1 January 1995, 3 months rent has been double counted on the move to the new system. The entire £6,000 was charged in 1994–95 and £3,000 of it is charged again in 1995–96.

A transitional adjustment of £3,000 should therefore be made subject to any other adjustments to be made.

Example 2
Taking the same facts as Example 1, insurance premiums are paid annually in advance on 1 January as follows:
£1,000 on 1 January 1995
£1,200 on 1 January 1996

Relief will be due as follows:

1994–95
£1,000
(the premium paid in the year)

1995–96
6 April 1995 to 31 December 1995:
£1,000 × 9/12 = £750
1 January 1996 to 5 April 1996:
£1,200 × 3/12 = £300

Page 271. Changes of accounting date in advance of the transition to current year assessing [2.24]

We have been asked by a number of practitioners why the example included in Tax Bulletin Issue 18 (August 1995) entitled 'Changes of Accounting Date in advance of Transition to Current Year Assessing' does not follow the practice set out in paragraph 3 of the Inland Revenue booklet IR26 'Changes of Accounting date'.

The practice described in the article is only relevant in cases where:

> '. . . the averaging calculations would normally include 1996–97 as a relevant year . . . [and where] . . . the "aggregate profit" could only be assessed by the use of ICTA 1988, s 60(4) to generate overlaps (or gaps) between the basis periods for 1995–96 and 1996–97.'

These will be cases which fall within the terms of **paragraph 7(a) of IR26**.

IR26 only provides an introduction to the Board's practice on changes of accounting date. Anyone seeking a more detailed description is advised to consult IM 1370 to IM 1400 of the 'Inspectors Manual', or seek advice from their Tax Office.

Page 271. Self assessment: Assessment of schedule A income arising to a partnership [5.55 and 5.56]

We have been asked to clarify the circumstances in which the income from jointly owned property constitutes partnership income within the terms of ICTA 1988, s 111 (as substituted by FA 1995, s 117(2)).

There are a number of possibilities. For example, consider Mr and Mrs Jackson who let a jointly owned property.

Where Mr and Mrs Jackson carry on a business in partnership, and that business comprises both a Case I Schedule D source and a Schedule A source, then ICTA 1988, s 111(7) & (8) would apply. The income from the Schedule A source will be assessable using the basis periods that apply for the Case I Schedule D source.

But it may be that these two activities have been arranged in such a way that there are two separate businesses and two separate partnerships, albeit partnerships between the same two individuals. In such circumstances ICTA 1988, s 111(10) would apply to the partnership with the Schedule A source. The income from the Schedule A source will be assessable on a tax year (6 April to 5 April) basis.

There is a further possibility. Joint ownership of property does not, of itself, create a partnership. There will only be a partnership if, exceptionally, the exploitation of the property constitutes the carrying on of a business jointly with a view to profit. Where the letting income is not ancillary to a Case I/II partnership source, and the letting activity cannot be described as the carrying on of a business, the income arising is not assessable as partnership income. Instead, each share will be assessable as the personal income of Mr and Mrs Jackson. In this context there is a distinction between the term 'business' as used in the Partnership Act 1890, and the new concept of a 'Schedule A business' introduced by FA 1995.

[ICTA 1988, s 111].

Issue 21, February 1996

Page 282. Farmer's averaging and the transition to self-assessment [4.20]

We have been asked about farmer's averaging and the transition to self-assessment.

At present, farmer's averaging works by adding the profits before capital allowances assessable for two consecutive years of assessment and assessing half the total each year.

It is profits assessable which are averaged not profits for periods of account. So the first step is to work out the profit assessable. For cases where 1996–97 is the transition year for self-assessment, the profit will generally be based on the results of *two* years of account reduced by self-assessment transition averaging (under FA 1994 Sch 20 para 2(2)). For example, a farmer's results are—

– Year ended 31 December 1994, Profit £55,000
– Year ended 31 December 1995, Profit £60,000
– Year ended 31 December 1996, Profit £10,000

The profits assessable are—

1995–96
£55,000 previous year basis

1996–97
£35,000 half the total profit for the two years ended 31 December 1996.

The profits assessable differ by more than 30% of the higher of them so farmer's averaging may be claimed. If a claim is made the profits assessable become—

1995–96 £45,000
1996–97 £45,000

We have seen it suggested that farmer's averaging can be claimed when the results shown by the accounts for the first of these two years (the year ended 31 December 1995 in the example) are known. This suggestion is incorrect. It is based on the misconception that it is profits for periods of account, rather than profits for years of assessment, which are averaged.

The way in which averaging is given will change fundamentally under self-assessment. This will be explained in detail in a later article [below] and in a Help Sheet which will be available to farmers to assist them with their self-assessment tax returns.

If 1996–97 is averaged with 1997–98 then new rules will apply—

– it is profits after capital allowances which are averaged, and
– claims will be at partner level not partnership level.

By contrast, if 1996–97 is averaged with 1995–96 then the present rules apply—

– profits before capital allowances are averaged, and
– if the farm is a partnership, averaging is dealt with at partnership level.

For cases which commenced for tax purposes after 5 April 1994 the new rules apply straightaway.

For further information see pages 188, 189 of Inland Revenue Guide SAT 1 (1995) 'The new current year basis of assessment'.

Page 283. Record keeping equipment

There has been an increasing number of queries over recent months about the Revenue's attitude towards the use of optical imaging systems to preserve taxpayers' records.

Until recently there were no specific requirements for either business or personal taxpayers to keep records or to retain them after their returns and accounts had been filed. Obviously, people have always needed to keep records in order to make a complete and correct return. Equally, it has always made sense for them to retain these records for a time afterwards. In that respect, nothing has changed.

However, legislation introduced in FA 1994 as part of the preparation for the self-assessment system for individuals (which will be introduced from the tax year 1996–7) has now helped to clarify the position by setting some clear rules. These rules will also apply in due course to companies, although the precise starting date has yet to be fixed.

The rules, drafted with computer held records in mind, say that the new duty to preserve records may be satisfied by preserving the information which they contain. In the Revenue's view, these rules will specifically permit for tax purposes the use of optical imaging systems, provided that what is retained on disc represents a complete and unaltered image of the underlying paper document.

Records relating to a taxpayer's obligations as an employer (for example, records of PAYE deductions etc) must still be retained in paper form and contractors in the construction industry must continue to keep the originals of subcontractor documents and vouchers (for example forms SC60).

Any vouchers which will be used as the basis of a claim to repayment (for example, dividend vouchers) must also be retained in the original paper form. However, there is no change for financial intermediaries which are already authorised to retain records on microfiche or similar media without retaining the originals.

The Revenue regards these rules as applying *now* to both individuals and companies.

Further information can be obtained from – Julia Hawkes, Room 538, SW Wing, Bush House, Strand, London WC2 4RD, Telephone number 0171 438 6196.

Further information on the new record keeping requirement can be found in the leaflet SA/BK3 'Self-assessment – a guide to keeping records for the self-employed'.

Page 283. Basis periods: partnerships with ancillary letting income – transition to new Schedule A

FA 1995 introduced new rules for calculating taxable income from UK property under Schedule A. These rules apply for income tax purposes only and apply for the 1995–96 tax year and later years. Inland Revenue Guide SAT 1 (1995) 'The new current year basis of assessment' explains the general approach to the transition from old to new Schedule A at para 9.94 onwards, but says nothing specific about ancillary letting income of trading and professional partnerships. This article covers several detailed points about basis periods.

Commencement of trade or profession after 5 April 1994

Where the trade or profession started after 5 April 1994, the partnership's rental income is immediately taxed on a current year accounts basis. The effect of this rule is that a partner's share of rental income will be assessed using the same basis period as that for trading or professional income. No special transitional problem arises and this article says nothing more about these cases.

Commencement of trade or profession before 6 April 1994

But if the partnership's trade or profession started before 6 April 1994, the current year accounts basis will not normally apply to Schedule A ancillary sources until 1997–98 and an extra transitional difficulty arises. Strictly, ancillary partnership rental income is taxed for 1995–96 and 1996–97 on a fiscal year basis. That is, taking the results of the years to 5 April 1996 and 5 April 1997 respectively. But for 1997–98 (and later years) the current year accounts basis must be used. In some cases this can mean that the Schedule A basis periods have to be changed from an accounts basis, to a fiscal basis and then back to an accounts basis again.

The rest of this article explains the way to avoid this problem.

Partnership used current year accounts basis for 1994–95

In Tax Bulletin Issue 18 (August 1995 p 241) we said that, where a partnership's trade or profession started before 6 April 1994, we will accept that ancillary partnership Schedule A or Case VI rental income previously assessed on a current year accounts basis, including for 1994–95, can retain the same basis for 1995–96 and 1996–97. A current year accounts basis will then apply under statute for 1997–98 and later years. This avoids the change of basis period for 1995–96 and 1996–97.

Partnership used previous year accounts basis for 1994–95

We have now been asked whether a similar approach may be used for trading or professional partnerships which started before 6 April 1994 and where Schedule A or furnished lettings income was assessed on a previous year accounts basis. It can. We will accept that a current year accounts basis may be used in 1995–96 and 1996–97 in these cases. This means that, for these cases, the transition to new Schedule A will include a change from a previous year accounts basis for 1994–95 to a current year accounts basis for 1995–96.

Partnership used fiscal year basis for 1994–95

The ancillary rental income of some partnerships may have been taxed up to 1994–95 on the current, fiscal year basis (that is, the year to each 5 April). Here, the 5 April basis should continue to be used for 1995–96 and 1996–97 and then the current year accounts basis must be used for 1997–98.

Transitional Schedule A adjustment for 1994–95 in partnership cases

SAT 1 (1995) explains how to work out any transitional adjustment needed because of gaps between the basis periods for 1994–95 and 1995–96 (para 9.94 onwards). The calculation must be made for 1994–95 and, ideally, made in 1994–95. Where, however, the 1994–95 assessment is final and is not capable of further amendment, any transitional adjustment (calculated as for 1994–95) should be made in the 1995–96 assessment. Tax Bulletin Issue 20 (December 1995) gave some examples at pp 268 to 271. Further guidance is set out below for trading and professional partnerships which started before 6 April 1994 and which have ancillary rental income.

Transitional Schedule A adjustment – current year accounts basis used for 1994–95

There are two separate cases where the partnership used a current year accounts basis for ancillary rental income in 1994–95 and earlier years.

First, there is the case where the partnership decides to stay on the current year accounts basis for 1995–96 and 1996–97. Here there will be no change of basis period and no transitional basis period adjustment will be needed on this account. This approach may be preferable because it is simpler and gets the transition over quickly.

Second, there is the case where the partnership decides to change to the fiscal year basis for 1995–96 and 1996–97. Here there will be a gap between the 1994–95 and 1995–96 basis periods and a transitional basis period adjustment on this account will need to be considered. The partnership will have to change back to a current year accounts basis in 1997–98. The 1997–98 charge will be based on the full profits of the current year accounts.

Transitional Schedule A adjustment – previous year accounts basis used for 1994–95

Where a previous year accounts basis has been used in the past for rental income, there will always be a gap between the basis period for 1994–95 and 1995–96. Any transitional adjustment because of the gap should be calculated using the principles explained in SAT 1 (1995) and Tax Bulletin Issue 20 (December 1995). There are two cases.

First, there is the case where the partnership decides to change at once to a current year accounts basis for 1995–96. Changing at once to the current year accounts basis may be preferable because it gets the transition over.

Second, there is the case where the partnership chooses to adopt the fiscal year basis for 1995–96 and 1996–97. Here, the partnership will also have to change to a current year accounts basis in 1997–98.

Transitional Schedule A adjustment – fiscal year basis used for 1994–95

In this case there will be no change of basis period after 1994–95 because the fiscal year basis will continue to be used up to and including 1996–97. Hence no 1994–95 transitional adjustment for a gap can arise.

Identification of transitional overlap profit, or genuine overlap profit, in 1997–98

We intend to publish a further note in a later issue of Tax Bulletin on the position in 1997–98.

Page 286. Due dates for payment of tax charged in composite partnership assessment for 1996–97

We have been asked to clarify the due dates for payment of the tax charged in a composite partnership assessment for 1996–97.

1996–97 is the first year of self-assessment for personal returns, including returns completed by individual partners. It will also be the first year in which self-assessment returns are required from partnerships. But for most partnerships the 1996–97 Schedule D Case I or II profits will be assessed by means of a composite partnership assessment (see Inland Revenue Guide SAT 2 (1995) para 5.12 'Self-assessment – the legal framework'). All the associated machinery provisions, for example in respect of the payment of tax or an appeal will apply to that assessment as they do now.

In particular, the notes to Table 23 of FA 1994 Sch 26 indicate that the repeal of TA 1988 s 5 does not apply to partnerships until 1997–98. Therefore the due dates for a 1996–97 composite assessment made at the normal time remain 1 January 1997 and 1 July 1997.

Each individual partner will have to include his or her share of the 1996–97 profit in his or her self-assessment return. But to ensure that these profits are not taxed twice, each partner will be able to treat the tax paid by the partnership on his or her share of partnership profit as if it were a tax credit for tax deducted at source (FA 1995 Sch 21 para 3 – see SAT 2 (1995) paras 3.123–3.125).

Page 286. Transitional issues – claims under TA 1988 s 383 for 1995–96 [3.9 and 4.2]

Under self-assessment capital allowances are treated as a trading expense of the period of account for which they are due. If the adjustment for capital allowances creates or augments a Schedule D Case I or II loss, this loss is available for relief in the normal way without the need for a special claim by the taxpayer (beyond the claim to the allowances themselves).

In contrast, under the existing rules a taxpayer is required to make a separate claim – under TA 1988 s 383 – if he or she wants to create or augment a Case I or II loss using capital allowances. Where such a claim is made, the resulting loss is available for set off against other income – subject to certain conditions – as if it were a Case I or II loss available for relief under TA 1988 s 380 or 381.

We have been asked to clarify how the special transitional basis period rules for 1996–97 affect the operation of TA 1988 s 383 for 1995–96 and 1996–97. (*Note*: if the trade or profession commenced on or after 6 April 1994 neither s 383, nor this article, are relevant, because the new self-assessment rules already apply from the date of commencement.)

The capital allowances that can be included in a s 383 claim are those of 'the year of assessment for which the year of loss is the basis year – s 383(1). For an established business this means that a Case I or II loss for any particular year of assessment can be created or augmented by the capital allowances that would otherwise be due for the next year of assessment.

For example, if the result of the accounting period, the 12 months to 30 April 1994, is a loss, then –

– year of loss is 1994–95.
– the basis period for capital allowances relevant to s 383 claim is 12 months to 30 April 1994.
– the year the allowances would have been given in an assessment is 1995–96.

But what of the next accounting period, the 12 months to 30 April 1995.

1995–96 is now the year of loss. But for a continuing business, the 12 months to 30 April 1995 do not form the basis period for 1996–97, or any other year of assessment. Instead the special transitional rules in FA 1994 Sch 20 apply. The assessment for 1996–97 will be based on the average profits of the 24 months 1 May 1994 to 30 April 1996 and the capital allowances due for 1996–97 will be calculated by reference to the qualifying expenditure in that same 24 month period (for example, see para 6.68 of Inland Revenue guide SAT 1 (1995) 'The new current year basis of assessment').

The intention was that the existing loss relief rules should operate unchanged for 1995–96 and 1996–97. This was to ensure that losses were not averaged in the transition to current year assessment. Therefore, we do not intend to refuse TA 1988 s 383 claims for 1995–96 providing –

- the claim is made in respect of the capital allowances that would have been available for such a claim if the existing preceding year basis of assessment had continued to apply for 1996–97, and
- the claim includes an undertaking that the capital allowances claimed and relieved under s 383 in 1995–96 will be deducted from any capital allowances available for claim in 1996–97, including any allowances to be given effect by set-off against any balancing charges arising in that year.

In effect, a s 383 claim for 1995–96 will be a claim for a portion of the capital allowances which, in our view, are only strictly due in 1996–97. Where the allowances advanced by such a claim exceed the allowances available for 1996–97, the excess will be recovered as if it were a balancing charge for that later year (see example 2 below).

EXAMPLE 1: Simple case; no additions or disposals
A trader has an annual accounting date of 30 September. The capital allowance computations for 1995–96 and 1996–97 are as follows –

	Capital allowance basis period	*Plant and machinery*	
1995–96	12 months to 30 September 1994	WDV b/f	12,000
		wda	(3,000)
			9,000
1996–97	24 months 1 October 1994 to 30 September 1996	WDV b/f	9,000
		wda	(2,250)
		WDV c/f	6,750

But the result for the 12 months to 30 September 1995 is a loss. If the trader wants to augment this loss under TA 1988 s 383 then he or she can do so in respect of the capital allowances that would have been available for such a claim if the existing preceding year basis of assessment had continued to apply for 1996–97.

If the existing preceding year basis of assessment had continued to apply, the Case I or II basis period for 1996–97 would have been the 12 months to 30 September 1995. The allowances that would have been due are £2,250 –

	Notional capital allowance basis period	*Plant and machinery*	
1996–97	12 months to 30 September 1995	WDV b/f	9,000
		wda	(2,250)

The allowances used to create or augment the 1995–96 loss must then be deducted from the claim made for 1996–97 –

1996–97	Allowances actually due	2,250
	Less: allowances used in 1995–96 loss claim	2,250
	Balance available 1996–97	0
	WDV c/f	6,750

EXAMPLE 2: Additions and disposals
A trader has an annual accounting date of 30 September. The capital allowance computations for 1995–96 and 1996–97 are as follows –

	Capital allowance basis period	*Plant and machinery*	
1995–96	12 months to 30 September 1994	WDV b/f	20,000
		additions	4,000
		disposals	(0)
		Total	24,000
		wda	(6,000)
		WDV c/f	18,000
1996–97	24 months 1 October 1994 to 30 September 1996	WDV b/f	18,000
	(12 months to 30 September 1995)	additions	2,000
		disposals	(4,000)
	(12 months to 30 September 1996)	additions	4,000
		disposals	(14,000)
		Total	6,000
		wda	(1,500)
		WDV c/f	4,500

But the result for the 12 months to 30 September 1995 is a loss. If the trader wants to augment this loss under TA 1988 s 383, then he or she can do so in respect of the capital allowances that would have been available for such a claim if the existing preceding year basis of assessment had continued to apply for 1996–97.

If the existing preceding year basis of assessment had continued to apply, the Case I or II basis period for 1996–97 would have been the 12 months to 30 September 1995. The allowances that would have been due are £4,000 –

	Notional capital allowance basis period	*Plant and machinery*	
1996–97	12 months to 30 September 1995	WDV b/f	18,000
		additions	2,000
		disposals	(4,000)
		Total	16,000
		wda	(4,000)

The allowances used in this way must then be deducted from the claim made for 1996–97 –

1996–97	Allowances actually due	1,500
	Less: allowances used in 1995–96 loss claim	(4,000)
	Balance available 1996–97	0
	Balancing charge 1996–97	2,500
	WDV c/f	4,500

EXAMPLE 3: No allowances available

A trader has an annual accounting date of 30 September. The capital allowance computations for 1995–96 and 1996–97 are as follows –

	Capital allowance basis period	*Plant and machinery*	
1995–96	12 months to 30 September 1994	WDV b/f	20,000
		additions	4,000
		disposals	(0)
		Total	24,000
		wda	(6,000)
		WDV c/f	18,000

1996–97	24 months 1 October 1994 to 30 September 1996	WDV b/f	18,000
	(12 months to 30 September 1995)	additions	2,000
		disposals	(24,000)
	(12 months to 30 September 1996)	additions	20,000
		disposals	(0)
		Total	16,000
		wda	(4,000)
		WDV c/f	12,000

But the result for the 12 months to 30 September 1995 is a loss. If the trader wants to augment this loss under TA 1988 s 383, then he or she can only do so in respect of the capital allowances that would have been available for such a claim if the existing preceding year basis of assessment had continued to apply for 1996–97.

If the existing preceding year basis of assessment had continued to apply, the Case I or II basis period for 1996–97 would have been the 12 months to 30 September 1995. But no allowances would have been due for that period –

	Notional capital allowance basis period	*Plant and machinery*	
1996–97	12 months to 30 September 1995	WDV b/f	18,000
		additions	2,000
		disposals	(24,000)
		Total	(4,000)
		wda	(0)
	notional balancing charge		4,000

In this example no TA 1988 s 383 claim would be possible for 1995–96.

Issue 22, April 1996

Page 293. Self Assessment and 1996–97 Partnership Assessing [12.26]

This article explains the relationship between the 1996–97 partnership assessment and the Self Assessment (SA) returns for that year issued to partnerships and partners. It expands on an earlier article, 'Self Assessment: New procedures for taxing partnerships', Tax Bulletin Issue 12 (August 1994, pages 146–148) and includes details of:

- the proposed arrangements for allocating partner's allowances, reliefs and rate bands;
- the effect of appeal and postponement applications against partnership assessments;
- the limited circumstances where profits can be agreed and appeals against 1996–97 partnership assessments determined prior to receipt of SA partnership returns;
- how tax and Class 4 National Insurance Contributions (NIC) assessed on the partnership will be taken into account in the partner's self-assessment;
- how we intend to deal with SA partnership returns in tax offices from April 1997 where there is a 1996–97 partnership assessment.

1996–97 is the first year of Self Assessment. New style SA returns will be issued to all partnerships requiring a return of partnership profits. In addition, every partner will be required to make a return of his or her share of any partnership profits and to include this share of partnership profits in his or her self-assessment for 1996–97. But, as part of the transitional arrangements for SA, most partnerships – '**old partnerships**' – will also receive a composite partnership assessment of total trading or professional profits for 1996–97.

Old partnerships

A partnership assessment will only be made for 1996–97 if the partnership is an 'old partnership'.

A partnership whose trade or profession commenced before 6 April 1994 is an 'old partnership' up to the date of any change in its membership which occurs after that date. The partnership will remain an 'old partnership' if at such a change in membership, the partners elect under Section 113(2) Income and Corporation Taxes Act (ICTA) 1988 for the continuation basis of assessment to apply. It will continue to be an 'old partnership' until there is a change of membership for which no election is made.

New partnerships

A 'new partnership' is a partnership whose trade or profession commenced on or after 6 April 1994 or one which commenced earlier, but whose trade or profession is treated as commencing on or after 6 April 1994 because on a change in membership no Section 113(2) ICTA 1988 election was made.

Payment of tax on profits made by 'new partnerships'

A partnership assessment will not be made on a 'new partnership' for 1996–97. Instead, the arrangements for individuals will apply and the partners will be required to make payments on account on their self-assessment, based on the relevant amount of tax and Class 4 NIC assessed on them for 1995–96. This includes the tax and Class 4 NIC payable on their share of the partnership's trade or professional profits. The payments on account will be due on 31 January 1997 and 31 July 1997 with any balancing payment having to be made by 31 January 1998.

Change in partnership during 1996–97

If during the period 6 April 1996 to 5 April 1997 there is a change in membership of an 'old partnership' and a continuation election is not made in respect of that change, then:

- for the period up to the date of change, the partnership is an 'old partnership'.
- for the period thereafter, the partnership is a 'new partnership'.

The rest of this article is concerned only with the new SA rules as they apply for 1996–97 to 'old partnerships' and the members of such partnerships.

1996–97 Partnership assessments

In the case of an 'old partnership', the 1996–97 partnership assessment is the means of collecting tax and Class 4 NIC due on the partnership's trade or professional profits. Because the assessment is on the partnership, each partner is jointly liable for the tax due. **1996–97 is the last year for which composite partnership assessments will be issued and for which the joint liability rule will apply. All of the relevant pre-Self Assessment rules apply to these assessments, including the existing 1 January and 1 July payment dates, arrangements for appeals, postponement applications and interest where payment is late.** But these rules must be operated in tandem with the new rules applying to SA partnership returns.

SA Partnership return

In April 1997, a Self Assessment return will be issued to every partnership requiring a return of the partnership's income, profits and disposals of capital assets and the allocation of those items between the partners.

SA Return for individual partners

In April 1997, each partner will also be issued with their own personal SA return. They will be required to send in their completed return by 30 September 1997 if they wish the Revenue to calculate the tax due, or by 31 January 1998 if they intend to do the calculation themselves.

If they are a member of an 'old partnership', they will have to include in their return their share of the trade or professional profits. But to ensure that these profits are not assessed twice, the partners will be entitled to a credit for their share of the income tax and Class 4 NIC assessed on the partnership against their individual liability. An explanation of how this will work is contained later in this article under the heading 'Partner's Tax Credit'.

In the simplest situation, where a partner's only source of income is his or her share of the partnership's trading or professional profits, all of the tax and Class 4 NIC due for 1996–97 will be collected through the partnership assessment.

Reason for partnership assessments

There are two main reasons why partnership assessments are being issued for 1996–97. First, the assessment will not be based solely on the profits of the current year, but will normally be an average profits figure. It was decided that tax should remain a liability of the partnership for 1996–97, so that the partners could decide amongst themselves the fairest way of dividing the tax bill between them.

Second, SA requires payments on account to be made. The amounts to be paid are based on the tax assessed for the previous year. The Revenue will normally notify the amount to be paid on account to tax payers but this is not practicable for continuing partnerships where the profits for the previous year were included in a partnership assessment. Therefore, partnership assessments are being issued for one last year. For 1997–98 we will be able to calculate payments on account from the partner's 1996–97 self-assessment, 1996–97 is the last year where allocation of the profit between partners is based on the tax year 6 April 1996–5 April 1997.

Issue of partnership assessments

Following our practice in previous years, the 1996–97 composite partnership assessments will normally be issued between August and November 1996.

They will initially be made in estimated figures because, although transitional rules apply, 1996–97 is the first year of 'current year' assessing. In other words, the basis period for 1996–97 in all cases will end in that tax year. Indeed, for many partnerships the basis period for 1996–97 will not have ended when the assessment is issued.

As now, partnership assessments will be supplemented by 'partner's statements'. These will show each partner's share of the partnership's trading or professional profits for 1996–97, the personal allowances and reliefs to which they are entitled and the income tax and Class 4 NIC due on that share of profits.

Allocation of personal allowances, reliefs and rate bands

Where there is a partnership assessment and a partner has another source of income, i.e. other than their share of the partnership's trading or professional income, a decision has to be made on how to allocate allowances, reliefs and rate bands to which the partner is entitled.

Legislation requires that some allowances and reliefs are to be given against specific classes of income. If these rules do not apply, the allowance or relief is given in such a way as to minimise the individual's tax liability. In addition, some income has to be treated as the 'top slice' of income for the purpose of allocating rate bands.

Personal allowances are an example of where legislation does not lay down rules as to how they are to be allocated. In the past our policy has been to allocate such allowances in accordance with the wishes of the taxpayer, or his or her agent, if such a request can be accommodated.

Where no request is made, allowances have been allocated against the income on which tax is first payable. This policy, which is designed to give a result which generally works to the taxpayer's advantage, will continue to apply for 1996–97.

Unless legislation specifies that another order should be applied, for 1996–97 allowances, reliefs and rate bands will be allocated:

- first against any Schedule E income,
- then against the share of profits included in the partnership assessment, and
- any balance will be taken into account in any further tax due in the partner's self-assessment.

This is a different order from that which we would normally have applied in previous years. A partner may have income from property, etc. which in past years has been covered by allowances or separately assessed. For 1996–97 the partner will need to make payments on account of the tax payable on this income on 31 January 1997 and 31 July 1997 and any balancing payment on 31 January 1998.

Since the SA payments on account are calculated by reference to the tax assessed for the previous year, there should be a timing advantage to the partner in having their allowances given against the partnership's trading or professional profits. This will reduce the tax payable by the partnership on 1 January and 1 July 1997 rather than the personal tax due under the SA rules at a later date.

When the estimated partnership assessments and partner's statements are issued in the autumn of 1996, they will reflect any allowances which partners have claimed in their 1996 tax return (or for which they have otherwise established their entitlement).

If a partner, or agent, wants the allowances, reliefs or rate bands to be allocated in a different way, they should inform the tax office when appealing against the partnership assessment. No objection will be made to any reasonable request.

Appeals and postponement applications

The mechanisms for appeals and postponement applications against 1996–97 partnership assessments will operate in the same way as in past years.

It may initially be difficult to make an accurate postponement application when an appeal is made against the partnership assessment. This is because the partnership liability for 1996–97 is based on the accounting period ending in that year. When the appeal is made, the accounting period may not have ended and even if it has ended it is unlikely that there will have been time to prepare accounts. Where accounts have been prepared, the postponement application should be made in line with these accounts.

If a postponement application proves to be inaccurate, a revised application should be made as soon as a clearer idea of the amount of the profits to be assessed for 1996–97 emerges. More than one postponement application may be needed.

Accounts and accounts information

Under Self Assessment, accounts information will be required in a standard format in the Partnership return. A completed return, including standard accounts information, will be required in every case. Submission of accounts and computations by themselves will not constitute a valid return, although their submission with the return may be necessary in some cases in order to make a full disclosure.

However there may be circumstances where the partnership may need to send in accounts and computations prior to the issue of Partnership return. Examples include situations where:

- the account ends after 5 April 1996 but must be used to determine the profit assessable for 1995–96 or an earlier year;
- the account shows a loss which is the subject of a claim to which effect can be given;
- one or more of the partners is a company.

In these cases, we will deal with them when they are submitted.

In addition, in the case of an 'old partnership', we will deal with any accounts and computations we receive before the issue of the partnership return in April 1997 as quickly as possible with a view to agreeing the partnership assessment at an early date.

Where computations are agreed and any other matters relating to the appeal are also settled, the Inspector will seek to determine the appeal against the partnership assessment under Section 54 Taxes Management Act (TMA) 1970 in the normal way. But the partnership will still be required to complete a SA partnership return for 1996–97 providing the information required in the prescribed format.

If we cannot agree the computations we may make enquiries, but these would follow the new approach for SA enquiries. In particular, reasons may not be given for commencing enquiries.

Where computations have been agreed in advance of submission of the partnership return, we will not subsequently enquire into the agreed partnership profits. The only basis on which such enquiries would be made would be under the discovery legislation.

The agreement of accounts and computations in one of these limited circumstances is designed to ensure that, where the pre-and post-SA legislation interact in respect of any period of account, we can deal with the effect of the old legislation as early as possible. This is a transitional arrangement and will not be continued for 1997–98 or later years.

Early filing of partnership SA returns

In order to ensure that the first year of SA runs smoothly, we hope that partnerships will file their 1996–97 partnership SA return as early as possible. These returns will be given priority in tax offices.

The return will be checked upon receipt and may be repaired. In cases where the trade or professional profits have not already been agreed on the basis of the prior submission of accounts and computations, we will agree the figures at this stage or raise enquiries. The appeal against the partnership assessment will also be determined if possible, although this may depend upon claims for allowances and reliefs in the partner's SA returns.

Once the SA partnership return has been filed and the assessment is final, the Revenue will not make any enquiries other than under the discovery legislation.

Early filing of the partnership SA return will have advantages for partnerships, partners, their agents and ourselves. It will:

- provide early certainty over the level of partnership profits, the partnership income tax and Class 4 NIC liability and consequently the credit to which each partner is entitled in his or her self-assessment;
- avoid the need to amend the partners' SA returns to reflect changes in the partnership tax position;
- assist us in processing partnership and partners' SA returns;
- spread processing work in the first year of SA.

There have been suggestions in the press that early submission of a Self Assessment return may increase the chance of it being selected for an enquiry. This is not the case. The Revenue policy is, and will continue to be under SA, to concentrate compliance activity on those areas where there appears to be a high risk of a loss of tax.

Partner's tax credit

For 1996–97, partners will be required to self-assess their total income in their SA tax returns. The partner's self-assessment will have to include items already dealt with in the composite partnership assessment, namely:

- his or her share of the partnership's trading or professional income;
- any allowances and reliefs taken into account in arriving at the partnership's tax liability;
- a notional tax credit for the partner's share of assessed tax.

The statutory rule for the notional tax credit is contained in para 3 Schedule 21 Finance Act 1995 which describes the credit:

> '. . . as if his share of any income tax to which the partnership is assessed for that year were income tax which in respect of that year had been deducted at source.'

We have previously described the credit as the tax **paid** by the partnership on a partner's share of partnership profit. (See leaflet SAT2 (1995) paras 3.123 to 3.125 and **Tax Bulletin** Issue 21 (February 1996 page 286.)) But strictly the credit arises in respect of the tax **assessed**. There is no restriction to this credit where some part of the partnership tax assessed is still unpaid when the partner completes his or her SA Return. But equally, the final credit figure may not be known when the partner completes his or her SA return, for example, because the composite partnership assessment is still in estimated figures.

Purpose of the partner's tax credit

The purpose of the tax credit in the partner's return is to eliminate from the tax liability arising from the partner's own self-assessment, the tax payable on the partnership's trading or professional income.

Where the partnership assessment is final, at the time the partner's SA return is completed, the tax credit to be claimed by the partner is his or her share of the tax shown in the partnership assessment. The total of the credits for all of the partners will equal the tax assessed on the partnership. It is not necessary to consider the payment position when claiming the credit.

Where the partnership assessment is not final, the credit claimed will be a provisional figure which will need to be repaired when the partnership's tax liability becomes final. The provisional figure should normally be the partner's share of the tax payable in accordance with the partnership's latest postponement agreement with the Inspector, or determination by the Commissioners, under Section 55 TMA 1970. But we recognise that there be circumstances where it may be appropriate to claim a different figure. A return containing a provisional figure of tax credit will not be regarded as incomplete. The return will be repaired when the tax credit is finally agreed.

The individual partner will only be given credit for tax on the share of the partnership profits attributed to him or her, less the allowances or reliefs taken into account in the partnership assessment. The credit cannot differ from that sum, regardless of what the individual partner may have paid.

This is because the individual partner's self-assessment must reflect the position in the partnership assessment.

References to tax credit apply equally to Class 4 NIC.

Example

The following example illustrates some of the principles set out in this article.

Mr Smith and Mr Brown have carried on business in partnership for many years. The partnership normally draws up its accounts to 30 June each year but for the transitional year 1996–97 draws up a two year account to 30 June 1996. This shows a trading profit of £80,000 and so the profit to be assessed for 1996–97 is £40,000 (£80,000 × 50%).

For 1996–97 profits must be allocated according to the profit sharing arrangements in force for the period 6 April 1996 to 5 April 1997. In that period profits were allocated 40% to Mr Smith and 60% to Mr Brown.

Each partner has no other source of income and is only entitled to the basic personal allowance.

The 1996–97 partnership assessment is as follows:

Profits	£40,000
less Capital Allowances	£4,000
Net Assessment	£36,000

Allocation between partners

Name of partner	**Share**	**Tax on share**	**Class 4 NIC**
Mr Smith	£14,400	£2,396.40	£452.40
Mr Brown	£21,600	£4,124.40	£884.40
Net amount payable		£6,520.80	£1,336.80

Both partners are jointly liable for the whole of the tax and Class 4 NIC payable. But to calculate the tax and Class 4 NIC due the profits must be allocated between the partners. The tax and Class 4 NIC due on each share is as follows:

	Mr Smith	**Mr Brown**
Share of profit	£14,400	£21,600
Personal Allowance	£3,765	£3,765
Net chargeable to tax	£10,635	£17,835

Mr Smith

3,900 × 20%	£780.00
6,735 × 24%	£1,616.40
Net tax payable	£2,396.40

Mr Brown

3,900 × 20%	£780.00
13,935 × 24%	£3,344.40
Net tax payable	£4,124.40

	Mr Smith	Mr Brown
Class 4 NIC Profit	£14,400	£21,600
Lower limit	£6,860	£6,860
Charged at 6% on	£7,540	£14,740
Amount payable	£452.40	£884.40

These calculations are shown in the 'partner's statements' which are issued to the partners, and their agents, at the same time as the partnership assessment.

In their 1996–97 personal Tax Return each partner will need to include their share of the partnership profits and to claim a credit for the tax and class 4 NIC payable on their share of that profit. The figures will be as follows:

	Mr Smith	Mr Brown
Share of Profit	£14,400	£21,600
Income Tax credit	£2,396.40	£4,124.40
Class 4 NIC credit	£452.40	£884.40

Issue of guide

A booklet called 'A Guide to your partnership tax assessment' will be issued with each 1996–97 partnership assessment and partner statement. The booklet will explain how the 1996–97 partnership assessment fits into the SA system.

If you have any enquiries arising from this article please write to:
Mr J. Pengelly
8th Floor
10 Maltravers Street
London WC2R 1LB.

Page 298. Self Assessment: carry-back of personal pension contributions made in 1996–97

This article explains how the Revenue will treat payments made to personal pension schemes and retirement annuity contracts in the tax year

1996–97, where the payments are carried back to the tax year 1995–96. It considers the consequences for:

- calculating the amount of tax relief
- repaying any tax overpaid
- setting the levels of payments on account for 1996–97.

Personal Pension and Retirement Annuity Relief

Taxpayers get relief for contributions to personal pension schemes and retirement annuity contracts by setting their payments against their earned income. The amount eligible for relief is calculated for a year of assessment by reference to certain percentage limits of the taxpayer's earnings for that year. Where relief is not fully used in a year, taxpayers may elect to have payments made in the following year, carried back (i.e. treated as if they had been made in the earlier one) to sweep up the unused relief. (Sections 619 (4) and 641 Income and Corporation Taxes Act 1988.)

Treatment of payments made up to 5 April 1996 (1995–96)

At present, where tax relief is available in year 1 and a payment made in year 2 is carried back to sweep up the unused relief, the Revenue:

- amend the assessment of year 1,
- set the tax reduction against any amount of tax outstanding or make a repayment.

For example, if the relief for year 1 amounted to £2,000 but only £1,000 was paid in the year, then a further payment of £1,000 could be carried back from year 2 to year 1. The Revenue would amend the year 1 assessment to give tax relief for the further £1,000 and repay tax and interest if appropriate. The election to carry-back must reach the Inspector of Taxes no later than the 5 July following the tax year of payment.

Treatment of payments made under Self Assessment

Some changes to the present arrangements have been made to take account of the introduction of Self Assessment. These changes were first introduced in Section 107 Finance Act 1995. The position was amended by Clause 128 and Schedule 17 Finance Bill 1996 and the new rules all start on 6 April 1996. In addition, Clause 135 and Paragraphs 17 and 18 of Schedule 21 to the Finance Bill 1996, extend the time limit for making an election to carry-back to 31 January following the tax year in which a payment is made. This will apply for payments made in 1996–97 and subsequent years.

The new rules mean that under Self Assessment where tax relief is available in year 1, carrying back a payment made in year 2 has the following effect:

- the tax relief due is calculated in relation to the income and tax rates for year 1;
- it gives rise to a tax credit which can be repaid or set against outstanding liabilities.

But it does **not**:

- amend the assessment for year 1, nor
- reduce the level of payments on account for year 2 which have been set by reference to the year 1 assessment.

If the rules under Self Assessment were applied to the example above, the relief for the additional contributions of £1,000 in year 2 carried back to year 1 would result in a tax credit for year 2 calculated at the tax rates of year 1. This tax credit could then be set against any outstanding tax liabilities or, if preferred, claimed as a repayment.

These changes maintain the flexibility of the current arrangements and the amount of relief. But under the Self Assessment rules, the earlier year's assessment will not be amended.

Representations and Press Commentary

The Revenue received representations from taxpayers, advisers and the Pensions Industry which indicated that they expected contributions made from 6 April 1996 to 5 April 1997 to amend the 1995–96 assessment and to affect payments on account for 1996–97, due on 31 January and 31 July 1997. They therefore expected to be able to continue to pay contributions throughout 1996–97 and have contributions affect the 1995–96 assessment, as they would now. Additionally, some press articles have led to further uncertainty about the exact way in which the new rules would operate.

Treatment of payments made in 1996–97

In response to the concerns expressed, the Revenue issued a Press Release 'Carry-back of personal pension contributions made in 1996–97' on 21 March 1996. It said that '. . . *where qualifying personal pension contributions are paid in the tax year 1996–97 but are carried back for relief to 1995–96, the Department will take those contributions into account when setting the level of any payments on account required for 1996–97 under self assessment. This change responds to representations from the Pensions Industry and others about the interaction between the personal pension rules and the introduction of self assessment.*'.

What this means is that where tax relief is available in the year 1995–96, a payment carried back from 1996–97 will:

- amend the 1995–96 assessment.

- reduce the level of the payments on account for 1996–97 to take account of the amendment, to the 1995–96 assessment,
- give rise to a repayment of tax or, where tax is owing, reduce the amount outstanding.

This treatment will not change the amount of relief obtainable, nor the dates upon which payments are required under Self Assessment. But by amending the 1995–96 assessment and changing the amounts of the payments on account that are payable for 1996–97 it maintains the current practice for a further year and gives taxpayers, their advisers and the Pensions Industry longer to become familiar with the new rules.

Page 299. Self assessment: deadline for new failure to notify chargeability – 5 October 1996

The Self Assessment agents' pack issued to all tax practitioners in June 1995 included an A3 'Timetable for Self Assessment'. The 1996 column had an entry as follows: –

'5 October 1996

- deadline to advise the Inland Revenue on all income for 1995/96 tax year.'

This is meant to explain the new time limit for notifying chargeability to tax under Section 7 Taxes Management Act 1970. We understand that this is being confused with the current deadline for sending in returns to avoid an interest charge i.e. 31 October 1996. We would like to clarify the position and are sorry if it was ambiguous before.

Paragraph 1, Schedule 19 Finance Act 1994 changes the time limit for notification of chargeability from 12 months after the end of the tax year to 6 months (i.e. by 5 October after the end of the tax year). This new limit applies for the tax year 1995–96 onwards.

The date in Statement of Practice 6/89 (Delay in rendering tax returns – Interest on overdue tax) is unchanged for this year at 31 October 1996. So it will continue to apply for 1995–96 returns. The 5 October date is relevant only in the context of the need to notify chargeability if a return has not already been issued by the Inland Revenue by that date.

Page 300. Effective dates of payment

As one of the changes in the move to Self Assessment, Finance Act 1994 introduced legislation specifying that where, after 5 April 1996, payment is made by cheque, it shall be treated as having been made on the day the cheque is received. This provision related to the calculation of interest and repayment supplement on income tax, corporation tax, capital gains tax and Class 4 NICs. Changes have also been made to Regulations to apply similar treatment, from 19 April 1996, to payments in respect of PAYE, the Subcontractor's Scheme, and Class 1 and Class 1A NICs, and from 22 April in respect of Gilt Interest.

Payments to the Inland Revenue are made in a variety of ways as well as by cheque. The following table identifies the different methods of payment and gives details of when payment will be deemed to have been made for each method.

These rules will apply to all payments of income tax, corporation tax, capital gains tax and NICs from **6 April 1996, (or 19 or 22 April 1996 as above)**, and were announced in an Inland Revenue Press Release on 1 April 1996.

Effective dates of payment

Payment method	Effective date of payment
Cheques cash, postal orders	
General, including payments handed in to the Revenue	*The day the Revenue receives the payment.*
Exceptions	
Where payment is received by post following a day when the office has been closed, for whatever reason, including a weekend	*The day that the office was first closed.*
Electronic Funds Transfer (EFT)	*One working day immediately before the date that value is received.*
Payments by CHAPS and BACS**	*A working day is defined as a Bank of England working day.*
Bank Giro payments	*Three working days prior to the date of processing.*
	This applies to both Bank Giro on tape and clerical Bank Giro payments.
Girobank payments	*Three working days prior to the date of processing.*

** BACS is an EFT System through which Bank-sponsored organisations make payments through BACS into accounts at any bank branch in the United Kingdom. CHAPS is also an EFT System providing same-day settlements for high value inter-bank payments and is used by the 12 settlement banks and the Bank of England.

The Revenue's practice on payments by BACS and CHAPS was announced in an Inland Revenue Press release of 1 April 1993 and will continue to apply for all payments of tax by EFT.

Appendix G

Income from self-employment – Standardised Accounts Information

Income and expenses

You must fill in this page if your annual turnover is £15,000 or more

Do the figures in boxes 3.16 to 3.51 include VAT **3.14** or exclude VAT **3.15**

Sales/business income (turnover) **3.16** £

Any disallowable expenses included in boxes 3.33 to 3.50		Total expenses	
3.17 £	Cost of sales	**3.33** £	
3.18 £	Construction industry subcontractor costs	**3.34** £	
3.19 £	Other direct costs	**3.35** £	box 3.16 less (boxes 3.33 + 3.34 + 3.35)
	Gross profit/(loss)		**3.36** £
	Other income/profits		**3.37** £
	Expenditure		
3.20 £	Employee costs	**3.38** £	
3.21 £	Premises costs	**3.39** £	
3.22 £	Repairs	**3.40** £	
3.23 £	General administrative expenses	**3.41** £	
3.24 £	Motor expenses	**3.42** £	
3.25 £	Travel and subsistence	**3.43** £	
3.26 £	Advertising, promotion and entertainment	**3.44** £	
3.27 £	Legal and professional costs	**3.45** £	
3.28 £	Bad debts	**3.46** £	
3.29 £	Interest	**3.47** £	
3.30 £	Other finance charges	**3.48** £	
3.31 £	Depreciation and loss/ (profit) on sale	**3.49** £	
3.32 £	Other expenses	**3.50** £	boxes 3.38 to 3.50
Put the total of boxes 3.17 to box 3.32 in box 3.53 below	**Total expenses**		**3.51** £
			box 3.36 + box 3.37 *less* box 3.51
	Net profit/(loss)		**3.52** £

Tax adjustments to net profit or loss

Disallowable expenses	boxes 3.17 to 3.32 **3.53** £	
Goods etc. taken for personal use and other adjustments (apart from disallowable expenses) which increase profits	**3.54** £	
Total additions to net profit (deduct from net loss)		box 3.53 + box 3.54 **3.55** £
Deductions from net profit (add to net loss)		**3.56** £
Net business profit/(loss) for tax purposes		boxes 3.52 *plus* 3.55 *less* box 3.56 **3.57** £

Now fill in page 3.

You must fill in this page ***(leave blank any boxes that do not apply to you)***

Capital Allowances - summary

	Allowances for this year	Balancing charge
Motor cars:- *(Separate calculations must be made for each motor car costing more than £12,000 and for cars used partly for private motoring.)*	3.58 £	3.59 £
Other business plant and machinery:-	3.60 £	3.61 £
Agricultural or Industrial Buildings Allowance *(A separate calculation must be made for each block of expenditure)*	3.62 £	3.63 £
Other capital allowances claimed *(Separate calculations must be made.)*	3.64 £	3.65 £
Total allowances/balancing charges	Total column above 3.66 £	Total column above 3.67 £

Adjustments to arrive at 1996-97 profit or loss for tax

Income tax basis period begins 3.68 / / **and ends** 3.69 / /

Did your business start before 6 April 1994? - tick either the 'Yes' or the 'No' box

Yes No

If 'Yes' complete this column		**If 'No' complete this column**	
Profit from box 3.13 or 3.57	3.70 £	Profit or loss from box 3.13 or 3.57	3.75 £
		Add balancing charge	3.76 £
		Deduct Capital Allowances	3.77 £
Adjusted profits for 1996-97	3.71 £	Adjustment to arrive at profit or loss for this basis period	3.78 £
Adjustment for farmers' averaging (show reductions in brackets)	3.72 £	Adjustment for farmers' averaging (show reductions in brackets)	3.79 £
Add balancing charge	3.73 £		
Deduct Capital Allowances	3.74 £		

Net profit for 1996-97 (if loss, enter '0' here) 3.80 £

Allowable loss for 1996-97 3.81 £

Loss offset against other income for 1996-97 3.82 £

Loss to carry back 3.83 £ Loss to carry forward (that is, allowable loss not claimed in any other way) 3.84 £

Losses brought forward from last year 3.85 £ Losses brought forward from last year used this year 3.86 £

Taxable profit after losses brought forward — box 3.80 *less* box 3.86 — 3.87 £

Any other business income (for example, Enterprise Allowance (Business Start-up Allowance) received in 1996-97) 3.88 £

Total taxable profits from this business — box 3.87 + box 3.88 — 3.89 £

Class 4 National Insurance Contributions

Tick this box if exception or deferment applies 3.90

Adjustments to profit chargeable to Class 4 National Insurance Contributions 3.91 £

Class 4 National Insurance Contributions due 3.92 £

Subcontractors in the construction industry

Deductions made by contractors on account of tax (remember to send us your SC60s) 3.93 £

Page 3 of 4 **CCO 2/96**

Summary of Balance Sheet

Leave these boxes blank if you do not have a balance sheet

		Box			
Assets	Plant, machinery and motor vehicles	3.94	£		
	Other fixed assets (premises, goodwill, investments etc.)	3.95	£		
	Stock and work in progress	3.96	£		
	Debtors/prepayments/other current assets	3.97	£		
	Bank/building society balances	3.98	£		
	Cash in hand	3.99	£		
				Boxes 3.94 to 3.99	3.100 £
Liabilities	Trade Creditors/accruals	3.101	£		
	Loans and overdrawn bank accounts	3.102	£		
	Other liabilities	3.103	£		
				Boxes 3.101 to 3.103	3.104 £
Net business assets represented by				Box 3.100 *less* box 3.104	3.105 £
	Capital Account				
	Balance at start of period*	3.106	£		
	Net Profit/(Loss)*	3.107	£		
	Capital introduced	3.108	£		
	Drawings	3.109	£		
	Balance at end of period*			Boxes 3.106 to 3.108 less box 3.109	3.110 £

** If the Capital Account is overdrawn, or the business made a net loss, show the figure in brackets.*

Additional information

Page 4 of 4 CCO 2/96

Index

Index